CW01676795

Science of Fat Loss

10 Habits To Maximise Health And Fat Loss

PHIL RICHARDS

I dedicate this book to my beautiful children who inspired me to write this book so that they could have a life of vibrant health and happiness.

I also want to thank my mum for helping me when I was on my knees. And lastly my research scientist on this book Jamie Pugh who put in an incredible amount of hard work and I will always be grateful for his contribution.

First paperback edition printed 2013 in the United Kingdom
A catalogue record for this book is available from the British Library.

ISBN 978-0-9927227-3-9

Published by Phil Richards Performance
For more copies of this book, please
email: enquiries@philrichardsperformance.co.uk
Tel: 01639 861593

Designed and Set by SWATT Design Ltd
Eastleigh, SO50 9DE

Printed by Zenith Media
Rhondda, CF40 2XX

Science of Fat Loss

The Most Comprehensive Book Ever Written On Fat Loss!

By Phil Richards

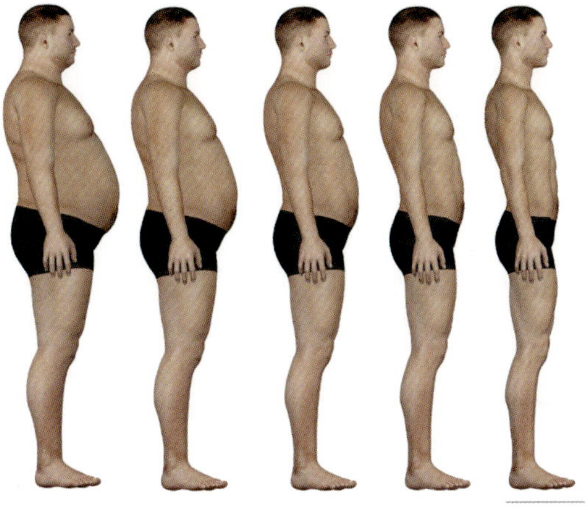

"Please let me take this opportunity to say thank you for purchasing Science of Fat Loss Book. Remember, without health, you simply won't have safe, effective and long term fat loss - and that I can guarantee. Today fat loss has become a science. No longer can it be thought of as simply eat less and exercising more. There are now so many other factors that contribute to obesity, as you will read extensively throughout this book.

If I'm honest with you, I wrote the book for myself as I was simply fed up of being overweight and not feeling healthy. I was overweight for many years and feel that this has given me a much greater insight into the difficulties of losing weight. I have always been fanatical about fitness and nutrition but, after my research, I realised that what was making me fat was not a lack of exercise or what I ate. In my case, it was stress and toxicity, which had a catastrophic effect on my health and inability to lose weight and I will explain in more detail throughout the book why this is the case for most people.

For several years I've had the privilege of being able to carry out full time research into nutrition and conditioning strategies for health, fat loss and performance. This is on the back of working as a Head Strength, Nutrition & Conditioning coach in professional rugby for 10 years. In my last year in professional sport I also worked as a consultant to three professional teams, at Premiership level, in three different sports, as a full time nutrition and fat loss expert.

The information I gathered over this period of time is quite literally astonishing. For example, I observed professional players train up to 8-12 times per week and still gain excess body fat. This helped me learn that exercise is just one part of the jigsaw in the fat loss puzzle and that's why this book is based on 10 different habits, with exercise being the last. The reason why exercise is last is that you will see very little effect from exercise unless you put the other 9 habits in place. It's like a domino effect; each habit contributes to the next habit, eventually having a very powerful effect on each other.

The domino effect

What I want you to do before we start this journey of education on how to lose fat and get healthy is to concentrate more on your body fat percentage and not your overall weight. Why? The only measurement that makes any sense from accurately understanding if you have a healthy weight or a unhealthy weight is your body fat %. I have tested thousands of athletes body fat percentage who have been exceptionally lean (5 – 10% body fat), but if I went by the body mass index (BMI) they would have been declared clinically obese. This is how backwards our medical profession is at assessing whether someone is obese or not, using a system which simply does not give you the correct answer.

There are no gimmicks in this book, it is based on my extensive research, experience and scientific facts. Trust me, there are no quick-fix measures to lose fat - it simply boils down to applying the 10 habits presented in this book. I would strongly advise that you read one habit per week and apply what is relevant for you into your life. This way you are not trying to make countless changes in a few days, which are certain to fail in the long term.

In this book I have tried to give credit to all sources, where possible. However, due to the extent of the research that I have undertaken I am sure you can appreciate that it may not have always been possible to track down original sources, although I have strived to do so at all times.

I have discussed and recommended a number of my supplements throughout this book. This is not meant as a sales pitch I have personally researched and developed every single one of the products over the last few years and have had excellent results with them personally and with the athletes/teams I consult for. Of course use whatever supplements/brands that you feel comfortable with. All of my products are available on my website

www.philrichardsperformance.co.uk

Please enjoy the book. If you do, please share it with as many people who you think will benefit from the information it contains."

Phil Richards

Amongst professional athletes, Phil Richards is regarded as one of the leading strength, conditioning and nutrition experts in the world. He has prepared professional boxers for title fights, led premiership rugby teams to league titles & cup finals and transformed the careers of professional athletes in many sports and disciplines.

Phil regularly lectures and consults for elite athletes and teams as well as running workshops and seminars based on the principles and knowledge he has gained over a 25 year career of working with some of the World's leading experts in his field. Phil has probably interned with more experts in the field of strength, conditioning and nutrition than any other coach in the world. Phil also holds various qualifications in clinical, medical and sports nutrition and is also an advanced cellular nutritional microscopist. Phil is also Europe's first Westside Barbell Certified Strength Coach which is like the Phd in the strength training world.

Phil applies this wealth of learning to a no nonsense approach to build health, strength and performance. Throughout Phil's successful career he has worked with and consulted for the 'who's who' in world sport including: Amir Khan (World Champion Boxer), Worcester Warriors (Professional Rugby), Worcester County Cricket, Somerset County Cricket, London Harlequins (Professional Rugby), Swansea RFC (Professional Rugby), Leicester Tigers, (Professional Rugby), Wigan Warriors (Rugby League), Hull KR (Rugby League), Bolton Wanderers (Professional Football), Glenn Ross (World Masters Strongest Man), Nick Dunn (World Triathlon Champion), Stuart Stokes (Olympian Steeplechaser) and many, many more. Phil Richards has dedicated his life to finding out exactly what really works in the field of nutrition, strength and conditioning - and his track record is undeniable. Phil gets results!

In 2009, Phil began applying this experience and knowledge into developing a range of nutritional products that would deliver health and performance to athletes and members of the general public alike. Since then, the range has grown to some 30+ products and is now being shipped worldwide to athletes, teams and clients across the globe. These products have been developed for one thing, RESULTS. Phil has been meticulous in ensuring every single ingredient in every single product is well sourced and is there only to benefit the product, and therefore the athlete and the general public.

www.philrichardsperformance.co.uk

The information in this book is not meant as medical advice. The training programs, nutrition plans and supplement plans were developed by the author as an adjunct to improved health and fitness. These programs may not be suitable for everyone. All individuals, especially those who suffer from any disease or are recovering from any injury or illness, should seek the advice from a qualified medical professional before making any lifestyle changes. The author has been thorough in his research. However, he is neither responsible nor liable for any harm, injury or illness resulting from any of the information provided in this manual. The views expressed in this book are that of Phil Richards and not of Phil Richards Performance Ltd.

Table of Contents

HABIT 6: Anabolism Vs Catabolism 313

HABIT 7: The Awesome Foursome: Growth Hormone, Insulin, Sunshine & Sleep 381

HABIT 8: Nutritional Cardiology 439

INTRODUCTION

As you read this book, begin to put the pieces of the 10 habits jigsaw in place. Put them in one piece at a time and eventually, when all of the pieces fit together, you will get that leaner, happier and healthier body.

When you read this book, you could easily become overwhelmed by the number of changes that you feel you may need to make in your life to become lean, happy and healthy. Let me give you another analogy which I have used for many years with my athletes and teams.

Chase one rabbit, and catch it.
Chase two, and you catch nothing!

Focus in on what is the most important change that you need to make. When you achieve that, move on to the next. For example, after reading the book you might recognise that your breakfast is making you fat and that you need to do more exercise. Spend one week changing your breakfast so that it becomes a habit. Then, the following week, start introducing some exercise. This way you will make changes very gradually and you will get into the habit of living a healthier lifestyle.

Learn to understand that the most powerful drugs on this planet are not those that pharmaceutical companies invented. These often do far more harm than good, and the evidence on this is truly staggering. However, I feel that we have become so dumbed down in our society that we don't question anyone in a white coat; if they say, "take this" most people usually do. There are no doubt an incredible amount of knowledgeable, caring doctors out there but the problem is they have literally ZERO training in nutrition, lifestyle, detoxification & emotional health which are usually the root cause for most illnesses and disease, including obesity. In fact these modalities are often thought in modern Westernised medicine as nothing more than 'quackery' - sad but very true. Treating people with a pill and not addressing these factors is, in a word, INSANE, yet every day this is how modern medicine goes about its business, driven by the greed of pharmaceutical companies. The sad truth is nobody questions this but I advise you to question everything to do with your health from both the allopathic field and alternative field for it is the most precious commodity you have along with time!

I'm not going to walk on eggshells or be politically correct whilst I write this book nor will I exaggerate the truth or use scare mongering tactics to get you to take action. My philosophy is quite simple; to tell the truth and it's time to get down to bare knuckle stuff for we are now living in a culture where political correctness is simply being afraid to tell the truth without upsetting people, well in my book a spade is a spade - simple!

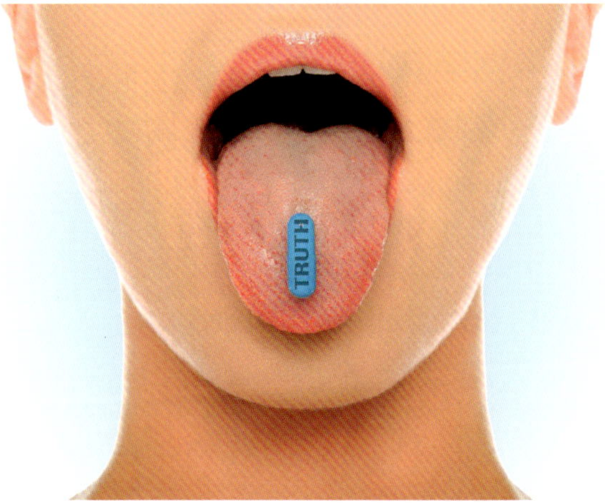

The pill that everyone wants

But can't seem to swallow

This is not a Diet Book: Why Diets Don't Work Long Term

I want to make it very clear that this book is not a 'fad' diet or anything like that. Why? Because they do not work. There are 4 main problems with many of the popular diet plans which millions of people follow worldwide and why they fail to lose weight safely, effectively and for the long term.

1) They are concerned with reducing weight rather than the correct approach of losing body fat.
2) They strip off vital muscle which is the major component that burns the fat in the first place. Nutrition scientists have known for decades that low calorie diets of 800 – 1200 calories per day can use up to 45% of muscle tissue for energy, this is a disaster long term for fat loss. Fat burns in the furnace of muscle and muscle is 15 - 20 times more metabolically active than fat. You must preserve your muscle at all costs!
3) They take off weight too fast, thereby throwing the body into a defensive, fat preserving condition. This literally causes hormonal chaos putting you in fat storage mode instead of fat burning mode.
4) They release toxins which have been stored in body fat which can decrease our fat burning hormones and inhibit our energy factories called mitochondria from burning fat efficiently.

So remember, the true purpose of weight reduction is to dispose of excess body fat while retaining lean muscle tissue. This is why many of the diet programs, run by the plethora of slimming clubs, fail - they reduce weight but also muscle. Like a boomerang, that weight is certain to come back on. This, though, is a great business model for the slimming clubs as you always get repeat business.

It's obvious that people differ widely in their inborn tendencies to store fat. But some researchers/trainers have overblown this to claim that each person is designed to be healthy only at a certain fat level, and that the body will always revert to that level. Well they are 100% wrong! The amount of fat you carry is not ordained by your genes. It is caused by what you eat, how much exercise you get and unfortunately today by the level of toxicity that you have been exposed to, even during pregnancy which you will read about in habit 1. Science has shown that neither the number of fat cells nor their size is fixed ***(Winick M, ed. Childhood Obesity. New York, NY: Wiley 1975).*** Body fat is much more dependent on nutrition, lifestyle and level of toxins within our body. Your body fat has no internal reference for a permanent level of fat, only for a habitual level.

When you remain at a particular level of fat for a year or more, your body develops all the adipose cells, capillaries, enzyme counts, peripheral nerves, hormone levels, and connective tissue to support it. It comes to recognize that level of fat and will defend it vigorously. That is your 'fat point'. The body constantly monitors its fat point with hormonal messengers, such as glycerol, which warn the brain to take defensive action if even one pound is suddenly used for fuel. This is why usual forms of dieting always fail as they slow metabolism, increasing fat storage, and increasing appetite.

How can you drop those excess pounds of fat off your body without putting your body on full alert that it's under threat? Easy. Reliable studies show that it takes years of overeating to grow fat. Body fat typically creeps on by only an ounce or so per day, a pound every two or three weeks. In a year you are 20 pounds over and in 3 or 4 years you gain 60 pounds of excess fat. Your body shifts its habitual fat point up very slowly and to shift it down, you have to operate the same way, very slowly. Otherwise the body will cannibalize your muscle, excite your fat storage enzymes and boost your appetite to ravenous.

This is also why I'm against fasting, because it will increase your fat storage hormones and decrease thyroid hormones. My definition of fasting is far more intelligent from a hormonal perspective than a lot of the nonsense out there which, in reality, is not do-able long term either. When you fast for 2 days and then eat quite ravenously for 5 days, for example, you will eventually turn yourself into a very efficient fat storage machine and that's exactly what nature intended. You will read in habit 7 and 9, the best way to fast, from a hormonal perspective, for fat loss is to not eat 4-5 hour before bed.

Severely reducing your calorie intake is also something that I am totally against. Research from Cambridge University studied 11 individuals who consumed a routine maintenance diet for 11 days. These diets amounted to approximately 1612 calories per day, including 807 calories of carbohydrate, 534 calories of fat, and 271 calories of protein. After the 11-day prelude, the participants went on to a starvation-regime of 405 calories per day using the ever-popular 'Cambridge Diet' (a powdery preparation which is mixed with water prior to consumption).

After four days of Cambridge starvation, the subjects lost an average of nine pounds! They were happy, until the researchers filled them in on what was really going on. Basically, about one of those lost pounds was pure glycogen (stored sugar). Another four pounds of water was lost with this solitary carbohydrate pound meaning that five out of the nine pounds dropped (56%) were good things that the dieters' bodies really needed. It's hard to know from the study how much protein (muscle) was converted to carbohydrate and then burned up for fuel, too, but when you do the appropriate calculations, it's very difficult to believe that the subjects lost more than two pounds of fat. So, at least 78% of the weight lost was good stuff (glycogen, protein, and water).

Now, let's say that these people were satisfied with their nine-pound weight-loss and decided to go back to normal - but not excessive - eating. One of the first things their bodies would do would be to re-stock that missing pound of glycogen (remember that although the body gives up carbohydrate rather freely, it will try desperately to get that glycogen back, if given a chance). That would mean that five pounds (one pound glycogen and four pounds water) would return to the dieters' carcasses in a very short period of time.

And that's the best-case scenario! Swedish studies have shown that when one follows carbohydrate depletion with adequate carbohydrate replenishment, glycogen storage can sometimes soar to more than twice normal ***('Diet, Muscle Glycogen, and Physical Performance,' Acta Physiologica Scandinavica, vol. 71, pp. 140-150, 1967).*** In the Cambridge case, that could mean up to two pounds of glycogen and eight pounds of water, or a total gain of 10 pounds within a short period of time. That would be a net gain of one pound for our Cambridge victims, despite their four days of starvation misery. Easy go, easy come!

The bottom line? Despite the rosy claims made by the marketers of quick weight loss products and diets, weight lost easily is weight regained even more readily. To lose weight properly, it's important to trim away fat slowly and steadily.

The danger of Excess Body Fat

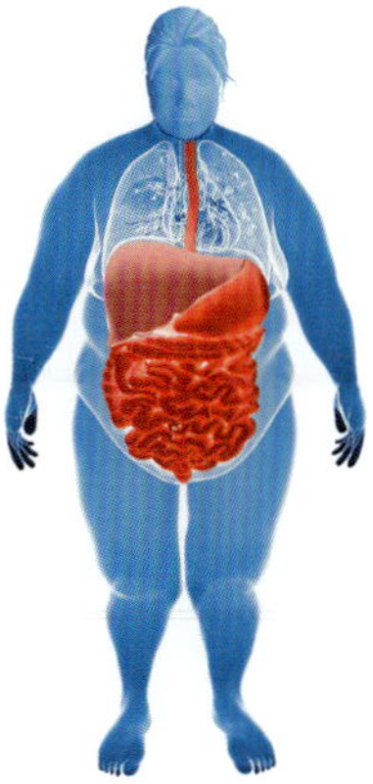

It is 100% impossible to be healthy and fat so don't get caught by the many magical nonsense pills, powders & lotions on the market offering fat loss because they are total nonsense. Unless they can do things like detoxify you, balance your hormones, enhance mitochondrial function, build healthy cells, balance pH, nourish the cardiovascular system, create better digestion, increase activity levels, decrease inflammation and optimise brain chemistry etc. then they will fail in the long run. This may all sound complex now but throughout this book I will show you the fundamentals of how building better health for yourself can turn you into a fat burning machine instead of a fat storage machine!

Before we start to look at some of the factors that have led to what has become an obesity epidemic in our society, it is important to examine the link between those who are fat and those who are sick so that you realise that carrying a little bit of extra fat can be devastating to your health. What's more, it doesn't even have to be a lot of extra fat that you are carrying; even a 10% increase above ideal weight causes a 6–7% increase in blood pressure. That's only 15lbs extra on a 150lb person. And losing that extra weight causes an immediate drop in blood pressure of 10–11%.

Being seriously overweight also causes rapid diabetes. Both men and women carrying 60 lbs or more, are 3000% more likely to develop diabetes. Even moderate overweight increases your risk of diabetes by about 100%. ***(Westlund K, Nicholayse R. Scand J Lab Clin Invest 1972;127 (S):1-22)***

Cancer also loves body fat. The American Cancer Society did a massive 20 year study involving over one million American citizens. Results showed that men who were 40% overweight, had higher rates of prostate cancer, colon cancer and rectal cancer. Women who were 40% or more overweight, had higher rates of breast cancer, ovarian cancer, uterine cancer, gallbladder cancer, cervical cancer, and endometrial cancer. ***(American Cancer Society, Cancer Prevention Study 1959 – 79. New York, NY: American Cancer Society, 1980)***

Dr. Mikhail Kolonin, lead study author noted *"Our earlier studies led us to hypothesize that fat tissue called white adipose tissue, which is the fat tissue that expands in individuals who are obese, is itself directly involved and that it is not just diet and lifestyle that are important."*

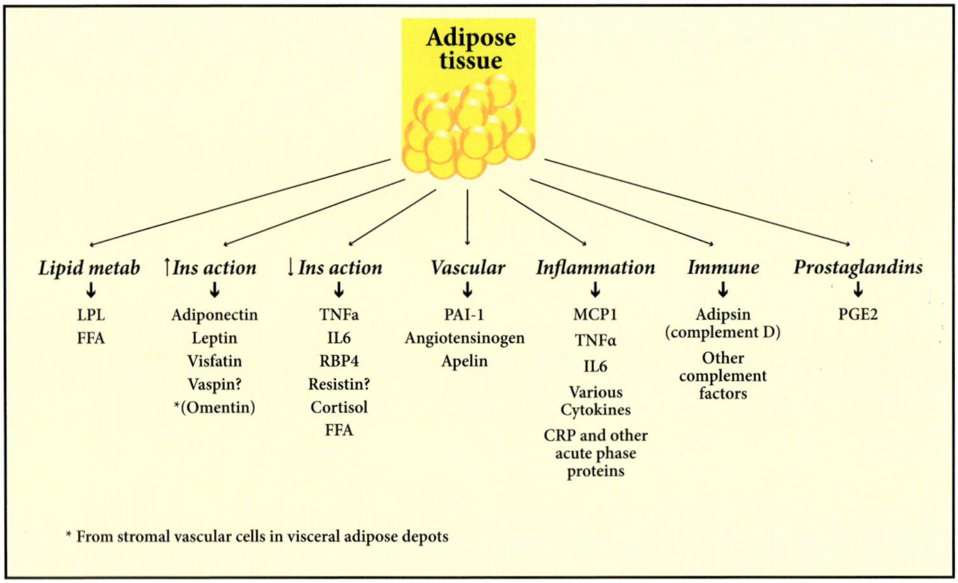

Researchers examined two groups of mice, one obese and the other lean, and observed that when both were fed the same diet, the obese mice developed tumours at a higher and more rapid rate as compared to their lean counterparts. The scientists also found that the obese mice had more adipose stromal cells (ASC's) that enter the circulation. When the stromal cells entered forming tumours, many of them turned into fat cells while others became part of the blood vessel network feeding the tumour growth. They concluded that adipose stromal cells contributed to angiogenesis, an essential component in tumour development that feeds nutrients and oxygen to fuel cancerous growth.

Dr. Kolonin concluded *"Our results suggest that ASC's recruited from endogenous adipose tissue can be recruited by tumours to potentiate the supportive properties of the tumour microenvironment."* In the past, researchers have associated overweight and obesity with increased risk for prostate, breast, ovarian, colorectal and renal cancers. This important study now explains the specific mechanism to explain how excess body fat is an independent risk factor in cancer development and progression.

Fat is the only organ with an almost unlimited ability to increase in size. For a long time, the conventional wisdom was that the number of fat cells in the body was fixed during childhood and remained constant throughout life. We now know that fat cells not only change in volume, they also change in number. In other words they get bigger and they also multiply.

A healthy adult who has healthy body fat has 25-30 billion fat cells, and an overweight adult has 75 billion, however with severe obesity, this number can be as high as 250 to 300 billion! That is 10 times what a healthy person has.

A child who has normal weight parents has a 7% chance of being overweight or obese. A child who has 1 overweight parent has a 40% chance of being overweight or obese. A child who has 2 overweight parents has a 70% chance of being overweight or obese. That is scary when you look at how many children today have 2 overweight or obese parents. As parents we set the example. Our children need to see us eating healthy and exercising. What we do speaks so much louder than what we say.

The fatter you are, the fatter you get. Simply stated, it appears that when a person accumulates body fat of an amount equal to more than about 20 lbs over ideal weight, the fatty tissues begins to act like a separate endocrine organ, secreting hormones such as cortisol, and other non-beneficial hormones. These hormones accelerate the fat-storage process, and through the catabolic, or muscle-wasting effects of cortisol, the body fat begins to take away the muscle stores while piling on the extra fat pounds. This is a runaway train that is very difficult to stop. So extremely obese people have toxic stores of fat that are beginning to take over the person's metabolism and make it almost impossible for them to lose fat.

You will read throughout the book the devastating effects excess body fat has on our health and the above, is simply a fraction, of fat's effect on health, but hopefully enough of an effect to wake YOU up and take action.

We also owe our children the right to be fit, healthy & lean because they are also being hit on multiple fronts in readiness for them to be the food industry and big pharma next customers. As a parent, do not rely on government policy to protect your children from the obesity crisis, as you have got the uninformed leading the uninformed. You must be 100% responsible for your child's health and I urge you to read this book cover to cover and start nourishing the most precious things in our lives, our children, with clean organic foods instead of junk foods. I suggest getting a reverse osmosis water filter system in the home to give them clean water and take out the multiple toxins found in our tap water.

No Excuses

For the contents of this book to work, so do you - it really is that simple. You have to be 100% committed to eating clean, drinking clean and thinking clean. Remember this, "a half - hearted commitment is worse than no commitment at all". You are either in or out. Don't kid yourself; if you want real results then you need real commitment. If you want half-hearted results then you only need half-hearted commitment.

> ***"In order to succeed, your desire for success should be greater than your fear of failure."***
>
> **Bill Cosby**

The reason for this first chapter on mental preparation is quite simple: if you fail with your new nutrition, lifestyle and exercise plan it's because mentally you were too weak to follow a new path to wellness. So please read this first chapter carefully and apply what's relevant to you to change your life for the better.

Everyday thousands of people are trying to lose weight by exercising and dietary control and this is obviously essential in our quest to drop excess body fat and get healthy. But let me tell you in plain language – unless you detoxify your mind, the chances of getting the body you want are very small, no matter how much exercise you do or how disciplined you are with your diet. Even if you do get the body you want, if you still have a toxic mind you will always feel unhappy and unwell. Remember that health and time are the two most important commodities that we have in life, you must never take them for granted because when they are gone so are you.

From my 30 years of training people from all walks of life, the first thing I look at today is how much love and happiness they have presently in their lives. Why? The more love and happiness in their lives, the more the body will respond to exercise and get outstanding results. When there is anger, hatred and hostility in one's life no exercise or nutrition program is going to get results in the long run. Why? The body is in a constant catabolic state where adding lean muscle onto the body and losing excess fat is virtually impossible. This is because the body will either use substrates to make cortisol, our stress hormone, or testosterone, our muscle building, fat loss hormone, depending on the stress of the body. If it's constantly under stress more cortisol, and less testosterone, will be made, making it very difficult to lose fat and build muscle and this is discussed in great depth in habit 6 of this book.

One of the biggest destroyers of our health as adults is undoubtedly toxic relationship: make sure if you are in one you get out of there as quickly as you can. I have had my fair share of toxic relationships, like most people my age, and the biggest lesson I have learnt is to get out when you know it's not right. I spent ten years with the wrong person and it crumpled me into the ground and literally took me ten years to get back up again. You can't out train a toxic relationship and that's a fact.

> ***"Keep away from people who belittle your ambitions. Small people always do that, but the really great make you feel that you, too, can become great."***
>
> **Mark Twain**

So before we get into the 10 habits to build health & lose weight I want to teach you some mental health tools, as well as inspirational stories which have helped me personally not only in my battle against the bulge but also my 30 year battle against depression. Never forget this fact "You deserve to be happy and lean, but you have to work at it!".

December 16th 2012 was a significant day in my life as this was the day I simply refused to leave toxic thoughts have any impact on me anymore, and as soon as I had a toxic thought after this day I eliminated it immediately. What was the catalyst for this? For as long as I can remember I had always had the dark cloud of depression hanging over me and would often be suicidal and on the evening of December 16th 2012 I was making my way up the stairs to my bed when I noticed a book on the stairs. The title of the book literally hit me smack between the eyes "Prisoners Of Our Thoughts". In the instant of those words engaging with my brain I realised that's exactly what I was; a prisoner of my thoughts. If only I could control my thoughts and not my thoughts controlling me, then I could live the life I want which was quite simple and that was just to feel happy. And my life hasn't been the same since!

Hatred paralyzes life;
Love releases it.
Hatred confuses life;
Love harmonizes it.
Hatred darkens life;
Love illumines it.

Martin Luther King, Jr.

What You Think About, You Bring About!

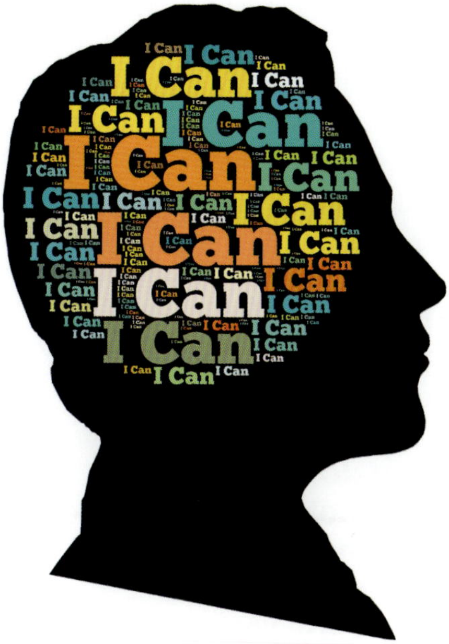

Another important fact for me during my research for this book was the realisation that our thoughts control our emotions, our emotions affect our hormones and our hormones affect our weight as well as our sense of well being. Why is this significant? Well first of all when you understand that your hormones control your weight and when you are constantly depressed, angry, hostile, jealous, anxious we are putting the body in fight or flight mode meaning this is no time to heal, this is time to break down our fat burning furnace muscle and use it as fuel instead. This is ok if it's done as nature intended during emergency situations only e.g. getting chased by a big muscular lion, but if it's constantly switched on because you are worrying about finances, sitting in traffic, relationships or job issues etc. and you couple this with poor nutrition and lifestyle habits then your stress hormones will do their job and literally break you down and turn you into a fat storing machine, making it virtually impossible to lose fat.

One study that found that the cortisol levels (a stress hormone we cover in detail throughout this book) of the depressed individuals was 68% higher than those without depression (this would make losing fat very difficult). That same study found that testosterone was significantly lower in these individuals and were negatively correlated with cortisol levels. To put it directly: the higher the STRESS, the lower the TESTOSTERONE and the less chance you have of dropping body fat.

So you can see depression and testosterone do not go together. If you want to increase your testosterone, you absolutely must get this under control: depression leads to lower testosterone levels which is essential to both men and women's ability not only to feel better but essential for fat loss. This would make adding muscle to burn fat virtually impossible if one is constantly depressed due to the cortisol testosterone ratio.

When you have someone who is going through an extremely stressful event in their life, there is very little stress that they can cope with. You must remember that exercise is in itself stress. When you put stress on top of more stress, something has to give eventually and it is usually results. The amount of people I see in the gym training at full speed ahead and making zero progress week after week, I guarantee that if they reduced stress in their life the exercise would yield significant results. How you feel emotionally is without doubt the best possible indicator you have of whether you are heading towards HEALTH or DISEASE.

To detoxify our body we must also detoxify our mind, because our mind can sabotage even the most scientifically sound nutrition & exercise plan.

"When things go wrong as they sometimes will;
When the road you're trudging seems all uphill;
When the funds are low, and the debts are high
And you want to smile, but have to sigh;
When care is pressing you down a bit-
Rest if you must, but do not quit.
Success is failure turned inside out;
The silver tint of the clouds of doubt;
And you can never tell how close you are
It may be near when it seems so far;
So stick to the fight when you're hardest hit-
It's when things go wrong that you must not quit."

~ Unknown

Remember even the most deadly snake bite doesn't kill you it's the venom running through your bloodstream which will eventually paralyse your body, but what if the venom was stopped by a tourniquet and the venom couldn't enter the bloodstream? This analogy is like the many stressful situations we face daily they can only do harm like the venom if allowed to run in our bloodstream where we release a chemical cascade of adrenaline and cortisol which can in excess cripple us. But thankfully you can change the venom into positive juice within a split second by simply changing our thoughts from NEGATIVE TO POSITIVE. Don't kill your results by NEGATIVE THINKING!

I loved what the late former South African President Nelson Mandela said, when asked how he survived years of imprisonment without growing bitter, and he replied, "Bitterness only hurts one's self. If you hate, you will give them your heart and mind. Don't give those two things away".

Do not dwell in the past,
Do not dream of the future,
Concentrate the mind
On the present moment.

Buddha

One of the biggest mistakes that we do as humans is worry about yesterday and tomorrow, when in reality yesterday is gone and tomorrow is guaranteed to no one. The most important time in your life is NOW. And a great analogy to this is if you were driving your car on the motorway and you kept looking in the rear view mirror then there is a very strong likelihood you will crash and if you kept looking at the cars way in front of you there is also a very strong likelihood you will crash. If you simply concentrated on the NOW there is a very strong likelihood you will get to your destination safe and well and this is the same in life and in reality the only thing you can control is NOW.

My son Mansel, who is now 7, has taught me many valuable lessons over the years but undoubtedly the most important one is that, as adults, we tend to forget about being in the NOW because we are often too busy worrying. I can be walking along a path with Mansel then he will shout, "Dad, look at this" and I will go running over to look down. I can't see anything then he points out, "see it Dad? The little ant carrying a leaf isn't it amazing."

When I pick Mansel up from school, the first question I usually ask him is, "what have you learnt today?" He usually replies, "I can't remember. Now can we go play." Brilliant, he is now *my* teacher.

"Your worst enemy cannot harm you as much as your own unguarded thoughts."
Buddha

Laughter could also be your best antidote to excess stress and absolutely no doubt help lose the fat off your gut. Dr. Lee Berk, of Loma Linda University Medical Center has written about the health benefits of laughter. He concluded that laughter boosts the immune system and reduces dangerous stress hormones in the body.

In one remarkable study involving sixteen men who watched a funny video, levels of stress hormone cortisol fell by 39% after a good belly laugh. Adrenaline levels fell by 70%, while levels of the feel good hormones endorphins rose 27%. Not only that, but growth hormone levels sky-rocked by 87%. Now if that doesn't get you putting laughter in your fat loss program nothing will.

Sigmund Freud identified the three parts of the emotional mind as the parent, adult and child. He noted that the child part of the mind is completely unconscious, while the parent part of the mind is completely conscious. The adult mind is partly unconscious, partly conscious. He concluded that too many people have locked away the child part of their emotional mind, sadly so, because when the parent or adult mind rules the emotions, life tends to be drained of joy, fun and adventure.

Never lose the child in you.

Never lose the child in you; take every opportunity to laugh, be silly or mischievous. I remember when my son Mansel told me when no one was looking, him and a friend decided to lick a tree. I asked him why they had done this and what they got out of this. He looked me straight in the eye and said, "It was fun Dad!"

Never Give Up On Your Childhood Dreams

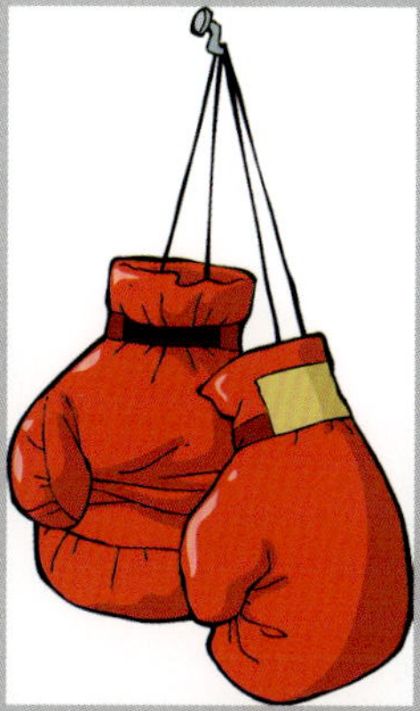

When I was in the sixth grade at Ford Boulevard Elementary School, my class was asked to write an essay on what we wanted to be when we grew up. We then had to get up and read our assignment aloud. Kids said they wanted to be doctors, policemen, firemen. I got up and said I wanted to be an Olympic gold medallist in boxing. The class burst into laughter. They thought I was kidding. One kid said, "Yeah, right, you're from East L.A. How are you going to be a gold medallist?" the teacher thought I wasn't taking the assignment seriously, so she punished me by keeping me after class. I started crying telling her, "I'm not kidding. That's what I want to be."

Oscar De La Hoya Olympic Gold Medallist Barcelona Olympics 1992

"Obstacles are those frightful things you see when you take your eyes off your goal."
Henry Ford

The Power Of Believing

If you want to change, stop thinking and believing that you are a product of your past and start acting and behaving like the person you want to be. Remember your brain doesn't know the difference. Start thinking and believing that you already are what you wish to be and in as much detail as possible. At first, this will take a strong constant conscious effort. Like most things though the more you do it the more natural it becomes. YOU CAN BE OR DO WHATEVER YOU THINK YOU CAN!

Cliff Young's Story

Every year, Australia hosts 543.7-mile (875-kilometer) endurance racing from Sydney to Melbourne. It is considered among the world's most gruelling ultra-marathons. The race takes five days to complete and is normally only attempted by world-class athletes who train specially for the event. These athletes are typically less than 30 years old and backed by large companies such as Nike. In 1983, a man named Cliff Young showed up at the start of this race. Cliff was 61 years old and wore overalls and work boots. To everyone's shock, Cliff wasn't a spectator. He picked up his race number and joined the other runners.

The press and other athletes became curious and questioned Cliff. They told him, "You're crazy, there's no way you can finish this race". To which he replied, "Yes I can. See, I grew up on a farm where we couldn't afford horses or tractors, and the whole time I was growing up, whenever the storms would roll in, I'd have to go out and round up the sheep.

We had 2,000 sheep on 2,000 acres. Sometimes I would have to run those sheep for two or three days. It took a long time, but I'd always catch them. I believe I can run this race."

All of the professional athletes knew that it took about 5 days to finish the race. In order to compete, one had to run about 18 hours a day and sleep the remaining 6 hours. The thing is, Cliff Young didn't know that!

When the morning of the second day came, everyone was in for another surprise. Not only was Cliff still in the race, he had continued jogging all night. Eventually Cliff was asked about his tactics for the rest of the race. To everyone's disbelief, he claimed he would run straight through to the finish without sleeping. Cliff kept running. Each night he came a little closer to the leading pack. By the final night, he had surpassed all of the young, world-class athletes. He was the first competitor to cross the finish line and he set a new course record!

The most important person to have belief in you, is you! You have to work hard to get good and then work harder to get better. It's that simple! There is no magic formula, just plain hard graft.

Natalie du Toit

In 2001 Natalie was riding on her motor scooter when she was hit suddenly on the side by a careless driver, causing her to lose her left leg just above the knee. Less than 2 years later she qualified for the finals of the 800 meter freestyle at the 2002 Commonwealth Games. In 2008 Natalie qualified for both the Paralympic and Olympic games.

Randy Couture

In March of 2007 Randy came out of retirement at age 43 and challenged 27 year old Tim Sylvia for the UFC heavyweight title. The insiders of mixed martial arts not only thought Randy didn't have a chance winning, but they thought he was actually going to get seriously hurt in the process. The result: Randy almost knocked out Tim Sylvia 8 seconds into the fight and completely dominated him for all 5 rounds... gives hope to all 30, 40, and 50 year old fitness warriors doesn't it!

James Buster Douglas

James stunned the world when he knocked out the then invincible Iron Mike Tyson. The first interviewer into the ring with the new champ was quick to try to explain to the world just how and why this mighty upset had occurred. His analysis went something like this, "Buster, you kept him at bay with double left jabs, you tied him up, you maintained a delicate balance of constant pressure etc what was your strategy? Is that what you planned to do tonight? "I planned to whip his ass," Buster replied, "and you know what? That's just what I did."

> ***Twenty years from now you will be more disappointed by the things that you didn't do than by the ones you did do. So throw off the bowlines. Sail away from the safe harbor. Catch the trade winds in your sails. Explore. Dream. Discover.***
>
> **Mark Twain**

In a Native American folk story, a Native American elder was transferring wisdom upon his grandson and described his daily conflict well. "I have two wolves fighting in my heart. One wolf is vengeful, fearful, envious, resentful, and deceitful. The other wolf is loving compassionate, generous, truthful, and serene." The grandson asked, "Which wolf will win the fight the wise elder responded, "The one I feed most."

Before Roger Bannister ran his first sub four minute mile experts were writing papers explaining why the human body could not run a mile in less than four minutes. Almost everyone except for Roger Bannister thought that running a mile in less than four minutes was impossible. As Roger Bannister said "The man who can drive himself further once the effort gets painful is the man who will win."

When Bannister broke the four minute barrier in 1954, other runners duplicated the feat within months. What changed in these elite runners? One word - belief. They now knew that if Roger Bannister could run a sub four minute mile so could they.

Don't blame your genes

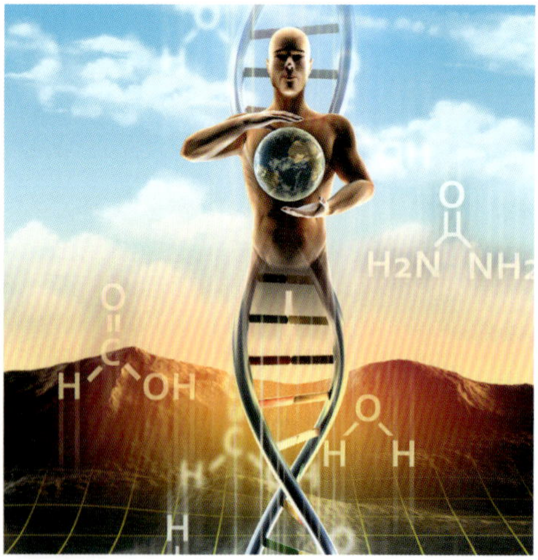

If I had a pound for every time I've heard someone blame their genes for their body shape, athletic ability or academic capability I would genuinely be a wealthy man. Unless you were born with a genetic disorder (which accounts for approximately 6% of the population) then trust me, you have the genetic potential to achieve truly outstanding achievements both physically and mentally.

Whether you hail from Russia, China, USA, UK or Nairobi, your genetic makeup is strikingly similar to that of every other person on Earth, analyses has shown. Although scientists have long recognised that, despite physical differences, all human populations are genetically similar, the new work concludes that populations from different parts of the world share even more genetic similarities than previously assumed.

All humans are 99.9% identical meaning that there is only 0.1% difference between you and someone you think is untouchable - now all of a sudden that untouchable person is touchable!

You achieve your goals with passion, desire, hard work, perseverance and BELIEF. As I was finishing this book, and as I look at the 30+ products I have developed, I can't help to have a wee smile. Why? I left school with ZERO qualifications and my teachers believed my life would amount to very little. As Mark Twain said, "Your education starts when you leave school". I love that quote along with Helen Keller's quote "A ship that never leaves the harbour is always safe but you never get to see the world".

You should never give up on what you feel you can achieve. You simply must DO IT or you will live a life that is not true to you or your true potential.

It does not matter if others do not believe in you but it does matter if you do not believe in you, remember all humans who do not have a genetic defect are 99.9% identical so there is absolutely no excuse to achieve your goals:)

Imagine the scene; there you are taking a stroll along the beach on a beautiful June morning, listening to the waves splashing against the shoreline, lost in your thoughts, when all of a sudden you hear a huge roar. You look round and there is a very muscular lion heading towards you from a distance. You then cover 100 meters in under ten seconds as you panic about the prospect of being lunch. What just happened to those untapped sprinting genes? THEY WOKE UP!

OK, you might not have done 100 meters in under ten seconds but I bet you it would be the fastest 100 meters you have ran in your life if the scenario was real. When you have purpose and desire you will achieve anything, and I mean anything, so next

time you are struggling to lose weight and get in shape don't blame your genes blame your thoughts and your environment!

Body and mind are intertwined – every thought, feeling and intention you have sends ripples throughout your body. They can be so powerful they can even affect your genes. It really is exciting to know that we can genuinely influence our genes with the way we think and the environment that we create internally and externally. You must remember that every cell in your body is tuned into every thought you have and they will react accordingly, good or bad. Cells are like little people; think of yourself as a community of little people (cells), over 50 trillion of them, and how you communicate with your little people and the environment you provide will determine how the little people (cells) look after the big person (you). Think positive thoughts, nourish yourself with nutritious foods, clean drinking water, create the right environment and your little people (cells) will make sure they look after the big person by becoming healthier, happier, more vibrant and leaner.

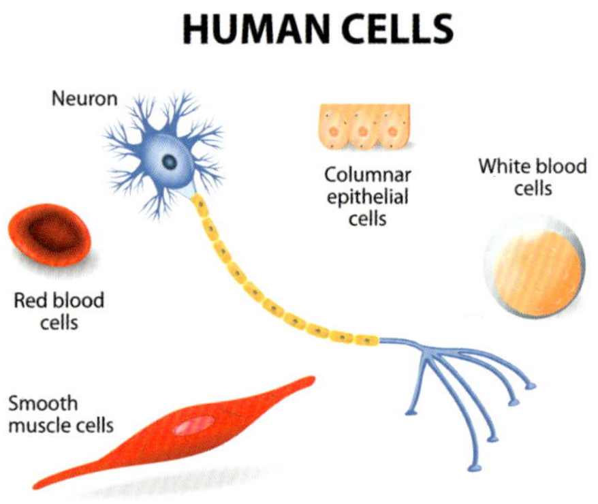

Our thoughts effect every cell in our body

Further support for the idea that our beliefs translate into physiological changes in our bodies comes from the laboratories of those studying the field of molecular biology called Epigenetics – meaning 'control above the genes'. What's above the genes when we talk about epigenetic control? The mind. While you cannot change your DNA, you may be able to utilise the power of your mind to alter how your DNA expresses itself and author Dr. Bruce Lipton asserted that you may be able to change how your DNA is expressed based on what you believe. So, changing your thoughts can actually change how your brain communicates with the rest of your body. Thereby altering the body's biochemistry.

Your genetic code is like a blueprint that can be interpreted in millions of different ways. Before the human genome project, biologists assumed that we had at least 120000 genes which would have equated for 1 gene for every protein made in the body. So researchers were baffled when they discovered that we only have approximately 25000 genes which can express themselves in a variety of ways. In fact, we now know that each of those 25000 genes can express itself in at least 30000 ways via regulatory proteins that are influenced by environmental signals.

Scientists are now learning that the genome is far more responsive to the environment of the cell than genetic determinism suggests. This means that the majority of disease processes can be explained by environmental factors to which the cells are exposed; things such as nutrition, pH imbalances, toxins, hormonal changes and even love, happiness, hate and anger.

Bruce Lipton, a cell biologist, worked with pleuripotential stem cells (cells that can become anything). He placed one of these in a petri dish where it was nourished with cell culture medium as it divided into many genetically identical cells. Lipton then split the cells into 3 petri dishes and exposed them to 3 different culture mediums (the environment). What he discovered was that the environment to which the cell was exposed determined whether the cell became a muscle cell, a fat cell or a bone cell – even though all of the cells were genetically identical, they expressed themselves differently. The final outcome of the same genetically identical DNA was expressed as radically different cells due to the environment. The cellular environment also determined whether or not the cell stayed healthy.

Cells exposed to a good environment enjoyed optimum health, while those exposed to a bad environment got sick. You must remember, we are no more than a petri dish full of 50 trillion plus cells covered by skin. If they are to perform, they need to be well nourished, have a well balanced pH level, detoxification and positive thinking. The environment to which the cell is exposed to determines the health of it, and what it becomes.

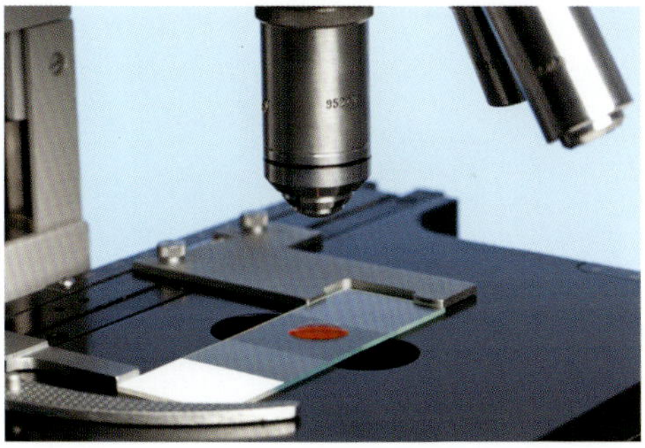

As a qualified advanced cellular microscopist I have observed thousands of live blood samples, I only need to look at the blood through my microscope and even without seeing the person can give you an exceptionally accurate description on how that person is feeling. A great example that I can use here is one of a natural female bodybuilder who I used to consult for. When I looked at her bloods in December of 2012 I knew that she was not following my nutrition and supplement plan as her blood cells looked very sick and tired and that's exactly how she was feeling. After I read her the riot act and told her to stick to my way or hit the highway, within 8 weeks I looked at her bloods (in front of a live audience) and it was a total transformation. As she explained to the audience, not only did she feel incredible but her training had gone up to a completely different level and the results followed.

"The truth could not be hidden...one prick of my finger and all was revealed. My blood was in a bad way. People don't realize what this means.... your blood is your river and transport network therefore if this is not in order then the network its delivering to will not be nourished with what's needed to not only build muscle but also to repair from the stress we put our body under through everyday life and training.

It was at this point I was saved by the man himself, Phil Richards, and the results have been phenomenal from the training programs Phil Richards has guided me. 3 main things that there's no denying have made significant improvements over the last 6 weeks....

1) A thorough Phil Richards Health Supplement plan
2) A clean diet with ZERO protein shakes and just 1 coffee a day and
3) Excellent training programs from Phil with great variety to combat the law of 'accommodation'....

If you want to get strong, lean, muscular & healthy you better listen to Phil Richards common sense approach with no BS."

Nina Ross (Natural Bodybuilder, and a great Mum & Teacher)

Placebo Healing Through Belief

A remarkable phenomenon in which a placebo - a fake treatment, an inactive substance like sugar, distilled water, or saline solution - can sometimes improve a patient's condition simply because the person has the expectation that it will be helpful. Expectation too, plays a potent role in the placebo effect. The more a person believes they are going to benefit from a treatment, the more likely it is that they will experience a benefit.

As many as one in three patients reported feeling better after receiving a drug that has no active ingredients. For decades, these findings were dismissed as purely psychological. Now new research indicates that placebos can cause real biological changes, a finding that is transforming how medicine is practiced. While treating wounded American soldiers during World War II, Henry Beecher ran out of pain-killing morphine. Desperate, he decided to continue telling the soldiers that he was giving them morphine, although he was actually infusing them with a saline solution. Amazingly, 40% of the soldiers reported that the saline treatment eased their pain. Today, scientists better understand why those soldiers felt better. Beecher gave the soldiers a placebo.

Exactly how placebos work to relieve pain and other symptoms remains a mystery, but neuroscientists have uncovered several important clues. They have learned that placebos help the brain release natural chemicals and change brain activity in ways that mimic the effects of real drugs and treatments.

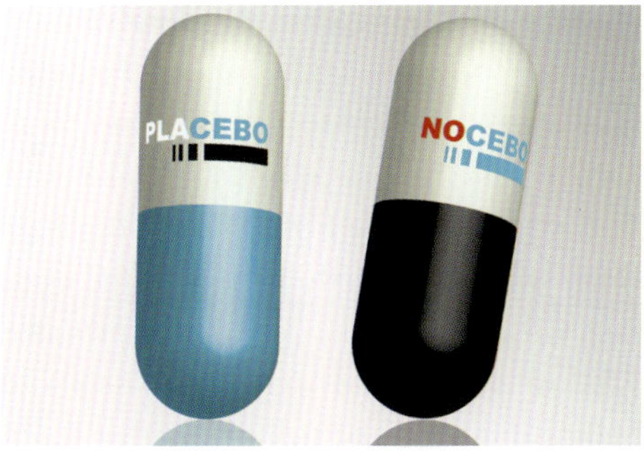

Placebo - the power of belief. Nocebo - the power of disbelief.

Dr. Bruce Mosely, an orthopaedic surgeon and renown for the surgeries he performed on people with debilitating knee pain, designed a study to prove how effective his knee surgery was. The patients in one group of the study got Dr. Moseley's famous surgery. The other group of patients underwent sham surgery, during which the patient was sedated, three incisions were made in the same location as the real surgery, and the patient was shown a pre-recorded tape of someone else's surgery on the video monitor. Dr. Mosely even splashed water around to mimic the sound of the lavage procedure. Then he sewed the knee back up. As expected, one third of the patients getting the real surgery experienced resolution of their knee pain. But what really shocked the researchers was that those getting the sham surgery had the same result! In fact, at one point in the study, those getting the sham surgery were actually having less knee pain than those getting the real surgery, probably because they hadn't undergone the trauma of the surgery. What did Dr Moseley's patients think about the study results? As one World War 2 veteran who benefited from Dr. Moseley's placebo knee surgery said, "The surgery was two years ago and the knee has never bothered me since. It's just like my other knee now."

In another example, a serious skin disease called congenital ichthyosiform erythrodermia results in a hardening and blackening of the skin. A 16 year old boy was seen with this incurable skin condition by Hypnotist Dr. Mason who offered mental imagery to relax him and help him learn to see his skin normal. In 10 days the skin had returned to normal and the results were published in the British Medical Journal and were later verified by other medical researchers.

In "Love, medicine and miracles", Dr. Bernie Siegel cites one study showing that patients in a control group for a new chemotherapy drug were given nothing but saline, yet they were warned it could be chemotherapy - 30% of them lost their hair. In another study, hospitalized patients were given sugar water and told it would make them throw up – 80% of them vomited.

The Nocebo: Negative Beliefs That Can Make You Sick!

Ten years ago, researchers stumbled onto a striking finding: Women who believed that they were prone to heart disease were nearly four times as likely to die as women with similar risk factors who didn't hold such fatalistic views. The higher risk of death, in other words, had nothing to with the usual heart disease culprits – age, blood pressure, CRP, weight. Instead, it tracked closely with belief. Think sick, be sick. In another study, a group of people with asthma breathed in a vapour that researchers told them was a chemical irritant or allergen. Nearly half of the patients experienced breathing problems, with a dozen developing full blown asthma attacks. They were treated with a substance they believed to be a bronchial dilation medicine, and they recovered immediately. In actuality, both the irritant and the medicine were a nebulised (reduced to affine spray) saltwater solution. In these studies it was simply the person's belief on what the outcome would be that led to the result but it also proves the point that your beliefs can change your physiology.

> ***"What you think means more than anything else in your life. More than what you earn, more than where you live, more than your social position, and more than what anyone else may think about you."***
>
> **George Matthew Adams (Author)**

"Be like water making its way through cracks. Do not be assertive, but adjust to the object, and you shall find a way around or through it. If nothing within you stays rigid, outward things will disclose themselves. Empty your mind, be formless. Shapeless, like water. If you put water into a cup, it becomes the cup. You put water into a bottle and it becomes the bottle. You put it in a teapot, it becomes the teapot. Now, water can flow or it can crash. Be water, my friend."

Bruce Lee

The power of visualisation

You must start visualising with true belief who you want to be and how you want to look. If you keep seeing yourself as an overweight person with no energy and low self - esteem you will keep getting that result. Start seeing yourself as lean, happy, vibrant, enthusiastic, intelligent and you know what your body will respond to those thoughts. Let's look at some incredible stories on visualisation.

Visualisation or mental practice can get you closer to where you want to be in life, and it can prepare you for success. For instance, Natan Sharansky, a computer specialist who spent 9 years in prison in the USSR after being accused of spying for US has a lot of experience with mental practices. While in solitary confinement, he played himself in mental chess, saying: "I might as well use the opportunity to become the world champion!" Remarkably, in 1996, Sharansky beat world champion chess player Garry Kasparov!

A study looking at brain patterns in weightlifters found that the patterns activated when a weightlifter lifted hundreds of pounds were similarly activated when they only imagined lifting. In some cases, research has revealed that mental practices are almost effective as true physical practice, and that doing both is more effective than either alone. For instance, in a study at everyday people, Guang Yue, an exercise psychologist from Cleveland Clinic Foundation in Ohio, compared "people who went to the gym with people who carried out virtual workouts in their heads". He found that a 30% muscle increase in the group who went to the gym. However, the group of participants who conducted mental exercises of the weight training increased muscle strength by almost half as much (13.5%). This average remained for 3 months following the mental training.

Brain studies now reveal that thoughts produce the same mental instructions as actions. Mental imagery impacts many cognitive processes in the brain: motor control, attention, perception, planning, and memory. So the brain is getting trained for actual performance during visualization. It's been found that mental practices can enhance motivation, increase confidence and self-efficacy, improve motor performance, prime your brain for success, and increase states of flow – all relevant to achieving your best life!

Remarkably, science has also demonstrated that your brain cannot tell the difference between a visualized image and reality. A Harvard study taught two groups a simple 5-fingered piano melody; one group physically practiced the melody for 2 hours a day over 5 days. The other group merely visualized playing the melody. As you can probably guess, the new neurological wiring that took place were almost identical between the two groups. So it is absolutely essential that you visualise what you want to look and feel like with 100% conviction and belief and start rewiring your brain for success and not failure.

'The power of visualization'

Let go of your stresses

A psychologist walked around a room while teaching stress management to an audience. As she raised a glass of water, everyone expected they'd be asked the "half empty or half full" question. Instead, with a smile on her face, she inquired: "How heavy is this glass of water?"

Answers called out ranged from 8 oz. to 20 oz.

She replied, "The absolute weight doesn't matter. It depends on how long I hold it. If I hold it for a minute, it's not a problem. If I hold it for an hour, I'll have an ache in my arm. If I hold it for a day, my arm will feel numb and paralyzed. In each case, the weight of the glass doesn't change, but the longer I hold it, the heavier it becomes." She continued, "The stresses and worries in life are like that glass of water. Think about them for a while and nothing happens. Think about them a bit longer and they begin to hurt. And if you think about them all day long, you will feel paralyzed – incapable of doing anything."

> ***"You've gotta dance like there's nobody watching, Love like you'll never be hurt, Sing like there's nobody listening, And live like it's heaven on earth."***
>
> **William W. Purkey**

It's important to remember to let go of your stresses. As early in the evening as you can, put all your burdens down. Don't carry them through the evening and into the night. Remember to put the glass down!

Gratitude is so important for you to lead a very rich and productive life and to be able to get what you want. When you keep complaining about everything then things usually get worse for you as you are signalling that you don't deserve anything. So, usually, you don't get anything and then you get more discontent and things just get worse.

Practice gratitude with everything you have in your life, for we truly have a gift and it's called life. Please use your gift wisely for not only yourself but for all living creatures. My life hasn't been the same since I stopped moaning, groaning and complaining and simply realised that this was strangling my life. Instead, at every opportunity I get, I practice gratitude with genuine enthusiasm so much so that the first thing I do when I get out of bed is to be grateful for another day. Please do not underestimate what I'm saying here and think it is a bit fluffy because trust me gratitude delivers results better than any drug ever could.

Dr. Victor Frankl's Story

Dr. Victor Frankl was a psychiatrist and a jew. The Nazis imprisoned him in the death camps during World War 2 in Germany where he experienced things so repugnant that he could scarcely reduce them to words. Frankl's parents, brother, and wife died in the camps or were murdered in the gas ovens. Of his immediate family, only his sister survived the camps. Frankl himself suffered torture and innumerable indignities, never knowing from one moment to the next if his captors would send him to the ovens or leave him among those who were left with the task of removing bodies or shoveling out the ashes of those who had been cremated while they were sill ALIVE.

One day, naked and alone in a small room, Frankl began to become aware of what he later called the "last of the human freedoms" - to choose one's attitude in any given set of circumstances, to choose one's own way. Frankl openly acknowledged that the Nazi captors could control his entire environment and do what they wanted with his body. They could not however destroy his inner identity. Frankl came face to face with the reality that his own choices, not his circumstances, defined his identity. No matter how horrifying the environment in which he lived, and no matter how much humiliation and degradation others heaped on him, he was still in control of how he choose to respond. And the same is true for each one of us.

Wild Bill Cody

This article was taken from the book 'Return from Tomorrow' by George G. Ritchie It is a true story of events in Dr. Ritchie's life while in the army during WWII, as recounted by himself.

"I was part of a group assigned to a concentration camp near Wuppertal, charged with getting medical help to the newly liberated prisoners, many of them Jews from Holland, France, and Eastern Europe. This was the most shattering experience I had yet had; I had been exposed many times by then to sudden death and injury, but to see the effects of slow starvation, to walk through those barracks where thousands of men had died a little bit at a time over a period of years, was a new kind of horror. For many it was an irreversible process: we lost scores each day in spite of all the medicine and food we could rush to them.

Now I needed my new insight indeed. When the ugliness became too great to handle I did what I had learned to do. I went from one end to the other of that barbed wire enclosure looking into men's faces until I saw looking back at me the face of Christ.

And that's how I came to know Wild Bill Cody. That wasn't his real name. His real name was seven unpronounceable syllables in Polish, but he had long drooping handlebar mustaches like pictures of the old western hero, so the American soldiers called him Wild Bill. He was one the inmates of the concentration camp, but obviously he hadn't been there long: his posture was erect, his eyes bright, his energy indefatigable. Since he was fluent in English, French, German, and Russian, as well as Polish, he became a kind of unofficial camp translator.

We came to him with all sorts of problems; the paper work alone was staggering in attempting to relocate people whose families, even whole hometowns, might have disappeared. But though Wild Bill worked fifteen and sixteen hours a day, he showed no signs of weariness. While the rest of us were drooping with fatigue, he seemed to gain strength. "We have time for this old fellow," he'd say. "He's been waiting to see us all day." His compassion for his fellow-prisoners glowed on his face, and it was to this glow that I came when my own spirits were low.

So I was astonished to learn when Wild Bill's own papers came before us one day, that he had been in Wuppertal since 1939! For six years he had lived on the same starvation diet, slept in the same airless and disease-ridden barracks as everyone else, but without the least physical or mental deterioration.

Perhaps even more amazing, every group in the camp looked on him as a friend. He was the one to whom quarrels between inmates were brought for arbitration. Only after I'd been at Wuppertal a number of weeks did I realize what a rarity this was in a compound where the different nationalities of prisoners hated each other almost as much as they did the Germans.

As for Germans, feeling against them ran so high that in some of the camps liberated earlier, former prisoners had seized guns, run into the nearest village and simply shot the first Germans they saw. Part of our instructions were to prevent this kind of thing and again Wild Bill Was our greatest asset, reasoning with the different groups, counselling forgiveness.

"It's not easy for some of them to forgive," I commented to him one day as we sat over mugs of tea in the processing center. "So many of them have lost members of their families." Wild Bill leaned back in the upright chair and sipped at his drink. "We lived in the Jewish section of Warsaw," he began slowly, the first words I had heard him speak about himself, "my wife, our two daughters, and our three little boys.

When the Germans reached our street they lined everyone against a wall and opened up with machine guns. I begged to be allowed to die with my family, but because I spoke German they put me in a work group."

He paused, perhaps seeing again his wife and five children. "I had to decide right then," he continued, "whether to let myself hate the soldiers who had done this. It was an easy decision, really. I was a lawyer. In my practice I had seen too often what hate could do to people's minds and bodies. Hate had just killed the six people who mattered most to me in the world. I decided then that I would spend the rest of my life... whether it was a few days or many years... loving every person I came in contact with."

Now if these stories doesn't teach you to forgive and move on with your life then nothing will.

> ***"Nothing can stop the man with the right mental attitude from achieving his goal; nothing on earth can help the man with the wrong mental attitude."***
>
> **Thomas Jefferson**

Build The Right Team Around You

If there was one thing that ten years in professional rugby taught me it was that it only takes one negative player or coach to affect the whole team. I was very fortunate to have worked with some great teams and won multiple league titles and cup finals. On the flip side I have been with teams where one member of the coaching team has brought the team to it's knees because of his negative/toxic attitude. Surround yourself with the right people and success happens automatically!

The next time you see geese heading south for the winter, flying along in a "V" formation, you might be interested in knowing what science has discovered about why they fly that way. It has been learned, that as each bird flaps its wings, it creates an "uplift " for the bird immediately following. By flying in a V" formation, the whole flock adds at least 71% greater flying range than if each bird flew on its own, so they can get where they are going quicker and easier, because they are traveling on the thrust of one another. When a goose falls out of formation, it suddenly feels the draft and resistance of trying to go it alone, and quickly gets into formation to take advantage of the lifting power of the bird immediately in front. The geese honk from behind to encourage those up front to keep up their speed. Finally, when one goose gets sick, or is wounded by a gunshot and falls out, two geese fall out of formation and follow him until he is able to fly, or until he is dead, then they launch out on their own, or with another formation to catch up with the group. The geese teach us an incredible lesson, surround yourself by people who will work as hard as you will, and with the same goals, and results will follow. This proves the acronym of T.E.A.M. (Together Everyone Achieves More).

Geese can teach us a lot about team work!

Goal setting

With no goal you'll never hit the target.

Set goals which challenge you but are reachable with the right training, nutrition, mind set and recovery. You will be absolutely amazed what you are capable of and you will soon realise that most of your limits are simply in your head. If your motivation to lose fat and get in great shape is not strong then you have little hope of seeing any results from the information presented in this book or your efforts in your training program. So stop procrastinating as time is like health, once it's gone so are you. Set a goal and go for it. Don't be one of those nauseating people you meet at a dinner party or on a night out and they start the sentence with "I could have been", no be the inspirational person that starts the sentence with "Yes I did".

Winners make things happen, losers let things happen remember that!

> ***"There is no passion to be found playing small in settling for a life that is less than the one you are capable of living."***
>
> **Nelson Mandela**

Inspirational Stories

Terry Fox was determined not to let cancer bring him down and to raise awareness for it's research. Terry Fox was born in Winnipeg, Manitoba on July 28th, 1958. At age 18 Terry was diagnosed with bone cancer and had his right leg amputated six inches above his knee. Determined not to let this stop him he went on to win three national championships in wheelchair basketball. During his cancer treatment Terry witnessed a lot of suffering especially amongst children, he decided to do something to help. On April 12th, 1980 he started his Marathon of Hope in St John Newfoundland to raise awareness for cancer research. He ran 26 miles every day 7 days a week for 143 days. He was forced to stop because of returning cancer in his lungs. He had stopped in Thunder Bay in 1980 and he asked to be brought to a hospital. On June 28th 1981 Terry lost his battle with cancer one month before his 23rd birthday.

Sean Swarner was the first cancer survivor to complete the 7-summits, the highest peaks of the 7 continents. The 29,035-foot giant known as Mount Everest tortures its challengers with life-threatening conditions such as 100 mph winds, the dramatic loss of oxygen, snowstorms, and deadly avalanches. Climbers of Everest are faced with incredible dangers, but for Sean Swarner the obstacles he overcame prior to his summiting make his story even more compelling. Sean isn't just a cancer survivor; he is truly a medical marvel. He is the only person in the world ever to have been diagnosed with both Hodgkin's disease and Askin's sarcoma. He was diagnosed in the fourth and final stage of Hodgkin's disease at the age of thirteen, when doctors expected him to live for no more than three months. He overcame his illness only to be stricken a second time when a deadly golf ball-sized tumor attacked his right lung. After removal of the Askin's tumor, Sean was expected to live for less than two weeks. A decade later and with only partial use of his lungs, Sean became famous for being the first cancer survivor to climb Mount Everest.

After the summit of Everest, Sean had the desire and dream to continue moving forward and reaching people around the world. Climbing the highest mountain on each continent became his next goal. Proving to others that anything is possible, Sean successfully summited Mt. McKinley, to be the first cancer survivor to complete the seven summits. You can read more about Swarner's story on his 2007 book. 'Keep Climbing: How I Beat Cancer and Reached the Top of the World'

When Wilma Rudolph was four years old, she had a disease called polio which causes people to be crippled and unable to walk. To make matters worse, her family was poor and could not afford good medical care. She was from a large family. She was the 20th child of 22 children. Her father was a railroad porter and her mother was a maid. Her mother decided she would do everything she could to help Wilma to walk again. The doctors had said she would not be able to walk. She took her every week on a long bus trip to a hospital to receive therapy. It didn't help, but the doctors said she needed to give Wilma a massage every day by rubbing her legs. She taught the brothers and sisters how to do it, and they also rubbed her legs four times a day. By the time she was 8, she could walk with a leg brace. After that, she used a high-topped shoe to support her foot. She played basketball with her brothers every day. Three years later, her mother came home to find her playing basketball by herself bare-footed. She didn't even have to use the special shoe.

A track coach encouraged her to start running. She ran so well that during her senior year in high school, she qualified for the 1956 Olympics in Melbourne, Australia. She won a bronze medal in the women's 400-meter relay. In 1959, she qualified for the 1960 Olympic Games in Rome by setting a world's record in the 200-meter race. At the Olympics that year she won two gold medals; one for the 100-meter race and one for the 200-meter race. Then she sprained her ankle, but she ignored the pain and helped her team to win another gold medal for the 400-meter relay! She retired from running when she was 22 years old, but she went on to coach women's track teams and encourage young people. Wilma thought God had a greater purpose for her than to win three gold medals. She started the Wilma Rudolph Foundation to help children learn about discipline and hard work. She died of brain cancer in 1994. Even though she is no longer alive, her influence still lives on in the lives of many young people who look up to her.

So next time you are looking for excuses not to train, eat correctly or feeling sorry for yourself remind yourself of these inspirational stories and move on.

> ***"If you can't fly then run, if you can't run then walk, if you can't walk then crawl, but whatever you do you have to keep moving forward."***
>
> **Martin Luther King Jr.**

The Important Things In Life

A philosophy professor stood before his class with some items on the table in front of him. When the class began, wordlessly he picked up a very large and empty mayonnaise jar and proceeded to fill it with rocks, about 2 inches in diameter.

He then asked the students if the jar was full. They agreed that it was.

So the professor then picked up a box of pebbles and poured them into the jar. He shook the jar lightly. The pebbles, of course, rolled into the open areas between the rocks.

He then asked the students again if the jar was full. They agreed it was.

The professor picked up a box of sand and poured it into the jar. Of course, the sand filled up the remaining open areas of the jar.

He then asked once more if the jar was full. The students responded with a unanimous "Yes."

"Now," said the professor, "I want you to recognize that this jar represents your life. The rocks are the important things – your family, your partner, your health, your children – things that if everything else was lost and only they remained, your life would still be full. The pebbles are the other things that matter – like your job, your house, your car. The sand is everything else, the small stuff."

"If you put the sand into the jar first," he continued, "there is no room for the pebbles or the rocks. The same goes for your life. If you spend all your time and energy on the small stuff, you will never have room for the things that are important to you. Pay attention to the things that are critical to your happiness. Play with your children. Take your partner out dancing. There will always be time to go to work, clean the house, give a dinner party, or fix the disposal."

"Take care of the rocks first – the things that really matter. Set your priorities. The rest is just sand."

5 Biggest Regrets of People on their Deathbeds

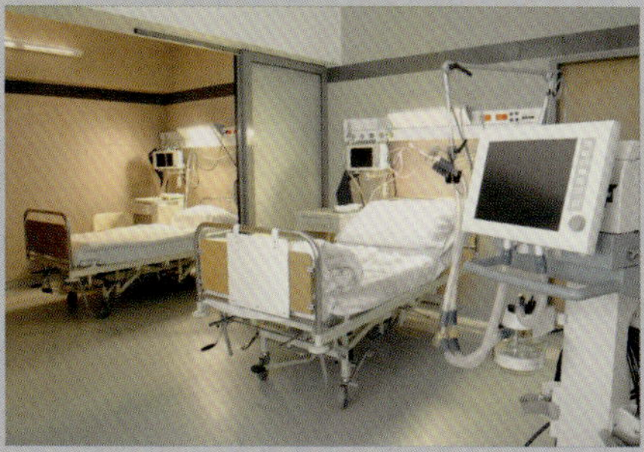

When one is faced with imminent death, there are always the expected regrets as to how one has lived life. A nurse by the name of Bronnie Ware, who worked for many years in palliative care, composed a list of the five largest regrets that people have on their deathbeds. "Some incredibly special times were shared," Ware said. "I was with them for the last three to twelve weeks of their lives."

1) **I wish I'd had the courage to live a life true to myself, not the life others expected of me.**

"When people realize that their life is almost over and look back clearly on it, it is easy to see how many dreams have gone unfulfilled. Most people had not honored even a half of their dreams and had to die knowing that it was due to choices they had made, or not made," Ware says.

2) **I wish I didn't work so hard.**
"This came from every male patient that I nursed. They missed their children's youth and their partner's companionship . All of the men I nursed deeply regretted spending so much of their lives on the treadmill of a work existence."

3) **I wish I'd had the courage to express my feelings.**
"Many people suppressed their feelings in order to keep peace with others. As a result, they settled for a mediocre existence and never became who they were truly capable of becoming. Many developed illnesses relating to the bitterness and resentment they carried as a result," Ware warns.

4) **I wish I had stayed in touch with my friends.**
"Often they would not truly realize the full benefits of old friends until their dying weeks and it was not always possible to track them down. Many had become so caught up in their own lives that they had let golden friendships slip by over the years. There were many deep regrets about not giving friendships the time and effort that they deserved. Everyone misses their friends when they are dying."

5) **I wish that I had let myself be happier.**
"This is a surprisingly common one. Many did not realize until the end that happiness is a choice. They had stayed stuck in old patterns and habits. The so-called 'comfort' of familiarity overflowed into their emotions, as well as their physical lives. Fear of change had them pretending to others, and to their selves, that they were content. When deep within, they longed to laugh properly and have silliness in their life again."

So I hope this chapter has given you some inspiration and also made it perfectly clear to you that it is essential to commit to being healthy, getting fit and dropping excess body fat. If you fall off the plan dust yourself down and get back on the plan, we all make mistakes but only fools keep repeating them. You are about to read probably the most advanced book ever written on fat loss, don't panic it's written in simple-to-understand language and I have included plenty of informative pictures and plans so you fully understand it. Read 1 habit at a time, apply what you learn, then move to the next habit.

"Promise Yourself"

To be so strong that nothing can disturb your peace of mind.
To talk health, happiness, and prosperity to every person you meet.
To make all your friends feel that there is something in them
To look at the sunny side of everything and make your optimism come true.
To think only the best, to work only for the best, and to expect only the best.
To be just as enthusiastic about the success of
others as you are about your own.
To forget the mistakes of the past and press on to
the greater achievements of the future.
To wear a cheerful countenance at all times and give
every living creature you meet a smile.
To give so much time to the improvement of yourself
that you have no time to criticize others.
To be too large for worry, too noble for anger, too strong for
fear, and too happy to permit the presence of trouble.
To think well of yourself and to proclaim this fact to
the world, not in loud words but great deeds.
To live in faith that the whole world is on your side so
long as you are true to the best that is in you."

– Christian D. Larson

HABIT 1

THE FURTHER WE MOVE AWAY FROM THE NATURE, THE FATTER WE BECOME

"If people let the government decide what foods they eat and what medicines they take, their bodies will soon be in as sorry a state as are the souls of those who live under tyranny."

Thomas Jefferson

There are many, many causes of obesity and illness that are a result of our modern way of life. From our unnatural, processed foods to our drinking water, cookware and cosmetic products. The more we can move back towards a natural way of life, the easier it will become to be lean and healthy.

- *how far have we moved from nature*
- *how we can feed our genes*
- *the biggest source of toxicity in the Western World*

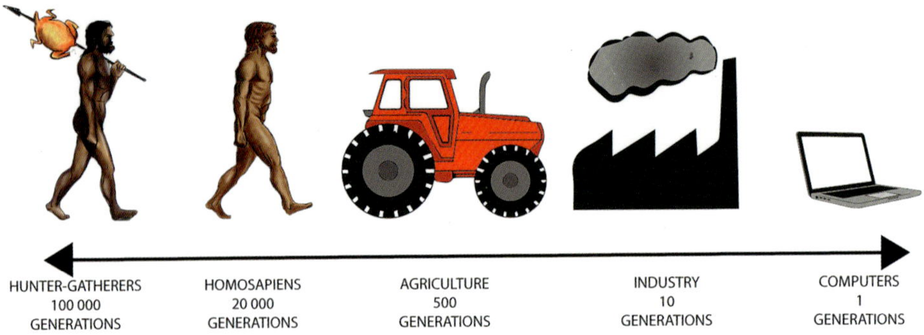

Our genetic constitution has changed little in 10,000 years its make-up evolved from biological processes eons earlier. Proto-humans evolved about 5 million years ago, began using stone tools 2 million years ago, and ate meat.

In this Habit let's look at the multiple ways in which our toxic world is making us sicker, fatter, dumber and more exhausted.

You Must Take Full Responsibility For Your Health!

What we must ask ourselves today is why obesity has skyrocketed so much in such a small amount of time. UK obesity levels were remarkably constant and small for decades. Indeed, throughout the tens of thousands of years before the 1966 data, there is no record of an obesity problem, let alone an epidemic. Can you imagine obese hunter gatherers trying to hunt their prey 10,000 years ago? Suddenly, in evolutionary terms, and dramatically, in amounts, obesity levels increased from 2-3% in the 1970's to today where two thirds of UK citizens are now overweight or obese.

Our ancestors had to be exceptionally fit and healthy to simply survive

Today, in the UK, it has been estimated that over 30% of children are overweight or obese. The real tragedy is that our children are being programmed to be fat even from gestation, as you will read later in this chapter. The information presented in this habit though will allow parents to make much more educated choices for their children and not having to rely on the misinformed medical and government officials, who are usually guided by the food and pharmaceutical industry and not the health of them or their children.

The sad truth today is that the more research I do on how to get healthy and lean in the 21st century, the more I realise that there are so many organisations that profit from sick, tired and overweight people. Why? There is no money to be made by big pharma by having a society of healthy, vibrant people; it really is that simple, cynical, but unfortunately true. And big pharma has a huge influence on what doctors prescribe. After all when was the last time your doctor prescribed clean organic foods, clean water, sunshine and fresh air? This is not an attack on doctors as there are plenty of caring doctors, but they usually just prescribe drugs and that is not the answer.

And the giant food companies need you to become addicted to their junk food by lacing them with sugar, salt, fat which we are genetically designed to become addicted to these foods. During our evolution these foods gave you the most calories which was essential to survival and the food companies know this. They also add a plethora of artificial ingredients like monosodium glutamate which are all exceptionally addictive substances to humans and make us sick and fat.

Are we becoming addicted to junk food?

If you are living in the Western World, look around you and try to spot lean healthy people who are full of energy. And, if you are lean and full of energy then those people who eat crap and take no exercise presume you must be on something like steroids. Yes lean, energetic people are usually on something; it's called energy from clean foods, drinking clean water, lots of positive thinking, sunshine and taking plenty of vigorous exercise which humans are designed for. So get off your couch potato ass, stop eating crap, and exercise, and you too could become lean and healthy.

We are always being told that we are living longer today than we have ever lived before. That is total nonsense. This is statistics to try and make our disastrous health care system look as if it's doing a great job when in reality it's doing an appalling job in the majority of cases. Humans are genetically programmed to live for up to 120-140 years old, depending on which research you read, and have been for thousands of generations. On average we do live longer, statistically, than our ancestors but only because we don't have the dangers that our ancestors had like childhood mortility, accidents, infections and famines etc. But are we healthier? I very much doubt it and the research clearly shows this.

Ask yourself this question; if we are healthier now than at any other time in human history, why can't you get a car parking spot in any hospital in the UK during the day or you have to wait months for operations etc. Why is your local GP surgery usually packed every morning Monday to Friday with sick people?

Why are we dying on mass from cancer, heart disease & brain diseases in our millions? Remember, you don't catch these diseases, we build them from within when our internal environment becomes polluted from the army of toxins we are exposed to every day from our food, water and environment and we also become overfed and malnourished due to the quality of food most people eat.

Remember this, the more deficient your food is in essential nutrients, the more food you will crave and the hungrier you will become, consuming more food than you really need looking for those essential nutrients. The ironic thing today in affluent societies, even though we have an abundance of food sources, we are usually malnourished due to eating too much processed food sources and this is another way we become sick, tired and obese. At every opportunity you get, choose certified organic fresh foods, it's not only good for your health but also your waistline!

How do you keep a wild animal healthy?

Say that you're a zookeeper in a zoo, and your job is to keep the animals happy and healthy - what would you do? Put them all in the same pen and feed them all dog chow?

No. You would replicate each animal's natural habitat as closely as possible, and feed them the diet that they would naturally eat in the wild. Feed raw meat to the lions, rodents to the snakes, and bamboo to the pandas. Give the monkeys trees to climb and give the birds space to fly. Make the penguin house cold, and the reptile house hot. Animals thrive in their natural habitat. They are healthier, often live longer, and fall sick less frequently. And the same general principle applies to human beings: to be happy and healthy, we should eat, move, and live in ways that resemble our ancestral habitat.

Re-creating the natural human habitat

But what is the natural human habitat? For most of human history on this earth, humans lived as hunter-gatherers in the wild. Wild humans, living in the wild. And we were good at it. We survived on flat grassy savannahs and on the sides of steep mountains, in parched deserts and in drenched rain forests, next to the sea and far inland, on the hot equator and in the eternal winter of the Arctic.

A picture tells the story!

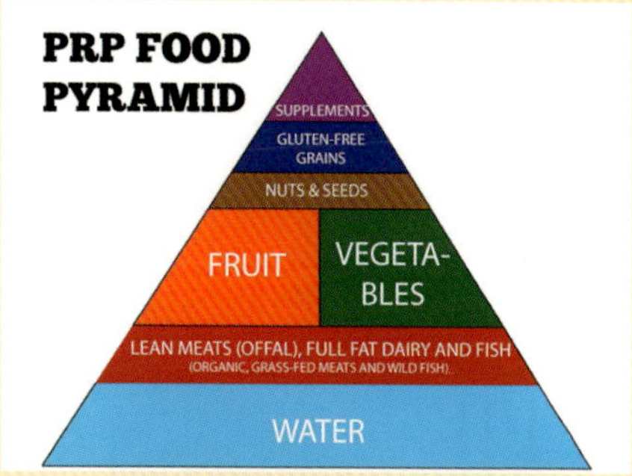

The diet of our Paleolithic ancestors was one that was made up of fresh, in-season, organic foods. It did not come in a packet and it was not produced in a factory. You must find the right ratios of food from the pyramid to suit your metabolic type. Some get lean on higher carbs, some on higher amounts of protein. Compare this to the recommended food plate (on the next page).

We accomplished all this without the help of domesticated plants and animals — just using language, primitive tools, and teamwork. But ten thousand years ago, we started to tame the wilderness: the Agricultural Revolution begun. The Agricultural Revolution ushered in a new set of foods into the human diet that previously had no place. We domesticated wild grains, turning them into wheat, corn, and rice. We domesticated wolves into loyal companions, and bred wild animals and raised them for their meat and milk. And at the same time that human civilization began to flourish, individual human health began to worsen.

Then approximately 200 years ago the industrial revolution which increased our ability to mass produce foods like sugar, flour and cereals emerged and this unfortunately increased obesity and disease.

The diet that made us human is the one that will keep us human. That diet was rich in fruits, vegetables, nuts, high quality animal protein, especially offal & fish. You will not see a fat hunter gatherer today or undoubtedly in our history so it would be wise to follow similar traits to them to understand that this is the optimum exercise & diet for health and fat loss. Remember we are still genetically hunter gatherers and we are meant to be active and eat the way mother nature wants us to! So stop blaming your genes if you are overweight and start blaming the junk you are putting down your throat and the lack of activity which is required to burn fat & build muscle.

The recommended "eatwell food plate". Follow this advice and most people will become obese due to excess carbohydrate intake.

There are races of people who are all slim, who are stronger and faster than us who have continued the diet of their ancestors. They all have straight teeth and perfect eyesight. Obesity is very rare amongst these people. From the research by Western-Price, it was confirmed that when people moved away from their natural diet, health deteriorated very quickly.

Weston-Price was a dentist in the early 20th Century who published a book titled "Nutrition and Physical Degeneration". In the book he described his global travels, which he spent studying the diets and nutrition of various cultures. The book concluded that aspects of a modern Western diet (such as flour, sugar, and modern processed vegetable fats) cause nutritional deficiencies that are a cause of many dental issues and health problems.

These people live by nature's rules and nourish themselves with unadulterated foods and drink clean water. They get natural sunlight, are grounded (have a close connection with the earth through barefoot walking) and are not swimming in electro magnetic frequencies. They live as close-knit communities that care for each other - the strong help the weak. Compare this to the westernised world of today where its dog eat dog mentality.

99% of our genetic heritage dates back to before the appearance of humankind. Only 1% of our biological makeup has appeared since human and great ape lines separated some four million years ago. The point is to reflect upon how little an opportunity there has been to for our body's to adapt to the age of agriculture and our present junk food, toxic diet. Looking at the scene of human nutrition from this perspective, it is obvious that, throughout human evolution, man relied on wild foods with a high nutrient ratio compared to today. Our physiology was initially adapted by, and is still adapted to wild, not modern, foods. We spent 99.8% of our existence as a species as hunter-gatherers and in a blink of an eye we are completely living against the way our genes evolved and that means we are in trouble.

What Palaeolithic people did not eat

- Cow's milk, cereal grains (introduced after 10 000 BC)
- Table salt (NaCl)
- White sugar (after 1800)
- Potatoes (after 1750)
- Highly processed foods (mostly after 1800)
- Pesticide residues (after 1930)
- Radioactive foods (after 1945)
- Artificial/synthetic additives (mostly after 1950)
- Vegetable oils
- Sugared drinks
- Alcoholic Beverages
- Processed Foods
- High Fructose Corn Syrup
- Medications

So when you study the diet that we evolved on for thousands of generations, where we had no obesity crisis, you realise it would be wise to follow the eating habits of our ancestors. If you want to be really smart you would eat according to what we ate pre-agriculture, which was around 3000-10,000 years depending on where you lived.

The data showing that our paleolithic diet is far healthier for us than our modern westernised diet comes from archaeological studies of ancient skeletons. Studies tell us that the Paleolithic humans were in remarkably good health. Paleolithic humans were tall and slender; cavities and signs of malnutrition or stress in bones were rare, muscle attachments were strong.

Cambridge University experts say that humans are past their peak and that modern-day people are 10% smaller and shorter than their hunter-gatherer ancestors. And if that's not depressing enough, our brains are also 10% smaller. You only have to listen to a politician waffle for ten minutes to confirm this. These findings reverse perceived wisdom that humans have grown taller and larger, a belief which has grown from data on more recent physical development. The decline has happened over the past 10,000 years.

The blame has been put on agriculture, with restricted diets and urbanisation compromising health and leading to the spread of disease. The theory has emerged from studies of fossilised human remains found in Africa, Europe and Asia.

Feed your genes

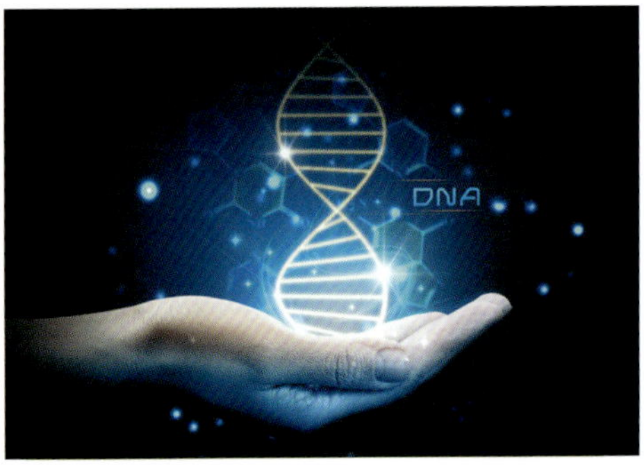

Genes, built from microscopic double-strands of deoxyribonucleic acid (DNA), direct the behaviour of your body's 50 trillion plus cells. They define your body's outward physical features, such as the colour of your eyes and hair, and how tall you are. When your genes work well, they enable you to live with total health and vitality, free of disease. When genes don't work well, they program us to become sick, tired and dysfunctional.

How does all this happen? The information in your genes is written in the chemical language of DNA. The letters in this alphabet are sequences of molecules called nucleotides. Each letter is constructed around one of four substances called DNA bases: adenine (A), cytosine (C), guanine (G), and thymine (T).

Different arrangements of these four nucleotides spell different words, and long strings of DNA (e.g., TACGACCTGA) form the genes that instruct cells to make specific enzymes and proteins. These enzymes, in turn, catalyze a host of other biochemical reactions, and the proteins form the structure of hormones and tissue.

All of this remarkable activity depends on nutrients. The DNA in the protein you eat is broken down and reconstructed into your own distinctive DNA. Vitamins B3 and B6 are needed for thymine synthesis, folic acid for guanine and adenine, and B3 for cytosine. When these nutrients are lacking, DNA cannot be synthesized – and its instructions cannot be carried out.

'We are made up of proteins and our genes make our proteins,' says Tim Spector, professor of genetic epidemiology at King's College London and author of 'Identically Different: Why You Can Change Your Genes'.

Although we can't change the structure of genes it is now possible to change the way our genes work – like with nutrients and positive thinking. Chemicals produced by our body or diet can switch our genes on and off, like a dimmer switch on a light, to produce more or less of these proteins. Food, exercise, toxins, deficiencies, stress and our emotions can all switch genes on or off.

What is DNA?

We all know that elephants only give birth to little elephants, giraffes to giraffes, dogs to dogs and so on for every type of living creature. But why is this so?

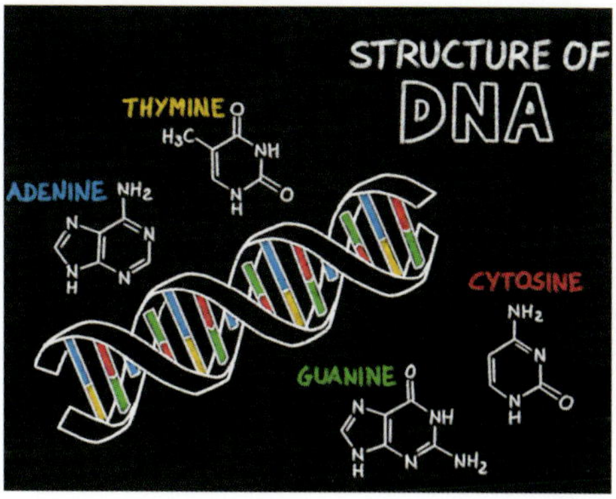

The answer lies in a molecule called deoxyribonucleic acid (DNA), which contains the biological instructions that make each species unique. DNA, along with the instructions it contains, is passed from adult organisms to their offspring during reproduction.

Where is DNA found?

DNA is found inside a special area of the cell called the nucleus. Because the cell is very small, and because organisms have many DNA molecules per cell, each DNA molecule must be tightly packaged. This packaged form of the DNA is called a chromosome.

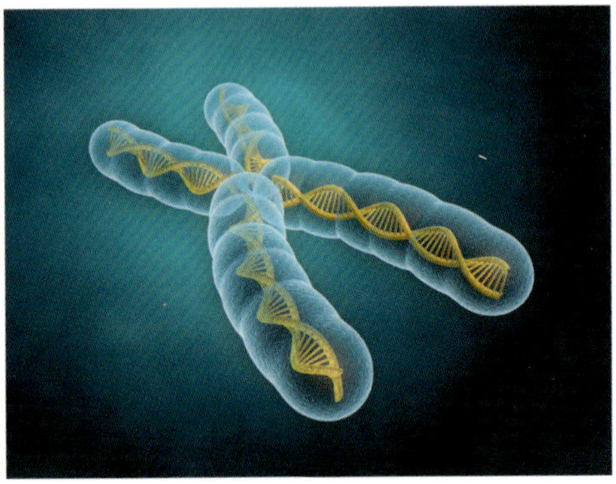

A chromosome

During DNA replication, DNA unwinds so it can be copied. At other times in the cell cycle, DNA also unwinds so that its instructions can be used to make proteins and for other biological processes. But during cell division, DNA is in its compact chromosome form to enable transfer to new cells.

Researchers refer to DNA found in the cell's nucleus as nuclear DNA. An organism's complete set of nuclear DNA is called its genome.

Besides the DNA located in the nucleus, humans and other complex organisms also have a small amount of DNA in cell structures known as mitochondria. Mitochondria generate the energy the cell needs to function properly.

In sexual reproduction, organisms inherit half of their nuclear DNA from the male parent and half from the female parent. However, organisms inherit all of their mitochondrial DNA from the female parent. This occurs because only egg cells, and not sperm cells, keep their mitochondria during fertilization.

What is DNA made of?

DNA is made of chemical building blocks called nucleotides. These building blocks are made of three parts: a phosphate group, a sugar group and one of four types of nitrogen bases. To form a strand of DNA, nucleotides are linked into chains, with the phosphate and sugar groups alternating.

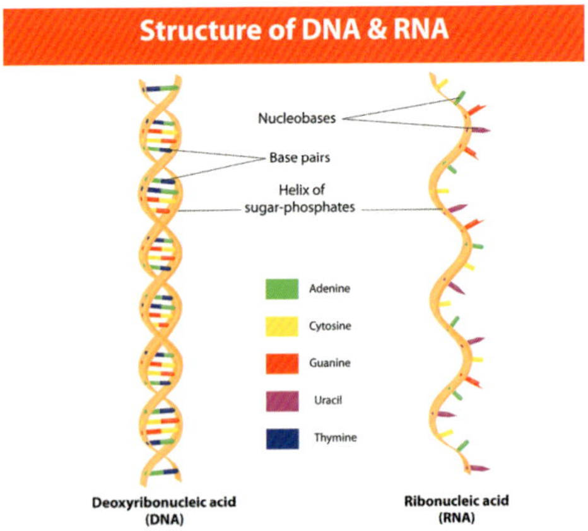

The complete DNA instruction book, or genome, for a human contains about 3 billion bases and about 20,000 genes on 23

pairs of chromosomes. We have literally unlimited ability you just need a purpose to tap into our incredible potential.

Because of the enormous complexity of the human body, organ function, cell structures and instinctive behaviors, it was once believed that humans must possess somewhere around 2 million protein-coding genes. The Human Genome Project was launched in 1990 with the widespread belief that when it was finished, it would "unlock" all the mysteries of the origins of disease in humans. It was also believed that when the human genome fully mapped, scientists would be able to create humans in any form they wanted, including humans with extra arms or legs, humans free of all disease, humans with "enhanced" physical powers, and so on.

At the start of the Human Genome Project, everybody "knew" that humans were far more complex than, say, a roundworm, which only has about 20,000 protein-coding genes. This is why estimates of the number of genes in a human ranged from 100,000 to 2 million. Scientists were absolutely sure that humans were far more complex than a tiny roundworm, and therefore humans needed far more genes.

The first draft of the Human Genome Project was published in the year 2,000. Far from being a breakthrough that would end all human disease, its findings utterly shattered the mythology of genetics as the sole explanation for all inheritance and physical development. Why? Because the Human Genome Project found that humans have only about 20,000 protein-coding genes, roughly the same number as the roundworm.

A human being has about the same number of protein-coding genes as a roundworm? By comparison, the common fruit fly has about 15,000 genes, only marginally less than a human. And yet it is obvious to any intelligent observer than a human being is considerably more complex than a fruit fly and a roundworm.

You've probably heard about how humans share over 98% of their genes with some chimps. It shows just how small differences in DNA can make a huge difference in the way life takes shape. Well, how about this one? We share 50% of our genetic make up with a banana and this could be as high as 100% if you are a politician. Scientists have found this thanks to the Human Genome project, which mapped all the genes in the human body and allowed them to compare our genes with other life forms. Here are some other interesting comparisons: We share 60% of genes with a Fruit Fly, 75% with a mouse and 80% with a cow!

It's interesting to think how little different all living things are. Scientists say that this is because plant and animal life separated about 1.5 billion years ago, and the genes we share are due to our common ancestors.

Epigenetics

Is it "nature" or "nurture" that influences behaviour and health outcomes? Researchers now know these factors are not independent: experience and environment ("nurture") modify genes ("nature") — a phenomenon known as epigenetics.

The environment affects genes, which are present in chromosomes, without changing the genetic code. This process is called epigenetics. "Nature vs. nurture" is often set as a conflict: is it genes or the environment that influences behaviours and health? Decades of research helped scientists learn how the environment has an enormous effect on genes and on subsequent generations — sometimes in ways they never imagined.

During the winter of 1944-45, the German army cut off food supplies to the western part of the Netherlands, resulting in a five-month famine. Decades later, researchers noticed something peculiar in the adult children born to mothers who were in the first trimester of pregnancy during the famine — higher rates of obesity and cardiovascular disease compared with the general population. These findings demonstrated that a mother's diet could influence the health of her offspring.

Experiments in mice show just how important a mother's diet is in shaping the epigenome of her offspring. All mammals have a gene called *agouti*. When a mouse's *agouti* gene is completely unmethylated, its coat is yellow and it is obese and prone to diabetes and cancer. When the agouti gene is methylated (as it is in normal mice), the coat color is brown and the mouse has a low disease risk. Fat yellow mice and skinny brown mice are genetically identical. The fat yellow mice are different because they have an epigenetic "mutation."

When researchers fed pregnant yellow mice a methyl-rich diet, most of her pups were brown and stayed healthy for life. These results show that the environment in the womb influences adult health. In other words, our health is not only determined by what we eat, but also what our parents ate.

Chemicals and additives that enter our bodies can also affect the epigenome. Bisphenol A (BPA) is a compound used to make polycarbonate plastic. It is in many consumer products, including water bottles and tin cans. When pregnant yellow agouti mothers were fed BPA, more yellow, unhealthy babies were born than normal. Exposure to BPA during early development had caused decreased methylation of the agouti gene. However, when BPA-exposed, pregnant yellow mice were fed methyl-rich foods, the offspring were predominantly brown. The maternal nutrient supplementation had counteracted the negative effects of exposure. Depletion of your body's methyl groups is how "bad" genes are expressed.

How are methyl groups in our body depleted? By consuming a poor diet loaded with "white death"—white sugar, white flour, and white salt, "bad oils"—trans-fatty acids and hydrogenated oils, produce loaded with pesticides and herbicides, junk food, drinks loaded with caffeine, high-fructose corn syrup and acid, genetically-modified foods, toxins and stress!

What helps create methyl groups? HCL or stomach acid! This is WHY it is vital for everyone to have the proper amount of stomach acid (HCL)! We create massive amounts of HCL when we are young but as we age, we make less and less. Again, further decreases in stomach acid or HCL are caused by excess stress and a poor diet.

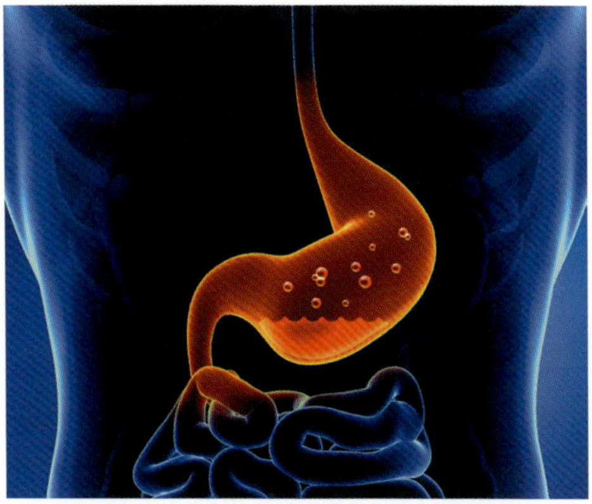

Stomach acid is essential for methyl groups.

Methyl groups are VITAL for normal cell replication at the level of the DNA! They literally turn genes "on" or "off. When you have depleted methyl groups, bad genes like cancer causing oncogenes are turned "on" and good genes, like cancer preventing tumor-suppressor genes, are turned "off.

When you have sufficient methyl groups, good genes, like tumor suppressor genes, are turned "on", and bad genes, like oncogenes, are turned "off.

Methyl groups are also vital for phase II liver detoxification, protein methylation, homocysteine metabolism (increasing the methyl groups decreases inflammation), neurotransmitter synthesis, and nucleic acid synthesis.

Inadequate methylation capacity can lead to birth defects, depression, cognitive decline, diseases and cancer. Impaired methylation has even been associated with autism.

To keep methylation running smoothly you need optimal levels of B vitamins. Without enough B vitamins methylation breaks down, and the results can be catastrophic. A breakdown in methylation also puts you at higher risk for conditions like osteoporosis, diabetes, cervical dysplasia and cancer, colon cancer, lung cancer, depression, pediatric cognitive dysfunction (mood and other behavioral disorders), dementia, and stroke.

Tips to Optimize Your Methylation Process

1) Eat more dark, leafy greens – You want to eat vegetables like bok choy, escarole, Swiss chard, kale, watercress, spinach, or dandelion, mustard, collard, or beet greens. These are among the most abundant sources of the nutrients needed for optimal methylation.
2) Get more Bs in your diet – Good food sources include sunflower seeds and wheat germ (vitamin B6); fish and eggs (vitamin B6 and B12); cheese (B12); beans and walnuts (vitamin B6 and folate); leafy dark green vegetables; asparagus, almonds, and whole grains (folate); and liver (all three).
3) Avoid processed foods and tinned foods – These are depleted in vitamins.
4) Too much animal protein in the diet. Too much methionine in some diets may negatively affect methylation.
5) Inflammation and infections in the body. These seem to use up more methyl groups needed to fight off these threats to life.
6) Metal toxicity, especially copper and mercury. These may interfere with methyl group formation.
7) Avoid caffeine – Excess amounts can deplete your B vitamin levels.
8) Limit alcohol to 3 drinks a week – More than this can deplete your B vitamin levels.
9) Don't smoke – smoking inactivates vitamin B6.
10) Keep the bacteria in your gut healthy – Take probiotic supplements and use other measures to make sure the bacteria in your gut are healthy so you can properly absorb the vitamins you need for methylation.
11) Improve stomach acid – Use supplemental HCl like PRP Super Digestive Enzyme. And take a comprehensive multi vitamin and mineral supplement loaded with B vitamins and ensure that B12 is methylcobalamin and not cynacobalim like PRP's Ultimate Multi Vitamin & Mineral.

Thanks to our genes, our bodies are programmed for taking in excess nutrients and storing them as fat. This ability is what allowed our hunter-gatherer ancestors to survive during times of famine, which were a fact of life for them. Back then, any number of circumstances like a change of season, drought or injury preventing one to hunt could have prevented a ready food supply, so it made good sense in time of plenty to store as much food in the body as fat.

Those humans who made large amounts of insulin (the key fat storing hormone) from their pancreas, and stored a lot of fat efficiently, would not die from starvation during the famine period. They lived to pass on their genetic tendency to make a lot of insulin, store fat and thus "survive." Those who were less good at storing fat starved during the "famine" periods and did not pass on their genes.

So we are a species designed and genetically "selected" to make large amounts of insulin in response to overeating. We have also, at some level, been programmed to the have an ability to override satiety, and overeat massively. Thus, in a world of constant and cheap high caloric food, buffets, etc., humans, now face an obesity crisis. We need to better understand our metabolism, and understand that connecting our brains (satiety and hunger) to our mouth can allow us to control what drives obesity. If we do that we will have some hope of dealing with this personal and societal health care crisis and get back to a population full of lean and healthy people, but you will have to be disciplined to fight against your instinct to eat more than you need because this is encoded in our genes so you must educate yourself (which is what this book is about).

You must remember that the ability to store fat has allowed the human race to survive for millions of years. No system is infallible though and unfortunately today we have an abundance of substances that have been artificially added to our water, food, environment and wash care products etc., which keeps us in fat storage mode. And, it doesn't matter how hard you hit the gym, you will get fatter, or make no improvement, unless you know how to play the fat loss game. It is a completely different game to that of even 50 years ago when there was not as much toxicity as we are exposed to today!

Most of the foods on supermarket shelves were not available even 100 years ago.

It has been estimated that about 80% of the food on the shelves of supermarkets today didn't exist a 100 years ago in its current format! If you look at most supermarkets, 80% of the produce in there is packaged for long life storage. If there is one thing I have learnt as a nutritionist, the quicker a food spoils, the more nutritious it is. You should look to eat food in its natural state. Buying food in boxes and tins, with a long shelf life, should instantly warn you this simply is last resort food if there has been a natural disaster or something , you should not be trying to nourish yourself with these empty toxic foods as you will pay a price eventually with your health.

Toxins & Toxicity

In the past 60 years approximately 87,000 man-made chemicals have been introduced into our food and water supply depending on what research you read. Can you imagine the effect multiple toxins have on our body over a period of time?

The rise in worldwide obesity rates parallels the increase in environmental toxicity. Synthetic chemicals that have been added to our environment, only in the last couple of decades which cause havoc with our hormones and mitochondria preventing us from using up our fat stores and stimulating us to store more fat. **This is hypothesised to happen in two ways, first by lowering our ability to generate heat, and secondly by reducing levels of hormones essential for releasing body fats from storage.**

Chemical damage appears to make people less able to raise body temperature, this can be seen in people who are severely damaged by chemicals, as they tend to have a lower than average body temperature. So if they produce less heat, they end up using less energy. Hypothyroidism causes the same symptoms as you will find out in habit 5.

The reason for this inability to convert existing fat stores into heat is that hormones that are essential for mobilizing fats, namely catecholamines, have been lowered. Because of this our fat stores cannot be exploited fully to produce heat energy or indeed energy for any other

Toxicity: the invisible killer

reason. So once our fat is in storage, it becomes very difficult to shift, creating ever increasing amounts of fat stores that our bodies simply cannot use up.

We know that toxicity can severely damage and alter physiology. For example, many industrial chemicals mimic the effects of the hormone oestrogen in the body and oestrogen encourages fat storage. We call these compounds xenooestrogens, and they are all around us, in the form of flame retardants, pesticides, plastics, and many thousands of other chemicals which we use and are exposed to on a daily basis. We also know that many man-made chemicals interfere with our ability to burn fat by inhibiting and decreasing mitochondrial function (bacteria within cells that burn fuel), which we will discuss in much greater depth in habit 4 of this book.

Several studies have shown that obese people have high levels of toxins stored in their fatty tissue. The theory resulting from this academic work is that the body is using fatty tissue, which has a relatively low level of metabolic activity, as a place to store the toxins away from the body tissues that have high levels of metabolic activity, such as blood, organs, and muscle. In effect, body fat becomes a storehouse of toxins in an attempt to "firewall" the body from toxicity.

There are many suspected links between xenooestrogens and precocious puberty. Children today are fatter than in years past, just as their parents and other adults are. Likewise, the bodies of young children contain more xenooestrogens from plastics, pesticides and other industrial sources. One theory states that these xenooestrogenic compounds act as signals to the developing endocrine system, helping to trigger an early puberty and obesity.

I first became alerted to the effects that cosmetics can have on my athlete's body fat levels when I was consulting for a number of elite teams. I was researching the subject of endocrine disruptors at the time whilst carrying out around 5000 body composition tests within a season with three different premiership sports teams. Due to the amount of training they were doing they were showering 8-12 times a week and using these products which, I found out, could increase oestrogen levels. I could see the effect this was having on the players as some of their body fat percentage increased as the season progressed.

This isn't limited to adult wash care products. If you look at the ingredient lists of most children's wash care products, shampoos etc., then you will find the same oestrogen promoting substances such as parabens.

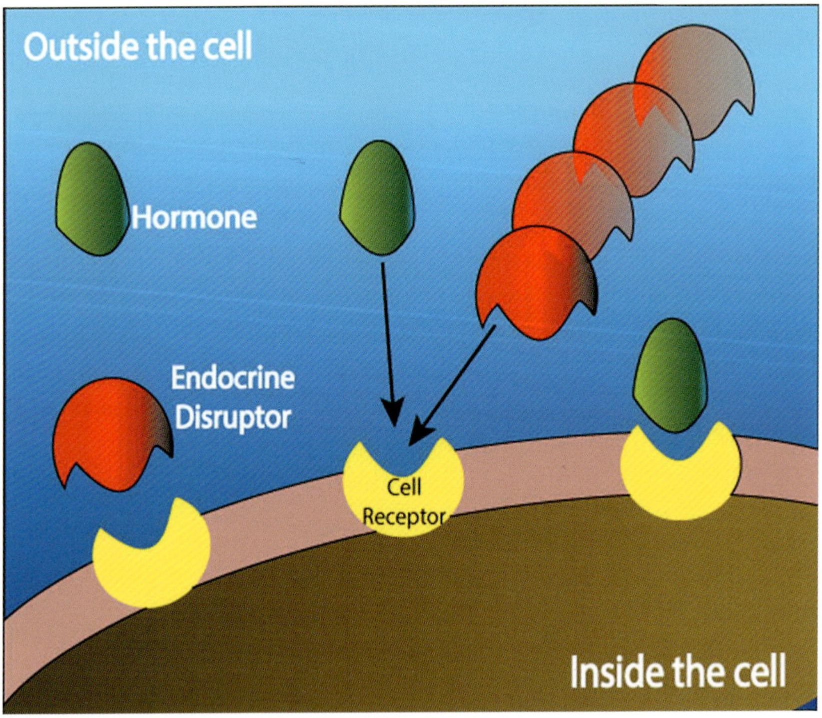

How endocrine disruptors work by interfering with cellular communication.

So which organ is primarily responsible for dealing with all of these toxins? The liver. What happens when the liver's detoxification system is overloaded? The answer is simple: when the liver does not function properly, toxins that we are exposed to accumulate in the body. When the liver cannot process (detoxify) toxins fast enough, because of overload, the toxins have to be stored in the body to be dealt with later. Guess where it is stored? Yes in our FAT!

The more toxins in your body, the more fat you will lay down to absorb the toxins. It is almost impossible to be lean with a high content of toxins in the body. And make no bones about it the more toxins you store not only are you more likley to lay down more fat to store those pesky toxins but you will overtime become sicker and sicker.

Scientists estimate that everyone alive today carries within her or his body at least 700 contaminants, most of which have not been well studied. This is true whether we live in a rural or isolated area, in the middle of a large city, or near an industrialized area.

In the month leading up to a baby's birth, the umbilical cord pulses with the equivalent of at least 340 litres of blood each day, pumped back and forth from the nutrient- and oxygen-rich placenta to the rapidly growing child cradled in a sac of amniotic fluid. This cord is a lifeline between mother and baby, bearing nutrients that sustain life and propel growth.

Not long ago scientists thought that the placenta shielded cord blood — and the developing baby — from most chemicals and pollutants in the environment. But now we know that at this critical time when organs, vessels, membranes and systems are

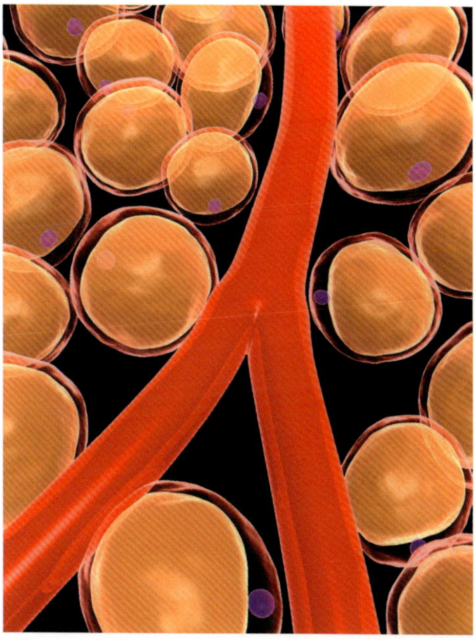

There are a variety of reasons toxins pose a major challenge to weight loss. A person who has too many toxins to process will make new fat cells and store those toxins along with fat in them. This is first a form of self-defense against being poisoned, and second, a strategy to get toxins out of the circulation and away from major organs. Fat cells act as the body's garbage dump. Toxins and other consumed, unusable garbage are stored there. The more that is consumed, the more waste there is, leading to more mass in fat cells. Fat cells can either grow in numbers, grow in mass, or both. This means that some people will not be able to lose any weight at all, regardless of how little they eat, until the acute nature of their detoxification problems are addressed. We cover detoxification in great detail in habit 2 of this book.

knit together from single cells to finished form in a span of weeks, the umbilical cord carries not only the building blocks of life, but also a steady stream of industrial chemicals, pollutants and pesticides that cross the placenta as readily as residues from cigarettes and alcohol. This is the human "body burden" — the pollution in people that permeates everyone in the world, including babies in the womb.

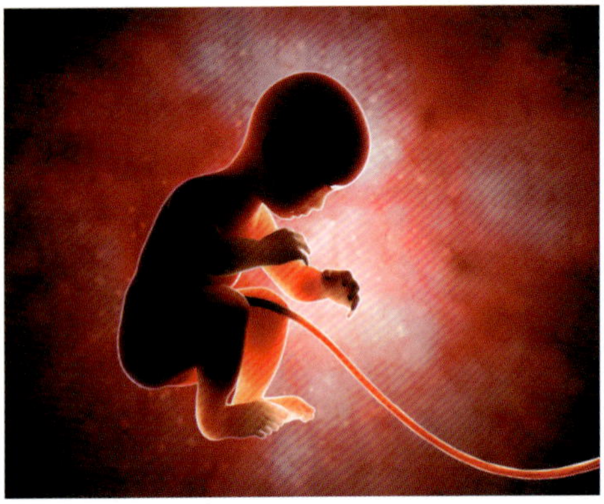

The umbilical cord can carry a stream of chemicals, pollutants and pesticides.

In a study spearheaded by the Environmental Working Group (EWG) in collaboration with Commonweal, researchers at two major laboratories found an average of 200 industrial chemicals and pollutants in umbilical cord blood from 10 babies born in August and September of 2004 in U.S. hospitals. Tests revealed a total of 287 chemicals in the group. The umbilical cord blood of these 10 children, collected by Red Cross after the cord was cut, harbored pesticides, consumer product ingredients, and wastes from burning coal, gasoline, and garbage.

This study represents the first reported cord blood tests for 261 of the targeted chemicals and the first reported detections in cord blood for 209 compounds. Among them are eight perfluorochemicals used as stain and oil repellents in fast food packaging, clothes and textiles — including the Teflon chemical PFOA, recently characterized as a likely human carcinogen by the EPA's Science Advisory Board — dozens of widely used brominated flame retardants and their toxic by-products; and numerous pesticides.

Of the 287 chemicals detected in umbilical cord blood, it is known that 180 cause cancer in humans or animals, 217 are toxic to the brain and nervous system, and 208 cause birth defects or abnormal development in animal tests. The dangers of pre- or postnatal exposure to this complex mixture of carcinogens, developmental toxins and neurotoxins have never been studied.

The scientific theory of how these chemicals cause weight gain and difficulty losing weight has now been established. They bind to gene signalling within adipose tissue and induce new fat cells to form while simultaneously increasing inflammation. Often, the newly formed fat cells are themselves damaged by the toxins so that they cannot metabolically perform, which includes an inability to make leptin normally (an appetite regulating hormone that will be discussed more in Habit 6).

These damaged fat cells can fill up with excess fat and toxins, but are not able to efficiently carry out normal functions of fat cells, leading directly to increased risk for type 2 diabetes via the suppression of the important fat cell hormone known as adiponectin, a protein hormone that modulates metabolism including glucose and fatty acid catabolism. High levels are associated with low body fat.

It is also very clear that toxins are released back into the circulation during weight loss. This is especially the case during significant weight loss. In one study, during a weight loss of 12% of body weight, toxins in the blood increased 23-51%, with the heaviest individuals releasing the most toxins. Over a one year period of weight loss, toxic exposure ranged up to an incredible 388%.

Scientists have shown that the toxins that are released can also interfere with thyroid hormone function during weight loss. Human data shows that as the toxins go up in the blood during weight loss, the levels of biologically active thyroid hormone triiodothyronine (T3) go down. This means that your detoxification systems must be in good working condition for healthy weight loss – or possibly even to engage weight loss - in order to excrete these toxins out of the body.

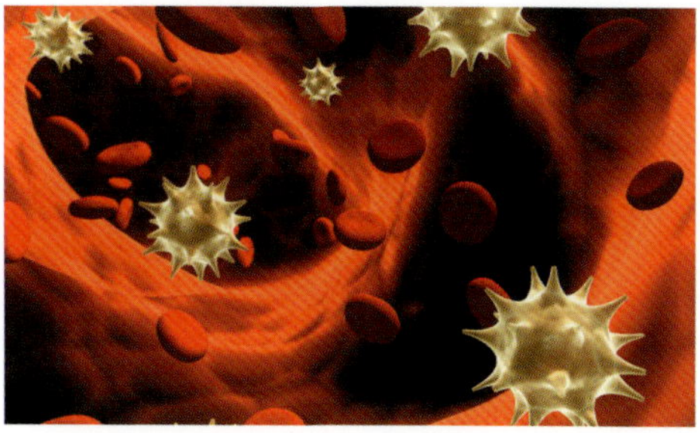

It is now understood that "toxic" blood triggers the formation of new fat cells.

"Toxic" blood also triggers the formation of new fat cells. This is because the inner lining of your circulatory system (endothelial cells) directly communicate to your baby fat cells and can tell them what to do. Keeping your blood as clean as possible and supporting your liver are vital steps to ensure that this process goes smoothly. I will cover how you can improve the health of your blood, in great detail, in Habit 8, "Nutritional Cardiology".

Dr. Paula Baillie-Hamilton, an expert on metabolism and environmental toxins, was one of the first to make a link between the obesity epidemic and the increase in environmental chemicals. Baillie-Hamilton argued that exposure to chemicals can damage your body's natural weight-control mechanisms. She calls toxic chemicals that act as endocrine disruptors "chemical calories." Environmental researchers now call these chemical calories "obesogens."

Here's the thing about hormones and toxic chemicals. Hormones communicate by travelling through the body and connecting with receptors. Receptors are like locks and hormones are the keys. The "keys" circulate through the body until they find the right "locks." When a hormone key enters into its correct receptor lock, the hormone/receptor complex bind to specific parts of DNA in the cell, which directs the cell's function. The problem is that certain toxic chemicals also fit the receptors.

As these chemicals circulate through the body, they enter the receptors as if they were hormones, blocking the way for the actual hormones to enter. The chemicals do not contain the vital information and the communication doesn't take place, thereby breaking the connection between hormone and receptor. For the hormone, it really is quite like a husband coming home to find that another man is already in bed with his wife and there is no room for him! Though research in this field is still relatively new, scientists believe that it takes a very small amount of these chemicals – even a single exposure – to disrupt normal functioning.

It is very important to understand how the organisations that produces the masses of man-made toxins found in our food, water, air & homes will stamp their feet and say very convincingly that the amounts found in our food, water, air and homes is so small that it would have little or no effect at all. Well when you understand the concentrations that hormones work within the body then you realise that this simply isn't true. Hormones within our bodies can work in concentrations at parts per trillion which is equivalent to ½ teaspoon of salt in 1000 size Olympic swimming pools.

The world wildlife foundation environmental group conducted a series of blood tests on people from all walks of life in the UK. In 2003, they tested the blood of individuals across the UK and found an average of 27 chemicals in every one of them. These compounds included long banned DDT and PCB's, from old electrical equipment and building materials, as well as more common chemicals found in everyday materials such as paints, glues, toys, electrical goods, furniture, carpets and clothing.

As these chemicals build up, they can alter our metabolism, cause enzyme dysfunction and nutritional deficiencies, create hormonal imbalances, damage brain chemistry, and cause cancer. Because the chemicals accumulate in different parts of the body, at different rates and in different combinations, this can result in a disturbingly large variety of different chronic illnesses.

There is now very strong evidence that our bodies mistake certain man-made chemicals used in plastics, food, wrappers, and fragrances, and many more items, for naturally occurring hormones that regulate the production and storage of fat cells. These chemicals are literally turning us into 24/7 fat storage machines.

Do toxins program us to be fat from early life?

"Evidence has been steadily accumulating that certain hormone-mimicking pollutants, ubiquitous in the food chain, have two previously unsuspected effects. They act on genes in the developing foetus and newborn to turn more precursor cells into fat cells, which stay with you for life. And they may alter metabolic rate, so that the body hoards calories rather than burning them..." Retha Newbold of the National Institute of Environmental Health Sciences.

One example of how toxins make us fat can be seen in the dramatic increase in obesity in babies. In 2006, Harvard scientists from the School of Public Health found that the rate of obesity in infants less than 6 months old has risen 73% since 1980! It appears it may be the load of environmental toxins they are exposed to in the womb which contributes to their obesity. Disconcertingly, studies on prenatal exposure to endocrine-disrupting chemicals showed that exposure in-utero (in the womb) could cause permanent changes that could predispose you to weight gain later in life.

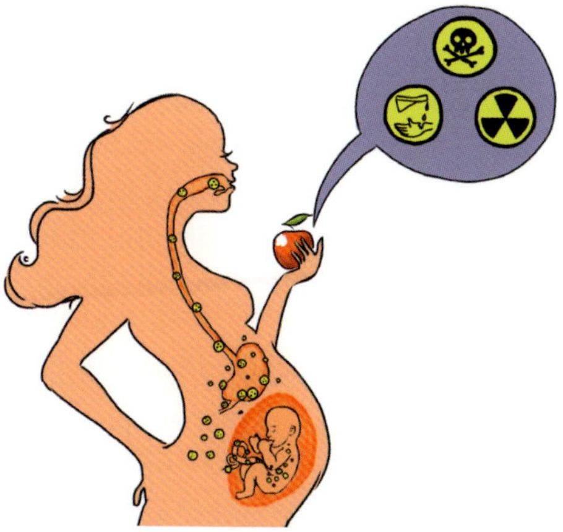

Children are exposed to environmental toxins before they are even born.

Infants are exposed to pesticides, phthalates, bisphenol-A, flame retardants, and heavy metals such mercury, lead, and arsenic. These compounds have a broad range of negative effects on human biology, as we have already seen. They damage the nervous system, increase your risk of cancer, and it has been shown they contribute to obesity. This is not a fringe idea of radical environmentalists. The National Institutes of Health, the Food and Drug Administration, the Environmental Protection Agency and the National

Academy of Sciences recently convened to examine this new phenomenon of "obesogens" - the toxins that cause obesity.

Vaccinations: could they be causing more problems than we are supposed to know about and contributing to a string of modern diseases like obesity and diabetes?

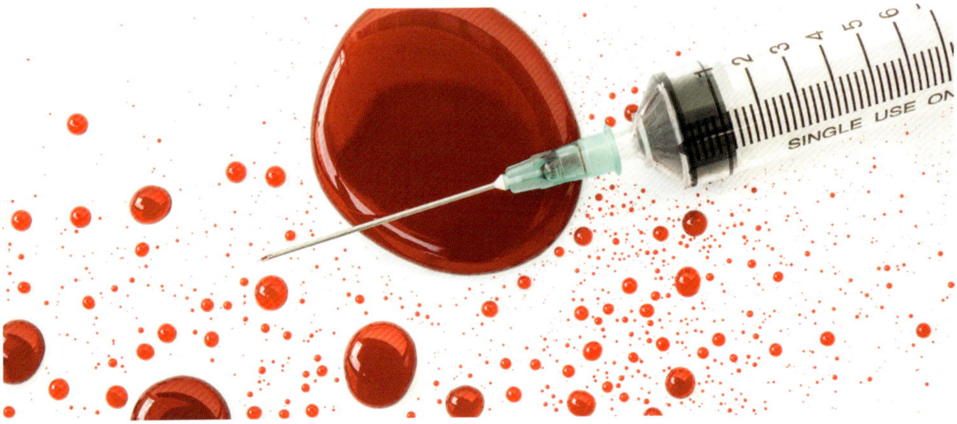

Comprehensive research compiled by expert immunologist Dr. J. "Bart" Classen has uncovered the disturbing fact that childhood vaccines are a **common cause of both type 1 and type 2 diabetes**, as well as the barrage of chronic illness symptoms typically associated with metabolic syndrome. Because they tend to overstimulate the immune system, vaccines have the potential to either inhibit the proper production of insulin, resulting in the development of type 1 diabetes, or spur the production of too much insulin, resulting in the development of type 2 diabetes.

Type 1 diabetes, as many people are already aware, is an autoimmune condition whereby the body attacks the pancreas and destroys the pancreatic cells responsible for producing insulin, a detrimental situation in which the body must be artificially injected with insulin. Type 2 diabetes, on the other hand, is actually a chronic inflammatory condition marked by the pancreas **producing too much insulin**, and the body being unable to properly absorb it.

According to Dr. Classen, most of the people who develop type 2 diabetes, although often overweight or obese, are not typically responsible for triggering the onset of this potentially deadly condition. Particularly in children, there is clearly another factor involved in the development of both type 1 and type 2 diabetes, and one that available science on the subject seems to confirm is related to childhood vaccines.

Vaccine Ingredients

Formaldehyde
Aluminum
Thimerosal (influenza vaccine)
Polysorbate 80
Monosodium Glutamate
Antibiotics: strepomycin, neomycin, gentamicin, polymyxin B
Allergens: soy, gelatin, egg, yeast
Human diploid cells or residual proteins from aborted fetal tissue
Animal by products: chick embryonic fluid, fetal bovine serum, guinea pig embryo cells, monkey kidney cells

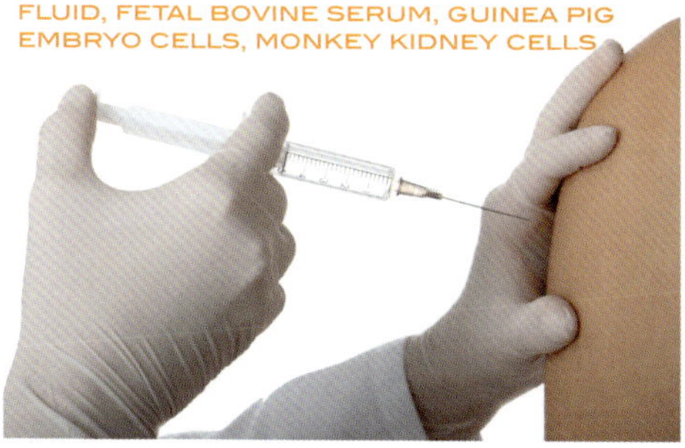

"Not only are vaccines causing an epidemic of autoimmunity including type 1 diabetes, but they are causing an epidemic of metabolic syndrome as the immune system acts to suppress the inflammation and autoimmunity caused by the vaccines," says Dr. Classen, who for many years has been researching the connection between vaccines and diabetes.

"Current data shows that vaccines are much more dangerous than the public is led to believe and adequate testing has never been performed even in healthy subjects. The current practice of vaccinating diabetics as well as their close family members is a very risky practice."

The human body naturally produces an adrenal hormone known as cortisol that is responsible for regulating proper carbohydrate and protein metabolism, and generally helping the body to adapt and deal with stressful situations. Excessive cortisol production is linked to type 2 diabetes and metabolic syndrome, while inadequate cortisol production is linked to type 1 diabetes.

It appears as though individuals who naturally produce slightly lower than normal levels of cortisol are more prone to develop type 1 diabetes as a result of vaccines, according to Dr. Classen's research, while vaccinated individuals who tend to produce higher than normal levels of cortisol are more prone to develop type 2 diabetes. In either case, vaccines seem to be the smoking gun in explaining why cases of both type 1 and type 2 diabetes have risen dramatically throughout the past half century.

The large percentage of the medical profession want members of the public to simply bury their heads when it comes to vaccination and simply do not want us asking questions on the possible dangers of vaccinations!

"Poor diet and low exercise can not explain many facets of the (diabetes) epidemic, including the onset in children six months of age, the protective effect of obesity on the incidence of type 1 diabetes, and the epidemic of type 2 diabetes/metabolic syndrome in grass fed horses," adds Dr. Classen, referencing a recent study he conducted that was published in the journal Current Diabetes Reviews.

"Poor diet and exercise also do not explain the epidemic of type 1 diabetes in children that resembles the epidemic of type 2 diabetes / metabolic syndrome" ***(http://www.ncbi.nlm.nih.gov/pubmed/22934546).***

Dr Robert S. Mendelsohn M.D is an expert with weighty research for parents looking deeper for answers to their children's problems. He lists quotes from many experts who state that childhood vaccinations are causing childhood diabetes. Here are a few of them:

1) "We found a large epidemic of diabetes. A 60% increase occurred in New Zealand following this immunization program." Dr. J. Bart Classen MD, former Researcher National Institute of Health, Classen Immunotherapies
2) "Four children...developed diabetes mellitus shortly after active mumps vaccination." ***K. Helme, et al Diabetogia, Vol. 29, Number 1/30-33, 1/1/86***
3) "Hepatitis B vaccine and Haemophilus influenzae type b vaccine have been respectively suspected to be responsible for neurological demyelinating disease and insulin dependent diabetes mellitus." ***Ovetchkine P., Arch Pediatr, 8(3):316-20 3/101***
4) "In 1992, 180 European doctors jointly noted that the mumps vaccine "can trigger diabetes which only becomes apparent months after vaccination." ***Albionico et al, JAM 192;9(1)***

Certain toxins can also cause mitochondrial damage. For example, one study showed that thimerosal-derived methylmercury (which is used as a preservative in certain vaccines, skin test antigens, and tattoo inks), inhibits mitochondrial respiration and leads to an increase in the formation of superoxide. The study found a fivefold increase in the levels of oxidant damaged mitochondrial DNA after Thimerosal treatment. As you'll read throughout this book anything that inhibits mitochondrial

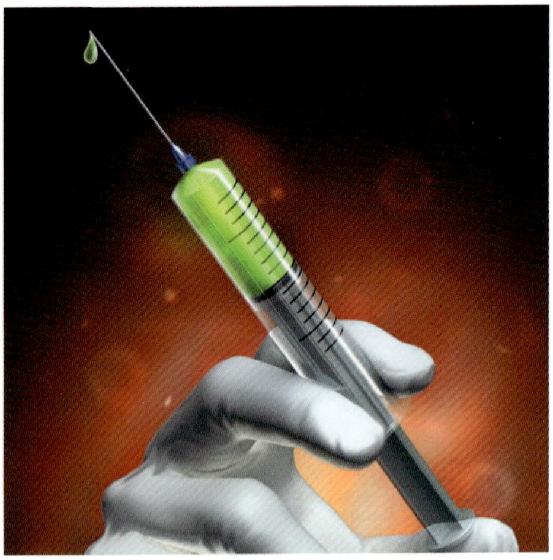

function also inhibits health & fat loss and we seem to be subjected to an enormous amount of vaccines today!

UK 2013 Immunisation Schedule

AGE	Immunisation (Vaccine Given)
2 months	• DTaP/IPV(polio)/Hib (diphtheria, tetanus, pertussis (whooping cough), polio, and Haemophilus influenzae type b) - all-in-one injection: Pediacel®; plus: • PCV (pneumococcal conjugate vaccine) - in a separate injection: Prevenar 13®. • Rotarix® (rotavirus gastroenteritis) - oral route.
3 months	• DTaP/IPV(polio)/Hib (2nd dose: Pediacel®); plus: • MenC (meningitis C) - in a separate injection: NeisVac-C® or Menjugate Kit®. • Rotarix® (rotavirus gastroenteritis) - oral route.
4 months	• DTaP/IPV(polio)/Hib (3rd dose: Pediacel®); plus: • PCV (2nd dose: Prevenar 13®) - in a separate injection.
Between 12 and 13 months	• Hib/MenC (combined as one injection) - 4th dose of Hib and 2nd dose of MenC: Menitorix®; plus: • MMR (measles, mumps and rubella) - combined as one injection: Priorix® or MMR II®; plus: • PCV (3rd dose: Prevenar 13®) - in a separate injection.
3 years and four months to 5 years	• Pre-school booster of DTaP/IPV(polio): Repevax® or Infanrix-IPV®; plus: • MMR (second dose: Priorix® or MMR II®) - in a separate injection.
Around 12-13 years (girls)	• HPV (human papillomavirus types 16 and 18) - three injections: Gardasil®. The second injection is given 1-2 months after the first one. The third is given about six months after the first one.

Around 13-18 years	• Td/IPV(polio) booster: Revaxis®. • MenC (booster dose: NeisVac® or Menjugate Kit®) - in a separate injection.
Adults	• Influenza and PCV for those aged over 65 years and also those in high-risk groups. • Td/IPV(polio) - for those not fully immunised as a child: Revaxis®. • DTaP/IPV(polio) - for pregnant women 28-38 weeks gestation. • Shingles (Zostavax®) for those aged 70-79 years (from Sept 2013).

Vaccines contain a combination of at least 39 different highly toxic metals, cancer causing substances, toxic chemicals, live and genetically modified viruses, bacteria, contaminated serum containing animal viruses and foreign genetic material, extremely toxic de-contaminants and adjuvants, untested antibiotics, none of which can be injected without causing any harm. Vaccine contaminants have included bovine (cow), avian (chicken) and monkey viruses and bacteria such as streptococcus in the DTP (diphtheria, tetanus and pertussis) vaccine *[Pediatrics, Vol. 75, No. 2, Feb 1985]* and Serratia marcescens in the influenza vaccines [2004 influenza season].

HIV/AIDS: Nobel Laureate Advocates Natural Cure

In an interview for the AIDS-documentary "House of Numbers", Dr. Luc Montagnier – Recipient of the 2008 Nobel Prize in Medicine for the discovery of the Human Immunodeficiency Virus (HIV) – spoke out for nutrition and micronutrients in the fight against HIV/AIDS:

In a filmed interview Dr. Montagnier stated that:

There are many ways to decrease the transmission of HIV just by utilising simple measures such as nutrition, giving antioxidants, hygiene measures and fighting the other infections that are present in patients.

If you have a good immune system your body can get rid of HIV naturally.

We should push for combinations of measures, such as antioxidants; nutrition advice; nutrition; fighting the other infections that are present in patients such as malaria, tuberculosis, parasitosis and worms; education and promoting genital hygiene.

People always think of drugs and vaccines because there is no profit in nutrition.

If you take a poor African patient who has been infected with HIV and you build up their immune system it should also be possible for them to get rid of HIV naturally.

All of the above constitutes important knowledge which has been completely neglected.

There is no scientific study to determine whether vaccines have really prevented diseases. Rather disease graphs show vaccines have been introduced at the end of epidemics when the disease was already in its last stages. In case of Small Pox the vaccine actually caused a great spurt in the incidence of disease before public outcry led to its withdrawal.

I am not advocating that you do not vaccinate. That is a personal choice and one that I personally decided to take by not vaccinating my youngest daughter, and the constant pressure from the medical profession to vaccinate is nauseating and nothing short of bullying. But when you ask your GP what's in the vaccine and what are the possible side effects they look at you as if "how dare you ask such a question". Why? Because they don't know the answer!

Well as a parent I have the right to ask that question on what is being injected directly into my child's bloodstream. And if I 100% believed that the vaccines would help my child I would administer it myself with 100% enthusiasm but for me presently I have ZERO faith in vaccinations in their present concoctions and believe in the future medicine will look back at what we are doing today and shake their head in shame.

Question everything that concerns your health or your child's health this is everybody's right. The medical profession should welcome this with open arms and not go into defensive mode when they get questioned - it's called professionalism!

You will neither find any doctor willing to sign a disclaimer that if a vaccination harms your child that you can take them to a court of law and sue them, and you can't sue the vaccination supplier either they are protected by law.

Cow's milk

"In lieu of the recent evidence that cow's milk protein may be implicated in the pathogenesis of diabetes mellitus, we believe that the Committee on Nutrition should clarify whether cow's milk is ever appropriate for children and whether or not infant formulas that are based on cow's milk protein are appropriate alternatives to breast milk." **Paediatrics, July, 1992: 89**

"Introduction of dairy products and high milk consumption during childhood may increase the child's risk of developing juvenile diabetes." **Diabetologia 1994;37(4):381-387**

Researchers in Maine report a new explanation for the mysterious link between consumption of cow's' milk protein in infant formula early in life and an increased risk of later developing Type-1 diabetes. A protein in cow's milk that triggers an unusual immune response appears to be the main culprit, they say.

In the study, Marcia F. Goldfarb points out that several studies have reported a possible link between the early introduction of cow's milk protein into an infant's diet and subsequent development of the disease. In Type-1 diabetes, the immune system erroneously appears to attack and destroy insulin-producing cells in the pancreas. It usually begins in childhood.

A meta-analysis of case-control studies by Professor Gerstein of the University of McMaster implied that early exposure to cow milk proteins (<4 month old) was a risk predictor of type

1 diabetes. Early exposure to cow milk is related to shorter duration of breastfeeding. In a Finnish national case-control study, when both the duration of breastfeeding and the age at introduction of cow milk were studied, early exposure to cow milk turned out to be the dominant risk determinant of type 1 diabetes.

A new intriguing hypothesis was proposed by the Finnish group, arguing that an early exposure to cow's milk formula results in an immune response to bovine insulin present in minute amounts in such formulas and that this could trigger an immune response to insulin, a key beta-cell antigen. The cow's milk theory is also compatible with the high diabetes incidence in milk-consuming countries such as Finland, Sweden, and Norway. The UK is now the 5th leading country in the World for type 1 diabetes.

Well when you consider the amount of cows milk most children drink coupled with the mountain of vaccinations then you can see why we are in a diabetes epidemic. Couple this with the amount of processed crap children eat and the future is not looking bright for their futures but least big pharma will make more profits!

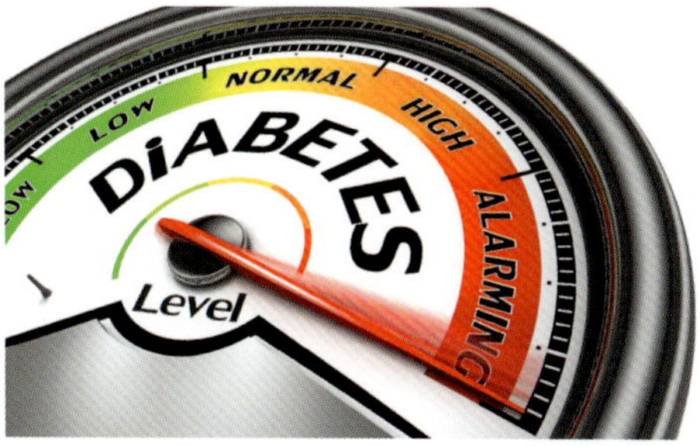

Remember, cow's milk is best kept for baby cows. However, I do believe that raw milk from a cow could be a nutritious food source for humans, due to its high enzyme content which have not been destroyed by pasteurisation and homogenisation.

Bottle-feeding small babies can set them up for a life of heart disease and obesity, according to a new study. While breastfed babies limit their own intake of milk because they have to work hard to get it, bottle-fed babies lie back and swallow what they are given. The danger, according to researchers, is that they will be offered more than they need, building up an appetite for the future. "When they are exposed to high-protein, high-fat foods, they are more likely to become obese," they concluded.

> ***"At least 20% of adult obesity is caused by over-feeding in infancy, according to Professor Atul Singhal from the MRC Childhood Nutrition Research Centre at the Institute of Child Health in London."***

Singhal and colleagues followed up children who were involved in two studies from the 1990s when they were new born babies. Some were given nutritionally enriched baby milk

– now only ever given to weak, premature babies – and others were given standard formula. Those who were given the extra nutrition had a fat mass by the age of five to eight that was 22%-38% greater than those who were fed standard formula. Increased fat in childhood is a known risk for being overweight in adulthood.

"This study robustly demonstrates a link between early nutrition and having more fat in later life in humans – a finding suggested by previous studies and confirmed in many other animals. Our findings are strong, consistent, show a dose-response effect, and are biologically plausible," said Singhal.

But the implications of the study go beyond the use of enriched formula milk, to the overfeeding of any baby. "In public-health terms, it supports the case in the general population for breastfeeding – as it is harder to overfeed a breastfed baby," Singhal said. He pointed out that formula milk is based on cow's milk – and that cows gain weight much faster than humans.

Protein is a prime example of how human milk is unique nutrition for human babies. Human milk is low in protein, at least when compared with the milk of other species, especially cow's milk. This isn't a nutritional deficiency; there are good reasons for this. Human infants are designed to grow slowly. While it's important for humans to develop strong bodies, even more important is brain development and the learning of social skills. The experiences that shape the brain come from close contact between mother and baby, when baby is held and carried. If human infants doubled their birth-weight in less than 50 days the way baby calves do, and then continued growing, how could their mothers carry them and talk to them and keep them close?

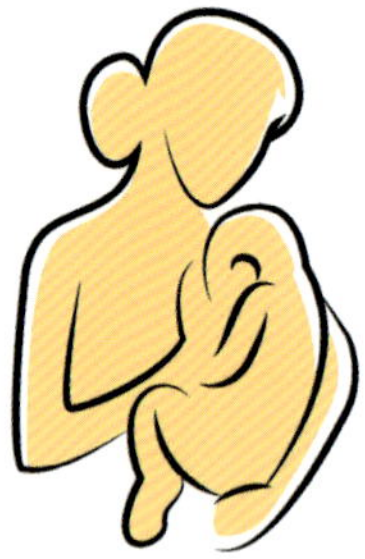

So, whilst breastfeeding is indeed the better alternative for newborns and babies, this also comes with a warning. DDT, PCBs, trichloroethylene, perchlorate, dibenzofurans, mercury, lead, benzene, arsenic...all found in breast milk. Because breasts store fat, they store toxic, fat-loving chemicals. When we nurse our babies, we feed them, in albeit minuscule amounts, paint thinners, dry-cleaning fluids, wood preservatives, toilet deodorisers, cosmetic additives, gasoline by-products, rocket fuel, termite poisons and flame-retardants.

The amount of chemicals that infants suckle through milk is not insignificant. Recent studies show that lactating mothers offload about 14% per month for dioxins, and up to 8% per month for PCBs, of their total body burden per month to their offspring, or about 30% if they nurse for a year. Therefore, mothers need to ensure that they are limiting their exposure to these chemicals.

Antibiotics could they be contributing to obesity?

Expanding waistlines may be caused by more than bad diets and sedentary habits. Antibiotics could be disrupting our gut bacteria, helping people pack on fat like farm animals. This scenario is, for now, a hypothesis, but one that's fleshed out in two new studies. In the first, mice given antibiotics experienced profound changes to internal microbe communities that process food and regulate metabolism. In the other study, body weight in children rose with antibiotic exposures as infants.

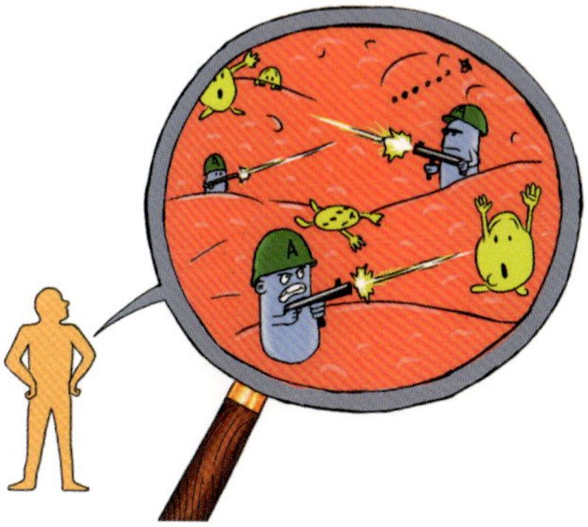

Antibiotics can have detrimental effects on gut bacteria

"Early life antibiotics are changing the microbiome (the totality of microbes, their genetic elements and environmental interactions in a particular environment), and its metabolic capabilities, at a critical time in development," said microbiologist Martin Blaser of New York University. "These changes have downstream effects on metabolism, including genes related to energy storage." For some reason, animals given steady low doses of antibiotics grow larger and faster than usual. Blaser wondered why this was, whether it was related to the animals' microbiomes, and whether something similar could happen in humans.

In the Nature journal, researchers, led by Blaser and fellow microbiologist Ilseung Cho, showed that steady, low doses of antibiotics added to the diets of lab mice, mimicked the exposures received by farm animals. Their mice didn't gain weight, but their body fat swelled by 15%, an effect that held for different types of antibiotics. When the researchers looked at their microbiomes, they found markedly different types of bacteria. Changes were also found in the genetic profiles of their mice, with unusual activity in genes linked to breaking down carbohydrates and regulating cholesterol levels.

According to Blaser, this could be a version of what happens inside people. That's difficult to study in gut-level detail, but an Aug. 21 International Journal of Obesity paper by Blaser and NYU paediatrician Leonard Trasande looked for population-level trends in 11,000 British children.

Among children exposed to antibiotics before they were six months old, the researchers found small but consistent average increases in body mass years later. Antibiotics appeared to have altered their metabolic trajectories. Blaser called the data preliminary, but said it fits the patterns seen in both farm animals and his mice.

It is estimated that the amount of antibiotics used in animal farming has skyrocketed in the last few years. In just over a decade it is estimated that their use has increased eight-fold in the UK.

Unnatural birth, unnatural weight (caesarian section)

Research conducted in 2012 and published in the Archives of Disease in Childhood, monitored the health of 1,255 pairs of mothers and children between 1999 and 2002. Each mother had voluntarily joined the study before 22 weeks of pregnancy, and their babies were measured and weighed once after birth, at six months, and then at three years.

The study found that the babies that were delivered by c - section (of which there were 284, or 22.6 percent of the total) were twice as likely to suffer from obesity by the age of three than those that were delivered vaginally. They also suffered noticeably higher BMI and skinfold thickness measurements.

The study also found that the mothers that delivered their babies via c - sections tended to be heavier and less inclined to breastfeed their babies than mothers that delivered naturally. While this could explain the disparity in body weight between the two groups of babies, the researchers believe that the difference between the composition of gut bacteria acquired at birth between the two delivery methods is also a significant contributing factor.

"An association between caesarean birth and increased risk of childhood obesity would provide an important rationale to avoid non-medically indicated caesarean section," concluded the study authors.

Pesticides are they contributing to the obesity crisis?

People are becoming a little bit more aware of the importance of reading labels when it comes to calories and macronutrients, but wouldn't it be interesting if the food suppliers had to list all the pesticides used during the production of the food, drink or cosmetic? You wouldn't get a big enough label in most cases. For example, according to the Environmental Working Group's analysis of USDA data, pesticides showed up on 98% of more than 700 non-organic apple samples tested (and yes, they were washed). And it wasn't just one pesticide either – apples from around the country, domestically grown and imported, were found to have up to 48 different kinds of pesticides on them.

Studies suggest that every single one of us in the Western world may consume around 4.5 litres of pesticides a year. According to researchers at Purdue University in Indiana, apples now top the list as the most contaminated by pesticides (see the table below), even after they are peeled and washed. Strawberries are the third most contaminated fruit and veg, and other popular fruits such as grapes, blueberries are not that far behind. According to the group, eating five servings a day of the most contaminated fruits and vegetables is akin to ingesting 14 different pesticides per day. This is why consuming organic foods is so important in our quest for long term health and fat loss as it decreases our exposure to these chemicals which are literally crashing our metabolism and fattening us up without us eating more foods.

A tractor spraying chemicals on to apple crops.

The 12 best and worst foods in regards to pesticide levels. (2012 results)	
Worst Offenders (Buy Organic)	**Cleanest of the Bunch**
1) Apples	1) Onions
2) Celery	2) Sweetcorn
3) Sweet Bell Peppers	3) Pineapples
4) Peaches	4) Avocado
5) Strawberries	5) Cabbage
6) Nectarines	6) Sweet Peas
7) Grapes	7) Asparagus
8) Spinach	8) Mangoes
9) Lettuce	9) Eggplant
10) Cucumber	10) Kiwi
11) Blueberries	11) Cantaloupe
12) Potatoes	12) Sweet Potatoes

Not only have we introduced an estimated 87000 man-made chemicals to the environment, we have also decreased the nutrient content of our soil leaving us with foods that are deficient in vital detoxification nutrients which organs such as the liver require. Remember our health starts with the soil and we are as only as healthy as the soil our foods have come from. Non organic crops have soils which are usually exceptionally deficient in nutrients essential for our health and well being.

The nutrient content of UK soil, between 1939-1991, fell, in some cases dramatically.

Vegetables: Sodium 49%, Potassium 16%, Magnesium 24%, Calcium 46%, Iron 27%, Copper 76%, Zinc 59%

Fruit: Sodium 29%, Potassium 19%, Magnesium 16%, Calcium 16%, Iron 24%, Copper 20%, Zinc 27%. The only mineral to rise was phosphorous, by 2%

Clear differences between organic and non-organic food, study finds:

Organic food has more of the antioxidant compounds linked to better health than regular food, and lower levels of toxic metals and pesticides, according to the most comprehensive scientific analysis to date.

The international team behind the work suggests that switching to organic fruit and vegetables could give the same benefits as adding one or two portions of the recommended "five a day".

The team, led by Prof Carlo Leifert at Newcastle University, concludes that there are "statistically significant, meaningful" differences, with a range of antioxidants being "substantially higher" – between 19% and 69% – in organic food. It is the first study to demonstrate clear and wide-ranging differences between organic and conventional fruits, vegetables and cereals.

The researchers say the increased levels of antioxidants are equivalent to "one to two of the five portions of fruits and vegetables recommended to be consumed daily and would therefore be significant and meaningful in terms of human nutrition, if information linking these (compounds) to the health benefits associated with increased fruit, vegetable and whole grain consumption is confirmed".

Those Pesky Pesticides Not Only Kill Pests They Can Also Make Us Sick, Tired & Obese!

More concerns of the damaging effects that pesticides have on our health and waistlines are growing, for example **at low doses organophosphates have been used to fatten up animals by severely reducing their ability to use up existing fat stores.** As the animal's fat burning abilities slow down, they gain weight and they have no doubt the similar effects in humans after all we are also an animal. Organophosphates are one of the most common pesticides and therefore continue to be found as residues in many of our foods.

PHIL SAYS
Organic Food

I always strive to buy organic fruits, vegetables, meats and fish wherever possible and advise my athletes and clients do the same and have done so for the last 20 years. With meat I also always look to buy grass-fed and always wild, not farmed, fish.

For example the reality of where our fish comes from is of paramount importance for our health! There is a vast difference between wild caught fish and farmed fish.

Fish farms produce supermarket protein with high concentrations of antibiotics, pesticides and lower levels of healthy nutrients. Research has found that farmed fish has less usable omega-3 fatty acids than wild-caught fish and a 20% lower protein content. A USDA review confirmed the findings. Farmed fish are fattier and have a high concentration of omega-6 fatty acids. Imbalances in the levels of omega-3 and omega-6 fatty acids create inflammation in the body.

Farm-raised fish are given antibiotics to stave off disease that results from crowded conditions and are also treated with pesticides to combat sea lice. **Sea lice from fish farms kill up to 95% of migrating juvenile wild salmon.**

The pesticides used to treat sea lice in fish farms circulate throughout the ocean. Pesticides that have been banned for decades have concentrated in the fat of much marine life.

This fat is used in the feed that fish farms use, and studies by the Environmental Working Group, along with those done in Canada, Ireland and the UK, have found that cancer-causing polychlorinated biphenyls (PCBs) exist in farm-raised salmon at 16 times the rate of wild salmon.

Dibutyltin is a chemical used in PVC plastics. Dibutyltin can interfere with normal immune responses and inflammation control in both animals and humans. A 2008 study found that dibutyltin may be contributing to the rise of **allergies, asthma, obesity and other metabolic and immune disorders in humans**. Scientists have found that dibutyltin in farm-raised mussels is more than 6 times higher than that of wild mussels.

Researchers have also found levels of polybrominated diphenyl ether (PBDE), a chemical used as a flame retardant, in high levels in farm-raised fish. PBDEs are endocrine disruptors that are thought to contribute to cancer. Scientists believe that both fish feed and increasing concentrations in the open oceans are contributing to high PBDE levels in fish and humans.

Another study, conducted at the University of New York at Albany found that dioxin levels in farm-raised salmon are 11 times higher than those in wild salmon.

Dioxins are one of the "dirty dozen," says the World Health Organization (WHO) because they are highly toxic and are stored for a long time in the body: their half life in fat cells is 7 to 11 years. **Dioxins impair the endocrine, immune, nervous and reproductive systems and are carcinogens**.

University of British Columbia professor Daniel Pauly calls aquafarms "floating pig farms" because tremendous amounts of fish feed and fish waste accumulate on the seafloor because of them, creating a perfect breeding ground for bacteria that threaten other marine life.

Researchers from the **George Mateljan Foundation** say that "a good sized salmon farm produces an amount of excrement equivalent to the sewage of a city of 10,000 people."

So think next time you order that nice salmon fillet in the restaurant thinking you are making a healthy choice, ask them is it wild or farmed and if they say farmed order something of a more healthy choice.

Another group of chemicals with very powerful weight gaining effects are the organochlorines. Studies show that the higher the level of these chemicals in the body, the greater the body weight will be. One animal study, found that one type of organochlorine, the pesticide and widespread pollutant, hexachlorobenzene (HCB), to possess such extreme fattening effects that when they're food intake was cut by 50%, animals treated with HCB still managed to gain more weight than did untreated animals on full rations!!!

This is just unreal when you truly grasp what these invisible chemicals on our foods are doing to our health and our poor children are truly getting it much worse than adults due to their inability to detoxify as efficiently as adults. Think about it, we have only been spraying our foods with this insane cocktail of pesticides, herbicides and fungicides for approximately 70 years and this also coincides not only with the gradual climb in obesity but also cancer.

A picture tells 1000 words! Always eat fresh organic foods wherever possible

Organochlorine pesticides are mostly used as insecticides. Specific uses take a wide range of forms, from pellet application in field crops, to sprays for seed coating and grain storage. Some organochlorines are applied to surfaces to kill insects that land there.

Many organochlorines are known or suspected hormone disruptors, and recent studies show that extremely low levels of exposure in the womb can cause irreversible damage to the reproductive and immune systems of the developing foetus. Dr Annette Pernille Hoyer, who has worked on many studies looking at pesticide use, said: "I fear that the link is significant. The use of pesticides should be reduced as much as possible in general. **Human beings are**

naive when they do not believe that a poison designed to kill living organisms does not harm them".

Many pesticides are deliberately designed to target mitochondria (mitochondria are responsible for 95% energy production in humans) as the stronger the ability of a chemical to poison the mitochondria, the more effective it is in killing. Organochlorines actually reduce the mitochondria's ability to convert food into readily usable energy in the form of ATP. Not only does this affect energy production in our mitochondria, but it affects all of the mechanisms used by our bodies to produce energy leaving us feeling exhausted and unable to drop body fat effectively.

This is why you must go certified organic foods at every opportunity for your health and that of your children.

Bisphenol A (BPA) and Phthalates could they be making us sicker and fatter?

Another endocrine-disrupting chemical that may be linked to obesity is Bisphenol A (BPA). It is used to make polycarbonate plastic water bottles, baby bottles, the linings of metal food and soft-drink cans, thermal receipt paper, and dental sealants. Studies show that mice and rats fed low doses of BPA during early development became more obese as adults than those that weren't fed the chemical. BPA leaches from food and beverage containers into what we eat and drink.

Bottled water can absorb the BPAs from the plastic

BPA first caught researchers' attention after normal mice began to display uncommon genetic abnormalities. The defects were linked to plastic cages and water bottles that had been cleaned with a harsh detergent, causing BPA to leach out of the plastic. After determining how much BPA the mice had been exposed to, the researchers realized even an extremely small dose of 20 parts per billion daily, for just five to seven days, was enough to produce effects.

Some laboratory research has found that, particularly in female animals, BPA exposure can lead to higher weight gain and greatly increased fat deposits. Exposed animals ate no more food, but gained more weight than unexposed animals. Cell culture studies show that BPA can suppress hormones that protect from insulin resistance and even trigger other types of cells to become fat cells. Analyses of BPA in U.S. residents have linked higher exposure to a greater likelihood of diabetes and heart disease.

Phthalates are also endocrine disrupting chemicals and are commonly found in personal care products such as moisturisers, nail polishes, soaps, hair sprays and perfumes. They are also used in adhesives, electronics, toys and a variety of other products. Researchers, lead by Tamarra James-Todd, Ph.D., a researcher in the Division of Women's Health at BWH, analysed urinary concentrations of phthalates in 2,350 women who participated in the National Health and Nutrition Examination Survey. They found that women with higher levels of phthalates in their urine were more likely to have diabetes. **Another study linked a type of phthalate that leaches into processed food with abdominal obesity and insulin resistance in men.**

Phthalates (or plasticizers) have an affinity for the testicles, which accounts for the ever worsening levels of testosterone in males. It is no surprise that the average male is producing less testosterone than 20 years ago, and it is getting worse. Phthalates are also known to block the receptor sites for thyroid.

Unfortunately the chemistry of phthalates resemble that of many hormones. As hormone mimickers, they are potent environmental endocrine disruptors. They can for example damage hormone receptors at the place on the cell membrane where our endogenous (produced within the body) hormones get transported into the cell to do it's work. By blocking the action of our natural hormones this often makes hormone replacement ineffective, that's why a lot of people for example on hormone medication feel no difference when they are on the medication.

One study of more than two thousand adults found at least 80% had detectable levels of six persistent organic pollutants that can remain in our tissues for up to ten years. Those people whose bodies had high levels of persistent organic pollutants such as dioxin, PCBs, and chlordane **were thirty eight times more likely to be insulin resistant than people with low levels - this is a recipe for obesity and diabetes.**

Cooking appliances could be causing you both obesity and health problems!

Perfluorooctanoic acid (PFOA) is used to make non-stick cookware. Such toxic cookware and their released gases threaten hormonal balance. One study has shown a link between thyroid disease, cancer and non-stick cookware. The study was published in the journal Environmental and reported that people with high levels of PFOA, were more likely to develop thyroid problems, as well as various types of cancers. So you need to carefully consider the cookware you use (see Phil says for my recommendations).

You also need to be aware of the dangers of microwaving food inside containers made of plastic, cellophane, cardboard and styrofoam which may leach toxins into the food and increases the levels of carcinogens being consumed. Since most containers do not visibly melt or get hot, consumers have the false notion that the synthetic boxes and wrappers are not releasing toxins, but new research shows they are, and at levels that are alarming. Consumers are guaranteeing a dose of poison when they buy processed food (which contains synthetic ingredients), "nuke" them in a microwave, and then consume the radiated chemicals and vapors from the packaging.

While plastics can be safely used to hold dry foods at room temperature, if they are carrying liquids or being used as containers to heat foods, they often leach BPA and other chemicals right into the food. BPA has been found to alter brain function, not just body hormone expression.

Levels of BPA in your blood rise 1200% after eating tinned soup, reports the Harvard School of Public Health. And the worst part of all is that BPA replacement chemicals such as BPS have been found to be twenty times more toxic than BPA. So if you're drinking out of plastic or heating foods out of plastic, you're very likely to be harming yourself and your waistline.

Professor Bernard Blanc of the University of Lausanne, and an independent researcher, Dr. Hans U. Hertel concludes "Food, heated by microwaves, causes pathogenic changes in the blood of individuals who consume such food, similar to what is seen in the initial stages of cancer."

PHIL SAYS
Cookware

When I'm buying cookware I avoid non-stick coated pans and instead select cast-iron or ceramic pans. I also always advise all of my athletes to do the same.

Microwaving food also reduces the nutrient quality of the food. A study published in the November 2003 issue of The Journal of the Science of Food and Agriculture found that broccoli "zapped" in the microwave with a little water lost up to 97% of its beneficial antioxidants. By comparison, steamed broccoli lost 11% or fewer of its antioxidants. Microwaving food also leads to unhealthy clumping, or agglutination, in the blood. Each time, the effect can last up to two hours or longer.

I can't believe now how many foods are available in supermarkets today which can only be cooked in microwaves. There are literally are rows of these products which, to the naked eye, look really healthy and yet again in reality are totally toxic to the human body. Do yourself a favour and never use your microwave again. It's one of the first pieces of advice I give to any athlete I consult for.

Chemicals in Everyday Products are probably not only costing you pounds to buy but adding pounds to your bodyweight!

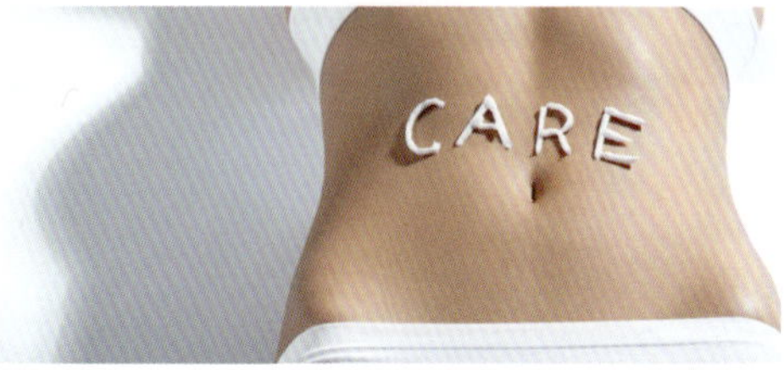

Many everyday items that we use are also full of hormone disrupting chemicals which can have an affect on our health and fat loss. Petrochemical compounds are found in general consumer products such as creams, lotions, soaps, shampoos, perfumes, hair sprays and room deodorizers. Such compounds often have chemical structures similar to oestrogen and indeed act like oestrogen in the body.

As much as 60% of any substance applied to the skin or scalp is absorbed into the body. This is facilitated further as there are detergents present in many products which improve skin absorption. These toxins go straight into the bloodstream and put tremendous strain on the kidneys and liver as they work to rid our bodies of these harmful chemicals. The use of these harsh chemicals would not be such a problem if the skin did not readily absorb them. Some chemicals can penetrate the skin in significant amounts, especially when left on the skin. A recent case that made headline news found traces of 350 man-made chemicals, including residues from personal care products, in human breast milk.

Even in most commercial tampons there are some other ingredients including;

- Dioxin and disinfection-by-products (DBPs) such as trihalomethane. These chemicals are present when the tampon is bleached, and are very toxic. Dioxin is also a hormone disruptor and a known carcinogen.
- Oestrogen. This encourages heavier flow.
- Pesticides, herbicides and synthetic fertilizers that are used in non-organic cotton.
- Phthalates. These are chemical plasticisers that are used in plastic tampon applicators and cardboard applicators.
- Polypropylene. This is a type of plastic which can withstand very high temperatures.
- Rayon. Made from wood or cotton pulp, rayon is an artificial fibre that is highly chemically processed and highly absorbent, making it particularly dangerous when used in a tampon as it can lead to Toxic Shock Syndrome.
- Viscose. Another type of wood pulp that is treated with toxic chemicals such as caustic soda and sulphuric acid.

The average woman absorbs 4lb 6oz of chemicals from toiletries and makeup every year, the industry magazine In-Cosmetics recently reported.

Many common sunscreen chemicals also increase oestrogen within us which is not good for our health or our weight. Margaret Schlumpf and her colleagues (Institute of Pharmacology and Toxicology, University of Zurich, Switzerland) have found that many widely-used sunscreen chemicals mimic the effects of oestrogen and trigger developmental abnormalities in rats. Her group tested six common chemicals that are used in sunscreens, as well as lipsticks and facial cosmetics. Five of the six tested chemicals (benzophenone-3, homosalate, 4-methyl-benzylidene camphor (4-MBC), octyl-methoxycinnamate and octyl-dimethyl-PABA) behaved like strong oestrogen in lab tests and caused cancer cells to grow more rapidly.

Another study has shown that a potent sunscreen ingredient, oxybenzone, may be a cause of endometriosis. This condition occurs when uterine tissue grows in abnormal sites in the abdomen and causes severe pain. Women are usually diagnosed because of severe cramping during their periods. In this study of 600 women, those with the highest levels of a form of oxybenzone in their urine had a 65% increased risk of endometriosis. Oxybenzone, like bisphenol-A (BPA), is a chemical that mimics oestrogen. And, endometriosis growth is fed by oestrogen.

This study should be another warning sign that oxybenzone should not be put on the skin. The highest levels of oxybenzone in the urine of women in this study occurred in the months of July and August, showing that the sunscreen ingredient is readily absorbed into the bloodstream. We have also become a society that is obsessed with covering up using sunscreen. However, this prevents us from getting our free fix of vitamin D from the UVB rays from sunlight which protects us from several types of cancer.

We will cover in much more detail the incredible healing benefits of the sun in habit 7 of this book.

Is What You're Drinking Making You Fat?

Our food is not the only thing that has become toxic over the last few decades. Our tap water is literally full of toxins and endocrine disrupting chemicals which is having a significant effect on our health. What we drink has changed significantly over the last few generations with many of our drinks today full of chemicals

Time and time again we get governments trying to convince us they care about public health when in reality it is about making us sicker, dumber and fatter. Be Warned! "Adding fluoride to water should be considered by councils in England to improve dental health", the government's public health advisory body says.

Public Health England (PHE) urged councils to act after reviewing the impact of water fluoridation on children in areas where it has been introduced. About 6m people - 10% of the country - currently live in areas with fluoridated water supplies. PHE said it was a "safe and effective" public health measure. Its review found it had reduced tooth decay and hospital admissions for dental problems.

Southern Ireland has unfortunately got mass fluoridation and I lecture there quite frequently and have observed countless times people with dental fluorosis.

When was the last time your doctor prescribed good nutrition, clean drinking water, sunshine, grounding and stress reduction? Probably never. Why? There is no return business for healthy people and big pharma DOES NOT want that to happen it kills their business model! Also doctors have virtually no training or knowledge on nutrition that's why you normally only leave the surgery with medication and not education on how to improve nutrition and lifestyle sad but very true.

NOW THE FACTS ON FLUORIDATED WATER!

Children who drink fluoridated water develop lower IQs. According to information compiled by the fluoride awareness group Fluoride Action Network (FAN), at least 34 published studies have identified a link between fluoride exposure and reduced IQ levels.

Fluoridated water is toxic to formula-fed babies. Did you know the U.S. Food and Drug Administration (FDA) recognizes fluoride as an "unapproved drug," which means those who receive it are being forcibly medicated against their will and without informed consent? Fluoridated water is particularly harmful for the development of formula-fed babies.

Water fluoridation has created an epidemic of dental fluorosis. Chronic exposure to fluoride can lead to a form of tooth decay known as dental fluorosis, which is marked by brown or white staining and corresponding mottling on teeth. It would be scientifically foolish to insist otherwise when acknowledging the fact that as many as 60% of all adolescents, and particularly those who live in fluoridated areas, now suffer from the permanent condition.

Water fluoridation is responsible for damaging bones, triggering arthritis. Back in 2006, the National Research Council (NRC) published a report showing that the federal government's maximum contaminant level for fluoride in water is a complete fraud. As it turns out, so-called "optimal" fluoride levels in water do not protect the health of children or adults, and regular exposure to fluoride in water can lead to brittle bones, preclinical skeletal fluorosis, and arthritis.

The fluoride added to most water supplies is an industrial waste product that can cause cancer. Unbeknownst to many is the fact that the fluoride chemicals added to most municipal water supplies are not naturally occurring elements in the earth, but rather waste byproducts of industrial production systems. Such chemicals have never been properly safety tested, and they most definitely do not benefit oral health in any way.

Robert Carton, former president of the Union of Government Scientists at the US Environmental Protection Agency – the body that oversees drinking water quality in the US – has described fluoridation as "the greatest case of scientific fraud of this century, if not of all time."

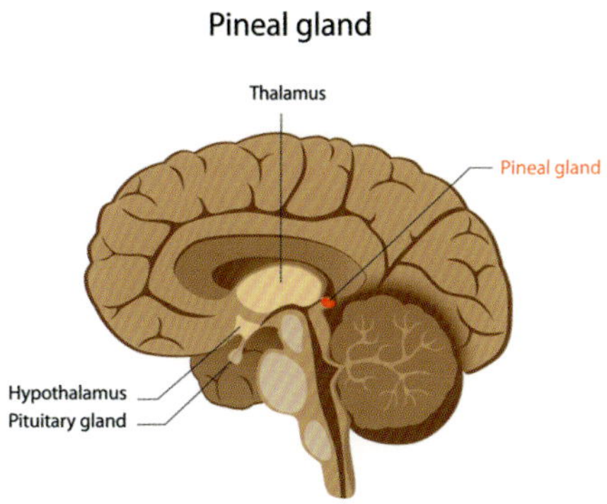

It is now known - thanks to the meticulous research of Dr. Jennifer Luke from the University of Surrey in England - that the pineal gland is the primary target of fluoride accumulation within the body. The pineal gland (or pineal body) is an important endocrine gland. It is a small, oval structure descending from the roof of the diencephalon, a section of the brain that relays sensory information between the brain's different regions. Although it's very tiny (only about six millimeters long) the pineal gland produces several important hormones. The most significant of these is melatonin, a hormone which regulates the circadian rhythm, or sleep cycle. Check if your tap water contains fluoride and, if it does, get a reverse osmosis water filter fitted (which I advise anyway) and use fluoride free dental products. I will talk more on the benefits of reverse osmosis throughout this book.

A study published in the journal, *Food Research International*, has revealed that millions of people across the globe are at serious risk of developing tooth decay, bone loss, and other serious health conditions as a result of over-exposure to fluoride. Many inexpensive, store brand black and green teas, it turns out, contain dangerously high levels of fluoride that far exceed even the government's over-inflated maximums for fluoride exposure.

Study has found that certain brands of tea have been found to have high fluoride levels!

Though it focused mainly on private label tea brands sold in the U.K., the study identified what is presumably a reality in many developed nations -- cheap teas generally contain levels of fluoride so high that drinking them may be considered unsafe. Based on an analysis of 38 different tea brands, Ph.D. student Laura Chan and her colleagues from the *University of Derby* found that fluoride levels averaged around six milligrams per liter (mg/l) in store brand tea.

"This study suggests that people drinking economy brands of tea may be exposed to high levels of fluoride, which can cause dental, thyroid and bone problems," admitted the U.K.'s *National Health Service* (NHS) in an announcement. "The researchers calculate that people drinking one liter of cheap tea a day may be consuming more fluoride than the daily recommended amount, as advised by U.S. experts."

Fluoride is not the only problem though. "Chlorine is so dangerous, that it should be banned. Putting chlorine in the water is like starting a time bomb. Cancer, heart trouble, premature senility, both mental and physical are conditions attributable to chlorine, used in treated water supplies. It is making us grow old before our time by producing symptoms of ageing such as hardening of the arteries. I believe if chlorine were now proposed for the first time to be used in drinking water it would be banned by the Food and Drug Administration." Biologist/chemist Dr. Herbert Schwartz

"We are learning the hard way that all the time we thought we were preventing epidemics of one disease, we were creating another. Two decades after the start of chlorinating our drinking water the present epidemic of heart trouble and cancer began." Dr. Joseph M. Price, PhD

"Drinking tap water that is chlorinated is hazardous, if not deadly to your health." US Council of Environmental Quality

"Chlorine gas was despicably used in WW1. When the war was over, the use of chlorine was diverted to poisoning germs in our drinking water. All water supplies throughout the country were chlorinated. The combination of chlorine (when in drinking water) and animal fats results in atherosclerosis, heart attacks and deaths." "Chemistry and Control of Modern Chlorination", Dr AT Palin, PhD, (OBE)

This makes you think, doesn't it? The next time you innocently drink a glass of water from your tap in the house you should be thinking "is this 100% safe and healthy?" We are naive as humans in that if we can't see it then it can't do any harm! Wrong! In habit 2 I talk about getting reverse osmosis water filters fitted to your house. This, to me, is absolutely essential for our health.

Chlorine in tap water has been linked to the rising number of people developing food allergies, a study has revealed.

The chemical, which is used to treat drinking water and is also present in commonly-available pesticides and household items, may weaken food tolerance in some individuals. Researchers found adults with high levels of dichlorophenol – a chemical by-product of chlorine – in their urine, were up to **80 per cent** more likely to have a food allergy.

In a study of 2,211 American adults with the chemical in their urine, 411 were found to have a food allergy, while 1,016 had an environmental allergy.

The research, published in a journal of the American College of Allergy, Asthma and Immunology, concluded: 'Excessive use of dichlorophenols may contribute to the increasing incidence of food allergies in Westernised societies. 'This chemical is commonly found in pesticides and consumer insect and weed control products, as well as tap water.' Lead author Dr Elina Jerschow added: 'Previous studies have shown that both food allergies and environmental pollution are increasing in the United States. "Our study suggest these two trends might be linked, and that increased use of pesticides and other chemicals is associated with a higher prevalence of food allergies.'

Pharmaceuticals are now being found in drinking water, according to a study conducted in England. The study looked at 12 pharmaceuticals thought to pose an environmental threat, including painkillers, antibiotics, and antidepressants, and it found traces of these pharmaceuticals in both sewage waters and drinking water. It also found traces in the rivers downstream from the sewage treatment plants.

This is shocking information -- apparently we are dosing ourselves with such high levels of pharmaceuticals that we are now collectively polluting the rivers, streams and even the drinking water for the mass public.

Once again, it seems that as long as there are profits to be made, everybody in the pharmaceutical industry is happy, regardless of the negative impact on the environment. In fact, I don't think you even hear much talk at all these days about pharmaceutical companies working to protect the environment. It's pretty much just, "Here, take this drug, pay us money for a pill, and then flush it down the toilet. After that, we don't want to think about it anymore."

It's not just our water either. A 2008 report by PAN Europe found that 100% of conventionally produced wines that they analysed, including wines made in France, Germany, Austria, Italy, Portugal, South Africa, Chile and Australia, were shown to contain pesticides. One bottle contained 10 different residues, while the average number of pesticides was more than four per bottle. Almost half of all conventional wines tested contained pesticides classified by the European Union as being carcinogenic, mutagenic, reprotoxic or disruptive to the endocrine system – including three French wines purchased at more than €200 per bottle.

The European Commission published a 10 year overview of the use of pesticides in European agriculture. The EU study shows that grapes receive 4.7kg of synthetic pesticides per hectare – a higher dose than any other crop except potatoes. In fact despite accounting for 3.5% of the total EU agricultural area, grapes receive 15% by weight of the synthetic pesticides applied to all major crops.

If you must have your glass of wine go ORGANIC!

Is that daily cup of coffee contributing to your waistline?

Most people are not aware that regular coffee consumption can be a significant source of pesticides. According to the CS Monitor, conventional farmers apply up to 250 pounds of chemical fertilizers per acre! So when you sip on your non-organic morning brew, you are also sipping on pesticide residues. Further, the UK has limited input and control over the type and quantity of pesticides used in the countries from which we import. Since the vast majority of coffee consumed in the UK is grown outside this country, a return to non-organic farming of coffee beans usually means a return to heavy use of pesticides.

Coffee also stimulates your adrenals - the hormones that activate your fight or flight response. If your adrenal hormones are stimulated too often, which is probably going to happen if you are a multiple daily coffee drinker, your adrenal glands may eventually burn out. When your adrenals no longer function effectively, your body will go in search of a replacement hormone - which happens to be progesterone. Progesterone has its own full-time job to do, part of which is to keep your body's oestrogen in balance. As your progesterone is used up compensating for your exhausted adrenals, you run the risk of becoming oestrogen dominant. Oestrogen dominance can lead to obesity, cancer and osteoporosis.

Coffee also raises the acidity level of your blood, causing calcium to be pulled from your bones and teeth for use as a buffering agent. The combination of oestrogen dominance and high blood acidity puts you at an even greater risk for osteoporosis. In fact, research has established an undeniable link between coffee consumption and hip fractures.

If you're going to drink coffee, going organic is the "healthiest" way to do it. Of course, coffee is really not healthy at all. Caffeine is a drug. It's a legal and widely available drug, but a drug nonetheless, and very powerful. I drink coffee very occasionally but always organic if I can get it. I cringe with sadness at the amount of women I see drinking latte's as if its some sort of nutritional drink. Listen to me - it will screw you up if you keep drinking this poison every day and, to add insult to injury, having a sugary snack with your coffee is a great way to increase anxiety, acidity as well as pack the excess fat on your butt, hips & guts!

Drinking more than two cups of coffee daily may boost oestrogen levels in women and could worsen conditions such as endometriosis and breast pain. According to researchers, women who drank the most coffee had higher levels of oestradiol, a naturally occurring form of oestrogen, during the early follicular phase, or days 1 to 5 of the menstrual cycle.

The study included nearly 500 women aged 36 to 45 who were not pregnant, breast-feeding or taking hormones. All women answered questions about their diets, smoking habits, height and weight. Researchers measured the women's hormone levels during days 1 to 5 of their menstrual cycle.

Women who consumed more than one cup of coffee a day had significantly higher levels of oestrogen during the early follicular phase of their menstrual cycle. Caffeine intake from all sources was linked with higher oestrogen levels regardless of age, body mass index (BMI), caloric intake, smoking, and alcohol and cholesterol intake. This study provides a basis for believing that coffee consumption increases oestradiol levels. While these effects are modest with one or two cups, they are more evident at higher levels of consumption. ***Fertility and Sterility October 2001;76:723-729***

Genetically Modified (GM) Foods could be making you fatter and you don't even know you are eating them because they don't have to say on the label!

In global terms the use of GM crops has increased steadily since the first commercial plantings in North America in the late 1990s. By 2012 over 17 million farmers in 28 countries were growing GM crops on 170 million hectares, which is more than 12% of the world's arable land, an area of land more than 5 times the size of the UK.

As part of a long-term project studying the health effects of GM foods, researchers from Norway fed food containing GM corn to one group of rats and food containing non-GM corn to another group. Over the course of 90 days, the rats on the GM-corn diet grew fatter and consumed more food than the rats on the non-GM diet.

The researchers also noticed that rats got fatter when they ate fish that had been raised on GM corn. They also tried the experiment on salmon and saw similar results: Fish eating GM corn grew faster, and they ate more, than fish eating non-GM corn. The salmon on GM corn were also less able to digest proteins, and experienced immune-system changes that didn't occur in non-GM-fed fish.

Monosodium Glutamate A Villain In Disguise And It Can Make You Fat And Dumb (MSG)

MSG is found in almost all convenience foods, fast foods and processed foods. It is used as a flavour enhancer in cheap, processed foods to make their taste more appealing. While making bland foods taste more appealing, this chemically structured ingredient is shown to cause neurotransmitter damage and is also linked to the skyrocketing cases of obesity we see today.

A team of scientists in the Faculty of Medicine at the Complutense University of Madrid has discovered that when given to rats, E-621 (AKA MONOSODIUM GLUTAMATE) produces a massive 40% increase in appetite. The scientists think the additive affects the arcuate nucleus area of the brain and so prevents proper functioning of the body's appetite control mechanisms. According to this hypothesis, people who consume foods with MSG just feel more and more hungry, the more they eat.

By directly stimulating the pancreas to release insulin, which drops the blood sugar, MSG can be considered an "anti-appetite suppressant". In other words, eating MSG makes you hungrier than you would have been, sooner than you would have been. Over-release of insulin can lead to obesity and insulin resistance - the start of Type II Diabetes.

People who use MSG as a flavour enhancer in their food are more likely than people who don't use it to be overweight or obese even though they have the same amount of physical activity and total calorie intake, according to a University of North Carolina at Chapel Hill School of Public Health study published in the journal Obesity.

If fried snack crisps had a warning printed right on the bag that said, "Warning: these chips will make you obese," would you still buy them? Would you still eat them?

Well, in a sense, you do see that warning on chips; just read the ingredient list. Research suggests that MSG causes obesity, making unhealthy snacks even unhealthier than you may have suspected.

Rats are not normally fat. When scientists inject the rodents at birth with MSG, like magic, they produce obese test subjects. Because MSG triples the amount of insulin the rat's pancreas creates, the results are perfect....MSG Treated Rats = Fat Rats. These findings are substantiated in over 100 studies and can be found at the National Library of Medicine, at www.pubmed.com. All you have to do is search under "MSG Obese."

Researchers at UNC and in China studied more than 750 Chinese men and women, aged between 40 and 59, in three rural villages in north and south China. The majority of study participants prepared their meals at home without commercially processed foods. About 82 percent of the participants used MSG in their food. Those users were divided into three groups, based on the amount of MSG they used. The third who used the most MSG were nearly three times more likely to be overweight than non-users.

"Animal studies have indicated for years that MSG might be associated with weight gain," said Ka He, M.D., assistant professor of nutrition and epidemiology at the UNC School of Public Health. "Ours is the first study to show a link between MSG use and weight in humans."

Because MSG is used as a flavour enhancer in many processed foods, studying its potential effect on humans has been difficult. He and his colleagues chose study participants living in rural Chinese villages because they used very little commercially processed food, but many regularly used MSG in food preparation. "We found that prevalence of overweight was significantly higher in MSG users than in non-users," He said. "We saw this risk even when we controlled for physical activity, total calorie intake and other possible explanations for the difference in body mass. The positive associations between MSG intake and overweight were consistent with data from animal studies."

MSG goes by many different names because the food industry knows the public is becoming more aware of the problems MSG causes so in their true colours of dishonesty they have come up with multiple disguises:

Names of ingredients that contain processed free glutamic acid (MSG)

(Last updated March, 2014)

Everyone knows that some people react to the food ingredient monosodium glutamate. What many don't know, is that more than 40 different ingredients contain the chemical in monosodium glutamate (processed free glutamic acid) that causes these reactions. The following list has been compiled over the last 20 years from consumer reports and information provided by manufacturers and food technologists.

Names of ingredients that always contain processed free glutamic acid:	**Names of ingredients that often contain or produce processed free glutamic acid during processing:**	**The following are ingredients suspected of containing or creating sufficient processed free glutamic acid to serve as MSG-reaction triggers in HIGHLY SENSITIVE people:**
Glutamic acid (E 620)[2] Glutamate (E 620) Monosodium glutamate (E 621) Monopotassium glutamate (E 622) Calcium glutamate (E 623) Monoammonium glutamate (E 624) Magnesium glutamate (E 625) Natrium glutamate *Anything* "hydrolyzed" *Any* "hydrolyzed protein" Calcium caseinate, Sodium caseinate Yeast extract, Torula yeast Yeast food, Yeast nutrient Autolyzed yeast Gelatin Textured protein Whey protein Whey protein concentrate Whey protein isolate Soy protein Soy protein concentrate Soy protein isolate *Anything* "protein" *Anything* "protein fortified" Soy sauce Soy sauce extract *Anything* "enzyme modified" *Anything* containing "enzymes" *Anything* "fermented" *Anything containing* "protease" Vetsin Ajinomoto Umami	Carrageenan (E 407) Bouillon and broth Stock *Any* "flavors" *or* "flavoring" Natural flavor Maltodextrin Oligodextrin Citric acid, Citrate (E 330) *Anything* "ultra-pasteurized" Barley malt Malted barley Brewer's yeast Pectin (E 440) Malt extract Seasonings	Corn starch Corn syrup Modified food starch Lipolyzed butter fat Dextrose Rice syrup Brown rice syrup Milk powder Reduced fat milk (skim; 1%; 2%) *most things* "low fat" or "no fat" *anything* "enriched" *anything* "vitamin enriched" *anything* "pasteurized" Annatto Vinegar Balsamic vinegar *certain* amino acid chelates *(Citrate, aspartate, and glutamate are used as chelating agents with mineral supplements.)*

(1) Glutamic acid found in unadulterated protein does not cause adverse reactions. To cause adverse reactions, the glutamic acid must have beenprocessed/manufactured or come from protein that has been fermented.

(2) E numbers are use in Europe in place of food additive names.

The following work synergistically with MSG to enhance flavor. If they are present for flavoring, so is MSG.		
Disodium 5'-guanylate (E 627)	Disodium 5'-inosinate (E-631)	Disodium 5'-ribonucleotides (E 635)

Contrary to popular belief, studies have found that artificial sweeteners such as aspartame can:

Stimulate your appetite
Increase carbohydrate cravings
Stimulate fat storage and weight gain

Artificial sweeteners like sucralose, aspartame and Acesulfame K also tend to do the opposite of what they are marketed as doing. Several studies have linked consumption of diet sodas, which are loaded with synthetic sweetening chemicals, to cause weight gain rather than weight loss, which may come as a surprise to many people.

A study, published in the January 2013 issue of the journal Appetite, was done by a Brazilian research team with the Faculty of Medicine of the Federal University do Rio Grande do Sul. Rats were fed plain yogurt sweetened with either aspartame, saccharin, or sugar, plus their regular rat chow, for 12 weeks. "Results showed that addition of either saccharin or aspartame to yogurt resulted in increased weight gain compared to addition of sucrose (sugar), however total caloric intake was similar among groups," the researchers write.

Aspartame is found in many drinks, foods and even childrens' multi vitamins. You, and your children, should be very cautious of this ingredient and avoid it at all costs.

Diet fizzy drinks can raise the risk of diabetes by 60%, startling research has revealed. A study of more than 66,000 women found those who drank artificially sweetened drinks were more likely to develop the disease than those who indulged in regular, 'full fat' versions. The findings, published in the American Journal of Clinical Nutrition, fly in the face of conventional thinking that regular versions of fizzy drinks are always worse for our health.

Studies have began to show that drinking these low calorie, sugar free drinks are linked to increases in weight. The San Antonio Heart Study looked at over 5000 men and found that those who drank these drinks had Body Mass Index (BMI's) over 40% higher than those who didn't even when other factors were taken into account.

Food additives and sweeteners are able to augment the addictive properties of food. As an example, on the relative sweetness scale, glucose, the primary sugar in blood, weighs in at a measly 0.8. Compare that with table sugar (sucrose) that is rated 1.0. High fructose corn syrup is 1.2 and fructose is 1.4 almost twice as sweet as glucose.

Food manufacturers understand this addiction all too well and that's why thousands of foods are loaded with artificial sweeteners to get us addicted to this junk food which makes the junk food industry billions of pounds whilst we also gain pounds unfortunately around our waistlines.

Where do artificial sweeteners fall on this same scale? Aspartame is listed 180, acesulfame K at 200, and saccharin at 300, while sucralose weighs in at 600. This means Splenda is 750 times as sweet as glucose. No wonder so many of us are addicted to foods containing these super sweet additives, many of which are already loaded with sugar and high-fructose corn syrup (HFCS). The sweet taste products deliver can change the way we perceive food, think about food, crave food and they can increase appetite and the secretion of the hormone insulin.

A 2010 scientific review published in the Yale Journal of Biology and Medicine (YJBM) discussed the neurobiology of sweet cravings and the unexpected effect of artificial sweeteners on appetite control. It cites several large scale prospective cohort studies that found positive correlations between artificial sweetener use and weight gain, which flies in the face of "conventional wisdom" to cut calories in order to lose weight.

Fructose is a cheap form of sugar used in thousands of food products and soft drinks, which can damage your, or your child's, metabolism. More than any other form of sugar, heavy fructose consumption can cause dangerous growths of fat cells around vital organs and can trigger the early stages of diabetes, heart and liver disease. Fructose, usually derived from corn, is fuelling the obesity crisis in a big way due to its heavy use by the food and beverage industry in the form of high-fructose corn syrup (HFCS) and crystalline fructose. If you or your child are consuming excess fructose daily, it can result in damage to your liver.

Dr. Richard Johnson's book, The Fat Switch, dispels many of the most pervasive myths relating to diet and obesity. He discovered the method that animals use to gain fat prior to times of food scarcity, which turned out to be a powerful adaptive benefit. His research showed that fructose activates a key enzyme, fructokinase, which in turn activates another enzyme that causes cells to accumulate fat.

Since all fructose gets shuttled to your liver, and, if you eat a typical Western-style diet, you consume high amounts of it, fructose ends up taxing and damaging your liver in the same way alcohol and other toxins do. And just like alcohol, excess fructose is metabolised directly into fat – not cellular energy, like glucose. While in times of complete glycogen depletion (i.e. post workout or true hunger), fructose can be used to replenish these stores, any excess will be converted to fat. So, eating fructose in excess of the very small amount our body can handle is really like eating fat – it just gets stored in your fat cells, which leads to mitochondrial malfunction, obesity and obesity-related diseases. I cover this in more depth throughout the book.

PHIL SAYS

READING LABELS

If you are buying packaged food/drink products, I strongly suggest that you become vigilant in reading labels. However, spotting some of this artificial sweeteners can be difficult as they can masquerade under a number of names. This is why I am a strong advocate of only buying foods in their natural state as most processed foods are loaded with an array of flavourings, artificial sweeteners, trans fats and a host of other nasties.

Two other studies have added more reason for concern that high-fructose corn syrup causes significantly more harm to the body than its mere sugar content would suggest. High-fructose corn syrup contains 55% fructose and 45% glucose. In contrast, table sugar (also known as sucrose) contains a 50-50 split. In the first study, published in the journal Pharmacology, Biochemistry and Behaviour, researchers from Princeton University found that rats consuming high fructose corn syrup gained more weight and developed more cardiovascular risk factors than rats consuming equivalent amounts of sucrose.

> ***"Some people have claimed that high-fructose corn syrup is no different than other sweeteners when it comes to weight gain and obesity, but our results make it clear that this just isn't true," researcher Bart Hoebel said.***

Hoebel and colleagues fed two groups of rats an identical diet, supplemented with one of two sweetened beverages. One beverage consisted of a sucrose solution in concentrations similar to those found in many sweetened beverages. The other consisted of a high-fructose corn syrup solution at roughly half the concentration of a typical soda. The researchers found that the rats consuming the corn syrup solution gained significantly more weight than the rats consuming the sucrose solution.

After six months, the rats in the corn syrup group had gained 48% more weight. They also underwent an increase in fat deposition (especially in the abdomen). Every rat consuming high-fructose corn syrup became obese. In contrast, rats fed a high-fat diet did not become obese in all cases.

After eating fructose, 100% of the metabolic burden rests on your liver - ONLY your liver can break it down. This is much different than consuming glucose, in which your liver has to break down only 20%, and the remaining 80% is immediately metabolised and used by the rest of the cells in your body.

Part of what makes excess fructose so bad for your health is that it is metabolised to fat in your body far more rapidly than any other sugar. For example, if you eat 120 calories of fructose, around 40 calories are stored as fat. But if you eat the same amount of glucose, less than one calorie may get stored as fat. Consuming fructose is essentially consuming fat!

One of the primary problems with fructose is that it is isocaloric but not isometabolic, meaning that while you can have the same amount of calories from fructose or any other nutrient, including glucose, the metabolic effect will be entirely different despite the identical calorie count. This explains why calorie counting doesn't work. You simply have to take the quality or source of the calories into account in order to successfully lose weight.

Fruit *juice* typically contains very high concentrations of fructose, which will cause your insulin to spike and may counter the benefits of the antioxidants. Previous studies have already clearly demonstrated that drinking large amounts of juice dramatically increases your risk of obesity. Children are at particular risk here, since so many children are given juice whenever they're thirsty instead of plain water. For example, research has revealed that 3- and 4-year-olds who carry extra weight and drink just one to two sweet drinks a day double their risk of becoming seriously overweight just one year later.

When buying commercial fruit juice, you need to check the label, as the majority of fruit juices contain high fructose corn syrup and artificial flavors in addition to concentrated fruit juice. But even freshly squeezed fruit juice can contain about eight full teaspoons of fructose per eight-ounce glass!

The drug addiction of sugar is actually more powerful than cocaine and the food manufacturers know this and that's why most of our processed foods are loaded with sugar. According to the 2007 Bordeaux University research study, refined sugar is far more addictive than cocaine - one of the most addictive and harmful substances currently known.

An astonishing 94% of rats who were allowed to choose mutually-exclusively between sugar and cocaine, chose sugar. Even rats who were addicted to cocaine quickly switched their preference to sugar, once it was offered as a choice. The rats were also more willing to work for sugar than for cocaine. The researchers speculate that the sweet receptors (two protein receptors located on the tongue), which evolved in ancestral times when the diet was very low in sugar, have not adapted to modern times' high-sugar consumption.

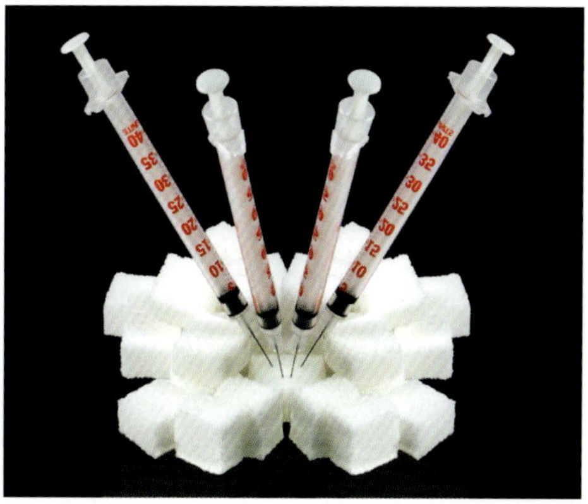

Therefore, the abnormally high stimulation of these receptors by our sugar-rich diets generates excessive reward signals in the brain, which have the potential to override normal self-control mechanisms, and thus lead to addiction.

Plastic Fats Found In Processed Foods Increase Fat On Your Gut!

"Do you think this has any trans fat?"

Trans fats (artificial fats) make you fatter than other foods with the same number of calories - but that's not all. Researchers at Wake Forest University found that trans fats increase the amount of fat around the abdomen. They do this not just by adding new fat, but also by moving fat from other areas to the abdomen.

"Trans fat is worse than anticipated," Wake Forest researcher Lawrence L. Rudel, Ph.D. says. "Diets rich in trans fat cause a redistribution of fat tissue into the abdomen and lead to a higher body weight even when the total dietary calories are controlled."

The Nurse's Health Study of 80,000 women found that a 2% increase in trans fat consumption increased a woman's risk of heart disease by 93%. Just a 2% increase in trans fats calories has been found to boost your risk of diabetes by 39%.

In the UK hydrogenated vegetable oil, otherwise known as trans fat, doesn't even have to appear clearly on ingredients labels (at the time of printing). Have a look, and you might find it called 'shortening', or 'hydrogenated fats', may be 'hydrogenated vegetable oils' (HVOs), perhaps 'partially hydrogenated vegetable oils' (PHVOs), or not mentioned at all.

MARGARINE MANUFACTURING PROCESS

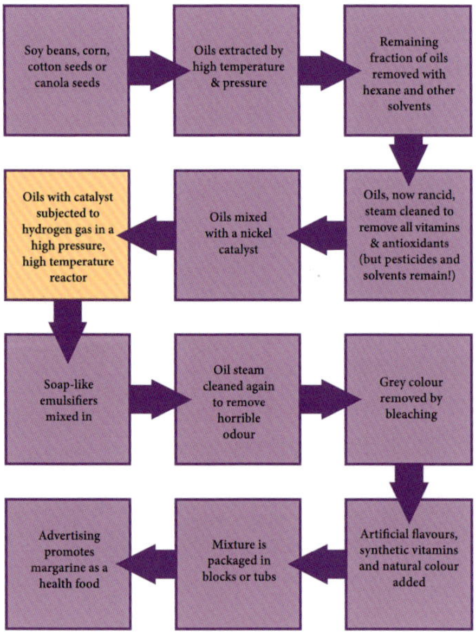

Margarine should genuinely have a health warning on the lid saying this is a non food that is simply not fit for human consumption, but due to some very clever marketing and scaremongering we have convinced millions to eat this shite at the expense of their health! The scientific evidence is compelling and totally at odds with decades of official advice that we should all be cutting down on our consumption of animal fats.

Taking a sample of middle-aged Australian men who had either experienced a heart attack or suffered from angina, half were advised to cut their animal fat intake and replace it with safflower oil and safflower oil margarine, while the other half continued to eat as normal.

If Government nutritionists and the food processing industry were right — and margarine really was better for you, as they've been claiming for decades — you'd expect the men who switched to safflower oil to live longer and have better health outcomes. The exact opposite turned out to be true. Those who ate more of the safflower-derived products were almost twice as likely to die from all causes, including heart disease. Suddenly, margarine isn't looking the healthy option that those expensive marketing campaigns claim it to be.

For a start, the once widely accepted wisdom that saturated fats are bad for you — an idea on which so much health advice is founded — is looking increasingly shaky.. Certainly, these saturated fats have already been identified as key components of cell membranes, essential for the production of steroid hormones and having an important role to play in the transport and absorption of certain vitamins and minerals.

Margarine should carry a health warning it is so repugnant to our health. As human beings you should promise yourself never to eat this non food and don't fall for the cholesterol lowering nonsense either. That is another massive food industry con which is causing more misery for people who have been massively misled that cholesterol is a killer just to fuel statin sales. In habit 4, 6 and 8 you will see why cholesterol is absolutely essential for our health and well being.

How margarine can be passed off as a health food has to go down as one of the biggest food frauds of all time.

EMFs

EMFs are electromagnetic frequencies and come from things such as wi-fi and mobile phones. Perhaps, one of the most serious consequences of EMFs exposure is its effects on our hormonal systems. Artificially created EMFs are estimated to be 100-200 million times greater than what existed just two generations ago. Every minute of every day, whether we are awake or asleep, we are exposed to a constant barrage of man-made EMFs.

Rajkovic et al. (2003) showed that after three months exposure to power line frequencies, the thyroid glands of rats showed visible signs of deterioration. They also lost their ability to produce the thyroid hormones, which they did not recover even after the fields were switched off. Esmekaya et al. (2010) found a similar visible deterioration of the thyroid gland in rats exposed to simulated 2G cell phone radiation for 20 minutes a day for three weeks. Eskander et al. (2012) found that people living for six years within 100 metres of a cell phone base station showed a significant reduction in the release into the blood of a number of hormones, including ACTH from the pituitary gland, cortisol from the adrenal glands, and prolactin and testosterone from organs elsewhere. However, the most highly significant loss was in their ability to produce the thyroid hormones. The expected consequence of this is hypothyroidism, the most frequent symptoms of which are fatigue and obesity.

A Swedish study on the use of wireless phones, including cell phones and cordless phones, has uncovered a link between electromagnetic radiation exposures and the risk of malignant and non-malignant brain tumours. **300% increased risk for long term users**. This new study reveals that people who used cell phones and cordless phones for more than a year were at a 70% greater risk of brain cancer compared to those who used cell phones and cordless phones for a year or less. Those who used cell phones and cordless phones for more than 25 years were found to have a 300% greater risk of brain cancer than those who used cell phones and cordless phones for a year or less.

The total number of hours of cell phone and cordless phone use was found to be as important as the number of years of use. A quarter of the study's subjects were found to have lifetime cell phone or cordless phone use of 2,376 or more hours, which corresponds to about 40 minutes a day over ten years. Heavier users were found to have a 250% greater risk of brain tumors compared to those who'd never used cell phones or cordless phones or used them for less than 39 hours in their lifetime.

Brain cancer risk highest on side of head used to phone

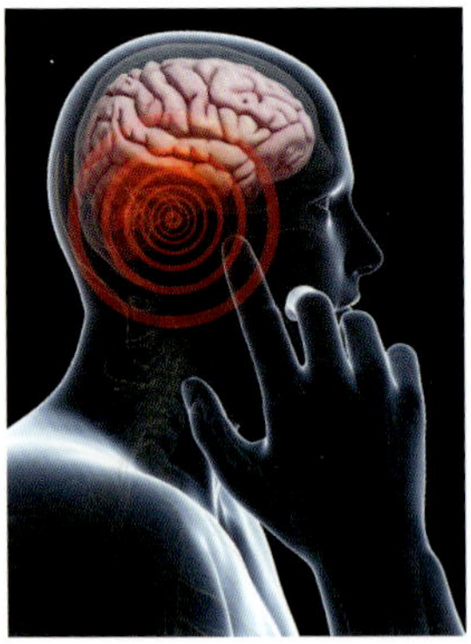

This new study echoes the previous study findings of the decade long 13-nation Interphone study, which found a 180% greater risk of brain cancer among those who used cell phones for 1,640 or more hours in their lifetime. But it also goes further.

In this latest study, for all types of cell phone and cordless phone use, brain cancer risk was found to be greater in the part of the brain where the exposure to cell phone and cordless phone radiation was highest, on the side of the head where people predominantly used their phones.

Given the consistent results from these studies, public health bodies from around the world are asking that the current wireless safety standards be reviewed.

The World Health Organization (WHO) recently classified radio frequency electromagnetic fields as a Group 2B possible carcinogen. Doctors groups are also sounding the alarm. The

American Academy of Environmental Medicine, the International Society of Doctors for the Environment (ISDE) and the Irish Doctors Environmental Association (IDEA) are all calling for improved standards.

Practice safe use of wireless phones

In the absence of sufficiently protective standards and legislation, individuals need to act now. This means:

- Limiting calls to those that are absolutely necessary on wireless devices
- Using a speaker phone or air tube headset whenever possible
- Keeping cell phones away from the body
- Turning your cell phone off when not in use
- Texting instead of talking
- Alternating from one side of the head to the other when phoning
- Avoiding using a cell phone when reception is poor
- Using a corded land line whenever possible
- Removing cordless phones from bedrooms

Minimizing the effects of these wireless exposures now instead of later is timely and crucial.

Your Dental Health Could Be Making You Fat, Sick & Exhausted!

Your dental health can make you fat, sick and tired. Amalgam fillings should be called DEATH by slow poison fillings. 50% of these are made from mercury which is a very toxic poison to humans as well as all living organisms. This is a tragedy and the dental profession should hold their head in shame in allowing this extremely toxic heavy metal to be place in men, women and children's mouths.

> ***"Scientific research has demonstrated that mercury, even in small amounts, can damage the brain, nervous system, heart, lungs, liver, kidneys, thyroid, pituitary and adrenal glands, blood cells, enzymes and hormones. Mercury is also known to suppress the T-cells of immune system by as much as 100%."***
>
> **Eastin Center for Modern Dentistry**

Approximately 8 million amalgam fillings are placed in our mouths every year in the UK. I will never forget asking a dentist, who attended one of my seminars in the UK, what is the youngest children will get MERCURY fillings put in their mouths? When she replied aged 4, I was literally blown away with this. Why? Read ON.

Scientific research has demonstrated that mercury, even in small amounts, can damage the brain, heart, lungs, liver, kidneys, thyroid gland, pituitary gland, adrenal gland, cells, enzymes and hormones and suppress the body's immune system.

The height of irony is that dental amalgam is shipped as a hazardous material to the dental office, and any amalgam leftover is also treated as hazardous and requires special precautions to dispose of. Yet most dentists will readily implant this hazardous material directly into your mouth, with assurances that it's perfectly safe and harmless. Yes it's INSANE!

According to the German Ministry of Health, "Amalgam is considered a health risk from a medical viewpoint due to the release of mercury vapour. "Everyday activities such as chewing and brushing the teeth have been shown to release mercury vapours from amalgams. Studies by the World Health Organization show that a single amalgam filling can release 3 – 17 mcg of mercury per day ***(Melillo, W. "How Safe is Mercury in Dentistry? The Washington Post Weekly Journal of Medicine, Science and Society, 1991,4).***, making dental amalgams a major source of mercury exposure.

Since mercury is a cumulative poison, building up in the body with repeated exposure, its effects can be devastating. It can prevent nutrients from entering the cells and wastes from leaving. Mercury can bind to DNA (deoxyribonucleic acid) of cells as well as cell membranes, distorting them and interfering with normal cell functions. ***(Vimy, M.J., et al. "Maternal – Fetal Distribution of Mercury Released from Dental Amalgam Fillings. "American Physiological Society 258 (1990) R939 – R945)***

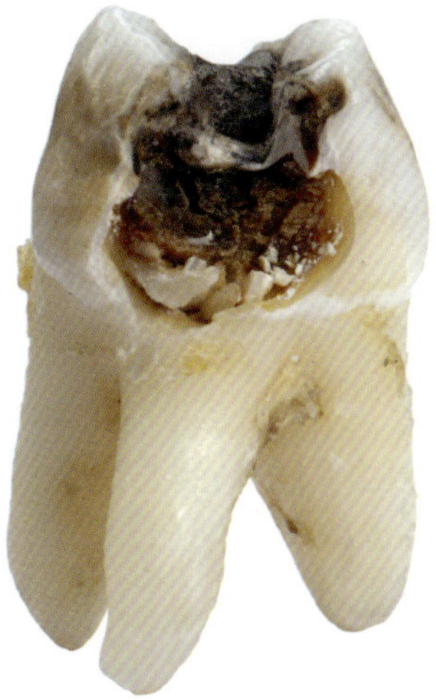

Mercury is a potent neurotoxin that can damage your brain, central nervous system and kidneys, and mixing it with other alloys and placing it in your mouth does NOT all of a sudden render it harmless. Children and foetuses whose brains are still developing are at greatest risk, but anyone can be affected. Naturally, the more amalgams you have, the greater your risk of experiencing health problems as a result of this mercury toxicity.

For many years the dental community maintained that mercury was tightly bound with other metal components and did not escape from amalgam fillings. This is a lie, research has proven that mercury vapours do escape during chewing, brushing and when contacted with hot or acidic foods. And, even if mercury didn't escape from amalgam fillings (which the evidence is 100% clear it does), does it still make sense to have such a toxic substance in your mouth a few inches from your brain?

One study reported on levels of mercury vapour measured in the mouth after chewing. The mercury level was 54 times higher in the mouth of an individual with amalgams than in the mouth of an individual without amalgams. It is physically impossible for mercury to be "locked in" the amalgam fillings once they are placed in the teeth.

A "silver" filling, or dental amalgam, is not a true alloy. Amalgams are made up of 50% mercury. The amalgam also consists of 35% silver, 9% tin, 6% copper and a trace of zinc. The mercury vapor from the amalgams is lipid soluble and passes readily through cell membranes and across the blood brain barrier. The vapor serves as the primary route of mercury from amalgams into the body. It is clear that amalgam mercury transfers to human tissues, accumulates with time, and presents a potential health threat. The mercury escapes continuously during the entire life of the filling primarily in the form of vapor, ions but also abraded particles. Chewing, brushing, and the intake of hot fluids stimulates this release.

Mercury can inhibit the action binding of happy hormones like serotonin at the synapse (nerve to nerve connection) leading to depression & carbohydrate cravings. Methylmercury has been shown to accumulate in the testosterone-producing Leydig cells of the testes decreasing production of testosterone. Several studies have shown workers occupationally exposed to mercury have lower testosterone levels. The enzyme thyroid peroxidase, converts T4 (inactive form of thyroid hormone) to T3 (active form of thyroid hormone) and this can be blocked by mercury in the body.

Today as well as being described the second most toxic chemical in the world, mercury has been categorised by Dr. Lars Friberg, M.D., Ph.D., a former head of toxicology of the World Health Organization (WHO), in this way: "There is no safe level of mercury and no one has actually shown there is a safe level and I would say mercury is a very toxic substance."

The overt clinical effects resulting from toxic exposure to mercury have been clearly described. The scientific literature shows that amalgam fillings have been associated with a variety of problems such as Alzheimer's Disease, autoimmunity, kidney dysfunction, infertility, polycystic ovary syndrome, neurotransmitter imbalances, food allergies, multiple sclerosis, thyroid problems, and an impaired immune system.

The nervous system is more sensitive to mercury toxicity than any other organ in the body. Mercury has recently been documented to be associated with arrhythmias and cardiomyopathies as hair analysis showed mercury levels to be 20,000 times higher in those with these cardiac abnormalities. Mercury exposure has also been associated with other neurological problems such as tremors, insomnia, polyneuropathy, paresthesias, emotional lability, irritability, personality changes, headaches, weakness, blurred vision, dysarthria, slowed mental response and unsteady gait.

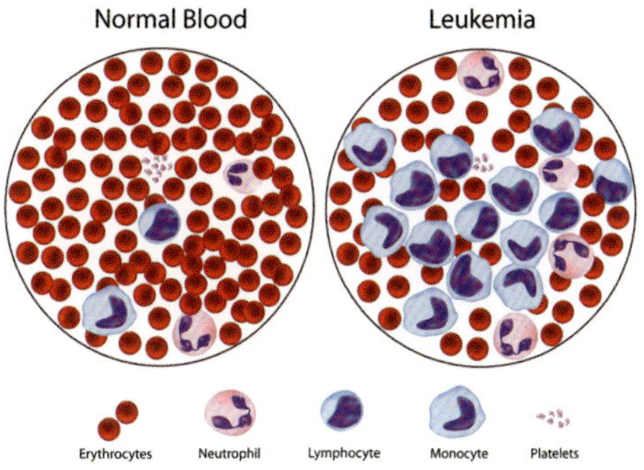

In 1973 Hal Huggins blew the whistle on amalgam fillings. Dr. Huggins found that when mercury came out of fillings it caused leukemia. He was at first surprised at this finding, and went on to try to prove that mercury didn't come out of the tooth. Dr. Hal Huggins, being an expert in body chemistry analysis, analyzed the blood of patients who were receiving mercury fillings. To his surprise, he found that mercury fillings were indeed poisoning the body. He brought his findings to the American Dental Association, who then proceeded to try to run him out of business.

Dr. Hal A. Huggins DDS, MSc has both a Dentistry degree and a Master's degree in Immunology, plus over 40 years of research and experience in Holistic Dentistry. Hal Huggins is an expert in blood chemistry and cellular chemistry. He looked at calcium, cholesterol, liver function tests and white blood cells. He found that blood cell counts changed all over the place from placing silver mercury fillings. He then devoted many years of his life spreading this information to the dental profession and the media.

Hal Huggins and many other researchers and dentists believe that mercury is poisonous; it shouldn't be in people.

It's no coincidence that someone I know who has had leukemia before and then given the all clear to have it return after a few months of having another amalgam filling placed in her mouth and this is after her telling her dentist that she did not want another amalgam filling for she already has a face full of them along with two root canals. I then looked at her live and dry blood through a microscope in front of a live audience and there was a high presence of heavy metals in her blood. She is now on a very comprehensive detoxification plan and as we get her healthy we will incorporate this with the removal of the amalgam fillings and root canals over a period of time.

Root-canaled teeth are essentially "dead" teeth that can become silent incubators for highly toxic anaerobic bacteria that can, under certain conditions, make their way into your bloodstream to cause a number of serious medical conditions—many not appearing until decades later. Most of these toxic teeth feel and look fine for many years, which makes their role in systemic disease even harder to trace back.

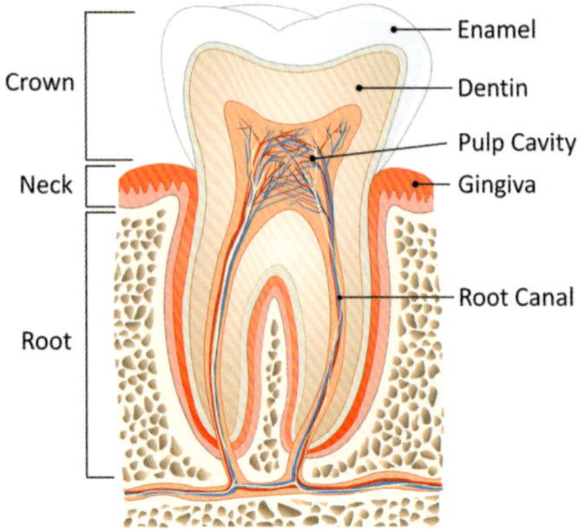

Sadly, the vast majority of dentists are oblivious to the serious potential health risks they are exposing their patients to, risks that persist for the rest of their patients' lives. Most dentists would be doing an enormous service to public health if they familiarized themselves with the work of Dr. Weston Price. Unfortunately, his work continues to be discounted and suppressed by medical and dental professionals alike.

Dr. Price was a dentist and researcher who traveled the world to study the teeth, bones, and diets of native populations living without the "benefit" of modern food. Around the year 1900, Price had been treating persistent root canal infections and became suspicious that root-canaled teeth always remained infected, in spite of treatments. Then one day, he recommended to a woman, wheelchair bound for six years, to have her root canal tooth extracted, even though it appeared to be fine.

She agreed, so he extracted her tooth and then implanted it under the skin of a rabbit. The rabbit amazingly developed the same crippling arthritis as the woman and died from the infection 10 days later. But the woman, now free of the toxic tooth, immediately recovered from her arthritis and could now walk without even the assistance of a cane.

Price discovered that it's mechanically impossible to sterilize a root-canaled (e.g. root-filled) tooth. He then went on to show that many chronic degenerative diseases originate from root-filled teeth — the most frequent being heart and circulatory diseases. He actually found 16 different causative bacterial agents for these conditions. But there were also strong correlations between root-filled teeth and diseases of the joints, brain and nervous system. Dr. Price went on to write two groundbreaking books in 1922 detailing his research into the link between dental pathology and chronic illness. Unfortunately, his work was deliberately buried for 70 years, until finally one endodontist named George Meinig recognized the importance of Price's work and sought to expose the truth by writing his book titled "The Root Canal Cover Up".

Remember your dentist gets paid by putting fillings and root canals in your mouth so he/she is going to be usually very defensive and agitated when you question them on the toxins they put in your mouth!

Dentists and their parent dental associations are loath to inform patients that the mercury they place in the mouth is a deadly poison that negatively influences not only their oral environments but total body physiology as well. This is a shame that the majority of dentists will take to their grave. "Mercury is one of the most potent chemical inhibitors of thiol-sensitive enzymes and mercury vapour easily penetrates into the central nervous system," writes Dr. Boyd Haley who goes on to say, "Amalgams leak mercury, this is a fact that any chemistry department can confirm. We have made amalgam fillings outside of the mouth, placed these fillings in sterile water for 15 minutes to several hours. We then tested this water for toxicity to tubulin and creatine kinase. The result was that the solutions in which amalgams were soaked (even for fifteen minutes) were extremely toxic. This work is supported by reports doing similar experiments at the University of Michigan Dental School where they described solutions in which amalgams were soaked as being 'extremely cytotoxic.'

> ***It is estimated that an amalgam filling will release up to half of its mercury content over a ten year period (50% corrosion rate).***
>
> **- Dr. Robert Gammal**

This is why I strongly advise my athletes to remove their amalgam fillings and root canals if they have any, as I truly believe it is a major stressor amongst all the other stressors that we face today in our stinking, polluted world. I cover in habit 2 the detoxification protocol that I recommend you have if you do decide to remove the amalgams from your mouth and only get it done by a competent dentist who is familiar with the risks of amalgam removal and ensure maximum safety precautions are used during the procedure.

When we fill our body & mind with hate, anger, jealousy, poor foods, alcohol, caffeine & toxins, losing body fat becomes an impossibility. Why? You have to be healthy before you can lose weight. The body can't and won't release fat until it is at a certain level of health. And this is why so many diets fail.

Conclusion

Now you can see that there is no single cause of obesity today in the 21st century and when you hear someone say that weight loss is simply a matter of using more calories than one needs to lose weight then unfortunately they simply do not understand the complexity of weight loss today. There are unfortunately multiple causes of obesity as we have just read, from constant stress, drinking water, coffee, tea, alcohol, medications, EMFs, dental products, pesticides, herbicides, fungicides, MSG, aspartame, trans fats, high fructose corn syrup, vaccinations, antibiotics, processed foods, phthalates, xenooestrogens, beauty care products, cookware and a host of other hormone disrupting products. This is why I say, when you move away from nature, the fatter you become!

So what is important from our first habit is to stay as close to mother nature as we possibly can as our ancestors have done for over thousands of generations. Habit 2 will concentrate on detoxification which will help us rid the body of the multiple factors that are making it 100% impossible to have vibrant health and to maintain a healthy body fat percentage.

Some authors that I recommend for you to read more around the subject of our natural diet and way of living are; Robb Wolf, Loren Cordain, Lindsey Berkson, Nora Gedgaudas, Jack Chalem and Dr Walter Crinnion.

PHIL SAYS
ACTION PLAN

Eat organic foods, get a reverse osmosis water filter fitted for clean drinking water, use chemical free washware products, use safe cookware, throw your microwave away, minimise mobile phone use (if at all), reduce stress as much as possible.

Make sure that you surround yourself with very positive, loving and caring people. This will have an incredible effect on your health and well-being.

These simplistic measures alone will have a monumental effect on your health and your ability to lose body fat safely, efficiently and for the long term.

Please enjoy the rest of the habits as all of the information you need are contained within these.

HABIT 2

DETOXIFICATION IS ESSENTIAL FOR OPTIMUM FAT LOSS

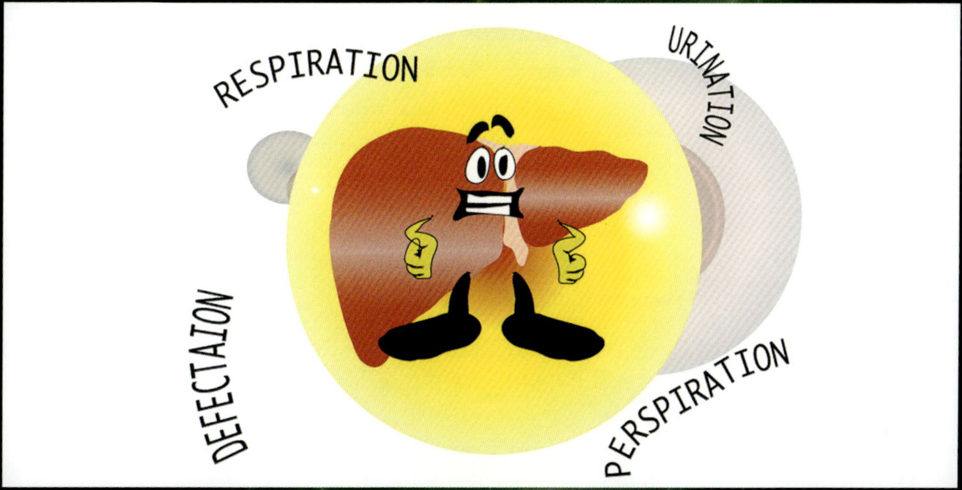

We are swimming in a sea of man-made toxins and chemicals which are crippling our ability to lose weight and reclaim our health.

But it is not all doom and gloom. If we can supercharge our detoxification pathways then at least we have got a chance of overcoming the insanity of the toxic 21st century, dropping excess fat with ease and reclaiming a healthy body and mind.

"Open your eyes, look within. Are you satisfied with the life you're living?"

Bob Marley

Detoxification Pathways

Well you can now see from habit 1 that we are swimming in a sea of man-made toxins and chemicals which are crippling our ability to lose weight and reclaim our health. This is exactly how the pharmaceutical companies want us to be so they have a ready made supply of sick customers. But it is not all doom and gloom. If we can supercharge our detoxification pathways then at least we have got a chance of overcoming the insanity of the toxic 21st century, dropping excess fat with ease and reclaiming a healthy body and mind, plus sticking one finger up to big pharma.

Before we look at physically detoxing our bodies remember from the mental preparation habit, at the beginning of this book, that the biggest toxin we face every day is our thoughts; so keep them on your side 100% of the time. I also want to add that another toxin that we face today is the media, who constantly bombard us, 24/7, with doom and gloom which I believe is done intentionally to keep us in constant fear and reduce our intelligence. I personally no longer watch television unless its something like a wildlife program, comedy or DVD. I urge you to get away from the moronic soaps and only watch the news if you need a dose of anxiety and depression.

Detoxification

Physically, we get rid of toxins through four pathways:

1) Perspiration
2) Respiration
3) Urination
4) Defecation

Researchers have found that dieting without detoxing is one of the best ways to poison yourself and get FATTER. In a study at Laval University, in Quebec, scientists showed that the rise in circulating toxins during weight loss led to a drop in the resting metabolic rate (the energy we expend during rest) and a reduction in the most active form of thyroid, T3, which drives metabolism! Another study from Lavel University, Quebec, found that those who released the most pesticides (organochlorines) from their fat stores during weight loss had the slowest metabolism after weight loss.

A study published in Obesity review 2003 concluded that pesticides and PCBs (from industrial pollution) are released from the fat tissue, where they are stored, and poison our metabolism preventing us from losing weight. Another study that was published in the

American Journal of Physical Endocrinology Metabase in 2002 stated that the increase in toxins during weight loss in men inhibited normal mitochondrial function and reduced the subjects ability to burn calories, retarding further weight loss.

Now you can see why detoxification needs to run in parallel if you want long term, successful weight loss. Toxins block nutrients from adequately nourishing the cells of your body. This can have a devastating effect on our hormones, energy and health of the cells which will cripple your metabolism.

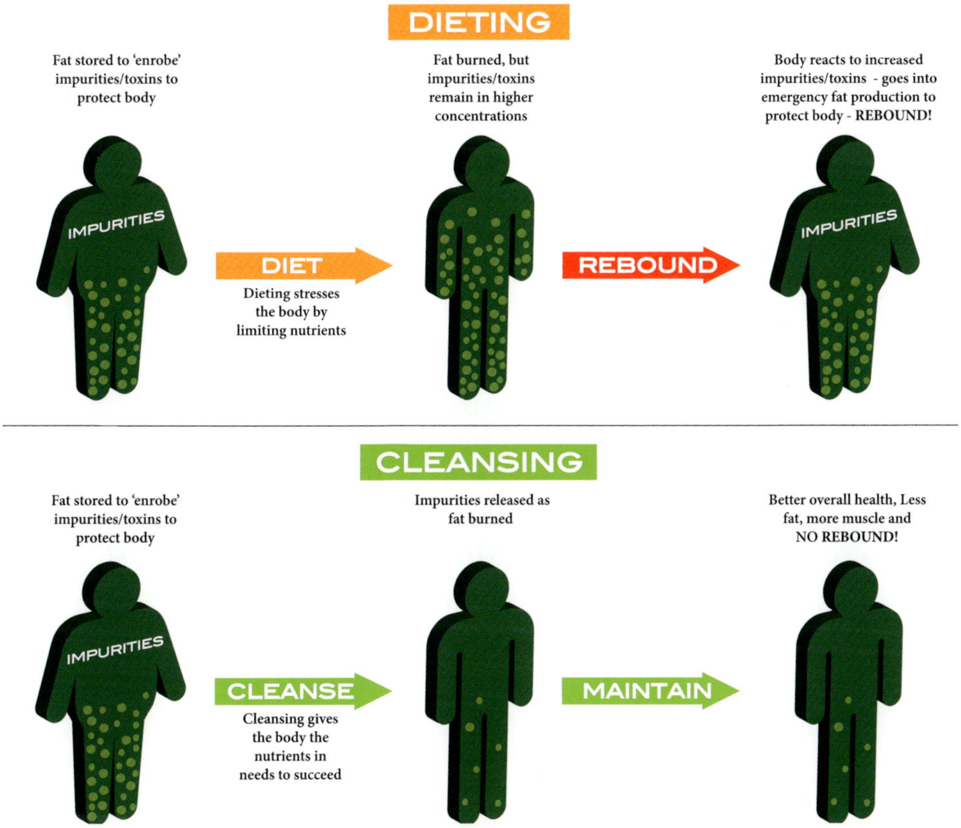

You must remember that you are only as healthy as your cells. You are a mass of 50 trillion plus cells. Cells make tissues, tissues make organs and organs make humans. LOOK AFTER YOUR CELLS!

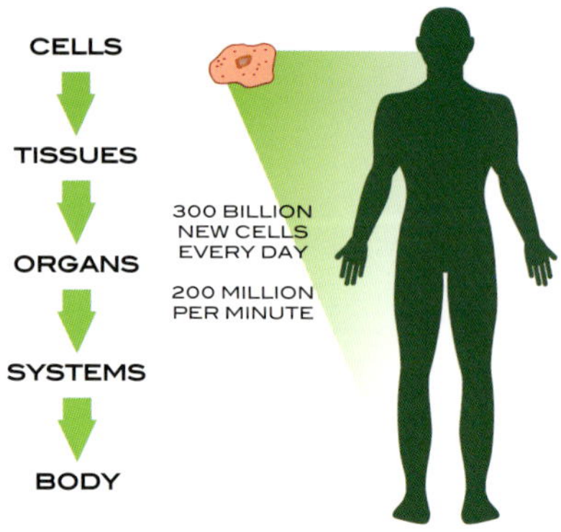

There are two sides of detoxifying: the first is to reduce the toxins your body is exposed to, and the second is to improve your body's ability to detoxify. Detoxification supports a healthy metabolism. By removing toxicity, you allow the cells to process nutrients in a more efficient way. This will significantly boost the rate at which you metabolize the foods you eat. When you clean up your diet at the same time as you detoxify, metabolism is further enhanced.

The importance of pH in our detoxification

First, let's look at the importance of pH levels whilst detoxifying as this should never be overlooked. Why? A healthy pH means you are well oxygenated and healthy. A low pH reading means you have low oxygen levels and are much more susceptible to low energy and illness.

The majority of the foods and drinks we consume are acidic, such as meat, grains and sugar, with colas, alcohol, coffee and other soft drinks being highly acidic. So unless you have been eating a very healthy diet, full of fresh vegetables, your body is more likely to be acidic, which creates an environment where disease can manifest.

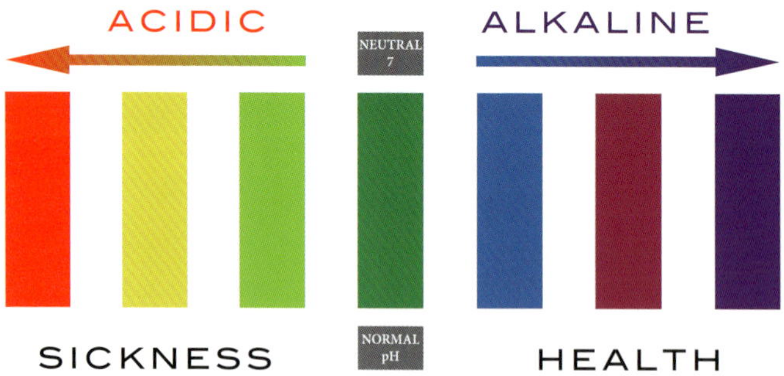

pH: What does it mean? pH is the abbreviation for potential hydrogen. The pH of any solution is the measure of its hydrogen-ion concentration. The higher the pH reading, the more alkaline and oxygen rich the fluid is. The lower the pH reading, the more acidic and oxygen deprived the fluid is. The pH range is from 0 to 14, with 7.0 being neutral. Anything above 7.0 is alkaline, anything below 7.0 is considered acidic.

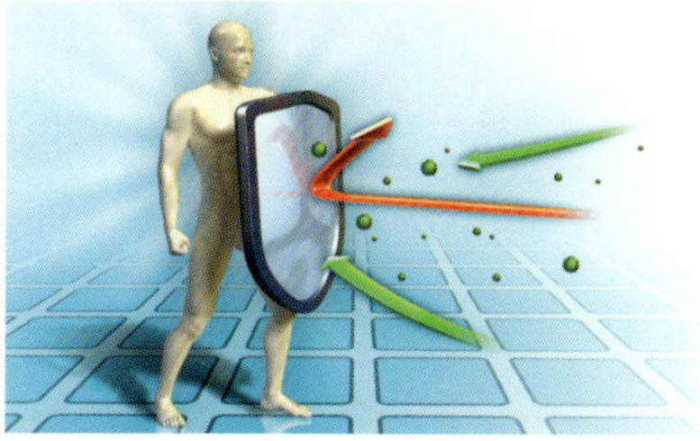

Raising pH increases the immune system's ability to kill bacteria, concludes a study conducted at The Royal Free Hospital and School of Medicine in London. Viruses and bacteria that cause bronchitis and colds thrive in an acidic environment.

In order to maintain a healthy immune system with a slightly alkaline pH, we need to consider detoxification to counter the "slow kill" from the myriad of toxins pervading every element of our environment which we saw from Habit 1. Arthur C. Guyton, M.D., who is considered one of the world's most recognized authors on human physiology, has spent the better part of his life studying the pH of the body. In his "Textbook of Medical Physiology", which is used to train medical students, he states that the first step in maintaining health is to alkalise the body.

In the 1860's Louie Pasteur's theory (see the picture below) became cemented in our minds, that germs cause disease. Hailed as one of the most important discoveries of modern science, we supposedly had found the real cause of disease. Disease arises from micro-organisms outside the body. These micro-organisms do not change, and anybody can be a victim of disease.

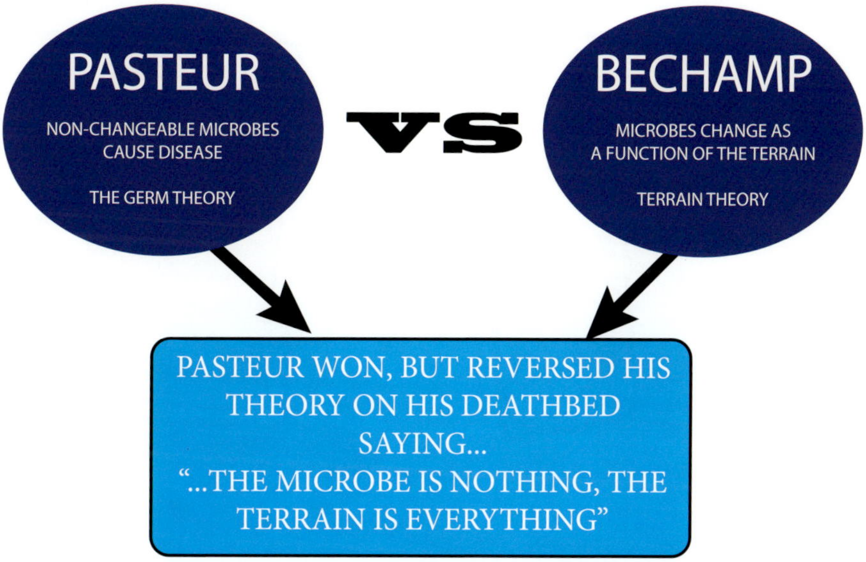

HOWEVER, THE ROAD WAS SET FOR THE GERM THEORY AND AS A RESULT, MEDICINE TODAY ALLEVIATES THE SYMPTOMS OF DISEASE BUT RARELY THE CAUSE

Antoine Bechamp was a French Physician and Biologist Professor of Medical Chemistry and Pharmacy at the Montpellier University and University of Lille. From examinations of an amputated arm and many examinations of frozen plants during a cold winter, these convinced him that, upon injury, bacteria developed internally without any outside influence due to terrain changes.

Bechamp believed that germs were pleomorphic, meaning that they changed depending on the terrain. This means that disease usually arises from within the body, that healthy micro-organisms exist within the body, and micro-organisms change and transform based on their environment. When you think logically about the biggest killers in the western world, e.g. heart disease and cancer, you realise that you do not catch these diseases. These diseases are built from within when we become too acidic and toxic.

Rudolph Virchow (a German doctor known as the 'Father of Pathology'), said: "If I could live my life over again, I would devote it to proving that germs seek their natural habitat, diseased tissue, rather than being the cause of the diseased tissue; e.g., mosquitoes seek the stagnant water, but do not cause the pool to become stagnant."

If you had a fridge freezer full of food and you accidentally hit the power switch off and then went away for a two week holiday. When you get back from and you open your fridge freezer, to your horror you would see mould, fungus, maggots and a horrific smell from the rotten meat. Well how did this occur after all the fridge was air tight door closed? Nothing could creep in from the outside. The answer is very simple the internal environment changed creating the ideal environment for germs to thrive this is pleomorphism.

What determines the state of micro-organisms in the body is a very simple matter. If you are continually acidifying your system, and if you have habits whereby you are acidifying your systems constantly, (heavy metals, toxins, downing coffee, tea, coke, acid thoughts, meat, dairy, pharmaceuticals, alcohol, pollution, pastries, relationship stress etc.) then you are creating an environment where disease can thrive. As our bodies become acidic, their oxygen level begins to drop, leaving us tired and fatigued and this is what allows fungus, mould, parasites, bad bacteria, and viral infections to flourish and gain a hold throughout the body which can then cause disease.

The health of the cell depends on the quality of the nutrients that it takes in, how well the nutrients are assimilated, the effectiveness of the cells detoxification and the fluids which the cell is bathed in. The following example by Nobel Prize winner Dr. Alexis Carrel is a perfect example of cell health and environment.

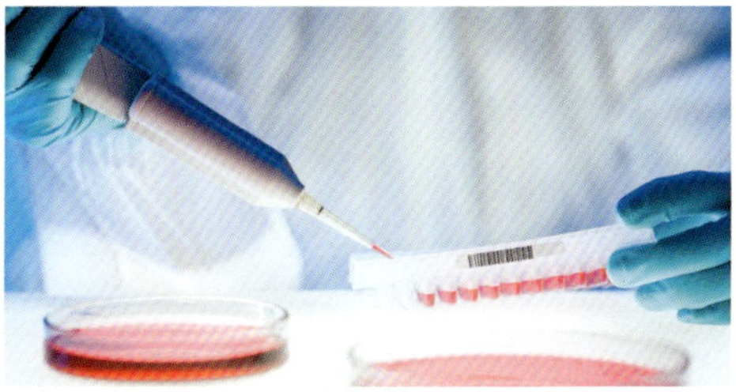

Dr. Alexis Carrel showed that the health of the cell is influenced by the environment it is in.

Nobel Prize winner Dr. Alexis Carrel did an experiment [1912-1940] to keep cells from a chicken's heart alive and reproducing new cells for 28 years! A chicken's life span is far less than this. So why did these chicken cells live so well and so long? Dr Carrel did this by placing the cells in a saline solution that was the perfect temperature, pH, and nutrient/mineral balance. He and his co-workers replaced this solution daily (cleaning away the toxic [acidic] wastes). Eventually, after 28 years the purpose of the experiment was achieved. The cells did not die of aging they simply stopped the experiment and Dr. Carrel concluded the following;

> ***"The cell is immortal. It is merely the fluid in which it floats which degenerates. Renew this fluid at intervals, give the cells what they require for nutrition and, as far as we know, the pulsation of life may go on forever."***

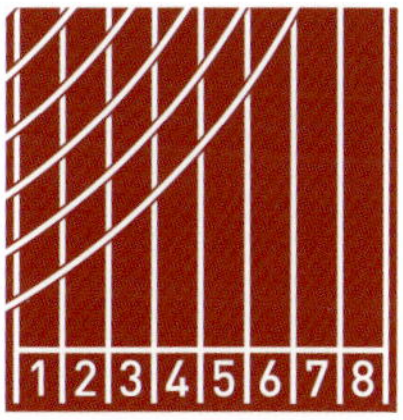

If I threw a grass seed onto a running track, it is impossible for the grass seed to take root. Why? Because the environment is not conducive for growth. However, if I threw that grass seed onto a lush patch of grass, it will inevitably take root. The environment allows this to happen. It is the same with us - we can only catch disease from outside sources if our internal environment is right for disease/germs to get a foothold due to an acidic terrain.

Bruce Lipton, cell biologist and author, said; "I will never forget a piece of wisdom I received in 1967, on the first day I learned to clone stem cells in graduate school. It took me decades to realize how profound this seemingly simple piece of wisdom was for my work and my life. My professor, mentor, and consummate scientist Irv Konisberg was one of the first cell biologists to master the art of cloning stem cells. He told me that when the cultured cells you are studying start ailing, you look first to the cell's environment, not to the cell itself, for the cause."

Dr. Otto Warburg, winner of the 1931 Nobel Prize for his studies in cell respiration, believed that a person's level of health and vitality has a direct correlation to the levels of oxygen in his or her bloodstream. Proving that viruses, bacteria and cancer cells can not survive in an oxygenated environment. Dr Otto Warburg noted that alkaline bodies absorb up to 20 times more oxygen than acidic bodies.

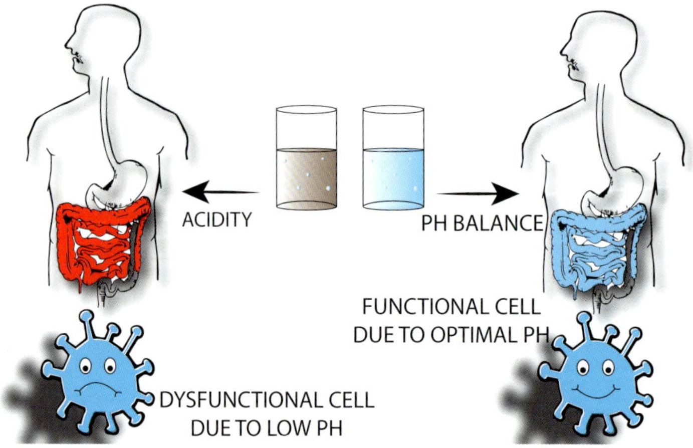

Creating the optimum pH levels within the body creates the right environment for cells to thrive

One of the best ways to assess whether your body has healthy pH levels is to check your 2nd urine of the day. A good reading would be between 6.8-7.2. Remember, the urine pH indicates the acidity of your tissues, not your blood.

Detoxification Through Respiration

The lungs are the organ responsible for bringing oxygen to the blood. It plays the crucial role as the first detox organ as it gets in contact with airborne toxins, chemicals, viruses, bacteria, and allergens. The lungs oxygenate the veins to bring new oxygen to the heart for distribution while removing toxic waste like carbon dioxide from the arteries to be expelled from the body.

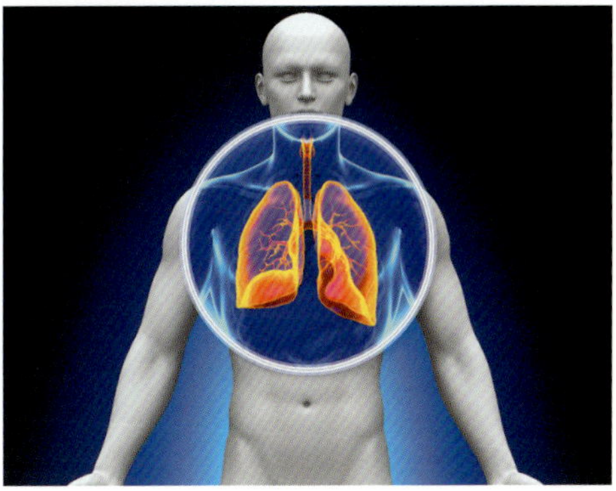

The lungs play a role in eliminating toxins from the body

A poor diet, air pollution, shallow breathing and habits like smoking all contribute to make our lungs less efficient and decrease their natural detoxification ability. Supporting our lungs with proper breathing techniques increases its effectiveness. A more efficient lung provides more oxygen for our bodies resulting in increased energy levels and a clear state of mind. Learning deep breathing techniques is an important aspect of lung detoxification. Proper breathing techniques allow more air into the lungs and improves its efficiency. This one of the reasons why exercise is so important during detoxification.

How to Detox with Deep Breathing

Oxygen is one of the most important substances in the human body. It is possible for the body to go months without food and days without water, but only a few precious minutes without oxygen before the body suffocates. Breath really is the source of life, even though we do it naturally and therefore do not give it much thought. Take a moment and focus on your breathing - you may be surprised at the shallowness of your breath.

Learning to breathe deeper and take in more oxygen can have wonderful health benefits. By bringing more oxygen into the body, deep breathing is one of the best ways to get more of the blood's waste, or carbon dioxide, out of the body. Deep-breathing techniques are extremely effective in handling depression, anxiety, and stress-related disorders. Just take a second and allow yourself to breathe deeply for a few moments. You will immediately notice your heartbeat slows and you will feel significantly more relaxed.

When people do not take in enough oxygen and exhale enough carbon dioxide, it can have consequences such as fatigue, mental fog and decreased tissue function. These problems are often thought to be problems with diet, but the brain cannot function properly if it is not receiving an adequate supply of oxygen. Shallow breathing (or chest breathing) causes a constriction of the chest and lung tissue over time, decreasing oxygen flow and delivery to your tissues. Deep, rhythmic breathing expands the diaphragm muscle, which expands the lung's air pockets, invoking a relaxation response within the body, and massaging the lymphatic system.

The lymphatic system acts sort of like the body's sewer system. Blood flow carries nutrients and ample amounts of oxygen to the body, while the lymphatic system carries away destructive toxins. The consequence of a sluggish lymphatic system is that you cannot detoxify properly. Deep breathing serves as a kind of pump for the lymphatic system. If you aren't breathing deeply or moving regularly, chances are your lymph fluid is not flowing as well as it could. This can lead to health problems, including weight gain, muscle loss, high blood pressure, fatigue, and inflammation.

Learning how to breath more deeply and fully is a vital way to keep the body's cleansing and detoxifying systems working at full capacity. Proper breathing is especially important when working out, because your body uses the oxygen as a source of energy. Shallow breathing when working out can cause a significant reduction in the amount of intensity and time your body can exercise. By taking a few moments in your day to really pay attention to the inhalation and exhalation that supports your life, you will balance and clean the body. Remember, small changes add up to big improvements.

Detoxification Through Perspiration

Sweating is one of the most effective methods for getting the most damaging toxins out of the body. There are no drugs, no surgery, no chelation, nor other detoxification methods with before and after measurements that compare to sweat. The skin is the largest organ of the human body. Usually nobody thinks of skin as being an organ. Skin is very thin and it takes only a few moments for some kind of liquid substance to be absorbed. Make a little experiment with garlic. You can rub it into your foot and wait. Very soon you can taste the garlic in your mouth. Here is the proof that skin easily absorbs most things and that's why you must be extremely cautious on your skin care and body wash products. It is wise that if you cannot pronounce the name on the ingredient list don't rub it on your skin. Remember this important point; you can absorb up to 60% of what you rub onto your skin. Our skin not only absorbs well, it excretes toxins as well. The human body has an important ability to sweat, which is a natural body reaction to expel various toxins, including heavy metals.

There are between 10-100 times more toxins in your fat than in your blood, so one of the best ways to remove toxins is to decrease your body fat. That really is your first defence. Choosing the right foods and exercise are key here. After that, one of the most effective detoxification strategies I know of, is the use of an infrared sauna. This can be done for about 30 minutes to one hour daily. Remember, it's important to hydrate well before and during the sauna treatment to avoid dehydration. Also, check with your healthcare provider that you are fit enough to use the sauna. Additionally, you can exercise for 30-60 minutes immediately prior to help liberate some of the toxins from your fat. I suggest that you do aerobic exercise to increase blood flow and perspiration.

Far infrared rays are part of the sun's natural spectrum. The radiant energy produced by an infrared sauna is the same as heat from the sun, with the exclusion of the ultraviolet rays. A heat source, (usually ceramic heating elements), emits infrared waves that penetrate and relax the body as increased blood circulation warms the skin. Sweat and toxins are released through the skin's open pores as the warm blood circulates deeper throughout the body. The infrared sauna is a powerful means of cellular cleansing as it increases metabolism and blood circulation. In addition to its use for detoxification it also relaxes muscles and rejuvenates the body.

Infrared saunas are an amazing way to help detoxify through perspiration and because of the softer heat, they are more tolerable than regular saunas

The far infrared sauna is also far safer and infinitely more tolerable than a conventional sauna because it uses a heat energy that penetrates tissues, triggering mobilization of chemicals from subcutaneous fat storage, directly into the sweat. This activating penetration allows for a much lower overall temperature to be used. Infrared saunas warm the body instead of heating the surrounding air. Traditional steam saunas heat the air and require temperatures ranging from 150 – 200 degrees Fahrenheit to promote perspiration, whereas a heat range of 110 – 140 degrees in an infrared sauna produces the same results.

The cooler air temperature is more tolerable to heat-sensitive individuals and allows for sessions of up to 45 minutes, nearly twice as long as in a typical steam sauna session. The softer heat of an infrared sauna also penetrates deeper into the skin - as much as 1 ½ inches - and draws out more toxins than a steam sauna, according to Dr. Aundrea Adams of the International Institute of Holistic Healing, who compared the detoxification findings of the two sauna types. Dr. Adams summarised a report which concludes that sweat from a traditional sauna was up to 97% water, while the sweat released in an infrared sauna was only 80 – 85% water. The remaining 15–20% was comprised of heavy metals, sulphuric acid, sodium, ammonia, uric acid and fat-soluble toxins.

PHIL SAYS

Infrared Saunas

I use the infrared sauna 4 – 5 times per week and have personally had outstanding results. I usually do 30 minutes after I've done an hours training in the morning. Before I begin, I take 1 teaspoon of PRP Alkalising Salts in 1 pint of water - this is loaded with electrolytes. When my sauna is finished, within ten minutes I then drink 1 pint of water with a tablespoon of PRP Ultimate Greens to ensure that I pull as many toxins out of my system as possible.

Since I've done this my body fat has reduced significantly. Remember before trying any supplements, exercise plan or use of modalities like sauna consult with a qualified medical practitioner. I am simply sharing with you what works for me.

Clearly the therapeutic advantages of the infrared sauna are considerable. In her book Detoxify Or Die, Sherry Rogers, M.D. extols the benefits of the far-infrared sauna. She cites a study done by specialists at the Mayo Clinic which proves the effectiveness of therapeutic infrared sauna use for patients of end-stage congestive heart failure. The individuals in this three-week study tolerated the infrared sauna heat without side effects, and experienced significant chemical detoxification. The toxic load was the underlying cause of their condition and the heart function of each of these patients improved as a result of the therapeutic cleansing. They were also able to eliminate some of their medications.

Run as close to nature as possible

Of course there are many other ways to sweat other than sitting in an infrared sauna. I regularly run most days, not only for fitness but especially for sweating; it's a great way for detoxing both chemically and emotionally. Try to run as close to nature as you can as this gives you a good karma and clears your head. I often get my best ideas whilst running. And you will still get benefits from using a normal sauna or steam room, the main thing is to simply sweat those toxins out.

Detoxification Through Urination

Your kidneys are two bean-shaped organs, each about the size of your fist. They are located in the middle of your back, just below your rib cage, on either side of your spine. Your kidneys weigh about 0.5 percent of your total body weight. Although the kidneys are small organs by weight, they receive a huge amount, 20 percent, of the blood pumped by the heart. The large blood supply to your kidneys enables them to do the following tasks:

Once toxins have been removed from fat cells, they need to be eliminated from the body. Chelating agents can help remove these toxins to be excreted from the body via the urine.

- Regulate the composition of your blood: Keep the concentrations of various ions and other important substances constant; Keep the volume of water in your body constant;
- Remove wastes from your body (urea,

ammonia, drugs, toxic substances); Keep the acid/base concentration of your blood constant

- Help regulate your blood pressure
- Stimulate the making of red blood cells
- Maintain your body's calcium levels

Your kidneys receive the blood from the renal artery, process it, then return the processed blood to the body, through the renal vein, and remove the wastes and other unwanted substances in the urine. Urine flows from the kidneys through the ureters to the bladder. In the bladder, the urine is stored until it is excreted from the body through the urethra.

The kidneys are among the body's most important detoxification organs, if it were not for their constant filtration of the blood, we would become poisoned by our own wastes. In order to clean toxins out of the blood effectively, the kidneys must function properly. If they become congested with toxins and bacteria they cannot filter the blood or regulate chemical and pH balance effectively. For this reason, looking after your kidney health is essential in any detoxification plan.

Taking care of your kidneys

Paramount to good care of the kidneys is reducing the toxic load they have to deal with, especially proteins and chemical contaminants which can build up in the kidneys, slowing their function, increasing acidity and raising blood pressure.

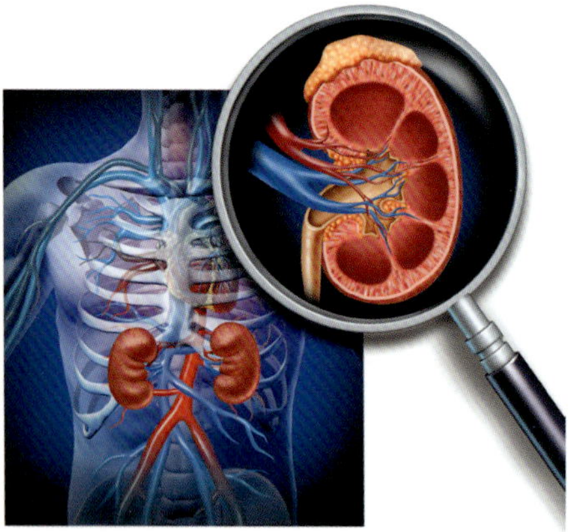

Drinking enough water so that the urine is a light color of yellow. A whole lot of water is not necessarily good for the kidneys, and it is always better to drink small amounts of water throughout the day, rather than gulping down a litre or two because you're thirsty. This just creates kidney stress.

Water is also very important during the final stage of elimination, lubricating the intestines and providing the basis for urine. Drinking more clean water during detoxification therefore is an obvious must. I strongly recommend reverse osmosis (RO) as the cornerstone of your drinking water.

Some Herbs useful for kidney detoxification:

Hydrangea root (*Hydrangea Arborescens*) The most common use for hydrangea is for the kidneys and bladder because of its effective diuretic property which helps increase the flow of urine. This removes impurities from the system and lessens the likelihood of infection along the entire urinary tract, which includes the kidneys, bladder, prostate (in men) and urethra. Hydrangea is also considered an anti-lithic herb, which prevents stones or gravel from forming in the kidneys and bladder. As an anti-lithic herb, it can also assist the body in removing stones and gravel from these organs.

Gravel root (*Eupatorium purpureum*) Gravel root also exhibits both diuretic and anti-lithic properties. Used primarily for kidney stones or gravel (which accounts for its name), it also helps with cystitis, dysuria, urethritis, and pelvic inflammatory disease. It can also play a role in the systemic treatment of rheumatism and gout as it encourages excretion of excess uric acid.

Marshmallow root (*Althaea Officinalis*) Marshmallow root aids in the passage of kidney stones and is used in combination with other diuretic herbs for kidney treatments which assist in the release of gravel and stones. It works very well for urinary problems.

Marshmallow has factors which combine with and eliminate toxins, helping the body to cleanse. This makes marshmallow an excellent herb to add to other formulas to help neutralize toxins that are the causative factors of arthritis.

Juniper berry (*Juniperus communis*) Juniper Berries are used to treat infections, especially within the urinary tract, bladder, kidneys, and prostate. Their antiseptic properties help remove waste and acidic toxins from the body, stimulating a fighting action against bacterial and yeast infections. Juniper Berries make an excellent antiseptic in conditions such as cystitis. But the essential oil present in this herb is quite stimulating to the kidney nephrons. Some texts warn that juniper oil may be a kidney irritant at higher doses, nonetheless, people with serious kidney disease probably shouldn't take juniper.

Contemporary herbalists primarily use juniper as a diuretic ("water pill") component of herbal formulas designed to treat bladder infections . The volatile oils of juniper reportedly increase the rate of kidney filtration, thereby increasing urine flow and perhaps helping to "wash out" offending bacteria. The volatile oils, particularly terpinen-4-ol, may cause an increase in urine volume. According to some sources, juniper increases urine volume without a loss of electrolytes such as potassium. It is recommended by the German Commission E for kidney ailments.

Uva ursi (*Arctosyaphylos uva ursi*) The chief constituent of Uva Ursi is a glycoside called arbutin. This is what is responsible for its diuretic action. During its excretion arbutin produces an antiseptic effect on the urinary mucous membrane and can therefore help eliminate urinary tract infections. Tannic acid is also contained in the leaves. This herb also helps to keep the pH balance of urine from being too acid. It actually strengthens the lining of the urinary tract and helps to relieve any inflammation in the system. It has a direct sedative effect on the bladder walls. For chronic inflammation of the bladder or kidneys Uva Ursi has no equal. Two studies report that urine from individuals given uva ursi is active against the most commonly involved bacteria in bladder and urinary tract infection.

This study supports the results of a double blind study of 57 women with recurrent cystitis. After one year, the placebo group had 20% incidence of recurrent cystitis, whereas the uva ursi group had no recurring infection. In addition it has anti-lithic properties that help in dissolving crystals not just in the kidneys, but throughout the body as well. It has, therefore, been used for arthritis and other painful joint problems.

Parsley root (*Petroselinum crispum*) An important diuretic, parsley root also helps clear uric acid from the urinary tract and helps dissolve and expel gallstones and gravel – and prevent their future formation. It also inhibits the secretion of histamine and is therefore useful in treating hives and relieving other allergy symptoms. A decoction of parsley root can help eliminate bloating and reduce weight by eliminating excess water gain. Note: the German Commission E, an advisory panel on herbal medicines, has approved parsley for use in the prevention and treatment of kidney stones.

Detoxification Through The Liver

The liver is the largest glandular organ of the body. It weighs about 3 lb (1.36 kg). The liver lies on the right side of the abdominal cavity beneath the diaphragm. The liver's ability to function and to rebuild and repair itself is absolutely dependent on the quality of nutrients that you consume and the less toxins consumed the quicker the liver can detoxify YOU!

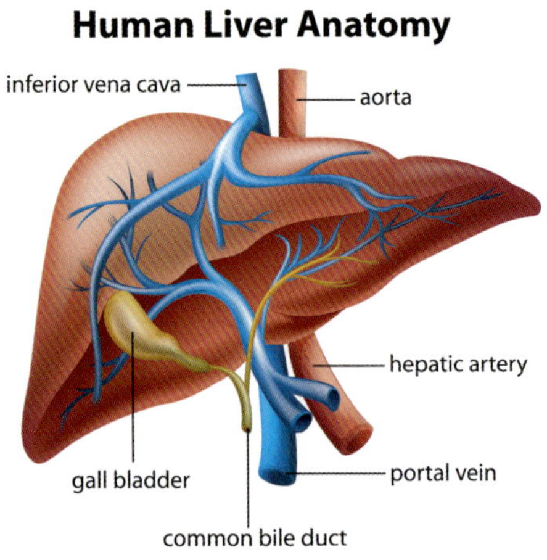

So the liver is essential for detoxification and fat loss, so pay attention on both the function and needs of the liver; it could help you drop excess fat quicker than any method that I know.

Your liver plays a central role in the metabolism of any type of calorie. During weight gain when your white adipose tissue is unable to store fat fast enough, it turns to the primary backup location for fat storage – your liver. Now when your liver gets clogged with excess fat, metabolism becomes even more strained, your waistline expands, and you are at risk for developing far more serious health problems.

If your liver cannot handle the excess fat and sugar coming at it from poor eating habits and drinking sugary drinks to excess, then fat and sugar will pile up in all the wrong places all over your body – hardening your arteries, your brain, and generally giving you the look of Humpty Dumpty. Your liver is also essential for hormone function as you will read throughout this book, when your liver is dysfunctional so are your hormones.

Having a fatty liver can also elevate the risk for type 2 diabetes by up to 500 percent. When your liver is clogged with fat, it has difficulty breaking down fat to use as fuel. Your liver and white adipose tissue are constantly breaking down and restoring fat (triglycerides). The problem is that once the liver is clogged then the process becomes imbalanced and tilts more toward fat storage than fat break down. This is reflected by elevated triglycerides in your blood. In fact, as your triglycerides begin to elevate from weight gain, they actually turn off gene function in your liver that causes fat to pile up in your liver.

Higher stress levels induce cortisol release and it has now been discovered that as cortisol levels rise, a protein (HES1) in your liver elevates, which turns off your liver's ability to break down fat. This also contributes to fatty liver and abdominal weight gain. Another reason why it is so important to de - stress to lose weight.

The Liver's Role Breaking Down Fats

The liver plays an active role in the process of digestion through the production of bile. Bile is a mixture of water, bile salts, cholesterol, and the pigment bilirubin. Hepatocytes in the liver produce bile, which then passes through the bile ducts to be stored in the gallbladder. When food containing fats reaches the duodenum, the cells of the duodenum release the hormone cholecystokinin to stimulate the gallbladder to release bile. Bile travels through the bile ducts and is released into the duodenum where it emulsifies large masses of fat. The emulsification

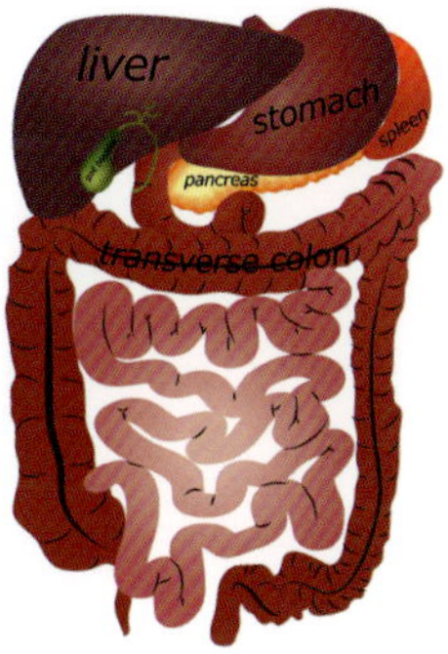

of fats by bile turns the large clumps of fat into smaller pieces that have more surface area and are therefore easier for the body to digest.

The liver is capable of turning one type of chemical into almost any other type of chemical. It can turn protein into sugar, sugar into fat, glycerol into glucose, etc. For example if you eat a great deal of carbohydrate and your glycogen (stored carbohydrate) stores both in the liver and muscles are already full the liver will convert the excess glucose derived from the carbohydrates into fat. That's why high carbohydrate diets, unless you are an elite athlete, can make you fat.

This is also another reason that high carbohydrate foods that market themselves as "low fat" give you false information in regards that these foods can make you extremely fat due to their action in the liver and muscles. If these are full with glycogen then they will turn the excess sugar into fat with a click of a finger.

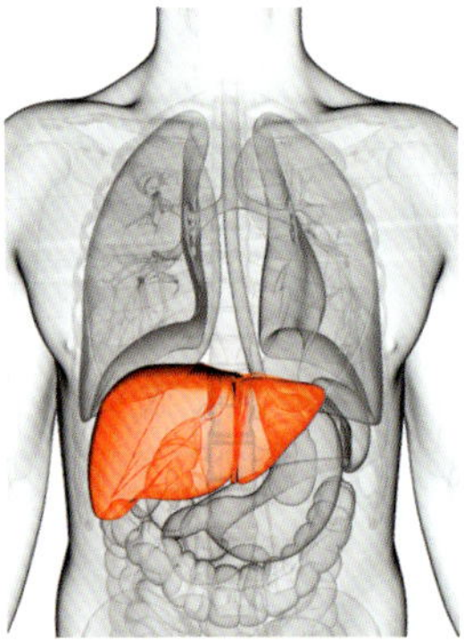

The liver can become congested from chemicals, alcohol, toxins, drugs, caffeine and heavy metals. Evidence of a "fatty liver" is often shown by a roll of fat at the waistline, which happens because the liver has stopped breaking down fat and started storing it. When the liver does not function properly, toxins that we are exposed to accumulate in the body and will stimulate the body to lay down more fat to store them.

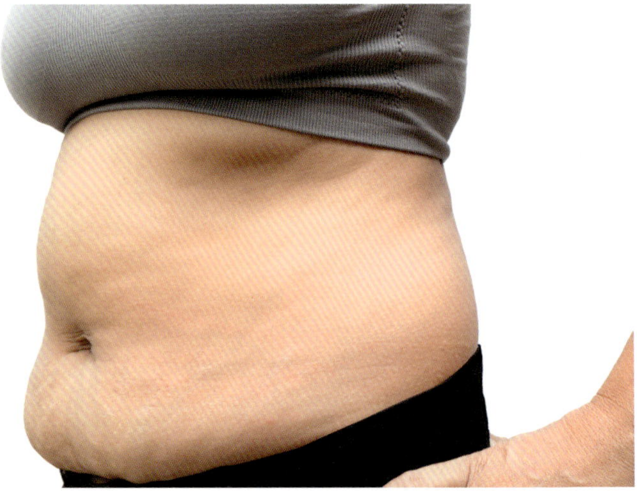

It is the external environment that contributes most to the load of toxins that the liver has to detoxify. Today, the burden on the liver is heavier than ever before in history. Additionally, nutritional deficiencies and imbalances from unhealthy eating habits add to the production of toxins, as do alcohol, our addiction to caffeine and many prescription drugs, further increasing stress on the liver and requiring a strong detoxification capacity.

There are many things today that accumulate and eventually over-burden the liver. Once this happens more fat cells are laid down in order to store excess toxins

Many of the toxic chemicals that enter the body are fat-soluble, which means they dissolve only in fatty or oily solutions and not in water. This makes them difficult for the body to excrete. Fat soluble chemicals have a high affinity for fat tissues and cell membranes, which are composed of fatty acids and proteins. In these fatty tissues of the body, toxins may be stored for years, being released during times of exercise, stress or fasting. During the release of these toxins, several symptoms such as headaches, poor memory, stomach pain, nausea, fatigue, dizziness and palpitations can occur.

The liver is responsible for removing toxins from the blood. Without a clean, efficient liver and healthy kidneys, blood is not filtered clean. "Dirty" blood, loaded with toxins or waste products, is heavier and more sluggish. This causes poor circulation and reduced capacity to carry oxygen and nutrients. A clean and efficient liver which produces cleaner blood would help energy production because clean blood can carry more oxygen and nutrients. Clean blood is also lighter; it flows better and results in better blood circulation.

The following are the most common symptoms of a toxic liver; being edgy, easily stressed, elevated cholesterol, skin irritation, depression, sleep difficulties, indigestion, kidney damage, heart damage, brain fog, hypothyroidism, oestrogen dominance, chronic fatigue, weight gain, poor memory, PMS, blood sugar imbalances, allergies, or obesity. Phew know you can see why the liver is so important in your sense of well being and ability to lose excess fat.

Nutrition is the most critical factor where detoxification is concerned. Like any of the body's functions, detoxification requires nutrients. If these nutrients are not present in sufficient quantity, detoxification is hindered or stalled completely. One reason many toxins are stored is because the nutrients are not available to complete the process of detoxification due to our processed foods and non organic food we eat this is why today nutritional supplementation is absolutely essential.

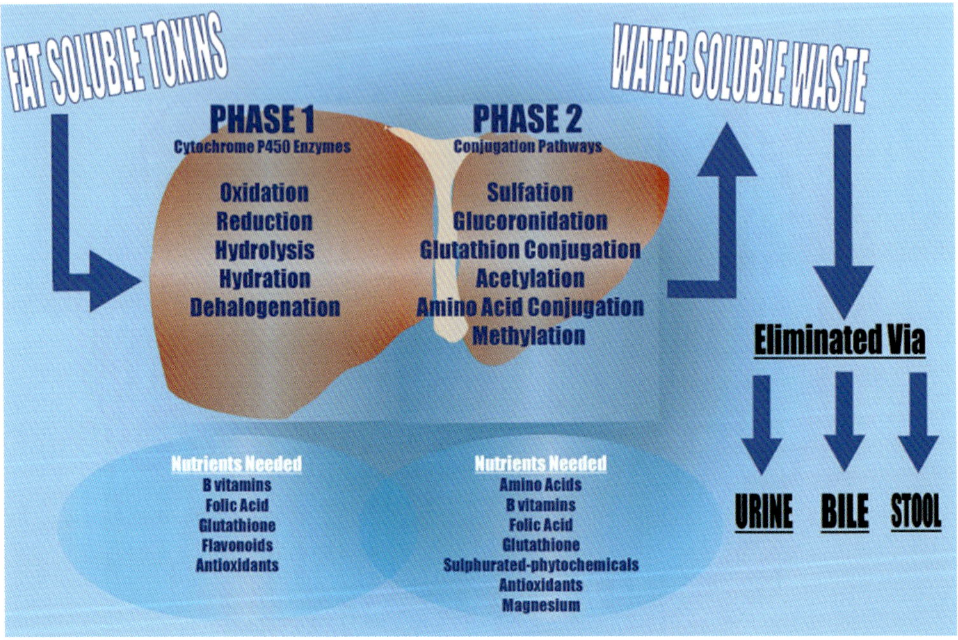

Here's how the two phase process works in the liver:

Phase 1: *Toxins such as environmental chemicals, drugs, and metabolic end products enter the body and activate a group of enzymes called cytochrome P450 mixed function oxidases. In this phase, the toxins are transformed into an intermediate state that can be broken down in phase 2.*

Phase 2: *in this step, the body adds specific nutrients to transform the toxin into a water soluble compound for a safe exit via urination or bowel movements.*

These foods are great for liver detoxification because of their high sulphur content.

Alcohol and the Liver

Alcohol is detrimental to the health of your liver and is also a notorious oestrogen increaser. It does this by affecting the liver's P450 enzyme subsystem in a negative way. Basically, it slows down your body's ability to process oestrogen, allowing it to build up in your bloodstream. The liver detoxifies alcohol by a few enzymes to break it down into harmless chemicals that can be excreted from the body. However, stores of these enzymes are not unlimited and the liver can become overburdened quickly. If too much alcohol is consumed then it cannot be broken down properly and acidic metabolites are formed.

Alcohol is terrible for our liver. Overwhelming evidence has shown that alcohol itself is toxic to the liver, even when nutrition is adequate. Alcohol interferes with the liver's ability to metabolize hormones.

In one study volunteers consumed the equivalent of at least a six-pack of beer a day, along with high protein diets enriched in minerals and vitamins. After one "weekend" of drinking, fat accumulation in the liver was already detectable by chemical analysis. In another study, baboons were given an adequate diet, but had alcohol as 50% of their total calories. All developed a fatty liver.

Five signs of a toxic or dysfunctional liver.

It has also been found that circulating oestrogen levels increase significantly in women who drink. In one study, blood and urine oestrogen levels increased up to 32 percent in women who drank just two drinks a day. Consequently, breast cancer risks are higher for women drinkers.

Caffeine and the Liver

Caffeine reaches its peak concentration thirty to sixty minutes after consumption, after which it is inactivated by the liver, with only half its peak level left four to six hours. However, during this time the liver has to work very hard to detoxify the caffeine and is consequently less efficient at detoxifying other toxins. If you are lean and healthy then having a cup of organic coffee with your breakfast every day is like throwing a marble at an elephant's ass trying to get it's attention - it isn't going to have any effect on your already super efficient liver. However if you are obese and tired constantly, give coffee a miss until you can see your toes again whilst standing!

Tips for a healthy liver

- Eat organically produced foods as much as possible to avoid toxic chemical residues.
- Avoid artificial flavorings and preservatives.
- Avoid damaged fats such as hydrogenated fats found in many processed foods.
- Use cold pressed oils and do not use them for cooking. Only a little butter, a saturated fat (coconut oil), should be used for cooking. Cooking with olive oil is still controversial. If used then do not heat it to a high temperature and add AFTER food has been removed from heat.
- Make sure your nuts and seeds are really fresh.
- Avoid excess saturated animal fat like sausage, bacon, salami, hot dogs, high fat dairy products like whole milk, ice cream and cheese.
- Alcohol is known to be a powerful toxin that will damage the liver. Avoid it or drink very occasionally!
- Do not overeat at meal time as this places an enormous added burden on your liver and detoxification pathways. Also chew your food thoroughly!
- Treating your liver well by following the above advice will have a huge impact on your body fat, health and longevity.

Thyroid Hormones and Liver

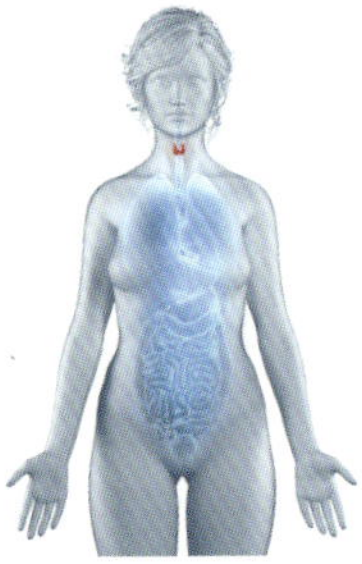

Your thyroid gland produces two main hormones which we will cover in great detail in habit 5 of this book: T4 (also called thyroxine) and T3 (also called triiodothyronine). These hormones help to control your metabolic rate, that is the rate at which your body burns calories. They also have a huge bearing on your energy levels and maintenance of normal body temperature. T4 is not the active thyroid hormone; it must be converted into T3 in your body in order to exert its effects. The majority of this conversion does not occur in your thyroid gland. Most T4 to T3 conversion happens in your liver, kidneys and muscles. **In fact, 60% of T4 is converted into T3 in the liver providing it is functioning at full effectiveness. Now you can see why a dysfunctional liver can lead to a cascade of hormonal problems.**

If you are taking thyroid hormone medication in the form of thyroxine, it too must be converted into the active form in your body. Therefore if you are taking thyroid medication but still not feeling much better, your liver could be to blame! It is vital that you work on improving the health of your liver if you want healthy thyroid hormone levels. If you have a fatty liver or a sluggish liver, this conversion will not be effective. This can leave you feeling tired, depressed, puffy, overweight and with dry skin and thinning scalp hair.

Indeed you could have a thyroid problem caused by a faulty liver. This relationship also works the other way. Thyroid hormones affect the liver cells responsible for detoxification. So, when thyroid function is low due to hypothyroidism the enzymes that carry out detoxifying tasks simply can't do their job efficiently.

Sugars, Insulin and the Liver

Insulin is also a fat storing hormone. So high levels of insulin can promote the storage of fat, especially in the abdominal area. The high levels of insulin also send a message to the liver to store more fat, so many people with a high insulin level develop a fatty liver. Avoid eating large amounts of sugar, especially refined sugars, as the liver will convert sugar into a type of fat called triglycerides. These fats can build up inside our cells causing fatty degeneration of organs or will be transported to areas for storage, such as the hips, thighs and stomach. This is why many people as mentioned earlier become fat on a high carbohydrate/low fat diet.

"Avoid the artificial sweetener aspartame found in diet drinks and diet foods as aspartame is also toxic to the liver. When you ingest the toxic chemical aspartame it is absorbed from the intestines and passes immediately to the LIVER where it is taken inside the liver via the liver filter. The liver then breaks down or metabolises aspartame to its toxic components – phenylalanine, aspartic acid and methanol. This process requires a lot of energy from the liver which means there will be less energy remaining in the liver cells. This means the liver cells will have less energy for fat burning and metabolism, which will result in fat storing.

Excess fat may build up inside the liver cells causing "fatty liver" and when this starts to occur it is extremely difficult to lose weight. In my vast experience any time that you overload the liver you will increase the tendency to gain weight easily". Sandra Cabot, M.D.

How Not to Help Your Liver

Those looking on the internet or local bookstores looking for information on ways to help detox their livers are likely to come upon various programs proclaiming a liver flush, liver detox, or some type of extended fasting. Fasting for longer than a few days can be extremely hard on your liver. The rationale behind it is that because your liver has been overloaded by eating too much, then not eating much of anything for an extended period of time will give it a break and help empty the liver of excess fat and toxins.

The problem when you don't eat protein due to fasting for a few days your liver actually slows down and you can seriously impair your metabolism and detoxification function. When scientists want to study animals with defunct liver function they simply take the protein out of their diets until their livers quit working. Even upon protein re-feeding it can take six months for their livers to recover.

The gallbladder/liver flush is quite simply stupid and dangerous. It typically involves fasting on apple juice for several days and then consuming large amounts of olive oil, citrus juice, and Epsom salts. The substances seen in the stool following this effort are not gallstones, but rather the oil itself forming soft complexes. I never recommend this for anyone unless I don't like them.

Exercise to Help Fatty Liver

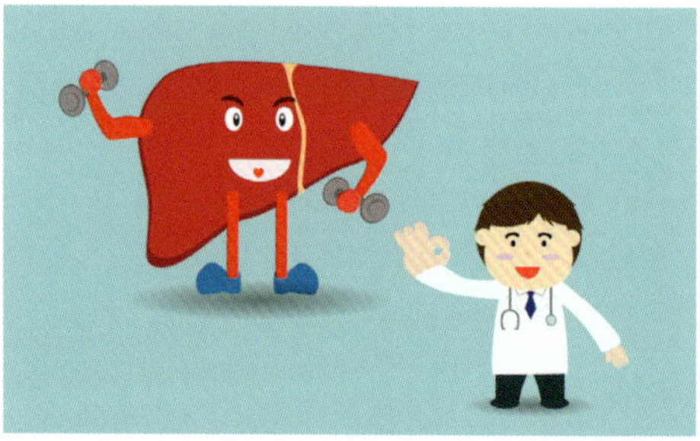

Consistent exercise is vitally important to resolving the issue of a fatty liver. This is because exercise creates a demand for nutrients to flow to muscles, helping your liver have preferred options regarding where to send nutrients and offload its cargo making room for more nutrients to come into the liver to be stored because remember when the liver is full of glycogen and it can only hold approximately 100 grams it will convert the rest into FAT. This is why I usually exercise early morning in a fasted state but loaded with amino acids this allows me to empty my liver regularly and this helps with fat loss.

If you are fit enough and get a good response to intense exercise, it will produce the best results. Remember the harder, more intense you exercise, the more glycogen you use and this is covered in great depth in both habits 9 and 10 of this book. However, a number of studies are showing that moderate consistent exercise can definitely improve this problem.

Obese individuals who walked on a treadmill for one hour per day improved insulin resistance, boosted adiponectin levels this hormone improves insulin sensitivity, lowered free radical damage, and improved fatty liver problems. Another study showed that placing sedentary obese adults on a four week aerobic cycling and stretching program cleared out 21 percent of their liver fat, clearly helping to unclog their livers.

An animal study seeking to document molecular mechanisms showed that three aerobic sessions per week were adequate to reduce weight gain, shrink belly fat, and clear out liver fat. In humans who lost weight and then exercised 40 minutes twice a week, even if they regained a slight amount of weight, they did not regain "dangerous fat" that is associated with fatty liver. I would always suggest more exercise than this study. However, the study shows that keeping up even a moderate exercise program can prevent sliding back into the fatty liver problem.

Strength training is also likely to help fatty liver. This is because fatty liver disturbs growth hormone signaling that also contributes to fatty liver. On the other hand, strength training along with reducing inflammation helps condition growth hormone signaling to be normal. Also strength training with higher repetitions can help deplete glycogen stores in muscles allowing the liver to release its stored glycogen to help fuel sessions when the muscles start to become depleted of their own glycogen stores.

Things the Liver Loves

Well it seems we have found a use for coffee! Coffee enemas help to remove the toxic mucoid plaque around the colon walls, thus killing parasites. Coffee enemas are better than water, because they stimulate the liver to create more glutathione. Studies have shown that coffee enemas can increase glutathione in the liver by almost 700%. The enema is the best way to gain beneficial effects before reaching the liver. Glutathione is one of the body's most important and powerful antioxidants, helping to detoxify toxins.

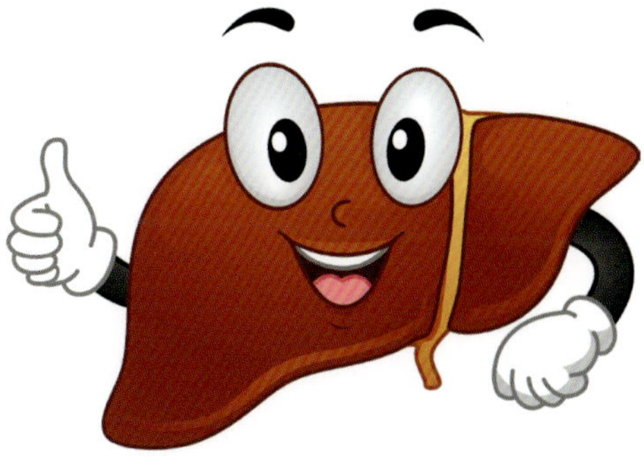

Coffee enemas, although often scoffed at today, were actually used as part of conventional medicine all the way up to the 1960s, and were included in the Merck Manual, which was a handbook for conventional medical treatments into the 1970s. **When you drink coffee, it tends to suppress your liver function, but when taken rectally as an enema, the caffeine stimulates nerves in your lower bowels, which causes your liver to release toxins as a reflex.**

Coffee enemas can help with a range of other health issues. They are used with amazing frequency in retreats and other health centers. For thousands of years, people have been using enemas to cleanse their colons. Dr. Max Gerson, whose meticulous application of coffee enemas, combined with a specialized diet, fresh juices and certain nutritional supplements, produced impressive results in patients with cancer and other degenerative and chronic conditions.

Coffee enemas reduce levels of systemic toxicity by up to 700%. According to the late Dr. Max Gerson, a pioneer of coffee enema therapy and its effectiveness as part of his famous Gerson Diet, caffeine and other beneficial compounds in coffee stimulate the production of glutathione S-transferase (GST) in the liver. GST is said to be the "master detoxifier" in the body, as this powerful enzyme binds with toxins throughout the body and flushes them out during the enema process. According to a 1982 study conducted by the *National Research Council* (NRC), the effect of green coffee bean consumption on the production of glutathione S-transferase (GST) in test mice was an astounding 600% increase in the liver, and a 700% increase in the small intestine. In humans, the effect is similar, if not amplified, during a coffee enema, as coffee is able to directly stimulate the liver without having to first run through the digestive tract. **The result is a powerful detoxifying effect that is unmatched by sheer diet alone.**

Coffee enemas cleanse and heal the colon and digestive tract, improving peristalsis. Besides detoxifying, coffee enemas also cleanse and flush the digestive tract and colon without substantially disrupting the beneficial flora that populate a healthy gut. By regularly taking coffee enemas, you will not only help keep your digestive tract clean and free of debris and toxic buildup, but you will also promote healthy peristalsis, which is the series of organized muscle contractions that move food through the digestive tract and the tubular organs that connect to the kidneys and bladder.

Coffee enemas boost energy levels, improve mental clarity and mood. As with any detox protocol, the body is effectively ridding itself of poisons that sludge up the blood; decrease oxygen transfer; and clog up the intestines, all of which generally leave a person feeling fatigued and ill. A coffee enema is a particularly effective detoxifier; however, as the direct absorption of caffeine and palmitates into the bloodstream stimulates the release of bile and the efficient removal of wastes from the body in one fell swoop. The end result is a detoxifying release so powerful that many people describe it as a "high" marked by significantly improved energy levels, enhanced mental clarity, and better moods.

A coffee enema can be done at least once a week for general health maintenance and up to four times a day for those with chronic disease. Use organic coffee boiled with pure water for 3 minutes. Simmer uncovered for about 15 minutes and let cool so the water is room temperature. The suggested ratio is 3 tablespoons of coffee to 1 litre of water. Place the mixture into an enema. Lie on your right side with your knees curled up or whatever position you feel comfortable with, insert the nozzle about 2 inches inside the rectum and deposit the coffee. After the enema has been deposited, move around a bit to shift the coffee around. It may be challenging, but try to hold the fluid in for 12-15 minutes but no more than 15 minutes. It is always a good idea to consult with a knowledgeable medical professional before doing enemas.

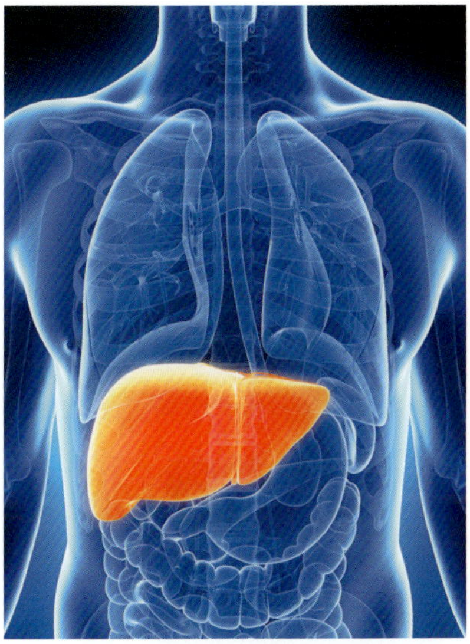

There are also nutrients and herbs that help to protect and detoxify the liver itself so that it can perform better to detoxify the entire body:

Apples contain pectin which helps to bind and excrete heavy metals through the intestines. This directly helps to reduce the load of filtration on the liver.

Beetroot, carrots, red onions and aubergine (eggplant) contain flavonoids and beta-carotene which are potent antioxidants. Beetroot also contains betaine which promotes the flow of fat and bile from the liver. Betaine also protects the liver from the toxic effects of alcohol.

Garlic contains allicin and the mineral selenium, both antioxidants. It assists the removal of heavy metals from the liver.

Eggs, brown rice and whole grains, broccoli and spinach contain B-complex vitamins which improve liver function and promote liver de-congestion. Vitamin B12 helps to metabolize fats and improves liver health.

Artichoke leaf promotes regeneration of the liver and promotes blood flow in that organ, stimulates bile flow.

Turmeric, one of the most powerful foods for maintaining a healthy liver, has been shown to actively protect the liver against toxic damage, and even regenerate damaged liver cells. Turmeric also boosts the natural production of bile, shrinks engorged hepatic ducts, and improves overall function of the gallbladder, another body-purifying organ.

Recent findings are demonstrating that the amino acid taurine is one of the major nutrients involved in the body's detoxification of harmful substances and should be a part of any liver detox plan. Taurine is found in high amounts in animal protein, organ meats and invertebrate seafood and is often deficient in vegetarians.

Increasing evidence suggests that taurine may help treat the most common cause of liver disease in the UK, non-alcoholic fatty liver disease (or NAFLD). Non-alcoholic fatty liver disease occurs when too much fat accumulates in the liver, and it can be caused by insulin resistance and metabolic syndrome. Over time, the end result is the loss of liver function, leading to liver cirrhosis. Studies show that taurine defends liver cells against free radicals and toxins, helping to reduce the severity of oxidative stress-induced liver injury. This is vitally important in alcoholic and non-alcoholic fatty liver diseases, both of which can progress to cirrhosis and liver failure

Human studies reveal the impact of taurine on liver disease. When 24 patients with chronic hepatitis took 2 grams of taurine 3 times daily for 3 months, serum markers of liver damage, as well as markers of oxidative stress, decreased significantly, as did their elevated levels of cholesterol and triglycerides

Vitamin C is also a very powerful antioxidant for the liver and reduces toxic damage to the liver cells from chemical overload. It neutralises free radicals generated during the phase 1 detoxification pathway in the liver. Toxic chemicals are far less dangerous if there is plenty of vitamin C in the liver. In a study on guinea pigs short term vitamin C deficiency reduced the levels of vitamin C in the liver by 25% and led to a 50% reduction in both the amount produced and the effectiveness of the bile.

Guinea pigs, like humans, can not produce any vitamin C.

Among foods, the brassica family, i.e. cabbage, broccoli, and Brussels sprouts, contains chemical constituents that stimulate both phase I and phase II detoxification enzymes. One such compound is indole-3-carbinol, which is also a powerful anti-cancer chemical. It is a very active stimulant of detoxifying enzymes in the gut as well as the liver. Cruciferous vegetables also contain glucosinolates which help the liver produce enzymes for detoxification.

Oranges and tangerines contain limonene, a phytochemical, a strong inducer of both phase I and phase II detoxification enzymes that neutralize carcinogens.

Lecithin is one of the best supplements to thin the bile so that toxins and chemicals can flow out of the liver more readily.

To date, findings from nine double-blind trials indicate phosphatidylcholine (PC) clinically supports liver recovery from toxic chemical attack or acute or chronic viral damage! The liver's parenchymal cells (the functional parts of an organ in the body) depend heavily on the membrane phospholipids to optimally process newly absorbed nutrients, assemble circulating lipoproteins (LDL and HDL cholesterol, among others) and detoxify thousands of potentially toxic incoming chemicals.

Other organs such as the lungs, skin and kidneys also have phase 1 and 2 enzymes. This is one of the reasons that deep breathing, sweating and drinking lots of water help the body detoxify.

Detoxification Through Defecation: Keep Our Bowels Healthy

The colon plays a vital role in the health of our entire body. The condition of this organ, also known as the bowel, affects every other organ in the body and, consequently, our overall health. An unhealthy colon can have a direct relationship on the dysfunction of the liver, heart or brain or any other organ. Having a healthy colon is essential for overall health and well being.

When the bowel becomes underactive, toxic wastes are more likely to be absorbed through the bowel wall and into the bloodstream. The blood then circulates these toxins to every cell in the body potentially altering cellular function. As the body becomes increasingly toxic, proper oxygenation cannot take place in the tissues. Without oxygen, the body loses energy and this becomes a downward spiral of health. A tired body has reduced ability to throw off toxins, which is why toxic, sick people are always tired people.

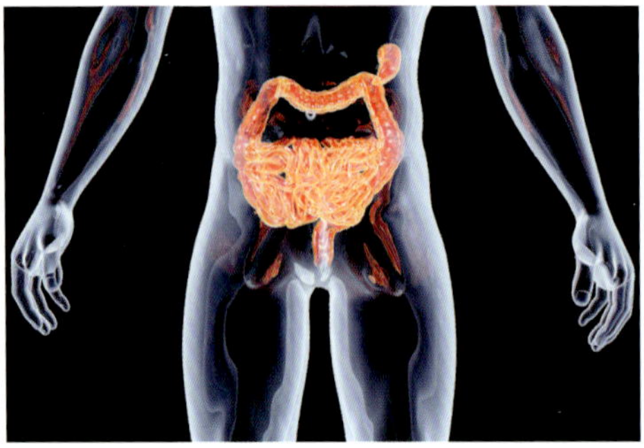

Your bowel health is critical for your fat loss goals. Ensure you have a good supply of pro- and prebiotics, keep hydrated and have a good supply of fibre in your diet.

The body depends on a clean bowel. Remember, the cleanliness of any tissue in the body depends upon the condition of the bowel. It is the source of most internal toxic material, which makes its way into the blood and the lymph through the bowel wall and is then carried to and deposited in the cells and tissues. A cleaner bowel leads to cleaner blood, which leads to cleaner cells and then onto cleaner tissues allowing metabolism to function optimally.

The bowel is considered to be a part of the digestive or gastrointestinal system. It is designed to help the body absorb nutrients and fluids from the foods we eat and drink. After taking out everything the body needs, the bowel then expels the leftover waste.

The colon is a 5-6 foot long muscular tube that delivers stool to the rectum. As the stool moves through the colon, the fluids are removed and absorbed into the body. The consistency of the stool is dependent upon many things, including how long the stool sits in the colon, how much of the water has been absorbed from the waste, and the amount of fibre and fluids in your diet. Stool consistency can vary from hard lumps, mushy, very loose to watery stool. The best and easiest consistency of stool is mushy, like toothpaste; this consistency may be obtained by adding fibre to your diet preferably from fruits and vegetables.

Your stool should be of a similar consistency to that of toothpaste.

Fibre helps move waste through the colon because it is indigestible by the human body. In other words, fibre adds 'bulk' to the stool. It is important to eat a diet high in fibre; however, most of us lack fibre in our diet. About 25-35 grams of fibre is required by the body to keep the bowels healthy and moving. If your bowel movements are too loose, fibre can make them firmer; on the other hand, if your stools are too hard, fibre can make them softer. A low-fiber diet causes oestrogen levels to be higher, while a diet high in fiber results in decreased oestrogen levels in the bloodstream. Why? Excess oestrogen is excreted in the bowel. When stool remains in the bowel for a longer time, as in constipation, the oestrogen is reabsorbed.

Studies have shown that women on a high-fiber diet have lower levels of circulating oestrogen. Lower levels of oestrogen mean less oestrogen stimulation of breast tissue, for example, which reduces the risk of breast cancer. So eat plenty of non starchy vegetables to get the most valuable forms of fiber and to not only keep bowel movements healthy but also to get rid of excess oestrogen. Don't eat high fiber breakfast cereals for fiber they will most likely cause obesity through insulin resistance as well as wheat and milk allergies!

Constipation is a way your body is telling you to consume more fiber and drink more water!

Another factor that helps to control the consistency of your stool is fluid. If the colon does not have enough fluids to absorb from the waste, the stool will be dehydrated, resulting in hard, lumpy stool that is difficult to pass. In most adults without bowel disease, a diet high in fibre and drinking 2-3 litres of water a day will produce soft stools that are easy to pass. Fluid and fibre work together to encourage healthy bowel habits. You must eat a diet high in fibre and drink plenty of water. Remember, "healthy" stools should be the consistency of toothpaste being squeezed from the tube – soft and free flowing.

One of the most frequent bowel problems that people experience today is constipation. A constipated system is one in which the transition time of toxic wastes is slow. The longer the "transit time," the longer the toxic waste matter sits in our bowel, which allows them to putrefy, ferment and possibly be reabsorbed. The longer your body is exposed to putrefying food in your intestines, the greater the risk of developing disease.

THINK YOU KNOW YOUR SHIT?

Separate hard lumps, like nuts
You're lacking fibre and fluids.
Drink more water and eat
some fruit and vegetables

Sausage-shaped, smooth and soft
Optimal shit!
Your getting things right!

Sausage-shaped but lumpy
Not as serious as hard lumps,
but you need to take on fluids
and plenty of fibre.

Watery, no solids, all liquid
You have diarrhoea!
Probably from some infection and
your bodies own 'clear out'.
Drink plenty of clean water to
prevent dehydration!

*Sausage-shaped but with
cracks on surface*
Pretty normal, but possibly
greater intake of fluids is
required here.

*Fluffy pieces with ragged edges, a
mushy stool*
Borderline normal, this shit tends
to lead to diarrhoea.

*Sausage-shaped but with
cracks on surface*
Pretty normal, but possibly
greater intake of fluids is
required here.

Soft and sticks to the loo
Presence of excess oil. Possibly means your
body is not absorbing fats properly.
Diseases such as chronic pancreatitis
prevent the body absorbing fats.

A highly processed diet and an unhealthy lifestyle can cause a dysfunctional bowel leading to intestinal toxaemia. When the intestinal tract is the recipient of an improper diet or when the colon is not evacuated in a timely fashion, the normal intestinal flora are replaced by more harmful bacteria, and intestinal toxaemia is the inevitable consequence.

In modern civilization, the greatest numbers of bowel disturbances are found in industrialized countries. Modern societies who still live as hunter/gatherers very rarely, if ever, encounter bowel problems, for example the research by British surgeon Denis P. Burkett M.D., has confirmed the lower incidence of several types of cancer amongst Eastern African natives eating a high fibre diet which reduces bowel transit time. One of the main differences between the African natives and the British, he also found, was the fact the British had much slower transit time through the colon compared to that of the African natives due to less fibre in the diet of the British.

The average Western diet contains 11.0 grams of fibre, as compared to 24.8 grams of fibre in the diet of Bantu tribesman. In rural eastern Africa and other primitive societies there is virtually no incidence of diverticulitis or colon cancer, unless the natives adopt a modern "civilized" diet, as they do when they move to urban areas.

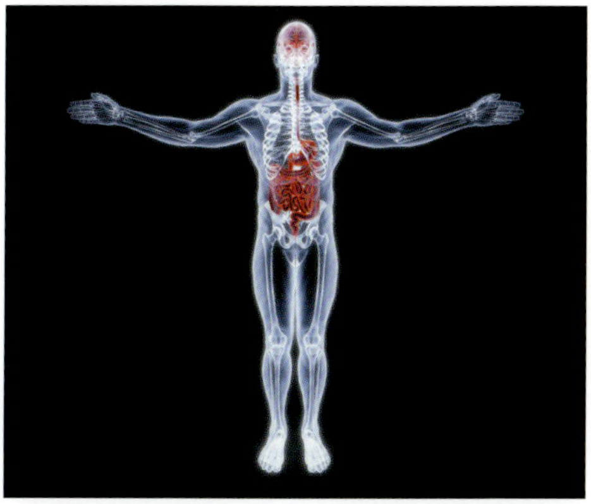

The brain communicates with the gut and the gut communicates with the brain. We will discuss this more in habit 3.

I strongly suggest that you relax before you eat any meal. When you sit down for a meal, instead of digging right in, perform a little relaxation ritual to start your digestion off right and be very grateful for your food. Before you even pick up your fork, take a slow, deep breath and try to release any tension in your muscles. Eat slowly and enjoy your food, chewing it thoroughly and focusing on the nutrients and energy your meal is providing you. I also suggest that whilst eating your food, you do not watch anything stressful on the TV (like the news) as this will increase your stress hormones. This will take blood from the gut and to the muscles as the body prepares for fight-or-flight. This will decrease your ability to digest foods and store more of it as fat.

Chew your food thoroughly as well and this is very important for better absorption from foods and will allow more efficient elimination.

Gut Bacteria

Your gut bacteria plays an essential part in regards to your health and your waistline.

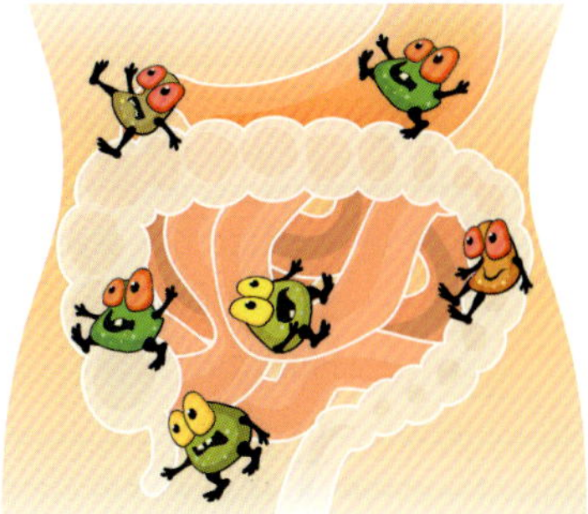

The human body consists of over 100 trillion microflora (bacteria), 80% of which live in our intestines and weighing between 1-2kg. The micro-flora in our gut can be good for the body (such as probiotics which can increase immune function) or potentially harmful to the body by causing illness and infections.

It is suggested that we should have between 50-85% "good" bacteria. Although, worryingly, those on a high meat diet have been found to have only 5%, meaning it is outnumbered by the "bad" bacteria 20 to 1.

Your diet plays a large role in determining the ratio of good and bad bacteria. Sugary foods and lots of meat help many harmful bacteria to thrive. A diet high in fibre (and therefore prebiotic, which feed good bacteria) gives probiotics the edge as they can digest fibre whereas many harmful bacteria cannot.

Examples of prebiotic foods include;

- Oats
- Tomatoes
- Onions
- Almonds
- Bananas
- Cottage cheese
- Goats milk

Microbes survive longer when they stick to cells of the intestine, and so escape being swept away by peristalsis (wave-like contraction of muscles which squeezes food through the digestive tract). Probiotics regulate peristalsis and compete with harmful microbes for access to these cells, which means more harmful microbes leave the body.

A study published in Environmental Health in 2005 randomly gave workers either drinking straws with probiotics or a plain straw. Over the next 80 days those with the plain straws had around 80% more days off due to illness. This occurred even though all those who took part described themselves as "healthy".

A double-blind study in Germany with around 500 people looked at the effect of supplementing with vitamins or vitamins plus probiotics in preventing colds over winter. Those who took the probiotics not only had fewer colds, their colds lasted for less time. And, when blood samples were analysed, it was found that their white blood cells numbers had increased from the start of the study. This is due to the fact that around 80% of the immune system is found in the digestive tract.

Probiotics thrive when fibre is present. The reason for this is that many fibrous foods have prebiotic qualities and so can be digested by probiotics but not by many harmful bacteria. Therefore it is essential that we get enough prebiotic foods . The prebiotic part of foods avoids digestion in the small intestine and is passed on to the large intestine where it is fermented by the probiotic bacteria.

One of the reasons why it is difficult for an overweight person to lose body fat may be because of their gut bacteria. Analysis of the microbiota of obese mice and humans have been shown to increase the number of short-chain fatty acids, which increase the energy harvest from food and promote fat storage as adipose tissue. Put simply, the gut bacteria in obese people may make them absorb more energy from food and store more of this energy as fat.

Our highly processed, high-sugar, high-fat, low-fiber diet - plus many drugs like antibiotics, steroids, anti-inflammatories, acid-blockers, and hormones - completely alter the bacterial ecosystem in the gut, leading to breakdown, inflammation, and a leaky gut.

Breast Fed Babies Have Healthier Gut Bacteria Than Formula Fed Babies

During the first few weeks of life, an baby's immune system is almost entirely dependent on the mother's breast-milk for immune protection from its environment. Breast-feeding during the first weeks and months of life is now recognized as an important strategy to ensure a healthy balance of good bacteria in an infant's gut.

You may not be aware that your gut is actually the center of 60-70% of your immune system and may play a crucial role in the development of chronic disease. The gut plays such an important role because it is a primary defense between the "outside" and "inside" worlds. When good bacteria line the gut, they prevent potentially harmful bacteria from lining it instead.

Breastfeeding Recommendations

The World Health Organization now recommends exclusive breastfeeding for at least 6 months to promote health. Additionally, the nutritional committees from the American Academy of Pediatrics, European Society for Pediatric Allergology and Clinical Immunology, & the European Society for Pediatric Gastroenterology, Hepatology, and Nutrition ALL recommend feeding babies breast milk for 18-24 months as hypoallergenic foods are introduced one at a time starting at 6 months.

More allergenic foods such as corn, wheat, dairy, soy, peanuts, eggs, & shellfish should only be introduced when the child is older and their immune system is more developed. Some practitioners recommend that mothers avoid these allergenic foods as well to prevent passing sensitivity on to their children.

Infant symptoms such as a atopic eczema can actually disappear upon a lactating mother's removal of allergenic foods from her diet. If a mother is looking for a supplement to her own breastmilk, she can take probiotics during pregnancy and breastfeeding which has been shown to promote infant immune health.

The Infant Immune System & Gut Health

Immunity is passed from the mother through her breast-milk which contains antibodies against specific antigens present in the immediate environment. Demonstrating the unique bond a lactating mother has with her baby, a baby's saliva actually communicates with the mother and literally affects the composition of the milk based on the baby's unique needs!

Mother's breastfeeding can help prevent and support gut problems and research suggests that breast milk can help re-establish a healthy balance of bacteria and antibodies even after use of antibiotics. Unfortunately, the process of re-establishing healthy levels of infant bacteria through breastfeeding may take as long as 2-4 weeks!

How Can Infant Gut Health Become Altered?

Because of high c-section rates and feeding with cow or soy milk formulas, "natural" infant gut development can be altered. Mothers who breastfeed may help reduce potential complications. For instance, research has shown that breastfed infants have a more acidic environment in their gut during the first six weeks of life. Their tiny guts become naturally full of healthy bifidobacteria and naturally low in potentially harmful bacteria such as E. coli, Bacteroides, Clostridia, and Streptococci. In addition to healthy bacteria, infants depend on something called sIgA from their mother's breast milk as a passive form of antibody protection that lines an infant's GI tract and protects them from potentially harmful antigens in their immediate environment.

sIgA continues to be the primary gut immune defense as we age…decreasing with physical, emotional, and chemical forms of stress. When sIgA levels are disrupted, we may become more susceptible to IgE and IgG reactions associated with food allergies, sensitivities, and intolerances to those with genetic susceptibilities.

Introducing allergenic foods too early & failing to breastfeed may "turn on" genes that make us susceptible to allergies later in life. Genetic susceptibility of gluten allergy alone may be present in up to 81% of Americans. These low-level food reactions can contribute to "leaky gut" – a condition where your intestines absorb proteins that the body sees as "foreign", initiating delayed immune reactions.

Disadvantages of Formula Feeding

Within as little as four days of life, the presence of bifidobacterium in the guts of breastfed infants can be over 300% higher than in formula-fed infants. Pathogenic bacteria tend to make up the dramatic difference in bottle-fed babies.

Supplementing breast milk with even just a little bit of formula can affect the acidity of the gut environment, possibly promoting the presence of harmful bacteria and threatening the integrity of the gut lining! In Habit 3 you will see the link between gut bacteria, brain function and autism link!

SO YES BREAST IS BEST FOR YOUR BABY'S HEALTH

Detoxification of heavy metals

We should now have an understanding on the incredible damage that heavy metals can do to our health and how they destroy cellular health and disrupt endocrine function, make no bones about it heavy metals are destroying every cell in our bodies.

Mercury, as discussed throughout this book, because of its debilitating effects on human health, is unfortunately one of many heavy metals we have to endure today. Remember amalgam fillings are in reality mercury fillings which are toxic time bombs in your mouth and I am not exaggerating that fact!

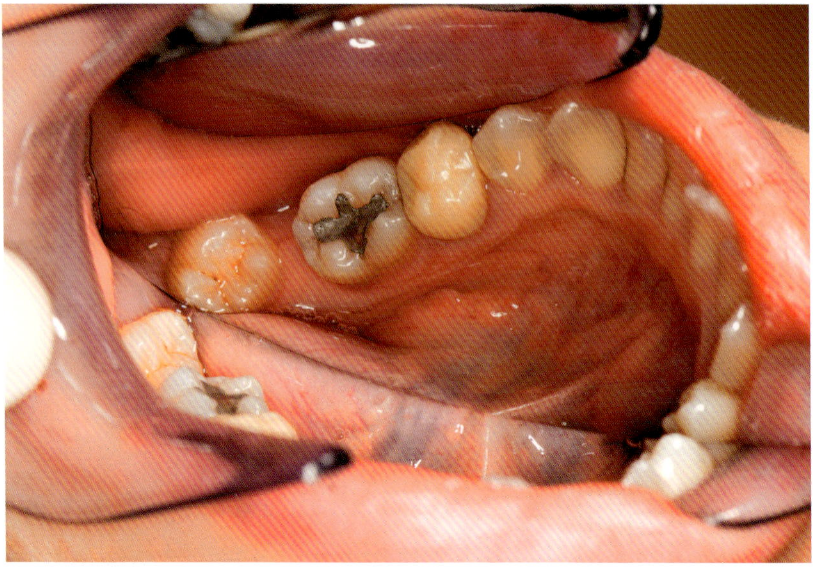

Cilantro

Cilantro is capable of mobilizing mercury, cadmium, lead and aluminium in both bones and the central nervous system. It is probably the only effective agent in mobilizing mercury stored in the intracellular space (attached to mitochondria, tubulin, liposomes etc.) and in the nucleus of the cell (reversing DNA damage of mercury). It mobilizes mercury so well, it could overwhelm your liver if you don't use one to five grams of chlorella daily to help flush the mercury out.

Cilantro, chlorella and spirulina are often difficult to get into our diets but can be taken in as powdered supplements.

Cilantro mobilizes mercury, aluminum, lead and tin stored in the brain and in the spinal cord and moves it into the connective tissues. The mobilized mercury appears to be either excreted via the stool, the urine, or translocated into more peripheral tissues. The mechanism of action is unknown. Cilantro alone often does not remove mercury from the body; it often only displaces the metals from intracellularly or from deeper body stores to more superficial structures, from where it can be easily removed with chlorella.

Chlorella

Chlorella is a "green food," a single-celled, microalgae that is about two to ten microns in size. It's very small. It is this small size combined with its unique properties that make it such a useful detoxification tool. Its molecular structure, allows it to bond to metals, chemicals and some pesticides.

When chlorella is taken into your body, its natural action will bind it to lingering heavy metals, chemicals and pesticides found in your digestive tract, which is your body's pathway to your bloodstream, where these harmful toxins are delivered and deposited into your body's cells. So chlorella first and foremost will help your body eliminate unwanted metals and toxins.

A book written for the mining industry, Biosorption of Heavy Metals, details how miners use these organisms to increase the yield of precious metals in old mines. The mucopolysaccharides in chlorella's cell wall absorb rather large amounts of toxic metals similar to an ion exchange resin.

Chlorella also enhances mobilization of mercury compartmentalized in non-neurologic structures such as the gut wall, muscles, ligaments, connective tissue, and bone. Chlorella is an important part of the systemic mercury elimination program, as approximately 90% of the mercury is eliminated through the stool. Using large doses of chlorella facilitates fecal mercury excretion. After the intestinal mercury burden is lowered, mercury will more readily migrate into the intestine from other body tissues from where **chlorella will effectively remove it.**

Studies in Japan have shown chlorella may help reduce body fat percentage and may be useful in fighting obesity and weight related diabetes. Chlorella's cleansing action on your bowel and other elimination channels, as well as its protection of your liver, also helps promote clean blood. And clean blood helps assure metabolic waste gets efficiently carried away from your tissues.

A three year double blind metal detoxification study, with over 350 people participating, was undertaken at a Russian metal foundry, where more than 20 natural compounds were used in trials to remove heavy metals from people who had been exposed at very high levels to four main metals - antimony, lead, cadmium and arsenic. What were the results of testing chlorella as a heavy metal detoxification agent? The Russian trial using chlorella combined with cilantro eliminated ALL heavy metals, including mercury, with no reported side-effects alone.

Many reports have come from Japanese research studies that followed the nuclear catastrophe resulting from atomic bombs being dropped on Hiroshima and Nagasaki in 1945. In a report on animals, authors noted that chlorella (8 grams daily) increased elimination of cadmium: 3-fold in faeces and 7-fold in urine (Ichimura 1973). Other researchers from Japan showed that chlorella helped detoxify uranium and lead (Horikoshi 1979).

Chlorella has detoxification potential for similar compounds, such as dioxin and polychlorinated biphenyls (PCBs) (i.e., chemical compounds used in plastics, insulation, and flame retardants, with potential to cause cancer and liver damage). Other research indicates that chlorella is useful in detoxification of high levels of mercury in the body caused by removal of mercury amalgam. Some dentists recommend chlorella to patients having mercury amalgams replaced (as well as to themselves and staff who can incur accidental exposure from day-to-day exposure to amalgam filling procedures).

In addition to its detox abilities, chlorella is one of nature's best superfoods. It contains all the amino acids, providing easy-to-digest protein. It also contains vital minerals such as magnesium and iron. The high level of chlorophyll in chlorella helps optimize oxygen into blood intake.

Spirulina has been shown as an effective chelating agent for removing toxins such as mercury, and radioactive substances from the body. It has also been used to remove cadmium and lead from waste water. Just as important as their ability to detox heavy metals, both spirulina and chlorella exhibit strong healing and regenerating capabilities. They are filled with beneficial vitamins, minerals, proteins and fats which work together in a synergistic way to provide energy and vitality.

From all of this information and research, I have developed a heavy metal detoxification plan that I have used numerous times. It includes a number of products that I specifically developed for heavy metal detoxification.

SUPPLEMENT PLAN: Mercury Detoxification				
20-30 Minutes Before Meals (Unless Training)	**Breakfast**	**Lunch**	**Dinner**	**1 Hour Before Bed On An Empty Stomach**
1/2 Teaspoons of **Alkalising Salts** In 500ml of water	2 x **Cordyceps**	1 x **Cordyceps**	1 x **Cordyceps**	2 Scoops of **Nitric Oxide Generator**
	1 x **Ultimate Multivitamin & Mineral Formula**	1 x **Ultimate Multivitamin & Mineral Formula**	1 x **Ultimate Multivitamin & Mineral Formula**	
	1 x **Oestro Detox Formula**	1 x **Oestro Detox Formula**	1 x **Oestro Detox Formula**	3 x **Magnesium Relax**
	1 Teaspoon of **Ultimate Fish Oil Liquid**	1 Teaspoon of **Ultimate Fish Oil Liquid**	1 Teaspoon of **Ultimate Fish Oil Liquid**	
	1 x **Iodine Forte Capsule**	1 x **Iodine Forte Capsule**	1 x **Iodine Forte Capsule**	
	2 Scoop **Collagen Formula**	2 Scoop **Collagen Formula**	2 Scoop **Collagen Formula**	
	2 x **Probiotic Gut Health**			
BETWEEN MEAL TIMES: In between breakfast, lunch & evening meals drink 500ml of reverse osmosis water or still mineral water with TWO heaped TEASPOONS of **Ultimate Greens**.				

Detoxification using oil pulling therapy

Oil pulling is a technique where a teaspoon of oil (sesame, coconut, olive or sunflower) is moved around the mouth and through the teeth with a swishing motion for 15-20 minutes, one to three times per day, always on an empty stomach. The premise behind the therapy is that oil attracts various pathogens in the mouth which are then suspended within the liquid and subsequently spat out. The oil also seeps into hard to reach pockets below the gum line where damaging bacteria tend to thrive. Remember the health of your mouth will determine the health of you!

Even with the best dental hygiene, germs can still get the upper hand over health. When our oral condition is in bad shape, it affects every system of the body. Take for instance cognitive decline. According to GreenMed Info, periodontal disease has been linked with stroke and cognitive impairment in numerous studies. Attikon University Hospital in Greece showed a clear correlation between periodontal disease and stroke. Likewise, the University of Alabama School of Dentistry discovered in a 9,853-participant study that tooth loss was strongly connected to cognitive decline.

Furthermore, bacteria such as Streptococcus mutans multiply within the mouth and secrete toxins into the bloodstream, thereby causing inflammatory disorders like heart disease. As reported by naturopath Case Adams in Cognitive Decline Linked to Periodontal Disease:

"A late 2011 study from the School of Dentistry at Italy's *University of Cagliari* studied forty men between 20 years old and 40 years old. Half of the men had periodontal disease and the other half did not. The researchers tested the subjects for parameters indicating developing cardiovascular disease among both groups.

The research found that the periodontal disease patients had higher levels of inflammation-associated IL-2. This suggested to the researchers, "the existence of an early endothelial dysfunction in young adults with atypical periodontitis." Oil pulling has been scientifically shown to substantially reduce problematic *Streptococcus mutans* bacteria. *Global Healing Center* states:

"Another study *[published in the African Journal of Microbiology Research]*, conducted in 2008 found a "remarkable reduction in the total count of bacteria" in the mouth, and an overall marked reduction in susceptibility dental cavities. The antibacterial activity of sesame oil was also studied and found to have an effect on the *Streptococcus mutans* in the mouth. In fact, these studies showed an overall reduction of bacteria from 10 to 33.4 percent in participants, and after 40 days of oil-pulling, participants were found to show 20 percent in average reduction in oral bacteria."

A Thai study published in the *Asia Journal of Public Health* in 2011 found that oil pulling with other edible oils could also decrease harmful oral bacteria to a comparable degree. In fact, the report notes that coconut and sunflower oil, along with sesame oil itself, are particularly effective at treating certain microorganisms: "It was found that coconut oil exhibited antimicrobial activity against *S. mutans* and *C. albicans*. Sesame oil had antibacterial activity against *S. mutans* whereas sunflower oil had antifungal activity against *C. albicans*.

This result might explain why oil pullers who change oils from time to time often report additional or renewed benefits. Since each oil used in oil pulling contains different anti-cavity properties, a temporary change can remove bacteria that the previous oil might be less effective against. Such coverage is far more natural, and cheaper, than that provided by commercial mouthwashes. The oil acts like a cleanser. When you put it in your mouth and work it around your teeth and gums it "pulls" out bacteria and other debris. It acts much like the oil you put in your car engine. The oil picks up dirt and grime. When you drain the oil, it pulls out the dirt and grime with it, leaving the engine relatively clean. Consequently, the engine runs smoother and lasts longer. Likewise, when we expel harmful substances from our bodies our health is improved and we run smoother and last longer.

Additional benefits

Not only does oil pulling boost oral, cognitive and cardiovascular health, but it also heals a host of other conditions. Mike Barrett of *Natural Society* reports:

"... Dr. F. Karsch, M.D., presented a paper to the All-Ukrainian Association outlining rather incredible possibilities oil pulling is capable of. Going by Dr. Karsch, oil pulling benefits can help with almost any illness or chronic condition, including:

Mouth and gum disease; stiff joints; allergies; asthma; high blood sugar; constipation; migraines; bronchitis; eczema; heart, kidney, lung diseases; leukemia; arthritis; meningitis; insomnia; menopause (hormonal issues); cancer; AIDS; chronic infections; varicose veins; high blood pressure; diabetes; cracked heels; acne, arthritis; bronchitis; dermatitis; sinusitis; and many more."

Oil pulling can work its magic almost instantly. Some people report relief from certain conditions after doing it only once. Minor problems often clear up within a few days. More serious, chronic problems may require a few weeks or several months or more depending on lifestyle issues. Toxins are pulled from the body the very first time you try it. One of the first cleansing symptoms you will experience is an increased flow of mucous from your throat and sinuses. Mucous drainage is one of the body's methods of removing toxins. While you are pulling, mucous may build in the back of your throat. You may even have to expel the oil and clear the mucous from your throat before reaching a full 20 minutes. That's okay, take another spoonful of oil and continue until you've pulled for a total of 15-20 minutes. You may also experience a little nausea and perhaps even need to vomit as your body expels toxic waste. Other symptoms may also arise temporarily. These symptoms will subside as your body becomes cleaner and you become more comfortable with oil pulling. Unlike other methods of detoxification that last for only a short time, oil pulling should become a regular part of your daily schedule, like brushing your teeth.

Oil pulling is incredibly effective in brightening teeth, healing gums, preventing bad breath, quenching inflammation, and healing oral infections. It is also effective in treating many systemic conditions throughout the body. In order to oil pull, you put between 1 teaspoon and 1 tablespoon of oil in your mouth, then swish it around for 15-20 minutes on an empty stomach. I do it three times a day, 20-30 minutes before meals. The used oil is discarded and the mouth rinsed out with water. The oil is never swallowed because it is loaded with bacteria, toxins, pus, and mucus.

Conclusion

Detoxification is simply about keeping the elimination channels operating efficiently. Eating nutrient dense foods and drinking plenty of clean reverse osmosis water. Taking sensible exercise in the fresh air with sunshine and getting a good sweat on whilst opening the lungs. Use infrared saunas to enhance the detoxification and eliminate, as much as you can, all man made toxins from multiple sources which we looked at in habit 1. It is of critical importance that if you are going to detoxify, do it properly ,or you will simply get sicker, fatter and more fatigued. Use all the techniques outlined in this habit and you will see significant improvements. Start off slowly and always consult with a knowledgeable medical practitioner before starting any detoxification protocol.

Some of the books that I have read in learning about detoxification, and which you may find helpful are;

- "The 7 Principles of Fat Burning" by Eric Berg
- "The Pure Cure" by Sharyn Wynters & Burton Goldberg
- "The pH Miracle for Weight Loss" by Robert Young & Shelly Young
- "The Detox Solution" by Dr Patricia Fitzgerald
- "Toxic Dentistry Exposed" by Drs Graeme & Lilian Munro-Hill
- "Detoxify or Die" by Shelly Rodgers
- "Oil pulling Therapy" by Dr Bruce Fife
- "The Gerson Therapy" by Charlotte Gerson & Morton Walker

HABIT 3

CHANGE YOUR BRAIN CHANGE YOUR WEIGHT

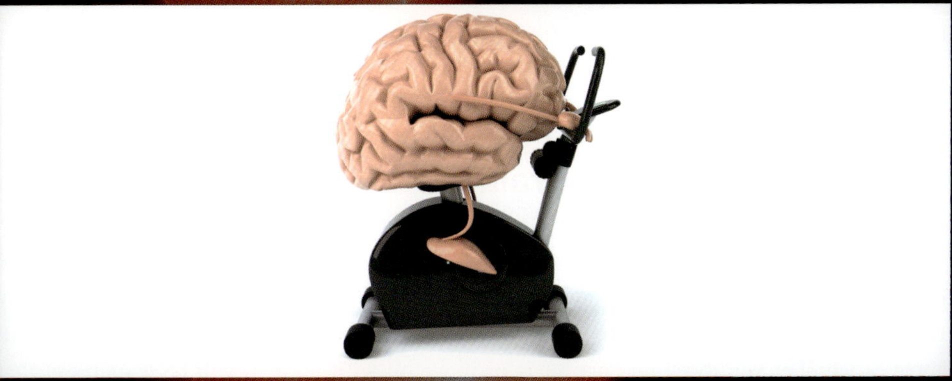

What organ decides on what you eat, drink or the effort you put into your exercise session? Yes of course it's your BRAIN. The brain has incredible nutrient requirements, it hates toxins, dislikes excess stress because excess stress can kill brain cells by the millions.

The brain is also the master controller of your hormonal system when your brain works right your hormones work right and when your brain doesn't work right your hormonal system can become dysfunctional. This is essential if your goal is to maximise your physical & mental performance.

- *how to develop a healthier brains*
- *what 'destroys' our brains*
- *the sorts of fats your brain needs*
- *how your gut is connecting to your brain*

"If you love life, don't waste time, for time is what life is made up of."

Bruce Lee

In this habit, we are going to discuss how you can develop a high-functioning brain through the correct nourishment and how to protect the brain from the multiple factors which causes it harm. Remember, it is the brain that makes the choices in your life and it can help you achieve not only a better quality of life, but also help you make the correct food choices, which will allow you to build a lean, healthy body.

Unfortunately today we have an epidemic of brain diseases. Take a look at the amount of people who are on antidepressants, drugs, alcoholics, are coffee addicts and this goes through to our children being prescribed drugs for behaviour and concentration. As you are about to read, your brain is an incredible organ with virtually unlimited potential. I am going to teach you how to look after your brain through nourishment and how to protect your brain from the multiple insults it has to face every day.

Nutrition & Lifestyle Factors For Developing A Healthy Brain

When you look to the fact that it is our brain that will tell us what to eat and drink or how we feel, then doesn't it make sense to look first at brain health if we want to maintain a healthy weight? For it will be the brain that will decide if you have a piece of chocolate cake over an apple or whether you dwell on past hurts or move on with hope. It will be your brain that decides whether you stick to your exercise regime or watch TV while munching on junk food.

Your brain is flesh and blood. The mind is simply a function of the brain. For you to understand this point with more clarity, think of someone with Alzheimer's. This terrible disease will cause this person to lose their mind. Why? Because their brain has become diseased and, therefore, dysfunctional.

Lets have a very brief look at the anatomy of the brain with Paul MacLean who is the former director of the Laboratory of the Brain and Behaviour at the United States National Institute of Mental Health. He developed a model of the brain based on its evolutionary development. It is referred to as the "triune brain theory" because **MacLean suggests that the human brain is actually three brains in one**.

Each of the layers, or "brains", were established successively in response to evolutionary need. The three layers are; the reptilian system (or R-complex), the limbic system, and the neocortex. Each layer is geared toward separate functions of the brain, but all three layers interact substantially.

PHIL SAYS

Brain Nutrition

I have personally been fascinated with brain nutrition for many years and have developed a number of nutritional products to enhance my own brain function which I know sell on my website.

When your brain is working at optimum efficiency, life is 100% more enjoyable. When your brain is broken you will struggle with emotion, addictions, relationships and life in general. This is why you need to know what's breaking your brain and how to rebuild it. I personally suffered for over 30 years with depression, suicidal thoughts, self sabotage and a host of other mental health problems.

Because of the high fat content of the brain it is very vulnerable to toxins which, as we know from habit 1, have a high affinity for fat. This is why it's crucial to decrease toxicity if you want a functional brain. As we have seen, we now know we are swimming in a sea of toxins which is undoubtedly why we are swimming in a sea of mental diseases in the western world. So apply what you learnt in habit 2 and put detoxification protocols in place that not only allow you to lose weight but to protect your brain.

The Reptilian Complex

The Reptilian complex consists of the brain stem and the cerebellum. Its purpose is closely related to actual physical survival and maintenance of the body. The cerebellum orchestrates movement. Digestion, reproduction, circulation, breathing, and the execution of the "fight or flight" response in stress are all housed in the brain stem. Because the reptilian brain is primarily concerned with physical survival, the behaviours it governs have much in common

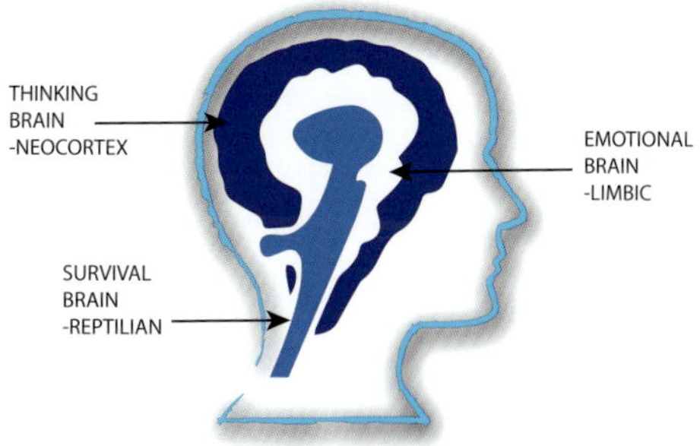

The brain has 3 major components; the neocortex, the limbic complex and the reptilian complex.

with the survival behaviours of animals. It plays a crucial role in establishing home territory, reproduction and social dominance. The overriding characteristics of R-complex behaviours are that they are automatic, have a ritualistic quality, and are highly resistant to change.

The Limbic System

The limbic system, the second brain to evolve, houses the primary centers of emotion. It includes the amygdala, which is important in the association of events with emotion, and the hippocampus, which is active in converting information into long term memory and in memory recall. Repeated use of specialized nerve networks in the hippocampus enhances memory storage, so this structure is involved in learning from both commonplace experiences and deliberate study.

LIMBIC SYSTEM STRUCTURES

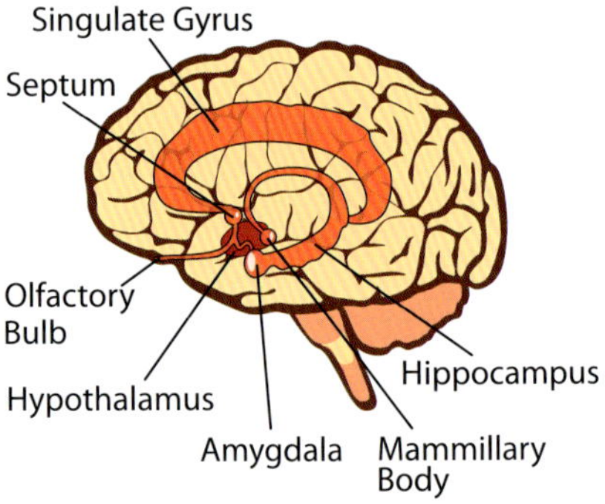

The limbic system is also involved in primal activities related to food and sex, particularly having to do with our sense of smell and bonding needs, and activities related to expression and mediation of emotions and feelings, including emotions linked to attachment. These protective, loving feelings become increasingly complex as the limbic system and the neocortex link up.

The Neocortex

Also called the cerebral cortex, the neocortex constitutes five-sixths of the human brain. It is the outer portion of our brain, and is approximately the size of a newspaper page crumpled together. The neocortex makes language, including speech and writing possible. It renders logical and formal operational thinking possible and allows us to see ahead and plan for the future. The neocortex also contains two specialized regions, one dedicated to voluntary movement and one to processing sensory information.

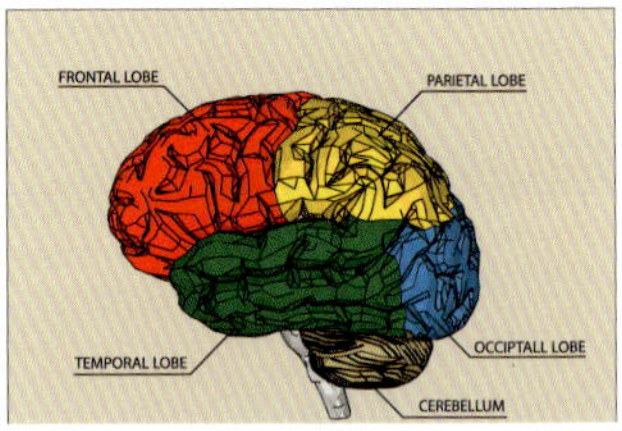

*The cerebral cortex of the brain. This is the part which separates us from other species. The cerebrum or **cortex** is associated with higher brain **function** such as thought and action. The **cerebral cortex** is divided into four sections, called "lobes": the frontal lobe, parietal lobe, occipital lobe, and temporal lobe.*

All three layers of the brain interact. The layers are connected by an extensive two-way network of nerves. On-going communication between the neocortex and the limbic system links thinking and emotions; each influences the other and both direct all voluntary action. This interplay of memory and emotion, thought and action is the foundation of a person's individuality. The full extent of this interconnectedness is unclear. However, it is incorrect to assume that in any situation one of our three "brains" is working and the others are not. What we can do, tentatively, is assume that at times one particular focus may be dominant while the rest of the brain acts in support and that education can influence which focus dominates.

Your brain is the most complex, mind blowing organ in the universe. It weighs only about three pounds, usually around 2 percent of the body's weight. Unbelievably it is 80% water. The brain uses 25% of the oxygen we breathe and up to 70% of the glucose we consume when at rest.

How the brain communicates

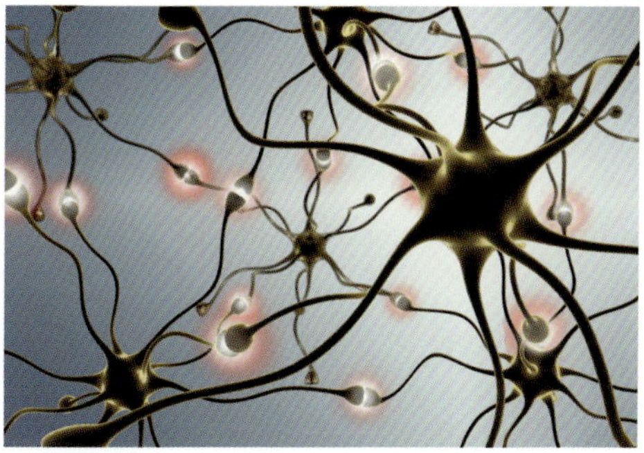

The brain is connected to every cell in the body through the nervous system. The signals and messages of the nervous system consist of chemical "runners" who deliver messages to and from the brain. These chemical runners are known as neurotransmitters. Nerve cells communicate through neurotransmitters, the endocrine system through hormones and the immune system through cytokines, and all three work together and we will cover all three in depth throughout this book as they are all essential in health and fat loss.

Our thoughts are transmitted by neurons. They gather information by transmitting electrical impulses along their elongated bodies. These impulses can cause chemical reactions. If you have lots of depressing thoughts you will experience depression. Similarly, lots of happy thoughts will help you experience happiness it really is that simple. We become our thoughts!

Hormones and brain function

The brain also contains receptors for thyroid hormones (those produced by the thyroid) and the six classes of steroid hormones, which are synthesized from cholesterol — androgens, oestrogens, progestins, glucocorticoids, mineralocorticoids, and vitamin D. The receptors are found in selected populations of neurons in the brain and relevant organs in the body.

Thyroid and steroid hormones bind to receptor proteins that in turn bind to DNA and regulate the action of genes. This can result in long-lasting changes in cellular structure and function. The brain has receptors for many hormones; for example, the metabolic hormones insulin, insulin-like growth factor, ghrelin, and leptin. These hormones are taken up from the blood and act to affect neuronal activity and certain aspects of neuronal structure.

In response to stress and changes in our biological clocks, such as day and night cycles and jet lag, hormones enter the blood and travel to the brain and other organs. In the brain, hormones alter the production of gene products that participate in synaptic neurotransmission as well as affect the structure of brain cells. As a result, the circuitry of the brain and its capacity for neurotransmission are changed over a course of hours to days. In this way, the brain adjusts its performance and control of behavior in response to a changing environment.

So our hormones are constantly communicating with our brains. In fact it has been calculated by scientists such as Candice Pert that 98% of brain communication is through our hormones and only 2% through neurotransmitters. This is why hormonal issues can lead to behavioural and mood disorders as we will cover in much more depth as we travel through this book. Hormones can also help neurotransmitters function more efficiently, for example, oestrogen enhances serotonin function and T3 thyroid hormone. The most biologically active form of thyroid hormone, T3, is actually a bona fide neurotransmitter that regulates the action of serotonin, norepinephrine, and GABA (gamma aminobutyric acid), an inhibitory neurotransmitter that is important for quelling anxiety.

When our brain is out of balance (whether that be too much or too little neurotransmitters or hormones), this can push you towards addictions; whether that being food, drugs or alcohol as well as violence, depression and suicide. All of our hormones and neurotransmitters work together as one dynamic system to help us maintain optimal health and keep us happy, focused, and peaceful. They are like a finely orchestrated symphony that must work together to keep everything in balance. This is why it is essential to nourish and look after your brain. Think of your hormones and neurotransmitters as your MESSENGER molecules.

Dehydration & Brain Function

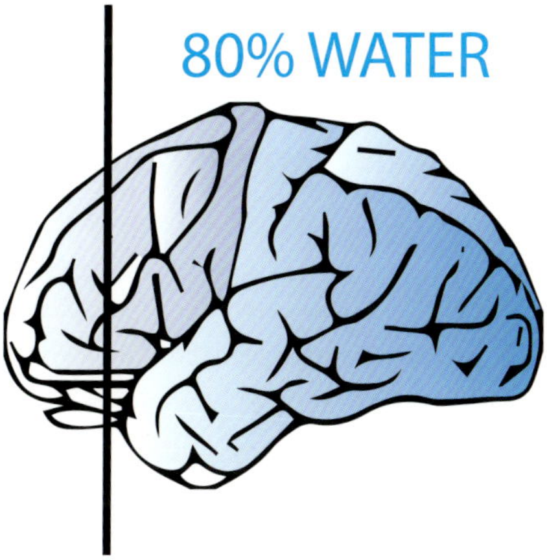

About 80% of the human brain consists of water

To understand the importance of hydration for brain health and function, you must first understand that about 80% of the human brain consists of water. So, you need to make sure you are getting plenty of H20. How much water you need though is very individualised. I am not going to tell you how much is optimum for you but, I have found that if I consume at least 1 litre of alkalised, filtered water for each 25kg of my body weight, then this is optimum for me. When I exercise, I will obviously then take on extra fluids, which I will go into further in Habit 9.

At 4-5 % below optimal fluid intake, you could experience a 20–30% decline in cognitive function. The decline in blood volume that occurs with even slight dehydration impedes the transport of oxygen and nutrients to the brain.

In one study men were subjected, on separate occasions, to each of three test conditions:

1) 40 minutes of walking on a treadmill with quite a steep incline (5%) at a speed of 5-6 km/hr in a temperature of about 28 degrees centigrade. The men were also treated with the drug frusemide – a diuretic that speeds dehydration.
2) Same conditions as above, but instead of being given frusemide, the men were treated with a placebo.
3) Same conditions as above, while the hydration status of the men was maintained (in other words, they were not allowed to become dehydrated).

Basically, conditions 1 and 2 were designed to induce dehydration of two severities (the one with frusemide being more severe), and condition 3 was designed to act as a control (where individuals expended about the same amount of energy in the same heat but did not suffer dehydration). The participants were then subjected to tests of mental function, fatigue and mood.

Dehydration was found to reduce vigilance and working memory (the ability to actively hold information in the mind needed to do complex tasks such as reasoning, comprehension and learning). Fatigue during exercise was worse during dehydration. Measures of tension and anxiety were greater too.

What this study shows is that dehydration does indeed have the capacity to affect brain function and mood, and therefore it pays to stay well hydrated. Our requirements for water vary according to a variety of factors including weather, temperature, how active we are, how much we sweat and how much water we get via what we eat. A good guide, in terms of water intake, is to drink enough to keep urine pale yellow in colour throughout the course of the day.

Brain Destroyers: Why Isn't My Brain Working?

Let's look at a number of factors that, unfortunately, are contributing to brain-drain and mental health disorders.

Mobile Phones

A Swedish study indicates that mobile phone use can raise the risk of brain tumours. In the study, 2,200 cancer patients, and an equal number of healthy control cases, were examined for mobile phone use. Among the cancer patients, about a tenth of the nearly 1,000 with malignant brain tumours were also heavy mobile phone users. Heavy use was defined as 2,000 or more hours, or about 10 years' use at an hour per day. Brain cancer patients also showed a significant increase in risk of tumour for the side of the head where they generally used the mobile phone. The researchers who conducted the study said that the figures demonstrate a 240% increased risk of a malignant tumour on that side of the head.

Intensive mobile phone users are at a higher risk of brain cancers, studies have shown. People who used their phones more than 15 hours each month found to be at two to three times higher risk of developing glioma and meningioma tumours. People who use mobile phones intensively appear to have a higher risk of developing certain types of brain cancer, French scientists have said.

Individuals who used their mobiles for more than 15 hours each month over five years on average had between two and three times greater risk of developing glioma and meningioma tumours compared with people who rarely used their phones, they found. The study, appearing in the British journal Occupational and Environmental Medicine, is the latest in a long-running exploration of mobile-phone safety.

Research has also indicated that children and teenagers are five times more likely to get brain cancer if they use mobile phones. Such studies are raising fears that today's young people may suffer an epidemic of the disease in later life. Swedish research has also reported more worrying news on mobile phone use and brain health at the first international conference on mobile phones and health. It came from a further analysis of data from one of the biggest studies carried out on the mobile phone/cancer link, headed by Professor Lennart Hardell. Professor Hardell told the conference that "people who started mobile phone use before the age of 20" had more than five-fold increase in glioma, a cancer of the glial cells that support the central nervous system.

The risk to young people from household cordless phones was almost as great. Cordless phones caused a fourfold increase in risk. Young mobile phone users were also five times more likely to get acoustic neuromas, disabling tumours of the auditory nerve that often cause deafness.

On June 1st, 2011 Scientists at WHO (World Health Organisation) classified mobile phones as carcinogenic. In a debate that has been ongoing with divisive opinions and inconclusive evidence, the WHO has come out and stated that the radiation emitted from mobile phones can "possibly" boost the risk of brain cancer.

So, could mobile phones be giving us brain cancer? And has the mobile phone industry spent years trying to bury the scientific evidence that it does in order to protect its $3 trillion, 4.6billion-customer, global business? According to Devra Davis, an eminent American scientist and one of the country's leading epidemiologists, the answer to both these questions is a resounding 'yes'. With mobile phone use soaring, especially among the young, Dr Davis says we could face a 'global public health catastrophe' in as little as three years if the problem is ignored. Mobile phones are low-powered radio frequency transmitters which produce microwave radiation. The debate over the cancer risks from this radiation has been going on for years. Yet the lack of any conclusive evidence has allowed the industry to claim phones are safe and led to sceptics being dismissed as scaremongers.

But now the alarm has been raised by an award-winning academic and toxicologist who was in the group that won the 2007 Nobel Peace Prize. In a book titled, "Disconnect: The Truth About Cell Phone Radiation, What The Industry Has Done To Hide It And How To Protect Your Family", Dr Davis says we have underplayed the threat from mobile phone radiation for too long. She says: 'Is it possible that the pervasive use of mobile phones is causing a host of subtle, chronic health problems, damaging our ability to have healthy children and creating long-term risks to our brains and bodies?

"The fact we do not have clear answers to this question at this point in the history of electronic technology is not an accident." Dr Davis says crucial scientific evidence, some of which has existed for decades, has been ignored - particularly that involving experimental research on animals and human cells. Her work includes supporting research from studies in the U.S., Sweden, Greece, France and Russia.

For example, a team at the University Of Washington found that just two hours of mobile phone-level radiation splintered the DNA of brain cells in rats, making them similar to cells found in malignant tumours. In Moscow, a study has found that while the brains of children who regularly use mobile phones look the same as the brains of those who do not, users have poorer memories and other learning problems.

Dr Davis, who is a grandmother, is worried about the effect on children, arguing that their thin, pliant skulls make them more vulnerable. The Finnish Radiation and Nuclear Safety Authority warned that regular use of mobiles could damage children's brains, confirming previous warnings in the UK, France and Israel. Dr Davis believes children are 'growing up in an unprecedented flood of radio frequency signals'. She says they should only use mobile phones in emergencies. 'The dangers for children are not definitively proven but do we really want to risk it?'

The most troubling research, she says, threatens male fertility. Research in seven countries, including the U.S., China and Australia, suggests that keeping a switched-on mobile in a trouser pocket can have a drastic effect on sperm count. All the research shows the same thing - if you take young men who are trying to become fathers, those who use mobile phones at least four hours a day have about half the sperm count of others,' says Dr Davis. 'Sperm exposed to mobile phone radiation in the lab is sicker, thinner and less capable of swimming. Using a mobile for four hours a day sounds a lot, but Dr Davis says 20 per cent of the young males in a 2008 study, by America's Cleveland Clinic, used their mobiles for this long. However, her most compelling evidence about the health dangers, and that mobile phone manufacturers are probably aware of the risks, is buried in the small print of the instructions that accompany every new phone.

Stress

Nothing kills brain cells (especially those in the hippocampus where memories are stored) faster than excess cortisol. Look after your stress levels if you want to look after your brain. Enduring a high stressor for over 30-60 minutes at a time has been shown to negatively impact the hippocampus in various ways which is the part of our brain where we have short term memory. Sustained exposure to higher than normal levels of cortisol results in the pruning back of the number of branches and synaptic connections of hippocampal neurons.

By a variety of mechanisms, these conditions also increase the rate of cell death in this region of the brain. As if this wasn't bad enough, research is also demonstrating that sustained increases in glucocorticoid levels also has negative effects, impairing the hippocampus' ability to create new neurons. All of this could result in the shrinking in size of the hippocampus, with associated declines in cognitive function, including the ability to retain new information and adapt to novel situations.

Even for healthy people, stressful moments can take a toll on the brain, a study from Yale University suggests. Researchers reported in the journal Biological Psychiatry that stressful occasions (like going through a divorce or being sacked) can actually shrink the brain by reducing gray matter in regions tied to emotion and physiological functions. This is important because these changes in gray matter could signal future psychiatric problems, researchers warned.

So it is essential to understand that by being a stress head you develop a dysfunctional brain so learn to reduce stress and this is also covered in habit 6 of this book but remember don't sweat over the small stuff!

Aspartame

The phenylalanine in the artificial sweetener aspartame depletes serotonin, leading to panic attacks, manic depression, rage and violence. There are over 92 different symptoms associated with aspartame consumption which is found in most diet products. Small amounts of aspartame can lead to the build up of formaldehyde (bound to protein) in the liver, kidneys, brain and soft tissues. Tests on rats show that they developed unusually high numbers of brain tumours when exposed to aspartame.

One study concluded that "Compared to other environmental factors putatively linked to brain tumours, the artificial sweetener aspartame is a promising candidate to explain the recent increase in incidence and degree of malignancy of brain tumours. Evidence potentially implicating aspartame includes an early animal study revealing an exceedingly high incidence of brain tumours in aspartame-fed rats compared to no brain tumours in concurrent controls" *J Neuropathol Exp Neurol. 1996 Nov;55(11):1115-23.*

It is interesting to note that the first experiments performed to test the safety of aspartame before its final approval in 1981 disclosed a high incidence of brain tumours in the animals fed the sweetener. In this study 320 rats were fed aspartame and 120 rats were fed a normal diet and used as controls. The study lasted two years. At the end of the study twelve of the aspartame fed rats had developed brain tumours, while none of the control rats had. This represented a 3.75% incidence of brain tumours in the rats fed aspartame, which was twenty-five times higher than the incidence of spontaneous brain tumours developing in rats (0.15%).

Aspartame was never tested on humans before its approval. Now, it is found in 6,000 products and consumed by more than 250 million people, with Americans consuming around half of the world supply. By default, we have now become the test subjects for aspartame's safety. Unwittingly we are providing evidence to aspartame's toxicity through the devastating effects it is slowly producing among its consumers.

A study published in the journal Appetite in 2013 found that compared to sucrose, a form of sugar, aspartame is actually worse in terms of promoting weight gain. Similar research published in the Yale Journal of Biology and Medicine found that aspartame alters the body's natural production of hormones, increasing both appetite and sugar cravings. Aspartame crosses the blood-brain barrier, potentially causing permanent brain damage.

Aspartame is composed of roughly 40% aspartic acid, a free-form amino acid that has the ability to cross the blood-brain barrier. When excess amounts of this compound via aspartame enter the body, brain cells are bombarded with an excess of calcium. The result is neural cell damage and even cell death, which can lead to serious brain damage. In extreme cases, exposure to aspartic acid, also known as aspartate, can cause neurological conditions like epilepsy and Alzheimer's disease, and is also implicated in causing diseases like multiple sclerosis (MS) and dementia. Endocrine disorders, or imbalanced or inadequate hormone production, are also linked to so-called "excitotoxin" exposure, or exposure to free-form amino acids like aspartate that overstimulate the brain.

You'll think twice, I hope, the next time you get tucked into a so called 'diet' product laced with aspartame proclaiming it to be good for your health!

Caffeine

The brain is critically dependent upon abundant blood flow, because it requires about 25% of all blood pumped by the heart. Therefore, any disruption of cerebral circulation has a profoundly negative effect upon the brain.

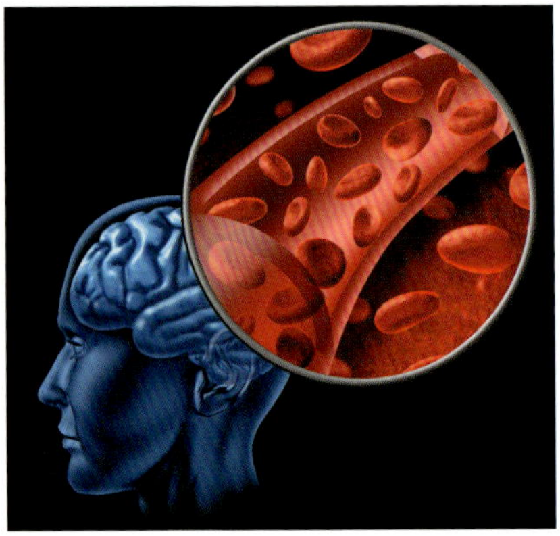

The brain needs a huge supply of blood. Around 25% of blood flow is directed to the brain

Caffeine though, can reduce blood flow to the brain because of its effects on adenosine. What is adenosine? How does adenosine affect blood flow to the brain? Why do nerve cells in our brains accept caffeine instead of adenosine?

As adenosine is created in the brain, it binds to adenosine receptors. This binding causes drowsiness by slowing down nerve cell activity. In the brain, this also causes blood vessels to dilate, most likely to let more oxygen into that organ. To a nerve cell, caffeine looks like adenosine: Caffeine binds to the adenosine receptor. However, caffeine doesn't slow down the cell's activity like adenosine would. As a result, the cell can no longer identify adenosine because caffeine is taking up all the receptors that adenosine would normally bind to.

So, what happens to the blood flow to the brain when caffeine is ingested? Caffeine causes the brain's blood vessels to constrict, because it blocks adenosine's ability to open them up. One regular cup of coffee can decrease blood flow to the brain by up to 30%.

To counteract the effect of caffeine, brain cells grow more adenosine receptors, which is the brain's attempt to maintain equilibrium in the face of a constant onslaught of caffeine, with its adenosine receptors so regularly plugged. This explains why regular coffee drinkers build up a tolerance over time - because you have more adenosine receptors, it takes more caffeine to block a significant proportion of them and achieve the desired effect.

If you have been taking caffeine every day and you stop, you can get an incredible headache because of the increased blood flow in your brain. The adenosine receptors are able to function properly again. Your brain is used to operating in one set of conditions (with an artificially-inflated number of adenosine receptors, and a decreased number of norepinephrine receptors) that depend upon regular ingestion of caffeine. Suddenly, without the drug, the altered brain chemistry causes all sorts of problems, including the dreaded caffeine withdrawal headache.

You only need to get through about 7-12 days of symptoms without drinking any caffeine though. During that period, your brain will naturally decrease the number of adenosine receptors on each cell, responding to the sudden lack of caffeine ingestion. If you can make it that long without a cup of coffee or tea, the levels of adenosine receptors in your brain reset to their baseline levels, and your addiction will be broken.

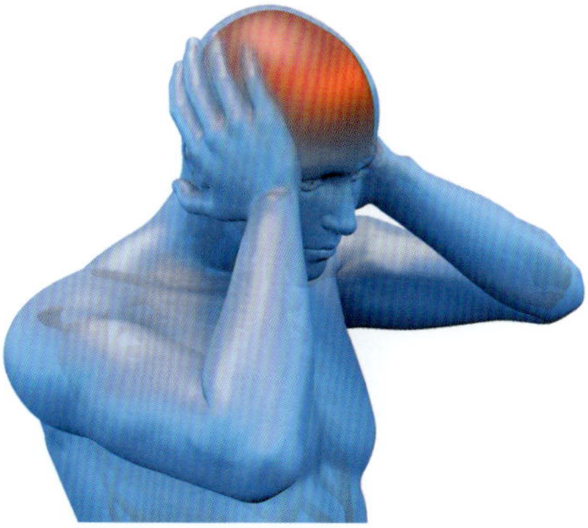

Do you want diminished blood flow to the brain as a result of consuming caffeine? Please consider this statement from Science Daily about the importance of the frontal lobes of our brain. "The frontal cortex of the brain has been long known to affect the internal control of behavior. It controls the capacity to plan, reason, conduct higher-level thinking and connect what we know about the world to how we behave." Blood gives this essential region of the brain oxygen, nutrition, and it takes away waste from the cells located there. Can we afford to decrease the blood flow to the area of our brains which helps us "plan, reason, and conduct higher level-thinking"?

Sugar

What do we usually put in our caffeinated drinks? Yes, SUGAR! Too much sugar, even healthy whole sugar leads to a decrease in blood flow to the brain. Sugar damages your brain and causes erratic neuronal cell firing. Too much sugar (no matter the kind) and processed sugar is an anti-nutrient and is toxic to your brain. Why? Because it causes increased level of inflammation. Recent research shows that sugar can be more addictive than cocaine.

Your brain runs almost EXCLUSIVELY on glucose and uses more than 20% of your body's total energy even though it only weighs a few pounds, yet your brain has no place where it can actually STORE glucose. We use approximately 120 grams of glucose per day for just brain function alone. However, overconsumption of sugar can have detrimental effects for the health of our brian. The brain can also run on ketones which is when fat is being broken down to be used as fuel.

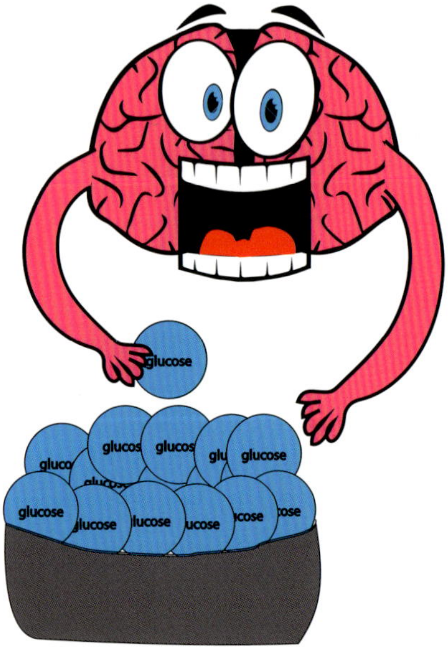

The brain is a glucose hog requiring around 120g of glucose per day

When insulin levels are high, glucose (the main fuel for the brain) is directed away from the brain and into other tissues, such as muscle. This elevation of insulin not only starves the brain of glucose but it keeps the fat switch well and truly on. So it is imperative for optimum functioning of the brain, and to keep lean, to maintain a steady blood glucose supply. And, if the brain is not receiving a steady supply of glucose, it will ramp your appetite up to make sure it gets its fix. The brain can also function very efficiently from a ketogenic diet which, I discuss in great detail in habit 9. A ketogenci diet is one of a high-fat, very low-carbohydrate diet. Instead of using glucose, the brain has no problems using ketones for brain function.

Historically, as hunter/gatherers, we ate the equivalent of 20 teaspoons of sugar per person per year. But just 200 years ago, we started consuming about 10 pounds of sugar per person per year - a 5,000% increase over our evolutionary ancestors! As if that weren't bad enough, we now eat approximately 150 pounds per person per year, or about 1/2 pound each day - that's the equivalent of drinking 6 cans of soda or eating 8 chocolate bars per day. What's worst, the average child consumes 34 teaspoons of sugar a day! That means that we are now eating 75,000% more sugar today than our ancestors did.

When blood sugar levels exceed the maximum threshold, the body experiences damaged nerve cells and stops them from working properly. This is referred to as glycation. Membranes become thicker and gunked up which slows down brain communication. This also creates inflammation in the brain, which is the body's way of saying something is wrong. We need carbohydrates for brain health, but we need the right ones. Your best bites are fresh fruits and vegetables.

There is actually another fuel that the brain can readily use and stop your food cravings almost instantly, the amino acid L-glutamine. Any absence of fuel for your brain's function is perceived correctly by your body as a code red emergency. Powerful biochemical messages then order you immediately to eat refined carbohydrates to fuel your brain quickly. L-glutamine reaches the starving brain within minutes and can often immediately put a stop to even the most powerful sweet and starch cravings. The brain feeds on L-glutamine instead of glucose and is satisfied and prevents you hopefully from destroying the chocolate cake in the fridge. When you have extreme carb cravings, which usually happen late in the evening, towards bedtime, you will find that glutamine will help curb these cravings.

Heavy Metals

Mercury causes damages to the brain and the central nervous system, causes psychological changes and can cause developmental changes in young children. Mercury is a toxic substance which has no known function in human biochemistry. It targets and kills neurons in specific areas of the nervous system.

Several mechanisms have been proposed to explain how mercury kills neurons:

- Protein inhibition
- Disruption of mitochondrial function
- Direct effect on ion exchange in a neuron
- Disruption of neurotransmitters
- Destruction of the structural framework of neurons

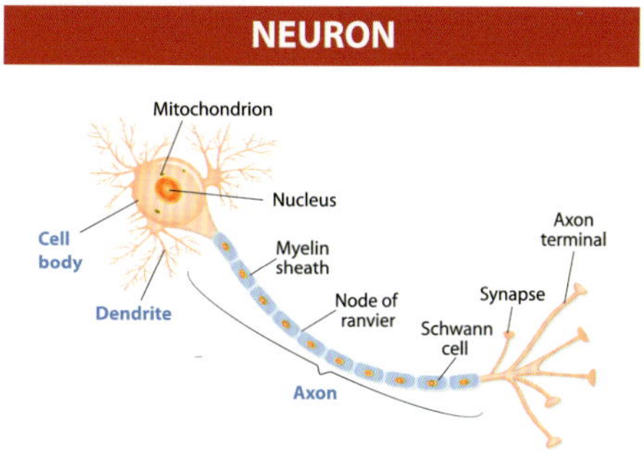

Methylmercury is especially dangerous to developing babies. This form of mercury is highly toxic and can cross the placenta and the blood-brain barrier. Mercury is concentrated in the brain of the developing foetus because the metal is absorbed quickly and is not excreted efficiently. Children exposed to mercury may be born with symptoms resembling cerebral palsy and other movement abnormalities, convulsions, visual problems and abnormal reflexes. The brains of children who have died as a result of mercury poisoning show neuron loss in the cerebellum and throughout the cerebral cortex. Mercury also appears to affect brain development by preventing neurons from finding their appropriate place in the brain.

You have to question pregnant mothers being offered the flu jab which can contain thimerosal (mercury). In 2001, the European Agency for the Evaluation of Medicinal Products advised doctors to use only vaccines without thimerosal for toddlers and infants, who are thought to be more likely to suffer harm from exposure to mercury. This followed a 1999 announcement by the U.S. Public Health Service and the American Academy of Paediatrics (AAP) that thimerosal should be reduced or eliminated in vaccines as a precaution.

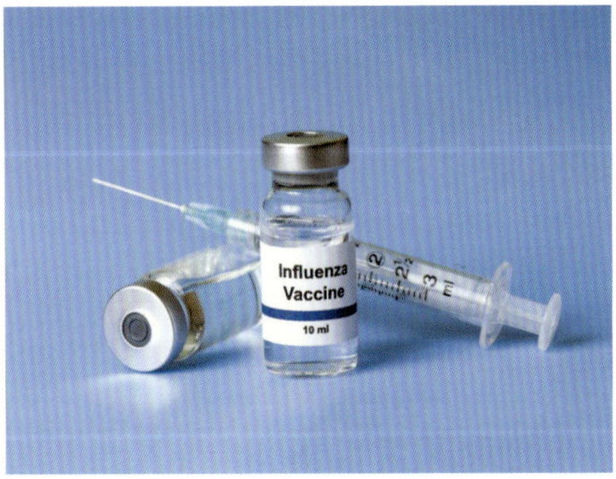

A study by the American Institute of Medicine concluded that a link between thimerosal in vaccines and neurodevelopmental disorders was 'biologically plausible'. In a related U.S. study, researchers found a statistically significant association between thimerosal in vaccines and children with problems such as attention deficit disorder (ADD) and speech and language learning delays.

A leading cause of ADHD (attention-deficit hyperactivity disorder) and autism in children could be the hidden chemicals lurking in the foods we eat, the water we drink and the products we consume, says a new study recently published in The Lancet. Researchers from the Harvard School of Public Health (HSPH) and the Icahn School of Medicine at Mount Sinai (ISMMS) found that, among other things, the fluoride chemicals added to many public water systems in North America directly contribute to both mental and behavioral disorders in children.

Building upon earlier research published in 2006 that dubbed fluoride as a "developmental neurotoxicant," the new review included a meta-analysis of 27 additional studies on fluoride, most of which were from China, that linked the chemical to lowered IQ in children. After thorough analysis, it was determined that fluoride obstructs proper brain development and can lead to autism spectrum disorders, dyslexia, ADHD and other health conditions, a "silent epidemic" that many mainstream health authorities continue to ignore.

According to the two main researchers involved in the study, Philippe Grandjean from HSPH and Philip Landrigan from ISMMS, incidences of chemical-related neurodevelopmental disorders have doubled over the past seven years from six to 12. The reason for this is that an increasing number of mostly untested chemicals are being approved for use without the public being told where and in what quantities such chemicals are being used.

"Since 2006, the number of chemicals known to damage the human brain more generally, but that are not regulated to protect children's health, had increased from 202 to 214," writes Julia Medew for The Sydney Morning Herald. "The pair said this could be the tip of the iceberg because the vast majority of the more than 80,000 industrial chemicals widely used have never been tested for their toxic effects on the developing foetus or child."

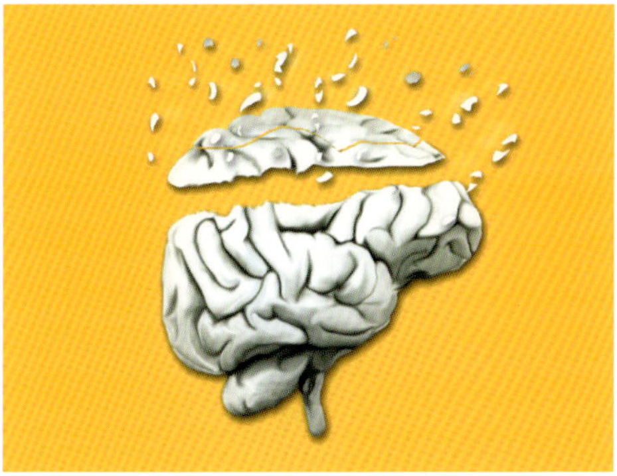

A recently-published Harvard University meta-analysis funded by the National Institutes of Health (NIH) has concluded that children who live in areas with highly fluoridated water have "significantly lower" IQ scores than those who live in low fluoride areas. The medical (and dental) communities are so stubbornly resistant to connect the dots when it comes to the skyrocketing increase of cognitive decline in adults and behavioral issues in children (ADD, ADHD, depression and learning disabilities of all kinds). In fact, there have been more than 23 human studies and 100 animal studies linking fluoride to brain damage. Fluoride can also increase manganese absorption, compounding problems, since manganese in drinking water has also been linked to lower IQ in children.

What is perhaps most surprising is that the harmful effects of fluoride have been known by conventional medical organizations for over half a century. For example, the Journal of the American Medical Association (JAMA) stated in their Sept. 18, 1943 issue that fluorides are general protoplasmic poisons that change the permeability of the cell membrane by certain enzymes. And, an editorial published in the Journal of the American Dental Association on Oct. 1, 1944, stated:

Drinking water containing as little as 1.2 ppm fluoride will cause developmental disturbances. We cannot run the risk of producing such serious systemic disturbances. The potentialities for harm outweigh those for good.

Long-lost research linking fluoride to cancer has resurfaced in a Dutch film clip featuring Dr. Dean Burk, who in 1937 cofounded the U.S. National Cancer Institute (NCI) and headed its cytochemistry department for more than 30 years. In the taped interview, he equates water fluoridation to "public murder," referring to a study that had been done on the 10 largest U.S. cities with fluoridation compared to the 10 largest without it. The study demonstrated that deaths from cancer abruptly rose in as little as a year or two after fluoridation began. This and other studies linking fluoride to cancer were government-ordered but were quickly buried once fluoride was found to be linked to dramatic increases in cancer.

This is, again, why I recommend getting a reverse osmosis water filter which will remove a lot of heavy metals and pesticides including fluoride if its in your water. I also recommend using fluoride-free dental health care products.

Aluminium is another metal that we should be concerned about in keeping our brains healthy! In 1988 one of the UK's most notorious pollution disasters occurred at a water treatment works on the edge of Bodmin Moor, 20 tonnes of aluminium sulphate leaked into the water supply serving the nearby town of Camelford. Years of bitter disputes followed, with people who had drunk the water complaining of health problems. There were government inquiries, accusations of a cover-up – and, in 2004, the death of Carole Cross. This 58-year-old Camelford resident died from a rare and aggressive form of Alzheimer's, and her brain was found to contain unusually high levels of aluminium.

Professor Chris Exley, who was called in nearly eight years ago to examine Mrs Cross's brain found it contained 23 micrograms of aluminium per gram of brain, compared to normal levels of 0-2mcg. But Prof Exley, a world-renowned expert on aluminium, hopes the inquest will do more than finally establish the truth about why Mrs Cross died (he is convinced that aluminium from the drinking water played a role in her mental deterioration). He also hopes it will highlight how little we know about the implications for our health of the most prolific metals on the planet. Aluminium, he argues, is now added to or used in almost everything we eat, drink, inject or absorb. At high levels, it is an established neurotoxin – yet no one knows whether the levels we are ingesting are safe.

"Hundreds of publications demonstrate that aluminium is not safe," he says. "But the accumulation of aluminium in the body has yet to become the subject of serious investigation and consideration in medicine." Exley, who is Professor of Inorganic Chemistry at Keele University, has been researching aluminium for a quarter of a century. His office is piled high with books on the subject, and he has contributed to scores of peer-reviewed papers and publications.

The metal is the most abundant in the Earth's crust, naturally absorbed from the soil by plants and foodstuffs. But while 50 years ago we may have ingested minute amounts from vegetables (and possibly from some of the pots they were cooked in), today aluminium is found in almost everything. In the form of salts, it has properties that make it a versatile and useful additive. "Aluminium sulphate is added to our water to improve clarity," says Prof Exley. "All foods that need raising agents or additives, such as cakes and biscuits, contain aluminium. Children's sweets contain aluminium-enhanced food colouring. It is in tea, cocoa and malt drinks, in some wines and fizzy drinks and in most processed foods.

"It is in cosmetics, sunscreens and antiperspirants, as well as being used as a buffering agent in medications like aspirin and antacids. It is even used in vaccines. We know aluminium can be toxic, yet there is no legislation to govern how much of it is present in anything, apart from drinking water."

"When the amount of aluminium consumed exceeds the body's capacity to excrete it, the excess is then deposited in various tissues, including nerves, brain, bone, liver, heart, spleen and muscle," he explains. "We call it the 'silent visitor' because it creeps into the body and beds down in our bones and brain."

Prof Exley's research has covered everything from the potential dangers of aluminium in antiperspirants and sunscreen to the high levels of the metal in vaccines and infant formula. In one study, his team tested 16 of the UK's leading formula milk brands for children up to the age of one. The results, published in 2010, showed that traces of the metal exceeded the levels legally allowed in water, and in some cases were more than 40 times that found in breast milk.

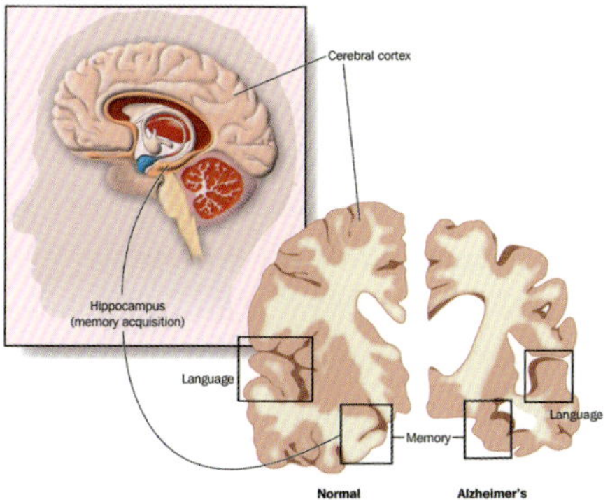

"Everyone has some aluminium in their bodies, but infants below the age of six months are especially prone to absorbing it and not so good at getting rid of it," he says. His research has led him to believe that accumulation of aluminium in the body is a risk factor not only for Alzheimer's disease but may also be linked to other neurological conditions such as Parkinson's and multiple sclerosis.

Aluminium is also used in 80% of vaccines as an adjuvant (to increase the vaccines effectiveness), which concerns Prof Exley. "Our research is looking at whether aluminium can cause an adverse reaction to a vaccine," he says. "Most children get about 14 vaccinations before the age of 13, so in susceptible individuals this could constitute an unacceptably high aluminium load."

Alcohol

Alcohol has access to all cells in the body. The body uses up DHA to deal with alcohol. Alcohol processing depletes the body of DHA and omega threes.

Research from the University College of London has estimated that the average Briton consumes 20 units of alcohol every single week. Autopsy studies have shown that patients with a history of chronic alcohol consumption have smaller, lighter, more shrunken brains than non-alcoholic adults of the same age and gender. This finding has been repeatedly confirmed in living alcoholics using a variety of imaging techniques. Structural imaging reveals a consistent association between heavy drinking and physical brain damage, even in the absence of medical conditions previously considered to be clinical indicators of severe alcoholism (e.g., chronic liver disease or alcohol-induced dementia).

Alcohol affects brain chemistry by altering levels of neurotransmitters. Neurotransmitters are chemical messengers that transmit the signals throughout the body that control thought processes, behavior and emotion. Neurotransmitters are either excitatory, meaning that they stimulate brain electrical activity, or inhibitory, meaning that they decrease brain electrical activity. Alcohol increases the effects of the inhibitory neurotransmitter GABA in the brain. GABA causes the sluggish movements and slurred speech that often occur in alcoholics. At the same time, alcohol inhibits the excitatory neurotransmitter glutamate. Suppressing this stimulant results in a similar type of physiological slowdown. In addition to increasing the GABA and decreasing the glutamate in the brain, alcohol increases the amount of the chemical dopamine in the brain's reward center, which creates the feeling of pleasure that occurs when someone takes a drink.

Is there hope we can enjoy a drink without shrinking our brains? Previous studies have suggested that long-term alcohol abuse causes brain damage and increases the risk of dementia. However, researchers from Loyola University Chicago Stritch School of Medicine in Illinois - who conducted this study - previously performed a meta-analysis that found drinking alcohol at moderate, social levels - a maximum of two drinks per day for men and one drink per day for women - may reduce risk of dementia and cognitive impairment during aging.

The team reasons that alcohol in moderate amounts "toughens up" brain cells, which makes them more resilient to damage, but that excessive amounts of alcohol overwhelms the cells, causing neuroinflammation and cell death. To investigate the extent to which omega-3 fish oil may protect against this damage, the researchers behind the meta-analysis - with collaborators at the University of Kentucky and the National Institute of Alcohol Abuse and Alcoholism - conducted a new experiment with cultures of adult rat brain cells. Over several days, they exposed the cell cultures to alcohol concentrations the equivalent of four times the legal limit for driving. This level of alcohol exposure is similar to that seen in chronic alcoholics.

The researchers then compared the brain cultures with other cultures that had also been exposed to the same levels of alcohol, but with the addition of the omega-3 docosahexaenoic acid (DHA) compound found in fish oil. The team observed that there was up to 90% less neuroinflammation and neuronal death in the brain cells that had been exposed to DHA than in the cells that had just been exposed to alcohol.

"Fish oil has the potential of helping preserve brain integrity in chronic alcohol abusers," says study author Michael A. Collins, PhD. "At the very least, it is unlikely that it would hurt them." However, the team states that further studies are needed to confirm their findings. They added that the best way for people abusing alcohol to avoid brain damage is to reduce their drinking to low or moderate amounts, or to give up alcohol altogether. "We don't want people to think it is okay to take a few fish oil capsules and then continue to go on abusing alcohol," says Collins

PHIL SAYS
ALCOHOL AND FAT LOSS

"If you want to drop body fat you MUST drop the booze until you shift a significant amount of the excess weight you want to lose. Why? Drinking in the evenings is a genuine disaster for fat loss as you increase insulin which stimulates fat storage, you also increase cortisol which breaks down muscles and interferes with how well you will sleep and to add insult to injury you drop growth hormone which is a hormone essential for deep sleep and fat loss.

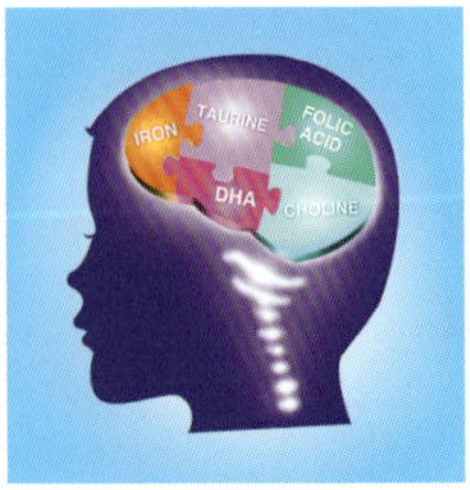

Now we are going to concentrate on building a healthy brain so you can function optimally, feel fantastic and make intelligent choices what to eat, drink and think to enhance your life, health and fat loss.

Your Brain Needs the Right Fats to Function Optimally

You must fully understand that when the brain is well nourished, well oxygenated, well hydrated and has a steady blood sugar supply, it is difficult to make the wrong food choices and just as importantly wrong life choices. We only choose the wrong foods and make wrong decisions when we have the wrong brain chemistry.

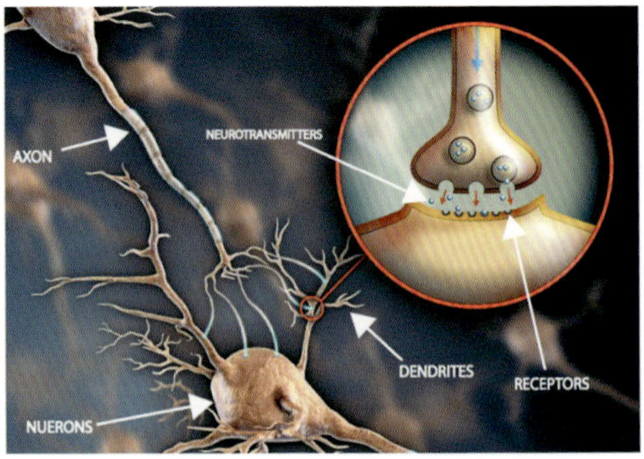

What our neurons look like. This is one way the brain communicates.

The brain has 3 major components which are totally dependent on what you eat and drink; neurons, neurotransmitters and receptors.

1) Neurons need an abundance of essential fatty acids and phospholipids.
2) Neurotransmitter are primarily amino acids therefore quality protein is required.
3) Receptors are proteins that receive the message.

Each neurotransmitter has to fit perfectly into the receptor of the neuron (much like a lock and key). If it does not fit exactly will not activate a clear transmission.

Nothing you put in your mouth is as agreeable or disagreeable to the intricate structures of your brain cells as fat. Your brain is the body's fattiest organ – 60% of the dry weight is made up of various fat like substances. This also makes the brain extremely vulnerable to toxins, as toxins have an ability for fat. A lack of omega 3, particularly DHA and EPA, combined with high levels of omega 6 is linked with deterioration of brain and visual function.

Which Fats are Fabulous

Omega 3 fatty acids (ALA, EPA, DHA) found in: • Flax oil • Hemp oil • Walnuts and Walnut Oil • Fish oil	Omega 6 fatty acids (GLA) found in: • Borage seed oil • Blackcurrant oil • Evening Primrose Oil	Omega 9 fatty acids found in: • Olive Oil • Rice Bran Oil • Avocados • Coconut Oil • Raw Milk & Butter	Phospholipids are the main structural component in biological membranes. Phospholipids maintains structural integrity and acts as boundary between the cell and between the compartments within the cells.

Denied the right fats, and flooded with the bad fats, your cerebral tissue may become partly starved - not a good picture. The outer membranes of your brain cells may stiffen and shrivel the dendrite tentacles that reach out to form patterns of communication with other cells may become stunted, the rich chemical flood of neurotransmitters may dry up or become short circuited, unable to gain entry to neurons and carry messages from neuron to neuron. It is a mess that nature never intended yet that is the state of many people's brains today.

We know that neurons can continue to grow and expand at all ages, even into old age. Such growth though requires rich supplies of essential fatty acids and adequate stimulation. Thus, the fat you eat throughout life is constantly moulding your brain. It's an exciting but sobering thought, considering that most brains are fed garbage fats throughout life. This usually results in garbage brains.

Cholesterol and it's essential role in brain function

One of the most crucial fats for your brain is CHOLESTEROL. Yes, you read that right. Don't choke on your statin tablets, read on and find out why low-fat, low-cholesterol diets make us sick, fat and dumb.

One of the many important roles cholesterol plays in the body is in our nervous system, enabling learning and memory to take place. In fact, one of the reasons that sleep is beneficial to our learning and memory is because it enables our brain to make more cholesterol - yes, make more cholesterol! Science is continually showing that cholesterol is one of the most important nutrients for our brains.

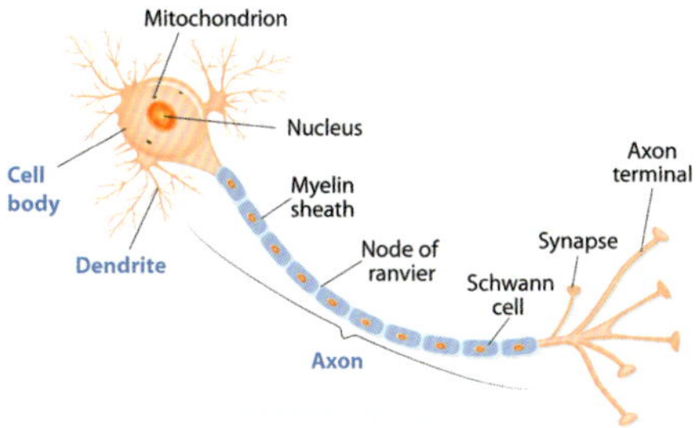

Cholesterol is abundant in the tissue of the brain and nervous system. Myelin, which covers nerve axons to help conduct the electrical impulses that make movement, sensation, thinking, learning, and remembering possible, is over one fifth cholesterol by weight. Even though the brain only makes up 2% of the body's weight, it contains 25% of its cholesterol. Yes - your brain is 25% cholesterol. One of the groups of genes that this study found to be upregulated during sleep were genes important for the synthesis and maintenance of myelin, including myelin structural proteins and genes relating to the synthesis and transport of cholesterol.

Evidence to date strongly supports the concept that sleep plays an important role in increasing performance of newly learned activities, consolidating memories, and increasing brain plasticity - which is the ability to form new, as well as break, connections between neurons called *synapses*. These benefits of sleep are not simply the absence of stress from sleep-deprivation, but an independent, critical role, in the actual process of learning and memory-formation.

But *why*?

Exciting research was published in the pages of Neuron in 2004, which identified about 100 genes that increase their activity during sleep. They found about as many that increased their activity during wake, and others whose activity varied with circadian rhythm, independent of sleep or wakefulness.

While there are many important cellular and molecular events that happen during sleep, and we are only cracking the surface in our understanding of them, one of the things this study showed is that **cholesterol** synthesis increases during sleep which, given the research described below, undoubtedly is part of the reason sleep is beneficial to mental functioning.

But the benefits of cholesterol extend beyond both sleep and myelin. **In fact, in 2001, cholesterol was found to be the most important factor in the formation of synapses, the basis of our learning and memory.** In the late 1990s and early 2000s, research was pointing to an unknown compound made by glial cells that was responsible for the ability of neurons to form synapses, or connections between each other. Thoughts, memories, learning, and all mental function is dependent on the formation of synapses, so the ability to form them will directly impact mental functioning and health. In the absence of this as yet unknown "glial factor," neurons formed few synapses, and the synapses they formed were inefficient and poorly functioning. In the presence of glial cells, which secrete the unknown factor, neurons formed many, highly efficient synapses.

So what is this "glial factor"?

Research in 2001, by Mauch, et al., published in volume 294 of Science magazine, determined that the unknown glial factor is cholesterol, which is released by the glial cells in a carrier called "apolipoprotein E." Initially, the researchers thought that the apolipoprotein E (apoE) may have been the glial factor itself. But it turned out that when neurons were treated with apoE, the beneficial effects on synapse formation were not observed. The researchers then reasoned that, since apoE fit the bill in some ways, but did not have the desired effect, some of the lipids it carried may have been the elusive glial factor. As it turned out, treating the neurons with a 10 mcg/mL solution of cholesterol increased synapse formation by **12 times!**

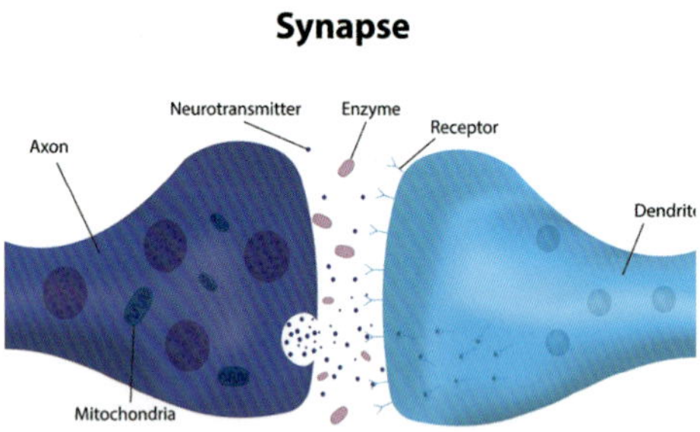

Cholesterol is essential for synapse health.

On the other hand, when *low-cholesterol* glial secretions were produced by using the cholesterol-lowering drug, mevastatin, the effect of the glial secretion on synapse formation was strongly diminished. When cholesterol was added back to the low-cholesterol secretion, the positive effect on synapse formation was *fully restored*. The authors identified cholesterol as a *limiting factor* of synapse formation. In other words, the need for cholesterol in the brain is large enough relative to the supply of cholesterol that the availability of cholesterol can directly limit the ability to form synapses.

We now know that the formation of synapses, or connections between neurons, is directly dependent on the availability of cholesterol. The formation of these synapses are what give us the ability to remember and learn. The benefits of sleep for memory formation and learning are in part a result of increased cholesterol synthesis during sleep. The implications are important and powerful. In our society's quest to lower cholesterol at all costs and without second thought, could some of the methods we use, such as taking cholesterol-lowering drugs, or eating low-fat, low-cholesterol diets, be limiting the availability of cholesterol to our nervous system?

The authors of the 2001 *Science* study described above concluded that the "results imply that genetic or age-related defects in the synthesis, transport, or uptake of cholesterol in the CNS may directly impair the development and plasticity of the synaptic circuitry." In fact, amnesia and cognitive dysfunction are reported as side-effects in some statin users. Dr. Duane Graveline, MD, former NASA scientist and astronaut, describes his bout of statin-induced memory loss,in which his wife caught him wandering aimlessly in his yard while he failed to recognize her.

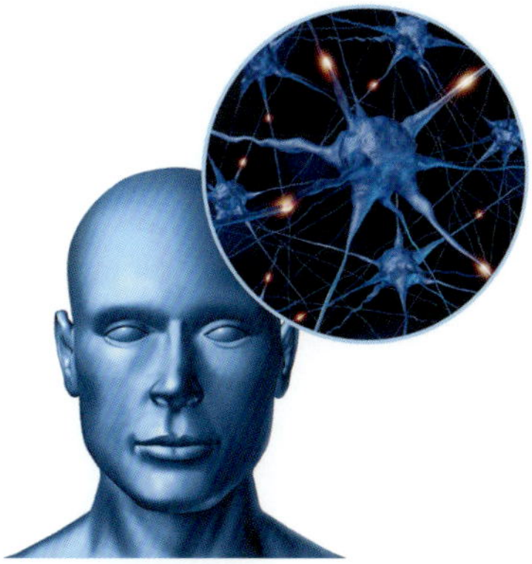

The neurons in our brain act like telephone lines, connecting to each other and sending messages all throughout the brain and the body.

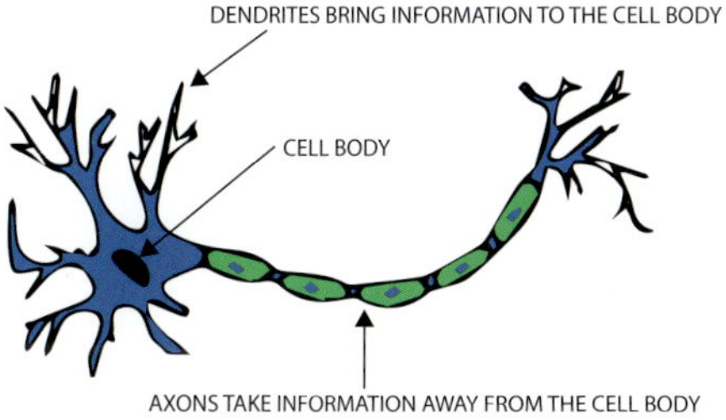

An illustration of a neuron. There are over 100 billion of these in your brain alone

In an article on the side-effects of cholesterol-lowering drugs, the Geriatric Times cites two randomized trials, several case reports, and one large case series pointing to memory loss as a result of statin drugs. Conversely, dietary cholesterol can help reverse the effects of declining memory with age. Mary Enig, PhD, cites a study in her book, *'Know Your Fats'*, that found that the cholesterol in eggs can help improve memory in the elderly.

Omega 3 and omega 6 - Why we went from dumb arse to smart arse

Somewhere in the evolutionary backwoods of the brain, something unprecedented happened in the story of life on earth. The human brain changed and was suddenly able to compute, manage and store information like never before. Why did this happen? Scientists think they have found the answer:-

Human life first originated in the sea, where there was an abundance of omega-3 fatty acids – the same fatty acids that now form the essential components of our eyes' photoreceptors and our brain's cell membranes. As time went on, flowering seed plants appeared and with them a brand new fatty acid family was introduced. The seed oils of these plants contained what we call omega-6 fatty acids. For the first time, the omega-3 and omega-6 fatty acid families existed on earth together and apparently this opened the door for an entire new set of species to arrive that would develop bigger brains.

How did the new species develop bigger brains? Human beings are thought to have lived on earth for millions of years, however the big brain change happened only in the last 200,000 years or so. What could have caused the change in human brains? And why did some human brains change and others stay the same? Could it have been what they ate?

The puzzle of the big brain change involved scientists putting together pieces that, at first look, had no relation. The first piece of the puzzle involved discovering early human populations that demonstrated greater intelligence. They found evidence in the East African Rift Valley and on the southern Cape of South Africa. The second piece of the puzzle was the discovery that docosahexaenoic acid (DHA) was a large contributor to brain growth. The third piece was the discovery that DHA was found in seafood. When scientists put all the pieces together they found that the early humans who lived near water sources and ate seafood experienced the big brain change!

People collecting shellfish could have easily provided themselves with a plentiful source of brain-specific nutrition, and their children would have naturally participated in the exploitation of this extremely rich resource. There must have been enough omega-3 and omega-6 fatty acids available in their diet to provide many generations with fuel for fetal/infant development as well as childhood and adult needs for the cardiovascular system and the brain.

A lot of the knowledge that I have gained on brain fats has been from Michael Schmidt and Dr Barry Sears and their excellent books.

Dr Donald Rudin, author of "The omega 3 phenomenon", has estimated that, over the past seventy five years, we have reduced our omega 3 fatty acid consumption by 80%. This explains why we are getting dumber, fatter and sicker. You must fully understand that without EPA & DHA primarily derived from fatty fish (salmon, mackerel, sardines, anchovies and tuna), or pharmaceutical grade fish oil, your brain cannot function at full efficiency; it is 100% IMPOSSIBLE.

Omega six fats and inflammation

During prehistoric days when our brains evolved, our ancestors ate equal amounts of Omega 3 and Omega 6. Omega 3 is found in seafood and our Omega 6 at that time came mostly from meat, fruits, vegetables, eggs & nuts. Today, unfortunately, a high percentage of our Omega 6's come primarily from processed vegetable oils and those idiotic margarine spreads which are promoted as health foods when in reality they should be promoted as death foods. Overeating Omega 6 and under eating Omega 3 oils can cause inflammation in our brains as well as our bodies. Most of us are filling our brain cells with the wrong kind of fat and ignoring the right type of fat - another reason why we are becoming dumbed down today and also aggressive as well as depressed!

One of the most fearful potential consequences of omega 6 dominance in brain cells is persistent inflammation of brain tissue. Such inflammation can injure cerebral blood vessels, set up processes that kill brain cells, warp nerve cell membranes disrupting normal functioning, interfere with neuronal message transmission, and promote strokes, Alzheimer's disease, and probably all degenerative brain diseases.

In 1999 evidence of chronic inflammation increased the odds of stroke by nearly 500% in a large group of men observed for twenty years as part of the Honolulu Heart Study. What's critical to the brain is not just the total amounts of omega 3 & 6 you eat but the relative amounts of each or the ratio. In fact the ratio is the critical factor that determines how well information is transmitted from neuron to neuron.

In a perfect world you would eat no more than one molecule of omega 6 fatty acid for every one molecule of omega 3 fatty acid for optimum brain function. Although research is showing that you can maintain excellent brain function with a ratio of 4–1 omega 6 & 3.

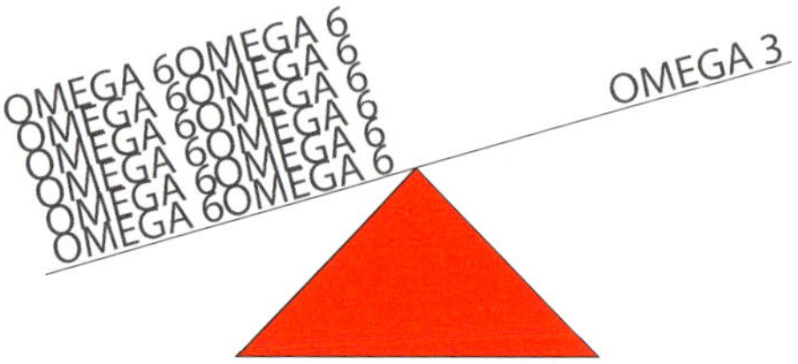

Our intake of omega-6 can often outweigh our intake of omega 3 which can have implications on our brain function

Excess omega six pushes us towards aggression, depression, impulsiveness, less cooperative spirit, lower intelligence, smaller brains, and illnesses all magnified by our inadequate intake of omega three fats. Capuchin monkeys on a high omega six diet deteriorated so badly that by the age of two, they were showing self mutilation behaviour. A study of violent offenders in the prison system showed that fatty acid abnormalities were common. Blood measurements revealed very low DHA in violent antisocial men. But,students supplemented with DHA exhibited lower stress and aggression during examinations.

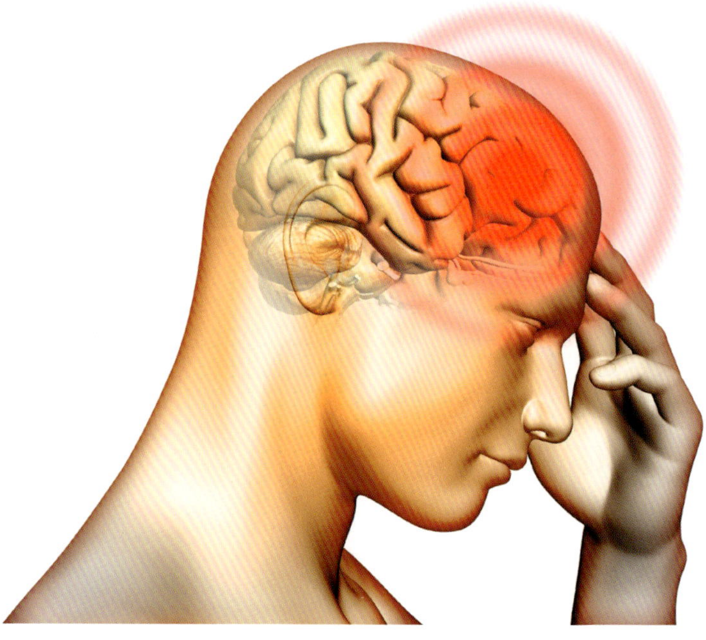

Omega six fats instruct the body to store fat.

Omega six fats tells the body to make bigger and make more fat cells available. Omega six switches down our metabolism. However, you can turn the "store fat" switch off with omega threes. Omega three encourages the body to burn fat and make small fat cells. So increasing your long chain omega three fats, and heavily cutting down your omega six fats, will switch off the "store fat" button. Your body will be pushed towards burn and store fat. Whilst the body is supplied with excess omega six fats, it will continue to store it.

Excess omega six fat is a fundamental factor in the rise of obesity. Once you have built up high stores of omega six in the body fat from years of eating lots of vegetable oils it can take up to two years to see a significant difference in adipose fat composition, that's why there is no such thing as quick fix diet plans you must work long term to build health and fat loss.

We store very little omega three fat and this tells us we must continually supply on a daily basis to provide this essential fat to the multitude of functions that the body uses it for. The body has a built in preference to burn omega threes, before omega sixes. Omega threes is better fuel than omega six. The body releases omega three in preference to omega six from fat stores. The body only stores 0.1 - 2% omega three fat by contrast, omega six storage rates are as high as 25%. So omega threes encourage the body to burn fat rather than store like omega six fats do. Omega threes increase metabolic rate and increase mitochondrial function which is essential to burn fat. A study showed that young adults on an energy restricted diet, lost more weight, when fish oil was added to their diet. Omega threes discourages fat cells from growing, and inhibits new fat cells from developing.

Take Fish Oils Without Antioxidant Protection And They Will Do More Harm Than Good, and why margarines and vegetable oils like sunflower and safflower cause heart disease, cancer and immune disorders!

I have been preaching about the benefits of fish oils for over 25 years but for the last ten years I have been warning about the dangers of taking fish oils without the antioxidant protection in the fish and why I put high dose antioxidant protection in PRP's Ultimate Fish Oils.

Polyunsaturated fats (PUFs) are greatly immunosuppressive. The first person to suggest that polyunsaturated fats suppress the immune system was Dr E A Newsholme of Oxford University, England.[i] What Newsholme wrote was that when our bodies get sufficient nutrition, our diet includes immunosuppressive PUFs which make us prone to infection by bacteria and viruses. When we are starved, however, our body stores of PUFs are depleted.

This allows our bodies' immune systems to recover which, in turn, allows us to fight existing infection and prevent other infections.

He was making the point that the immunosuppressive effects of PUFs in sunflower seeds are useful in treating autoimmune diseases such as multiple sclerosis,[ii] and that the same fatty acids could be used to suppress the immune system to prevent rejection of kidney transplants.

It was during the early days of kidney transplantation that doctors first encountered the problem of tissue rejection as their patients' bodies destroyed the alien transplanted kidneys. If transplantation were to be a success, they had to find a way to suppress the immune system. Newsholme had said that there was no better way to immunosuppress a renal patient than with sunflower seed oil. So kidney transplant doctors fed their patients linoleic acid.[iii] (Linoleic acid is the major polyunsaturated fatty acid in vegetable oils.) But the transplant doctors were then astonished to see how quickly their patients developed cancers and the treatment was stopped.

This was in line with heart trials using diets that were high in PUFs which also reported an excess of cancer deaths from as early as 1971.[iv].

By the early 1980s, we were being exhorted by doctors and nutritionists to eat more PUFs because they were 'good for us' despite the fact that Oncology Times carried a paper in January 1980 from the University of California at Davis that mice fed PUFs were more prone to develop melanoma. In May 1980, the same publication carried a similar report from Oregon State University which said that PUFs fed to cancer-prone mice increased the numbers of cancers formed.

In 1989 there was a report of a 10-year trial at a Veterans' Administration Hospital in Los Angeles. In this trial half the patients were fed a diet which had twice as much PUFs as saturated fats. In the half of patients on the high PUF diet there was a 15% increase in cancer deaths compared to the saturated fat group.[v] The authors of the report said that the PUFs had been the cause of the increase in cancer deaths. The 6 October 1973 issue of the British Medical Journal asked if PUFs were carcinogenic and came to the conclusion that they were.

The late American cancer researcher, Wayne Martin, liked to tell a story which suggests just how cancer-causing are PUFs. In 1930 in the USA 80% of men smoked cigarettes and the tar content of cigarettes was much higher than it is today. The death rate at that time from lung cancer was very low. In 1955 doctors decided that PUFs were beneficial in terms of heart disease protection. After this lung cancer deaths increased dramatically. By 1980 although the number of American men who smoked had dropped to only 30%, three times as much PUF was being eaten — and there were 60 times as many lung cancer deaths.[vi]

In 1990, Martin called Newsholme's Oxford University office but by then Newsholme had retired. Martin spoke to his successor to find that they were still treating autoimmune diseases with PUFs. By then they were using fish oil. The Oxford doctor said the reason for the fish oil was that the degree of immunosuppression increased with the degree of unsaturation and fish oil was much more unsaturated than sunflower oil. Martin asked the doctor why they were not talking about PUFs causing cancer. The doctor replied that if he did that he would be run out of Oxford.

It is from all of the research I have done over the years, that I have found again and again that, without anti-oxidant protection, fish oils easily oxidise and go rancid. My research (like that above) has shown that high dose fish oils can in fact be detrimental to our health.

That's why I have added the anti-oxidants vitamin A, D, E, K2 & CoQ10 – to protect the fish oils and to give you far greater health benefits that these vitamins have to offer.

References

From the book Trick and Treat by Barry Groves PhD

[i]. Newsholme E A. Mechanism for starvation suppression and refeeding activity of infection. Lancet 1977; i: 654.

[ii]. Miller JHD, et al. Double blind trial of linoleate supplementation in the diet in multiple sclerosis. BMJ 1973; i: 765-8.

[iii]. Uldall PR, et al. Unsaturated fatty acids and renal transplantation. Lancet 1974; ii: 514.

[iv]. Pearce M L, Dayton S. Incidence of cancer in men on a diet high in polyunsaturated fat. Lancet 1971; i: 464.

[v]. American Heart Association Monograph, No 25. 1969.

[vi]. Nauts HC. Cancer Research Institute Monograph No 18. 1984, p 91.

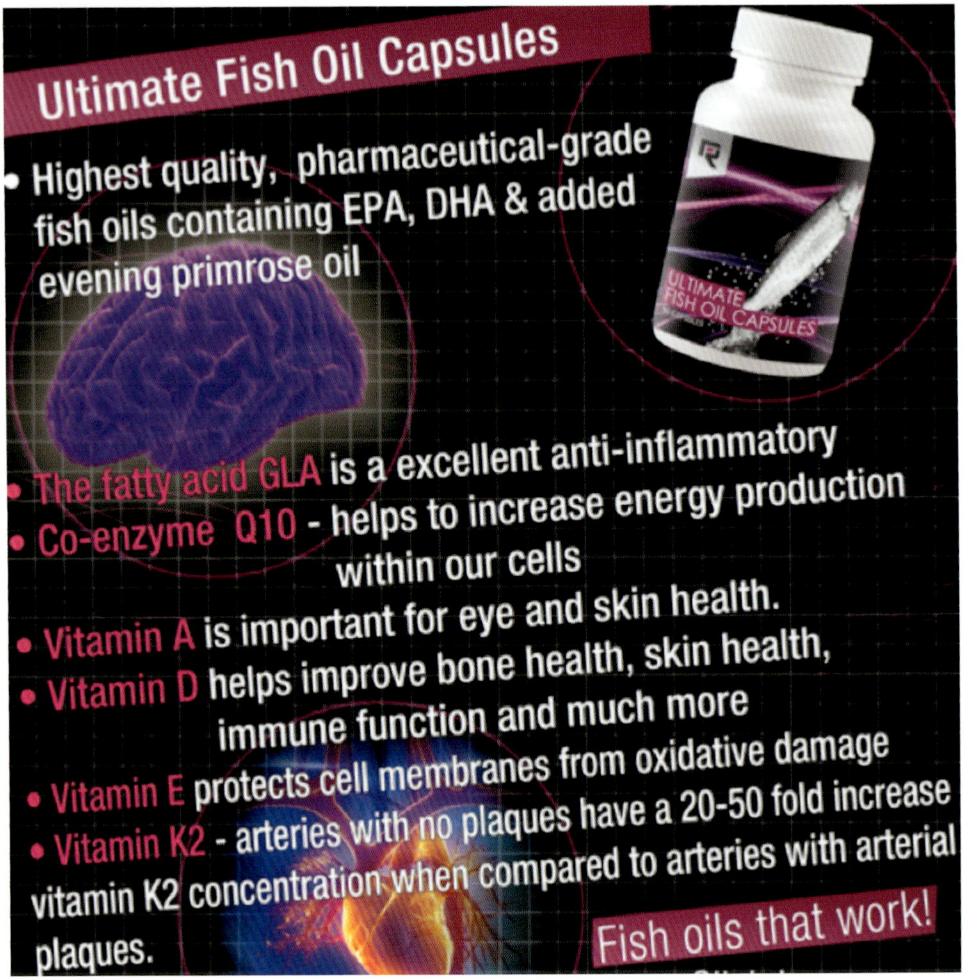

Omega 3 fats and brain chemistry

We can now see that the chemistry of the fat we eat can profoundly influence the very architecture of our brain cells; the profusion or scarcity of all-important dendrites and synapses the linchpins of intelligence, learning, memory, attention, concentration and mood. Essentially, the membrane consists of two layers of fatty molecules (phospholipids), and the membranes flexibility depends on the consistency of its fat. If the fat is hardened like lard, the membrane is stiff and rigid or if the fat is more fluid like fish oil, the membranes is soft and pliable. Cell membranes must be pliable and in constant flux to perform the communication miracles of the brain, says Dr. Joseph Hibben, a research psychiatrist at the National Institute Of Health in Bethesda, Maryland. That is especially true, he says, in the synapses of brain cells the junctions where nerve cells converge to pass their messages

A single nerve cell may make up to 20,000 connections with other cells. The place where these cells connect is the synapse. The portion of the nerve making the connections is called the synaptic membrane. This part of the nerve has the highest concentration of DHA than almost any other tissue in the body. These synaptic gaps, where signals jump from one cell to another, are the source of the brain's awesome powers. The more of these transmission centres or synapses on brain cells and the smoother the communication between them, the better the brain functions and the better sense of well-being that you will feel. Moreover, the number and quality of synaptic connections determine intelligence and optimal brain function even more than the total number of brain cells.

Omega 3 fish oil, more precisely the part called DHA (docosahexaenoic acid), is the building material for synaptic communication centres. You can't create more synapses, dendrites, or receptors that increase your brain's potential without a robust supply of DHA.

Like a growing tree, any time a nerve cell makes a new branch it requires new raw materials. Without adequate DHA available, branching out cannot happen. If brain fats are not available in needed amounts you will not grow new dendrites and axons and have a very hard time learning new material. Millions of messages pass through the synapses of a cell hourly. To accomplish that, a chemical messenger a neurotransmitter is cast adrift into a watery void by one nerve cell to find its way into the receptors of a nearby nerve cell. If the neurotransmitter does not fit perfectly into the receptor of the waiting neuron, the attempted communication fails. When a neurotransmitter does lock in, it activates the cell to fire and release more neurotransmitters to traverse thousands of synapses in a perpetual chain reaction of tiny sparks amongst billions of brain cells that ultimately form our universe, our thoughts, actions and mood. Each neurotransmitter, such as serotonin or dopamine, has a unique shape that must fit into the receptor embedded in the cellular surface of the membrane. For the perfect fit needed to activate clear transmission, the receptor alters its shape slightly.

If the membrane is made of fluid fat, such as fish oil, the receptor can easily change configuration. But if the membrane is made of rigid, hard fat like from trans fats, the receptor is immobilized, unable to wiggle or expand to let the neurotransmitter lock in. Then the communication between cells is not activated, in fact is short circuited, garbled, muted, or instantly terminated. Thus, how efficiently neurotransmitters pass from one neuron to another depends on the fluidity of the synapses. You can amplify message transmission across synapses a thousand fold by altering fat membrane consistency.

Even if you have an ample supply of chemical neurotransmitters, the message can't get through if the receptors don't function properly. You can send out all the neurotransmitters you want but, if only 50% of the normally functioning receptors are in a state to activate the messengers, only 50% of the message gets through. In short, a receptor sitting in a cell membrane filled with rigid fat is a dead or mute receptor. It can't sense or transmit much of anything. That is something to remember the next time you set out to solidify your cell membranes with too much trans fats and omega 6 fats. This is also another reason why those who take antidepressants don't see the results because the antidepressant can release more neurotransmitters but if the receptors are deaf or inhibited then the neurotransmitters can't work their magic.

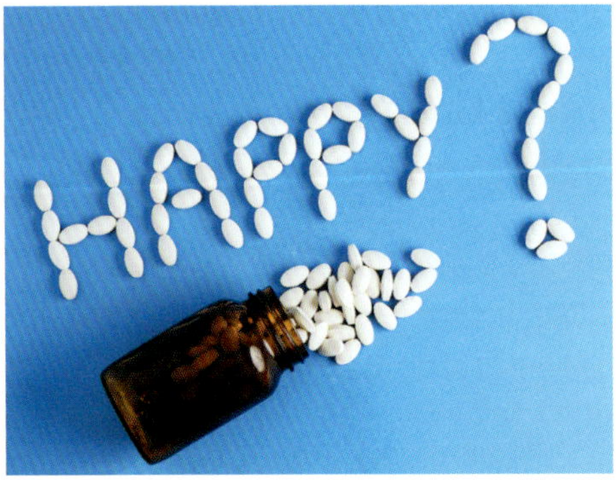

Pharmaceutical grade fish oils are excellent for enhancing mood.

An intriguing way fish oil seems to influence mood and behaviour is by boosting brain levels of the feel good neurotransmitter serotonin. It's well documented that many people with abnormally low brain and blood levels of serotonin are depressed, at high risk of suicide, and criminally impulsive. However, if you have high levels of DHA fish oil in your blood, you're apt to have high amounts of serotonin in your brain. Precisely how fish oil manages to boost serotonin is not well understood currently, but scientists speculate it may happen in several ways. Changing the fat composition of membranes which alters the actions of critical enzymes that, for example, convert tryptophan (an amino acid) to serotonin and control its breakdown and reuse or re-uptake. There's also recent evidence that eating fish creates more serotonin simply because the body uses DHA to manufacture more synapses, with more nerve endings, that in turn produce more serotonin. It's like building more serotonin factories, instead of just increasing the efficiency of the serotonin.

UCLA neuroscientists have shown that a diet high in the omega-3 fatty acid DHA helps protect the brain against the memory loss and cell damage caused by Alzheimer's disease. The new research suggests that a DHA-rich diet may lower one's risk of Alzheimer's disease. The journal Neuron reported the findings on Sept. 2004.

"This is proof that our diets affect how our brain cells communicate with each other under the duress of Alzheimer's disease," said Greg Cole, senior author and a professor of neurology at the David Geffen School of Medicine at UCLA. "We saw that a diet rich in DHA, or docosahexaenoic acid, dramatically reduces the impact of the Alzheimer's gene."

It used to be taught as fact, in medical schools, that the human brain in an adult is not capable of further growth. Since then, it has been proven that the adult mammalian brain does have the capacity to regenerate its cells though we still know little about this process. Neurogenesis is the term used to describe the recently discovered capacity of the human brain to grow new neurons. That's right, our brain is not physically fixed, it is constantly changing, losing some neurons, growing some neurons, making or deleting connections, and we all have the potential to achieve outstanding things in our lives, simply by nourishing and challenging our brains. This will force our brains to become smarter

Other fats for a healthy brain

Cell Membranes are made of the following:

- Fatty Acids from wild fish and fish oil, the omega 3 fats DHA and EPA.
- Phospholipids from foods like egg yolk, liver, soya beans, sardines, lentils, sesame seeds, flaxseed.
- Cholesterol from eggs, liver, poultry. This is the glue between molecules.
- Protein from high quality meat sources etc.

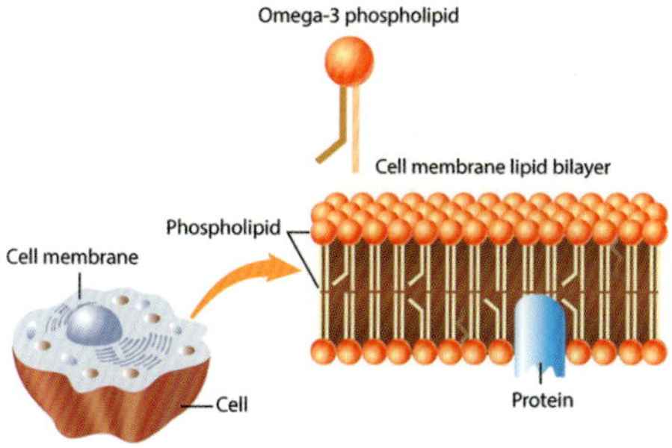

Receptors, transporters, gates, signal transducers etc. The most abundant fats in your cell membranes are the phospholipids. There are three main kinds of phospholipids - phosphatidylcholine, phosphatidylserine and dimethylamylamine, abbreviated DMAE.

Super Brain Builder – Phosphatidylcholine

Phosphatidylcholine is a substance which can be derived from the nutrient compound lecithin that consists of; phosphate, fatty acids and choline. The components of phosphatidylcholine, particularly the fatty acids and choline, make it valuable as a brain-promoting agent.

Supplementing phosphatidylcholine has some very positive benefits for your brain. Research on rats at Duke University Medical Centre in the USA, demonstrated that giving choline during pregnancy creates the equivalent of super brains in the offspring. The researchers fed pregnant rats choline halfway through their pregnancy. The infant rats whose mothers were given choline had vastly superior brains with more neuronal connections and, consequently, improved learning ability and better memory recall. All of which persisted into old age. This research showed that giving choline during pregnancy helps restructure the brain for improved performance in the long term.

"Choline does dramatically change the very structure of memory centres in the hippocampus of the developing foetal brain," declares Dr Stephen Zeisel, a world expert on choline. Dr Zeisel and colleagues found that when choline is lacking, cell division in the foetal brain is reduced. Cells migrate abnormally. An increasing number of brain cells die prematurely. If your brain does not get enough phosphatidylcholine, nutritionally, it will literally cannibalise brain cells to obtain this nutrient according to Dharma Singh Khalsa, M.D., "Brain Longevity: The Breakthrough Medical Program that Improves Your Mind and Memory".

Phosphatidylserine

Over 3,000 published research papers and more than 60 clinical trials have established that phosphatidylserine can help to rejuvenate your brain cell membranes. Phosphatidylserine increases communication between cells in your brain by increasing the number of membrane receptor sites for receiving messages. Phosphatidylserine modulates the fluidity of cell membranes - essential to your brain cells' ability to send and receive chemical communication. Phosphatidylserine also stimulates your brain to produce dopamine and this is likely why patients diagnosed with clinical depression have shown marked improvement in their symptoms as a result of taking phosphatidylserine daily.

One of the best known and most effective ways to lower excess cortisol levels is with the nutrient phosphatidylserine. Phosphatidylserine is believed to facilitate the repair of the cortisol receptors in the hypothalamus. It is believed that the cortisol receptors get damaged by high cortisol levels reducing the ability of the hypothalamus to sense and correct high cortisone levels. Because phosphatidylserine helps repair the feedback control apparatus, it is useful in correcting both high and low cortisol levels.

Phosphatidylserine can also help reduce increases in exercise-induced cortisol levels. In a double-blind, crossover study conducted at California State University, 10 men were given 800 mg of phosphatidylserine a day and then put through a vigorous whole-body workout (designed to elicit a cortisol response) four times a week. Each participant received phosphatidylserine for two weeks and then repeated the workout program for another two weeks with a placebo, after a washout period of 3 1/2 weeks. Blood samples were taken 15 minutes after each workout. This study found that phosphatidylserine reduced cortisol levels after exercise by 20%. The researchers also found that testosterone levels, which normally decline after intensive exercise, were not reduced.

Phosphatidylserine also boosts acetylcholine levels and contributes to healthy brain cell membranes, with benefits for cognition and mood. Phosphatidylserine may be even more effective when combined with the omega-3 fatty acid DHA. Substantial laboratory research suggests that phosphatidylserine ability to improve cognitive skills is greatly increased in the presence of DHA.

Phosphatidylserine helps to increase communication between cells. This is required by all cells, especially brain cells.

Furthermore, the combination of DHA and phosphatidylserine powerfully supports energy production in brain cells. Scientists from the National Institutes of Health believe that phosphatidylserine, with attached DHA, is among the most critically important molecules for healthy brain function, and that phosphatidylserine works optimally in the presence of abundant levels of DHA.

Dimethylamylamine (DMAE)

Research shows that supplementing with DMAE (another phospholipid) increases choline levels in the brain better than using choline itself. Having higher choline levels increases acetylcholine, a critical neurotransmitter involved in brain processes and muscle contraction. Boosting this neurotransmitter results in better mental function, better focus and drive in the gym, better muscle endurance and strength, improved mood and a greater sense of well being.

DMAE provides numerous benefits, one being that is protects the integrity of cell membranes. This helps prevent premature aging. Other benefits of DMAE include its ability to elevate mood, counteract depression and boost memory and concentration. Unless you eat a lot of organ meats, like liver, kidney and brains (the richest sources of phospholipids), often prized in traditional cultures, you will need to supplement with phospholipids if you want to achieve optimum brain function. This is why I developed a product called Cognitive Care. Please do not think that I am trying to sell you this supplement (or any others mentioned in this book, at that). I developed these products so as I could regain my own health.

Nutrition for Neurotransmitters

You have more brain cells in your head than the number of trees in the Amazon rainforest. You have more connections between brain cells than the number of leaves on all the trees in the Amazon rainforest. The fact is, it's not the size of the brain that mostly determines intelligence, but the number of connections between neurons. The connections are physical entities, and can therefore be nurtured and stimulated with various measures.

However, neurons differ from other cells in the body in some ways. Neurons have specialized projections called dendrites and axons. Dendrites bring information to the cell body and axons take information away from the cell body. Neurons communicate with each other through an electrochemical process. Neurons form specialized connections called "synapses" and produce special chemicals called "neurotransmitters" that are released at the synapse.

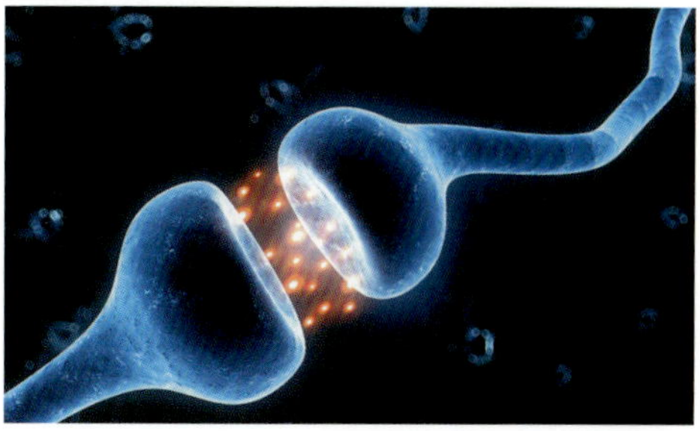

Neurotransmitters being sent from one neuron to another. This is how neurons communicate.

There are approximately 1 quadrillion synapses in the human brain. That's 1,000,000,000,000,000 synapses!

Neurotransmitters are the runners that race to and from the brain, telling every organ inside of us of us what to do. Neurotransmitters touch the life of every cell. Amino acids are the precursors to neurotransmitters, and the production of these substances can be directly affected by your diet. So it is essential to eat quality protein with each meal so that we have the substrates available to make our messenger molecules (neurotransmitters). There are many types of neurotransmitters, but our focus in this book is on the importance of dopamine, acetylcholine, GABA (gamma-Aminobutyric acid) and serotonin:

- Dopamine is derived from the amino acids tyrosine and phenylalanine.
- Acetylcholine is derived from the B-vitamin choline.
- GABA is derived from the amino acids taurine, theanine and glutamine.
- Serotonin is derived from the amino acid tryptophan.

Neurotransmitters affect mood, sleep, concentration, weight, and can cause adverse symptoms when they are out of balance. So the key to what's going on in our skull are special brain chemicals called neurotransmitters. They are the messengers of mood.

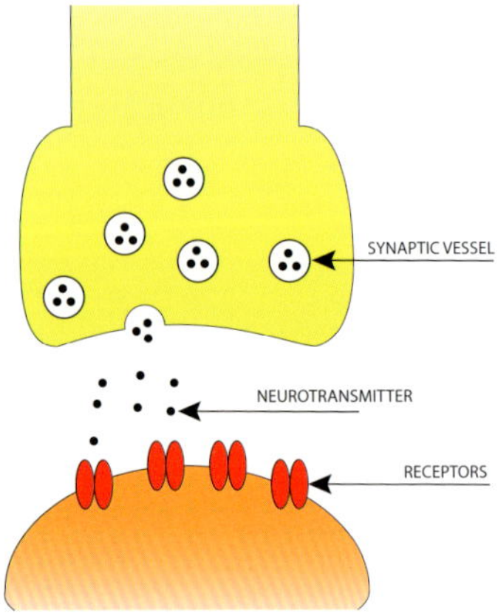

Synaptic gaps are where signals jump from one cell to another to pass on the body's electrical messages. The more of these transmission centres or synapses on brain cells and the smoother the communication between them, the better the brain functions.

The body also produces its own uplifting chemicals, known as endorphins, by breaking down food, and it is therefore possible to raise the levels of these substances in the brain by eating foods containing a combination of nutrients which release endorphins. Low endorphin levels can be caused by certain vitamin and mineral deficiencies. Certainly, a lack of B vitamins (particularly B12) and vitamin C, or of minerals such as iron, potassium and zinc, can cause you to feel low.

The four key neurotransmitters that can help with mood , inhibit cravings and addiction can be subdivided into two major categories. Think of them as ON & OFF switches for your brain. Those that excite and activate you, and those that make you calm & happy.

On Switches

Both dopamine and acetylcholine are on switches that create our ability to focus and learn. Dopamine is often thought of as the pleasure, motivation, and reward neurotransmitter in the brain. Cocaine and stimulants like caffeine boost dopamine in the brain that's why these substances often become addictive and eventually dumb down your receptors to dopamine meaning you have to consume more each time to get a hit.

Dopamine is built from the essential amino acids phenylalanine and tyrosine. Eating foods rich in protein, or supplementing your diet, with both these amino acids can help mood, energy, and attention. Dopamine levels are usually low in addicts, in people with low energy, depression and in ADHD.

DHA shortages may result in low dopamine, serotonin and melatonin (our sleep hormone), leading to depression and sleep problems. Impaired serotonin function has been linked to long term aggression, violent behaviour and sleep disorders in humans. It turns out that, among other things, omega-3 is an MAO (monoamine oxidase) inhibitor, meaning it paralyzes the MAO enzymes that destroy mood-boosting brain neurotransmitters like serotonin and dopamine.

Off Switches

GABA and serotonin are our off switches and create a calming effect on the mind and body helping us sleep and relax. Because their functions are similar, similar symptoms may occur when either is deficient. One of the most reliable predictors of alcoholism is a chronic under secretion of GABA. People who don't have enough GABA almost invariably experience high levels of tension. They often self medicate with alcohol.

New research published in the Journal of Alternative and Complementary Medicine shows that an hour of yoga raises levels of the inhibitory neurotransmitter GABA in the brain. Increased GABA levels reportedly help counteract anxiety and other neuropsychiatric disorders. The research, carried out at Boston University School of Medicine (BUSM) and McLean Hospital, used magnetic resonance spectroscopic imaging to examine two groups of people both before and after a one hour activity. One group practiced yoga, while the other read a book. Participants in the yoga group had a 27% increase in GABA levels, while those in the reading group remained unchanged. Co-authors Chris Streeter from BUSM and Domenic Ciraulo pointed out that this research shows a method of treating low GABA states.

Green tea is also an ingredient that could help your GABA production. Naturally, green tea has L-theanine which when taken moderately can produce a calming effect to avoid drowsiness.

For a solid dose of GABA, always include fresh citrus fruits in your diet. Foods that are high in glutamine can assist in GABA production. Some very helpful foods are beef liver, citrus, broccoli, halibut and lentils. As much as possible, include this in your daily diet with at least one to two servings every time you eat.

Another good addition to your diet are nuts such as walnuts and almonds. Foods rich in L-theanine such as oats, spinach, whole grains can also assist in the production of GABA. These foods can literally lower stress, while it provides other health benefits such as lowering the blood sugar.

Serotonin our happy neurotransmitter

Serotonin plays a crucial role in maintaining our overall happy feeling. Serotonin deficiency or a decrease in the serotonin level is most likely to blame for depression, aggression, anxiousness, and elevated pain sensitivity. Serotonin can be the easiest deficiency of all to develop.

The amino acid tryptophan is the only nutrient the body can use to make serotonin. According to the Lancet a 1997 study revealed that tryptophan is one of the first nutrients to be depleted by weight loss dieting. This could be another reason why dieting can cause anxiety and depression.

Stress and high cortisol levels can decrease serotonin levels. Cortisol increases the activity of enzymes that break down tryptophan which leaves less substrate to make serotonin.

High protein foods tend to lower brain tryptophan which in turn will lessen serotonin levels. Because carbohydrate consumption stimulates the uptake of tryptophan for the manufacture of serotonin. **Carbohydrate cravings in many cases is really a craving for serotonin. In many species, its directly tied to appetite – deplete serotonin, and they act like they are starving.**

The Gut-Brain Connection

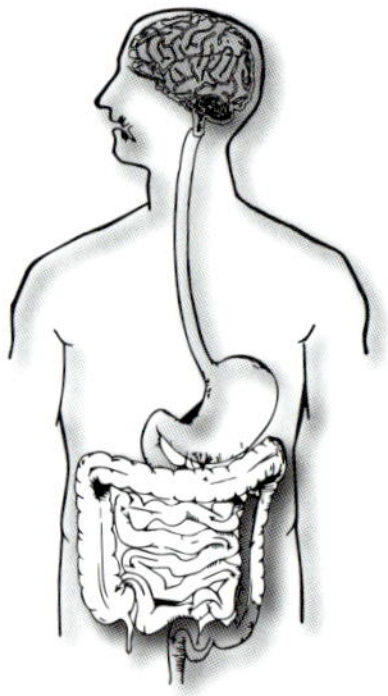

Our gut and our brain originate early in embryogenesis from the same clump of tissue which divides during fetal development. The health of your gut can have a huge influence on the health of your brain.

Our gut bacteria significantly influences the communication between the brain and the gut. When the gut is full of healthy bacteria, it has the potential to regulate mood and positive feelings. Beneficial bacteria in the gut, for example, will increase GABA receptors in the brain to alleviate mood disorders like chronic depression.

For you to have a fully functioning well nourished brain you must first have a fully functional digestive system. After all if you can't digest the nutrients the brain needs to function you will suffer from brain drain no doubt about that. Remember the brain is totally dependent on what you eat and digest!

Nearly every chemical that controls the brain in the head has been identified in the gut, including hormones and neurotransmitters According to Dr. Michael Gershon, M.D., author of `The Second Brain' and a neurobiologist at New York's Columbia-Presbyterian Medical Center, the stomach is our second brain with an independent network of over 100 million nerve cells in the gut.

Gut Bacteria Autism Link

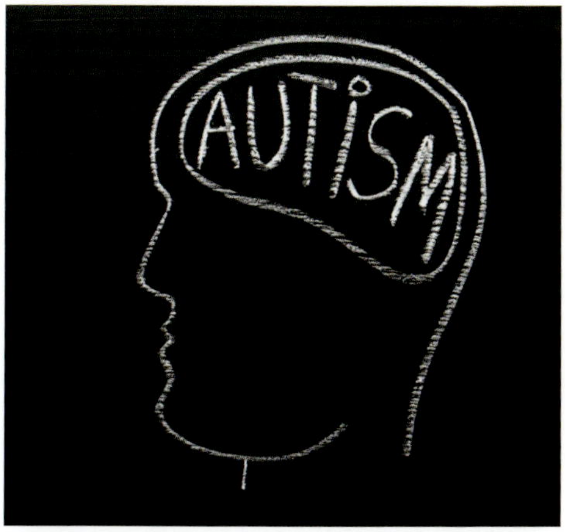

A new study showing that feeding mice a beneficial type of bacteria can ameliorate autism-like symptoms is "groundbreaking," according to University of Colorado Boulder Professor Rob Knight, who co-authored a commentary piece about the research appearing in the current issue of the journal Cell. The autism study, published in the same issue of Cell, strengthens the recent scientific understanding that the microbes that live in your gut may affect what goes on in your brain. It is also the first to show that a specific probiotic may be capable of reversing autism-like behaviors in mice.

"The broader potential of this research is obviously an analogous probiotic that could treat subsets of individuals with autism spectrum disorder," wrote the commentary authors, who also included CU-Boulder Research Associate Dorota Porazinska and doctoral student Sophie Weiss.

For the new Cell study, led by Elaine Hsiao of the California Institute of Technology, the researchers used a technique called maternal immune activation in pregnant mice to induce autism-like behavior and neurology in their offspring. The researchers found that the gut microbial community of the offspring differed markedly compared with a control group of mice. When the mice with autism-like symptoms were fed *Bacteriodes fragilis*, a microbe known to bolster the immune system, the aberrant behaviors were reduced.

Scientific evidence is mounting that the trillions of microbes that call the human body home can influence our gut-linked health, affecting our risk of obesity, diabetes and colon cancer, for example. But more recently, researchers are discovering that gut microbes also may affect neurology - possibly impacting a person's cognition, emotions and mental health, said

Knight, also a Howard Hughes Medical Institute Early Career Scientist and an investigator at CU-Boulder's BioFrontiers Institute.

The research of Dr. Andrew Wakefield was among the first to uncover the connection between a gut problem, chronic bowel inflammation, possibly caused by the presence of MMR vaccine strain of measles in the digestive tract, and symptoms of regressive autism.

Dr. Natasha Campbell-McBride is a Russian neurologist who has successfully treated her own son and she treats children from all over the world in her English clinic. Her research shows there's a profound dynamic interaction between your gut, your brain, and your immune system. She has developed what might be one of the most profoundly important treatment strategies for preventing autism, as well as a wide range of other neurological, psychological, and autoimmune disorders - all of which are heavily influenced by your gut health. In her research, Dr. Campbell-McBride discovered that nearly all of the mothers of autistic children have abnormal gut flora, which is significant because newborns inherit their gut flora from their mothers at the time of birth.

Establishing normal gut flora in the first 20 days or so of life plays a crucial role in the maturation of your baby's immune system. Babies who develop abnormal gut flora are left with compromised immune systems, putting them at higher risk for suffering vaccine reactions. If your baby has suboptimal gut flora, vaccines can become the proverbial "last straw" - the trigger that "primes" his/her immune system to develop chronic health problems.

Dr. Campbell-McBride's Gut and Psychology Syndrome, and Gut and Physiology Syndrome (GAPS) Nutritional program is vitally important for MOST people, as the majority of people have such poor gut health due to poor diet and toxic exposures, but it's particularly crucial for pregnant women and young children. According to Dr. Campbell-McBride, in children with GAPS, the toxicity flowing from their gut throughout their bodies and into their brains continually challenges their nervous system, preventing it from performing its normal functions and process sensory information. GAPS may manifest in a wide range of symptoms, fitting the diagnosis of either autism, or attention deficit hyperactivity disorder (ADHD), attention deficit disorder (ADD) without hyperactivity, dyslexia, dyspraxia, or obsessive-compulsive disorder, just to name a few possibilities. As Dr. Campbell-McBride states, she has yet to find an autistic child with normal bowel flora.

Wheat & Dairy

Recognized world authorities on gluten sensitivity have reported that gluten sensitivity can be primarily and, at times, exclusively a neurological disease. That is, people can manifest gluten sensitivity by having issues with brain function without any gastrointestinal problems whatsoever. The antibodies that a person has when they are gluten sensitive can be directly and uniquely toxic to the brain.

Gluten & Casein proteins are known to exert opioid-like effects on the brain. These proteins attach to receptors in the brain. They are nearly identical in structure to natural opioid-binding peptides (can have morphine-like effects). You must remember that wheat and dairy are very new to the human diet and we are now eating it on a mass scale and it is undoubtedly causing us MULTIPLE HEALTH PROBLEMS both physical and mental. The inflammation and toxic effects of gluten and casein (derived from wheat and dairy) are so powerful in derailing our brain function that they can lead to everything from brain fog, to depression, to ADHD, autism and dementia.

I also want to make the very strong point that not everyone is not allergic to wheat and dairy. You can easily get tested but ensure that you use a very reputable lab.

Israeli doctors recently found that two women previously diagnosed with Alzheimer's actually had an inherited autoimmune diseases, an allergy to gluten. The women were put on a gluten free diet and miraculously their memories came back and the Alzheimer's disappeared. This obviously doesn't mean this would happen in every case but very interesting nonetheless.

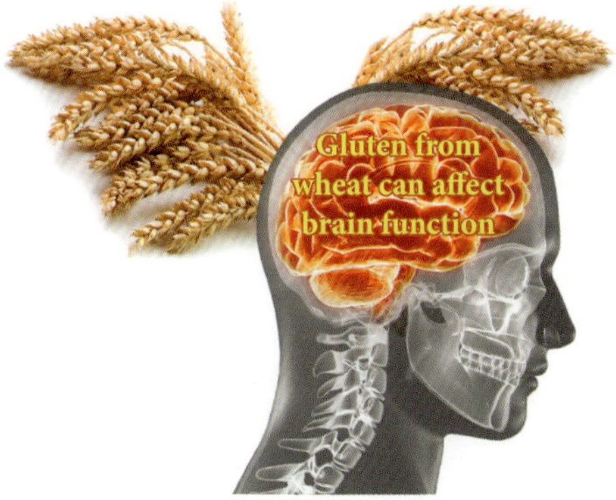

Gluten and casein proteins are also known to exert opioid-like effects on the brain. These proteins attach to receptors in the brain. They are nearly identical in structure to natural opioid-binding peptides. (Can have morphine-like effects and become addictive) 57% of patients with neurological dysfunction (including Autism and ADD patients) were shown to have antibodies to gluten (a component of wheat and other grains.) *Lahat E, et al. Prevalence of celiac antibodies in children with neurological disorders. Pediatr Neurol. 2000 May;22(5):393-6.* A unique type of enterocolitis (infection of the colon) was found in 93% of individuals with developmental disorders. *Wakefield AJ, et al. Enterocolitis in children with developmental disorders. Am J Gastroenterol. 2000 Sep;95(9):2285-95.*

Dr. Maios Hadjivassiliou, a recognized world authority on gluten sensitivity, has reported in the journal, The Lancet, that "gluten sensitivity can be primarily and at times, exclusively a neurological disease". That is, people can manifest gluten sensitivity by having issues with brain function without any gastrointestinal problems whatsoever. Dr. Hadjivassiliou indicates that the antibodies that a person has when they are gluten sensitive can be directly and uniquely toxic to the brain.

20% of children with coeliac disease have white matter lesions of the brain and the incidence is high enough that some authorities suggest that coeliac disease should be positively ruled out in all learning disabled children *(J Ped, Dec 2001, Vol. 108)*. Cognitive decline and underachievement in post secondary education is 400% more likely in gluten sensitivity (*Scandinavian Journal Of Gastroenterology, 2005)*.

Your Brain Thrives with the Right Exercise!

Our ancestors were the ultimate athletes. Can you imagine the effort it took to hunt wild game, to gather fruits, nuts & plants etc. Their strength and endurance levels would be equivalent to any professional athlete today that I have absolutely no doubt about. Everything today is so easy for us in the Western world we piss moan and groan today if someone has moved our remote control for the T.V. and we have to get up and find it. We are designed to be physically active and this has an enormous effect on our brains as you are just about to find out.

Why Is Exercise Good For Mood?

Exercise has amazing effects on our moods. This is not just a psychological phenomenon. There are also physiological processes behind it including;

- Increased blood flow to the brain and more efficient oxygen and glucose metabolism.
- Neuron response to stress is improved (especially in the hippocampus at least)
- Increases in serotonin to the brain
- Brain is protected against molecules that over excite it, including free radicals, high glucose levels, and high

glutamate levels

- Exercise produces BDNF which stands for "brain-derived neurotrophic factor. It's a protein actually, dubbed a master molecule and referred to as "Miracle-Gro for the brain".

BDNF is like miracle-grow for the brain!

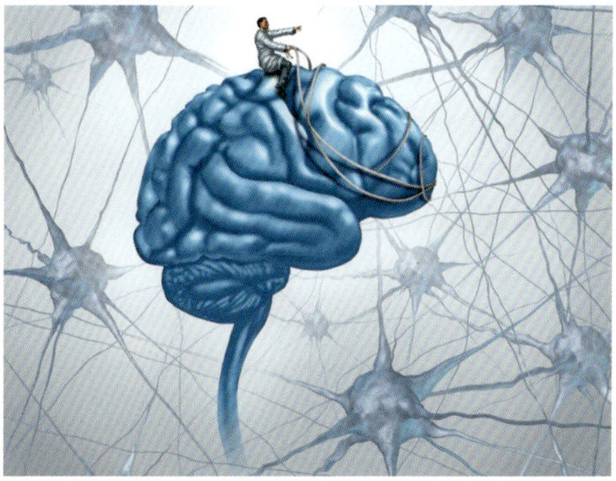

BDNF binds to receptors in the synapses between neurons, increasing voltage (yes your brain is electric!) and improving signal strength. BDNF inside the cells activates genes that increase production of more BDNF and other important proteins as well as serotonin. Low levels of BDNF have been associated with depression and even suicide. Serotonin has a reciprocal relationship with BDNF, i.e. BDNF boosts serotonin production and serotonin signalling stimulates BDNF expression.

One of the most exciting changes that exercise causes is neurogenesis, or the creation of new neurons. The new neurons are created in the hippocampus, the center of learning and memory in the brain. There also seems to be a role for neurogenesis in the treatment of depression. Studies show that the hippocampus of depressed women can be up to 15% smaller than normal.

This damage may be reversed by BDNF-stimulated neurogenesis. BDNF as the key chemical underlying exercises impact on the hippocampus. Perhaps it is not exercise that has the curative power, but rather BDNF, and exercise is only the trigger.

Exercise for a bigger brain

Humans start to lose nerve tissue beginning at age 30. Aerobic exercise reinforces neural connections by increasing the number of dendrite connections between neurons, creating a denser network, which is then better able to process and store information. Norman Doidge, MD, author of "The Brain that Changes Itself", writes: The idea that the brain is like a muscle that grows with exercise, is not just a metaphor. Just like a muscle, the brain grows thicker as we use it.

Endurance exercise appears to increase the brain's capacity to concentrate. After rigorous exercise people are more attentive and ,because they can concentrate better, they have the ability to process and retain more information.

Exercise is great for our brain health and helps increase blood flow to the brain, increase serotonin levels and produces BDNF.

In a German study volunteers who did two 3 minute sprints (separated by 2 minutes of lower intensity) during the course of a forty-minute treadmill session demonstrated higher increases in BDNF than non-sprinters. Not only that, the sprinters learned vocabulary words 20% faster than non-sprinting exercisers. It seems even a small amount of high-intensity exertion can have a profound effect on your brain.

Conclusion

From the information you have just read on the brain, I hope dearly that you nourish your brain with the correct nutrients to allow it to function at optimum efficiency. When the brain is well nourished, you must programme it with healing thoughts, positive thinking and not allow negative emotions affect your life.

I highly recommend the books written by David R. Hamilton and "Deadly Emotions" written by Don Colbert. I also recommend;

- "Change your thoughts change your life" - Dr Wayne Dyer
- "Change your brain change your body" - Dr Daniel Amen
- "Your miracle brain" - Jean Carper
- "The Natural Way to Beat Depression" - Dr Basant Puri & Hilary Boyd
- "Brain Longevity" - Dharma Singh Khalsa
- "The UltraMind Solution" - Mark Hyman
- "Spontaneous Evolution" - Bruce Lipton & Steve Bhaerman
- "Molecules of Emotion" - Candace Pert
- "The Biology of Belief" - Bruce Lipton
- "The Omega Diet" - Artemis Simopoulos & jo Robinson
- Dr. Mercola Website
- "Gut and Psychology Syndrome" Dr. Natasha Campbell - McBride

HABIT 4

HORMONES, MITOCHONDRIA AND METABOLISM: THE KEYS TO FAT LOSS SUCCESS

Hormones and mitochondria can have a profound effect on our metabolism and therefore our fat loss. Optimising our metabolism can help us burn more calories and help us select the correct fuels to burn for energy.

- ***what are hormones and mitochondria***
- ***is a calorie just a calorie***
- ***what hormones are important for fat loss***
- ***what causes damage to our mitochonria***

"You only live once, but if you do it right, once is enough."

Mae West

Metabolism from the Hormonal Perspective

The Fat "Storer"		The Fat "Burner"	
Hormone Levels		Hormone Levels	
Glucagon	Low ▼	Glucagon	High ▲
Cortisol	High ▲	Cortisol	Low ▼
Human Growth Hormone	Low ▼	Human Growth Hormone	High ▲
Insulin	High ▲	Insulin	Low ▼
Leptin	High ▲	Leptin	Low ▼
Adiponectin	Low ▼	Adiponectin	High ▲
Testosterone	Low ▼	Testosterone	High ▲
Thyroid Hormone	Low ▼	Thyroid Hormone	Optimum
Oestrogen	High ▲	Oestrogen	Low ▼
Progesterone	Low ▼	Progesterone	High ▲
DHEA	Low ▼	DHEA	High ▲

Take a look at the table for a summary of which are our fat storing hormones and which are our fat burning hormones.

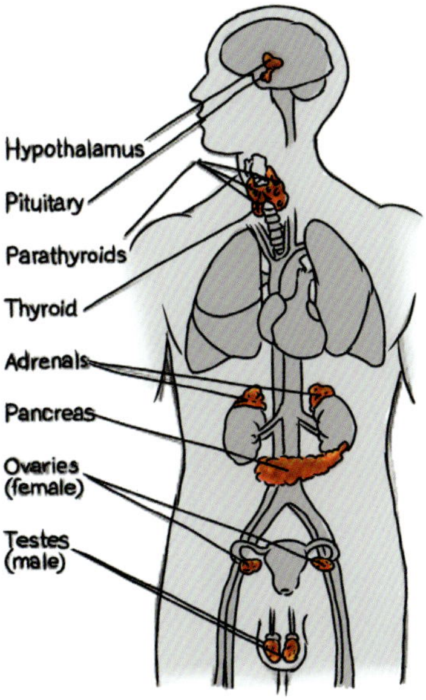

As this book talks a lot about hormones and mitochondria I thought it would be wise to dedicate a habit so that you become familiar with the terminology of endocrinology (study of hormones) and our little energy factories (mitochondria). When you understand the fundamentals of hormones and mitochondria you will never look at fat loss the same; you will quickly realise that, for example, counting calories is simply ineffective for fat loss.

Remember there are two things which can either make us fat, tired and depressed or lean, energised and happy? They are hormones and mitochondria.

Why is it that two people can eat the same amount of food and one gains weight while the other one does not? It's **METABOLISM**!

What regulates metabolism? Your **HORMONES & MITOCHONDRIA.**

Unfortunately, as you read in habit 1, there are so many endocrine disrupting hormones and heavy metals which interfere with both our hormones and mitochondria. That's why it's essential, in the toxic world of the 21st century, to detoxify correctly and eat organic foods, drink clean water and use washware products free from endocrine disrupting chemicals.

Hormones and mitochondria will determine whether you are lean or obese - it really is that simple.

However, be aware of the metabolism myth - because we equate thinness with health, you may think that because someone can eat what they want and not put on weight, they must have a healthy metabolism. However, this is not always true because the physiological definition of a healthy metabolism refers to all the processes of efficient regeneration, building up and using functional and structural proteins and fats and not just the ability to burn off sugar and stored fat as energy. Someone may not gain any weight and eat a truck load of food every day simply because they have very inefficient digestive systems and genuinely could be starving of nutrients due to a malfunctioning gut.

The Calorie Myth

Food as a profound effect on your hormonal response in regards to weight gain or weight loss and you should be more concerned with your carbohydrate, protein and fat ratios, and how this can affect your metabolism, more so than the amount of calories on your plate. Why? The whole weight loss industry is based on the myth of counting calories. From a hormonal perspective all calories are not alike and recent studies confirm this point.

A study led by Walter Willett, M.D., and his group from Harvard School of Public Health designed a study to determine whether low fat or low carbohydrate diets were better for losing fat. The results were startling. For twelve weeks, the researchers fed their group of overweight patients three different diets, all carefully controlled and prepared in a Boston restaurant.

- The first group ate a low fat diet of 1500 calories (55% carbohydrate, 30% fat, 15% protein) for the women and 1,800 calories for the men.
- The second group ate the exact same number of calories but from a low carbohydrate diet (5% carbohydrate, 30% protein, 65% fat).
- The third group also consumed a low carbohydrate diet, but they ate 300 more calories a day than the other group 1,800 for the women and 2,100 for the men.

The researchers discovered that the low carb group eating the same number of calories as the low fat group actually lost more weight. The low carb group lost on average 23 pounds, compared to 17 pounds for the low fat group, despite consuming exactly the same number of calories. What was more startling was the group eating 300 more calories a day than the low carb diet lost more weight than those eating the low fat diet, even though they consumed

25,000 more calories - which should have amounted to 7 pounds of increased weight. They actually lost an average of 20 pounds, or 3 pounds more than the low fat group, who ate 25,000 fewer calories during the 12 weeks.

In another study from the University of Washington School of Medicine, 19 subjects were fed each of three diets sequentially. For two weeks they followed a weight-maintenance diet comprising 15% protein, 35% fat, and 50% carbohydrate. For the next two weeks they followed a high-protein diet of equal calories. The macronutrient breakdown of this diet was 30% protein, 20% fat, and 50% carbohydrate. Finally, the subjects switched to a high-protein diet with the same macronutrient breakdown but no calorie restriction - subjects were allowed to eat as much or as little as they pleased. They stayed on this last diet for 12 weeks.

The authors of the study reported that when subjects switched from the low-protein weight maintenance diet to the high-protein weight maintenance diet, they started feeling much fuller despite the fact that they were consuming the same number of calories. Even more significant, during the unrestricted high-protein diet phase, the subjects voluntarily reduced their daily eating by 441 calories per day and lost almost 11 pounds, including more than eight pounds of body fat, on average.

Getting an adequate amount of fat in the diet is essential for effective and permanent weight loss. When people get hungry soon after a meal, they tend to overeat at the next. One of the reasons why fat is necessary for successful weight loss is that it satisfies hunger, thus reducing appetite and lowering total food consumption. Fat slows down the emptying of the stomach so that you feel full longer. When you are less hungry during the day, you will cut down on snacks and eat less at mealtimes. As a result, you consume fewer calories. Even though fat contains more calories than either protein or carbohydrate, its effect on curbing appetite more than makes up for the extra calories it contains.

The appetite-suppressing effect of fat has been shown in many studies. For example, in one study, a group of women were given a mid-morning yogurt snack and then later served lunch and dinner. There were two choices of yogurt. One was regular full-fat and the other was low-fat. Each was labeled, but there was no mention of total calorie content. Each, however, contained the same number of calories. The only difference was the fat content. Participants were allowed to choose whichever one they wanted. When the women were later served lunch, those who had the high-fat yogurt ate less than those who ate the low-fat variety. The extra fat in the yogurt snack satisfied their hunger longer and encouraged them to eat less at lunch.

Researchers also wanted to learn if those who ate less at lunch would eventually make up for it at dinner. But at dinner the ones who ate the high-fat yogurt and less food at lunch didn't eat any more than the others. They weren't any hungrier for eating less at lunch. So at the end of the day those women who ate the high-fat yogurt ended up consuming fewer total calories than those who ate the low-fat snack. ***(Rolls, B.J. and Miller, D.L. 1997. Is the low-fat message giving people a license to eat more? Journal of the American College of Nutrition 16:535.)***

One study evaluated the body weight and fat storage for three different diets – a low-fat diet, a high-fat diet containing long chain triglycerides (LCTs), and a high-fat diet containing medium chain triglycerides (MCTs). Calorie content in the diets were elevated to induce weight gain. The testing period lasted for 44 days. At the end of that time, the low-fat diet group had stored an average of 0.47 grams of fat per day, and the LCT group 0.48 grams/day, while the MCT group deposited only 0.19 grams of fat per day. The MCT group had a 60 percent reduction in the amount of body fat stored as compared to the other diets. ***(Crozier G. et al. 1987. Metabolic effects induced by long-term feeding of medium-chain triglycerides in the rat. Metabolism 36:807-814.)***

Because MCTs are used by the body as a source of fuel to produce energy, they have a stimulatory effect on metabolism. Studies have shown that MCTs boost metabolism, thus increasing the body's use of calories. As a result, calories obtained from all the foods we eat are burned up at a higher rate, so that fewer remain to be packed away as body fat. This boost in metabolism remains elevated for as long as 24 hours after eating a meal containing MCTs. So you enjoy an increased level of energy and continue to burn calories at an accelerated rate for many hours after the meal.

This increase in metabolism also leads to a rise in body temperature. People with low thyroid function report that after using coconut oil which is very rich in medium chain triglycerides (MCT), their body temperature rises, often to normal levels, and remains elevated for many hours. Temperatures in such people can rise 1 or 2 degrees or more depending on the amount of oil they consume. Those people who are overweight because of low thyroid function can utilized the metabolic stimulating action of coconut oil to help them shed excess pounds.

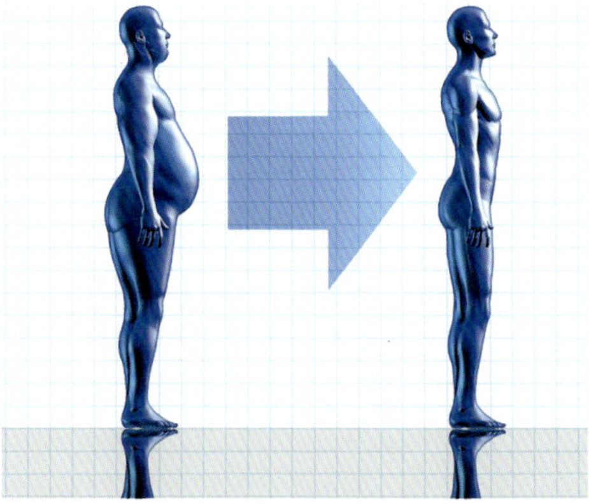

Because MCTs are used by the body as a source of fuel to produce energy, they have a stimulatory effect on metabolism.

Another interesting feature about coconut oil is that it helps to decrease total food and calorie consumption. Coconut oil is more satisfying than other fats. When added to meals people tend to eat less food and feel fuller longer, so they don't eat as much at the next meal. For example, in one study women were given a drink which contained either MCTs (from coconut oil) or an oil with LCTs. Thirty minutes later, they were offered lunch in which they could choose and eat as much as they wanted. The women who had the MCT oil before the meal ate less food, and as the authors of the study stated, "significantly decreased caloric intake in the lunch." ***(Rolls, B.J. et al. 1988. Food intake in dieters and non dieters after a liquid meal containing medium-chain triglycerides. Am. J. Clin. Nutr. 48(1):66.)***

In another study, a group of normal-weight men were fed a meal for breakfast differing only in the type of fat used. Later, food intakes at lunch and dinner were measured. Those eating breakfasts containing MCTs ate less at lunchtime. At dinner there was no difference. This study showed that when MCTs were eaten at one meal, hunger is forestalled for longer and less food is eaten at the next. Also important was that even though subjects ate less at lunch, they did not make up for it by eating more at diner. Total daily food intake decreased. ***"Van Wymelbeke, V., et al. 1998. Influence of medium-chain and long-chain triacylglycerols on the control of food intake in men. Am. J. Clin. Nutr. 68:226-234."***

Now let's look at what happens when one of the world's leading weight loss experts, Professor Jennie Brand-Miller from the University of Sydney, fed rats exactly the same number of calories; except one group of rats calories came from high glycaemic load (GL) foods and the other group of rats came from low GL foods. At the end of the 32 week trial **the low GL rats gained no weight whilst the high GL rats gained weight week on week, pound after pound.** By the end of the 32 weeks, the high GL group were not only 16% heavier but they had gained 40% more body fat on the same number of calories proving that all calories are not equal when it comes to increasing weight!

Example of some effects of certain foods on the glycaemic load!

Low Glycaemic Load	Medium Glycaemic Load	High Glycaemic Load
• apples • carrots • peanuts • beetroot • strawberry • watermelon	• bananas • wild rice • pineapple	• white rice • white potato • raisins

What is Glycaemic Load?

It's a unit of measurement that tells you exactly what a particular food will do to your blood sugar. Foods with a high GL have a greater effect on your blood sugar, which isn't desirable. Foods with a low GL encourage the body to burn fat, which is what we're aiming for. Keeping your blood sugar balanced is the concept at the heart of the low GL diet – sustainable weight loss will follow.

When your blood sugar level increases, the hormone insulin is released into the bloodstream to remove the glucose (sugar). Some glucose goes to the brain and muscles where it's used as an energy fuel, but any excess goes to the liver where it's turned into fat and stored, causing you to gain weight. Insulin is known as the fat-storing hormone.

GL is based on the glycaemic index (GI). Put simply, the glycaemic index of a food tells you whether the carbohydrate in a food is fast or slow releasing (fast is bad, slow is good). What it doesn't tell you is exactly how much of the food is carbohydrate. GL on the other hand tells you both the type and amount of carbohydrate in the food and what that particular carbohydrate does to your blood sugar.

A study by a Harvard professor Dr. David Ludwig, studied three groups of overweight children, in which they fed each group a breakfast containing an identical number of calories. One group ate instant oatmeal, one group ate steel cut oats, and the third group had a vegetable omelette and fruit.

Their blood was measured before they ate and every 30 minutes afterwards for the next 5 hours. Then they ate a lunch that was identical to the meal they had eaten for breakfast. After finishing lunch, they were told to eat whenever they were very hungry for the rest of the afternoon. What happened was very interesting. The group that ate the instant oatmeal (the breakfast that entered the bloodstream and turned to sugar the fastest) ate 81% more food in the afternoon than the group that had the omelette and fruit. Not only were they hungrier, but their blood tests looked entirely different. The instant oatmeal group had higher levels of insulin, blood sugar, blood fats, and adrenaline even though they had consumed the same number of calories as the omelette group. The steel cut oats group also ate 51% more food in the afternoon than the children who ate the omelette and fruit.

The conclusion here is that the kinds of calories you consume have a big impact on how much weight you gain, because different foods are metabolised in different ways. Also, the foods you eat will have an effect on which hormones are stimulated and if your mitochondria function optimally. This can have a profound effect on body fat composition as well as physical and emotional well being. This is why any diet which bases its philosophy on calories is one you should look at with extreme caution because in reality counting calories simply doesn't work long term.

Hormones

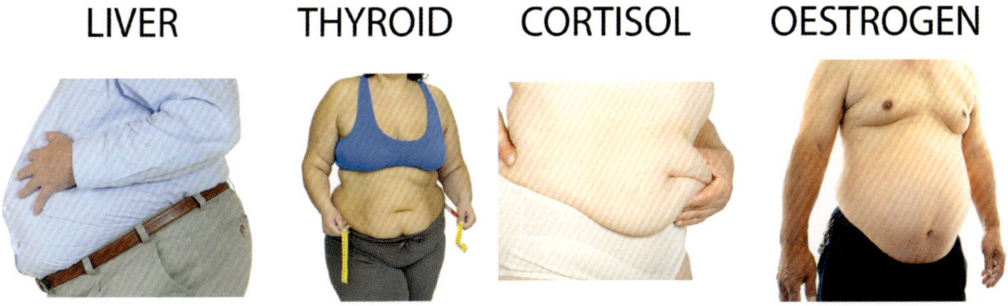

The outside of the body gives clues as to what's going on inside from a hormonal perspective and how/where you carry your fat. For example in the case of the adrenals if they are constantly bombarded with stress then as the result of excess cortisol you will tend to store fat around the abdominals (belly fat) and have skinny arms and legs. If there is an excess of oestrogen you'll see excess fat accumulate around the hips and thighs and if you are a man you get the added bonus of moobs. When there is an weakness in the thyroid gland there will be an appearance of excess weight all over due to the effect of the thyroid on metabolism. The liver can also indicate a pot belly look alike symptom which could signal liver toxicity which will also affect your ability to lose excess weight.The liver can actually swell to the size of a football. When you become insulin resistance you tend to resemble an apple shape due to excess fat storage on your gut!

For us to know how to optimize hormone and mitochondrial function, it is important for us first to know how hormones and mitochondria work at making our metabolisms function efficiently. But, you must always remember that for hormones & mitochondria to work at full efficiency they are both at the total reliance of the health of our cells and the environment of the cells. Look at cells like little people; keep them happy, feed them optimally and create the right environment and they will do an incredible job for you in return. Piss them off with negative thoughts, junk food and an hostile acidic environment and you will have a rebellion on your hands and your metabolism will grind to a halt and you will become sick, tired and obese.

Within the body there are various type of hormones which can have various effects;

- We have anabolic hormones like testosterone and growth hormone which increase muscle mass and decrease our fat stores.
- We have catabolic hormones like cortisol and glucagon which can break down muscle and convert it into energy during times of calorie restriction, high protein diets and excess stress.
- We have lipogenic hormones such as oestrogen and insulin which stores fat. Insulin can also be anabolic; it can wear two hats, which I will get into later.
- We have lipolytic hormones which help us burn fat such as glucagon, growth hormone, leptin, testosterone and the master blaster thyroid hormones.

Hormones tell your body whether to burn fat or to store fat and they also tell your body either to build muscle or cannibalise muscle. Therefore understanding how to get hormones on your side is essential if losing fat and gaining lean muscle tissue is your goal.

Men and Women have exactly the same hormones, only in different amounts.

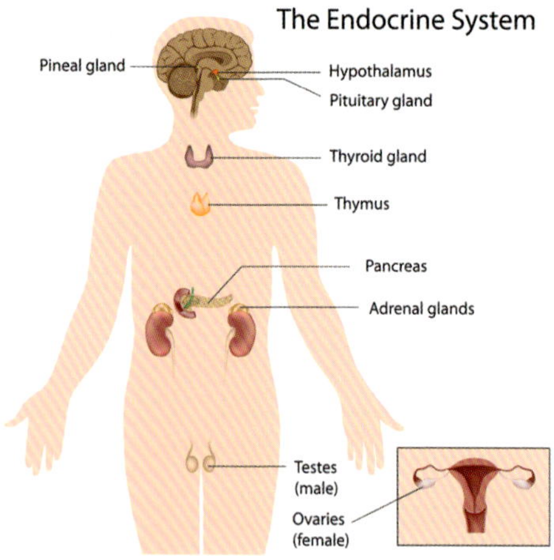

Hormones are secreted by the various cells, tissues and organs of the endocrine system. Natural hormones, the hormones our body makes, are usually short lived, staying in the blood stream for only a few minutes, or at most a few hours.

This is just long enough to deliver their message. After the hormone has delivered its message, enzymes from the liver break up the hormones into pieces that are either flushed out as waste or re-used to build other molecules.

Put simply, hormones are the body's chemical messengers that relay a signal from cell to cell. As profound orchestrator of all of life's processes, maintaining hormonal balance is imperative for optimum health. The entire hormonal system is interconnected. Therefore a change in one hormone equals a change in all hormones.

Remember, natural hormones are so potent that they can produce very dramatic changes in cellular activity with very small amounts known as part-per-billion, or even parts-per-trillion, so minute that only extremely sensitive tests can measure them. **Parts per trillion is equal to half a teaspoon of salt in 1000 Olympic sized swimming pool.**

All endocrine glands are ultimately controlled by the hypothalamus located deep within the brain. The hunger centre in the brain is also located in the hypothalamus and is the main site of action for leptin, adiponectin and other hunger hormones. The hypothalamus therefore is the main appetite centre in the brain as well as being in control for most of our endocrine system.

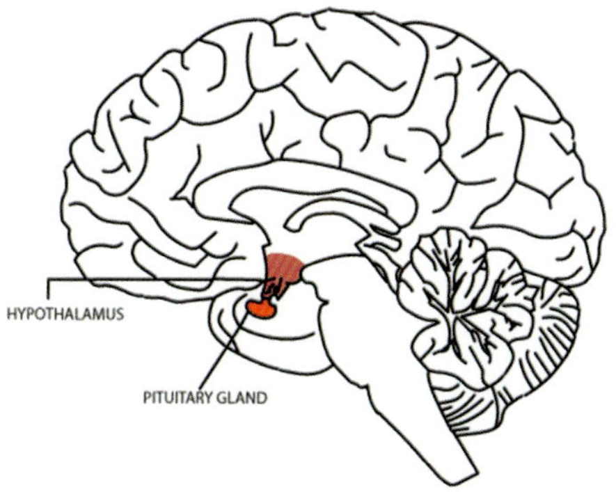

The hypothalamus and pituitary gland

The hypothalamus produces two types of regulating hormones, releasing ones and inhibiting ones, all of which act on the pituitary.

The portal system within the stalk carries these command hormones from the hypothalamus to the front end of the pituitary, which is called the anterior pituitary. There are also some hormones which are produced by the hypothalamus and then stored in the posterior pituitary gland prior to being released into the bloodstream. These are: Anti-diuretic hormone which controls water balance and blood pressure. It is made by the hypothalamus but is stored in the posterior pituitary gland prior to being released into the bloodstream. Oxytocin which stimulates uterine contractions during labour and milk secretion during breastfeeding. It is made by the hypothalamus but is stored in the posterior pituitary gland prior to being released into the bloodstream.

The pituitary and hypothalamus effectively function together as one unit, known as the hypothalamic – pituitary axis.

The hypothalamus is in control because it is wired directly into its ultimate master, the brain. Everything you experience or perceive from running from an hairy arsed tiger, to a hot romance, to seeing no food in the fridge (where you thought there was a cream cake);

the brain gets to know first that it has to make decisions about what to do next and what hormones to release.

Our Thoughts Control Our Emotions And Our Emotions Control Our Hormones.

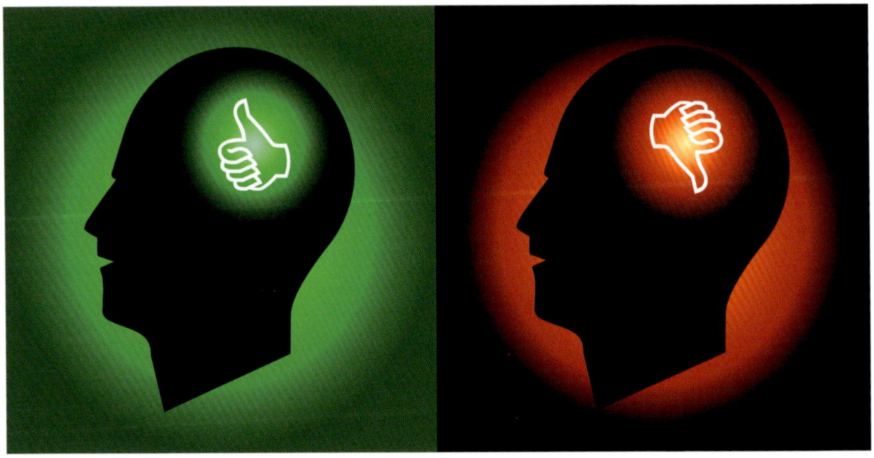

What are hormones made of?

Hormones can be subdivided into groups based upon the dietary precursors from which they are derived. Polypeptide hormones are derived from amino acids, steroid hormones are derived from cholesterol and eicosanoids are generated from essential fatty acids. Therefore, you can see that your diet has a major impact on providing the building blocks for making these critical signalling agents.

As well as our hormones being derived from food, food also has a massive influence on how our hormones behave as we have just read about earlier in this habit. For example carbohydrates stimulate insulin, protein stimulates glucagon and fat is neutral but the building material for our steroid hormones.

There are nine known groupings of endocrine hormone glands: three in the brain (pineal, pituitary and hypothalamus); three more in the throat (thyroid, parathyroids and thymus); two are in the abdominal region the adrenals and the pancreas; then the gonads testes for males, ovaries for females. But we also now know that fat cells. heart, kidneys and stomach produce hormones as well, remember endocrinology the study of hormones is still in it's infancy as a profession and no doubt over the coming decades many more hormones and functions will come to light.

What types of hormones are there? Hormones can be divided up on the basis of their chemical structure into 6 groups:		
1. Those derived directly from the amino acid tyrosine, including: • thyroxine • triiodothyronine • adrenaline • noradrenaline	2. Those made up of short chains of amino acids, including: • adrenocorticotropic hormone (ACTH) • corticotropin releasing hormone (CRH) • thyrotropin releasing hormone (TRH)	3. Those made up of long chains of amino acids, including: • insulin • growth hormone (GH) • prolactin • parathyroid hormone (PTH) • cholecystokinin (CCK) • secretin
4. Those made up of proteins linked with glucose molecules forming glycoproteins, including: • thyroid stimulating hormone (TSH) • follicle stimulating hormone (FSH) • luteinising hormone (LH)	5. Those derived from cholesterol thus forming lipid soluble steroid hormones, including: • oestrogen • progesterones • testosterone • androstenedione • aldosterone • cortisol	6. The essential fatty acids omega-3 and omega-6 are transformed in the body into hormones called eicosanoids. They control other hormones and practically all important functions in the body.

Fat is also part of endocrine system!

Fat is actually the largest endocrine gland in the body. Fat cells up until not so long ago were simply seen as primarily biological storage bins for excess calories. Today we know that fat cells do much more than simply store excess calories for a rainy day, body fat forms a complex, sophisticated hormonal system that is very much involved in human physiology.

As they say when you are purchasing a property - location matters! It can mean the difference to the value of the property and the quality of facilities near you. It's the same with body fat; where you store it has a significant effect on your health, from cardiovascular problems, the development of diabetes, arthritis and cancer. Body fat can be divided into two categories one being essential fat and the other storage fat. Essential fat is just that - it's necessary for normal, healthy functioning and is found in relatively small amounts in your bone marrow, organs, central nervous system and muscles. In men, essential fat constitutes approximately 3% of their body weight, whereas women is about 12%. This is because women's essential fat is critical for reproduction function, it's found in the breasts, pelvis, hips, and thighs. Storage fat, on the other hand, is the fat you accumulate beneath your skin (subcutaneous fat), in your muscles, and in specific areas inside your body.

Carrying excess fat around your abdominal region puts you at greater risk for disease than fat stored on your butt, hips, upper arms, and thighs. Why is visceral fat the medical term for abdominal fat such a problem to our health? Excess body fat is a silent killer; this type of fat actively releases fatty acids, inflammatory compounds, aromatase (an enzyme which converts testosterone into oestrogen), hormones that lead to increased blood fats, blood glucose, and blood pressure. One of the explanations for visceral fat toxicity has been it's related to an overactive stress response in the body.

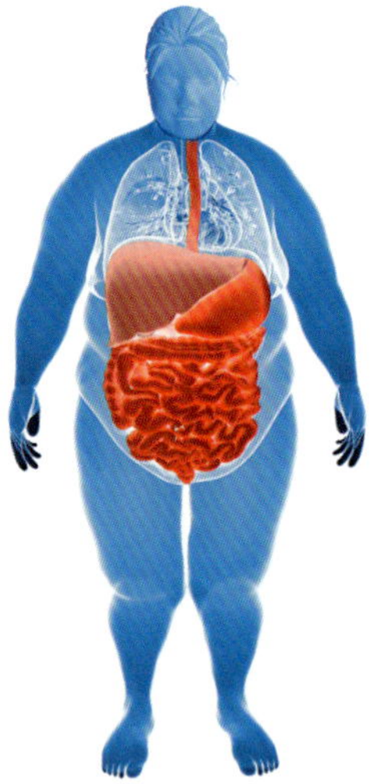

Excess fat, especially around your abdominal region, is very detrimental to your health.

Unlike other body fat, visceral fat cells are unique in that they release their metabolic products directly into what's called the portal circulation which is the passage of blood from the gastrointestinal tract and spleen through the portal vein to the liver. As a result, visceral fat cells that are enlarged and weighed down by excess triglycerides pour free fatty acids straight into the liver which creates more work for an already overworked liver.

According to a Mayo Clinic observational study involving nearly thirteen thousand Americans over about fourteen years, led by Dr. Francisco Lopez-Jimenez, people who are normal weight but have a high waist to hip ratio (belly fat) have an even higher risk of death than people who are considered obese based on BMI (body mass index) alone.

How to calculate waist-to-hip ratio

Working out the risk to your health is simple. Using a tape measure, take the following steps:

- Measure your hips
- Measure your waist
- Divide the waist number by the hip number

A ratio of 1.0 or more in men or 0.85 or more in women indicates that you are carrying too much weight around your middle. This puts you at increased risk of diseases that are linked to obesity, such as type 2 diabetes and heart disease.

Ideal Waist Measurement
For women:

- Ideal: less than 80cm (32")
- High: 80cm to 88cm (32" to 35")
- Very high: more than 88cm (35")

Ideal Waist Measurement
For men:

- Ideal: less than 94cm (37")
- High: 94cm to 102cm (37" to 40")
- Very high: more than 102cm (40")

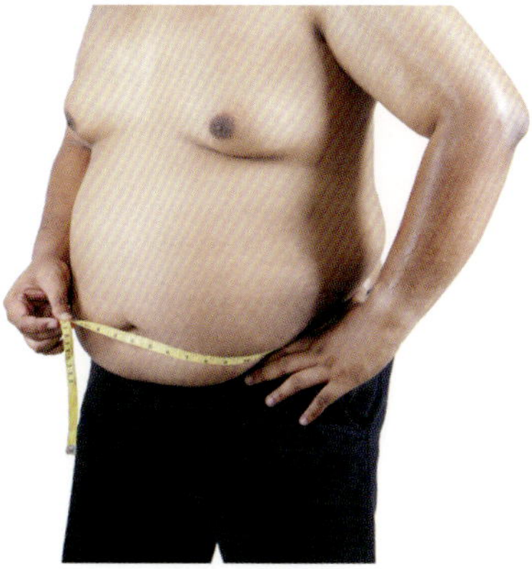

The risk of cardiovascular death was 2.75 times higher, and the risk of death from all causes was 2.08 times higher in people of normal weight with central obesity, compared to those with a normal body mass index and normal waist to hip ratio. The increased mortality risk accompanying higher ratios of visceral fat is at least part due to increased insulin resistance. And we know that insulin resistance in general is one of the primary problems underlying virtually all diseases.

As I said at the beginning of this book, measuring body fat % is the most intelligent way to see if you are carrying excess fat, but the waist to hip and waist ratios show us once again it's not necessary how heavy or fat you are, it's where you carry the fat that could be your problem. You will find out in habit 6 why we tend to store more fat on our stomachs and what the best solution is to shift this excess body fat and trust me, it's not situps.

Adipocytes (fat cells) function to store calories in the body. When energy is needed, specific command signals mobilize adipocytes to release their stored fat. The adipocyte is the primary site for fat storage. Under the microscope, adipocytes appear bloated with triglycerides, which is the form which most fat exists in the body.

Weight gain occurs when adipocytes (fat cells) accumulate a large amount of triglycerides and become enlarged. Obesity is characterized at the cellular level by an increase in the number and size of adipocytes in fat tissue. Adipocytes accumulate excess triglycerides due to overeating, insufficient physical activity, hormone imbalance, toxins and other causes. The fat cells give many command signals to the body but lets look at three which are very important for decreasing body fat to a healthy level.

Three important adipocyte command signals for fat loss

1) Adipocytes regulate their size and number by secreting command signals. One such signal is the hormone leptin, which is derived from the Greek term "leptos", meaning thin. Leptin is released by adipocytes to perform two critical functions. First it signals the brain that enough food has been ingested and shuts down appetite. It then seems to exert a process whereby triglycerides stored in adipocytes are broken down into fatty acids that can be used in energy production
2) The second command signal released by adipocytes is a hormone called adiponectin. This hormone is an important modulator of insulin sensitivity. High circulating levels of adiponectin have been shown to protect against coronary artery disease, whereas low adiponectin levels are observed in overweight individuals. The insulin-sensitizing effects of adiponectin represent a novel treatment target for insulin resistance, Type 2 diabetes, and obesity.
3) The third adipocyte command signal is glycerol-3-phosphate dehydrogenase. This enzyme is produced in adipocytes to help convert blood sugar into triglyceride stores in fat cells.

Leptin

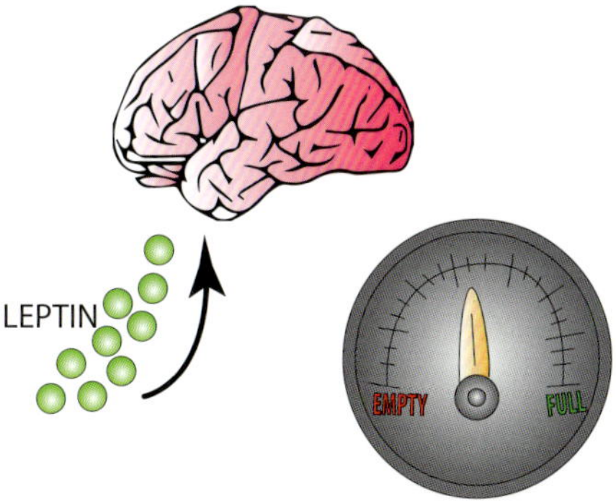

The word leptin derives from the Greek word "leptos" meaning thin. It sends a signal to your brain about how much fuel you have within your body.

Eating in harmony with leptin is essential for healthy metabolism. When released by adipocytes, leptin performs two critical roles. First, it stimulates centres in our brain to give us the signal of satiety. This means, we "feel full", and stop eating. The other important job that leptin has is to help us access and utilize fat stores for fuel in our body. In other words, leptin helps us burn our stored fat.

Leptin is actually made in your white adipose tissue or stored fat. This finding alone has revolutionized the entire field of endocrinology – as previously stored fat was just thought to be a warehouse for extra calories. Our new understanding means that your stored fat is actually a metabolic organ, much like your thyroid gland or adrenal glands.

Leptin is one of the most important hormones that regulates your body weight. It works with thyroid hormone, insulin, growth hormone, and adrenal hormones (like cortisol). Following a meal leptin is released from your fat, enters your blood, and travels to your brain. It delivers a message that you are full and also lets your brain know how much fuel you have on hand (like the petrol gauge in your car).

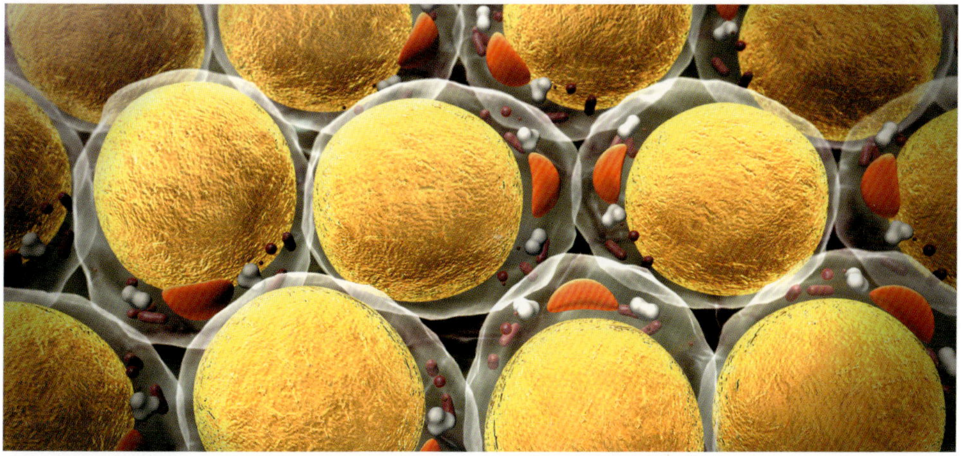

Leptin, when working efficiently, signals to fat cells to release fat which is then used as fuel.

So, given that leptin gives the "stop eating" message, it may seem illogical that leptin is much more abundant in the blood of obese individuals, but this is because obese people have more adipocytes that secrete leptin and C-reactive protein. C-reactive protein (CRP) is a marker of systemic inflammation and predictor of cardiac risk. As our abdominal girth increases, pro-oxidant cytokines, such as CRP, react with fat and create oxidized free radicals which can lead to atherosclerosis (hardened arteries), heart attack, stroke and cancer.

In fact the hormone leptin actually reacts and binds with the pro-inflammatory marker CRP. CRP binds with leptin and blocks both the leptin transport across the blood-brain-barrier to signal satiety and also blocks the leptin signalling at a cellular level to break fatty acids down for energy expenditure. Hence, the release of CRP by adipocytes is a leptin-binding protein and neutralizes the natural adipocyte-controlling effects of leptin. The result is a vicious fat cycle, where more leptin accumulates in the blood of obese individuals because it is not able to be picked up by leptin receptor sites on cell membranes. This is leptin resistance. In habit 8 there are effective protocols for lowering CRP levels.

How Do You Become Leptin Resistant?

You become leptin-resistant by the same general mechanism that you become insulin-resistant – by continuous overexposure to high levels of the hormone. If you eat a diet that is high in sugar (particularly fructose), grains, and processed foods – the same type of diet that will also increase inflammation in your body – as the sugar gets metabolised in your fat cells, the fat releases surges in leptin. Over time, if your body is exposed to too much leptin, it will become resistant, just as your body can become resistant to insulin. The only known way to re-establish proper leptin (and insulin) signalling is to prevent those surges, and the only known way to do that is via diet. **As such, diet can have a more profound effect on your health than any other known modality or medical treatment.**

You must keep leptin in a state of healthy balance for your metabolism to work correctly and your appetite to be under control. This is not a situation where you take leptin hormone as a substance. This is a case wherein diet, exercise, lifestyle (stress management in particular), restful sleep, and various nutrients all help to optimize leptin function in your body.

Allow 11-12 hours between dinner and breakfast. Never go to bed on a full stomach. Finish eating dinner at least three hours before bed. One of leptin's main rhythms follows a 24-hour pattern. Leptin levels are highest in the evening hours. This is because leptin, like the conductor in the orchestra, sets the timing for night time repair. It coordinates the timing and release of melatonin, thyroid hormone, growth hormone, sex hormones, and immune system function to carry out rejuvenating sleep. It does this while burning fat at the maximum rate compared to any other time of the day. And it does this only if you will allow it, by not eating after dinner.

Allow 5-6 hours between meals. Do not snack. It is vital to create times during the day when triglycerides (fats) are cleared from your blood. If triglycerides build up during the day they physically clog leptin entry into your brain, causing leptin resistance – meaning that leptin cannot register properly in your brain to signal satiety. **Your metabolism is not designed to deal with constant eating and snacking. Doing so confuses your metabolism and results in you eating much more than you really need.**

Yes, you are supposed to get a snack between meals – but it is supposed to come from your liver. **Snacking turns out to be one of the worst things you can do for fat loss. It doesn't matter how many calories you snack on, when you snack you throw powerful hormonal switches that cause leptin to malfunction and insulin will always remain high, which means you can not burn fat.** The fictitious idea that snacking is needed to stoke your metabolism or maintain your blood sugar is in no small part behind dietary advice that has helped cause an epidemic of obesity.

Drink water or a green drink in between meals. This keeps hunger at bay and gives the body incredible nutrition without hormonal spikes. However, if you participate in intense physical exercise, then I can categorically say that you must snack in between meals. You will achieve outstanding body composition results whilst following such a regime and I cover this in great depth in Habit 9 of this book on nutrient timing and digestion.

Do not overeat at meals!!!

DO NOT EAT LARGE MEALS. Always try to finish a meal when slightly less than full. The "full" signal will usually catch up in 10-20 minutes after completing your meal. Eating slowly is important for improved digestion and for sending "I'm full" signals to your brain.

So you can now see it is very important getting leptin on your side in you ability to drop body fat. Properly working leptin permits fat burning to occur. It is the hormone that controls the rate of fat burning in the liver, muscles, pancreas, and heart. Once fat utilization is disturbed, carbohydrates also turn into fat. This means that insulin resistance can be a consequence of leptin resistance. If you are leptin resistant then there is a very strong likelihood that carbohydrates will be converted into fat, because of the body's inability to burn fat. I must credit Byron Richards and his book "Mastering Leptin", which allowed me to understand the real truth about leptin and its role in fat loss and health.

Adiponectin and Inflammation

Adipose tissue contains immune cells that in overweight people crank out inflammatory signals, TNFa and IL-6, twenty four hours a day, seven days a week. This is a relentless form of stress and not only do overweight people have to deal with the stress of life, they have to deal with the stress of highly inflammatory immune signals being generated by the extra pounds of fat they carry.

Changing the type of fat in your diet can have a profound effect on these inflammatory signals dampening them down so you can overcome leptin resistance, reduce CRP and cortisol levels and this my friend makes losing body fat possible. Omega 3 fats, such as fish oil, for example, can reduce TNFa and IL-6 (inflammatory signals) from the white adipose tissue. Individuals in inflammatory states such as rheumatoid arthritis can reduce their inflammatory signals by a large percentage using pharmaceutical grade fish oil. For example, in a recent study, fish oil and GLA demonstrated the ability to reduce pro-inflammatory immune cell activity by up to 65% percent within four weeks. And, this was one reason I added GLA to my ultimate fish oil products.

Adiponectin, like leptin, is a hormone secreted from your adipose tissue. It is a powerful hormone that regulates insulin function and reduces inflammation in your circulatory system. High levels of adiponectin are associated with low levels of body fat. As the amount of fat tissue increases, the level of adiponectin decreases making you more likely to become insulin resistance. Larger fat cells naturally produce less adiponectin. Levels of adiponectin also appear to be directly related to abdominal fat.

While a variety of nutrients have been shown to support healthy levels of adiponectin, a new study points out that the basics of increased fibre, fish oil intake, and regular exercise all help raise your adiponectin levels. A review of the scientific literature regarding the influence of diet and adiponectin levels showed that daily intake of fish or omega-3 supplementation increased adiponectin levels by 14-60%. A 60-115% increase in adiponectin levels was also obtained with fibre supplementation.

How Hormones Affect Cells

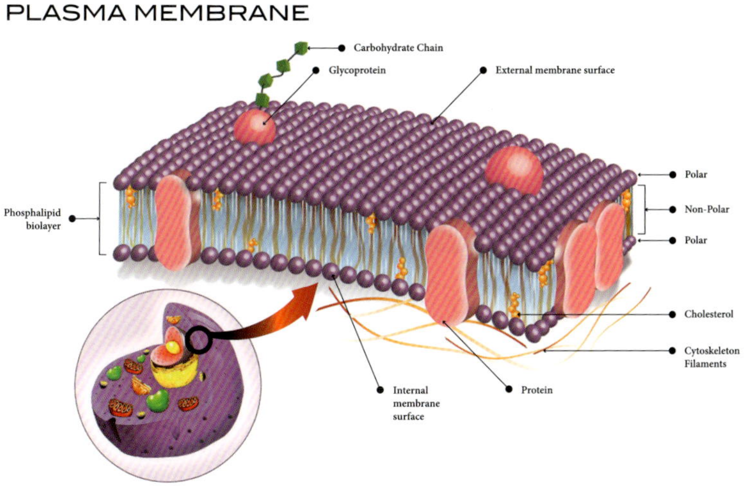

On the surface of cells are receptors that hormones joins with. These receptors and the hormones are created so specifically for one another that the hormone dispatched never adheres to the wrong receptor.

Every hormone thus resembles a key, and the receptor affected by it resembles a special lock that only that key can open. Virtually every cell in the body is studded with thousands of tiny structures called receptors. Think of receptors like our eyes, ears, nose, smell and sense of touch. Their job is to pick up signals coming at them from the surrounding space. **They are so important that, 40% of our DNA is devoted to making sure that they're perfectly reproduced from generation to generation.**

Once the receptors receive a signal, the information is transferred deep within the cell's interior. The information coming in directs things like cell division, cell migration for attacking enemies, making repairs and cell metabolism, to name but a few of the myriad of activities that are going on in our incredible cells.

The signal comes from other cells and is carried by our hormones, neurotransmitters and peptides referred to as ligands. The term ligand comes from the Latin word "to bind", and is used because of the way the substances latch so tightly to the cell's surface receptors. Information carrying ligands are responsible for 98 % of all data transfer in our body and brain. The remaining 2% of communication takes place in the synapse, between brain cells firing and releasing neurotransmitters across a gap to attach to receptors and unload their information.

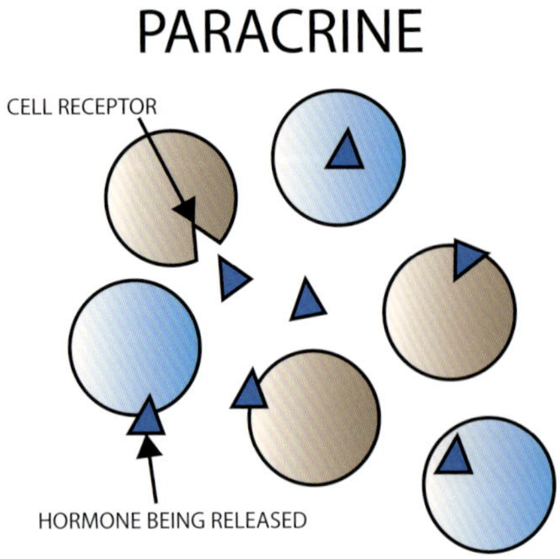

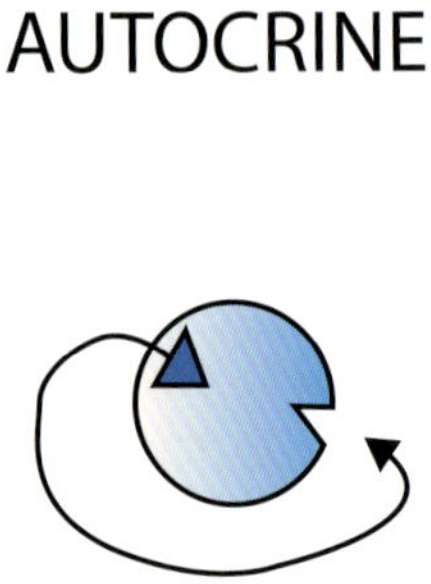

There are three distinct classes of hormone communication:
1. Endocrine - glands produce and release these hormones into the bloodstream, where they will travel and bind with a specific receptor.
2. Paracrine - these hormones don't travel randomly in the bloodstream. They are cell-to-cell regulators that have very defined constraints on how far they can travel. Examples of paracrine hormones are histamines which are released as local responses to stress and injury.
3. Autocrine - These hormones are sent out from the cell to test the immediate environment and then come back to report to that cell what lies just outside its perimeter. The most important autocrine hormones are the eicosanoids which are derived from essential fatty acids.

If the hormone can't get to its target site, it's as if it weren't there in the first place, even though there may be higher than normal levels of the hormone in the blood stream. This is why a lot of blood tests for hormones today simply don't tell you what's happening at the cellular level where it matters!

Endothelial cells that line blood vessels act as a barrier to either prevent or allow things, such as hormones, from entering target cells.

Getting to a target cell is no easy task for a hormone since most cells (muscles, heart tissue, lungs, and especially the brain) are protected from the bloodstream by the endothelial cells that line the blood vessel walls. These cells act as a potent barrier to prevent many things (based primarily on size) passing from the bloodstream into the space known as the interstitial space between the endothelial cells and the actual target tissues of the hormones.

If the endothelial cell barrier is functioning well, hormones are not impeded from reaching target cells. Any dysfunction to the endothelial cells will cause dysfunction of your hormonal system by decreasing the concentration of the active hormone in the interstitial space. We will discuss the health of the endothelium in greater detail in Habit 8.

Fat-soluble vitamin E and coenzyme Q10 protect the fatty cell membrane and the mitochondria, while water-based vitamin C and glutathione protect the cell interior. R-Lipoic acid has the unique ability to go anywhere.

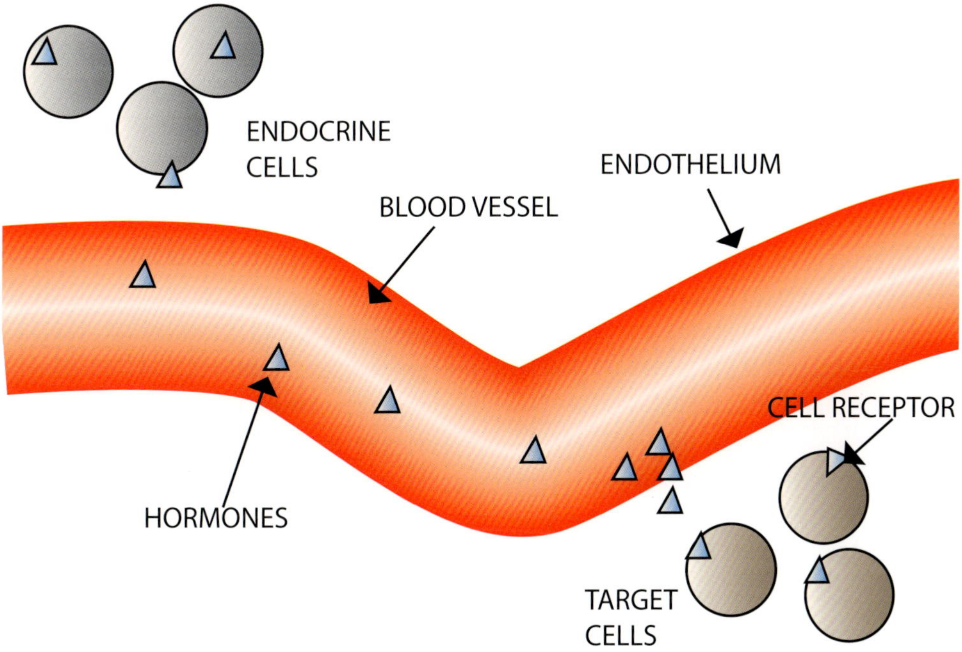

Free radicals, hydrogenated fat (trans fats), toxins and hormone disruptors have a combined effect of deafening the cell receptors to the talkative hormones. And this creates multiple health problems. Avoiding this is therefore a must for your hormonal health and quest for fat loss.

Cyclic AMP

Peptide hormones are composed of amino acids. A peptide hormone binds to a cell-surface receptor, it does not enter the cell. The resulting complex activates an enzyme that catalyses the synthesis of cyclic AMP from ATP. Cyclic AMP activates other enzymes that are inactive. Cyclic AMP is a second messenger; the hormone is the first messenger.

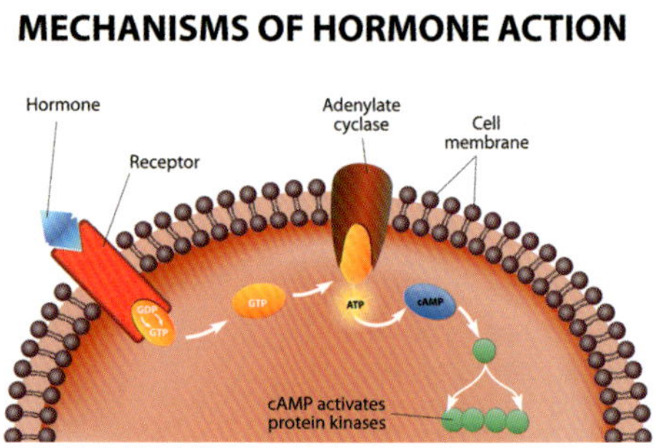

These are the key points of peptide hormone action and act through the following sequence of events:

1) A hormone, like insulin, docks on a cell receptor.
2) The receptor, which spans the membrane of the cell, undergoes a change that is transmitted to the interior of the cell.
3) Depending on the receptor and the hormone that has activated it, another molecule is synthesized within the cell that completes the message.
4) These new molecules are called second messengers of which there are two primary kind: Cyclic AMP, which is considered the "green light" for cells. "Good" eicosanoids interact with receptors that produce this second messenger. Inositol triphosphate is the equivalent to the "red light" for the cell and usually has a physiological action opposite to that of cyclic AMP. Bad eicosanoids use this pathway.
5) If the green light and red lights are balanced and working smoothly the result is wellness. If you have excess of red lights, then your traffic signals are out of balance, the result is the development of chronic disease.
6) The great complexity of your biological Internet comes down to maintaining the appropriate balance of green and red lights in each of the trillions of cells throughout the body.

Cyclic AMP levels are chronically diminished by elevated insulin levels! Growth hormone release and release of thyroid stimulating hormone need cyclic AMP before they can be released from the pituitary gland. Thyroid hormone will not be released into the bloodstream without cyclic AMP and the sleep inducing melatonin hormone will not be produced from serotonin without cyclic AMP. This is another crucial reason to control your insulin levels to enhance growth hormone and thyroid hormone two key hormones for FAT LOSS!

Eicosanoids

Eicosanoids are hormones that last for only a few seconds and are produced by every cell in your body. Since eicosanoids are produced in every cell, not one specific one, it is as if you had 50–100 trillion separate eicosanoid glands capable of making these exceptionally powerful hormones. We know that all forms of inflammation are ultimately controlled by eicosanoids. It is the balance of eicosanoids in your body that is so important to your health. Simply stated good eicosanoids promote cellular health and bad eicosanoids produce cellular destruction. Remember that anything that causes inflammation will, in turn, cause insulin resistance and can increase body fat!

All eicosanoids are derived from dietary fat, in particular the polyunsaturated essential fatty acids that must be supplied by the diet. There are only three such essential fatty acids that can be made into eicosanoids:

1) dihomo gamma linolenic acid (DGLA)
2) arachidonic acid (AA)
3) eicosapentaenoic acid (EPA)

DGLA and AA are omega 6 fatty acids, and EPA is an omega 3 fatty acid. The really good eicosanoids that accelerate cellular rejuvenation come from DGLA, the really bad eicosanoids that accelerate cellular destruction come from AA and EPA helps maintain a dynamic balance between DGLA and AA as well as diluting out any excess of AA in the cell. Omega-6 fats in excess are readily converted to arachidonic acid, a precursor to pro-inflammatory prostaglandin E2 (PGE2).

As powerful as eicosanoids are, they are ultimately controlled by the diet. All pro inflammatory eicosanoids are derived from the long chain omega 6 fatty acid AA. What's interesting to understand is that the more the ratio favours high AA, from omega 6, the more inflammation that will occur which increases cortisol levels and decreases testosterone! Gamma linolenic acid (GLA) is found in plant sources like evening primrose and borage oil. Its functions and benefits are very similar to DHA and EPA. Like DHA, GLA maintains the permeability and flexibility of cell membranes, creating cells that can obtain the needed nutrients for proper functioning.

GLA improves cell sensitivity to insulin, reducing our chance of developing diabetes, heart disease and excess body fat. This is why I added GLA to my Ultimate Fish Oils, so that it works synergistically with EPA & DHA to help dampen down inflammation within our bodies.

GLA goes to DGLA almost automatically. Once at DGLA, there are two biochemical paths available. One path leads to good eicosanoids and the other leads to the bad eicosanoids. To go down the bad road, DGLA is converted by the delta 5 Desaturase (D5) enzyme to arachidonic acid, which is the precursor to bad eicosanoids. So we see D5 is key. If we can inhibit this enzyme, the less arachidonic acid, the less bad eicosanoids and thus the less problem with our health, i.e. the less pain, inflammation heart disease, stroke, obesity, etc. What controls D5? It is activated by insulin. So yet again you can see controlling your blood sugar is also very important in controlling your eicosanoids and your inflammation levels. Another key to the puzzle is EPA which is a key inhibitor of D5. This shows that fish oils have many remarkable benefits to our health.

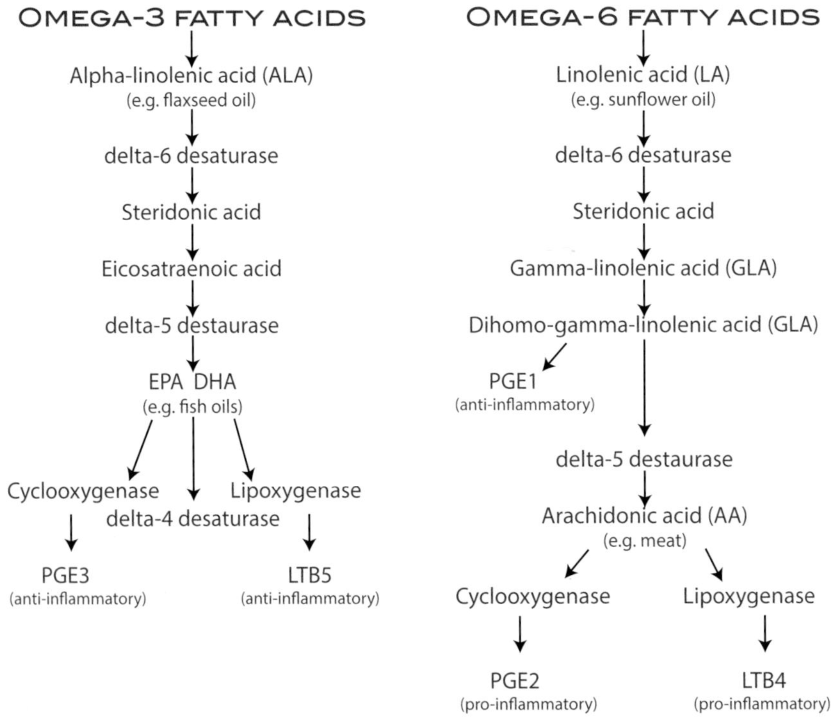

The AA/EPA ratio in the blood is the best marker of our future state of wellness because it measures the level of cellular inflammation in the body. Cellular inflammation is the type of inflammation that is below the perception of pain. What it does is disrupt hormonal signalling at the cellular levels that leads to increased fat accumulation, acceleration of the development of chronic disease, and decreased physical performance. You can't feel cellular inflammation, but you can measure it. The only way to measure cellular inflammation is by testing the ratio of two essential fatty acids (AA and EPA) in your blood. High levels of cellular inflammation do not mean you have a disease state, but it does indicate that you are not as well as you could be. Your future state of wellness can be determined by the levels of cellular inflammation in the blood as shown below.

AA/EPA Ranges	Cellular Inflammation	Future state of wellness
1.5 to 3	Low	Excellent
3 to 6	Moderate	Good
7 to 15	Elevated	Moderate
> than 15	High	Poor

The higher your levels of cellular inflammation, the more likely the future development of chronic disease will be accelerated. A recent study from Italy has demonstrated that the AA/EPA ratio is always greater than 15 in patients with chronic diseases. ***Rizzo AM, Montorfano G, Negroni M, Adorni L, Berselli P, Corsetto P, Wahle K, and Berra B. "A rapid method for determining arachidonic:eicosapentaenoic acid ratios in whole blood lipids: correlation with erythrocyte membrane ratios and validation in a large Italian population of various ages and pathologies." Lipids in Health and Disease 9:7 (2010)***

There are no drugs that can change the AA/EPA ratio. This is because AA/EPA ratio is a consequence of the diet. One method of lowering the AA/EPA ratio is to increase the intake of high-purity omega-3 fatty acid concentrates rich in EPA. This will increase the EPA content in the blood. This represents the fastest way to reduce the AA/EPA ratio. However, the best long-term method is also to reduce the AA levels in the blood. This is best achieved by following a strict anti-inflammatory diet reducing the amount of omega 6 vegetables oils.

So I hope you have a basic understanding of hormones and how they communicate with the cells as the more efficient the messages from the hormones can be heard by the cell, the easier it will be to lose fat and gain lean muscle tissue. It was the work of Dr Barry Sears which educated me on the importance of eicosanoids and I must give him huge credit for sharing this information in his books.

Now, let's look at the other part of the equation for enhancing our metabolism so that we can stay lean & healthy. Please enter, the mitochondria.

Mitochondria

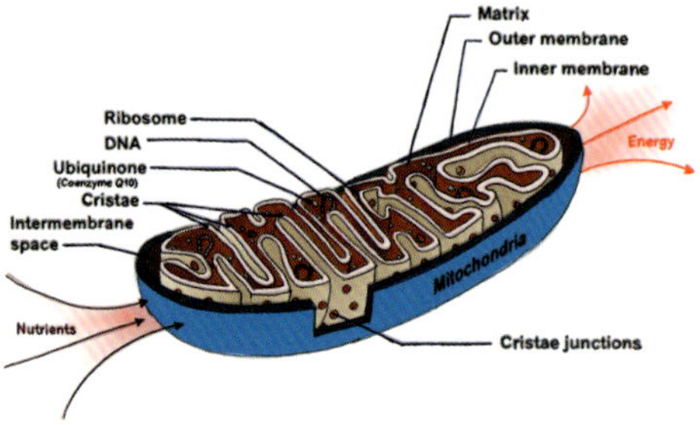

The anatomy of our mitochondria

Most fat utilization occurs in the cell's mitochondria. The greater the number of mitochondria, the more efficient fat utilization will be. Because muscle is the largest mitochondria containing tissue, muscle composition directly affects fat utilization. Any intelligent fat loss program should include a strength training program to increase muscle and improve our anabolic hormones. Remember exercise not only stimulates mitochondria, it also enhances our hormones and habit 10 gives you plenty of example training sessions showing you how to ramp your mitochondria and hormones up to increase fat loss and build lean muscle tissue. This is why many slimming programs, that do not take into account the essential role that muscle plays in increasing our metabolic rates, often fail in the quest for fat loss long term. These programs are mostly based on calorie deficits which cause the body to become highly catabolic, meaning that we lose a load of muscle and end up becoming a smaller, fatter and more toxic version of ourselves.

The primary role of mitochondria is to extract energy from nutrients to produce adenosine triphosphate, or ATP, which our body uses to create energy for a whole host of cellular processes. We are constantly using ATP, whether we're running, walking, thinking, breathing, pumping blood through our cardiovascular system, or singing a song. Think of a physiological process, and ATP is involved. Without mitochondria, then, we wouldn't be able to get much of anything done. We simply wouldn't be alive. The role of your metabolism is to take the oxygen you breathe and the food you eat and process it to make energy, the fuel of life. This energy is made in tiny little factories in our cells called mitochondria.

Mitochondria are responsible for approximately 95% of all energy produced within the human body. According to Professor Enzo Nisoli the average adult possess approximately 10 million billion mitochondria, which corresponds to approximately 10% of our body weight. That is some serious energy generating capacity.

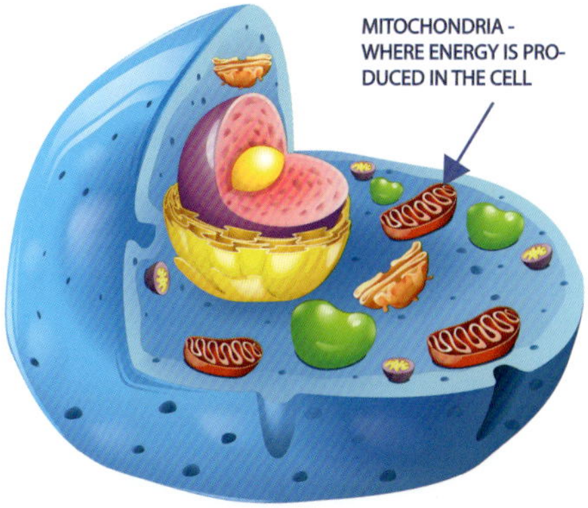

Mitochondria are the only places inside your muscle cells where carbohydrate, fat, and protein can be broken down in the presence of oxygen to create the energy you need to exercise.

When the mitochondria are not working to full capacity, you suffer all the symptoms of low energy, fatigue, slow metabolism, weight gain, memory loss, inability to put muscle on and the list goes on. It comes down to a simple numbers game: the more mitochondria you have, and the more efficient they work, the more fat you will burn as well as building more muscle.

What causes mitochondria to be less efficient

It is clear that obese people have fewer and more poorly functioning mitochondria than leaner people do. Perhaps that is why lean people stay lean and obese people stay obese. So you can see increasing and enhancing mitochondria is essential for fat loss.

Mitochondria are very sensitive to damage. And when they aren't working properly, you suffer all the symptoms of low energy - fatigue, memory loss, pain, rapid aging and more. Fatigue is the most common symptom of poorly functioning mitochondria. At the moment our understanding is that the causes fall into two main groups: either nutritional deficiencies or toxins.

Pesticides, just like toxic metals, can have devastating effects on our mitochondria. Many pesticides are developed to target the mitochondria specifically.

When toxins enter the body and move throughout the tissues, they come into contact with the mitochondria and damage them. The toxins can prevent ATP production and in one study, for example, 48% of the mercury that was found inside the individual cells were found in the mitochondria themselves. Mitochondrial damage caused by toxicity, ageing, or lack of essential nutrients and antioxidants can lead to lower mitochondrial capacity, which may result in steroid hormone decline, loss of muscle, gain in fat, general weakness and metabolic decline.

In a 2009 report submitted to the U.S. Department of Agriculture (USDA) on behalf of the Institute of Science in Society (ISIS), researchers Dr. Mae-Wan Ho and Brett Cherry identified how even very low concentrations of Monsanto's Roundup (glyphosate) herbicide are extremely toxic to human cells. Specifically, the research identified how Roundup obstructs both cell respiration and energy production in mitochondria.

Mercury in our body has the ability to strangle our mitochondria and making them less efficient.

A published paper (co-authored by the UCSD Statin Study director) suggests that statin-induced damage to the body's mitochondria is the true cause of the commonly-reported side effects of statin use. Mitochondria are essential to energy. CoQ10 in the mitochondria help produce energy and fight free radicals. Unfortunately for statin-users, CoQ10 travels along the same pathway as some types of cholesterol. Following its scorched-earth policy to a tee, statins block that pathway, meaning CoQ10 can't get through to help mitochondria destroy free radicals. More free radicals running rampant means more inflammation– which is the true cause of heart disease.

Another major factor to consider when looking at damage of the mitochondria are eating too many calories and not enough nutrients in your diet. Anything that causes inflammation also causes damage to the mitochondria.

We have our own anti-oxidant systems to protect us but these are easily overwhelmed by a toxic, low nutrient, high calorie diet. The endogenous anti-oxidants we make, called superoxide-dismutase, catalase and glutathione peroxidase, are dependent on essential dietary nutrients to help them work well including; zinc, copper, manganese, vitamin c and selenium which are often deficient in our processed food diets of today.

What causes your mitochondria to be more efficient

The more mitochondria you have, and the more efficiently they consume oxygen, the faster your metabolic rate, the easier it is for your body to burn calories and the more energy you have.

Important substrates that are needed for the mitochondria to function efficiently are;

- CoQ10
- L-Carnitine
- D-Ribose
- Magnesium

CoQ10, L-carnitine, D-ribose, and magnesium, individually and collectively help increase energy, or ATP, production in your body by supporting mitochondria within cells.

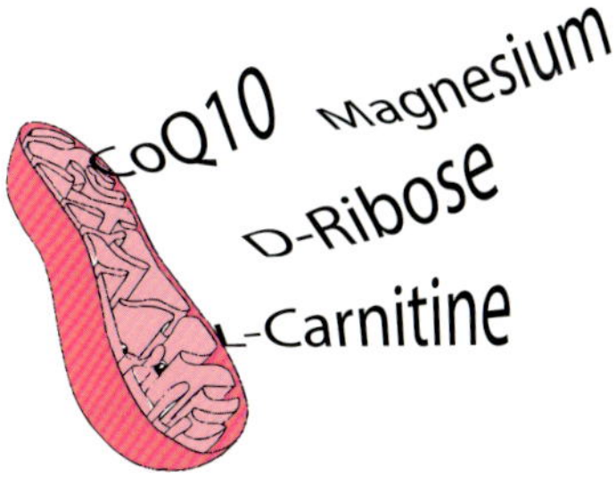

Fuel your mitochondria with The Fantastic 4 - magnesium, CoQ10, D-ribose and L-carnitine. I gained this information from the excellent work of Dr Stephen Sinatra and his book "Metabolic Cardiology"

CoQ10

CoQ10 supplementation also improve performance. For example, in one study, Dr J. Van Fraechem gave a group of healthy young men 60 mg of CoQ10 per day for 8 weeks. They did not change their usual level of daily exercise or diet yet increased their maximum exercise capacity by 28%! High intensity exercise has been shown to lower CoQ10 most probably due to the consequence of an excess of free radicals caused by increased metabolic demands of chronically exercising muscles. So, if you are regularly taking part in strenuous exercise you may need to think about supplementing with CoQ10

Carnitine

Carnitine is the gatekeeper for fat burning, it picks up fat and transports it into the mitochondria for burning to create ATP. The more Carnitine present the more fat burnt and this is essential for effective fat loss.

In a study by Dr Norris Siliprandi and colleagues at the University of Padua, Italy, gave athletes 2 grams of L-carnitine or a placebo, one hour before maximal exercise on the bicycle ergometer. Carnitine reduced post exercise levels of lactate and pyruvate, and significantly increased maximal work output. In another Italian study, normal subjects who were not athletes, were given L – carnitine supplements or placebo and tested for submaximal exercise on the ergometer bicycle. The carnitine trials showed a significant improvement in endurance. So there is evidence that L – carnitine can boost both anaerobic and aerobic performance. A dose of 2 – 4 grams taken for 2 weeks, one hour before exercise appears to be effective.

During long endurance training fats become a major energy source. You will not run out of fats to burn but you might run out of L-Carnitine, which is essential for fats to be used as energy. Endurance exercise rapidly depletes the pool of L-Carnitine in muscle, so the amount of carnitine available is a limiting factor on the energy supply of endurance athletes. Carnitine also increases maximum use of oxygen in athletes. This effect was first observed by Dr. Brian Liebovitz at the University of California. It has been confirmed by two Italian studies. Both gave athletes 4 grams of L-carnitine daily and V02 max increased significantly.

Dr. Bruce Ames, the world renowned scientist from the University of California at Berkeley, has spent the last decade discovering how we can give ourselves a metabolic tune up. In one study he gave old rats who were tired, wouldn't get on the treadmill anymore, and couldn't find the cheese in the maze, or swim very far, two molecules that boost metabolism, that make the mitochondria run better. They are alpha lipoic acid and L-carnitine. Overnight these rats became like young rats. They got up on the treadmill themselves, swam long distances without fatiguing and could easily find the cheese in the maze like young healthy rats. How could that happen? Well, he simply gave the cells the raw materials they need for optimal function.

D-ribose

D-ribose is essential as a building block of ATP (adenosine triphosphate), it rapidly restores depleted energy by providing substrate for ATP production. Strenuously exercised muscle may have lowered levels of ATP by 20%. It may take 3-4 days to replenish these ATP levels. Supplementing with ribose can increase the replenishment of ATP by up to 4 times Supplemental D-ribose absorbs easily and quickly through the gut and into the bloodstream. About 97% gets through. Doses should be between 5–15 grams depending on activity and heart problems.

Since all enzymatic reactions involving ATP have an absolute requirement for magnesium, it makes perfect sense to include magnesium to any program which wants to enhance ATP production within the mitochondria.

As you can now see you need a cocktail of micro-nutrients for the mitochondria to produce ATP efficiently they are magnesium, coenzyme Q10, L-carnitine and D-ribose. This is why I developed Cardio Fuel to boost mitochondrial function. We cover nutrients and mitochondria function much more in habit 8 of this book.

Exercise for Enhancing Mitochondria

Scientists were somewhat surprised to learn that mitochondria contain their own genetic material - and that all the mitochondria in an individual's body are inherited from one's mother, not father (this is because the egg contains mitochondria, while sperm cells are mitochondria-free). This may seem strange, since the egg is rather immobile and the sperm are distance swimmers, but the bottom line is that sperm are so tiny that mitochondria would weigh them down excessively on their harrowing passage toward the egg. The consequence of this, of course, is that you tend to inherit your exercise capacity from your mother, not your dad.

Of course, scientists began experimenting with ways to increase mitochondrial densities. At first, it was believed that the mitochondria might be under hormonal control and early research efforts were indeed able to show that mitochondrial numbers were increased when levels of a key hormone produced by the thyroid gland (thyroxine) increased. In laboratory rats, the simple addition of desiccated thyroid to normal rat food caused an explosive increase in mitochondrial size and density in both the heart and liver. This clearly shows how important a fully functional thyroid is in energy metabolism and fat loss.

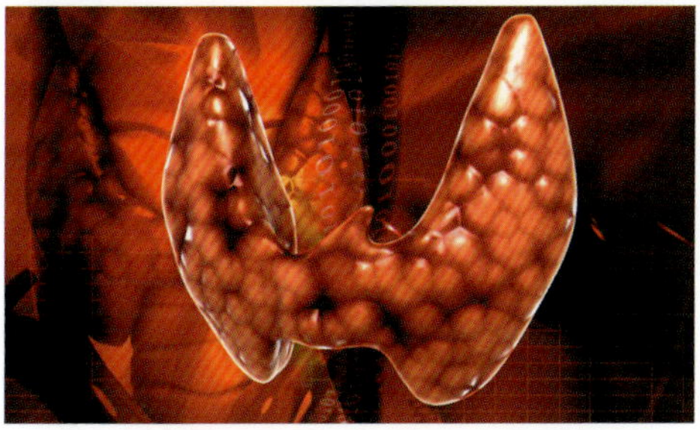

Thyroid hormone is essential for mitochondria and metabolic functions.

Exercise physiologist John Holloszy, of the Washington University School of Medicine in St. Louis, showed that chronic exercise could put mitochondrial numbers on the upswing. Holloszy simply had one group of lab rats to run on treadmills for up to 120 minutes per day at intensities of about 50-75% of VO2max for a period of 12 weeks, while a second group lolled in their cages. At the end of the 12-week period, Holloszy found that the running rats had increased their mitochondrial densities by approximately 50-60% and had also doubled their concentrations of 'cytochrome c,' a key compound found inside mitochondria which is crucially important in aerobic energy production ***('Effects of Exercise on Mitochondrial Oxygen Uptake and Respiratory Enzyme Activity in Skeletal Muscle,' The Journal of Biological Chemistry, vol. 242(9), pp. 2278-2282, 1967).***

Of course, exercise physiologists then began wondering which type of training was best for perking up mitochondrial numbers. Should one train fast? Long and slow? Mix fast efforts with slow ones? How long should one exercise (how many miles per workout and week) in order to optimise mitochondrial density?

Holloszy and his co-workers at Washington University were the first to really tackle this question. In a fairly simple piece of experimental work, Holloszy et al had one group of rats running 10 minutes per day, another running for 30 minutes, a third group exercising for 60 minutes, and a fourth working for 120 minutes per day. Training took place five days a week for 13 weeks, and training intensity was fixed at about 1.2 mph (or about 32 meters per minute and 313 minutes for the 10K, which is an intensity of around 50-60% VO2max for a healthy lab rat).

Not too surprisingly, the two-hour per day runners turned out to have the best mitochondrial set-ups. For example, compared to sedentary rats, the 10-minute per day exercisers had about 16%t more cytochrome c, while the 30-minute workers boosted cytochrome c by 31%. However, rats who ran for an hour expanded cytochrome c by 38%, and the two-hour rats increased it by 92%!

Holloszy's study provided nice support for the specificity of training principle, too. During a rugged endurance test staged at the end of the research period, the 10-minute rats lasted 22 minutes, the 30-minute ones for 41 minutes, the hour-long rats ran strenuously for 50 minutes, and the two-hour trainees stayed on the treadmills for a whopping 111 minutes! Of course, run time to exhaustion was directly related to cytochrome c concentration; the more c a rat had, the longer it could run at a tough pace. ***('Skeletal Muscle Respiratory Capacity, Endurance, and Glycogen Utilization,' American Journal of Physiology, vol. 228(4), pp. 1029-1033, 1975).***

Studies in humans, and animals, have shown that aerobic exercise and increase mitochondrial number and function.

Other researchers wanted to explore the intensity question, and Gary Dudley and his colleagues at the State University of New York at Syracuse did just that. Like Holloszy, Dudley had his rats training five times a week and used a variety of different workout durations, from five minutes up to 90 minutes per day. However, unlike Holloszy, Dudley restricted his study to only eight weeks and used a range of different training intensities - 100% VO2max, 85% VO2max, 70% VO2max, 50% VO2max, and 40% VO2max. Dudley also looked at how different intensities and durations influenced different muscle fibre types (fast twitch, aerobic fast twitch or 'intermediate', and slow twitch), which no one had ever done before. ***('Influence of Exercise Intensity and Duration on Biochemical Adaptations in Skeletal Muscle,' Journal of Applied Physiology, vol. 53(4), pp. 844-850, 1982).***

In contrast to what Holloszy had found, Dudley was able to show that training beyond about 60 minutes per workout was without benefit in terms of increasing cytochrome. In other words, a rat training at about 70-75% VO2max could upgrade cytochrome c by expanding workout duration from 30 to 60 minutes - but not by increasing workouts from 60 to 90 minutes. This was true at all intensities studied by Dudley - and also with all three muscle fibre types. Progressing beyond about 60 minutes per workout simply didn't have much value when it came to the mitochondria.

The faster you train, the better?

However, Dudley's most interesting findings were those related to intensity of training. He was able to show that in fast-twitch muscle fibres, just 10 minutes of fast running (at close to 100% VO2max) per day was enough to roughly triple cytochrome c concentrations over an eight-week period. In contrast, running for 27 minutes at 85% VO2max daily only hoisted cytochrome c by 80%, while 60 to 90 minutes at 70-75%

Interval training stimulates the mitochondria to become more efficient as well as increasing their numbers. This will increase fat loss.

VO2max nudged cytochrome c upward by just 74%. So much for the theory that intense exercise can hurt mitochondria.

So what's the bottom line? As Dudley and his colleagues put it, "an increase in the intensity of training brings about the greatest adaptive response in the mitochondria".

Expressing the crucial importance of intensity another way, Dudley and co-workers said, 'For the same adaptive response, the length of daily exercise necessary to bring about the change becomes less as the intensity of exercise is increased.' **In other words, 10 to 15 minutes of running at close to 100% VO2max in a workout can do much more for you than running for 60 to 90 minutes at slower intensities.**

World class endurance athletes might have up to 10% of their cells composed of mitochondria instead of 2% for sedentary person. So essentially they have five times as many little energy factories as the average person and this is why they can run so fast for so long. Muscle biopsy studies have shown that there are two major changes associated with mitochondrial energy production following endurance training: an increase in the number and the size of the mitochondria. Endurance training also increases the number of red blood cells that deliver oxygen to muscle cells with more efficiency.

AMPK - the marker of mitochondrial biogenesis

Getting your body to create new mitochondria requires a stressor, a challenge to the system. Well, the presence of AMPK (or amp-activated protein kinase) is how we know that such a stressor has been applied. AMPK is a metabolic regulator that increases mitochondrial biogenesis (formation of new mitochondria). Many things can stimulate AMPK, like caloric restriction, fasting, ketosis, and exercise. What do you notice about all four? Caloric restriction requires restricted caloric intake, fasting removes caloric intake entirely, ketosis restricts glucose intake, and exercise depletes stored energy; the common thread is that these are all energy-depleted states.

So, **AMPK increases mitochondrial biogenesis as a response to the lack of cellular energy and an adaption to the applied stress.** AMPK is the marker to look for when assessing mitochondrial enhancement potential. This is why I believe it is good to do high intensity interval training (HITT) and cardio training on empty stomach just loaded with PRP amino work capacity and cardio fuel this forces the mitochondria to burn fat, but remember you have got to work hard. As the saying goes; no pain, no gain!

So let's dig into the research and see how specific types and intensity levels of exercise influence AMPK expression. Most research into exercise and mitochondria has revolved around traditional endurance training. Classic stuff – long slow distance, jogging, cycling. And endurance exercise works. In fact, **"cardio" is the best way to increase AMPK and induce mitochondrial biogenesis.** It's quite basic, actually. Slow twitch muscle fibers, the ones used in endurance training, contain the most mitochondria, so it's natural that training that targets slow twitch fibers will also target more muscle mitochondria.

However, long, slow cardio may not be the only way to increase AMPK. Gibala et al provided an interesting study in which four 30 second "all-out" cycling sprints interspersed with four minutes of rest activated AMPK signaling. The authors speculate (but didn't test) that the increased AMPK probably resulted in mitochondrial biogenesis and improved glucose and fat oxidation. In another study, that same group of researchers confirmed that the same sprint training protocol – 30 sec on, four minute rest, four times – does increase mitochondrial biogenesis through activation of AMPK.

So we don't make new mitochondria or improve our existing ones just for kicks, just like we don't build lean muscle mass by sitting around. We have to give our bodies a reason to do it. We have to challenge our cells through purposeful aerobic and anaerobic conditioning. Make sure that your training is very challenging and purposeful because you can't con the mitochondria to become more efficient with mediocre effort.

One study, from scientists at Canada's McMaster University, adds to the growing evidence for the benefits of short term high-intensity interval training (HIIT) as a time-efficient but safe alternative to traditional types of moderate long term exercise. Astonishingly, it may be possible to get more by doing less!

"We have shown that interval training does not have to be 'all out' in order to be effective," says Professor Martin Gibala. "Doing 10 one-minute sprints on a standard stationary bike with about one minute of rest in between, three times a week, works as well in improving muscle as many hours of conventional long-term biking less strenuously."

HIIT means doing a number of short bursts of intense exercise with short recovery breaks in between. The authors have already shown with young healthy college students that this produces the same physical benefits as conventional long duration endurance training despite taking much less time (and amazingly, actually doing less exercise!) However, their previous work used a relatively extreme set-up that involved "all out" pedaling on a specialized laboratory bicycle. The new study used a standard stationary bicycle and a workload which was still above most people's comfort zone -about 95% of maximal heart rate - but only about half of what can be achieved when people sprint at an all-out pace.

This less extreme HIT method may work well for people (the older, less fit, and slightly overweight among us) whose doctors might have worries about them exercising "all-out." We have known for years that repeated moderate long-term exercise tunes up fuel and oxygen delivery to muscles and aids the removal of waste products. Exercise also improves the way muscles use the oxygen to burn the fuel in mitochondria, the microscopic power station of cells.

Running or cycling for hours a week widens the network of vessels supplying muscle cells and also boosts the numbers of mitochondria in them so that a person can carry out activities of daily living more effectively and without strain, and crucially with less risk of a heart attack, stroke or diabetes. But the traditional approach to exercise is time consuming. Martin Gibala showed that the same results can be obtained in far less time with brief spurts of higher-intensity exercise

It's not all about cardiovascular training though. You must remember the importance of weight training. Loss of muscle is actually one of the reasons yo-yo dieters can not seem to lose weight. They lose and gain over and over again but the big problem is that when they lose weight, they also lose muscle. Since muscle is much more metabolically active and burns 70x as many calories as fat cells, losing muscle slows down their metabolism, making it easier to gain weight and harder to lose it. You must gain muscle to lose fat

Weight training is essential for fat loss due to increased muscle which increases metabolism.

The loss of muscle has a tremendous impact on your ability to lose weight. This is why it is absolutely paramount that a well designed strength training plan is at the core of your fat loss plan.

For enhanced fat loss mix weights, endurance, speed, power and bingo you are in the exercise fat loss game. I give you all the information you need in Habit 10 to design your own exercise plan to gain lean muscle and improve cardiovascular fitness. So when you train next make sure you give your mitochondria a workout so they become more efficient at burning fat 24/7.

Conclusion

I hope you can now see the importance of understanding hormonal health, cellular health and enhancing mitochondrial function in your quest for a lean and healthy body. The rest of the habits will cover hormones and mitochondria, as well as cellular health, so you know how to manipulate these factors to optimize metabolism and become a fat burning machine instead of a fat storing machine.

If you want to learn even more about this topic then I suggest that you start with such books as "The Hormone Cure" by Sara Gottfried, "The Hormone Solution" by Thierry Hertoghe, "Sexy Hormones" by Lorna Vanderhaeghe & Alvin Pettle, "The Truth About Hormones" by Vivienne Perry" and "Natural Hormonal Enhancement" by Rob Faigin, "Omega Six The Devil's Fat" by Robert Brown

HABIT 5

THYROID: MASTER OF METABOLISM

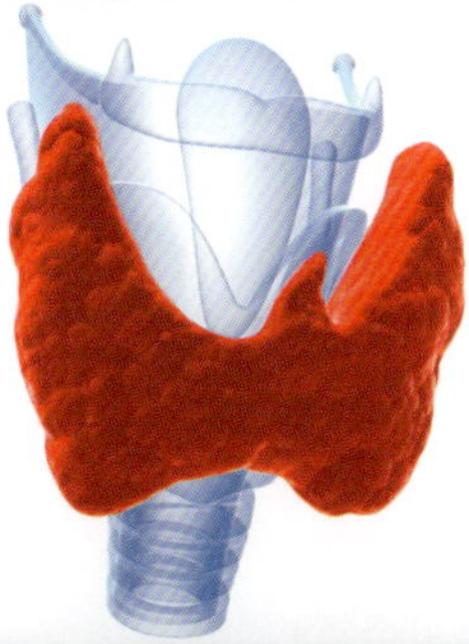

Because the thyroid has its fingers in so many bodily processes, when its function diminishes, so does that of many other systems like digestion, energy production, interactions with other hormones, our mood and an inability to lose weight no matter how much exercise you do or how clean your diet is. It can seem to be like a vicious cycle when the thyroid becomes dysfunctional. The conventional approach is usually to medicate if it's hypothyroidism (low thyroid function) which occasionally works but very often increases the problem. This is because for thyroid hormones to work, there are multiple factors that need to be addressed and simply popping thyroid medication very often FAILS as the millions of people worldwide know only too well.

For the past 33 years, I have looked in the mirror every morning and asked myself: 'If today were the last day of my life, would I want to do what I am about to do today?' And whenever the answer has been 'No' for too many days in a row, I know I need to change something.

Steve Jobs

In this habit I will teach you about the things that can destroy thyroid function and what steps you can take to get this gland back to working order. Because if the thyroid gland isn't functioning correctly neither will you and it will be incredibly difficult to lose weight, no matter how much you drop your caloric intake or how much exercise you do and the ironic thing is these two factors often contribute to thyroid problems. We will also look at why blood tests for thyroid hormones often do not give you a true picture of your thyroid health.

Unfortunately thyroid disorders are quite common and it is estimated that one in 20 people will experience a thyroid disorder in their lifetime. This figure is one in 14 for women, probably due to oestrogen being antagonistic to thyroid hormones, as you will read in this habit.

Thyroid Hormone Production

Thyroid secretion is essential for the operation of the cells and, in effect, determines how hot the fire gets in the cell and the speed of activity in the cell. The influence of thyroid secretion on body processes and other organs is incredibly widespread and important. When the thyroid gland is removed from an otherwise normal animal, all metabolic activity is reduced. After removal of the thyroid gland, excess amounts of water, salts, and protein are retained within the body. Blood cholesterol also goes up.

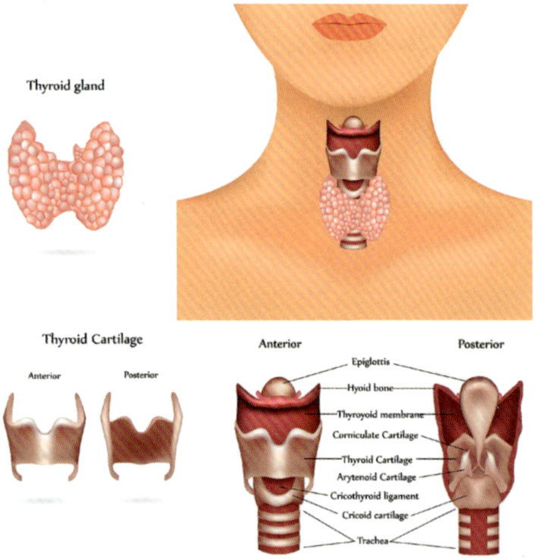

The thyroid, the body's thermostat, secretes two hormones that regulate body temperature, energy usage, and calorie burning. The thyroid has many effects on all the cells in the body, including the synthesis of RNA protein and consumption of oxygen by cells, affecting overall bodily metabolism. Thyroid function influences and is influenced by the pituitary, adrenals, parathyroid, and sex glands, all of which work together. The pituitary produces TSH (thyroid-stimulating hormone), which helps regulate thyroid hormone production. Thyroid malfunctioning is also influenced by abnormal immune responses and the adrenals. People with type-O blood are said to be genetically prone to hypothyroidism and low levels of iodine. Approximately 46% of people are blood Type-O.

Sitting at the base of the throat, the thyroid gland produces hormones that regulate basal metabolic rate, the speed at which our bodies burn food for energy. The thyroid gets its directions from the hypothalamus, at the base of the brain, by way of the pituitary gland. On a signal from the hypothalamus which releases thyrotropin releasing hormone to the pituitary which then sends thyroid-stimulating hormone (TSH) into the bloodstream. TSH travels to the thyroid gland and causes the release of thyroxine (T4), which is partly converted into triiodothyronine (T3).

Through a feedback mechanism, the hypothalamus determines when levels of T4 and T3 are low and alerts the pituitary to supply more TSH. The thyroid gland can store two to three months worth of thyroxine (T4).

The Physiologic Effects of Thyroid Hormones

It is likely that all cells in the body are targets for thyroid hormones. Thyroid hormones have profound effects on many "big time" physiologic processes, such as development, growth and metabolism, and deficiency in thyroid hormones is not compatible with normal health.

Metabolism: Thyroid hormones stimulate diverse metabolic activities most tissues, leading to an increase in basal metabolic rate. One consequence of this activity is to increase body heat production, which seems to result, at least in part, from increased oxygen consumption and rates of ATP hydrolysis. By way of analogy, the action of thyroid hormones is akin to blowing on a smouldering fire.

A few examples of specific metabolic effects of thyroid hormones include:

- **Lipid metabolism:** Increased thyroid hormone levels stimulate fat mobilization, leading to increased concentrations of fatty acids in plasma. They also enhance oxidation of fatty acids in many tissues. Finally, plasma concentrations of cholesterol and triglycerides are inversely correlated with thyroid hormone levels - one diagnostic indication of hypothyroidism is increased blood cholesterol concentration.
- **Carbohydrate metabolism:** Thyroid hormones stimulate almost all aspects of carbohydrate metabolism, including enhancement of insulin-dependent entry of glucose into cells and increased gluconeogenesis and glycogenolysis to generate free glucose.

vThyroid hormones also have a significant effect on how our mitochondria work by not only increasing their efficiency but also their numbers and this is significant for our energy levels and especially our ability to burn fat.

Triiodothyronine (T3) promotes weight loss by increasing metabolic rate. T3 increases basal metabolic rate by increasing the rate at which the body breaks down all food groups. It unlocks significant energy for the body to use, and it can produce very dramatic results especially in overweight people with diagnosed or silent hypothyroidism.

When the amount of thyroid hormones produced in the body falls, the rate of metabolism falls with it. Because of the reduced metabolic rate, low thyroid functioning results in difficulty in reducing body weight. When overweight individuals adopt healthy diets and take up regular exercise but still cannot shed weight, one of the most likely reasons is low metabolic rate caused by low T3 levels, or an inability of the body to convert T4 to its more active T3. Also of importance here, as you will read further on in this habit, is that most people who have thyroid problems don't actually have a problem with their thyroid; it's their immune system attacking their thyroids which causes hypothyroidism.

Growth: Thyroid hormones are clearly necessary for normal growth in children and young animals, as evidenced by the growth-retardation observed in thyroid deficiency. Not surprisingly, the growth-promoting effect of thyroid hormones is intimately intertwined with that of growth hormone, a clear indication that complex physiologic processes like growth depend upon multiple endocrine controls.

Development: A classical experiment in endocrinology was the demonstration that tadpoles deprived of thyroid hormone failed to undergo metamorphosis into frogs. Of critical importance in mammals is the fact that normal levels of thyroid hormone are essential to the development of the fetal and neonatal brain.

Low Thyroid Function

One of the main reasons why you may have the symptoms of poor thyroid function is a lack of nutrients that are vital for the normal function of thyroid hormone. Nutrient deficiencies place a major stress on the thyroid gland itself, helping to lock in sluggish and inefficient metabolism of calories. Various nutrients are needed to form thyroid hormone, activate thyroid hormone, and protect the thyroid and liver during this process.

For example, the thyroid gland has multiple small narrow cavities called follicles that are filled with a clear material known as thyroglobulin that is produced by a layer of thyroid epithelial cells known as thyrocytes. This material contains tyrosine, an amino acid that is the starting material used for thyroid hormone synthesis. Any deficiency in tyrosine may lead to a lack in the building materials to these epithelial cells.

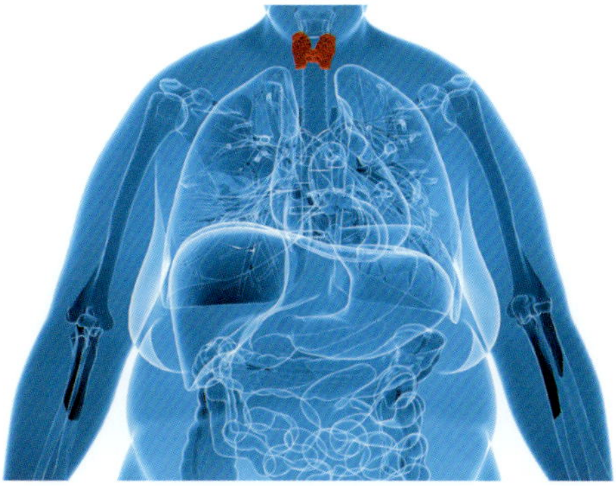

One of the most frustrating symptoms (as anyone with hypothyroidism will tell you) is undoubtedly losing weight. No matter how much exercise they do or how much they restrict calories they usually gain weight. Hypothyroidism as we know simply slows down the body's overall metabolism and fat burning ability. **For instance, the adrenal hormones adrenaline and noradrenaline that enhance fat burning lose power when the thyroid is underactive.** What's more, low thyroid function makes it harder for the body to burn fat by closing the sites on the cells that respond to lipase, an enzyme that metabolizes fat.

Thyroid hormones also affect the liver cells responsible for detoxification. When thyroid hormones are low, the enzymes that carry out detoxification simply don't mature, hindering detoxification which, as we learnt from habit 2, is essential for our health and ability to lose excess body fat. Again, this is one of those vicious cycles, as healthy liver function is integral to converting thyroid hormones into a form the body can use. Remember a functional liver converts as much as 60% of T4 into T3 so liver health optimises thyroid hormones.

Stomach acid production is also dependent on the hormone gastrin, which unfortunately diminishes with hypothyroidism. This can cause digestive complaints such as heartburn, bloating, gas; hinder the absorption of such vital nutrients as B12 and iron. Hypothyroidism and low HCL (hydrochloric acid) often go hand in hand. This is why hypothyroidism can

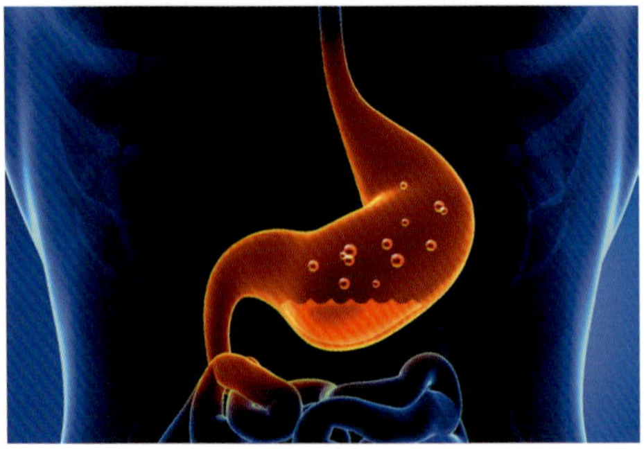

Low stomach acid can lead to hypothyroidism.

lead to anaemia in three different ways. Firstly anemia resulting from B12 and folic acid deficiency can develop from low stomach acid, one possible consequence of hypothyroidism.

Secondly, about 12 % of people with hypothyroidism have pernicious anaemia, an autoimmune disorder in which the body's immune system destroys a compound in the stomach lining necessary for the absorption of B12 and this compound is called intrinsic factor. Given that the vast majority of hypothyroid cases also have an autoimmune disorder in which the body destroys its own thyroid gland, it's not surprising that a hyperactive and malfunctioning immune system can lead to both pernicious anemia and hypothyroidism. **Lastly, since hypothyroidism leads to a deficiency in stomach acid, iron absorption is going to be significantly reduced.**

Biologically, insufficient iron levels may be affecting the first two of three steps of thyroid hormone synthesis by reducing the activity of the enzyme "thyroid peroxidase", which is dependent on iron. Thyroid peroxidase brings about the chemical reactions of adding iodine to tyrosine (amino acid), which then produces T4 and T3. Insufficient iron levels also alter and reduces the conversion of T4 to T3, besides binding T3. Additionally, low iron levels can increase circulating concentrations of TSH (thyroid stimulating hormone). Even worse, good iron levels are needed in the production of cortisol via the adrenal cortex. This reveals that an iron-containing protein is present in high amounts in the adrenal cortex and is involved in the synthesis of corticosterone. So by having low iron, you can potentially lower your cortisol levels which is essential for thyroid hormones to function efficiently. Iron, in addition to iodine, selenium and zinc, are essential for normal thyroid hormone metabolism.

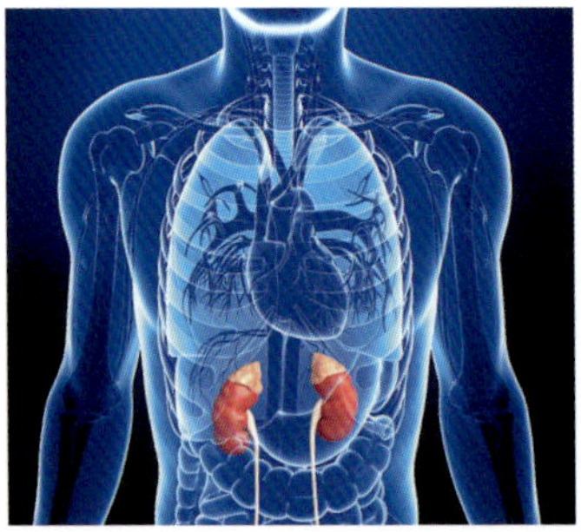

The adrenal glands sit on top of your kidneys and are essential for thyroid hormones to work effectively.

Crash dieting can also crash your thyroid gland by reducing your metabolic rate, which makes total sense when you think about it. Why? The body reacts to reduced calories as a starvation 'code red' and the thyroid's role, as we know, is to optimise metabolism. This would be a disaster during starvation (calorie restriction) as the body would literally cannibalize itself. So, as a safety precaution, when you cut the calories to what the body would sense as starvation mode, between 800 - 1200 calories, you will also significantly reduce thyroid metabolism.

And, if you keep doing the yo-yo dieting, over decades there is a very strong probability that you will inhibit your thyroid so significantly to the point where losing weight is virtually impossible. The negative effect of reverse T3, which inhibits active T3 (our fat burning hormone), on weight loss was demonstrated in a 1984 paper published in the journal, Metabolism. In this study, researchers compared the basal metabolic rates in two groups of volunteers with the similar weights. Individuals in the first group had previously experienced weight loss by dieting while those in the second group had not experienced weight loss or adopted dieting.

The results of the study showed that the basal metabolic rates of people who had lost weight by dieting was 25% lower on average than those in the second group.

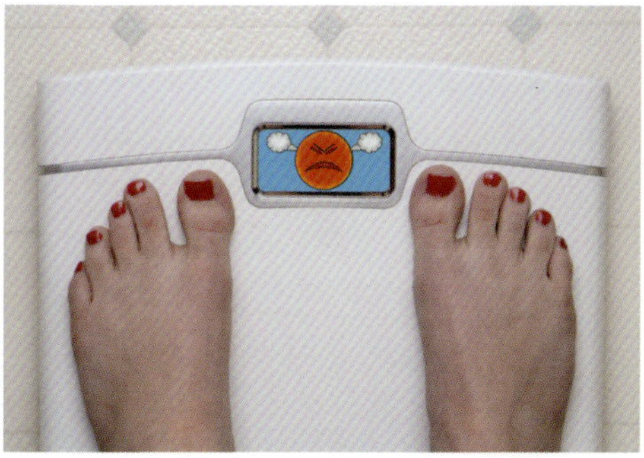

The study demonstrates the lasting effect of reverse T3. Those who had used dieting to experience weight loss had increased levels of reverse T3 because their bodies ramped up the production of the anti-thyroid hormone when faced with starvation. This led to a significant reduction of basal metabolic rate which makes it difficult for such people to lose more weight or for them to shed weight at all if they ever regained the lost weight.

Researchers at the University of North Carolina found that lengthy bouts of strenuous exercise can cause the body unnecessary stress - and lead to higher cortisol levels and lower levels of thyroid hormones 24 hours after exercise. So do not become an obsessive exerciser but I do recommend at least an hour a day and cover this in great detail in habit 10.

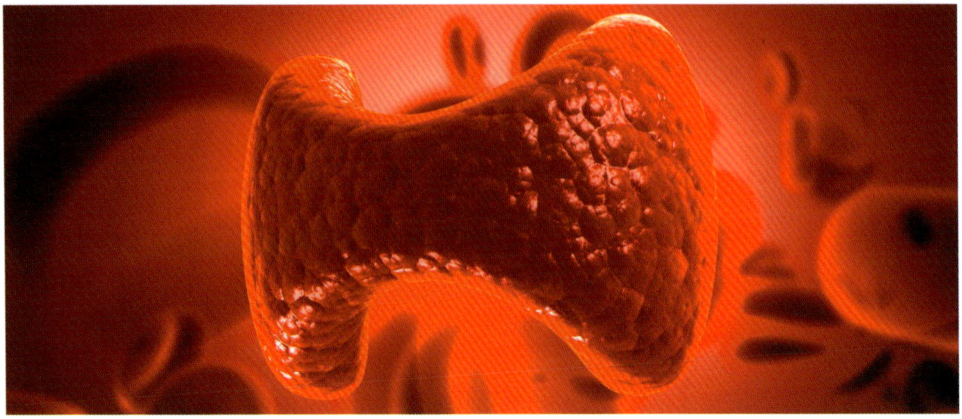

Excessive exercise can crash the thyroid.

Thyroid Hormone Receptors and Mechanism of Action

Receptors for thyroid hormones are intracellular DNA-binding proteins that function as hormone-responsive transcription factors, very similar conceptually to the receptors for steroid hormones.

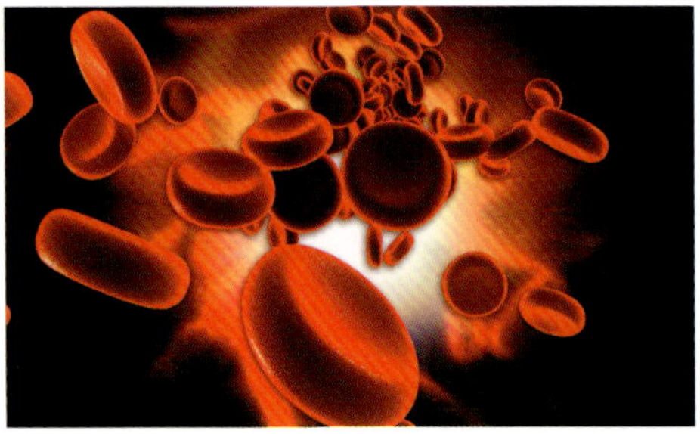

Thyroid hormones enter cells through membrane transporter proteins. A number of plasma membrane transporters have been identified, some of which require ATP hydrolysis; the relative importance of different carrier systems is not yet clear and may differ among tissues. Once inside the nucleus, the hormone binds its receptor, and the hormone-receptor complex interacts with specific sequences of DNA in the promoters of responsive genes. **The effect of the hormone-receptor complex binding to DNA is to modulate gene expression, either by stimulating or inhibiting transcription of specific genes.**

In order for the thyroid hormones to travel through the blood to reach the cells, a transport protein is needed. The three transport proteins are thyroxine-binding globulin, albumin and transthyretin (thyroxine-binding pre-albumin). All these transport proteins are produced by the liver, though transthyretin is also produced in the choroid plexus and thus is the main thyroxine-binding protein in the brain and spinal cord. In the rest of the body, transthyretin carries about 10% of the hormone while albumin binds around 15-20% and thyroxine-binding globulin carries about 70% of the thyroid hormones.

Protein malnutrition, alcoholism and liver disease can impair the production of these carrier proteins. T3 binds more weakly (is more easily released into cells) than T4. Thyroid hormones are thought to easily penetrate cell membranes.

How does T4 become metabolically active in the cell?

The active form of thyroid hormone is T3 but the thyroid gland releases 14 times more T4 than T3. Thus in the cell, the T4 must be converted to T3 by type l 5"-deiodinase, a selenium-dependent enzyme. (Selenium deficiency in rats decreased enzyme activity by 90%).

Type ii 5"-deiodinase is most active in the anterior pituitary, the central nervous system, placenta and brown (high mitochondrial content) fat. T4 can also be converted to reverse T3 (rT3) by the enzyme, 5" deiodinase (especially type l 5' deiodinase in the liver). Reverse T3 is an inactive form of the molecule. The production of rT3 is thought to be a way the body prevents the accumulation of excess T3. Both T3 and rT3 are further reduced to T2 (two iodine molecules), T1 (a single iodine molecule) and T0 (thyronine without any iodine). The half-life of T3 is one day while the half-life of T4 is about a week. The released iodine and thyronine return to the thyroid gland for re-assembly into T4 and T3.

Having thyroid problems is like dragging a weight around with you - something just doesn't feel right. You know life shouldn't be this tough

Every cell in the body has receptors for thyroid hormone. These hormones are responsible for the most basic aspects of body function, impacting all major systems of the body. **The activity of the Krebs cycle within the mitochondria is very thyroid dependent.**

The production and release of thyroid hormone in the thyroid gland is regulated by a feedback system in your brain - the hypothalamus and pituitary glands - which make TRH (thyroid-releasing hormone) and TSH (thyroid- stimulating hormone), respectively. If everything works as designed, you will make what you need and the T4 will be converted to T3. The hormones work in a synchronous feedback loop, creating a state of dynamic balance. There really is no start-and-stop place in the system; however, you may understand it better in this way: the brain's central command centre, the hypothalamus, detects a need for more thyroid hormone and releases TRH, which sends a signal to the pituitary (the second in command in the brain) to release more TSH, which is then released into the bloodstream, goes to the thyroid gland, and stimulates the production of T4 and small amounts of T3.

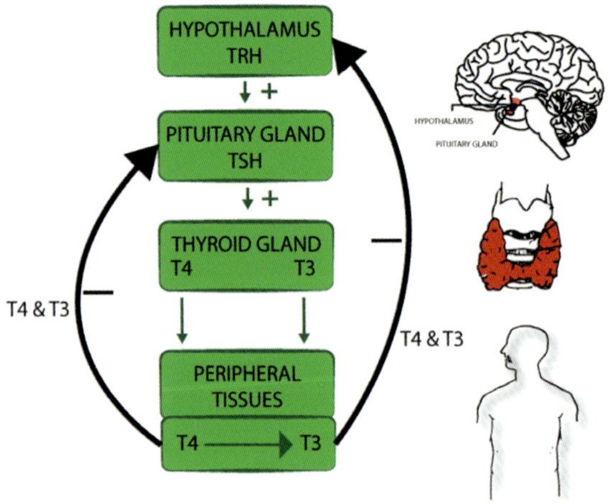

The thyroid hormone feedback loop. The hypothalamus and pituitary gland have created the signal to produce more T4 & T3. As this occurs, there is a negative feedback loop to signal a reduction in TRH and TSH release from the hypothalamus and pituitary.

What the Thyroid Needs

The function of the thyroid gland is to take iodine, found in foods, and convert it into thyroid hormones: thyroxine (T4) and triiodothyronine (T3). T3 and T4 are then released into the bloodstream and are transported throughout the body where they control metabolism (conversion of oxygen and nutrients to energy).

Food Item	Quantity	Iodine Content
Iodized Salt	100 grams	3000 mcg
Cereals and Breads	100 grams	10-11 mcg
Meat	100 grams	26-27 mcg
Vegetables	100 grams	32-33 mcg
Fruits	100 grams	4-5 mcg
Haddock	100 grams	Almost 300 mcg
Malt bread	100 grams	29-30 mcg
Cod	100 grams	More than 90 mcg
Boiled Egg	1 egg	23-24 mcg
Yogurt	1 cup	87 mcg

Strawberries	1 cup	13 mcg
Kelp	0.25 cup	415 mcg
Cheddar Cheese	1 ounce	5-20 mcg
Cottage Cheese	0.5 cup	25-70 mcg
Raw Oyster	13 grams	21-22 mcg

The thyroid gland needs iodine and the amino acid L-tyrosine to make T4 and T3. A diet deficient in iodine, selenium and poor protein sources can limit how much T4 & T3 the thyroid gland can produce and lead to hypothyroidism.

The thyroid needs protecting from free radicals. Most people do not realize that the natural process of making and activating thyroid hormone is highly oxidative, meaning a lot of free radicals are made even when the thyroid is running normally. Once the thyroid starts to struggle the increase in free radicals and related inflammatory signals (like TNFa and IL6) is significant and may induce stressful wear and tear on metabolic processes.Free radicals are neutralized by antioxidants. Once your antioxidant reserves are depleted your thyroid function must slow down otherwise there will be too much metabolic friction and health-deteriorating inflammation. Unfortunately, the modern diet is lacking in antioxidants and other nutrients needed to support thyroid health.

Selenium is Vital to Thyroid Function

Selenium is highly concentrated in the thyroid gland, more so than in any other organ in the human body, indicating its vital need in normal thyroid function. It acts as an antioxidant that protects the thyroid gland, a cofactor nutrient that facilitates the production of thyroid hormone, and as a nutrient that is required to facilitate the conversion of T4 to T3 (triiodothyronine, active thyroid hormone that works inside cells to set the pace of metabolism).

Manganese, a Thyroid and Liver Protector

Manganese has long been known as the anti-pear nutrient. New science is showing the vital role of manganese in liver function, fat metabolism, and liver anti-oxidant status. This relates to thyroid hormone activation, as most activation occurs on cell membranes in the liver.

If the liver is suffering from excessive free radical stress, then cell membranes are not as functional and the activation of thyroid hormone may become distressed.

Manganese is a mineral that is required to form a special antioxidant enzyme called manganese-dependent superoxide dismutase (MnSOD). It is a key part of the cell engine's antioxidant defense system that enables the cell engine to produce energy and heat efficiently. Poor function of this enzyme reduces the ability of cells to make energy and heat.

MnSOD is now found to be a primary protector of the thyroid hormone. This enzyme naturally rises as thyroid hormone activity is increased, acting as a protective buffer to support increased metabolic rate. If this enzyme is lacking, then activation of thyroid hormone generates friction and stress in the form of excessive free radicals. This results in wear and tear to the thyroid gland, liver, and nerves. A lack of manganese is clearly associated with reduced function of thyroid hormone in the body.

Guggul A True Friend of Healthy Thyroid Function

The thyroid gland likes the Ayurvedic herb called Commiphora mukul, known as guggul. The thyroid stimulating properties of guggul have been reported for the past twenty years. Animal studies show it works partly by stimulating thyroid hormone production and partly by increasing liver antioxidant status.

The active component in this herb is gugglesterone. Intense research is now being conducted with gugglesterones as they have been found to naturally regulate a gene receptor called farnesoid X receptor (FSX). As it turns out, FSX specifically turns on and off fat burning in the liver.

Gugglesterones have been used in traditional Ayurvedic medicine in India for several thousand years to help weight management. Any nutrient that enhances the burning of fat will at least have an indirect benefit to thyroid function, since obesity itself is a major stress to the thyroid gland.

Iodine and the Thyroid

Since iodine is needed for the production of thyroid hormone, and the body does not make iodine, we have to get it through what we eat. Worldwide, the number one cause of hypothyroidism is iodine deficiency, which remains a public health problem in 47 countries; about 2.2 billion people (around

38% of the world's population) live in areas with iodine deficiency. An article in The Lancet in 2008 stated that, "According to WHO, in 2007, nearly 2 billion individuals had insufficient iodine intake, a third being of school age. Thus iodine deficiency, as the single greatest preventable cause of mental retardation, is an important public health problem."

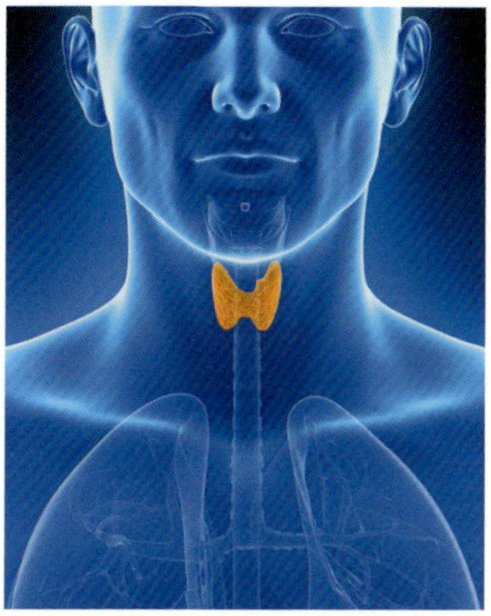

Thyroid cells are the only cells in the body which can absorb iodine. These cells combine iodine and the amino acid tyrosine to make T3 and T4. T3 is critically important because it acts on special receptors on the nucleus of the cells that send messages to your DNA to turn up your metabolism, to increase the fat burning in your mitochondria, and to generally make every system in your body work at the right speed. This is why T3 lowers your cholesterol, improves your memory, keeps you thin, promotes regrowth in cases of hair loss, relieves muscle aches, relieves constipation etc.

If you produce too little T3, or if the T4 you produce is not being properly converted into this active thyroid hormone (which can happen when any step in the process is inhibited), your whole system goes haywire: your metabolism and mitochondria don't get the proper signals, you gain weight and you suffer from the symptoms of hypothyroidism.

Thyroid peroxidase (TPO) is the enzyme responsible for making thyroid hormones. It liberates iodine to be added to tyrosine for T4 & T3 production. This process involves many cofactors, including iron, selenium, copper, magnesium, niacin, riboflavin, vitamin B6 & zinc. Therefore, a deficiency in any of these vitamins and minerals could lead to thyroid problems.

Thyroid hormones

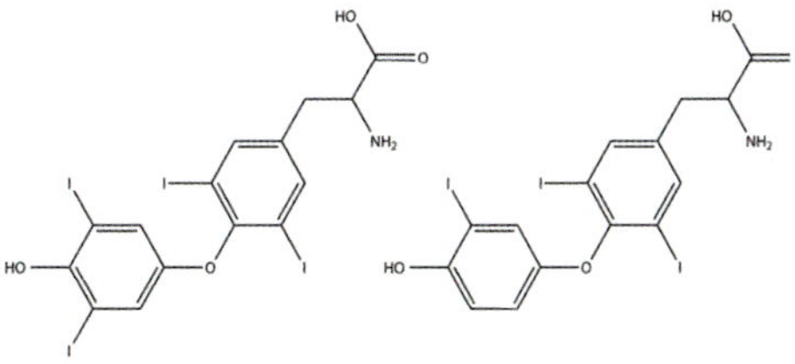

Thyroxine (T_4)   Triiodothyronine (T_3)

"Iodine deficiency may lead to an underactive thyroid and ultimately to a goitre, and goitres have been clearly associated with an increased risk of breast cancer." ***Breast Cancer: A Nutritional Approach by Carlton Fredericks, Ph.D.***

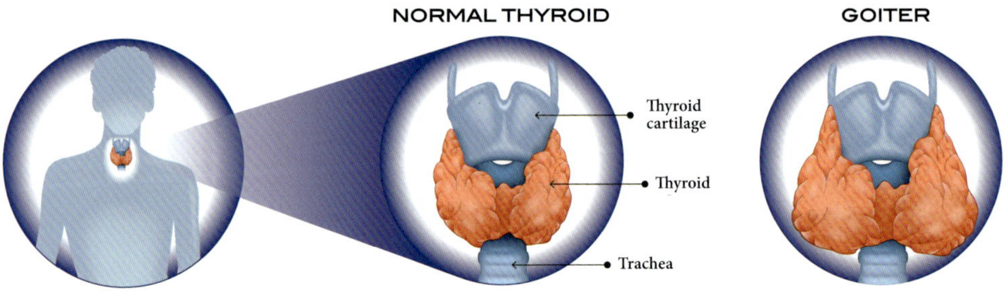

"At iodine sufficiency, the largest amounts of iodine are found in fat tissue and muscle (striated) tissue. If obesity is present, the body's need for iodine increases, as the fat cells of the body would require more iodine. Women's breasts are major sites for iodine storage. Maintaining adequate iodine levels is necessary to ensure an adequately functioning thyroid gland and normal breast architecture. I believe it will also lower the incidence of breast cancer and help women overcome breast cancer." ***Iodine: Why You Need It, Why You Can't Live Without It by David Brownstein, M.D.***

What Else Can Affect the Thyroid?

Soy and Your Thyroid

Genistein is particularly harmful for people who have pre-existing low or marginally low thyroid function. Genistein is one of several known isoflavones. Isoflavones, such as genistein and daidzein, are found in a number of plants, with soybeans and soy products like tofu and textured vegetable protein (such as margarines) being the primary food source. A daily dose of genistein as low as 30mg can affect normal thyroid function. High consumption of isoflavones such as soy burgers can bring the total daily genistein intake to over 200mg.

Soy also acts like oestrogen in your body, which also adds to issues of oestrogen dominance which creates further thyroid problems.

Soy should be taken out of your diet if you value your thyroid health.

Goitrogens And Thyroid Health

Most goitrogens are naturally-occurring chemicals that are ingested in foods or drugs. These chemicals can interfere with thyroid function in different ways. Some compounds induce antibodies that cross-react with the thyroid gland; others interfere with thyroid peroxidase (TPO), the enzyme responsible for adding iodine during production of thyroid hormones. Either way, the thyroid isn't able to produce as many of the hormones that are needed for regulating metabolism.

For people with healthy thyroid function, the thyroid simply compensates and makes more of the hormones as they're called for. But in some people whose thyroid function is already compromised, the thyroid gland may actually grow more cells as it tries to make up for inadequate hormone production, eventually forming a goiter (a swelling or enlargement of the thyroid gland).

You may be surprised by how many common foods contain goitrogenic compounds, but the good news is, in most cases you don't have to cross them off your grocery list. Let's take a look at some of them and discuss how you can keep them in your diet, even if you have hypothyroidism.

Gluten

Gluten sensitivity contributes to a wide range of autoimmune responses aside from celiac disease (the one for which it's best known). Gluten sensitivity has been found to go hand-in-hand with autoimmune disorders such as type 1 diabetes, Addison's disease, Sjögren's syndrome, rheumatoid arthritis, and autoimmune thyroid disease. If you have autoimmune hypothyroidism, you might want to consider limiting your intake of wheat, barley, and rye, or even going completely gluten-free (you will see the connection between gluten and Hashimoto's later in this habit). I also suggest that people with autoimmune thyroid disease consider screening for celiac disease, because undetected celiac can be one reason that people continue to have hypothyroid symptoms despite higher and higher doses of thyroid replacement hormone.

Soy isoflavones

Soy does contain goitrogenic compounds, specifically the soy isoflavone genistein. This compound, just like thyroid hormones, accepts iodine molecules from the thyroid peroxidase (TPO), which again, is the enzyme that also transfers iodine to the thyroid hormones. Some researchers have suggested that genistein and similar isoflavones may compete with thyroid hormones for iodine or alternatively may "block" the action of TPO.

Isothiocyanates

These compounds are primarily found in cruciferous vegetables, such as cabbage, Brussels sprouts, broccoli, broccolini, cauliflower, mustard greens, kale, turnips, and collards. Isothiocyanates, like soy isoflavones, appear to block TPO, and they may also disrupt signaling across the thyroid's cell membranes. But no one would argue that these vegetables are bad for you, given that they are filled with vitamins, minerals, antioxidants, and a variety of nutrients we all need. People with thyroid problems definitely should not avoid them instead, enjoy them steamed or cooked, as the heat alters the isothiocyanates' molecular structure and eliminates the goitrogenic effect.

Thimerosal

The enzyme thyroid peroxidase, converts T4 to T3 and is blocked by mercury in the body, primarily from dental mercury amalgam fillings and thimerosal, a mercury preservative found in vaccinations and other medicines.

Hypothyroidism

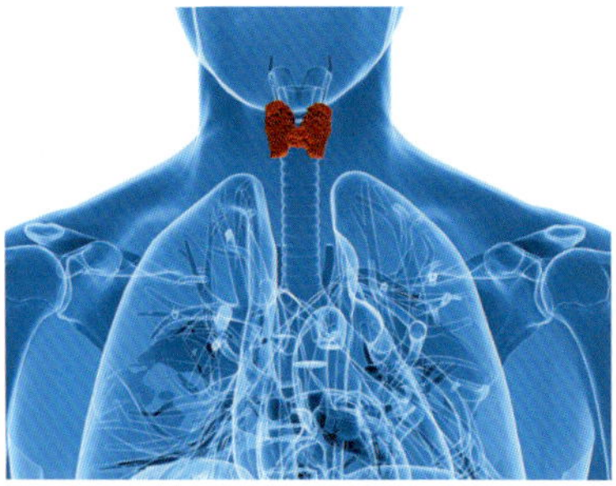

Do you feel fatigued, lethargic, and sluggish, especially when you wake up in the morning? Do you have poor-quality, cracked nails? Are you cold all the time? Do you have dry skin, coarse hair, or hair loss? Are you depressed? Are you constipated? Do you have muscle and joint pains? Have you lost the outer third of your eyebrows? Do you have trouble losing weight no matter what you do?

If you answer yes to any of these questions, you may be suffering from hypothyroidism, a potentially dangerous health condition that occurs when the production, conversion, or action of the thyroid hormones in your body is inhibited, resulting in too little active thyroid hormone in your blood. Take a look at the table below for a summary of symptoms which are common in those with hypothyroidism.

THYROID DYSFUNCTION

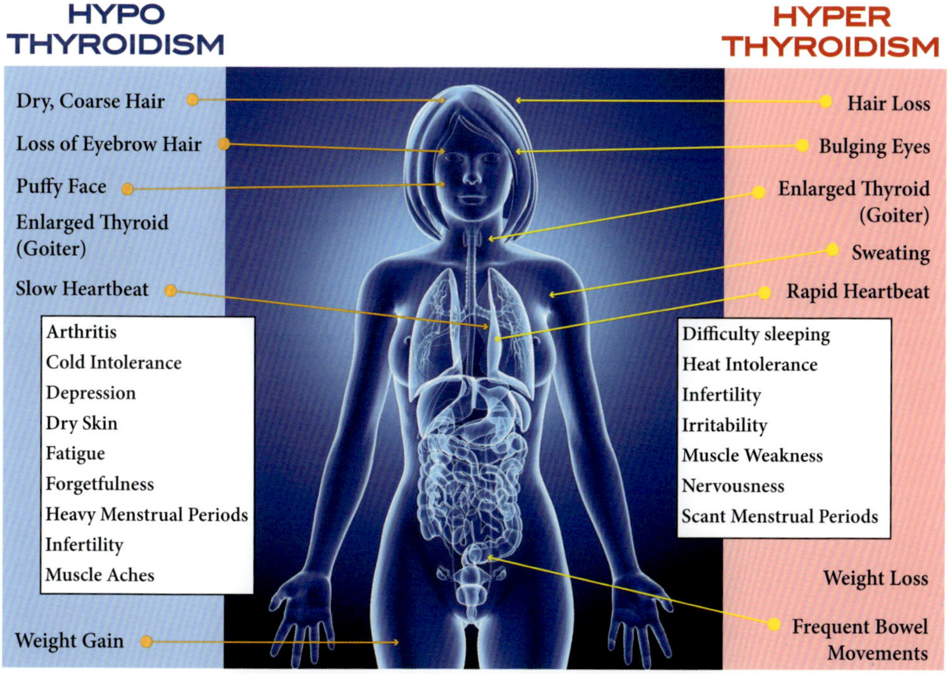

Thyroid Blood Tests

The diagnosis of hypothyroidism by laboratory methods is primarily based on the results of total T4, free T4, T3, and TSH levels. The typical blood tests measure thyroxine (T4), which accounts for approximately 93% of the hormone secretion by the thyroid. The most important blood tests to look at is T3 and reverse T3 (rT3)

If the cells are not able to convert T4 to the four-times more active T3, a person can have normal levels of thyroid hormone in the blood, yet be thyroid-deficient. This is why blood tests can be inaccurate and you need to look at symptoms as much as the blood tests! If for example you're taking prescription thyroxine (T4) but are not feeling any better, it's likely that the T4 is not converting to active T3 hormone.

The blood tests that may be done as part of a thyroid diagnosis include the following:

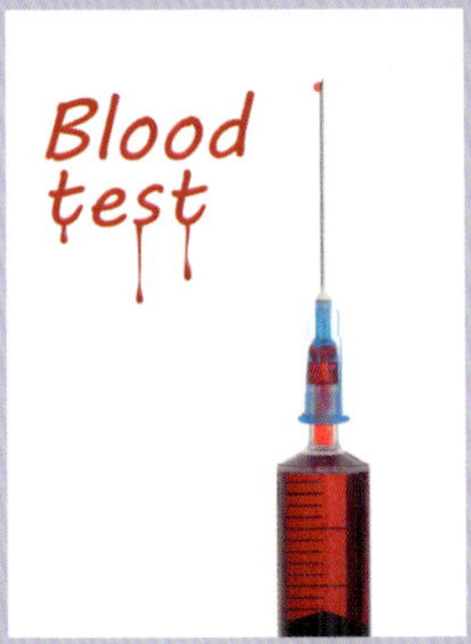

- Thyroid Stimulating Hormone (TSH) Test
- Total T4/ Total Thyroxine
- Free T4 / Free Thyroxine
- Total T3 / Total Triiodothyronine
- Free T3 / Free Triiodothyronine
- Thyroglobulin/Thyroid Binding Globulin/TBG
- T3 Resin Uptake (T3RU)
- Reverse T3
- Thyroid Peroxidase Antibodies (TPOAb) / Antithyroid Peroxidase Antibodies
- Antithyroid Microsomal Antibodies / Antimicrosomal Antibodies
- Thyroglobulin Antibodies / Antithyroglobulin Antibodies
- Thyroid Receptor Antibodies (TRAb)
- Thyroid-Stimulating Immunoglobulins (TSI)

3 important tests from the above is:

- Free T3 reference range 4 to 8.3
- Reverse T3 less than 25ng/dl
- TSH 1mlU/ml

It is possible, however, to go overboard with thyroid medication. Too much thyroid medication can stress out the adrenal glands, which will then overproduce cortisol as well as deregulate (impair) the ratio of cortisol and DHEA and epinephrine and norepinephrine. This will leave you more fatigued than you were in the first place, because the rest of your body's systems will not be able to produce the energy needed to keep up with your now revved-up thyroid.

It is possible for individuals to be hypothyroid and have elevated levels of T4. This is sometimes seen in liver disease. The liver utilizes large amounts of thyroid. If liver cells are not able to use all the thyroid brought to them by the blood stream, the thyroid backs up and the blood levels of thyroid hormone rise, similar to when a stream is dammed.

The single most important test for thyroid function is basal temperature. The reason for this is that thyroid hormone increases the conversion of ATP to ADP to power all the metabolic functions of the cell. In that conversion, a large % of the energy is released as heat. That heat is needed to maintain bodily functions by maintaining the proper temperature range for enzymatic activities necessary for life. Body temperature is a good measure of basal metabolic rate and is cheaper and simpler to perform than measuring the rate of conversion of oxygen to carbon dioxide, which is the "gold standard" measure of metabolic activity.

Thyroid Self-Test:

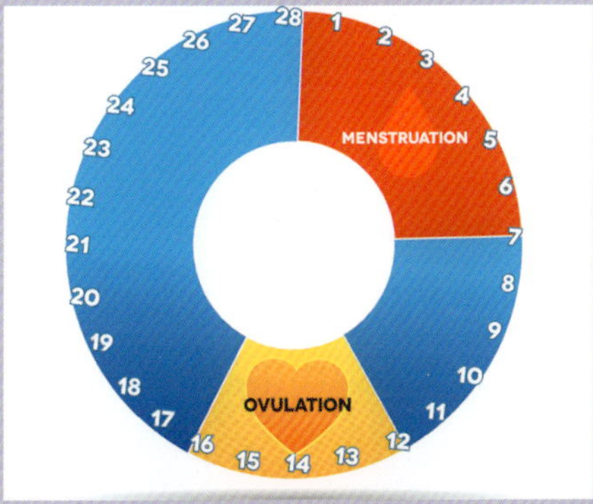

The basal temperature in menstruating women is most accurately measured on the 1st, 2nd, 3rd or 4th day of the menstrual cycle (preferably beginning on the 2nd day). Males, pre-pubertal girls, and postmenopausal or non-menstruating women may take basal temperatures any day of the month. You should take your temperature 3 days in a row.

To test yourself for an underactive thyroid, keep an electronic thermometer by your bed at night. When you wake up in the morning, place the thermometer in your armpit and hold it there for about 10 minutes. According to Broda Barnes, MD (a pioneer in thyroid metabolism), if the average temperature is below 97.8 Fahrenheit, then the diagnosis of a low functioning thyroid system is likely. An average temperature between 97.8 and 98.2 is considered normal.

An average temperature above 98.2 is considered high and might reflect an infection or a hyperthyroid condition. At least three days of measurement are necessary for an average.

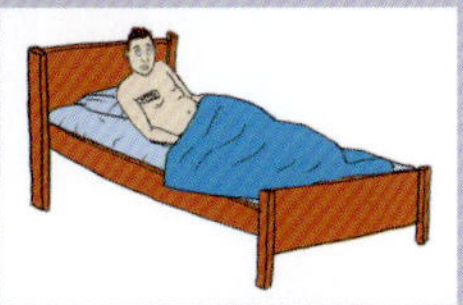

You can use a thermometer to check your waking temperature. This will help you assess whether you have an underactive thyroid.

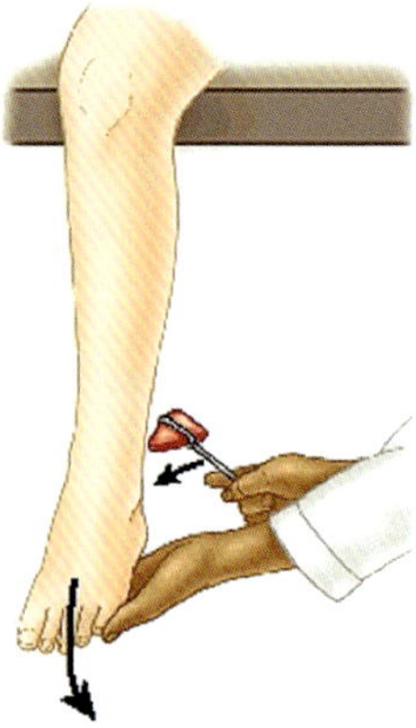

Another Functional test for the thyroid is the Achilles return reflex

- A delayed Achilles return reflex is a classic sign of hypothyroidism.
- In the absence of spinal lesions, a delayed Achilles return reflex bilaterally indicates the strong likelihood for low thyroid activity.

Another interesting test is to check the iodine status in your body, which is essential to thyroid function.

- The iodine skin test is a functional assessment for iodine status in the body.
- By applying on the skin a 2% solution of iodine we can see how quickly the body absorbs the available iodine.
- The quicker the iodine fades, the greater the deficiency can be assumed.

Cortisol and Adrenal Function

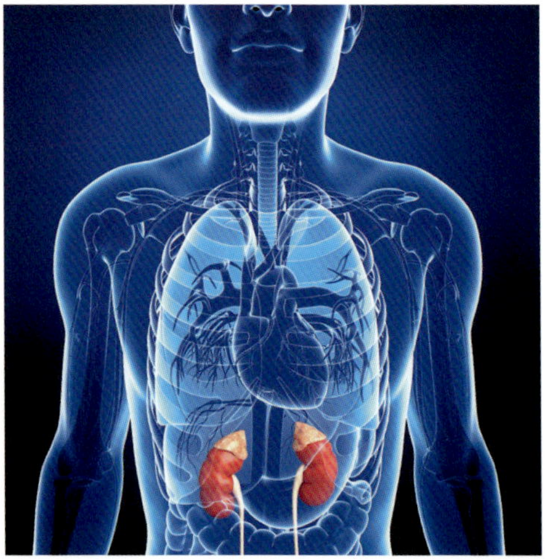

Cortisol is a key factor in setting the temperature of the body, so with high cortisol levels the body temperature in the morning will also be low. Why? **High cortisol levels reduce the thyroid hormone T3.** When T3 is low, metabolism slows and body temperature dips, hence the connection between thyroid and adrenals.

High cortisol also inhibits the messenger hormone thyroid stimulating hormone (TSH) – which is sent from the pituitary gland to the thyroid gland to release T4 – T3.

Low adrenal function often leads to low thyroid function, classically evidenced by high levels of thyroid binding globulin (TBG), low free T4, low free T3, high TSH, slow ankle reflex and low body temperature.

The adrenal glands main purpose is to produce and release certain regulatory hormones and chemical messengers, and the connection between thyroid and adrenal gland is a very important clinical consideration.

Cortisol produced by your adrenal glands helps enable thyroid hormones pass from your blood into your cells. Cortisol raises your cellular level of glucose which works with your cell receptors to receive T3 from the blood to the cells.

Cortisol affects the thyroid gland in three ways:

1) Cortisol is required to facilitate release of TSH from the pituitary gland.
2) Cortisol facilitates conversion of the inactive T4 hormone to the active T3 form.
3) Cortisol allows each T3 cell receptor to more readily accept T3.

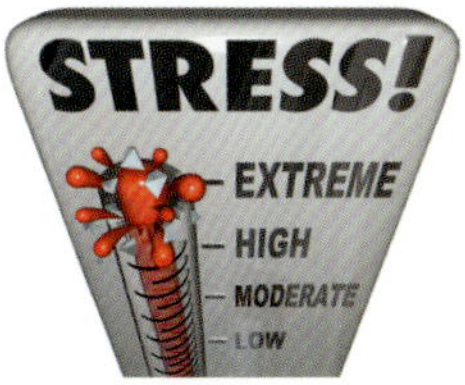

Stress is one of the worst thyroid offenders.

Your thyroid function is intimately tied to your adrenal function, which in turn is intimately affected by how you handle stress. Many of us are under chronic stress, which results in increased adrenaline and cortisol levels, and elevated cortisol has a negative impact on thyroid function. Thyroid hormone levels drop during stress. When stress becomes chronic, the flood of stress chemicals (adrenalin and cortisol) produced by your adrenal glands interferes with thyroid hormones and can contribute to obesity, high blood pressure, high cholesterol, unstable blood sugar, and more. A prolonged stress response can lead to adrenal exhaustion (also known as adrenal fatigue), which is often found alongside thyroid disease

Administering thyroid medication in cases of advanced adrenal fatigue without concurrent attention to adrenal recovery will often fail. In many cases, it is analogous to pouring oil onto a fire. An already weak adrenal system, in a low energy state, may not be able to carry the burden of extra

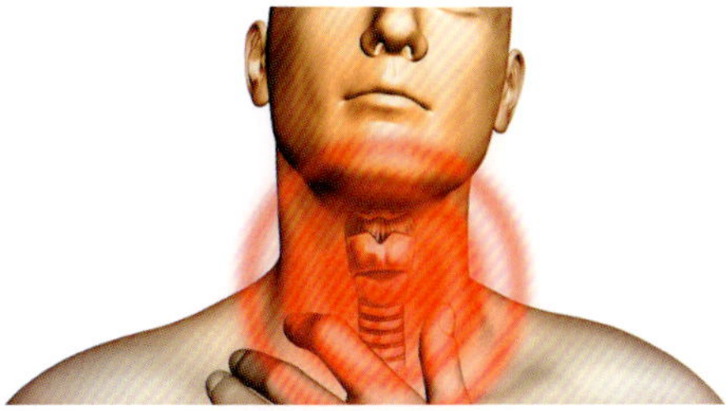

energy output that the thyroid hormones are demanding. What the adrenals need is rest, not extra work.

Because thyroid hormone raises metabolism, which results in increased cortisol clearance and if the body cannot produce the amount of cortisol needed for the higher metabolism, it can result in a low cortisol symptoms including fatigue, weight gain/loss, low blood pressure, dizziness and more. In habit 6 I give you information on how to help get your adrenals healthy which as you know realise are absolutely paramount to thyroid function, remember hormones work in synergy.

Cortisol is necessary to produce thyroid hormones, and also necessary for your body to convert T4 to the active T3, as well as thyroid receptor function. When your thyroid hormone receptors aren't working properly, any thyroid hormones you do make can't get into your cells. **Without enough cortisol, the thyroid receptors can eventually even disappear, until you correct the deficiency.** This is why a lot of people on thyroid medication don't see any benefits; because the doctor doesn't address adrenal function as part of the treatment.

Hypocortisolism, or low cortisol, occurs when the adrenal glands are unable to make a normal amount of the main stress hormone, cortisol. Often those with hypothyroidism are suffering from low cortisol levels. If the hypocortisolism is undiagnosed, or inadequately treated, thyroid medication may work only temporarily or completely fail to help with symptoms or even make the problems worse.

Your adrenals rely heavily on your thyroid to function correctly. None of the adrenals vital activities can be accomplished without adequate thyroid support. In fact, virtually every cell in your body has receptors for both cortisol and thyroid hormones. You must have adequate levels of both in your cells for your body to do its job and be healthy.

Hypothyroidism slows your adrenal glands and also stresses your body; increasing adrenaline output and further taxing the adrenals. In addition, hypothyroidism leads to an increase in cortisol binding globulin, a protein that binds cortisol and makes it unavailable to the body. This then becomes a vicious cycle, with low thyroid function leading to low adrenal function, which leads to even lower thyroid function. **Get your adrenals and thyroid working in harmony together which will give you vibrant health and optimum body fat levels.**

When you're dieting, or under a lot of stress and making high levels of cortisol in response to the situation, your body converts T4 to reverse T3 instead of the dynamo T3. **Reverse T3 ties up your thyroid receptors and prevents you from using the active T3 which enhances metabolism and fat burning.** This results in symptoms of hypothyroidism, no matter what your actual levels of thyroid hormones are. That's why its so hard to lose weight by extreme dieting or when you are under extreme stress or both. Your body goes into survival mode and drops metabolism and that's why rT3 increases at the expense of it's fat burning brother T3.

Hypothyroidism can be primary or secondary. **If hypothyroid symptoms, such as low body** temperature, fatigue, dry skin and weight gain persist despite thyroid replacement therapy regardless of laboratory values, one must look elsewhere for the cause of the low thyroid function.

Secondary hypothyroidism is low thyroid function caused by malfunction of another organ system. One of the most frequently overlooked causes is adrenal fatigue, as we have just discussed and oestrogen dominance.

Signs and Symptoms of Adrenal Fatigue:

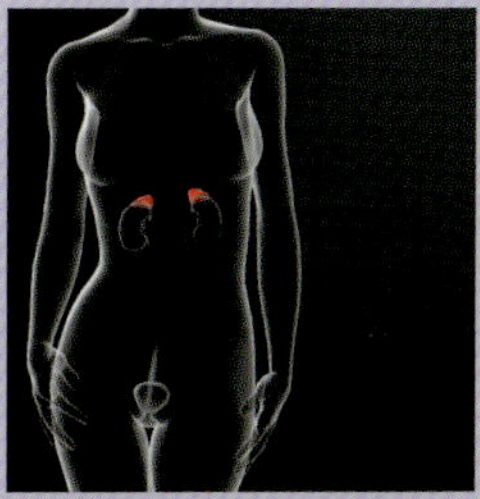

- Tendency to gain weight and unable to lose it, especially around the waist.
- High frequency of getting the flu and other respiratory diseases and these symptoms tend to last longer than usual.
- Tendency to tremble when under pressure.
- Reduced sex drive.
- Lightheaded when rising from a horizontal position.
- Unable to remember things.
- Lack of energy in the mornings and in the afternoon between 3 to 5 pm.
- Feel better suddenly for a brief period after a meal.
- Often feel tired from 9 - 10 pm, but resist going to bed.
- Need coffee or stimulants to get going in the morning.
- Cravings for salty, fatty, and high protein food such as meat and cheese.
- Increased symptoms of PMS for women; periods are heavy and then stop, or are almost stopped on the 4th day, only to start flow again on the 5th or 6th day.
- Pain in the upper back or neck with no apparent reason.
- Feels better when stress is relieved, such as on a vacation.
- Difficulties in getting up in the morning.
- Lightheaded.

Other signs and symptoms of adrenal fatigue include:

- Mild depression
- Food and or inhalant allergies
- Lethargy and lack of energy
- Increased effort to perform daily tasks
- Decreased ability to handle stress
- Dry and thin skin
- Hypoglycemia
- Low body temperature
- Nervousness
- Palpitation
- Unexplained hair loss
- Alternating constipation and diarrhea
- Dyspepsia

So you can see the very similar side effects of adrenal fatigue to hypothyroidism, this is why it's crucial to treat them both together because they work together.

Researchers at the University of North Carolina have found that lengthy bouts of strenuous exercise can cause the body unnecessary stress – and lead to higher cortisol levels and lower levels of thyroid hormones 24 hours after exercise.

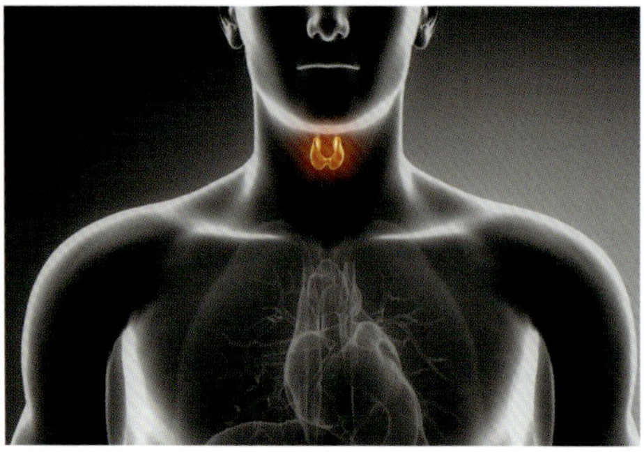

Those who take part in regular strenuous physical activity can end up having thyroid troubles and subsequent drops in performance and health.

The first key thing to understand is that thyroid function is highly responsive to stress – so it's natural to expect that heavy training would affect it. Studies demonstrate beyond any doubt that excessive cardio chronically shuts down the production of the thyroid hormone, T3.

Those who do endless hours per week doing cardio training unknowingly put themselves into the hypothyroid condition because excessive cardio inhibits their most precious fat burning hormone T3. In the quest to lose body fat, T3 levels can grant outstanding success or an absolute failure because of how it influences other fat-regulating hormones and our fat burning machines aka mitochondria which turn food into energy and this is obviously essential for both fat loss and performance.

There are multiple elite athletes who have crashed their thyroid glands and are now on thyroid medication. So extreme training over long periods of time undoubtedly down-regulates the thyroid.

Oestrogen Dominance and Thyroid Function

Oestrogen dominance is often associated with high levels of fat around the thighs and buttocks.

Oestrogen causes food calories to be stored as fat. Thyroid Hormone causes fat calories to be turned into usable energy. Thyroid Hormone and Oestrogen therefore have opposing actions.

High oestrogen levels lead to excessive production of thyroid-binding globulin (TBG) by the liver. If the TBG levels are high it will bind more thyroid hormones, thus reducing the free thyroid hormones available in the blood. Therefore, thyroid hormones cannot be used by the cells that require them for maintaining the body's metabolism.

Although there are enough thyroid hormones in the blood, they are not taken up by the body's cells, as they are inactivated by TBG. Oestrogen dominance therefore often leads to thyroid problems. This is one of the reasons why blood tests reveal 'normal' levels of thyroid hormones in such situations, but some people still show classical symptoms of thyroid problems.

Oestrogen has also been found to bind to thyroid binding sites within the cell. So excess oestrogen thus also decreases thyroid function by tying up its binding site with ease.

At puberty, in pregnancy, and at menopause, the thyroid gland often enlarges, probably as a result of oestrogen dominance.

Thyroid function stimulates the liver to deactivate oestrogen for secretion, so oestrogen dominance can create a vicious circle, in which excess oestrogen (or deficient progesterone) blocks thyroid secretion, causing the liver to allow oestrogen to accumulate to even higher levels. Progesterone can break the cycle and we cover how to increase progesterone and balance oestrogen in detail in habit 6.

Normally, the active thyroid hormone [T3] is released from the thyroid gland and travels in the blood stream. In the following illustrations, the active thyroid hormone [T3] is shown as a key, and every cell in the body is shown to have a receptor or keyhole in this analogy.

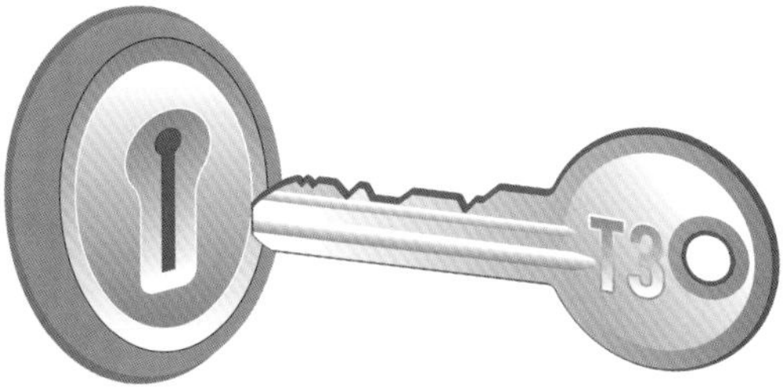

The nucleus in every cell has a keyhole and needs the key [the active thyroid hormone [T3) to be inserted into the keyhole to make a cell work. This can be seen in the following illustration.

However, if a person has oestrogen dominance for example [excess oestrogen, deficient progesterone, or a combination of the two], this is like putting a piece of duct tape over the keyhole. This can be seen in the following illustration.

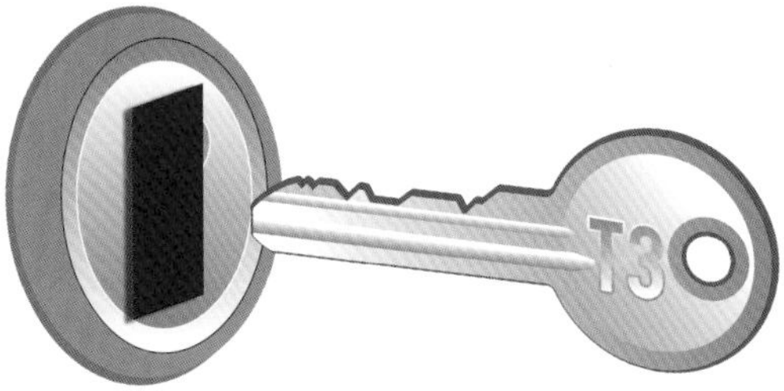

As the key [the active thyroid hormone [T3]], can't get into the key hole to turn on the cell so it can work, symptoms of hypothyroidism [under active thyroid] can appear. Lab tests in this situation would show that the thyroid is functioning normally and making the needed hormones.

Therefore, in this situation, even giving thyroid medication will not help a person with oestrogen dominance [excess oestrogen, deficient progesterone or the two], to feel better or help their body to work better. A person's oestrogen must be properly counterbalanced with the proper amount of progesterone before the active thyroid hormone [T3] can turn on the cells so that they can work.

Thyroid hormone and appetite

Without an optimum balance of leptin and ghrelin in your brain, you simply cannot achieve or maintain a normal weight. The intimate relationship between leptin and thyroid hormones is amazing. First, leptin promotes thyroid growth and thyroid hormone production. Leptin signals the hypothalamus to send the message to the pituitary to tell your thyroid to produce the right amount of hormone needed for metabolism.

Without leptin, or when leptin is inefficient, the communication between your hypothalamus, pituitary and thyroid gland fails to produce the right amount of hormones. Leptin also tells the cells in your body to convert enough T4 to T3. When leptin signalling is not at its best, thyroid hormones become less efficient in your cells and your body burns even less energy and fat.

Just as leptin influences the thyroid, thyroid hormone itself affects leptin levels and leptin efficiency. Leptin requires thyroid hormone to carry out its healthy metabolising, energy producing, fat burning benefits.

If your T3 is low, leptin will not efficiently spark your metabolism. So you can now see that you can not just take one hormone like thyroid and expect the pounds to melt away; all hormones work synergistically and if you want them to function efficiently - you must work on getting healthy by following the 10 habits in this book.

Thyroid hormone also has a profound effect on hunger hormone, ghrelin, levels. Low thyroid causes ghrelin to rise, making you hungrier and slowing metabolism even further. Restoring thyroid hormones to normal levels causes ghrelin to drop.

Amazingly, thyroid hormone has the ability to convert fat cells into calorie burning, heat producing cells. The hormones leptin, ghrelin and thyroid hormone work on the mitochondria to either enhance calorie burning and heat production (leptin and thyroid hormone) or slow heat production, which slows metabolism (ghrelin).

The Liver-Thyroid Connection

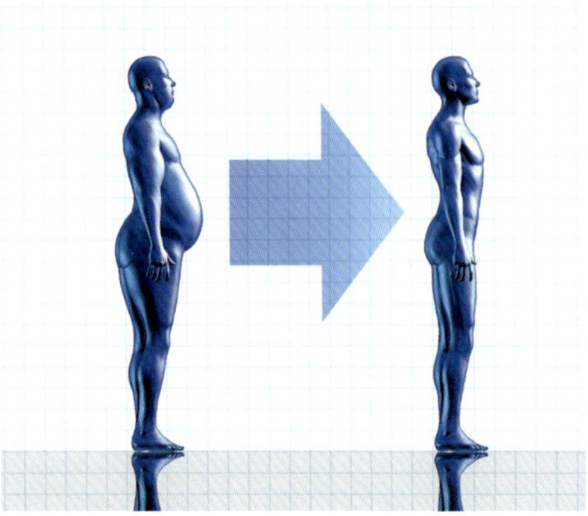

The amount of glucose in liver cells regulates the enzyme that converts T4 to T3. This means that hypoglycemia or diabetes (in which glucose doesn't enter cells efficiently) will cause hypothyroidism, when T4 can't be converted into T3.

When the liver is the main cause of hypothyroidism, your temperature (and especially the temperature of your nose, hands and feet) will fall when you are hungry, and will rise when you eat carbohydrates.

The thyroid gland secretes about 3 parts of thyroxin to one part of triiodothyronine, and this allows the liver to regulate thyroid function, by converting more of the T4 to the active T3 when there is an abundance of energy. Glucose is essential for the conversion, so during fasting there is a sharp decrease in metabolic rate, and in experiments, 200 or 300 calories of carbohydrates can added to the diet without causing fat storage.

When a person is fasting, at first the liver's glycogen stores will provide glucose to maintain T3 production. When the glycogen is depleted, the body resorts to the dissolution of tissue to provide energy. **Eating small amounts of carbohydrates (30 - 50 grams) can allow the liver to resume its production of T3.**

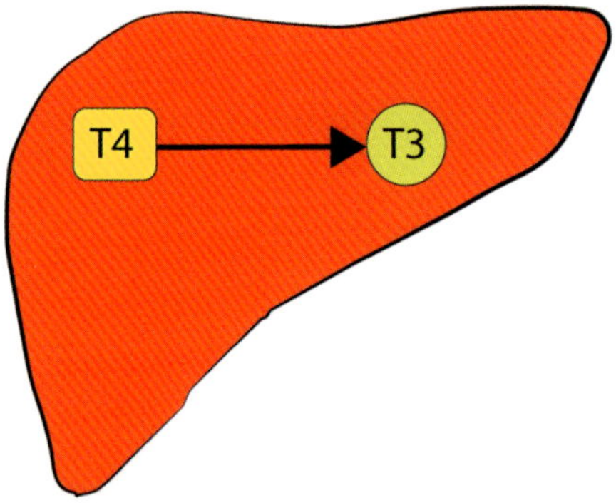

60% of the conversion of T4 into T3 takes place in the liver, provided that the liver is healthy and as adequate glycogen stores.

Thyroxine, increases insulin response. Hypothyroidism threatens the supportive role and contributes to hyperglycemia and poor insulin response.

The exact effects of thyroid hormone on insulin secretion remains poorly understood. However, a clinical trial demonstrated that a hypothyroid state resulted in a reduction in both insulin binding and a number of insulin receptors in the livers of experimental rats.

Most T4 to T3 conversion happens in your liver, kidneys and muscles. In fact, 60% of T4 is converted into T3 in the liver providing it is functioning at full effectiveness. Now you can see why a dysfunctional liver can lead to a cascade of hormonal problems.

If you have a fatty liver or a sluggish liver, this conversion will also not be effective. This can leave you feeling tired, depressed, puffy, overweight and with dry skin and thinning scalp hair. Indeed, you would have a thyroid problem caused by a faulty liver.

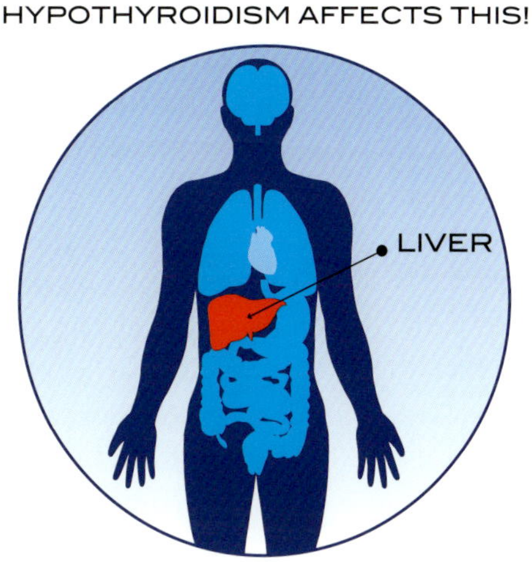

The Gut-Bacteria-Thyroid Connection

Gut bacteria plays a role in converting T4 into T3.

One little known role of the gut bacteria is to assist in converting inactive T4 into the active form of thyroid hormone, T3. About 20% of T4 is converted to T3 in the gastrointestinal tract (GI), in the forms of T3 sulphate (T3S) and triiodothyroacetic acid (T3AC). The conversion of T3S and T3AC into active T3 requires an enzyme called intestinal sulfatase. For this to happen you need lots of healthy bacteria.

Studies show that 90% of people with hypothyroidism are producing antibodies to thyroid tissue.

This causes the immune system to attack and destroy the thyroid, which over time causes a decline in thyroid hormone levels. What the vast majority of hypothyroidism patients need to understand is that they may not have a problem with their thyroid, they have a problem with their immune system attacking the thyroid.

An Italian study found that those with a significant allergy to gluten also developed a significant allergy to their own thyroids, which disappeared when the gluten was removed for three to six months. Several studies also show a strong link between autoimmune thyroid disease (AITD), both Hashimoto's (hypothyroidism) and Graves (hyperthyroidism), and gluten intolerance. The link is so well-established that researchers suggest all people with Autoimmune Thyroid Disorder be screened for gluten intolerance.

What explains the connection? It's a case of mistaken identity. The molecular structure of gliadin, the protein portion of gluten, closely resembles that of the thyroid gland. When gliadin breaches the protective barrier of the gut, and enters the bloodstream, the immune system tags it for destruction. These antibodies to gliadin also cause the body to attack thyroid tissue. This means if you have AITD and you eat foods containing gluten, your immune system will attack your thyroid.

Even worse, the immune response to gluten can last up to 6 months each time you eat it. This explains why it is critical to eliminate gluten completely from your diet if you have AITD.

The Thyroid Heart/Cholesterol Connection

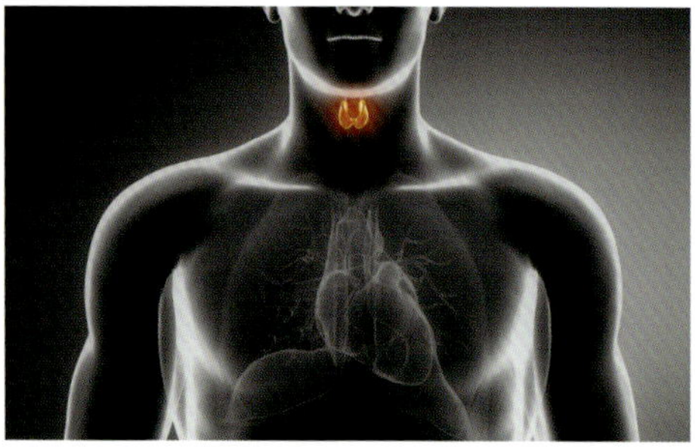

Thyroid hormone is very important for normal cardiovascular function, so when not enough thyroid hormone is present neither the heart nor the blood vessels function normally. Furthermore, hypothyroidism reduces the amount of nitric oxide in the lining of the blood vessels, causing them to stiffen.

T3 improves contraction and thus cardiac output, for one. So if it's low, output goes down. T3 also helps clear out excess arterial fatty deposits. So if its low, cholesterol and fatty acids go up. When the thyroid gland produces too little hormone, metabolism can slow, having a direct impact on the body's ability to clear cholesterol from the bloodstream. As a result, the risk of cholesterol being deposited in the arteries, especially around the heart, is increased, thereby increasing the risk for heart disease.

Even if your thyroid is underactive, and not true hypothyroidism, there can be an increase in total cholesterol levels, in addition to an impairment of your heart's ability to pump efficiently. Hypothyroidism can also lead to an enlarged heart and heart failure.

Tests from the University of Texas-Southwest Medical School, Dallas, TX underscore a clear correlation between hypothyroidism and hypercholesterolemia, (high blood cholesterol.) Ninety percent of patients with overt hypothyroidism have increased cholesterol and/or triglycerides. Once hypothyroidism is treated with a thyroid hormone replacement, and the TSH level is restored to normal, the majority of patients show an estimated 20 to 30 percent reduction in cholesterol levels.

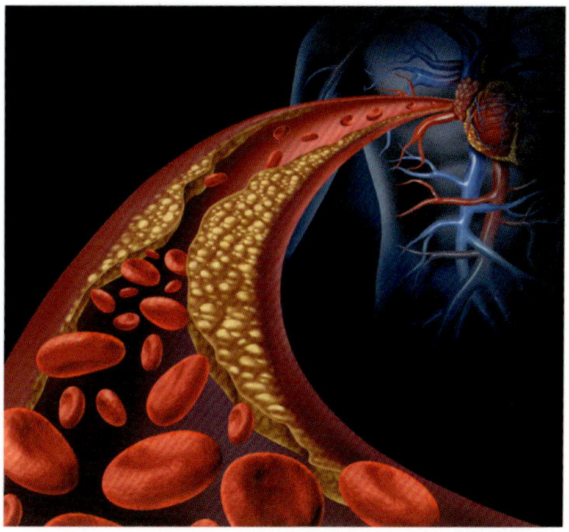

The Hunt Study is a population-based cohort study begun in 1984 and carried out at the Norwegian University of Science and Technology in Trondheim, Norway. It recruited participants from the local population of about 130,000 people. Since the entire Hunt Study involved the participation of more than 100,000 of these people, the results represent a complete and highly statistically significant cross section of almost an entire population.

This examination of Hunt Study findings, reported in the Archives of Internal Medicine, involved the prospective study of the associations between thyroid stimulating hormone (TSH) and fatal coronary heart disease (CHD) in 17,311 women and 8002 men without known thyroid or cardiovascular disease or diabetes mellitus. All participants had "normal TSH" levels, meaning the TSH values were in the lab reference range of 0.5 to 3.5. The women were stratified into three groups reflecting lower TSH, intermediate TSH and upper TSH levels. Mortality from heart disease was recorded over an 8 year observation period.

Researchers found that the group with the highest TSH had a 70% increased mortality from heart disease compared to the lowest TSH group, even though all these TSH values were in the range considered to be normal. Another report from the Hunt Study showed LDL cholesterol to be linearly associated with TSH level. As LDL cholesterol goes up, so does TSH.

Environmental Chemicals

The affinity of mercury for the pituitary gland was first identified by Stock in 1940. Autopsy studies in 1975 revealed that, contrary to accepted belief that the kidney was the prime accumulator of inorganic mercury, the thyroid and pituitary retain and accumulate more inorganic mercury than the kidneys. It has been well documented that mercury is an endocrine system disrupting chemical in animals and people, disrupting function of the pituitary gland, thyroid gland, enzyme production processes, and many hormonal functions at low levels of exposure.

People with high mercury levels in their bodies have more hormonal disturbances, immune disturbances, recurring fungal infections, hair loss and allergies. Hormones that are most often affected by mercury are thyroid, insulin, oestrogen, testosterone, both anterior and posterior pituitary, and adrenaline. Almost all hormones have binding sites capable of connecting to metabolic cofactors, but mercury can bind here, too. Mercury frequently has a stronger affinity for these binding sites than the normal activators; even though the hormone is present in the bloodstream, it may not be able to act as it is supposed to act.

Most mercury toxic patients have lower than optimum body temperatures. The most toxic persons may have temperatures as low as 96.2. When the amalgam fillings are removed correctly, there is a trend for the temperature to approach 98.6, sometimes within 24 hours of removing all of the amalgams. The thyroid gland is controlled by the pituitary gland. When the thyroid is influenced by mercury, there is a high incidence of unexplained depression and anxiety. A person may have adequate levels of T3 and T4 hormones, but if the hormones are contaminated, the person is functionally thyroid deficient. Thyroid imbalances cause chronic conditions such as clogged arteries and chronic heart failure. People who test hypothyroid usually have significantly higher homocysteine and cholesterol--documented risk factors in heart disease.

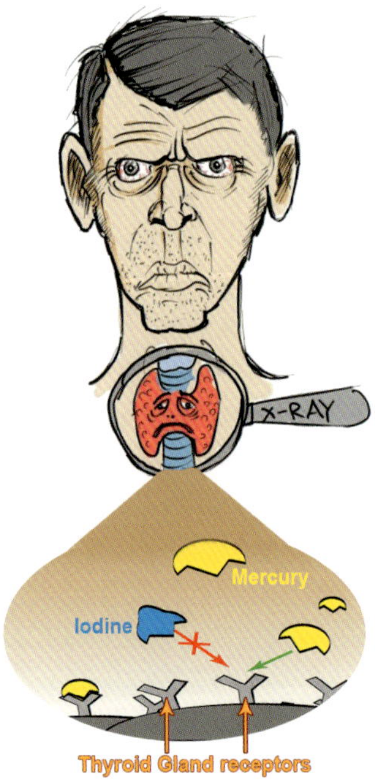

Mercury can sit on the iodine receptors in the thyroid gland therefore inhibiting thyroid hormones from being made.

Perfluorooctanoic acid (PFOA) studies have shown that people with the highest 25% of PFOA concentrations (above 5.7ng/ml) were more than twice as likely to have thyroid disease than those with the lowest 50% of PFOA concentrations (below 4.0ng/ml). PFOA is found in non-stick cookware, stain-resistant clothing and carpeting, food packaging and other consumer goods.

Scientists generally agree that Polychlorinated biphenyls (PCBs) alter thyroid hormones in the human body. PCBs have a shape very similar to thyroid hormones, which allows them to interfere or compete with normal hormones. Food can be a major source of human PCB exposure, usually from fish and animal fat. Bottom feeders and other aquatic organisms ingest and accumulate PCBs, resulting in bio-concentration upward in the food chain.

Farmed Salmon have been shown to contain high levels of PCB's

A study by the FOOD Safety Authority of Ireland, for example, found that farmed salmon has an average of four times more PCB's, dioxins, and other persistent chlorinated contaminants than wild salmon. In another study researchers tested more than seven hundred salmon totaling 2 metric tons of farmed salmon around the globe. The results: 13 persistent chlorinated pollutants were found in significantly higher levels in the farmed salmon than the wild salmon.

Another serious problem toxins create is a reduction in thyroid hormone levels and an increase in the excretion of thyroid hormones by the liver. Toxins induce a liver enzyme (Hepatic UDPGT), which promotes T4 excretion in the bile. This leaves you with less around to do the job of boosting your metabolism. In addition to all this, toxins compete with thyroid hormones by blocking your receptors and vying for thyroid transport proteins (the proteins which carry thyroid hormones around the body), making it even more difficult for your thyroid hormones to do their job.

Your thyroid hormones are very vulnerable to chlorine, fluorine and bromine (which are halides like iodine). This means that they compete for your iodine receptors. If you are exposed to a lot of these halides, you will not hold on to the iodine you need.

Bromine is present in many places in your everyday world - plastics, pesticides, hot tub treatments, fire retardants, some flours and bakery goods, and even some soft drinks. Bromide binds to the body's receptors and block the absorption of iodine receptors primarily in the thyroid and stomach.

The list of bromine is long, varied and frightening:

- Used in most grains
- Used in bleached and enriched flour
- Used as a retardant in furniture, carpets and clothing
- Used as a preservative in nuts and oils
- Sprayed on strawberries and vegetables
- Used as a fumigant for termites
- Used as an antibacterial agent along with chlorine in hot tubs and pools
- Used in Paxil and Prozak
- Used in carbonated drinks
- Used in computers and automobiles

Chlorine also blocks iodine in the body, so chlorinated water (both drinking and bathing) should best be avoided when possible to maintain a healthy thyroid.

Dental products containing fluoride could also be contributing to your thyroid problems.

Fluoride, a common additive to your water supply, and an ingredient in the toothpaste you and your children use, may be contributing to the increased rates of hypothyroidism and other health concerns without improving dental health. Dr. John Yiamouyiannis examined the raw data from a large study that was conducted by the National Institute for Dental Research (NIDR). He concluded that fluoride did not appear to have any decay preventing success, as there was little difference in the DMFT values (the mean number of decayed, missing or filled teeth) for approximately 40,000 children. It did not matter whether they grew up in fluoridated, non-fluoridated or partially fluoridated communities. ***(Yiamouyiannis, J.A. "Water Fluoridation and Tooth Decay: Results from the 1986-87 National Survey of U.S. Schoolchildren", Fluoride, 23, 55-67, 1990).***

Most developed nations, including all of Japan and 97% of western Europe DO NOT Fluoridate

FLUORIDE

BIOLOGICAL EFFECTS OF SODIUM FLUORIDE:

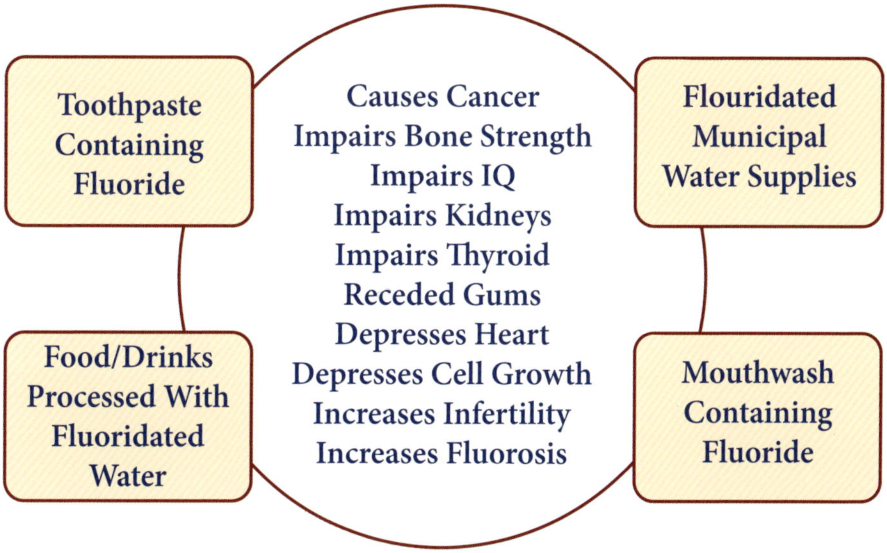

A larger study has been conducted in New Zealand. There, the New Zealand National Health Service plan examined the teeth of every child in key age groups, and have found that the teeth of children in non-fluoridated cities were slightly better than those in the fluoridated cities. ***(Colquhoun, J. "Child Dental Health Differences in New Zealand", Community Health Services, XI 85-90, 1987).***

Up until the 1950s, European doctors used fluoride to reduce the activity of the thyroid gland for people suffering from overactive thyroid (hyperthyroidism). Up to half of those drinking fluoridated water also suffer 'dental fluorosis' - a mottling of the teeth thought to be caused by its effects.

It has been established since the 1930s that the thyroid hormones control tooth eruption. Fluoridation delays the eruption of teeth because of its hypothyroid effect. Dental fluorosis is a sign of thyroid dysfunction. Any anti-thyroid substance administered during the time of enamel formation will produce the effects seen in dental fluorosis. Fluorides actually cause cavities. There are countless papers--some of them found in the York Report--clearly state that the dental defects seen in fluorosis predispose to caries. Hyperthyroidism, caused after iodine was added to public water supplies in the early 1920s, led to the use of fluorides as anti-thyroid medication. Fluorides are the worst endocrine disruptor imaginable.

In concentrations as low as 1ppm, fluorides damage the thyroid system on 4 levels:

1) Manufacture of thyroid hormones within the thyroid gland itself. The process by which iodine is attached to the amino acid tyrosine and converted to the two significant thyroid hormones, thyroxine (T4) and triiodothyronine (T3), is slowed.
2) The stimulation of certain of the G proteins whose function is to govern uptake of substances into each of the cells of the body, from the toxic effect of fluoride, has the effect of switching off the uptake into the cell of the active thyroid hormone.
3) The thyroid control mechanism is compromised. The thyroid stimulating hormone output from the pituitary gland is inhibited by fluoride, thus reducing thyroid output of thyroid hormones.
4) Fluoride competes for the receptor sites on the thyroid gland which respond to the thyroid stimulating hormone; so that less of this hormone reaches the thyroid gland and so less thyroid hormone is manufactured.

These damaging effects, all of which occur with small concentrations of fluoride, have obvious and easily identifiable effects on thyroid status. The running down of thyroid hormone means a slow slide into hypothyroidism. Already the incidence of hypothyroidism is increasing as a result of other environmental toxins and pollution together with wide-spread nutritional deficiencies.

In 1991 Robert Carton, former president of the Union of Government Scientists at the US Environmental Protection Agency – the body that oversees drinking water quality in the US – has described fluoridation as **"the greatest case of scientific fraud of this century, if not of all time."**

Fluoride-based pesticide chemicals such as cryolite (sodium hexafluoroaluminate) are commonly used on non-organic food crops because they are highly effective at both killing pests and protecting crops against pest damage. But these same chemicals tend to persist in, and on, produce, where unsuspecting consumers regularly consume them with their everyday meals. About one-third of the average person's fluoride exposure comes from non-organic food grown using fluoride chemicals.

Cryolite is actually sodium aluminum fluoride ... this sodium aluminum fluoride is especially effective at killing bugs. It's also very sticky, so when they spray it,it's more likely to stick on your produce, unless you're ... really working at trying to get it off of it.

Iodine intake immediately increases the excretion of bromide, fluoride, and some heavy metals including mercury and lead. **Bromide and f**luoride are not removed by any other chelator or detoxifying technique other than iodine.

Fats And Thyroid Function

Oh dear, this is going to throw another spanner into the works for all those low fat spreads on the supermarket shelves. They promise to reduce your weight and your cholesterol levels (which in reality is crucial for life but bad for statin and low cholesterol food sales). What they should also put on the label is that these fats make you sick, dumb, fat and tired as well - BOOM!

Read the ingredient list on these margarine products and you will usually find sunflower, corn or soy as the main ingredient which are omega 6 polyunsaturated fatty acids, which are often fed to pigs to fatten them up. In the late 1940s, chemical toxins were used to suppress the thyroid function of pigs, to make them get fatter while consuming less food. When that was found to be carcinogenic, it was then found that corn and soybeans had the same antithyroid effect, causing the animals to be fattened at low cost. The animals' fat becomes chemically similar to the fats in their food, causing it to be equally toxic, and equally fattening.

There are many changes in hormones caused by unsaturated fats. Their best understood effect is their interference with the function of the thyroid gland. Unsaturated oils block thyroid hormone secretion, its movement in the circulatory system, and the response of tissues to the hormone. When the thyroid hormone is deficient, the body is generally exposed to increased levels of oestrogen. The thyroid hormone is essential for making the "protective hormones" progesterone and pregnenolone, so these hormones are lowered when anything interferes with the function of the thyroid. The thyroid hormone is required for using and eliminating cholesterol, so cholesterol is likely to be raised by anything which blocks the thyroid function.

Vegetable oil is recognized as a drug for knocking out the immune system. Vegetable oil emulsions were used to nourish cancer patients, but it was discovered that the unsaturated oils were suppressing their immune systems. The same products, in which vegetable oil is emulsified with water for intravenous injection, are now marketed specifically for the purpose of suppressing immunity in patients who have had organ transplants. Using the oils in foods has the same harmful effect on the immune system. ***(E. A. Mascioli, et al.,Lipids 22(6) 421, 1987).***

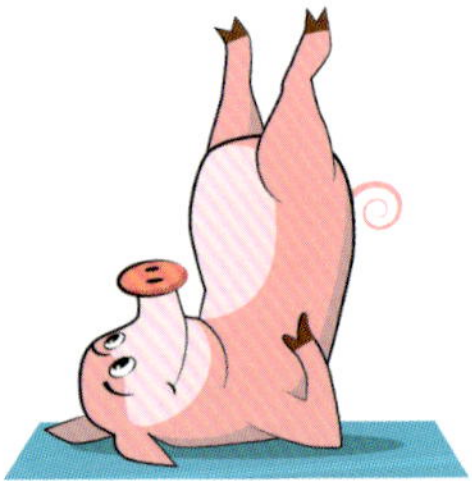

Coconut oil is unique in its ability to prevent weight-gain or cure obesity, by stimulating metabolism. It is quickly metabolized, and functions in some ways as an antioxidant. Isn't coconut oil fattening? Coconut oil is the least fattening of all the oils. Pig farmers tried to use it to fatten their animals, but when it was added to the animal feed, coconut oil made the pigs lean so they discontinued this practice very quickly.

Coconut oil is also a wonderful food to help stimulate the metabolism and aid with weight loss efforts. The mechanism of coconut oil's effects is by stimulating the thyroid gland and by reducing the appetite. The medium-chain fatty acids in coconut oil are instantly burned when consumed, which results in a boost in thyroid levels for hours. Furthermore, coconut oil helps you feel full and satisfied earlier in a meal and helps with satiety for hours afterwards. This combination makes it a perfect supplement to the diet in those wishing to lose weight.

One of the most outstanding benefits of consuming medium chain fatty acids is that they do not require the liver and gallbladder to digest and emulsify them. This means instant energy and increased thermogenesis (increased metabolic rate in the body) which leads to more heat production as well as improved circulation. For anyone with impaired fat digestion or a removed gallbladder, coconut oil is the only oil to consume as it is very easily digested.

Thyroid and Mental Function

There is an old medical saying that just a few grains of thyroid hormone can make the difference between an idiot and an Einstein. It aptly characterizes the thyroid as a quickener of the tempo of life.

Dr. Barry Durant-Peatfield, in his book "Your Thyroid and How to Keep It Healthy", states; "Brain cells have more T3 receptors than any other tissues, which means that a proper uptake of thyroid hormone is essential for the brain cells to work properly."

Thyroid hormones are one of the major "players" in brain chemistry disorders. And, as with any brain chemical disorder, until treated correctly, thyroid hormone imbalance has serious effects on the patient's emotions and behaviour.

Furthermore, because the brain requires sufficient thyroid hormones to function optimally, a low thyroid hormone status can contribute to overall loss of function and degeneration in the brain, including the areas of the brain that govern mood (Davis 2007). Overt hypothyroidism has also been shown to disturb serotonin signalling in the brain, which can contribute to depression (Stipcevic 2009). Findings that T3 is tery highly concentrated near the junctions between brain cells strongly support the concept of T3 as a brain chemical transmitter that is essential for maintaining normal mood and behaviour.

Thyroid Hormone is essential for brain function.

Extensive human research has led scientists to conclude that serotonin levels in the brain decrease if T3 is not delivered in the right amount. Thyroid hormone in the brain has the ability to enhance the production of serotonin in brain cells. The potent thyroid hormone T3 is found in greater quantities in the limbic system, a region of the brain that regulates mood, emotions, and perception of happy and sad events.

Hashimoto's (an autoimmune disease of the thyroid) can cause a person's metabolism to swing between overly active to overly depressed. These swings can mimic the symptoms of bipolar disorder and cause misdiagnosis and inappropriate treatment ***(Chang 1998; Kupka 2002; Cole 2002; Frye 1999).***

Any patient suffering from depression should be routinely assessed for hypothyroidism. There should be no exceptions; between 30-50% will be found to be hypothyroid, and as a result of treatment, their depression will begin to lift in weeks. Conventional medicine will turn with little thought to psychotropic antidepressants. The problem with these is that they are sometimes difficult to stop taking and is not targeting the problem, especially if it related to thyroid problems.

Here is a frightening thought: patients have been diagnosed with dementia and Alzheimer's disease, when in reality what they had was a thyroid disorder. A 2008 study, published in the Archives of Internal Medicine, found that older women who had levels of TSH that were either too high or too low had more than twice the risk of Alzheimer's disease than those with more moderate levels (the same was not true of men). This is another reason that testing your thyroid become part of your standard testing routine as you get older!

In terms of immunology, the thyroid gland acts as a gatekeeper: every 17 minutes all the blood in the body passes through the thyroid, where this gland's secretion of iodine kills germs that have come into the body (through absorption of food in the digestive tract, skin injury, respiratory intake, etc.)

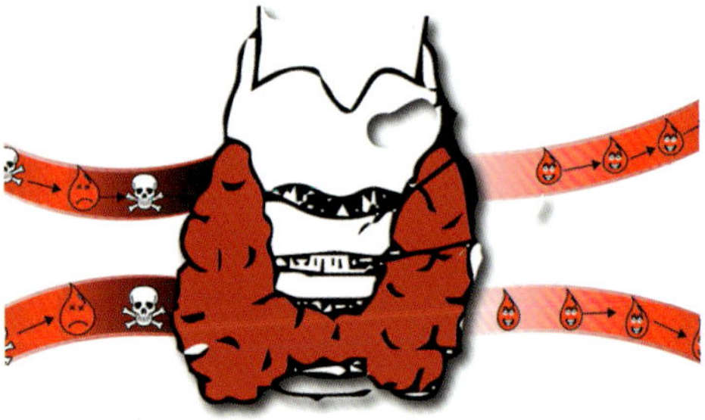

Pathogenic micro-organisms, the primary causative agent for disease in the body, are made weaker during their passage through the thyroid gland. With each "17 minute passage" they are made still weaker until most are killed, provided the thyroid has its normal supply of iodine.

Conclusion

Well now you can see how important the thyroid is for health and fat lost and, the huge number of factors which can inhibit the thyroid from working efficiently, leaving you often piling on the pounds and feel extremely tired and negatively effecting your mood.

Hopefully from this chapter you are now more knowledgeable on maintaining a healthy thyroid and, remember all hormones work in synergy.

If you want to know more about your thyroid gland and thyroid hormones then the books that I suggest that you read are;

- “Ultra Metabolism” - Mark Hyman
- “The Anti-Ageing Zone” - Barry Sears
- “Master Your Metabolism” - Jillian Michaels
- “Hormonal Balance” - Scott Isaacs
- “Thyroid - Guardian of Health” - Philip Young
- “Why Do I Still Have Thyroid Symptoms?” - Datis Kharrazian
- “The Thyroid Solution Diet” - Ridha Arem
- “Hypothyroidism - the unsuspecting illness” - Broda Barnes & Lawrence Galton

HABIT 6

ANABOLISM VS CATABOLISM

GET YOUR STEROID HORMONES BALANCED RIGHT FOR OPTIMUM FAT LOSS AND HEALTH

Are you still under the impression that cholesterol is a dietary villain and a primary cause of heart disease? And do you avoid eating healthy animal foods like eggs, butter and grass-fed beef because of "high-cholesterol" fears? All of our steroid hormones are made from cholesterol.

"The weak can never forgive. Forgiveness is the attribute of the strong."

Mahatma Gandhi

After reading this habit and habit 8 you will never look at cholesterol the same and you will realise how much we depend on this vital nutrient for our health and well being. You will also realise that everything you have been told about how bad cholesterol is for our health is simply a lie.

There are basically 6 types of steroid hormones: mineralocorticoids, glucocorticoids, androgens, oestrogens, progestagens and Vitamin D. The three steroidal hormones that are produced by the adrenals are:

- Mineralocorticoids
- Glucocorticoids
- Androgens

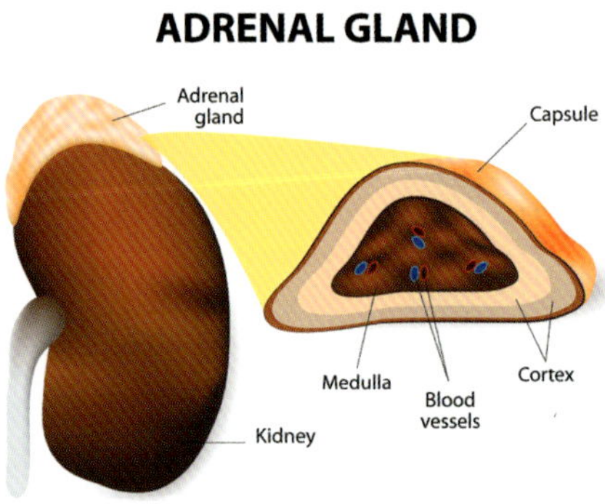

It is the family of 50 powerful enzymes known as Cytochrome P450 that is responsible for converting cholesterol into the 'master' steroid hormone, pregnenolone. Pregnenolone is often referred to as the 'master hormone' because it is converted into numerous other vital hormones. Without cholesterol which in synthesized in the liver, pregnenolone cannot be made. Drugs and foods that inhibit the liver's production of cholesterol may have a very damaging effect upon the cascade of hormones of the endocrine system.

Consider the vitally important functions of the 6 steroidal hormones, all of which are derived from cholesterol:

1) Glucocorticoids are vitally important for the metabolism of carbohydrates. The most important glucocorticoid is cortisol, a powerful adrenal hormone that has multiple functions in the body. Cortisol is also a powerful anti-inflammatory hormone that opposes immune hyperfunction.
2) Mineralcorticoide hormones such as aldosterone are hugely responsible for water/electrolyte dynamics through the control of sodium and potassium.
3) Androgenic hormones such as DHEA and testosterone are critical for libido, cardiovascular health as well as maintaining bone density. Studies have shown that low levels of DHEA correlate with poor bone density and osteoporosis. DHEA is also critical for memory and anti-aging.
4) Progestogens such as progesterone are vitally important for regulating women's menstrual cycles and are the 'gestation' hormones.

5) Oestrogens such as oestradiol are critical for sexual development and have various functions for bone and brain health.
6) Vitamin D is technically a sterol, but functions as a steroidal hormone. Vitamin D is converted in the liver and has hundreds of vital immune supporting functions. Vitamin D is also critical for calcium regulation in the blood.

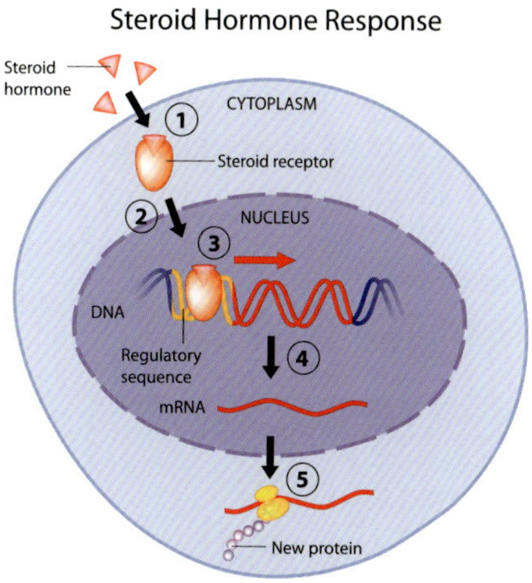

How a steroid hormone effects a cell.

So YES all of our steroid hormones are made from cholesterol. Steroid hormones have pregnenolone and progesterone as basic precursors. Some of the hormones in this pathway can be converted into others, and some can convert back, while others cannot.

In this habit we will look at the connection between pregnenolone, cortisol, testosterone, DHEA, oestrogen and progesterone in helping to decrease body fat composition and improve our overall health and vitality. We will also look at the insanity of cholesterol lowering foods and drugs.

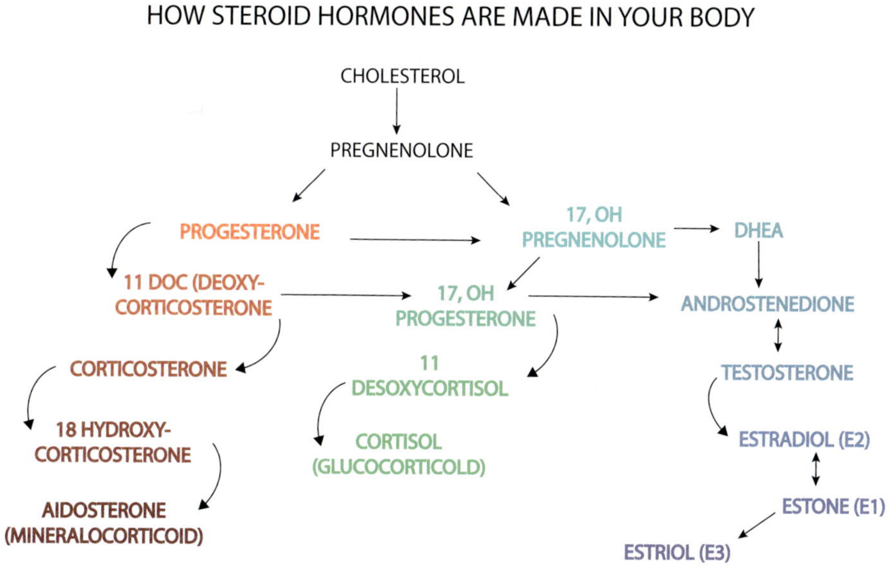

The Cholesterol Con

Are you still under the impression that cholesterol is a dietary villain and a primary cause of heart disease? And do you avoid eating healthy animal foods like eggs, butter and grass-fed beef because of "high-cholesterol" fears?

When you really understand the multiple functions of cholesterol in the human body you will soon realise the obsession by the medical profession and pharmaceutical companies to lower cholesterol to levels they deem as safe is one of the biggest medical frauds of all times driven purely for their profits and at the expense of your health. A multiple billion food and drug industry is literally booming on lowering one of the most vital nutrients that the human body needs for optimum health based on fraudulent information and yes that nutrient is cholesterol.

First of all let's analyse how the cholesterol theory (FRAUD) manifested into a multi-billion pound industry and be prepared for your jaw to hit the floor! Could it be possible that nearly everything your doctor and the media is telling you about high cholesterol and how it relates to heart disease and strokes is wrong? Absolutely!

If high cholesterol and high-fat diets are really NOT the cause of heart disease, then how did this massive misinformation campaign start? It actually started more than 100 years ago when the Cholesterol Theory was developed by a German pathologist named Rudolph Virchow. After studying arterial plaques from corpses, he theorized that cholesterol in your blood led to the development of plaques in your arteries.

Then in 1913 in St. Petersburg, Russia, Nikolaj Nikolajewitsch Anitschkow fed rabbits cholesterol and determined that it led to atherosclerotic changes which is narrowing of the arteries (apparently no one questioned the fact that rabbits are herbivores and do not naturally consume cholesterol!). This started the notion that eating cholesterol leads to plaque deposits in your arteries, and at that time it was believed that all cholesterol in your blood was due to dietary sources. This, of course, is not true, as it's now known that your liver makes about 85% of your body's cholesterol.

Plants do not contain any cholesterol. Animals are the only source of cholesterol, and herbivores do not eat animal products. Rabbits, being a herbivore, are not designed to digest animal fat and cholesterol, so when it is fed high doses of cholesterol one should not be surprised if the cholesterol winds up getting stuck in any part of the poor rabbit, including its blood vessels. Feeding high doses of fat and cholesterol to omnivores, like rats and dogs, does not produce atherosclerotic lesions in them.

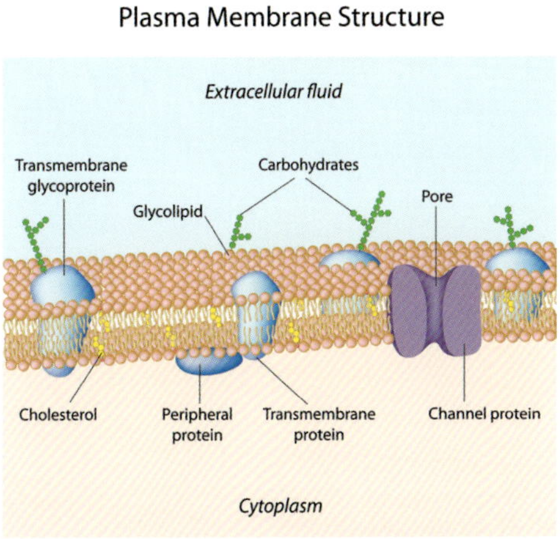

You will see cholesterol embedded in our cell membranes. Why? It's crucial for cells to maintain structure and aides in cellular communication.

That's right! Even if you didn't eat any cholesterol, you would still have cholesterol in your body, which is a good thing considering it's needed by every one of your cells to produce cell membranes. And you can't make steroid hormones without cholesterol or synapses in your brain which allow you to learn as well as main good emotional health.

For example, most people also do not realize that the best way to obtain vitamin D is from safe exposure to sun on your skin. The UVB rays in sunlight interact with the cholesterol on your skin and convert it to vitamin D. Bottom line? If your cholesterol level is too low you will not be able to use the sun to generate sufficient levels of vitamin D. And Ironically one of the most effective ways to lower cholesterol is to get sun on your skin but again we now live in an age where we slap the sunscreen on and miss out on naturally lowering cholesterol so we can use this substrate to make vitamin D which as you will read in habit 7 is crucial for health and fat loss.

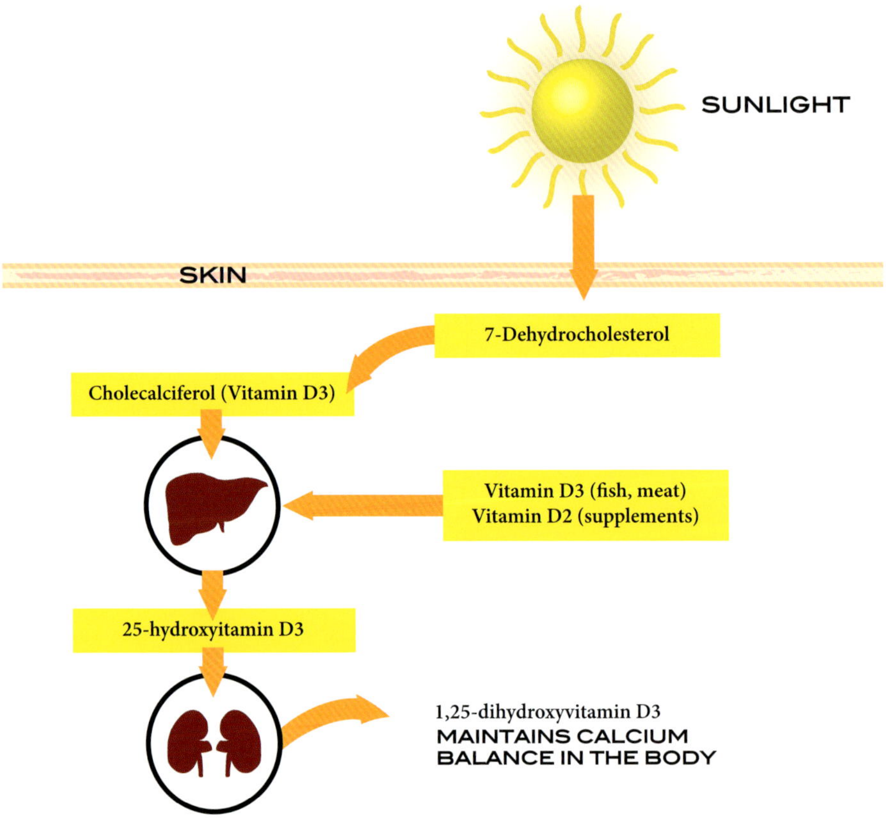

Additionally, it provides some intuitive feedback that if cholesterol were so dangerous, why would your body use it as precursor for vitamin D and virtually all of the steroid hormones in your body? Makes you think that there is a conspiracy against health doesn't it and in reality there is as like I keep saying unfortunately there is no money for big pharma, the modern medical system and giant food corporations if we had a society of vibrantly healthy people it's bad for profits!

Seven Countries Study

In the early 1900s, the Cholesterol Theory was already taking root, but it received even more completely flawed support in the 1950s and subsequent years thereafter. The string of research that effectively solidified the cholesterol myth we know all too well today.

The cholesterol theory of heart disease is nothing more that a fraud on a massive scale!

In 1953, Dr. Ancel Keys published a seminal paper that serves as the basis for nearly all of the initial scientific support for the Cholesterol Theory. The study is known as the Seven Countries Study that linked the consumption of dietary fat to coronary heart disease. What you may not know is that when Keys published his analysis that claimed to prove the link between dietary fats and coronary heart disease (CHD), he selectively analyzed information from only seven countries to prove his correlation, rather than comparing all the data available at the time - from 22 countries.

As you might suspect, the studies he excluded were those that did not fit with his hypothesis, namely those that showed a low percentage fat in their diet and a high incidence of death from CHD as well as those with a high-fat diet and low incidence of CHD. If all 22 countries had been analyzed, there would have been no correlation found whatsoever; it should have been called the 22 Countries Study!

The nutrition community of that time completely accepted the hypothesis, and encouraged the public to cut out butter, red meat, animal fats, eggs, dairy and other so called "artery clogging" fats from their diets - a radical change at that time that is still very much in force today. And unfortunately this information is having an incredible effect on people's health for these foods are some of the most nutritious foods we can eat and let me tell you this the more STRESS in your life the more cholesterol rich foods you MUST eat. Why? You need the cholesterol to help supply the adrenal glands so it can make more steroid hormones.

Dr. Keys' fraudulent research was pivotal for perpetuating the low-fat approach to health which 60 plus years on is still ingrained into the misinformed medical profession who pass this false information on to the public at a huge cost to health and huge profits to the low fat/cholesterol food industry and of course big pharma in their huge push to literally get everyone on their statin drugs!

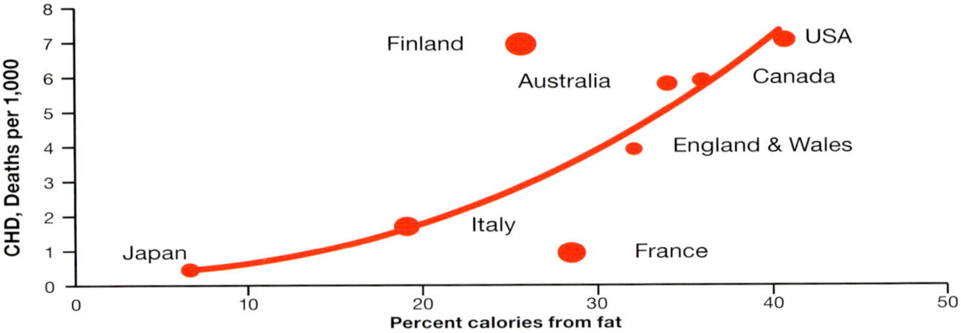

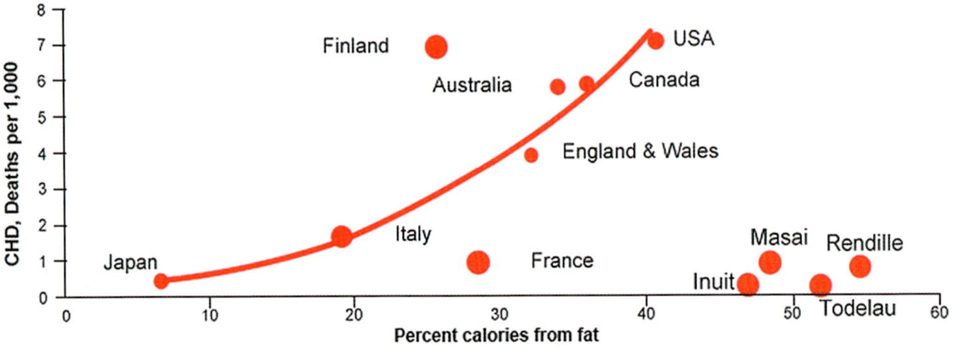

The top graph shows that the published study was nothing more that propaganda and a fraud to support Ancel Keys diet/heart hypothesis which was 100% INCORRECT! The bottom graph shows the true graph which shows that some countries had the highest percentage of their diet coming from fat but low rates of CHD.

More Flawed "Proof": The Framingham Study

The next major support for the cholesterol theory came from a study you have likely heard of called the Framingham Heart Study, which is often cited as proof of the lipid hypothesis. This study began in 1948 and involved some 6,000 people from the town of Framingham, Massachusetts who filled out detailed questionnaires about their lifestyle habits and diets. The study is credited with identifying heart disease risk factors, such as smoking, high blood pressure, lack of exercise and, yes, high cholesterol.

The cholesterol link was weak, as researchers noted those who weighed more and had abnormally high blood cholesterol levels were slightly more at risk for future heart disease, but widely publicized. What you don't hear about is the fact that the more cholesterol and saturated fat people ate, the lower their cholesterol levels.

In a 1992 editorial published in the Archives of Internal Medicine, Dr. William Castelli, a former director of the Framingham Heart study, stated:

> ***"In Framingham, Mass., the more saturated fat one ate, the more cholesterol one ate, the more calories one ate, the lower the person's serum cholesterol. The opposite of what... Keys et al would predict...We found that the people who ate the most cholesterol, ate the most saturated fat, ate the most calories, weighed the least and were the most physically active."***

The U.S. Multiple Risk Factor Intervention Trial (MRFIT), sponsored by the National Heart, Lung and Blood Institute, is another study that is highly misleading. It compared mortality rates and eating habits of over 12,000 men, and the finding that was widely publicized was that people who ate a low-saturated fat and low-cholesterol diet had a marginal reduction in coronary heart disease.

What did they leave out? Their mortality from all causes was higher! As Mary Enig and Sally Fallon stated in The Truth About Saturated Fat:

> ***"The few studies that indicate a correlation between fat reduction and a decrease in coronary heart disease mortality also document a concurrent increase in deaths from cancer, brain hemorrhage, suicide and violent death. After 10 years of lowering fat intake and not smoking, they found no significant difference in death from heart disease or total death compared to the control group of smokers, poor diet etc."***

Let's look at some studies which, rightfully, completely ridicule the low-cholesterol/low-fat hypothesis and heart disease connection.

The Indigenous Samburu and Masai tribes in Kenya largely subsist on meat, fat, milk and blood, they eat very little plant matter. Professor George Mann, from Vanderbilt University in Nashville, and other researchers have studied these people for many years. They found them to be free from any modern disease, including heart disease. Their blood cholesterol levels was very low, despite the fact they literally gorged on fat and cholesterol every day. However, when these same people moved to the city of Nairobi and adopted a modern lifestyle with a modern low fat diet, they became prone to heart disease, just like anybody else.

Diets in People with the Lowest Risk of Heart Disease – Masai, Inuit, Rendille, Todelau

The diet of the Maasai tribe in Kenya and northern Tanzania consists of meat, milk, and blood from cattle. It is 66 percent saturated fat.

The diet of Inuit Eskimos in the Artic, consisting largely of whale meat and blubber, is 75 percent saturated fat; and they live long healthy lives free of heart disease and cancer.

The Rendille tribe in the Kaisut Desert in NE Kenya subsist on camel milk and meat, and a mixture of camel milk and blood, known as "Banjo." Their diet is 63 percent saturated fat.

The Tokelau live well, without cardiologists, on three atoll islands that are now a territory of New Zealand. Their diet consists of fish and coconuts, which is 60 percent saturated fat.

German Ministry of Research and Technology showed that no exact link exists between food cholesterol and blood cholesterol. Even more surprising, in Japan, the cholesterol levels have risen during recent years, yet the number of heart attacks has dropped. The largest health study ever conducted on the risks of heart disease took place in China. Like so many similar studies, the Chinese study found no connection between heart disease and the consumption of animal fats.

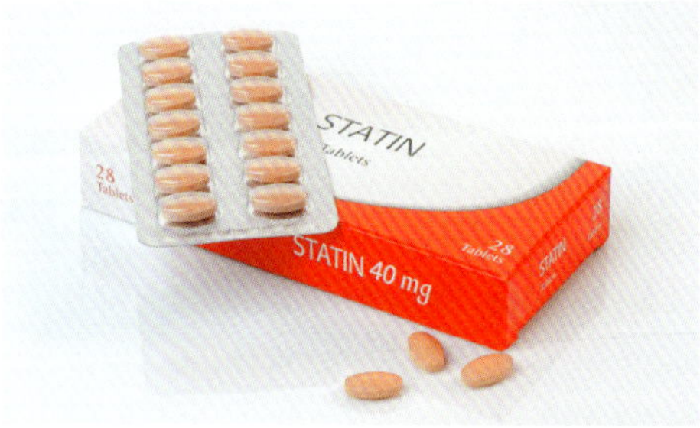

When your cholesterol levels are high it is not because you have a statin deficiency. It is usually because your body is trying to repair itself, for which cholesterol is a very important repair material.

In an 8-year long heart study, researchers observed 10,000 people with high cholesterol levels. Half of them received a best-selling statin drug. The other half were simply told to eat a normal diet and get enough exercise. The results stunned the researchers. Although the statin drug did indeed lower serum cholesterol, this had no impact whatsoever on death rate, non-fatal heart attacks and fatal arterial disease. In other words, the statin-users had zero advantage over those who received no treatment at all. However, they had just spent eight years taking a costly drug with hideous side effects - risking liver failure, muscle wasting, even sudden death. Lowering cholesterol either through drugs or low fat diets does not lower the risk of developing heart disease.

Eating margarine can increase heart disease in women by 53% over eating the same amount of butter, according to a recent Harvard Medical Study. While actually increasing LDL cholesterol, margarine lowers the so called beneficial HDL cholesterol. It also increases the risk of cancers up to five times.

Contrary to most people's belief a vegan diet is one of the worst diets you can follow for the prevention of heart disease and very detrimental as you will see in later research in this habit for testosterone production.

The proponents of the fraudulent diet-heart hypothesis have promoted vegetable oils in order to reduce cholesterol. The unfortunate surprise for them was study after study found that instead of reducing cholesterol, these oils increases it. They also cause atherosclerosis in experiments. Despite all this data vegetable oils and margarines are still being promoted as health and heart protective when in reality nothing could be further from the truth.

In India, studies by Dr. S L Malhortra of Bombay have demonstrated that people in Madras, who eat very little fat and no animal fat at all, die from heart disease seven times more, and at a younger age, than people from Punjab, where traditionally a lot of animal fat is consumed. So again, animal fat appears to be heart protective.

Large clinical trials where patients were put on low fat, low cholesterol, high carbohydrate, vegetarian diet created a drastically increased risk of heart disease. The author of one study at Harvard Medical School, Dr L Gould, one of the United States leading cardiologists, concluded: "I do not recommend a high carbohydrate strict vegetarian diet as it incurs substantial risk of coronary events".

Study after study, in many countries, have demonstrated that is IMPOSSIBLE to reduce your blood cholesterol, or the death rate from heart disease, by a low fat, low cholesterol diet. In fact animal fat and cholesterol in the food we eat have virtually no effect on the level of our blood cholesterol. Why? Because every organ and every cell of the body produces cholesterol – the body produces less when we eat cholesterol and yes the body produces more when we eat cholesterol rich foods. Of course the food industry that produces the low fat/low cholesterol foods do not wish you to know this FACT as it's not good for their business!

The Biologic Importance of Saturated Fat

There is good reason why 54 percent of the fat in mother's milk is saturated fat. Cell membranes need saturated fatty acids to function properly and be "waterproof." The heart prefers saturated long-chain 16-carbon palmitic and 18-C stearic acid (over carbohydrates) for energy. Bones need them to assimilate calcium effectively. They protect the liver from the adverse effects of alcohol and medications like Tylenol. Lung surfactant is composed entirely of saturated 16-C palmitic acid, and when present in sufficient amounts prevents asthma and other breathing disorders. Saturated fats function as signaling messengers for hormone production.

There is no such thing as good and bad cholesterol.

These terms are fictitious. In fact LDL the so called 'bad' cholesterol and HDL the so called 'good' cholesterol are not even cholesterol, they are lipoproteins, transporters for cholesterol. Remember, cholesterol isn't water soluble. As a result, they need to be carried by something else to travel in the blood. Those things are lipoproteins, so named because they're a mix of fat (lipo-) and protein. As it turns out, there are different types of lipoproteins. So, when you hear about different types of cholesterol, what they're really referring to is lipoproteins that carry both cholesterol and fat to cells. This association of lipoproteins with both fat and cholesterol has led to the idea that cholesterol is a fat, but that is also untrue.

HDL the so called 'good' cholesterol is the lipo-protein which transports cholesterol from the bloodstream back to the liver. And LDL the so called bad cholesterol transports cholesterol from the liver to wherever the body needs it. So, in reality, cholesterol is cholesterol; there is no such thing as good or bad. It is essential to life.

Cholesterol has many other health benefits. Many research studies have revealed, for instance, that cholesterol plays a key role in regulating protein pathways involved in cell signalling and may also regulate other cellular processes. It's already known that cholesterol plays a

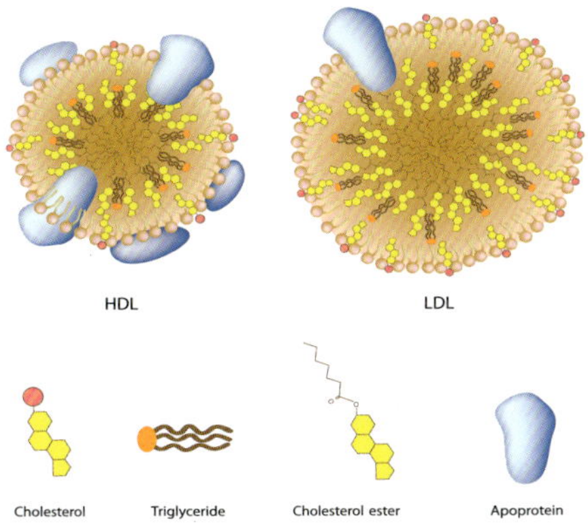

critical role within your cell membranes, but research suggests cholesterol also interacts with proteins inside your cells, adding even more importance. Your body is composed of trillions of cells that need to interact with each other. Cholesterol is one of the molecules that allow for these interactions to take place. Also, cholesterol is the precursor to bile acids, so without sufficient amounts of cholesterol, your digestive system can also be adversely affected.

So I hope that's cleared up a lot of nonsense about cholesterol. In habit 8, which is about nutritional cardiology, you will unfortunately see more misinformed information about this essential nutrient but fortunately there is a truckload of information on how to acquire a healthy cardiovascular system whilst eating sensible amounts of foods rich in cholesterol and saturated fats.

Let's look at Pregnenolone

Pregnenolone is a natural hormone, produced primarily by the adrenal glands, but also in the brain, liver, skin, testicles and ovaries. In the body, pregnenolone is used either as pregnenolone itself, or it is converted to DHEA (dehydroepiandrosterone), which in turn is converted into androgens (e.g. testosterone), oestrogens and other steroids, and through another pathway, it is converted into progesterone.

There are over 150 different steroid hormones which are made from pregnenolone in the body in total – it generates a whole symphony of hormones – in short it is "The Symphony of Life".

It is interesting to note that there is a clear difference in the metabolism of pregnenolone in human males and females – in males the metabolic pathway seems to favour conversion into testosterone and in females the conversion into ooestrogens.

Pregnenolone is called the mother of all steroid hormones for a good reason. It is a steroid hormone at the top of the hormonal production cascade. During periods of stress, the output of adrenal steroids such as cortisol will increase, which will put a great demand on pregnenolone production. This may lead to pregnenolone deficiency, which in turn may lead to reduction of both glucocorticosteroids and mineralocorticoids such as cortisol and aldosterone respectively.

Pregnenolone is synthesized directly from cholesterol and is responsible for countless functions in our bodies. By the age of 75, however, the body's production of this valuable hormone has declined by as much as 60%, and levels of the hormones for which pregnenolone is a precursor have also diminished.

Numerous studies have shown the effects of pregnenolone on the body and brain. In normal people, pregnenolone will boost energy, elevate mood and improve memory and mental performance. Pregnenolone will also create a sense of well being while improving the ability to tolerate stress. Furthermore, pregnenolone has a host of other benefits, which include the ability to influence cerebral function, the female reproductive cycle, immune defences, inflammation, mood, skin health, sleep patterns, stress tolerance, and wound healing.

Production of pregnenolone decreases with stress, aging, depression, hypothyroidism and exposure to toxins. It can also be depleted when levels of other hormones, such as cortisol, are low, as it is used to replenish those supplies.

During periods of stress, the output of adrenal hormones increases. Increased output of these hormones has been associated with increased fatigue in army pilots, resulting in poor performance. In a study of pilots under stress, 50 mg of pregnenolone daily improved performance with no adverse side effects.

Pregnenolone has been studied extensively since the 1940. One of its most important actions is to counter damage caused by the natural stress hormone called 'cortisol.' Cortisol is helpful in modest amounts, but is toxic at higher levels. Pregnenolone's ability to block excess cortisol levels may be one of the main reasons for its known memory-enhancing and mood-boosting benefits.

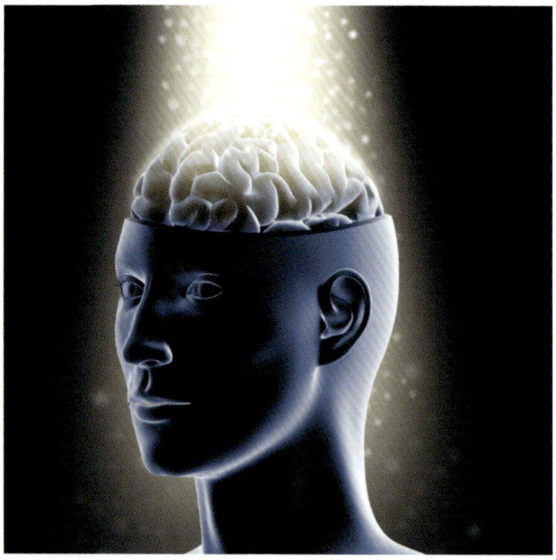

Pregnenolone is essential for brain function.

Pregnenolone also appears to help people approach life's daily challenges with a more positive mental outlook. According to the respected biologist and author Dr. Ray Peat,

PhD, "When using pregnenolone, men and women alike report feeling a profound mood of resilience and an increased ability to confront challenges successfully."

In the book, The Mood Cure, by Julia Ross, M.A., pregnenolone supplementation is highly recommended for helping overcome adrenal fatigue and reversing even the most devastating forms of exhaustion, emotional distress and depression. And in the book, Pregnenolone: A Radical New Approach to Health, Longevity, and Emotional Well-Being, author Dr. Gary Young, N.D., points out that pregnenolone enhances mental performance, facilitates learning, helps the body adapt to stress, increases one's overall feeling of happiness and well-being, and helps induce a change of attitude in which we actually become more appreciative of life.

Cortisol: the steroid hormone for stressful times

Cortisol is a steroid and one of the primary stress hormones. Production is stimulated within the endocrine system's hypothalamic-pituitary-adrenal (HPA) axis. Secretion comes from the adrenal glands.

Ironically named the master "stress" hormone, cortisol regulates the way your body uses various fuel sources and is essential for recouping energy following stress. When your adrenals are healthy, you will produce 35–40 mg of cortisol per day.

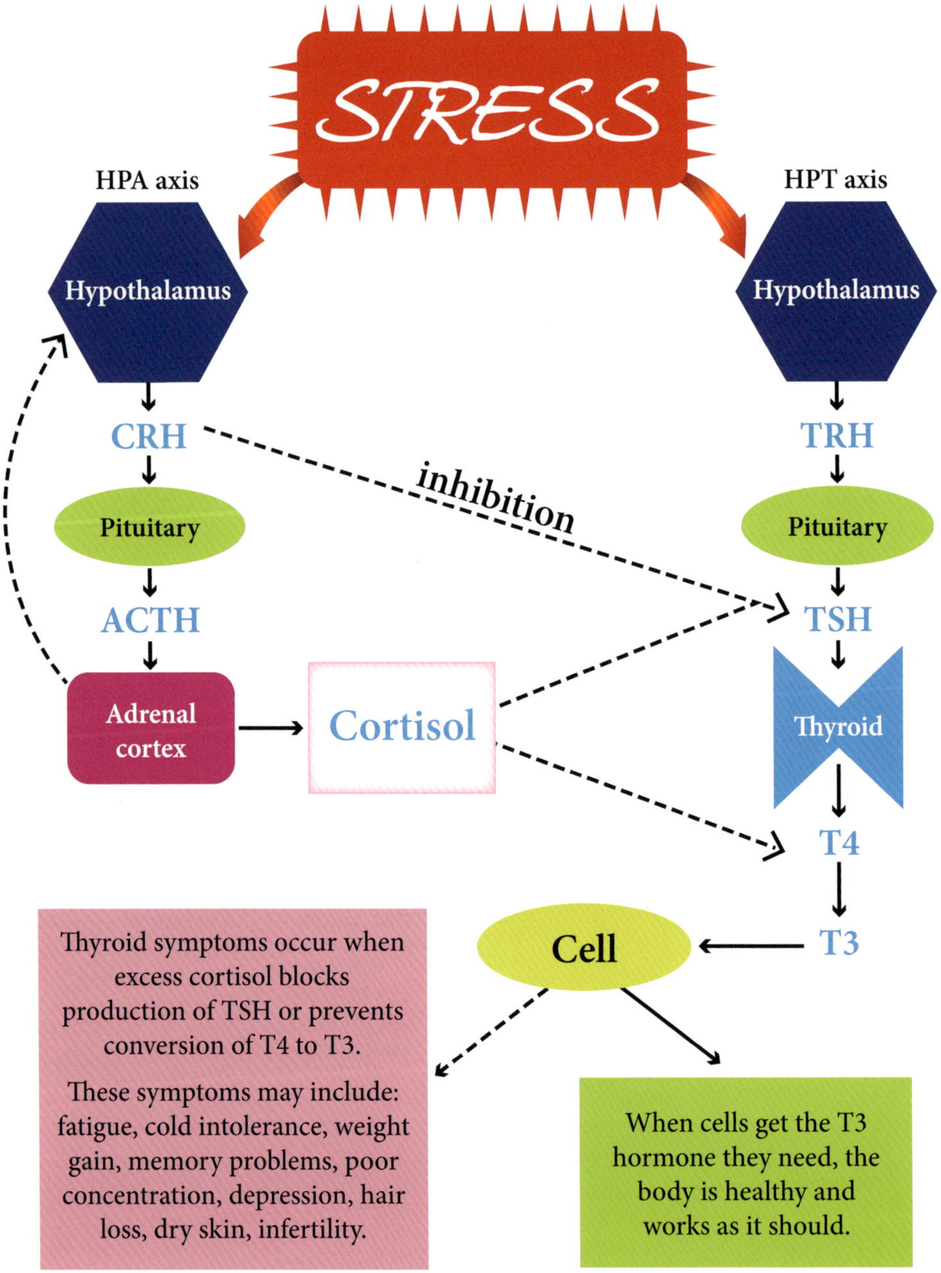

The HPA response begins when the hypothalamus secretes corticotropin releasing hormone (CRH) which directs the pituitary gland to release the hormone adrenocorticotropic hormone (ACTH). ACTH then directs the adrenal glands to secrete more hormones, including epinephrine, norepinephrine, and cortisol.

Normal cortisol hormone levels tend to follow a 24-hour circadian rhythm; the lowest level being at night during sleep that gradually increase to when you need to wake up and get moving. The high cortisol levels present in early morning rapidly drop off and then continue to decline for the remainder of the day. Under ideal conditions, your cortisol levels should be neither consistently high nor low, but fluctuate in a fairly rhythmic pattern.

A diagram of "normal" daily cortisol rhythm

The primary role of cortisol is to help mobilise energy for fuel.

Excess cortisol impedes the entry of amino acids into muscle cells for protein synthesis, and instead transports them to the liver to be used as energy. This is why individuals involved in strength training may experience a decrease in muscle mass and increases in body fat if they do not take the necessary steps to reduce/control cortisol levels. Cortisol is one of the main reasons athletes at all levels take one step forward & two back, unless they know how to manage their stress/cortisol levels.

If there is a true anti–muscularity drug, it is chronic stress. This was demonstrated in one experiment with young soldiers undergoing Army Training. **At the peak of training, their testosterone levels dropped by 30%.**

Within weeks after the course ended, thus removing the psychological and physical stress, their testosterone levels returned to their pre–training levels. Stress is one of the most serious threats to testosterone production, and chronic stress is unfortunately an epidemic in our 21st century way of life.

Studies have also shown that when cortisol is released into the bloodstream you become less sensitive to leptin, the hormone that tells your brain you are full. When this happens you tend to eat more, and crave more, sugar. This is why most of us when we are stressed crave some form of quick releasing sugar foods or beverages like alcohol, chocolate or ice cream.

So this is another reason to reduce stress and we cover the cortisol - leptin link in more depth in habit 7.

Controlling Stress Is The Key To Your Fat Loss Success

Remember this very important point: the less stress in your life, the more material you have for growth and repair. The more stress in your life, the less material you will have for growth and repair. It is exceptionally difficult to be lean and healthy when you can't control stress.

Whether they signal attack, retreat or surrender, every cell responds accordingly, and you feel the results. It is through the actions of the adrenal hormones that your body is able to mobilize its resources to escape or fight off danger (stress) and survive. In a more primitive society that would mean being able to run away quickly, fight or pursue an enemy or game, endure long periods of physical challenge and deprivation, and store up physical reserves when they are available.

Short, intermittent bursts of cortisol helped our ancestors survive in the wilderness and still come to our aid today. But unlike our ancestors, we face chronically stressful situations such as job loss, traffic jams, relationship stress, and financial insecurity. Additionally, there are new biological stressors such as obesity and environmental toxins.

The biological stress response is designed to be short term so, if it is aroused too often or lasts too long, it can potentially affect your overall health and well being. If you are constantly bombarded by stressors your cortisol and adrenaline will remain elevated; this is a disaster if trying to lose body fat! If your adrenals remain in a state of heightened alert and continue to produce adrenaline and cortisol, you're exposed to chronically

Stress is all around us learn good stress management skills to cope or you will become sick, tired and often gain weight.

elevated blood sugar, which raises insulin levels and can result in insulin resistance and type II diabetes. As well as this, excess cortisol breaks muscle tissue down, to be used as fuel, and this then lowers metabolism.

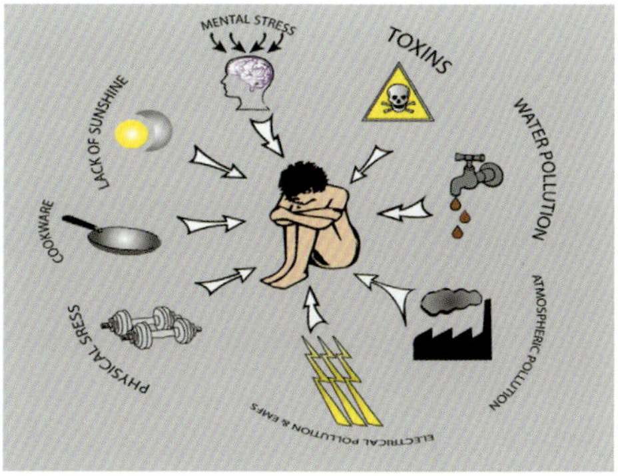

Stresses can be physical, emotional, nutritional, chemical, physiological or hormonal. Your body responds identically to all of these stressors, because it cannot distinguish the differences between them – stress is stress no matter what the source is. If you want to have a lean, healthy body then you must control stress. If you don't control stress, stress will control you - which usually means becoming sick, tired and obese.

Stress and abdominal fat

The link between cortisol and abdominal fat comes from the signal the hormone sends for fat storage to your abdominal fat cells. The fat cells in your abdominal area have four times more cortisol receptors than fat located elsewhere in the body, making them more sensitive to cortisol and causing them to respond more strongly to fat storage.

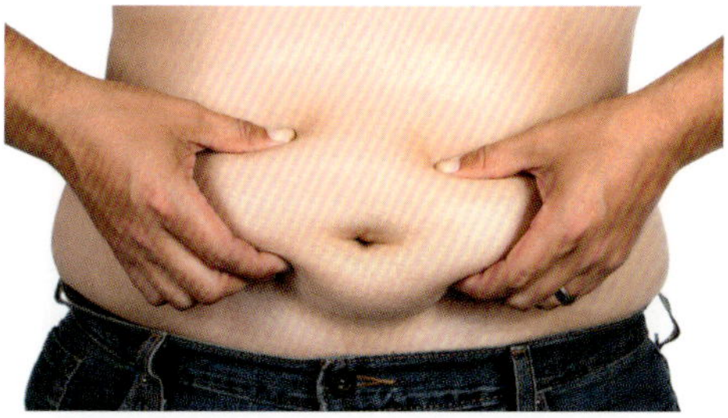

Elevated cortisol causes your body to store more of our calories as fat, especially around your stomach and the sides of your face and this increases the breakdown or catabolism of muscles. The physical profile associated with chronic high cortisol is a bit like Humpty Dumpty - you have a rounded moon face, large belly and skinny arms and legs.

Excessive cortisol can also stimulate your appetite, causing overeating, and cravings for sugary and high calorie fatty foods that are too strong to fight. Another key issue in weight gain is the relationship between insulin, a hormone made in your pancreas, and cortisol. When your body is stressed, cortisol is released to raise levels of fat and glucose (blood sugar) in your bloodstream and thereby increase energy and muscle strength. The increased blood sugar stimulates increased insulin, which has the job of keeping blood sugar levels within a very narrow range.

When Insulin is raised it blocks your body from using fat as a fuel. So, continuous levels of stress makes it almost impossible to lose fat!

When insulin is released continually, your cells eventually become desensitized to it, and high levels of blood sugar and insulin build up in the blood. This can cause insulin resistance and eventually type 2 diabetes. The reason fat accumulates around your middle is because it is close to the liver, where it can be quickly converted back into energy if needed.

The connection between stress and obesity cannot be overlooked. Cortisol signals a metabolic shutdown that makes losing weight almost impossible. It's as if the body feels it is under an attack, such that it must hoard all its resources, including fat stores, and won't let go of them under any inducement.

Stress can have a huge impact on your hormones, turning you into a fat storing machine.

Stress makes you burn fewer calories and cortisol can actually reduce the body's ability to release fat from its fat stores to use for energy! Stress hormones cause increased body fat in the abdominal region, exactly where we don't need or want it.

PHIL SAYS
Emotions

Our deadly emotions play havoc with our cortisol levels for example I get bombarded everyday with messages on what are the best supplements to reduce cortisol and I reply;

When you are on your knees from life's stressful events, those who help you in these situations, are your true friends.

"Be happy and have a positive attitude towards life is the quickest way to drop cortisol, and put yourself in an anabolic state. You and only you can choose how you will think and feel in any circumstance, event, relationship in your life. When you react with hostility, hatred, jealousy, anger and aggression this just sends your cortisol levels through the roof and you have to decide is it worth having such feelings every time you are faced with a stressful situation. Yes, of course, there will be times when situations agitate you but learn to control the situation instead of the situation controlling you. Life is often said to be 10% what happens to us and 90% how we respond to it."

So how does stress lower testosterone? Most of the research in this area was done through Population Council endocrinologist Matthew Hardy and his work on rats. He and his teams found out how stress lowers your testosterone: through a tricky little enzyme called 11ßHSD-1 (11-beta-hydroxysteroid-dehydrogenase-1).

In males, the body produces most of its testosterone in the Leydig Cells of the testes and this enzyme keeps cortisol from pushing down your testosterone. It literally puts the brakes on cortisol from destroying your testosterone. However, in times of stress, there is simply too much cortisol compared to 11ßHSD-1 and this leads to a decrease in your testosterone production.

HSD functions to convert inactive cortisol (called cortisone) back into active cortisol, which then functions as a potent fat-storage signal within fat cells, especially abdominal fat cells.

Recent research tells us that HSD activity is higher in abdominal fat cells than it is in fat cells in other parts of the body - which may be the reason why cortisol exposure is associated with higher levels of fat in the abdominal region, as compared to fat levels in other parts of the body, such as the thighs or buttocks.

Researchers in Berlin, Germany, have suggested that the regulation of cortisol levels within cells by HSD is just as important as cortisol levels in the plasma. This means that the adrenal glands are not the only place in the body for "production" of cortisol; fat cells can produce their own fat-storing cortisol via reactivation of inactive cortisol by the HSD enzyme.

This leads to higher cortisol levels within fat cells and a further increase in fat storage and the size of fat cells. Overall, according to the German scientists, it is this mechanism of "self-production" of cortisol within individual fat cells that may represent the most important pathogenic signal for central (abdominal) obesity.

Researchers from the University of Birmingham, in England, have some especially depressing news for people trying to lose weight by extreme dieting. Studying the metabolic effects of a very low calorie diet (eight hundred calories per day) for ten weeks, they found that the stress of the diet significantly increased cortisol levels throughout the body, but also increased HSD activity within fat cells by 3.4 times.

In a series of experiments conducted by researchers from Harvard University, the British Heart Foundation, Merck pharmaceuticals, and a Swedish biotechnology firm, not only has HSD over-activity been identified as a cause of obesity and diabetes, but reducing its activity has been shown to reduce belly fat - despite a high-fat and high-calorie diet!

Danish scientists have found that higher levels of growth hormone are associated with reduced HSD activity, a finding that may explain some of the primary effects of growth hormone in reducing body fat (especially abdominal fat) and increasing muscle mass.

Flavonoids have been found to help balance HSD activity. The most potent of the flavonoids for balancing HSD activity are found in the form of substances known as polymethoxylated flavonoids (PMFs) found in oranges (nobiletin and tangeretin), which can be up to three to five times stronger than other flavonoids. However, PMFs come from citrus peels, which you're probably not eating very many of.

Limit alcohol if you want to get your cortisol levels back to a healthy level as alcohol raises cortisol, and the effect persists for twenty four hours in men and probably longer in women.

Drinking too much alcohol is a forced chemical stressor; your body secretes cortisol to overcome the toxic effects of alcohol just as it would a lethal poison. Too much alcohol blocks your liver from breaking down glycogen into sugar for brain energy, and cortisol helps your body bypass this blockage by breaking down your muscles to turn into glucose to make new sugar a process called gluconeogenesis. So, not a situation you want if you are after a leaner body.

Eliminate caffeine from your diet. It's the quickest way to reduce cortisol production and elevate the production of DHEA, which is a very important steroid hormone involved in reducing body fat. 200 mg of caffeine (one 12 oz mug of coffee) can increase blood cortisol levels by 30% in one hour! Cortisol can remain elevated for up to 18 hours in the blood. This is the easiest step to stop fat storage and increase fat burning drop the coffee it's a myth that it drops body fat it doesn't.

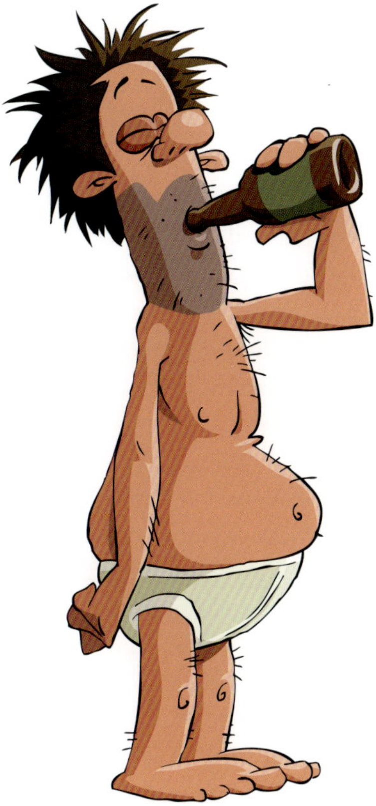

There is no easy way to say this – drop the booze if you want to drop the fat, it's that simple. When you get lean then occasionally have a drink.

Adrenal Fatigue

FACTORS AFFECTING THE ADRENALS

No bigger than a walnut and weighing less than a grape, each of your two adrenal glands sits like a tiny pyramid on top of each kidney ("ad" "renal" means "over" the "kidneys"). But don't let their size fool you; these powerful little endocrine glands manufacture and secrete steroid hormones such as cortisol, oestrogen and testosterone that are essential for life, health and vitality. They modulate the functioning of every tissue, organ and gland in the body to maintain homoeostasis (a constant internal environment) during stress and keep you alive.

The main purpose of the adrenals is to enable the body to deal with stress from every possible source, ranging from injury and disease, to work and relationship problems. They largely determine the energy of your body's responses to every change in your internal and external environment.

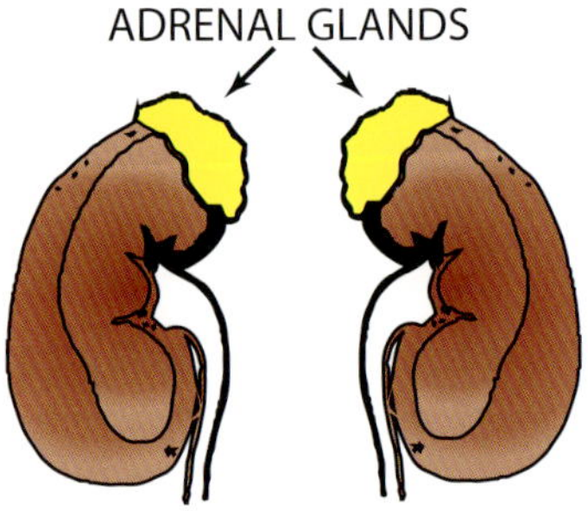

The adrenal glands sit on top of the two kidneys. The make and release steroid hormones.

In adrenal fatigue, more cortisol is secreted during the early stages. In the later stages of adrenal fatigue (when the adrenal glands become exhausted), cortisol output is reduced. Normally after many years on the roller coaster of stress when initially the adrenals are spewing out cortisol to help counteract the stress response they then become exhausted like all things in life when you keep pushing them into the ground. Then you are faced with low cortisol which is an issue you won't hear your mainstream doctor discussing unless you are flat on your back, in adrenal crisis, with blood pressure so low that you can't send oxygen to your brain and wanting to faint all the time.

Signs of adrenal fatigue:

- Do you have a hard time falling asleep at night?
- Do you wake up frequently during the night?
- Do you have a hard time waking up in the morning early, or feeling refreshed?
- Do bright lights bother you more than they should?
- Do you startle easily due to noise?
- When standing from sitting or from lying down, do you feel light-headed or dizzy?
- Do you take things too seriously, and are easily defensive?
- Do you feel you don't cope well with certain people or events in your life?

Any of the above sound familiar? If so, it may be time to heal those adrenal glands.

Testing Adrenal Function

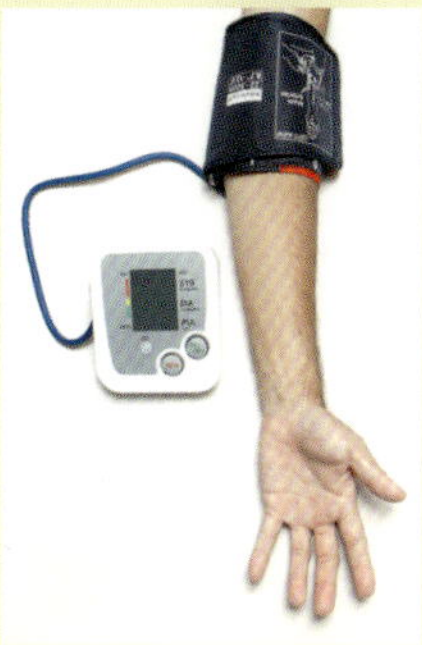

Take and compare two blood pressure readings—one while lying down and one while standing. Rest for five minutes in recumbent position (lying down) before taking the reading. Stand up and immediately take the blood pressure again

If the blood pressure is lower after standing, suspect reduced adrenal gland function the degree to which the blood pressure drops while standing is often proportionate to the degree of hypoadrenalism.

An interesting study showed that light exposure in the early morning has a strong impact on the morning cortisol peak. For those who awoke to bright light, cortisol levels about half an hour after waking were 35% higher than for those who awoke during darkness (Frank, Scheer, and Buijs 1999). One easy way to help normalise your production pattern if your cortisol levels are low is to increase your exposure to light during the day, especially in the early morning.

Nutrients that help alleviate adrenal fatigue

A full English Breakfast will regenerate adrenals whereas a bowl of breakfast cereal and a cup of coffee will be more likely to exhaust the adrenals.

One of the most essential nutrients for healing our adrenals is cholesterol yes cholesterol. Why? After our brain the organs most hungry for cholesterol, are our adrenals and sex glands. As we now know steroid hormones are made from cholesterol. Our stressful modern lives consume a huge amount of our steroid hormones leading to adrenal exhaustion. So when under a lot of stress eat more cholesterol rich foods like offal, caviar, cod liver oil, full fat dairy products and of course egg yolks to give the adrenals the materials it needs to make more cortisol and steroid hormones. You will read in habit 9 that it's best to have your high fat/cholesterol meals after training and not before, otherwise it will interfere with nitric oxide production, which is very important for physical performance.

Ginkgo biloba

For the last 5,000 years, leaves of the ginkgo tree have been used to treat various medical conditions. While ginkgo is currently used to help combat the debilitating effects of memory decline and dementia, emerging evidence suggests that it may be useful in treating the impact of stress and elevated cortisol levels. A recent double-blind, placebo-controlled study, published in the Journal of Physiology and Pharmacology, examined ginkgo's effects in modulating cortisol and blood pressure levels in 70 healthy male and female subjects. When subjected to physical and mental stressors, subjects who were given 120 mg per day of a standardized ginkgo extract saw smaller increases in their cortisol levels and blood pressure than did their counterparts who were given a placebo.

Vitamin C

After cholesterol rich foods, vitamin C is the most important nutrient for adrenal function and regeneration. When you are faced with a stressful situation, your vitamin C is rapidly used up in the production of cortisol and related stress-response hormones. In two separate studies about vitamin C supplementation (1,000–1,500 mg per day for one week), ultra-marathon runners showed a 30% lower cortisol level in their blood when compared to runners receiving a placebo.

It is interesting to note that, humans do not produce vitamin C. There are 3 other species that don't either; guinea pigs, fruit bats, and other primates. Those animals who do produce vitamin C, do so whilst under extreme stress; under times of stress they release a large amount of vitamin C.

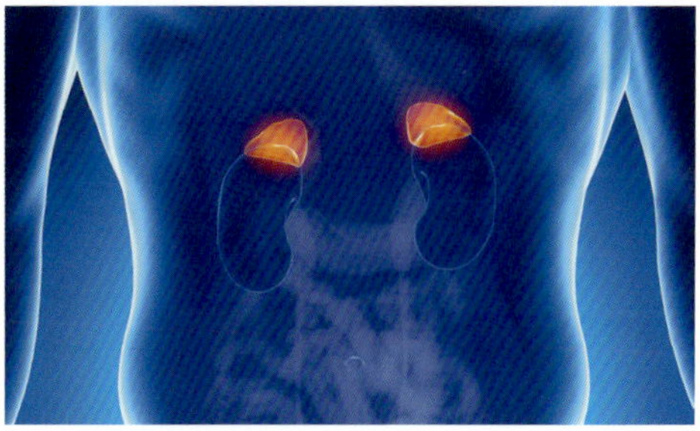

Vitamin C is utilized by the adrenal glands in the production of all the adrenal hormones, most notably cortisol.

In those animals who can produce vitamin C, glucose is one of the main substances used. From my research, it is best to take vitamin C at least 2 hours away from carbohydrate sources. This is because glucose competes with vitamin C at the same cell receptor sites.

I recommend that you take a minimum of 1000mg of vitamin C a day, in divided doses throughout the day. The more stress that you have in your life (physical, mental, chemical or emotional), the more I would increase the dosage. A good rule of thumb is that, you will know if you are taking too much vitamin C because you will be shitting through the eye of a needle!

Testosterone: required for men and women

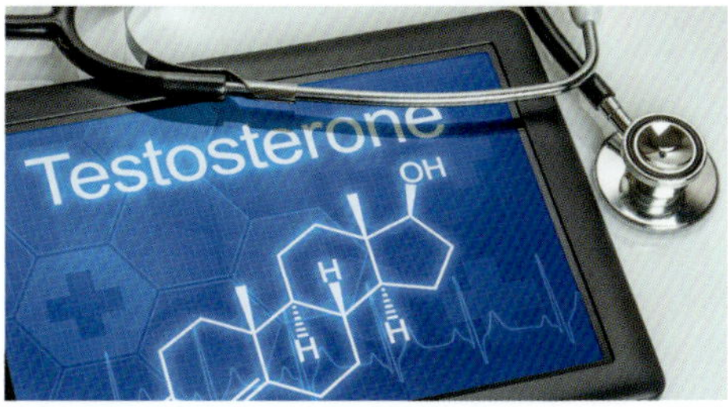

Often referred to as the "hormone of desire," testosterone is involved in maintaining muscle mass, mood, sex drive, and energy levels in both men and women.

Testosterone is actually produced by an intricate chain of events beginning in the hypothalamus. The hypothalamus secretes gonadotropin-releasing hormone (GnRH) to the pituitary gland in controlled pulses or bursts, which in turn causes the release of luteinizing hormone from the pituitary gland.

And it is luteinizing hormone that stimulates the Leydig cells of the testes to create testosterone. Why the science lesson? Because it is important to know that disease or damage to anything in this physiological chain, i.e. the hypothalamus, pituitary or testes, can cause hypogonadism, or low testosterone and will make it very difficult for you to significantly increase your testosterone.

THE INFLUENCE OF TESTOSTERONE

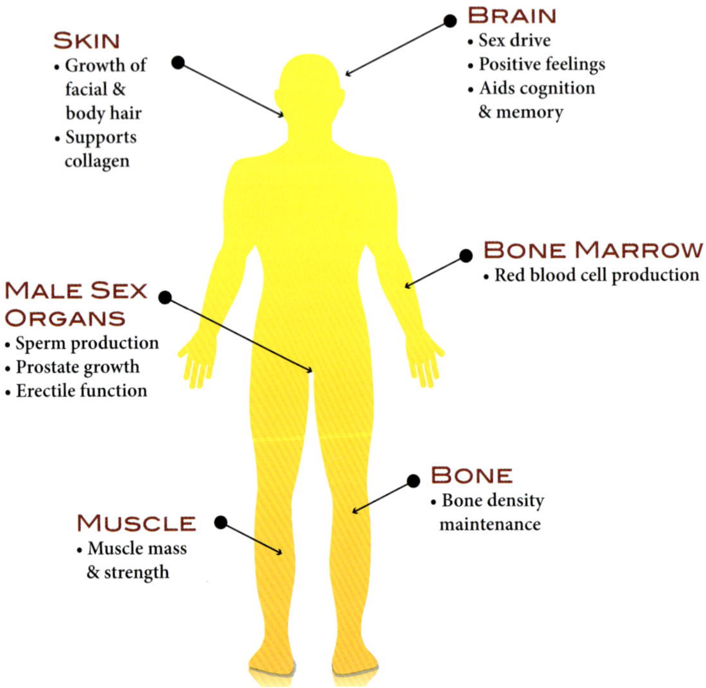

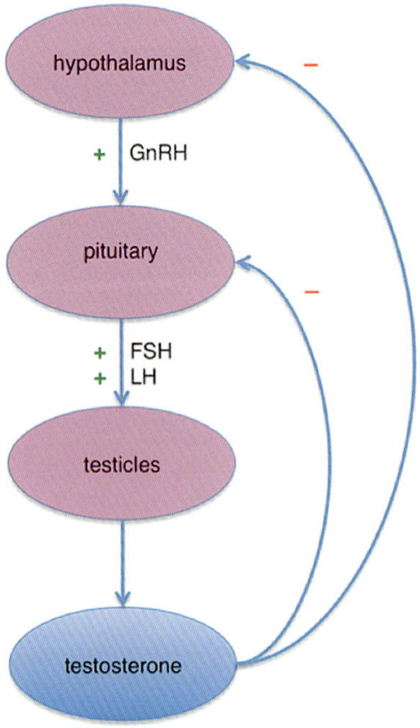

If you've sustained a blow to the head or a traumatic brain injury, caused by a stroke, heart attack, or loss of oxygen for long periods of time, low testosterone may result.

Large study documents the association between lower testosterone and higher mortality:

Normally testosterone is 30% higher in the morning than the evening. This may explain why men are more interested in sex in the morning and is part of the reason for spontaneous morning erections. In fact, the loss of morning erections is a sure sign that testosterone is declining and heart disease could be taking a grip.

As reported in the Archives of Internal Medicine, researchers at the VA Puget Sound Health Care System and the University of Washington at Seattle, evaluated whether low testosterone levels are a risk factor for mortality in male veterans. They studied the relationship between hormone levels and death in a total of 858 males over the age of 40. All participants received care in the VA Puget Sound Health Care System and had their testosterone levels checked at least twice between 1994 and 1999, with no more than two years elapsing between testing. These men were followed for average period of 4.3 years, with some followed for the full eight years of the study. None of the men had been diagnosed with prostate cancer.

19% of the men were classified as having low testosterone levels. 28% were classified as equivocal, meaning they had an equal number of test results in the low and normal ranges. 52.7% were classified as having testosterone levels in the normal range. Men who died during the first year of the study were excluded from the data. Results were adjusted for such co-variates as age, and medical morbidity.

Men in the low testosterone group had an 88% increased risk of death compared to the group who had normal testosterone levels. This is a highly statistically significant result that persisted after the other variables that may have influenced risk of death, such as age, other illnesses and body mass index were considered.

Testosterone levels are known to decrease following a traumatic or highly stressful event, and this may increase the risk of death during such periods. However, in a follow up analysis of the data, this factor was also adjusted for. Men with low testosterone levels were still found to be 68% more likely to have died. This finding points to the conclusion that the association between low testosterone and mortality is not simply due to acute illness, and cannot be easily justified or ignored by men in denial.

A study that measured free testosterone and 25-hydroxyvitamin D blood levels in a large group (2,069) men who were referred for coronary angiography. The results were nothing short of startling for those who fail to maintain optimal blood ranges of vitamin D and testosterone.

The researchers conducting this study carefully adjusted for confounding factors like age, body-mass-index, active smoking, physical activity, diabetes, C-reactive protein, prevalent coronary artery disease, serum calcium, and parathyroid hormone.

After study researchers corrected for these confounding factors, they found that in comparison with people having higher levels of 25-hydroxy-vitamin D and free testosterone in the body:

- Deficiencies of free testosterone and 25-hydroxy-vitamin D resulted in a 111% increased risk for all-cause mortality.
- Deficiencies of free testosterone and 25-hydroxy-vitamin D resulted in a 77% increased risk for cardiovascular mortality.
- Deficiencies of free testosterone and 25-hydroxy-vitamin D resulted in a 133% increased risk for non-cardiovascular mortality.

These sharp increases in mortality in response to deficiencies of testosterone and/or vitamin D reveal how far behind mainstream doctors and cardiologists are in treating patients with coronary artery disease. This study makes it abundantly clear that aging men should strive to achieve optimal blood levels of vitamin D and free testosterone. ***Lerchbaum E, Pilz S, Boehm BO, Grammer TB, Obermayer-Pietsch B, März W. Combination of low free testosterone and low vitamin D predicts mortality in older men referred for coronary angiography. Clin Endocrinol (Oxf). 2012 Feb 22. doi: 10.1111/j.1365-2265.2012.04371.x.***

Recent medical studies have shown that individuals who are on statins for a long period of time are becoming vitamin D-deficient. Why is this? In simple terms, the amount of Vitamin D your body absorbs from food and the sun is affected by the amount of cholesterol in your system. When the cholesterol is reduced by the statins, the amount of Vitamin D the body can absorb also decreases. For this reason, it is important for patients who are prescribed a statin to talk to their doctor about taking a vitamin supplement to bring their levels back into a normal range.

The tragic thing here is that a lot of middle-aged men are prescribed statin drugs which decrease both testosterone and vitamin D levels. Now, if that's not a medical disgrace, I don't know what is.

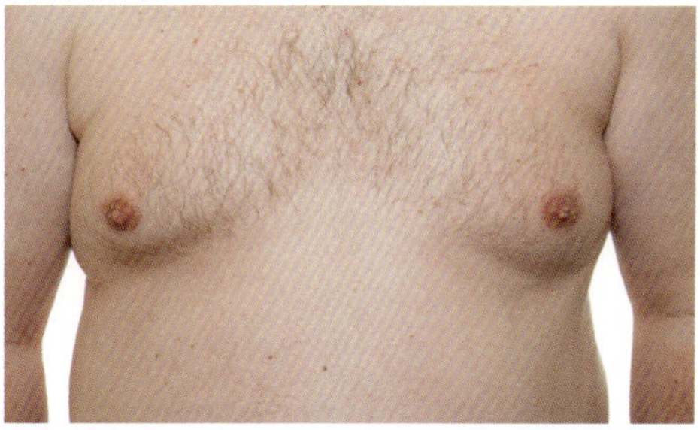

A man can become oestrogen dominate just as a woman can. Other symptoms of excess oestrogen that will sound very familiar to women are hair loss, headaches, irritability, bloating, knickers too tight and puffiness. Men also experience these symptoms.

Men in andropause exercise but see little to no improvement in muscle development or definition. This was definitely my personal problem I had become a total non responder to exercise no matter how hard or how often I pushed myself I just became fatter. My testosterone levels when I had them tested was lower than a worm's penis. Without payback from exercise most men with low testosterone gradually give up their exercise along with other aspects of their lives. Testosterone is what sends the signal to nature saying this man is still young and virile, the kind of guy that needs to be kept around.

As we read in habit 1, today's world is a toxic minefield of feminizing chemicals like bisphenol A (BPA) and parabens that overload men's systems with oestrogen, potentially leading to low testosterone. And a new study has revealed that men's exposure to such chemicals while in the womb can permanently alter their baseline testosterone levels as adults, leading to a lifetime of hormone-induced health problems.

The flabby stomach and enlarged breasts of middle aged men are a signal that their oestrogen levels are too high. Many men who are overweight can have oestrogen levels that are even higher than those of women of a healthy weight. This elevated oestrogen level along with declining testosterone can increase the risk of heart attack and stroke. Too much oestrogen can also suppress testosterone production.

Males produce a small amount of progesterone that is essential to their health. Progesterone along with testosterone helps balance the build-up of oestrogen. Progesterone is a precursor for cortisol, testosterone, and other hormones. Levels of progesterone fall off too as men age, and this drop causes a drop in other hormone levels.

A team of scientists from the Medical Research Council Centre for Reproductive Health at the University of Edinburgh in Scotland made the discovery after undertaking an investigation into why some men have much higher testosterone levels than other men, even when living relatively similar lifestyles as adults. Recognizing that high testosterone is essential for men's physical and mental health, the researchers decided to take a closer look at how this hormone is affected during pregnancy.

They looked specifically at Leydig cells, which live in men's testes and begin generating the testosterone hormone at puberty. Men's Leydig cells don't work as well when mother is exposed to too much oestrogen! As it turns out, men whose mothers do not have proper testosterone levels during pregnancy tend to inherit lower-functioning Leydig cells later, resulting in reduced production of this necessary hormone throughout their lives. Consequently, many of these men end up suffering from perpetual hormonal imbalance, which makes them more prone to obesity, diabetes, heart disease and even mental illness.

"There is increasing evidence that a mother's diet, lifestyle and exposure to drugs and chemicals can have a significant impact on testosterone levels in the womb," stated Professor Richard Sharpe, one of the study's lead authors. "We need a better grasp of these factors so that we can give reliable advice to pregnant women to protect the health of her unborn child."

Man with optimal testosterone

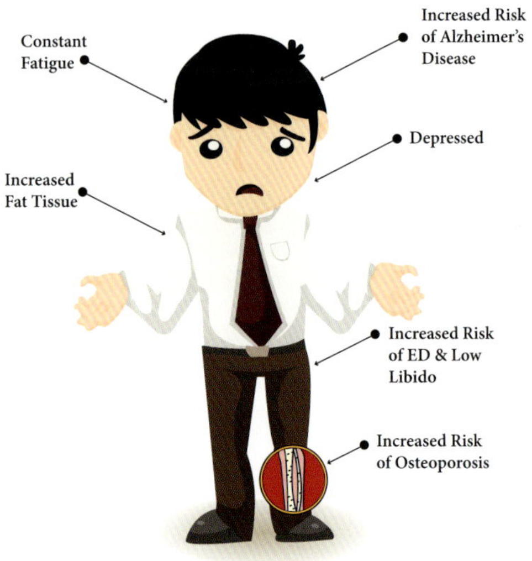

Man with deficient testosterone

An easy and non-invasive measurement, it could give you and doctors a quick way to gauge how much testosterone you were exposed to in the womb.

The ratio of the length of a man's index finger to that of his ring finger may seem like a strange thing to measure, but new research suggests that it's linked with penis size and the amount of testosterone he was exposed to during fetal development. The lower the ratio, the longer the penis.

HOW TO MEASURE YOUR FINGER

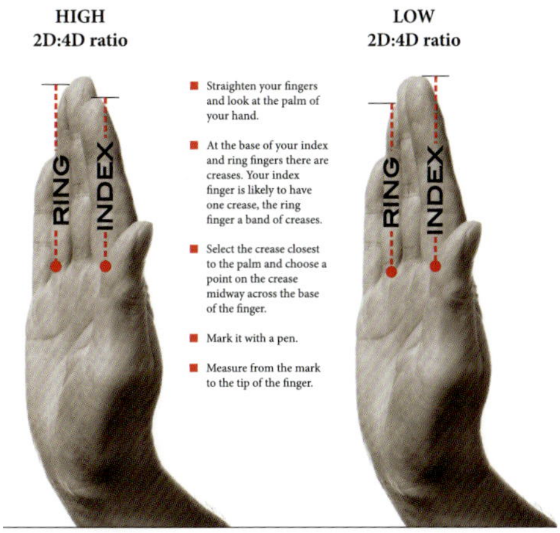

The new study was conducted on 144 Korean men who were hospitalized for urological surgery. A researcher measured the patients' penile length — flaccid and stretched — just after they went under anesthesia for their operations. A different researcher measured the men's finger lengths, in order to prevent knowledge of one measurement unconsciously affecting the other.

The data suggested that those with a lower ratio, whose index finger (or second finger, 2D) was shorter than the ring finger (or fourth finger, 4D), had a longer stretched penis length, which is well correlated with erect size.

"Based on this evidence, we suggest that digit ratio can predict adult penile size," the researchers, led by Dr. Tae Beom Kim of Gachon University in Incheon, Korea, wrote.

Previous studies have linked the so-called 2D:4D ratio of finger length with exposure to the sex hormones oestrogen and testosterone in the womb. So it's plausible that the same exposure may affect penis length.

Higher testosterone levels during fetal development are associated with a lower 2D:4D ratio, while higher oestrogen levels are connected with a higher one. Most men have index fingers that are shorter (low ratio) than their ring fingers, while most women's index fingers are the same size or longer (high ratio) than their ring fingers. Research has shown, however, that lesbians and female-to-male transgendered people are more likely to have more "male" ratios.

Finger-length ratios have been linked previously with a variety of other characteristics: in both males and females, lower ratios are associated with better athletic performance. In men, one study found that a lower ratio was connected with more success at high-frequency financial trading, while another study associated it with better performance on medical school entrance exams; women were not included in those studies.

Men with lower 2D:4D ratios were also more likely to have more "masculine" features, to have more symmetrical faces, and to be considered attractive by women, according to another study.

How Testosterone is Stored in the Body

On average, a man's body produces about 6-8 mg of testosterone a day, but not all of that testosterone floating in our bloodstream can be used by our bodies. Our total testosterone can be broken down into the following three sub-types:

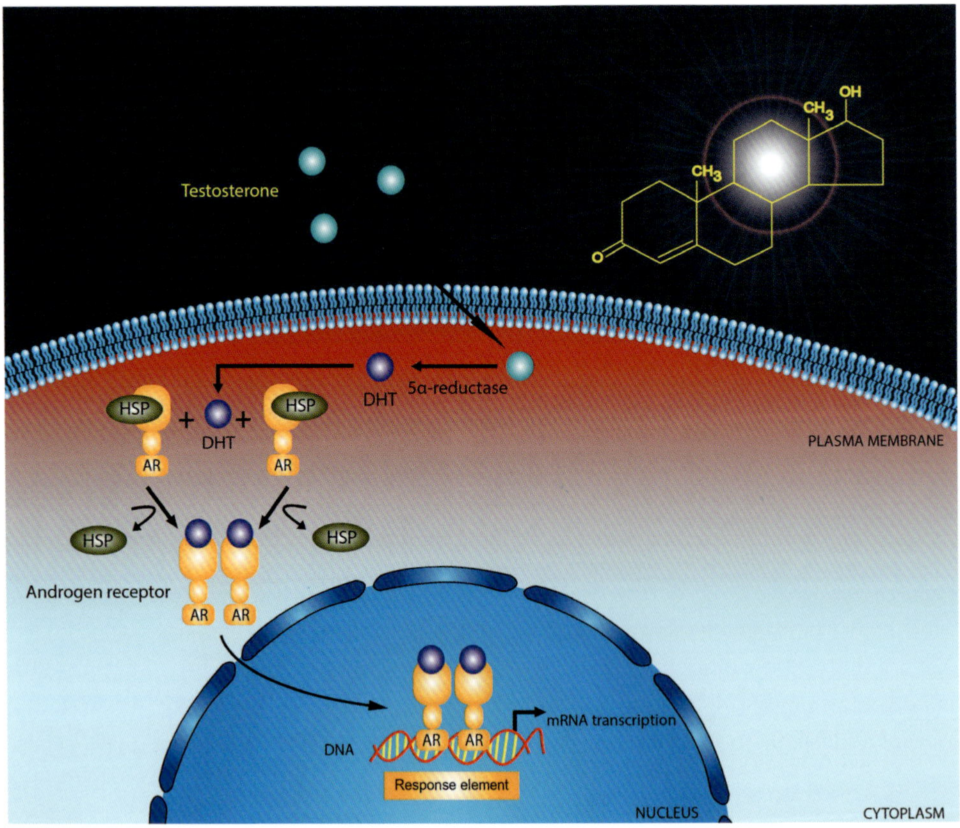

1) Free Testosterone.
This is testosterone in its purest form. The reason it's called "free" is because there aren't any proteins attached to it. Unbound to other molecules, free T can enter cells and activate receptors in order to work its virile magic on your body and mind. Despite free testosterone's benefits, it makes up only 2-3% of our total testosterone levels. To maximize the benefits of T, we want to do what we can to increase the amount of free testosterone in our bloodstream.

2) SHBG-bound Testosterone.
About 40-50% of our total testosterone is bound to a protein called sex hormone binding globulin (SHBG). SHBG is produced in our livers and plays an important role in regulating the amount of free testosterone in our bodies. The downside to SHBG-bound T is that it's biologically inactive, meaning our bodies can't use this type of testosterone to help build muscles, lose fat or boost our mood. SHBG isn't bad, but too much of it is. Excess SHBG is why it's possible to have high total testosterone levels, but still suffer symptoms of testosterone deficiency — the SHBG binds itself to too much testosterone and doesn't leave enough of the pure stuff. Research suggests that diet and lifestyle changes can help reduce the amount of SHBG in our system, making more free T available.

Fish oil has been shown to lower SHBG. Again, this is anti-andropause because andropause is known for slowly raising SHBG levels with age, which means that more SHBG is bound to your testosterone leaving you less free testosterone. The net effect of taking fish oil, then, is the opposite and will leave you with more free testosterone. Fish Oil has also been shown in one study to increase Luteinizing Hormone which triggers testosterone production.

3) Albumin-bound Testosterone.
The rest of our testosterone is bound to a protein called albumin. Albumin is a protein produced in the liver, and its job is to stabilize extracellular fluid volumes. Like SHBG-bound testosterone, albumin-bound testosterone is biologically inactive. However, unlike SHBG-bound T, the bind between albumin and testosterone is weak and can be easily broken in order to create free testosterone when needed. Because albumin-bound testosterone is easily converted to free T, some labs lump it together with free testosterone whenever you get tested.

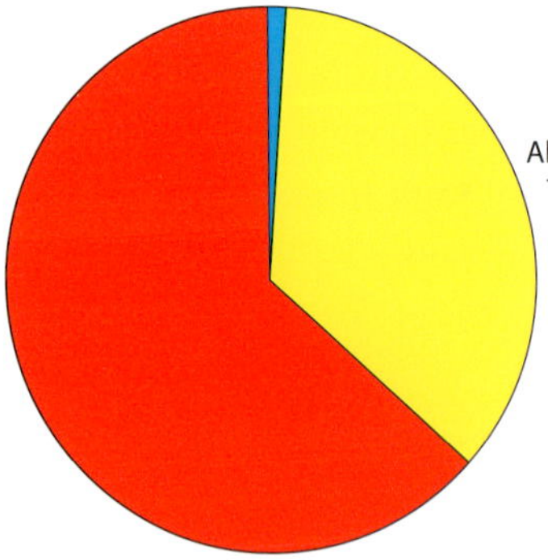

Only around 2% of the testosterone in the body is free. The rest is bound to either albumin or SHBG.

Studies have found that after age 30, testosterone levels in men may decline an average of 2% a year.

Average Testosterone Levels by Age in Men	
AGE	AVERAGE
15-24	750NG/DL
25-34	700NG/DL
35-44	650NG/DL
45-54	600NG/DL
55-64	550NG/DL
65-74	500NG/DL
75-84	450NG/DL
85-89	400NG/DL

The usual normal range for testosterone levels in serum samples is 300–1000 ng/dL (10– 35 nM/L) Estimate of the blood production rate of testosterone in normal adult men ranges from 5.0-7.5 mg/day. The testosterone content of the adult human testis is only about 50 µg (1 µg/g testis), indicating that nearly all of the synthesized testosterone is released into the circulation.

Men must aim to maintain their free testosterone in the range of 20 to 25 pg/mL of blood. This, from my research, is an optimum level. Conventional blood labs, on the other hand, say aging men are ok with as little as 6.6 pg/mL of free testosterone in their blood. This is an absurdly low level and I believe to be dangerous for one's health and keep their oestrogen from getting too high. Ideal oestrogen (oestradiol) levels in men have been shown to be between 20 and 30 pg/mL of blood.

Mainstream medicine's ignorance regarding the need to maintain free testosterone in the higher ranges is a significant cause of premature disability and death in aging men. Free testosterone is the biologically active form of this hormone measured in the blood. When looking at total testosterone blood levels, one should strive for a moderately youthful range of 700-900 ng/dL, though conventional reference ranges state that levels as low as 193 ng/dL are sufficient, a range that I believe is woefully inadequate.

My personal testosterone levels were as low as 220 ng/dl. At this time, I was on my knees. I have now trebled this number through a high fat diet and reduced stress in my life and feel and look like a completely different person. My body fat is <10% my mood is 100% positive and that is at 47 years young as I write this.

There are 8 reasons as to why free testosterone levels may be low:

1) Low fat low cholesterol diet.
2) On statin medication.
3) Too much stress in one's life.
4) Too much testosterone is being converted to oestrogen through the activity of aromatase.
5) Too much free testosterone is being bound by SHBG. This would be especially apparent if a male's total testosterone levels are high but free testosterone levels are low.
6) The pituitary gland is not secreting enough LH to stimulate gonadal production of testosterone. In this case, total testosterone would be low.
7) The gonads have lost their ability to produce testosterone, despite adequate amounts of LH. In this case, the level of LH would be high despite a low testosterone level.
8) DHEA is abnormally low.

Although women produce only about one-tenth the testosterone of men, women produce 300 micrograms per day, whilst men produce 6 – 8 milligrams per day. You can see how little testosterone a woman produces, this is a major reason as to why a woman should never fear putting on large amounts of muscle whilst doing strength training. Let me make it clear - for a woman to carry large amounts of muscle on her frame, she would either need to have a severe hormonal problem or be taking performance enhancing drugs. A woman's levels of testosterone drop by about 50% by the age of forty-five compared to the amount she produced at age twenty.

In a scientific review by the North American Menopause Society, nine out of ten studies on testosterone in women showed increasing testosterone levels to be effective in improving sexual desire, energy levels, body composition changes, and overall emotional outlook.

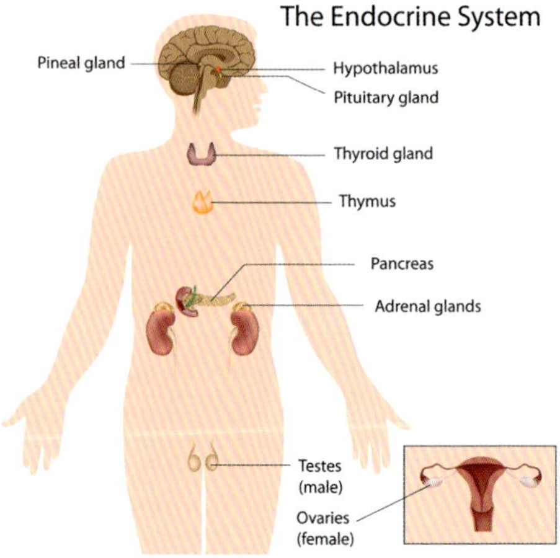

Most testosterone production in women comes from the ovaries and in men from the testes, but in both genders a substantial amount of testosterone also comes from the adrenal glands—the same gland responsible for cortisol production.

One study, published in 1996 in the Journal of Clinical Endocrinology and Metabolism, showed that obese women who boosted their testosterone levels lost significantly more abdominal fat and gained more muscle mass compared to women who were given a placebo and whose testosterone levels remained suppressed.

Researchers at the University of Washington, in Seattle, have shown that among women who lose weight using dietary restriction alone, each 2% loss of body weight is associated with a fall in testosterone levels of 10-12%. This is another reason which shows that dieters who focus on calorie restrictions are not only misinformed, but, in the long term, will have a negative effect on your hormones and increase your body fat.

Testosterone and your heart

In one study published in the Journal Metabolism in March of 2004, researchers found that low testosterone levels posed the greatest risk for men and was the greatest predictor of heart attacks and clogging of the arteries.

NOT high cholesterol, not diabetes, not smoking, not high blood pressure, not even being fat or having a statin deficiency!

It has been shown that men with lower levels of testosterone have poorer endothelial function. In a study of 187 males, researchers found that those men in the highest quartile of testosterone levels had 1.7 fold greater flow mediated dilation, a marker of endothelial function ***(Akishita, 2007).***

In another study, researchers examined the correlation between testosterone levels and mortality in over 900 men with coronary heart disease. The team found that the mortality rate in patients with testosterone deficiency was 21%, while only 12% of subjects with normal testosterone levels died. The authors of the study concluded that "in patients with coronary disease testosterone deficiency is common and impacts significantly negatively on survival" ***(Malkin, 2010).***

Researchers analyzed 30-day survival data for 126 men who had suffered a heart attack. All of the men who did not survive were found to have low total testosterone levels (<= 300 ng/dL). The team went on to conclude that "a low level of testosterone was independently related to total short-term [post-heart attack] mortality ***(Militaru, 2010).***

Testosterone levels are also inversely associated with the development of coronary artery disease. In a study of men 45 years of age or younger, researchers found that subjects with diagnosed coronary artery disease had significantly lower levels of free testosterone than did healthy, age-matched controls. The researchers went on to caution that, based on their findings, "a low level of free testosterone may be related to the development of premature coronary artery disease" ***(Turhan, 2007).***

In a study of over 11,000 men, followed for up to 10 years, baseline testosterone concentrations were inversely associated with cardiovascular and all-cause mortality. Men with total testosterone levels of 481 ng/dL or greater at baseline were significantly less likely to die of cardiovascular disease or any cause during the follow-up period compared to men with testosterone levels below 481 ng/dL. The correlation held even after adjustment for various other confounding factors. The authors of this study declared that "low testosterone may be a predictive marker for those at high risk of cardiovascular disease" ***(Khaw, 2007).***

Statins have been shown to reduce testosterone: A 2010 study in which testosterone levels in men treated with statins and non-statin-treated men were compared. This research is relevant because testosterone is a major driver of libido and sexual functioning. It turned out that those taking statins had lower levels of testosterone, and they also had higher scores of symptoms suggestive of 'hypogonadism' (low male hormone production). ***Corona G, et al. The effect of statin therapy on testosterone levels in subjects consulting for erectile dysfunction. J Sex Med 2010;7(4 Pt 1):1547-56***

So why in the hell are so many doctors prescribing statins which are known to lower testosterone levels to middle aged man?

In one, just 12 weeks of treatment with 80 mg of the statin simvastatin each day lowered bioavailable testosterone (testosterone that can have effect in the tissues) by about 10%, a change that was statistically significant. In another study, 12 weeks of simvastatin at a dose of only 20 mg a day was also found to have a testosterone-lowering effect too. ***Dobs AS, et al. Effects of high-dose simvastatin on adrenal and gonadal steroidogenesis in men with hypercholesterolemia. Metabolism2000;49:1234–8.***

How is it that statins may suppress testosterone levels? Well, as we now know cholesterol is the essential primary building block in the making of testosterone yes lower cholesterol you lower testosterone. It's another example of the critical role that cholesterol plays in the body.

Testosterone and the diabetes connection

Recent studies have demonstrated that low testosterone in men is strongly associated with metabolic syndrome, type 2 diabetes, cardiovascular disease (Miner and Seftel 2007), and an almost 50% increase in mortality over a seven year period (Malkin et al 2010).

In yet another body blow to the claimed benefits of statin drugs, more published research has found that statin drug use leads to accelerated coronary artery and aortic artery calcification, both of which greatly contribute to cardiovascular disease and mortality. The new study comes on top of findings that led the FDA to mandate adding "diabetes risk" to the warning label of statin drugs.

Restoring testosterone to youthful ranges in middle-aged, obese men resulted in an increase in insulin sensitivity as well as a reduction in total cholesterol, fat mass, waist circumference and pro-inflammatory cytokines associated with atherosclerosis, diabetes, and the metabolic syndrome (Kapoor et al 2006, Malkin et al 2004, Heufelder et al 2009). Testosterone therapy also significantly improved erectile function (Fukui 2007) and improved functional capacity, or the ability to perform physical activity without severe duress, in men with heart failure (Malkin et al 2007).

Low testosterone and excess oestrogen (in men): Numerous studies link low testosterone (and excess oestradiol) with increased heart attack and stroke risk ***(Wranicz, 2005; Abbott, 2007; Tivesten, 2006; Dunajska, 2004).***

Testosterone is intimately involved in the *reverse cholesterol transport* process, which *removes* cholesterol from the arterial wall by HDL. Excess oestrogen is linked with higher C-reactive protein and a greater propensity for abnormal blood clots to form in arteries, causing a sudden heart attack or stroke (Stork, 2008; Zegura, 2006). **Men should keep their free testosterone in a range of 20 – 25 pg/mL and their oestradiol levels between 20 – 30 pg/mL** *(Jankowska, 2009).*

The latest discovery makes it clear that statin drugs not only carry a significant risk of developing type 2 diabetes, they also accelerate the cardiovascular complications associated with diabetes. This has to be particularly disconcerting to the pharmaceutical companies since they have been marketing statins to reduce cardiovascular morbidity and mortality, not accelerate it.

According to Dr. Arthur Agatston, cardiologist and author of the South Beach diet books, coronary calcium is the best predictor of who will have a heart attack and who will not. A recent study published in the Journal of the American Medical Association found that coronary calcium was six times more accurate in predicting an impending heart attack than the risk factor of a family history of coronary heart disease.

In the new research, published in the journal Diabetes Care, researchers looked at patients with type 2 diabetes and advanced atherosclerosis and found that coronary artery calcification "was significantly higher in more frequent statin users than in less frequent users." Further, the researchers looked at a subgroup of participants who were not initially receiving statins and found that "progression of both CAC [coronary artery calcification] and AAC [aortic artery calcification] was significantly increased in frequent statin users."

The initial premise used to market statin drugs was that they lowered cholesterol and cholesterol led to clogged arteries and heart attacks. **That premise has been roundly discredited and the fact is that there has never been a single study which has proven that increased cholesterol levels cause heart attacks or other coronary problems.**

Another study where researchers analysed 3,484 Italian men who were already being treated for erectile dysfunction (ED). **They found that those who were taking statins for their cholesterol had significantly lower testosterone levels than men who weren't on statins.**

The researchers also found an increased incidence of hypogonadism in those taking statins. Hypogonadism is a condition in which the body doesn't produce enough testosterone, which may lead to erectile dysfunction, as well as a decrease in muscle mass and body-hair growth. Another study, published in November 30, 2007, has also concluded that - "High endogenous levels of testosterone in men are associated with low mortality from all causes, cardiovascular causes, and cancer".

The authors suggest that low testosterone may be a predictive marker for those at high risk of cardiovascular disease.

Lead author Dr Kay-Tee Khaw (University of Cambridge School of Clinical Medicine, UK) commented to heartwire : "This is the largest study of testosterone levels ever conducted. We don't know whether the association shown between higher levels of testosterone and lower mortality is causal or just a marker of something else, but regardless of this, it appears that low testosterone levels do identify a group at increased risk of cardiovascular death."

Fat cells convert testosterone into oestrogen. Furthermore, low testosterone is correlated to being overweight. Fat cells are loaded with aromatase, the enzyme that converts testosterone to oestrogen. The higher your percentage of body fat, the more oestrogen you can produce and the fatter you will become, unless you control your diet and use supplements plus exercise to lower oestrogen production.

To increase your testosterone levels, you must, I repeat you MUST, decrease your stress levels. The reason for this is that testosterone and cortisol are both made from cholesterol. The more stress in your life, the more cortisol that is required (using up this substrate) and so the less substrates you have to make testosterone. Remember, excess stress, whether you are a male or female, will make you tired, dumb and flabby.

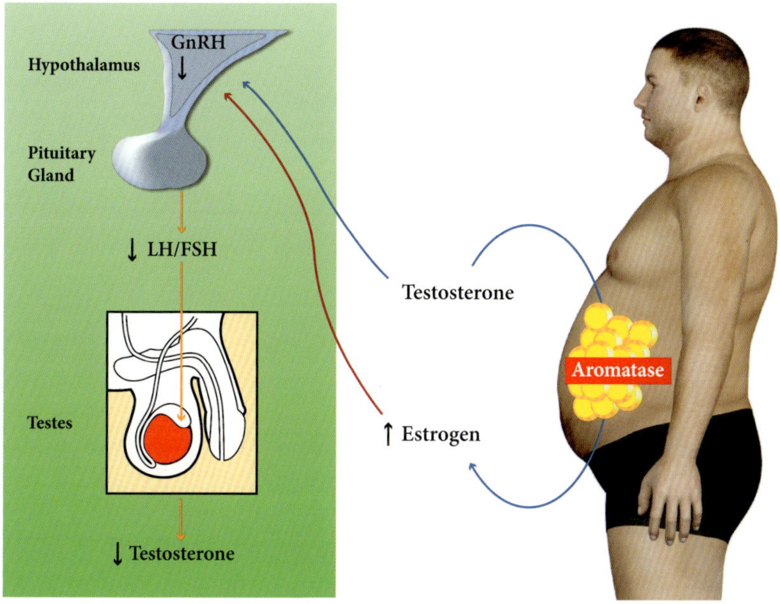

The more belly fat you have the more oestrogen you will produce and the fatter you will become!

Sunshine Increases Testosterone

Vitamin D, a steroid hormone, is essential for the healthy development of the nucleus of the sperm cell, and helps maintain semen quality and sperm count. Vitamin D also increases levels of testosterone. In one study, overweight men who were given vitamin D supplements had a significant increase in testosterone levels after one year.

By increasing circulating levels of vitamin D, sunbathing may help increase men's testosterone levels and thereby their sex drive, according to a study conducted by researchers from the Medical University of Graz, Austria, and published in the journal Clinical Endocrinology.

Researchers tested vitamin D and testosterone levels of 2,299 men over the course of several months. They found that like vitamin D levels, testosterone levels peaked in the summer and dropped during the winter. They also found that men who had at least 30 nanograms of vitamin D in every millilitre of blood had the highest levels of circulating testosterone.

Vitamin D deficiency is currently at epidemic proportions in the UK, and many other regions around the world, largely because people do not spend enough time in the sun to facilitate this important process of vitamin D production due to the moronic advice often given by misinformed doctors, dermatologists and government agencies. I cover the critical importance of vitamin D in more detail in habit 7.

So the first step to ensuring you are receiving all the benefits of vitamin D is to find out what your levels are using a 25(OH)D test, also called 25-hydroxyvitamin D. This test should be available by asking your doctor to perform a routine blood sample. Or you can find a lab that will also do this test for you.

A few years back, the recommended level was between 40-60 ng/ml, but more recently the optimal vitamin D level has been raised to 50-70 ng/ml. To get your levels into the healthy range, sun exposure is the BEST way to optimize your vitamin D levels; exposing a large amount of your skin until it turns the lightest shade of pink, as near to solar noon as possible, is typically necessary to achieve adequate vitamin D production.

If sun exposure is not an option, a safe tanning bed can be used (Always read the instructions). I personally use a UVB sun bed three times per week for 2 minutes, skin colouring will determine exposure. I only use the UVB sun bed during the winter months, or days in the summer where there is no sun exposure. Otherwise, if it is a nice sunny day (which is extremely rare in the UK) I will bare my body and get my free vitamin D.

Remember, you only get the maximum exposure of UVB rays between 12-3pm between April and October in the UK & Ireland. The darker the skin colour, the more time needed require sun exposure. I am whiter than white, so, after 10-15 minutes of sunshine, I put my t-shirt and cap on, I'm done.

A vitamin D3 supplement can be taken orally, but research suggests the average adult needs to take 8,000 IU's of vitamin D per day in order to elevate their levels above 40 ng/ml, which is the absolute minimum for disease prevention. So it pays to get your Vitamin D levels checked regularly to get yours to an optimum level to maintain health and vitality.

Research has also shown the close connection between vitamin A and vitamin D. They work synergistically. If you take too much of one then you will deplete the other. This is why I advise that you do your own research before consuming any high dose supplements. This is why I have added vitamin A and vitamin D to my Ultimate Fish Oil supplements; vitamin D protects omega-3 fats, but I was conscious of the fact that excess vitamin D can deplete vitamin A.

Remember; Stress Kills Testosterone

When you're under a lot of stress, your body releases high levels of the stress hormone cortisol. This hormone actually blocks the effects of testosterone, presumably because, from a biological standpoint, testosterone-associated behaviours (mating, competing, aggression) may have lowered your chances of survival in an emergency (hence, the "fight or flight" response is dominant, courtesy of cortisol).

Exercise is just another form of stress. Too much or the wrong type can wreak havoc with our hormones. Beasting yourself or others may not always be the most appropriate way to train for fat loss.

You must do everything in your power to be happy and focus on what's good in your life and ignore the negatives. This will have a big impact on increasing testosterone levels.

Eating too much protein has been shown to decrease testosterone. The research indicates that you do not need to eat more than 1 gram of protein per pound of body weight, unless you are doing multiple training sessions a day! Excess intake of carbohydrates, especially those that raise blood sugar rapidly, create chronically elevated levels of the hormone insulin and cortisol. These two hormones oppose the action of testosterone and can diminish it's production by up to 25%, according to some research. But, as you will read in habit 9, there will be a time like after intense physical exercise when you need carbohydrates.

Unless you are following a ketogenic diet which is an incredibly effective way of dropping excess body fat for those who simply fail with exercise and diet alone!

Cholesterol is the building block of testosterone as we now know, so it would make sense that a meat-eating, cholesterol-consuming diet would yield more of the big T than a vegetarian diet would. And indeed, that's what a 1985 study found when it looked at a large cross-section of omnivores and vegetarians. What was surprising was how significant the difference was: The meat-eaters actually had 36% more T than the guys who stuck to rabbit food.

A 1989 study found pretty much the same thing: The meat-eaters ate more fat, more cholesterol, more saturated fat, and less fibre than the vegetarians and had 31% more testosterone. A Dutch study published in 1992 looked at changes in T levels on these two diets. A group of young male endurance athletes ate and trained on each diet for 6 weeks (Half started on the meat-rich diet, half on the vegetarian diet; then they switched). Total testosterone declined 35% when the athletes used the vegetarian diet. Dutch research shows that athletes had higher testosterone levels when eating meat-based protein, compared with other sources, such as dairy and eggs. So even an ovo-lacto-vegetarian diet would not be good for T levels. And this shows that it is not just the fat and cholesterol in meat that raises T levels as these are found in dairy and eggs. It has something to do with meat itself.

I can relate to this as I was a vegan for 3 years after becoming a cellular microscopist. The research that I followed to become a cellular microscopist was all based on veganism and unfortunately I fell for the idiotic advice adhered too on these courses, which I now realise was completely flawed, which was based on a vegan diet promoting healthy blood and an alkaline body. I followed this diet to the letter and I can honestly say that I had the strength levels of a pregnant goldfish and I also became sick and fat. The first time I ate meat after three years was an interesting experience I can tell you I had a steak and a few hours later I had an erection which would have taken a skyscraper out it was as if boom my testosterone was back!

Many years on, after extensive research on how to build healthy blood, I realise that you must have quality animal meat and fat in your diet. Also, when you understand the hormonal system, especially steroid hormones, you realise how you need cholesterol in your diet as the precursor to all of our steroid hormones. You will find zero cholesterol in a plant based diet. This may also explain why I had the testosterone levels of a pregnant woman.

Anyone who advocates a vegan/vegetarian diet for health, fat loss and performance genuinely does not understand the nutritional requirements for humans. For example we WOULD NOT have evolved as a species if we did not eat meat and animal fats, our brain would not have developed and we would still be living in the jungle munching on leaves, fruits and the occasional bit of cannibalism.

And trust me, if you were on a survival expedition for a few weeks in the wild when you get really hungry and I mean really hungry a few days without food you will not be craving carrots with a hummus dip you will crave meat and fat which are obviously energy dense and delivers nutrients quickly to the starving body nature knows best!

Creatine and testosterone

One study followed a group of college athletes during a ten week exercise program. The athletes were divided into 3 groups: one group received a placebo, one group received creatine, and the third group received a mix of creatine and beta-alanine. The results showed that in the creatine group, testosterone levels and power output increased significantly. (Int J Sport Nutr Exerc Metab. 2006 Aug;16(4):430-46. Effect of creatine and beta-alanine supplementation on performance and endocrine responses in strength/power athletes. ***Hoffman J1, Ratamess N, Kang J, Mangine G, Faigenbaum A, Stout J.)***

Another impressive creatine study had 17 men who were doing some serious short-term overtraining in the gym. They were divided into 2 groups, the first one got 0.3 grams of creatine per kg of bodyweight, and the second group received a placebo. The results showed that during overtraining, the creatine group was able to preserve their power output much better than the placebo group, and the creatine group had continuously higher total and free testosterone levels thorough the study when compared to the placebo group. ***Eur J Appl Physiol. 2004 May;91(5-6):628-37. Epub 2003 Dec 18. The effects of creatine supplementation on muscular performance and body composition responses to short-term resistance training overreaching. Volek JS1, Ratamess NA, Rubin MR, Gómez AL, French DN, McGuigan MM, Scheett TP, Sharman MJ, Häkkinen K, Kraemer WJ.***

The researchers in this short-term study conducted on swimmers, saw that creatine supplementation was able to increase the swimming speed of a 50 meter sprint by 4.6% and testosterone levels by at least 15% when compared to placebo. The effects of creatine supplementation on performance and hormonal response in amateur swimmers. ***Science & Sports, Volume 26, Issue 5, Pages 272-277 D. Sheikholeslami Vatani, H. Faraji, R. Soori, M. Mogharnasi***

This study examined the long-term safety effects of creatine. Athletes who had ingested creatine for up to four years were found to have no adverse health effects, but a trend to increase testosterone levels was noted. ***Med Sci Sports Exerc. 2001 Feb;33(2):183-8.Creatine supplementation and health variables: a retrospective study. Schilling BK1, Stone MH, Utter A, Kearney JT, Johnson M, Coglianese R, Smith L, O'Bryant HS, Fry AC, Starks M, Keith R, Stone ME.***

Calcium-D-Glucarate

Calcium-D-Glucarate can be found in the skin of certain berries, like blueberries for instance. Calcium-D-Glucarate in a nutshell is a fiber that binds into oestrogen molecules and then "flushes" those molecules out of your body through the intestines. The way that this compound can be labeled as a testosterone booster is easy. Lowered oestrogen levels that follow the use of Calcium-D-Glucarate could lead to a boost in testosterone.

Calcium D-Glucarate includes the patented compound glucarate which has been shown to enhance the major detoxification pathways in the body. Animal studies have shown that high doses of calcium D-glucarate inhibit beta-glucuronidase, thereby enhancing the process of glucuronidation, in which foreign organic compounds, fat-soluble toxins and excess steroid hormones such as oestrogen are detoxified and excreted from our bodies.

Magnesium role in increasing testosterone

60% of your total testosterone is bound into SHBG (Sex Hormone Binding Globulin) which makes it "unavailable" for your body to be directly used. Magnesium however is one of the best supplements for lowering your SHBG count, which means that you'll have some more testosterone in the "free testosterone" form.

Geriatricians at the University Hospital of Parma, found out that older men who had more magnesium in their body, also had higher concentrations of serum testosterone and growth hormone.

University of Selcuk, Turkey, found out that athletes who supplemented with one gram of magnesium, increased their testosterone levels by 25% after 4 weeks of supplementation.

Fu-Jen Catholic University in Taipei found out that supplementation with magnesium significantly lowered their subjects fat percentage, when compared to placebo.

DIM or Diindolylmethane

DIM or Diindolylmethane is a breakdown product of indole 3-carbinol (I3C) which occurs naturally in cruciferous vegetables. DIM has been shown to have some benefits for our testosterone levels by effectively removing oestrogen from our liver, by the action called "oestrogen metabolism".

Research has also shown that this phytochemical compound lowers SHBG count while also increasing free testosterone levels. So we have here a nutrient that helps detoxify excess oestrogen, lowers down our SHBG count, and also increases free testosterone levels.

You can either get DIM by eating tons of cruciferous vegetables such as broccoli, cauliflower and brussel sprouts, but if you really want to reap out the benefits of DIM, use it as a supplement as well with Calcium-D-Glucarate to effectively flush out oestrogen from your body.

Cordyceps Sinensis - testosterone booster

Much of what is known about Cordyceps sinensis we owe to the research of Dr. Georges Halpern, a physician and professor emeritus with the University of Hong Kong, and author of several books about Cordyceps. His interest and commitment have resulted in making available to the Western world the many research studies conducted by Chinese scientists published in various Chinese scientific journals. These investigations with Cordyceps sinensis have been summarized in the following scientific articles: *1. Zhu, J.S., Halpern, G.M., and Jones, K. (1998): The Scientific Rediscovery of an Ancient Chinese Herbal Medicine: Cordyceps sinensis. Part I. Journal of Alternative and complementary Medicine 4(3), pp 289-303 2. Zhu, J.S., Halpern, G.M., and Jones, K. (1998): The Scientific Rediscovery of a Precious Ancient Chinese Herbal Regimen: Cordyceps sinensis. Part II. Journal of Alternative and complementary Medicine 4(4), pp 429-457.*

- Cordyceps is a medicinal mushroom that contains compounds that have been performing outstandingly well in latest clinical trials.
- Research on rat leydig cells (almost identical to ours) show that Cordyceps Sinensis has some benefits of stimulating those T boosting cells to release more testosterone.
- Oral supplementation with rats show that Cordyceps Sinensis increases testosterone levels in a matter of 3 hours, which tells us that this medicinal mushroom will survive the harsh conditions of our gastrointestinal system.
- Cordyceps contains super antioxidants, known for nourishing the leydig cells to preserve testosterone molecules from oxidization.
- In a double blind placebo study, Cordyceps Sinensis increased ATP levels by 50%.
- Cordyceps contains high amounts of mannitol, which increases blood flow to the pelvic region and improves sexual performance.
- **Cordyceps increases cellular Oxygen Absorption by up to 40%** *(Lou Y, Liao X, Lu Y. Cardiovascular pharmacological studies of ethanol extracts of Cordyceps mycelia and Cordyceps fermentation solution. Chinese Traditional and Herbal Drugs 1986;17(5):17-21,209-213)*
- Chronic obstructive pulmonary diseases improvement of 40% after Cordyceps supplement. *(Wang WQ. J. Administration Traditional Chinese Med 1995;5 (supp;):24)*
- **Improvements in the Immune System.** The improvements in the Immune System were so impressive that Dr. Zhu at the Journal of Alternative and Complementary Medicine 1998 stated: "Because of the above profound influence on immune functions, natural Cordyceps products have been used in many clinical conditions in patients with altered immune functions."
- Several studies with animals have demonstrated that *Cordyceps sinensis* increases the cellular energy production and oxygen supply. A double blind, placebo controlled investigation showed a marked reduction in fatigue in elderly patients when they were given three grams of Cordyceps daily. In another study, *Cordyceps sinensis* improved shortness of breath and reduced fatigue in patients suffering from chronic heart failure *(Reference 1, Chapter "Improvement of physical performance and quality of life", pages 293 – 295).*
- Cordyceps improves stamina and athletic performance. Several studies with animals have shown that Cordyceps sinensis increases the cellular energy production and oxygen uptake *(Reference 1, Chapter "Improvement of physical performance and quality of life", pages 293 - 295).* A study with mice demonstrated their improved swimming capabilities after

six weeks of Cordyceps supplementation compared with a control group.

- Cordyceps radically increases cellular energy. Cellular energy, which is also known scientifically as the ATP/IP ratio. Cordyceps has been clinically proven to increase cellular Bio-Energy by as much as 55% *(Reported XU C.F et al in ZHU J-S, Halpern GM, Jones K. The Scientific rediscovery of a precious ancient Chinese herbal regimen: Cordyceps sinensis: Part I. J Alt Comp Med 1998;4(3):289-303.)*
- Three separate Chinese double blind and placebo-controlled studies with over 200 men with "reduced libido and other sexual problems" showed remarkably similar results. On average, 64% of the Cordyceps-users reported significant improvement at the conclusion of the experimental period compared with 24% of the placebo group. In another double blind, placebo controlled study conducted with 21 elderly women with similar complaints, 90% reported improvements of their condition following the use of Cordyceps, compared with none in the control group.
- **Hormones – Adrenal Thymus, Mitochondrial energy** Dramatic Natural Improvements are seen in endocrine hormone levels, in fertility, and in Sexual Libido for men and women.

Dosage - Dosing varies between people but the average reported Cordyceps sinensis dose is between 2 and 5 grams. Always read the label before consuming.

Factors that can inhibit testosterone

In a journal found in the National Library of Medicine, studies have shown that in doses as low as 3 mg per day, fluoride has produced toxic effects on male reproductive hormones.

Studies on animals have consistently found, with a few exceptions, that high exposures to fluoride can seriously damage the male reproductive system, as measured by increased oxidative stress, altered sperm morphology, reduced testosterone, reduced sperm quality, reduced sperm motility, and reduced fertility. Studies of highly-exposed human populations have found similar associations with reduced testosterone and fertility. Consistent with these findings, carefully controlled in vitro studies have found that direct exposure of fluoride to the testes or semen inhibits testosterone production and damages sperm.

Flouride is a serious hazard for decreasing testosterone levels which is a genuine disaster for both males and females.

While researchers have known since the 1930s that mega concentrations of fluoride can completely (but reversibly) immobilize sperm, it was not until the 1970s and 1980s that researchers found that relatively modest concentrations of fluoride could cause damage prior to complete immobilization. ***(Haesungcharern 1978; Kanwar 1983; Chubb 1985a,b).***

The most notable findings to date, however, were published in 2002 and 2006 by a team of Polish researchers. The researchers reported that exposing ram semen to just 0.38 parts per million (20 umol/L) of fluoride for five hours was sufficient to "cause a statistically significant decrease in the motility of spermatoza and the number of intact acrosomes." ***(Zakrzewska 2002).*** The authors noted that these changes "undoubtedly affect the physiological function of the sperm."

"The activities of androgen-dependent enzymes—acid phosphatase (ACP), lactate dehydrogenase (LDH), and gamma-glutamyl transferase (y-GT-10S)—decreased significantly when the ejaculate was treated with NaF at concentrations of 20, 100, 200 µmol/L (0.38; 1.9; 3.8 ppm F-), but they returned to the initial value of the control at 0.1 mol/L (1900 ppm F-)... These changes undoubtedly affect the physiological functions of the sperm." ***Zakrzewska H, et al. (2002). In vitro influence of sodium fluoride on ram semen quality and enzyme activities. Fluoride 35: 153-160.***

"Fluoride-treated sperm [4,750 ppm for 20 minutes] exhibited a high percent of morphologic abnormalities, including a large number (10.59%) of elongated heads and 2.1% amorphous heads. The tail also revealed splitting (2.19%), coiling (11.6%) and deflagellation (22.43%). A few sperm had bent necks, and 16.75% of spermatozoa showed a diminutive acrosome. . . . These changes may have caused loss of membrane integrity and reduced metabolic activity, which ultimately resulted in deterioration of forward progression rating. The treatment

caused a significant enhancement in poor to fair forward progression and failure of good and excellent forward progression, leading to a significant decline in sperm motility. . . . The depleted sperm GSH in the present investigation strongly suggests that, like several exogenous compounds, fluoride is largely dependent upon glutathione for detoxification."
Chinoy NJ, Narayana MV. (1994). In vitro fluoride toxicity in human spermatozoa. Reprod Toxicol. 8(2):155-9.

"Our studies indicate that 3 ppm fluoride ions significantly inhibit testosterone secretion by rat testes perfused in vitro. . . . In conclusion, Oxypherol-E.T. contains contaminants that are toxic to endocrine organs. Fluoride ion may be the primary endocrine toxicant."
Chubb C. (1985a). Reversal of the endocrine toxicity of commercially produced perfluorochemical emulsion. Biology of Reproduction 33(4):854-8.

So if you believe the conspiracy theory to be true governments and powers to be who control the governments are working on a mass sterilisation program and nothing could be easier to do this than through our drinking water but also at the huge cost to people's health. Nobody is going to fuck with my testosterone that's why I follow what I present to you in this book!

Zinc inhibits levels of aromatase, the testosterone to oestrogen converter and declining levels of zinc are extremely common in the western diet. Zinc is also necessary for normal pituitary function, without which the proper hormonal signals will not be sent to the testicles to stimulate the production of testosterone.

One study has shown that cell phone usage may lower male fertility levels. Researchers have not yet isolated an underlying cause, but a likely culprit is alterations in the brain's pituitary output, since the men had lowered levels of Luteinizing Hormone which is required for testosterone production.

Don't Over Train

Researchers from the University of Connecticut have shown that overtrained athletes have elevated levels of sex hormone–binding globulin (SHBG, which binds testosterone, making it unavailable to the body) and reduced testosterone levels—both of which could be prevented by a well planned nutrition, training and recovery program.

A low testosterone person needs to be careful with their training program: study after study has shown that over-training significantly reduces testosterone levels for 1-4 days afterward! And, by the way, it doesn't matter whether it's endurance or weight training – the downward effect on testosterone levels is the same.

Rest and regeneration will help you increase your testosterone. If you don't, your circulating testosterone levels can plunge by as much as 40%, as was discovered by studies performed at the University of North Carolina.

Overtraining goes beyond just excessive endurance training or too many hours spent at the gym. Certain high-intensity exercise routines may push the body's stress response too far, leading to a cascade of biochemical responses that can cause serious damage to one's health in both the short and long term.

While short, intense workouts can be great for inducing fat loss, increasing aerobic capacity, and reducing risk for cardiovascular disease, excessively intense exercise can cause a variety of health problems, especially for those dealing with other concurrent stressors such as autoimmune disease, gut dysbiosis, or adrenal fatigue.

One short term study of 8 young men with an average age of 17 showed significant increases in baselines testosterone (7.5%) in only 11 weeks. This is a nice increase in testosterone when you consider that it occurred in less than three months! What did these young pups do to increase their already abundant testosterone? They simply engaged in "explosive strength training" for these 11 weeks. ***Eur J of Applied Physio, 2004, 91(5-6):698-707***

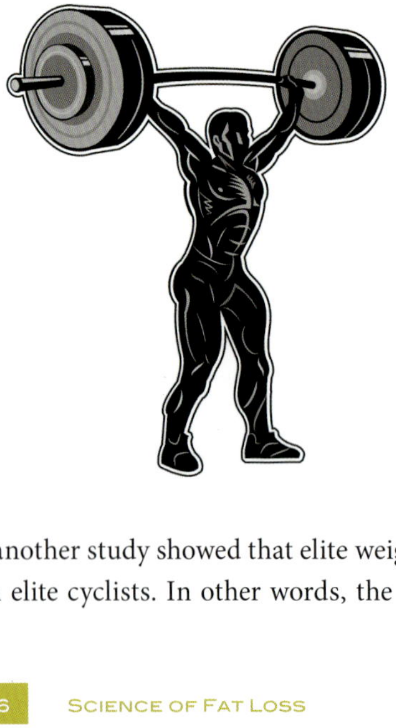

Are there any studies showing that this extrapolates to longer time frames? Yes! One study of nine elite weight lifters over a two year period showed significant increases in testosterone, luteinizing hormone and the ratio of testosterone to SHBG. The authors concluded that "the present results suggest that prolonged intensive strength training in elite athletes may influence the pituitary and possibly hypothalamic levels, leading to increased serum levels of testosterone". ***J Appl Physiol, 1988, 65:2406-2412***

Yet another study showed that elite weight lifters had significantly higher testosterone levels than elite cyclists. In other words, the body seems to adapt to the kind of exercise placed before it. In everyday language that means that weight lifting and weight training very likely lead to increases in testosterone over time. *J of Sports Sciences, 2004, 22(5):465-478*

Sports scientists often use the ratio between cortisol and testosterone as an indicator of how easily the body builds up muscle. That's why some sports scientists advise athletes to do power training early in the evening: testosterone levels may well be somewhat lower than earlier in the day, but cortisol levels are radically lower at this time of the day.

Strength training is really a kind of hormone therapy, write researchers at the Spanish University of Extremadura in the European Journal of Applied Physiology. According to the researchers, regular weight training raises testosterone levels by 40%.

DHEA: The fountain of youth

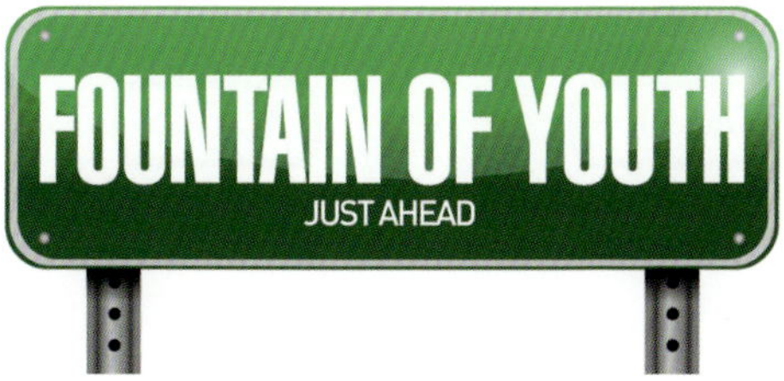

DHEA (dehydroepiandrosterone) is one of the critical hormones that scientists are calling the "fountain of youth". This hormone is made from **cholesterol** by the adrenal glands and is a precursor to 18 steroid hormones including oestrogen and testosterone. Healthy DHEA production is critical for lean muscle development, fat burning, bone growth, skin health, and immunity.

DHEA is a naturally produced pro-hormone and is the most abundant basic building block for hormones in the human body. From birth men and women alike gradually produce more and more DHEA until about age 25. After age 25 we produce about 2% less per year each year. So by age 35 we make about 20% less than we did at age 25, and by age 50 we are making half as much. By age 70 most people make minimal amounts of DHEA.

In 2009, scientists confirmed that low DHEA levels in men were linked to diabetes and coronary heart disease. DHEA powerfully modulates gene expression to shift the metabolic balance in favour of energy utilization and away from storage as fat.

Many researchers believe that DHEA's anti obesity effects are due to its ability to block a specific enzyme called glucose-6-phosphate-dehydrogenase (G6PD). Scientists believe that DHEA, by inhibiting G6PD, actually blocks the body's ability to store and produce fat.

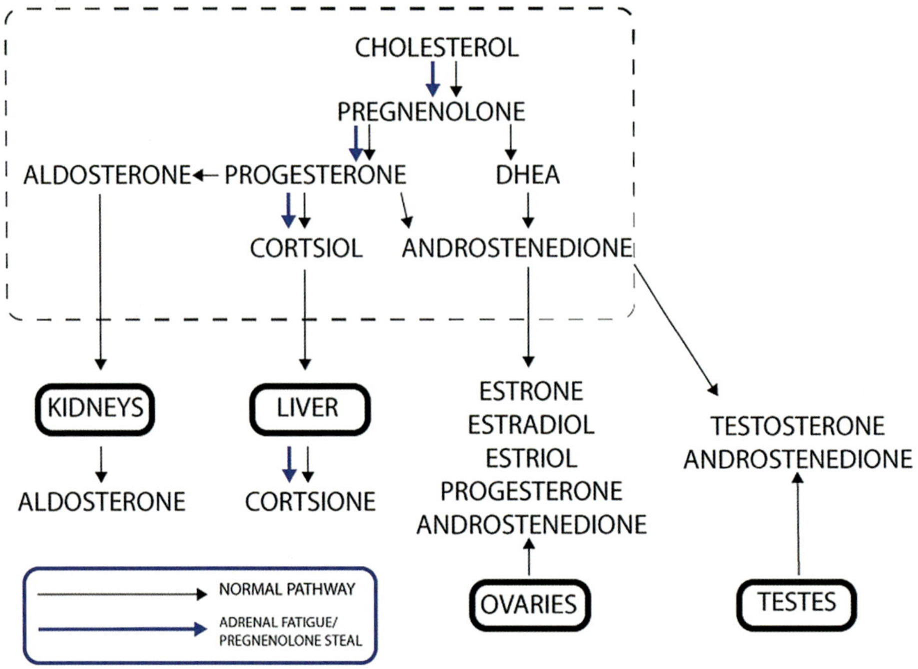

High stress and poor sleeping habits also cause increased cortisol levels. When these issues become chronic they cause a phenomenon called `pregnenolone steal. Pregnenolone is a by product of cholesterol metabolism that is necessary to produce both cortisol and DHEA. High stress causes this process to shift towards cortisol production. This shift essentially `steals` the necessary pregnenolone from the DHEA production pathway to produce more cortisol. This process depletes DHEA levels. This is known as the pregnenolone steal.

DHEA Cortisol Saliva testing procedure

There are a number of labs which will test your DHEA/Cortisol levels. You will be sent four tubes to collect the saliva;

- Collect the first sample immediately upon awakening or within 30 minutes after waking. For most, this will be between 7:00 AM and 9:00 AM. Circle "AM" on the collection tube label.
- Collect the second sample between 11:00 AM and 1:00 PM. Circle "NOON" on the collection tube label.
- Collect the third sample between 4:00 PM and 6:00 PM. Circle "PM" on the collection tube label.
- Collect the fourth sample between 10:00 PM and 12:00 AM. Circle "NIGHT" on the collection tube label.

You should then send the samples away as soon as possible to be analysed.

When our cortisol levels are managed through stress reduction the raw materials from which our bodies manufacture our DHEA are freed up to manufacture this essential fat busting hormone. So one of the most effective ways to increase DHEA is to manage stress, I have learnt to do this after being a stress head all my life and I've seen my body fat literally dropping off once I reduced all of the stress in my life, no amount of exercise or healthy eating did that for me.

High sugar and carbohydrate consumption increases blood sugar and insulin levels. **Elevated insulin causes a decreased production of DHEA in the adrenals.** Blood sugar imbalances also create critical vitamin and mineral imbalances that stress the adrenals and reduce DHEA production. Alcohol and caffeine consumption also decrease DHEA levels.

Many people rush out and look for DHEA boosting supplements; however, lifestyle factors that deplete DHEA levels should be addressed first. The most important factor includes reducing/eliminating adrenal stressors such as relationship stress, toxicity, leaky gut syndrome, parasites and other infectious agents, chronic inflammation, physical stress, nutrient deficiencies, poor sleep, & blood sugar imbalances.

Eliminate/reduce caffeine from your diet. It's the quickest way to reduce cortisol production and elevate the production of DHEA, the leading anabolic youth hormone.

An anti-inflammatory diet is also critical part to de-stressing the body and boosting DHEA levels. This diet should be very low in sugar and very rich in phytonutrients (chemical compounds found mostly in coloured fruits and vegetables) and trace minerals from fresh, raw or lightly steamed vegetables. Powerful anti-inflammatory herbs such as turmeric, ginger, rosemary, thyme, oregano, & cinnamon should be generously consumed on a regular basis.

Healthy fat consumption is an essential part of creating cholesterol which is needed to produce DHEA. Healthy fat sources include coconut products, avocados, olive oil, nuts, seeds, & purified omega-3 fish oil supplements. Healthy protein sources to boost DHEA production include wild-caught fish, grass-fed red meat, liver and free range chicken, turkey, and organic eggs.

Other lifestyle factors that are critical for healthy DHEA levels include regular sun exposure and/or supplementation to maintain vitamin D (25-OH) levels between 70-100 ng/ml.

Meditation is often used as an antidote to stress and has been found to increase DHEA levels. In fact, in a meditation study, a group of 45 year old males who regularly meditated were found to have 23% more DHEA than a smaller group who didn't meditate. In women, the meditators had 47% more DHEA. Another scientific study found that for every 20% increase in DHEA, there was a 48% drop in heart disease and a 36% drop in death from any cause.

Female Hormones for Health & Fat Loss

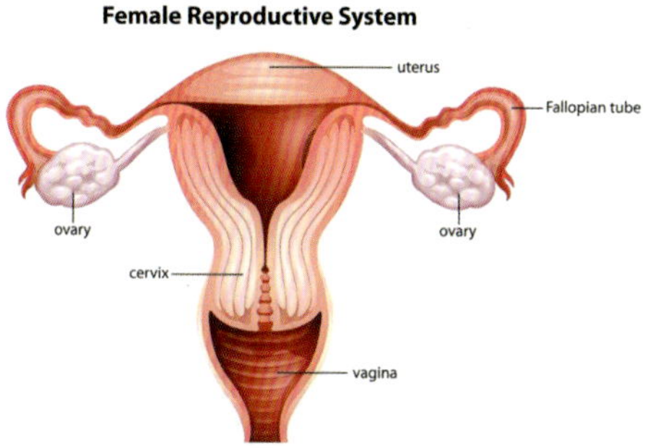

The two primary female hormones secreted by the ovaries are oestrogen and progesterone. The properties of one offsets the other and together they are maintained in optimal balance in our body at all times. Too much of one hormone or the other can lead to significant medical problems.

In non pregnant premenopausal women, only 100 - 200 micrograms of oestrogen is secreted daily. But during pregnancy, much more is produced. About 20 - 25 mg of progesterone is produced daily during a woman's monthly cycle. Up to 300 - 400 mg is produced daily during pregnancy which indicates how important progesterone is during pregnancy.

Oestrogen is produced in the ovaries. It regulates the menstrual cycle, promotes cell division and is largely responsible for the development of secondary female characteristics during puberty, including the growth and development of the breast and pubic hair.

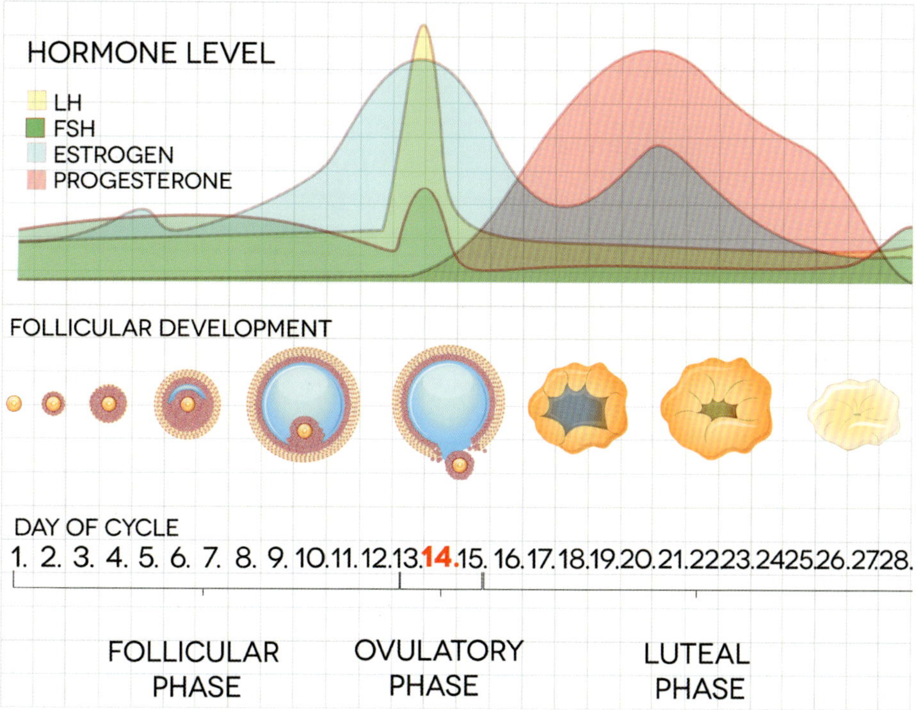

Men produce some level of oestrogen, though on a much smaller scale than women. In men, small levels of oestrogen are produced in the testes, but can also be produced in the liver, adrenal glands and fat cells. It has been shown that excess fat can lead to raised oestrogen levels in men.

When oestrogen levels start to get high in men, health problems start to arise. Elevated oestrogen levels in men have been shown to contribute to prostate cancer, heart disease, and gynecomastia (man boobs). Since high levels of oestrogen are typically accompanied by lower levels of testosterone levels in men, other changes also occur including; loss of muscle mass, fatigue, depression, low libido and erectile dysfunction.

Excessive oestrogen in men raises body fat and can contribute to a host of other problems. Aromatase is the enzyme that is responsible for converting testosterone into oestrogen and is found most prominently in fat cells. This is the link; the more body fat a man (and a woman) has, the more aromatase, and therefore oestrogen, they are likely to have.

What Exactly is Oestrogen?

Oestrogen is a naturally occurring human hormone. In fact, it is not a single hormone, but a collective name for several variants.

Oestradiol is the most potent, with estrone and estriol, its much weaker sisters. In healthy young women, the typical mix approximates 15/15/70% respectively. This is the combination worked out by Mother Nature as optimum for human females.

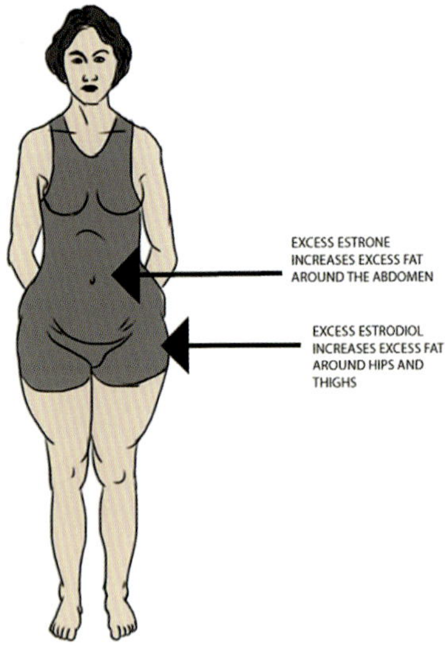

Oestradiol is produced by the ovaries, and promotes fat storage around the hips and the thighs.

Estrone is produced by fat cells from the conversion of male hormones (androgens). This type of oestrogen promotes the storage of fat around the middle.

Estriol is a weak form of oestrogen, the liver converts oestradiol and estrone into estriol to be excreted from the body. Oestrogen is a pro-growth hormone. Since too much of anything is generally not good, the body has another hormone to offset and counterbalance the effects of oestrogen. It is called progesterone. Oestrogen and progesterone work in synchronization with each other as checks and balances to achieve hormonal harmony in both sexes.

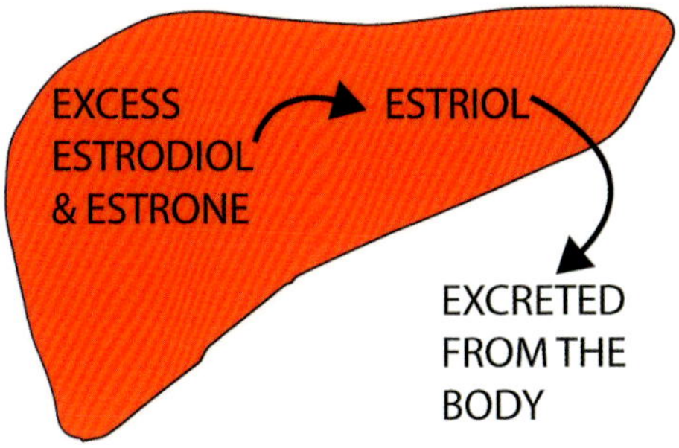

The liver converts oestradiol and estrone in to estriol to be excreted from the body provided it is functioning properly and not congested with toxins or you have a fatty liver.

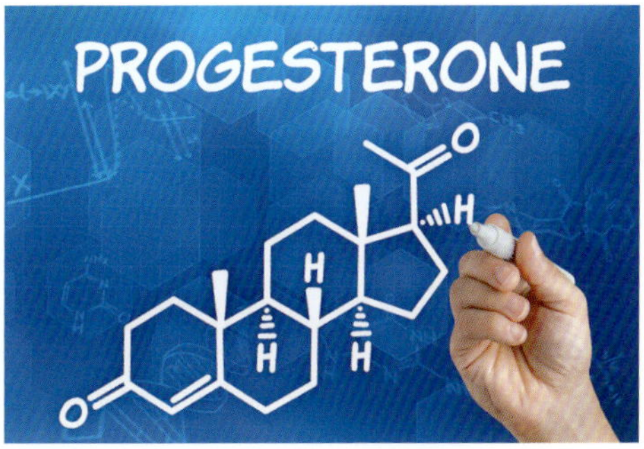

Progesterone, as its name implies, is a progestational hormone. In other words, it favours the growth and well-being of the foetus. Without a proper amount of progesterone, there can be no successful pregnancy. It protects us against the “growth effect” of oestrogen.

Progesterone is made from pregnenolone, which in turn comes from cholesterol. Production occurs at several places. In women, it is primarily made in the ovaries, just before ovulation, and increasing rapidly after ovulation. It is also made in the adrenal glands in both sexes and in the testes in males. In women, its level is highest during the luteal period (especially from day 19 to 22 of the menstrual cycle).

Functions of Progesterone

Progesterone acts primarily as an antagonist (opposite) to oestrogen in our body. For example, oestrogen can cause breast cysts while progesterone protects against breast cysts. When the hormonal balance between oestrogen and progesterone is off, the following symptoms of such imbalance include: hot flashes, vaginal dryness, water retention, weight gain, insomnia, mood swings, short-term memory loss, wrinkly skin and osteoporosis.

It is not the absolute deficiency of oestrogen or progesterone but rather, the relative dominance of oestrogen and relative deficiency of progesterone that is the main cause of health problems when they are off balance. From age 35 to 50, there is a 75% reduction in production of progesterone in the body. Oestrogen, during the same period, only declines about 35%.

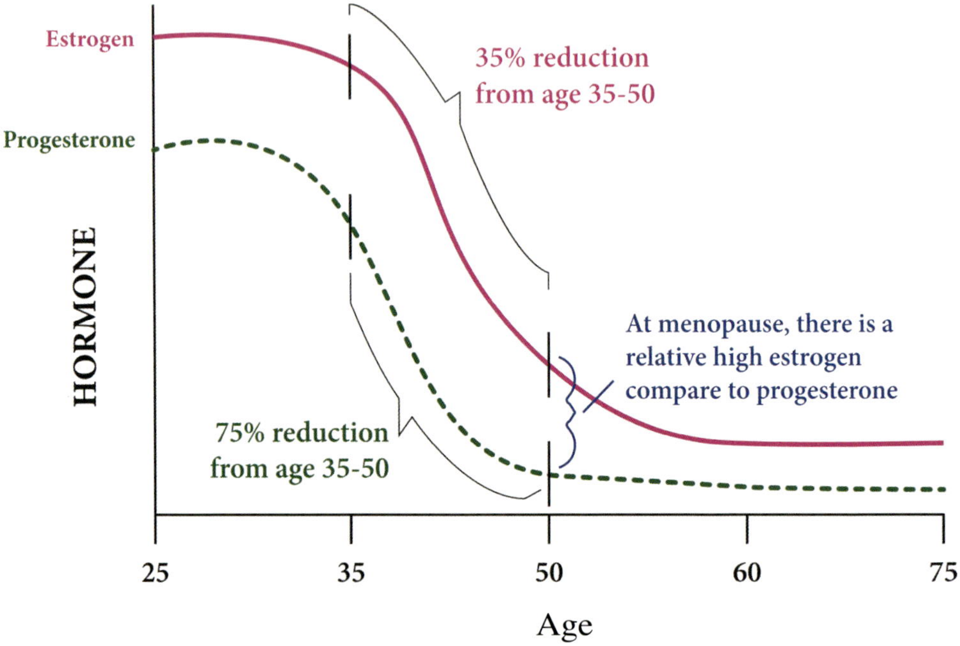

Stress causes adrenal gland exhaustion as well as reduced progesterone output. This tilts the oestrogen to progesterone ratios in favour of oestrogen. Excessive oestrogen in turn causes insomnia and anxiety, which further taxes the adrenal glands. This leads to a further reduction in progesterone output and even more oestrogen dominance. After a few years in this type of vicious cycle, the adrenal glands become exhausted. This dysfunction leads to blood sugar imbalance, hormonal imbalances, and chronic fatigue.

According to the late Dr. John Lee, the world's authority on natural hormone therapy, the key to hormonal balance is the modulation of progesterone to oestrogen ratio.

For optimum health, the progesterone to oestrogen ratio should be between 200-300 to 1.

Vitamin C comes to the rescue for low progesterone and it has been clinically proven to be effective. At doses of 750 mg/day, vitamin C has been shown to raise progesterone. In a randomized trial, women were randomly assigned to receive either vitamin C or a placebo. Within three menstrual cycles, the group receiving vitamin C saw progesterone levels increase on average from 8–13 ng/ml. The goal with progesterone is to get your levels between 10–25 ng/ml.

Also, drop the coffee if you want to raise your progesterone levels. Why? Caffeine increases cortisol and high cortisol can block progesterone receptors, a number of studies have linked caffeine with PMS symptoms.

What is so bad about oestrogen dominance? It is the root cause of a myriad of illnesses. Conditions associated with this include weight gain, fibrocystic breast disease, PMS, uterine fibroids, breast cancer, endometriosis, infertility problems, endometrial polyps, PCOS, autoimmune disorders, low blood sugar problems, and menstrual pain, among many others.

Anything that impairs liver function or ties up the detoxifying function will result in excess oestrogen levels, whether it has a physical basis, as in liver disease, or an external cause, as with exposure to environmental toxins, drugs or dietary substances. Not only is oestrogen produced internally, it's also produced in reaction to chemicals and other substances in our food. When it is not broken down adequately, higher levels of oestrogen build up. This is true for both men and women, although the effects are more easily recognized in men.

Women tend to suffer less from cardiovascular disease than men, but this difference becomes less marked post-menopause. This observation is behind a great deal of received wisdom, where oestrogen is assumed to have a beneficial effect on the heart and blood vessels. Today, new data seems to question these assumptions. A study has been conducted by a team of researchers at Paris-based Inserm (Institut national de la sante et de la recherche medicale – National Institute of Health and Medical Research), led by Pierre-Yves Scarabin, on 6,000 women aged over 65. The results demonstrate, for the first time, that women with high levels of oestradiol (one of the oestrogen hormones) in their blood are exposed to a greater risk of myocardial infarction (heart attacks) or strokes, the Journal of the American Heart Association reports.

Oestrogen hormones play a key role in sexual development and reproduction in women. Its blood levels are particularly high during the active reproductive period, according to an Inserm statement. After menopause, the ovarian function ceases, leading to a significant drop in oestrogen levels in the blood. However, low concentrations of these hormones do continue to circulate and may still exert biological actions.Throughout their lives, women are less exposed to the risk of cardiovascular disease than men. For many years, this relative immunity displayed by women was attributed to oestrogen undertaking a 'protector' role in terms of atherosclerosis (hardening of arteries) and its complications.

Now for the first time, the Inserm results demonstrate that high oestrodial levels in the blood lead to an elevated risk of myocardial infarction or strokes.This new data questions the beneficial role of oestrogen on the heart and vessels. "Fresh studies must confirm this harmful effect and establish whether these results can be applied to younger menopausal women," stated Pierre-Yves Scarabin.

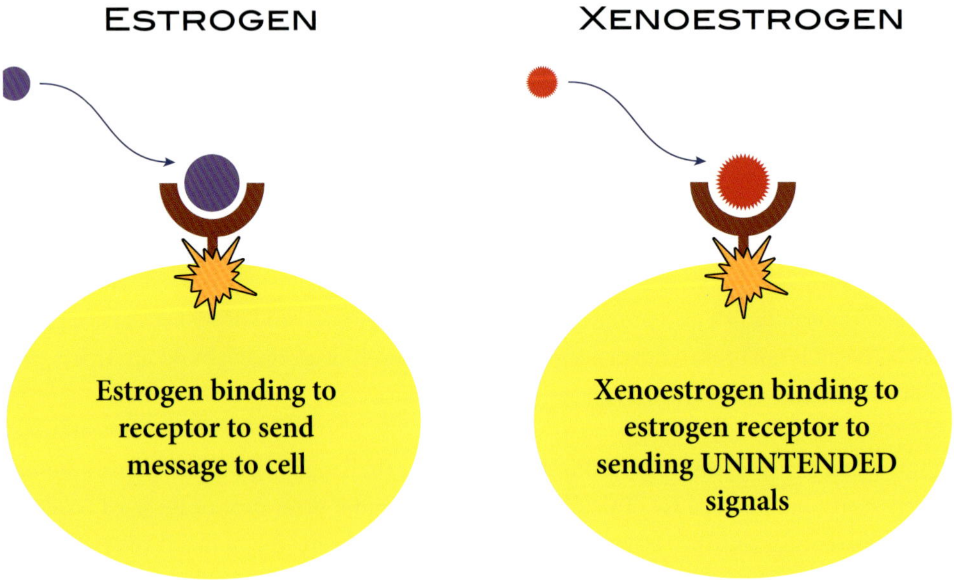

It has been found that circulating oestrogen levels increase significantly in women who drink alcohol. In one study, blood and urine oestrogen levels increased up to 32% in women who drank just two drinks a day. Consequently, breast cancer risks are higher for women drinkers.

High oestrogen relative to normal progesterone is a combination that is common in overweight women, and in women who have been exposed to xenooestrogens. Ovaries are the main source of oestrogen in females, but unfortunately fat cells also make oestrogen, as we have already discussed.

According to the research, women who gain more than 20lbs from age 18 to mid-life double their risk of postmenopausal breast cancer. That's only a few pounds per year! Oestrogen is 50-100 times greater in overweight menopausal women than in lean women, because as we now know fat cells produce oestrogen, and that probably accounts for the greater risk in breast cancer associated with being overweight.

With regards to thyroid health, taking "the Pill" will suppress the production of progesterone, which does a great job of preventing a woman from becoming pregnant, but also will create chaos with the endocrine system. People with thyroid conditions often have the condition oestrogen dominance, which can be caused by an excess in oestrogen, but is more commonly caused by a progesterone deficiency. And so a person who is taking oral contraceptives will frequently develop this condition, which not only can affect their thyroid health, but their overall health as well.

Birth control pills lower free thyroid hormones and testosterone. Birth control pills increase thyroglobulin, a protein that binds thyroid hormone. If you are on thyroid medication, you may need to adjust your dose accordingly. Additionally, birth control pills raise sex hormone binding globulin, a protein that binds free testosterone and may make it biologically inert.

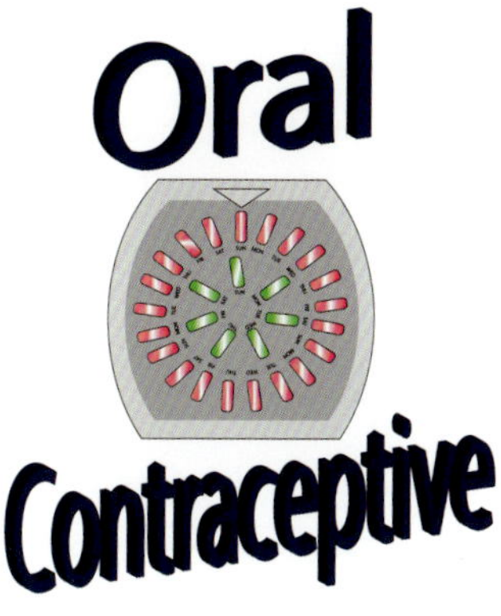

A report, from the Universities of Southern California and Hawaii, published in the British Journal of Cancer, states that eating grapefruit can increase the risk of breast cancer by nearly a third. The fruit is believed to boost blood levels of oestrogen, the hormone associated with increased risk of the illness. The researchers claim that postmenopausal women who eat as little as one quarter of a grapefruit per day (or juice equivalent) could see their chances increase by 30%.

Caffeine intake from all sources is linked with higher oestrogen levels regardless of age, body mass index (BMI), caloric intake, smoking, alcohol, and cholesterol intake. Studies have shown that women who consumed at least 500 milligrams of caffeine daily, the equivalent of four or five cups of

coffee, had nearly 70% more oestrogen during the early follicular phase (days 1 to 5 of their menstrual cycle) than women who consume no more than 100 mg of caffeine daily, or less than one cup of coffee.

According to a 1976 article in Environmental Quality and Safety, some steroids were so good at increasing levels of body fat that when oestrogens were given to broiler chickens, they caused such an increase in body fat that the practice had to be stopped. The levels of fat in the hen's bodies jeopardized their lives.

Foods from the brassica family (e.g. broccoli, cauliflower, spinach) help the liver enzymes detoxify excess oestrogen.

A low-fiber diet causes oestrogen levels to be higher, while a diet high in fiber results in decreased oestrogen levels in the bloodstream. Why? Excess oestrogen is excreted in the bowel. When stool remains in the bowel for a longer time, as in constipation, the oestrogen is re-absorbed. Studies have shown that women on a high-fiber diet have lower levels of circulating oestrogen. Lower levels of oestrogen mean less oestrogen stimulation of breast tissue, for example, which reduces the risk of breast cancer. And by fiber I mean non starchy vegetables & low glycaemic fruits and not those ridiculous fiber breakfast cereals and bars they cause more problems stay away from them nature didn't intend for us to eat these garbage foods and anything that comes in a box with a shelf life of 2 - 3 years you should be dubious of anyway!

Researchers have found that certain flavonoids such as green tea polyphenols and quercetin, found in onion and garlic, have shown anti-ooestrogenic activity. Research has also concluded that turmeric could be used to inhibit the ooestrogenic effects of pesticides and environmental xenooestrogens. Turmeric has also been shown to counter the proliferative effect on oestrogen on cancer cells.

It is known that the ovaries concentrate a large amount of iodine. After the thyroid, the ovaries have the second largest concentration of iodine in the body. Iodine deficiency produces changes in the ovarian production of ooestrogens as well as changes in the oestrogen receptors of the breasts. In an iodine deficient state, research has shown that ovarian oestrogen production increases, while oestrogen receptors in the breast increase their sensitivity to ooestrogens. Both of these conditions can increase the risk of developing pathology of the breasts, including breast cancer. Iodine affects oestrogen metabolism, reported to transform estrone and oestradiol into estriol.

Conclusion

Wow! I bet you didn't realise how important cholesterol was in providing the raw materials for all your steroid hormones, which you now understand includes your sex hormones. The key here is to eat high quality proteins, good fats and low glycaemic carbohydrates to optimise your steroid hormone balance. When it comes to stress this must be controlled at all times otherwise your cortisol levels are always going to be high and that is a disaster for your health and body fat levels.

If you want to learn more about these topics then I suggest that you start with the following books;

- "The Testosterone Revolution" - Malcolm Carruthers
- "The Secret Life of Your Cells" - Whitford Press
- "Revitalize Your Hormones" - Theresa Dale
- "The Anti-Oestrogen Diet" - Ori Hofmekler
- "Oestrogen - the killer in our midst" - Chris Woolliams
- "The Cortisol Connection" - Shawn Talbott
- "Overcoming Adrenal Fatigue" - Kathryn Simpson
- "Super T" - Karlis Ullis
- "The Testosterone Edge" - Brian O'Neill
- "The Complete Doctor's Stress Solution" - Penny Kendall-Reed & Dr. Stephen Reed
- "The Great Cholesterol Myth" - Jonny Bowden & Stephan Sinatra
- "Oestrogen Dominance" Michael Lam

HABIT 7

THE AWESOME FOURSOME: GROWTH HORMONE, INSULIN, SUNSHINE & SLEEP

Growth hormone, insulin, sunshine & sleep are 4 major players in your ability to lose fat and keep it off for good. That's why I call them the awesome foursome for fat loss. Get it right and the excess fat will literally drop off you, get it wrong and it will pile up on you - the choice is yours. So lets look how to get the awesome foursome on our side, starting with growth hormone.

"It is health that is real wealth and not pieces of gold and silver".

Mahatma Gandhi

Growth Hormone

Growth hormone is a protein hormone made up of about 190 amino acids that is synthesized and secreted by cells called somatotrophs in the anterior pituitary. It is a major participant in control of several complex physiologic processes, including growth and metabolism. Production of growth hormone is modulated by many factors, including stress, exercise, nutrition, sleep and growth hormone itself. However, its primary controllers are two hypothalamic hormones and one hormone from the stomach. Growth hormone-releasing hormone (GHRH) is a hypothalamic peptide that stimulates both the synthesis and secretion of growth hormone. Somatostatin (SS) is a peptide produced by several tissues in the body, including the hypothalamus. Somatostatin inhibits growth hormone release in response to GHRH and to other stimulatory factors such as low blood glucose concentration.

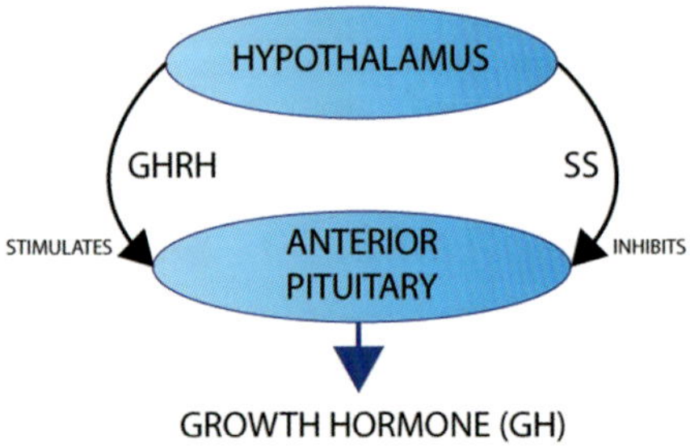

Growth hormone (GH) stimulates lipolysis (fat breakdown) and seems to regulate lipid deposition in adipose tissue. Patients with GH deficiency (GHD) have enlarged fat depots due to higher fat cell volume. The treatment of these patients with GH results in a loss of body fat. However, whereas GH replacement in patients with GHD leads to specific depletion of intra-abdominal fat.

In obese individuals the GH secretory response to a variety of stimuli (e.g. insulin, sleep, exercise...) is impaired compared to normal individuals.

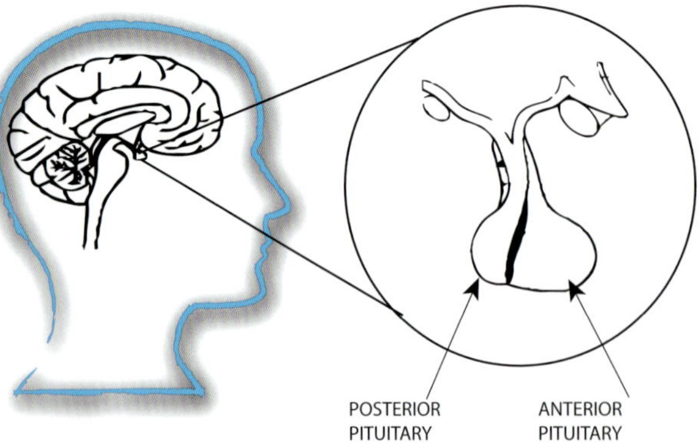

Growth Hormone is synthesised and secreted in the anterior pituitary gland

Physiologic Effects of Growth Hormone

Growth hormone is often considered an anabolic hormone. However, it has both anabolic and catabolic actions on different tissues in the body. For example, GH stimulates protein synthesis in muscle but in fat tissue it promotes lipolysis (fat breakdown). Another critical concept in understanding growth hormone activity is that it has two distinct types of effects:

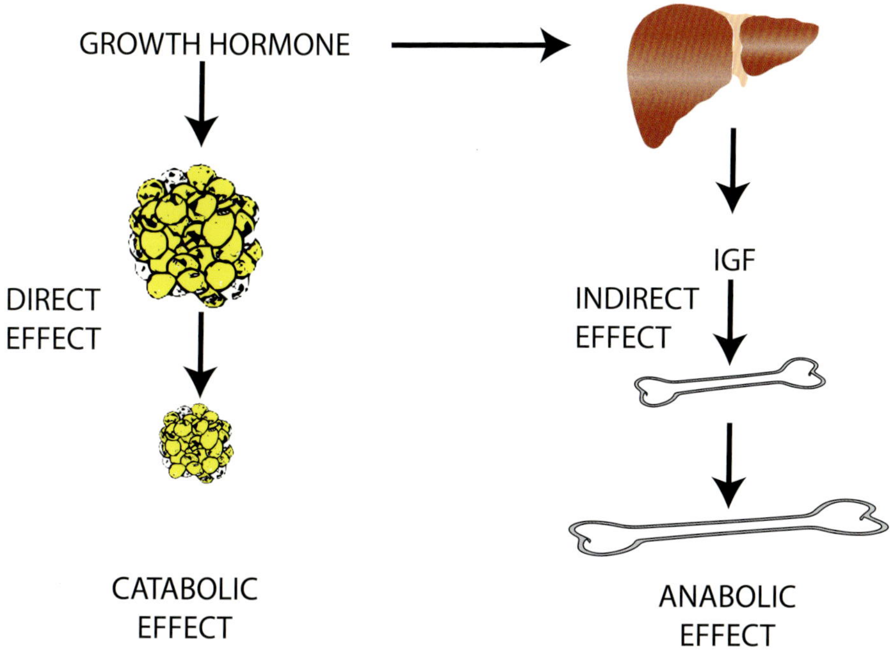

Growth hormone can have both direct and indirect, as well as anabolic and catabolic effects, in the body.

- **Direct effects** are the result of growth hormone binding its receptor on target cells. Fat cells (adipocytes), for example, have growth hormone receptors, and growth hormone stimulates them to break down triglyceride and suppresses their ability to take up and accumulate circulating lipids.
- **Indirect effects** are mediated primarily by an insulin-like growth factor-I (IGF-I), a hormone that is secreted from the liver and other tissues in response to growth hormone. A majority of the growth promoting effects of growth hormone is actually due to IGF-I acting on its target cells.

Metabolic Effects: Growth hormone has important effects on protein, lipid and carbohydrate metabolism.

- **Protein metabolism:** In general, growth hormone stimulates protein anabolism in many tissues. This effect reflects increased amino acid uptake, increased protein synthesis and decreased oxidation of proteins.
- **Fat metabolism:** Growth hormone enhances the utilization of fat by stimulating triglyceride breakdown and oxidation in adipocytes.
- **Carbohydrate metabolism:** Growth hormone is one of a battery of hormones that serves to maintain blood glucose within a normal range. Growth hormone is often said to have anti-insulin activity, because it suppresses the abilities of insulin to stimulate uptake of glucose in peripheral tissues and enhance glucose synthesis in the liver. Somewhat paradoxically, administration of growth hormone stimulates insulin secretion, leading to hyperinsulinemia.

The secretion of Growth Hormone decreases by 10 – 15% in each decade of life, but the body can still make large amounts of GH as we age; we have just got to know how to optimise growth hormone naturally so we can stay lean and healthy.

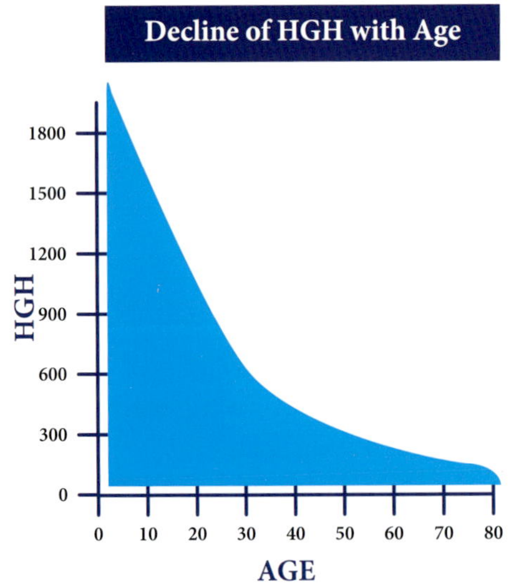

Unfortunately our bodies ability to produce growth hormone diminishes considerably as we age beginning immediately after puberty. Studies show that as early as age 26 your body may be producing less than half of the growth hormone that it did at 18 years of age. By age 35 hGH production may be down a full 75% from peak levels.

Growth Hormone Releasing Hormone (GHRH), is produced by the hypothalamus and induces the anterior pituitary to release Growth Hormone. To promote anabolism, first you have to increase output of growth hormone from the anterior lobe of the pituitary gland.

The four most effective ways to increase growth hormone naturally are; high quality sleep, intense physical exercise, controlling blood sugar and the use certain amino acids, such as arginine, glycine and glutamine. These can all be achieved easily with a bit of discipline and a real focus to decrease body fat.

Growth hormone is released into the bloodstream in bursts. Some of each burst goes directly to bone and muscle cells where it initiates growth. The rest is neutralized by the liver within 60–90 minutes. Before it is neutralized, the growth hormone causes the liver to manufacture somatomedins also called insulin like growth factor (IGF). IGF is made by the liver and is triggered by growth hormone. When the liver is damaged or overworked, through our enormously toxic environments, then this potent anabolic hormone decreases so this is another reason to work on liver detoxification.

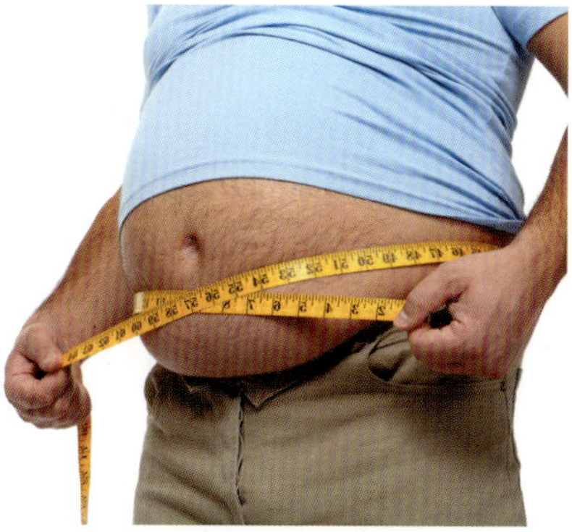

If you happen to suffer from fat stores concentrated centrally around abdominal region, growth hormone secretion will be even more impaired. Fortunately, research indicates that declining GH due to body fat gain is partially reversible with fat loss. So, lose fat to regain your growth hormone benefits.

As we now know, excess cortisol from stress stimulates the formation of excess fat in the abdominal area. Growth hormone and leptin have a see-saw effect; when leptin levels are high, growth hormone levels are generally low. Thus, leptin and growth hormone have an ebb and flow relationship, leptin's main effect on growth hormone is to restrict it. Once growth hormone is lacking, there is no metabolic factor to help reduce abdominal fat, and it will keep accumulating as part of leptin and insulin resistance. During fasting, growth hormone levels rise, but this is not because the brain is stimulating growth hormone production, rather in a fasting state the hunger hormone ghrelin promotes extra growth hormone production. Ghrelin acts to stimulate growth hormone and it loses its effectiveness in overweight individuals. It does this because leptin is too high as soon as leptin levels come down, ghrelin levels goes back into natural balance. This information means we can restore natural growth hormone function by lowering leptin and getting it back into natural balance.

Your stomach secretes ghrelin when it's empty, signaling the hypothalamus to turn on your appetite. As a society, we've come to fear hunger and avoid it like the plague. As soon as we feel hungry, we look for ways to satisfy our desire for food. But what if you could make friends with hunger and actually learn to enjoy the feeling? There are benefits to prolonging eating and staying hungry for a while. You see, ghrelin is a potent stimulator of growth hormone, and growth hormone has profound effect on fat burning and building lean muscle. It is also often considered an anti-aging hormone. So the next time you get hungry, remember that the longer you hold out (within reason) the more you rev up your fat-burning furnace. But what effect does our food have on growth hormone?

Ghrelin The Hunger Hormone

Ghrelin is a hunger hormone released from the stomach that travels to the brain and induces hunger. Ghrelin has also been shown to do a few other things not beneficial to dieters. Ghrelin causes the brain to crave sugary, salty, and fatty foods, so is also implicated in cravings.

Ghrelin also makes us more efficient at storing fat once we do eat. This is because ghrelin stimulates messenger RNA (mRNA) activity of the fat storing hormone lipoprotein lipase (LPL). For those who are not biochemists, mRNA is how the genes replicate the proteins they encode for. So, mRNA makes proteins, and the more mRNA activity you have, the more protein you make.

In the case of ghrelin, it stimulates the mRNA to make more LPL (the major fat sotring enzyme), and therefore makes you far more likely to store fat quickly and efficiently once you resume eating. So dieters and fasters beware. Ghrelin also directly stimulates LPL activity.

Growth Hormone and Protein

GH is released after the consumption of protein. This might signify to the body that it is now an opportune moment to build. Moreover, hormonally, protein intake is positively correlated with growth hormone, IGF-1, and glucagons. These hormones collectively, exert an anabolic and lipolytic effect (fat burning).

Increased protein intake will increase GH levels, and increased GH levels will increase the need for protein. Moreover, frequent protein feedings will increase absorption of protein and produce frequent GH spikes. So an ideal GH raising diet would include frequent feedings of high quality protein from animal sources (grass fed meat and wild fish). REMEMBER YOU CAN'T ABSORB MORE THAN 30–50 GRAMS OF PROTEIN PER SERVING. Otherwise, if you try to eat a cow at each meal, the excess protein will be converted into fat and the excess acid will lower your pH levels.

Growth Hormone and Blood Sugar

The most important point in regards to growth hormone and diet is that growth hormone levels increase significantly when insulin levels are low. Glucose inhibits the secretion of growth hormone by acting on specific areas of the hypothalamus. Consequently, during the day, when food is consumed periodically, growth hormone secretion by the pituitary is suppressed, and insulin release by the pancreas is increased. What this means is that consuming foods constantly throughout the day will limit growth hormone's fat burning effect and increase insulin's fat storage effect. So, when it comes to growth hormone, you want low insulin.

However, we need insulin to promote the benefits of growth hormone. Studies show that growth hormone fails to cause growth in diabetics and it also fails if carbohydrates are restricted from the diet. The reason for this could be that a strict low carbohydrate diet would lead to chronically low insulin levels, and insulin is needed to drive amino acids into the muscle cells. Moreover, IGF-1 is produced in the body through the combined actions of GH and insulin. IGF-1 is at least as powerful an anabolic agent as either of its parents but a low carbohydrate diet would lead to a reduction in IGF-1 levels. So a low carb diet is not the answer either. In fact, this relationship of insulin, growth hormone, and IGF-1 is one reason why those following a low carbohydrate diet also often plateau after a period of time. The key word here is TIMING. Time your carbohydrates to enhance insulin's effect on growth hormone by producing IGF-1 to ensure it gets transported from the liver to the tissues to do its magic of burning fat and building muscle. The most beneficial time for this is your pre, during & post workout meal and breakfast. We cover this in great detail in habit 9.

There is also a relationship with thyroid hormone here as well. Raising GH has a profound effect on normalizing thyroid function.

Growth Hormone, Potassium & Sodium Relationship

The next dietary nutrient to be looked at is potassium. Medical science has known for some time that even modest potassium deficiency causes growth hormone and IGF-1 suppression. The reason for this is related to cellular hydration, which is more complex than simply guzzling water for hydration. Fluid is constantly moving in and out of the cell across an electrical gradient bisected by the cell membrane. The key to obtaining the positive benefits of "cell volumization" is to maximize intracellular fluid. Water moves in and out of cells with electrolytes. The mineral sodium is the chief extracellular (outside) electrolyte, whereas the mineral potassium is the chief intracellular (inside) electrolyte.

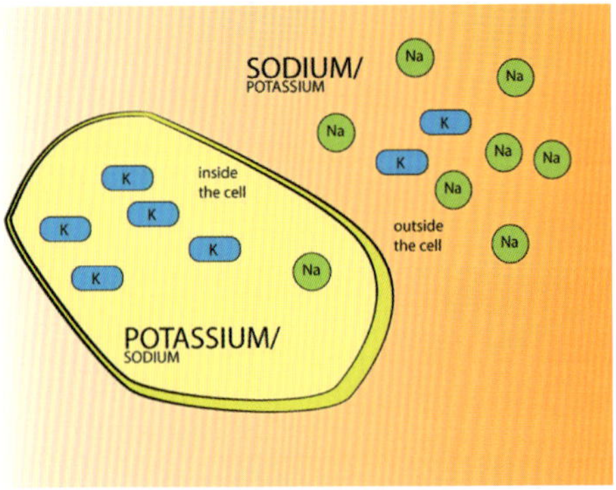

There is naturally more potassium than sodium in the cell. By increasing your potassium intake, and lowering your sodium intake, then you can shift fluid into the cell.

By increasing your potassium intake and reducing your sodium intake, you can shift water from the extracellular compartments of your body into the intracellular compartments. An increased intracellular hydration increases HGH release. And historically, human beings consumed far more potassium than sodium. The reason for a change in the potassium to sodium ratio is two fold. First, the best source by far for potassium is vegetables, and second fruit. But there has been a trend towards consuming less fruit and veggies than historically were eaten.

Researchers at the University of Aarhus in Denmark showed that growth inhibition occurs only after a few days of reduced potassium intake - long before there is any significant decline in muscle potassium.

Potassium deficiency causes profound inhibition of growth because potassium deficiency is required for the development of muscle cells themselves. When serum levels of potassium decline, as they almost do immediately on a potassium deficient diet, it is likely that this decline signals your brain to reduce growth hormone output and slow down muscle growth and recovery. That way your body avoids forming defective muscle cells because of an inadequate potassium supply.

Research has also established that activation of the growth hormone releasing hormone, somatocrinin, requires another enzyme called alpha – amidating monooxygenase, which is absolutely limited by the amount of vitamin C available for use as a cofactor. So you better have plenty of vitamin C around if you want to maximize growth hormone output.

Exercise and Growth Hormone

Exercise is a significant, natural optimizer of GH secretion. The type of exercise you do, as well the intensity and duration of your workouts, all play an important role in determining to what degree your training regimen contributes to GH secretion. Growth hormone is released under intense exercise. You can get some growth hormone release from strength work but it's primarily from lactate driven exercise and that is most potent with exercises of a novel variety. Once you've acclimated to a particular type of exercise you tend to get less hormone signaling. So get plenty of variety in your training. I will cover this in greater depth and what are the best exercise to stimulate growth hormone in habit 10.

It is also important to drink plenty of water during exercise, as dehydration has been shown to significantly reduce the exercise-induced human growth hormone response.

Bedtime Growth Hormone Release

It is well documented that inadequate sleep, irregular sleeping patterns, and poor quality sleep can substantially inhibit GH secretion. To optimize sleep; keep to a regular bedtime and wake up time; **do not consume alcohol or caffeine 4-6 hours before bedtime; and keep excess light and noise out of the bedroom.**

The largest burst of GH is released during the early hours of sleep - hence our eating habits are crucial to maximizing this night time secretion. More specifically, growth hormone is especially dependent on sleep, because a major growth hormone surge occurs during the first episode of slow-wave sleep, approximately 30-70 minutes after falling asleep.

Sleep is a prime fat burning time especially when one has not eaten at least 3 - 4 hours before bedtime.

Ideally, you should be slightly hungry and tired before bedtime and resist the urge to attack the fridge and eat it's contents.

The fastest way to disrupt sleep is to eat after your evening meal, too close to bedtime. When you go to bed with food still in the digestive system this forces the body to digest food when it should be performing other functions such as fat burning and body repair. Also, leptin resistance sets in, it causes higher amounts of adrenaline during sleep hours. This causes insomnia, light sleep, restless sleep and a general feeling of unrest. Put alcohol on top of late night eating and from a fat loss perspective it is a disaster. So if you want to drop the fat, drop late night eating and the booze and this in itself will be a massive step in your quest for optimum health and fat loss.

Avoid emotional stress before bed and this includes watching the doom and gloom of the news. Watch things that make you laugh, don't get into arguments or deep emotional discussions as this will simply put you in fight or flight mode and not into sleep mode. Read a relaxing book or listen to some soothing music before bed because if you get your sleep right you will not get anything more important for dropping excess fat!

Try to go for a 30 minute brisk walk after your evening meal. This will help with your sleep and, personally, some days I will not eat after 4 P.M. then do some cardio at about 8 P.M. for around 30-45 minutes and then go to bed about 90 minutes later after consuming my Nitric Oxide Generator drink which is loaded with certain amino acids which have been shown to enhance growth hormone production.

Eating before bed

Plan your last meal of the day carefully. Your last meal of the day is the most important for maintaining a robust GH/IGF-1 axis. A high fat, medium-protein, low-carbohydrate meal 3-4 hours before bed helps minimize insulin release and allows for maximum endogenous GH secretion. Consumption of carbohydrates at bedtime can blunt this crucial release of growth hormone. And the greater the amount of carbs and the higher the glycaemic rating of the carbs, the greater will be the increase in blood sugar and the greater the suppression of growth hormone.

In order to benefit from the night time release of HGH, it is important for you to sleep normally. However, alcohol-induced sleep is not normal. Unlike other hormones, HGH is tied to human circadian rhythms. When alcohol is consumed 1-6 hours before bedtime, it has a disruptive effect on the second-half of sleep. Alcohol can suppress the release of HGH during sleep, and decrease, or eliminate the benefits of the HGH.

Thus going to bed with a belly-full of carbohydrates is hormonally unwise and may diminish, if not nullify, nocturnal growth hormone release.

Nutrients for enhancing Growth Hormone

For the millions of sleepless among us, there may be good news—in the form of an inexpensive, naturally occurring amino acid known as glycine. Within the central nervous system, glycine functions as an inhibitory neurotransmitter, playing a well-documented and critical role in initiating normal patterns of REM sleep. Now, a new study of chronic insomniacs demonstrates that glycine administered orally just prior to bedtime significantly improves sleep quality, shortening the latency between sleep onset and initiation of slow-wave (deep) sleep as measured by polysomnography. Volunteers also reported less daytime sleepiness, a subjective finding that was objectively corroborated by improved performance on cognitive tasks testing memory recognition.

L - Glycine also has a calming effect on the brain and has been found to be an effective in releasing growth hormone.

L-arginine and Glutamine have been found in many studies to increase levels of growth hormone. The effect is accentuated when there is a relatively low blood glucose levels such as after the consumption of a low carb meal. This is why a good time to supplement is late in the evening, a few hours after consuming your last meal of the day

There are a variety of nutrients and supplements that have demonstrated to increase the release of growth hormone. For instance the amino acid **L – Glutamine has been shown to increase growth hormone by 15%.**

L - Arginine is an amino acid that is known as a growth hormone releaser and a precursor of the vital substance nitric oxide. The decrease of growth hormone in the human body with aging is a major reason why muscle mass tends to decrease with age and body fat tends to increase with age. Decreases in growth hormone also are partially responsible for the slower rate of skin growth with aging, which results in thinner and less flexible skin.

The effectiveness of arginine in releasing growth hormone is greatly diminished if foods have been consumed that cause other amino acids or significant amounts of insulin to be present in the bloodstream along with the arginine. That is why arginine should be taken on an empty stomach (i.e., at least one hour before or three hours after a meal). Arginine enhances exercise performance because it is one of the main ingredients, along with glycine, that goes into the biosynthesis of creatine in the liver. This means that arginine provides a two-fold boost in exercise performance by stimulating growth hormone levels and creatine synthesis.

The most abundant amino acid in the body is glutamine. Consuming even a relatively small amount of glutamine (2,000 mg) has been shown to increase plasma GH levels. Glutamine has also been shown to help preserve muscle mass in individuals vulnerable to losing lean body mass due to inactivity following surgery. This suggests that glutamine may provide important benefits in maintaining lean body tissue.

When 9 healthy subjects consumed two grams of oral glutamine 45 minutes after a light breakfast, 8 of the 9 subjects experienced elevated plasma growth hormone within 90 minutes. These findings demonstrate, the study authors wrote, that a surprisingly small oral glutamine load is capable of elevating plasma growth hormone. How does it work? In the small intestine, glutamine is converted into citrulline, which in turn triggers the synthesis of arginine, an amino acid shown to release growth hormone.

A study on glutamine that produced the most significant elevation of growth hormone administered the amino acid using carbonated water.

A study published in the *American Journal of Clinical Nutrition*, a relatively small amount of glutamine significantly increased growth hormone levels. The study subjects were given either a placebo or 2 grams of glutamine to drink. At 30 and 60 minutes after supplementation, their blood samples were analyzed for plasma growth hormone levels. Those who consumed glutamine had markedly increased growth hormone levels, while the placebo group exhibited no change in growth hormone levels. These findings demonstrate, the study authors wrote, "a surprisingly small oral glutamine load is capable of elevating... plasma growth hormone".

Another study adds to the evidence that that glutamine boosts growth hormone levels. In a randomized, double-blind, placebo-controlled trial of 42 healthy middle-aged and elderly adults, the subjects consumed either a placebo or 5 grams of a nutritional supplement composed mainly of glutamine, glycine, and niacin. The supplement was ingested twice daily for three weeks. At baseline and at the study's end, the investigators analyzed the participants' blood. Ingesting the supplement led to a 70% increase in serum growth hormone levels compared to placebo, leading the researchers to conclude that an oral mixture of glutamine, glycine, and niacin can enhance growth hormone secretion in healthy adults. *(Arwert LI, Deijen*

JB, Drent ML. Effects of an oral mixture containing glycine, glutamine and niacin on memory, GH and IGF-I secretion in middle-aged and elderly subjects. Nutr Neurosci. 2003 Oct;6(5):269-75)

How Important is Sleep?

The longest recorded period that a person has gone without eating is over 40 days. Most people can survive around 3 weeks without food. When it comes to sleep, the longest recorded period a person gone without sleep is just 11 days before death occurred. However, after just 2 days without sleep, concentration levels will be extremely poor and after 4 days, hallucinations occur. From this, it seems to make no sense that more attention is often focused on what goes in our mouth than how many hours snooze we get each night. Maybe because there's no money in sleep!

There are many, many studies showing that sleep deprivation can lead to overeating. In one of them, 26 healthy, normal-weight men and women participated in which they spent either 4 h/night (restricted sleep) or 9 h/night (habitual sleep) in bed. Each phase lasted 6 d, and functional magnetic resonance imaging was performed in the fasted state on day 6. Overall neuronal activity in response to food stimuli was greater after restricted sleep than after habitual sleep. In addition, a relative increase in brain activity in areas associated with reward, including the putamen, nucleus accumbens, thalamus, insula, and prefrontal cortex in response to food stimuli, was observed. The findings of this study link restricted sleep and susceptibility to food stimuli and are consistent with the notion that reduced sleep may lead to greater propensity to overeat. *St-Onge MP, McReynolds A, Trivedi ZB, Roberts AL, Sy M, Hirsch J. Sleep restriction leads to increased activation of brain regions sensitive to food stimuli. Am J Clin Nutr (2012)*

In humans, sleep deprivation has been associated with higher ghrelin levels, increased hunger and higher BMI.

Even a single night of sleep deprivation appears sufficient to increase ghrelin (an appetite stimulating hormone) and hunger. Spiegel et al. found that restricting sleep increased ghrelin as well as hunger and appetite, especially for calorie-dense, high-carbohydrate foods.

Studies have also repeatedly shown that sleep deprivation is strongly correlated with decreased insulin sensitivity and unwanted weight gain. One study has shown that one week of sleep deprivation (5 hours sleep a night) can significantly reduce insulin sensitivity. ***Buxton OM, Pavlova M, Reid EW, Wang W, Simonson DC, Adler GK. Sleep restriction for 1 week reduces insulin sensitivity in healthy men. Diabetes. 2010;59(9):2126-33***

One study even found that insulin sensitivity was reduced after only 1 night of partial sleep. ***Donga E, van Dijk M, van Dijk JG, Biermasz NR, Lammers GJ, van Kralingen KW, Corssmit EP, Romijn JA. A single night of partial sleep deprivation induces insulin resistance in multiple metabolic pathways in healthy subjects. deprivation. J Clin Endocrinol Metab. 2010 Jun;95(6):2963-8***

Just one night of sleep deprivation can have detrimental effects on many hormones. Animal and human studies have shown that just 4 hours sleep for 1 night leads to a reduction in testosterone and growth hormone and increases cortisol levels.

A research team from Chicago University compared normal sleepers (7.5-8.5 hours per night) to short sleepers (around 6.5 hours per night). **They found that those with less sleep secreted 50% more insulin and were 40% less sensitive to insulin compared to the group of longer sleepers.**

A lack of sleep also has an affect on the inflammatory processes of exercise. In a 2013 study, 30 healthy football players performed 4 interval sprints on a treadmill at 8am after both a regular night's sleep and a restricted night's sleep. Blood samples showed that plasma concentrations of IL-6 and TNF-α (Pro-Inflammatory Markers) were higher after restricted sleep both during the exercise (i.e., the first and the fourth run) and remained elevated during the recovery period (i.e., 60 min after the exercise). These results showed that sleep restriction increases the pro-inflammatory effect of exercise.

Before the invention of electric light in 1879, it was estimated that the majority of people got around 10 hours sleep a night. However, since then average nightly sleep time has been reduced by 20% to around 8 hours a night. One of the reasons for this may be the effect light has on melatonin. When the sun goes down and darkness occurs, the pineal gland is "turned on" begins to actively produce melatonin, which is released into the blood and you begin to feel less alert. Melatonin levels in the blood stay elevated for about 12 hours - all through the night - before the light of a new day when they fall back to low daytime levels by about 9 am. Daytime levels of melatonin are barely detectable.

Bright light directly inhibits the release of melatonin. Even if the pineal gland is switched "on" late in the evening, it will not produce melatonin unless the person is in a dimly lit environment. In addition to sunlight, artificial indoor lighting can be bright enough to prevent the release of melatonin. It is well established that short-wavelength or "blue" light is the most melatonin-suppressive; this is the type of light typically emitted by devices such as televisions, computer screens, and mobile phones. To produce white light, these electronic devices must emit light at short wavelengths, close to the peak sensitivity of melatonin suppression. This means that products such as tablets, smartphones, and other devices with self-luminous electronic displays are major sources for suppressing melatonin at night, thereby reducing sleep duration and disrupting sleep.

If you are looking for a good nights rest then you need to ensure that you switch off the T.V. or computer at least one hour before you hit the pillow.

Keys to a Good Night's Sleep

1) Establish consistent sleep and wake schedules, even on weekends
2) Create a regular, relaxing bedtime routine such as soaking in a hot bath or listening to soothing music – begin an hour or more before the time you expect to fall asleep
3) Create a sleep-conducive environment that is dark, quiet, comfortable and cool
4) Sleep on a comfortable mattress and pillows
5) Use your bedroom only for sleep and sex (keep "sleep stealers" out of the bedroom – avoid watching TV, using a computer)
6) Finish eating at least 3 - 4 hours before your regular bedtime
7) Exercise regularly
8) Avoid caffeine and alcohol products at least 4 - 6 hours before bed
9) Eliminate restless partners to another bedroom.

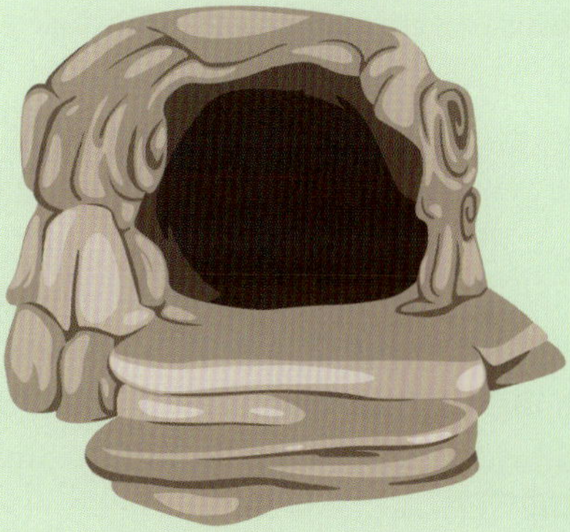

Your bedroom need to be like a cave - dark and quiet - in order to get a good nights sleep.

10) If your bedroom isn't pitch-black, you're not optimizing your output of melatonin. Banish any light-emitting electronic devices (cell phones, laptops, TVs) and try an eye mask or invest in black-out window shades.
11) Ditch your bra and leggings and sleep au naturel: Studies show that tight clothing can curb melatonin production by up to 60%.

Melatonin is essential for sleep, health & fat loss

Melatonin is a hormone that is produced from the amino acid tryptophan in tiny quantities by the pineal gland when the eyes detect no light (i.e., in darkness or blindness, or during sleep). Melatonin also is produced by the retina and, in vastly greater amounts, by the gastrointestinal system. Light at night, regardless of duration or intensity, inhibits melatonin secretion and phase-shifts the circadian clock, possibly altering

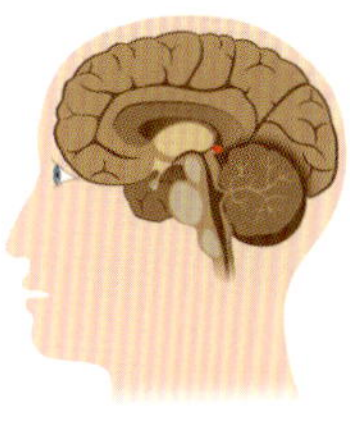

The pineal gland is essential for melatonin production which is the hormone of sleep and repair.

the cell growth rate that is regulated by the circadian rhythm. Circulating levels trail off during the early morning hours to help us awaken. Research demonstrates that melatonin exerts control over metabolic functions that determine fat accumulation, obesity and lipids and helps prevent cardiovascular disease.

Researchers from the University of Granada reporting in the Journal of Pineal Research have found that melatonin helps to control unnatural weight gain without reducing the intake of food. The hormone was shown to improve blood lipid profiles, to lower triglycerides and oxidized LDL cholesterol and to boost health-promoting HDL cholesterol. Researchers broke test subjects into three groups where one cohort was supplemented with melatonin. They found that the melatonin supplemented group experienced a significant reduction in body weight with no difference in calories consumed as compared with the non-supplemented subjects. The researchers publishing the result of this study believe this is the first proof that melatonin can act as a critical hormonal agent in the fight against cardiovascular disease and lipid dysfunction. The study authors concluded "administration of melatonin and intake of food containing melatonin might be a useful tool to fight obesity and the risks associated to it." In addition to natural food sources, many health-minded individuals will want to supplement with 1 to 3 mg of melatonin each night, taken 30 minutes before bed, to promote sound sleep, and avoid help with fat loss. Melatonin is naturally found in some fruits and vegetables including; mustard, Goji berries, almonds, sunflower seeds, cardamom, fennel, coriander and cherries.

You can't buy melatonin over the counter in the UK, you can in the USA. We can enhance our ability to make more melatonin by taking 5 HTP (found in PRP's Amino Relax) and exposing ourselves to more natural light during the day. It's ironic though that you can buy medications over the counter which can cause severe health problems but you can not buy something as beneficial as melatonin. Be warned there are a number or organizations which will try and ban the use of many nutritional supplements especially in the European Union.

It must also peak at the proper time in order to ensure adequate deep sleep. Melatonin levels decline with age and melatonin released correctly during the night is essential for proper leptin rhythm during the day. When melatonin is released incorrectly, leptin is thrown out of balance. It has been shown that supplementing with melatonin can restore normal leptin levels. An animal study showed that melatonin prevents accumulation of stomach fat and lowers leptin, independence of diet. Melatonin improves diabetes in animal studies by eliminating insulin resistance.

Simple strategies to maximize your melatonin secretion:

1) Go to Sleep Early: Hormone secretion, body temperature, digestion and tissue restoration are governed by 24 hour cycles linked to natural light exposure. Up to 80% of human growth hormone secretion takes place between the hours of 11pm and 1am. Individuals that are in bed by 10pm are maximizing this restorative hormone`s ability to heal and regenerate body tissues.
2) Practice intentional quiet time before you go to bed: Utilizing present moment mindfulness or meditation helps boost melatonin. This process speeds up the time from lying down to falling asleep and boosts the quality and satisfaction of the sleep. Take 15-20 minutes before bed and relax your mind and concentrate your breathing.
3) Reduce sugar, artificial flavorings & preservatives, processed foods, alcohol, caffeine and any other sort of stimulant. These reduce melatonin and growth hormone secretion in the body.
4) Hydrate effectively: Dehydration causes chronic stress responses in the body that minimize healthy melatonin and growth hormone secretion.
5) Keep Your Room Dark: Any sort of light stimulation will inhibit the pineal gland from forming melatonin. This will disrupt sleep and minimize melatonin's beneficial effects in the body.

This is all part of my personal bedtime routine:

- No food for at least 3 hours before bed and the meal will be high fat, medium protein and low carbohydrate. Something like this: Liver & Onions (cooked in coconut oil), Steamed Vegetables (with lots of organic butter over them) and that's it.
- The room is pitch black when I go to sleep
- One hour before bed I take 2 scoops of Nitric Oxide Generator , 2 Amino Relax capsules (great for serotonin and GABA production plus liver detoxification) and 3 Magnesium Relax capsules (great for relaxation and enhancing insulin sensitivity)

Insulin: the storage hormone

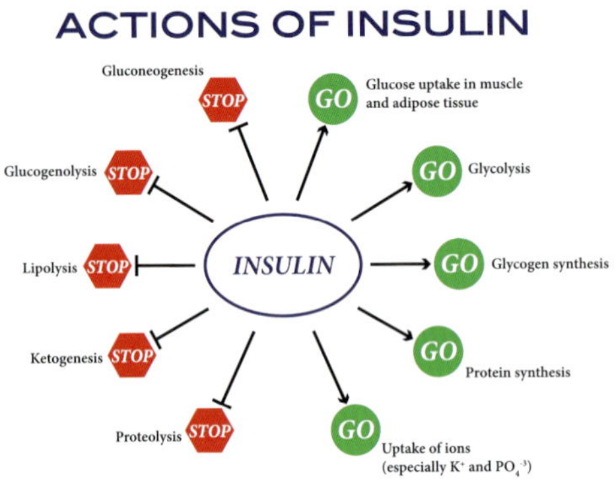

There are many conditions in Western industrialised societies today that were unheard of, or at least very rare, just a century ago. The same conditions are still unheard of in primitive peoples who do not have the 'benefits' of our knowledge. There is a very good reason for this: they eat what Nature intended; we don't. The diseases caused by our incorrect and unnatural diets are why we have become sick, tired and obese. Carbs appear to be the worst food group that increases body weight. I know this is contradictory to the 'healthy eating' low fat, high carbohydrate diet guru's, but it is demonstrably true and that's why the government food pyramid is a diet tragedy in regards to obesity as it could or should be renamed the government "obesity pyramid".

> ***"If people let the government decide what foods they eat and what medicines they take, their bodies will soon be in as sorry a state as are the souls of those who live under tyranny."***
>
> **Thomas Jefferson**

Humans are the only animals on the planet who destroy the nutritional value of their food before eating it. All other animals consume food in its natural, unprocessed state, but humans actually go out of their way to render food nutritionally worthless before eating it. No wonder humans are the least healthy mammals on the planet. Most of the food we eat, because it's grown in depleted soils and has little to no nutritional value. Even if we wanted to, we could never get every essential vitamin and mineral our bodies need through the foods we eat. Nutritional supplementation is therefore incredibly necessary today if our bodies are to maintain a healthy state.

There are 90 nutrients essential to human health. A deficiency in any one of these nutrients can lead to or cause, many diseases. For example, a deficiency in copper can lead to premature grey hair, an aneurysm and stroke. The 90 essential nutrients fall into four broad categories: amino acids; fatty acids; vitamins; and minerals. If you eat a disciplined, well rounded diet you can get all the amino acids, fatty acids and vitamins you need. It is practically impossible to get all of the minerals you need though, regardless of what kind or what quantity of food you eat. Human beings ideally get minerals by eating foods such as vegetables & fruits.

However, such foods are grown in soils which are usually massively deficient in minerals. Minerals serve as catalysts for the body's ability to use amino acids, fatty acids and vitamins. Therefore, without the necessary mineral co-factors it is unlikely that we are getting the maximum benefit from these nutrients. We can also get our minerals from meat and fish products also providing their diet is natural and not eating pesticide laden food fed by food manufacturers to simply fatten them as quickly as they can to make more money and get the produce to the market place.

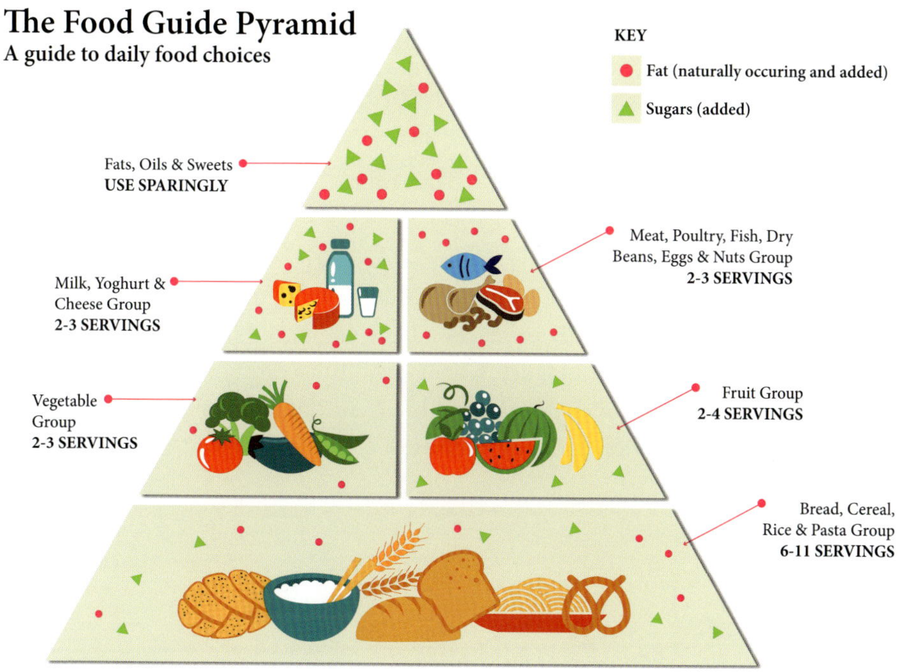

The Food Guide Pyramid is in reality The Food Diabesity Pyramid meaning follow these recommendations and there is a very strong liklihood you will become diabetic, obese and as a bonus will have a physique resembling a pyramid!

Carbohydrates - it doesn't matter whether these are in sugar, jam, bread, pasta, breakfast cereals, fruit or vegetable - are all exactly the same as far as your body is concerned: they are all ultimately converted to the blood sugar, glucose. All carbs are digested very quickly within a few minutes. This means that within a very short time after a carb-rich 'healthy' meal the level of glucose in your bloodstream will rise rapidly as is demonstrated in the graph at Figure 1. (Note that this shows very clearly that eating fat does not raise blood glucose).

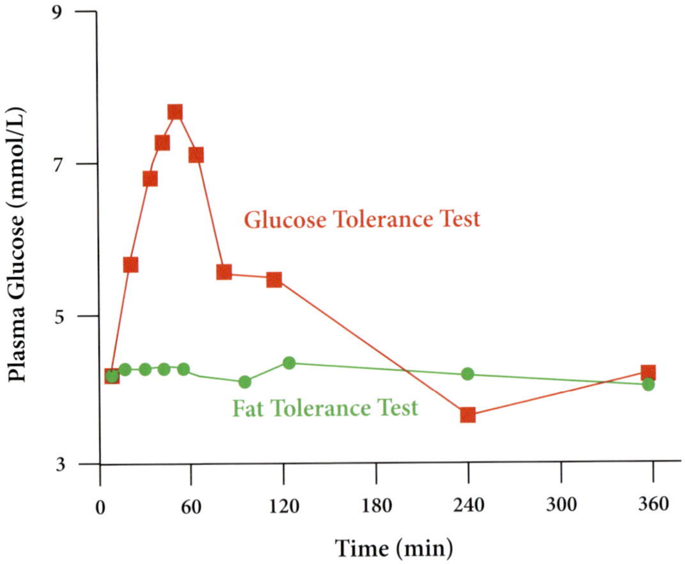

High blood glucose levels are dangerous and, as levels of glucose rise rapidly in the bloodstream, your pancreas rapidly produces a large amount of insulin to take the excess glucose out as is demonstrated in Figure 2. Note that just as eating fat does not raise blood glucose, it doesn't raise insulin levels either. This is an important point as insulin is the hormone ultimately responsible for body fat storage.

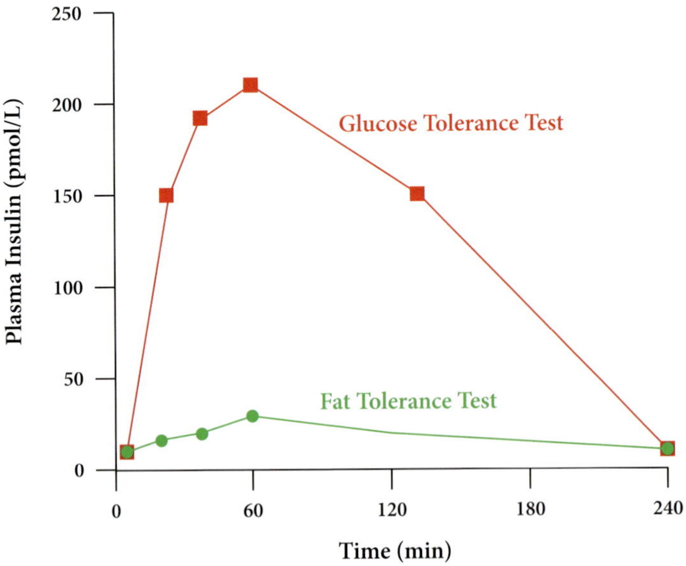

Insulin takes the glucose out of the bloodstream. It is converted first into a form of starch called glycogen which is stored in the liver and in muscles. But the body can store only a limited amount of glycogen in this way (around 400 grams in the muscles and 100 grams in the liver of the average person and up to 900 grams in elite athletes). All other excess glucose is stored as body fat. Key point - if you do little exercise eat little carbs, if you do a lot of exercise eat a lot of carbs. Otherwise they will be converted to fat!

There is also a further aspect to be considered: There is an inevitable time delay between cause and effect. When your blood glucose level is back down to normal, about 90 minutes after food, the insulin level in your bloodstream is still near its maximum and continually stacking glucose away in your fat cells. As a result, the levels of glucose in your blood fall below normal, and you soon feel hungry again. So you have a snack, usually of more carbohydrates and start the whole process over again. You're getting fatter but feeling hungry at the same time. The next problem is that insulin resistance caused by the continual high insulin levels in your bloodstream impairs its ability to satisfy a satiety centre in the brain. This contributes even more to overeating, obesity, and diabetes. Not surprisingly, a high insulin response to glucose has been shown to be a risk factor for long-term weight gain, and this effect is particularly so in people who are insulin-resistant.

For you to lose fat, your body must use that fat as a fuel; there is no other way. And the only way your body will use its stored fat as a fuel is if you force it to. That means depriving it of its present supply of glucose so that it has no choice in the matter.

What is the purpose of insulin in humans?

You may say that purpose of insulin is to lower blood sugar. Insulin's evolutionary purpose, as is known right now, is to store excess nutrients. Let's go back 40,000 years ago. Food was scarce, it was almost always "feast or famine." If the hunters brought back a massive beast to eat, humans had only a few days to eat as much as they could and store all of the massive excess calories as fat in order to fend off the starvation (famine) until the hunters brought back the next kill to eat. There were no refrigerators or freezers to store the food for a few months to "level out" the eating opportunity. The food would spoil quickly and, if they did not eat it in a few days, they could die of bacterial food poisoning. They had to eat a lot and quickly and store it as fat. So, we come from a time of feast and famine when if we couldn't store the excess energy during times of feasting, we would not be here because all of our ancestors encountered famine on a regular basis. We are only here because our ancestors were able to store nutrients, which they were able to do because they were able to elevate their insulin in response to any elevation in energy that the organism encountered.

When your body notices that sugar is elevated, it is a sign that you've got more than you need; you're not burning it so it is accumulating in your blood. So insulin will be released to take that sugar and store it. How does it store it? Glycogen? All the glycogen stored in your liver and muscle wouldn't last you through one active day. Once you fill up your glycogen stores that excess sugar is stored as saturated fat as previously mentioned. So the idea of government trained dieticians advocating a high complex-carbohydrate, low-saturated-fat diet is insane if health and fat loss is the goal. A high-complex-carbohydrate diet is nothing but a high-glucose diet, or a high-sugar diet. Your body is just going to store the excess glucose as saturated fat, and the body makes it into saturated fat quite readily.

Fruit can and will make you FAT! Yes fruit is one of the most fattening sources that we consume, yes it's full of vitamins, minerals, fiber and unfortunately FRUCTOSE. Sugar (sucrose) fructose and high fructose corn syrup both supply a significant portion of the total calories in a standard western diet. They both consist of two simple sugars - glucose and fructose. Glucose also comes from starches like potatoes, rice, pasta and our bodies produce it and every cell. Glucose is a molecule absolutely vital to life. Fructose however, is not. Humans don't produce fructose and throughout evolutionary history have never consumed it except seasonally when fruit were ripe and it helped to fatten us up in readiness for the winter months.

Glucose and fructose are metabolized very differently by the body. The key thing to realize, is that while every cell in the body can use glucose, the liver is the only organ that can metabolize fructose in significant amounts. When people eat a diet that is high in calories and high in fructose, the liver gets overloaded and starts turning the fructose into fat. Many scientists believe that excess fructose consumption may be a key driver of many obesity and type II diabetes.

Eating a lot of fructose in the form of added sugars may:

- Make your liver synthesize fats, which are exported as VLDL cholesterol, which leads to dyslipidemia (blood triglycerides and cholesterol), fat around the organs and ultimately, heart disease.
- Increase blood levels of uric acid, leading to gout and elevated blood pressure.

- Cause deposition of fat in the liver, potentially leading to non-alcoholic fatty liver disease.
- Cause insulin resistance, which ultimately leads to obesity and type II diabetes.
- Insulin resistance leads to elevated insulin and insulin like growth factor (IGF-1) in the entire body, which may ultimately cause cancer.
- Fructose doesn't affect satiety in the same way as glucose, making you eat more total calories automatically if your fructose intake is high.
- Excess fructose consumption may cause leptin resistance, throwing body fat regulation out of whack and contributing to obesity

A study investigated the possible role of insulin levels as a risk factor of heart disease. The study included 7,246 non - diabetic, working men, aged 43 - 54 years, initially free from heart disease, and followed for 63 months.

Pierre Ducimetiere the author of the study published in Diabetologia. Volume 19, November 3, 205-210 found that insulin levels were associated with heart disease and concluded: "high insulin levels may constitute an independent risk factor for coronary heart disease in middle aged non - diabetic men".

Pancreatic Health

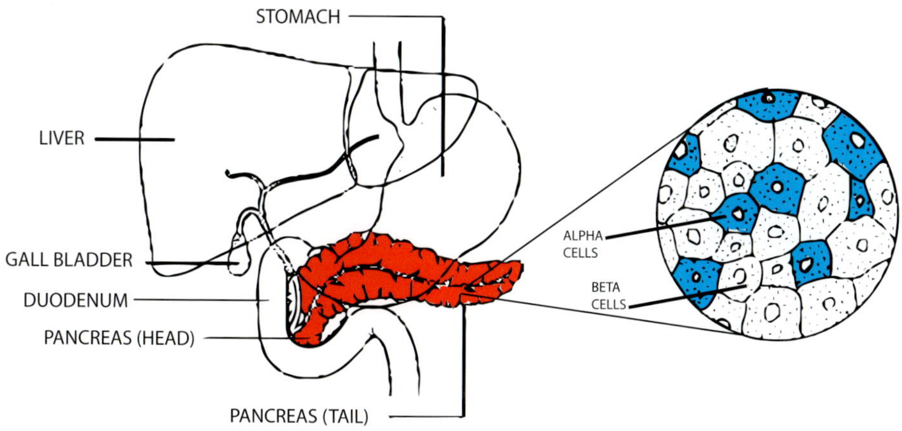

The pancreas is in the upper half of the abdomen. It lies behind the stomach and just in front of the backbone. It's about 15cm (6 inches) long and is shaped like a tadpole. The alpha cells secrete glucagon and beta cells secrete insulin.

Lets now look at pancreatic health and function, as well as insulin and glucagon in their role for fat loss.

The pancreas has digestive and hormonal functions:

- The enzymes secreted by the exocrine gland in the pancreas help break down carbohydrates, fats, proteins, and acids in the duodenum. These enzymes travel down the pancreatic duct into the bile duct in an inactive form. When they enter the duodenum, they are activated. The exocrine tissue also secretes a bicarbonate to neutralize stomach acid in the duodenum.
- The hormones secreted by the endocrine gland in the pancreas are insulin and glucagon (which regulate the level of glucose in the blood), and somatostatin (which prevents the release of the other two hormones).

Most people have about one million islets of Langerhans (which secrete insulin) that in total weigh 1 to 2 grams and constitute only 1-2% of the mass of the pancreas.

Pancreatic enzymes are natural chemicals that help break down fats, proteins and carbohydrates. A normally functioning pancreas secretes about 8 cups of fluid, called pancreatic juice, daily into the duodenum, the portion of the small intestine that connects with the stomach. This fluid contains pancreatic enzymes and helps neutralize stomach acid as it enters the small intestine.

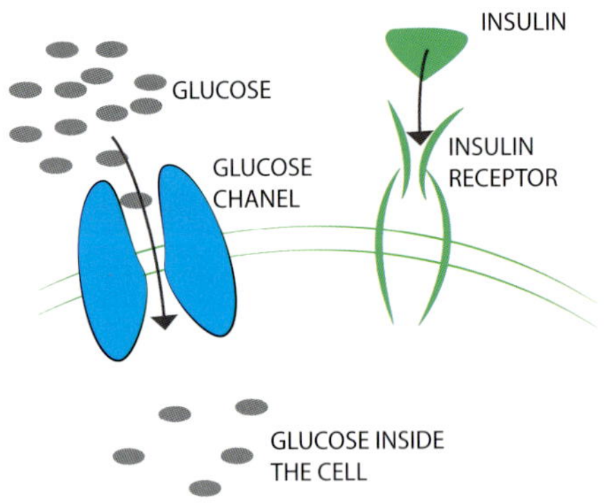

Insulin is the key that unlocks the body cell's glucose channel, allowing glucose to enter the cell. Without the insulin key, glucose is locked out of the cell and must remain in the bloodstream.

Dr. Humbart Santillo, M.D., states in his book Intuitive Eating that: "A human being is not maintained by food intake alone, but rather by what is digested. Every food must be broken down by enzymes to simpler building blocks. Enzymes may be divided into 2 groups, exogenous (found in raw food) and endogenous (produced within our bodies). The more one gets of the exogenous enzymes, the less will have to be borrowed from other metabolic processes and supplied by the pancreas. The enzymes contained in raw food actually aid in the digestion of that same food when it is chewed. One can live many years on a cooked food diet, but eventually this will cause cellular enzyme exhaustion which lays the foundation for a weak immune system and ultimately disease."

Lita Lee, PhD, in her book The Enzyme Cure, explains that food enzymes spare the pancreas from having to compensate for inadequate predigesting." In other words, consuming a predominantly "enzymeless" diet of over-cooked foods taxes the pancreas and, eventually, it will become less efficient at enzyme production.

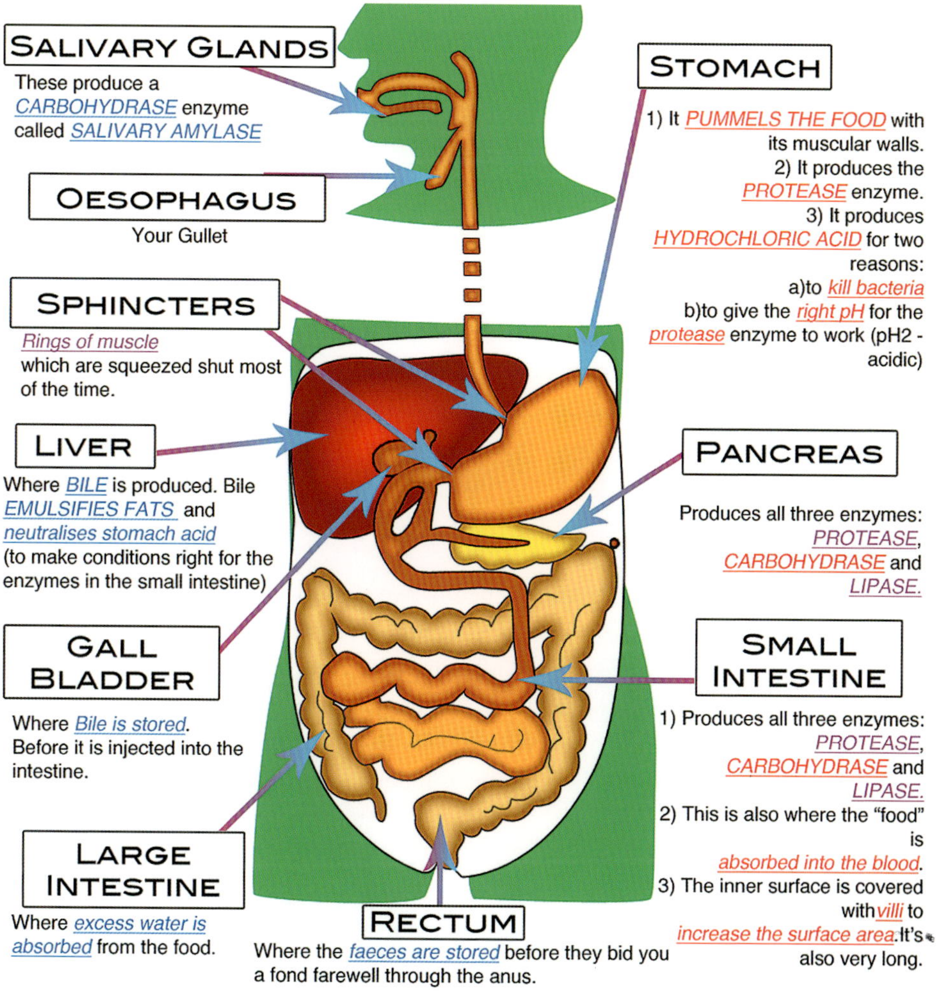

The more cooked food you eat the more you deplete your endogenous enzyme supply so try to consume foods also in their natural state as well as natural non cooked foods supply the enzymes to digest the food and this saves your endogenous enzyme supply.

An autoimmune process, whereby the body's immune system attacks the insulin-producing cells of the pancreas, is the defect behind type 1 diabetes. This is a different process from so-called 'adult-onset', or type 2, diabetes. Type 2 diabetes in adults represents a metabolic imbalance of both insulin secretion and insulin action at the cellular level, as opposed to the absolute deficiency of insulin observed with type 1 diabetes. In patients with type 2 diabetes, a number of factors lead to a poor response to insulin in muscle, fat, and liver. In essence, tissue cells become less responsive to insulin. This triggers the pancreas to overcompensate by producing greater quantities of insulin. Blood levels of insulin double, triple, even quadruple as the pancreas struggles to overpower the body's poor responsiveness to insulin. This is the situation called "insulin resistance.

For reasons that have yet to be understood, an overworked pancreas cannot meet the increased demand for insulin for long. After just a few years, the insulin-producing beta cells of the pancreas begin to "burn out" and blood sugar rises. Rising blood sugar is therefore a sign of insulin resistance. Insulin resistance is present in 90% or more of people with diagnosed diabetes. In all practicality, adult-onset, or type 2, diabetes is synonymous with poor sensitivity to insulin. Insulin resistance is an underlying cause of a number of metabolic abnormalities that are grouped together in a condition called the metabolic syndrome. This disorder is associated with a host of undesirable consequences such as rising blood sugar, increased triglycerides, which lead to a reduction in beneficial high-density lipoprotein (HDL) and an increase in dangerous, small low-density lipoprotein (LDL) particles, greater risk for blood clotting, and high blood pressure

Metabolic Syndrome

Metabolic syndrome is known by a number of different names - insulin resistance syndrome, syndrome X, borderline diabetes, among others and is typically associated with increased triglycerides, reduced HDL, heightened inflammation, three-fold or greater risk of heart attack, greater risk for stroke, and diabetes. Metabolic syndrome can drive the growth of atherosclerotic plaque even when everything else, like LDL, is corrected to perfect levels. Even with excellent LDL levels, for instance, hidden atherosclerotic heart disease can continue to grow at an alarming rate.

Blood Glucose Levels

	HbA_{1c} Test Score	MEAN BLOOD GLUCOSE mg/dL	mmol/L
ACTION REQUIRED	14.0	380	21.1
	13.0	350	19.3
	12.0	315	17.4
	11.0	280	15.6
	10.0	250	13.7
	9.0	215	11.9
GOOD	8.0	180	10.0
	7.0	150	8.2
EXCELLENT	6.0	115	6.3
	5.0	80	4.7
	4.0	50	2.6

A blood glucose meter can be a useful addition to your home health tools. The fasting blood sugar level is basically the level of glucose that is measured when a person does not eat for approximately 8 hours. The fasting sugar (or glucose) levels should be around 70 mg/dl. A blood glucose levels chart says that the blood sugar level after a meal should not normally increase 200 mg/dl. If a person wishes to check whether he is in good control of his glucose level or not, then the glucose level in the blood shouldn't be more than 120-150 mg/dl when checked 2 hours after a meal. Leptin and insulin resistance almost always occur together most people who are overweight have very high levels of both insulin and leptin. The best treatments for overcoming insulin and leptin resistance is to focus on improving the receptor that is alleviating the resistance. We will look at some nutrients which help the receptor become more sensitive to the call of leptin and insulin later in this habit.

Insulin acts on nearly every cell and influences energy storage, cell growth and repair, reproductive function and blood sugar levels. Consuming too much glucose from a high sugar-diet can make our cells become deaf to insulin's message, making us insulin resistant. When this occurs our appetite increases, we are more likely to be leptin resistant, and our metabolism slows. The more body fat an individual has, and particularly the more abdominal fat they have, the more likely they are to be insulin resistant.

BLOOD SUGAR MODEL

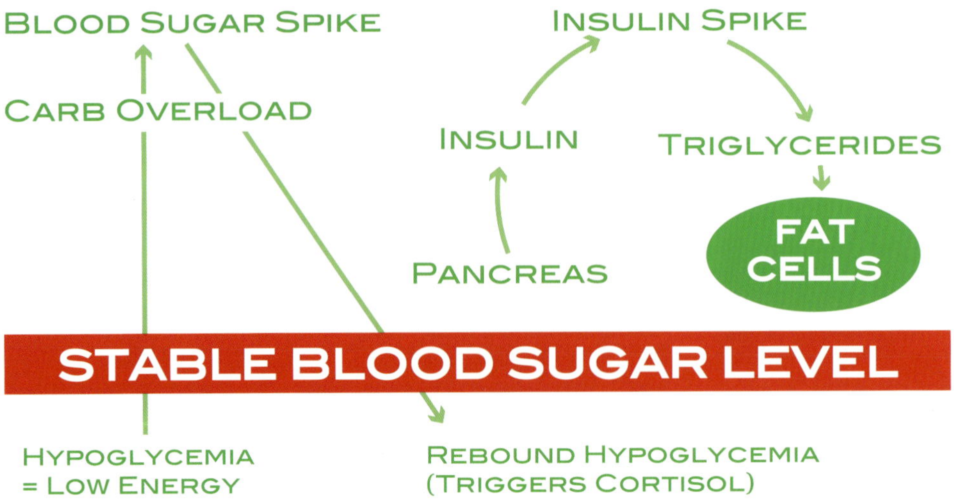

Consuming too much glucose from a high sugar diet can make our cells "deaf" to insulins message. When this happens, no matter how much or how loud insulin shouts its message, the cells can not hear it.

Insulin resistance makes fat cells produce TNF (tumor necrosis factor), a toxic hormone that causes inflammation. Excess fat, especially in the belly, causes insulin resistance, elevated blood sugar, dyslipidemia, and high blood pressure and increased inflammation. Therefore obesity causes inflammation and inflammation causes obesity so you must reduce body fat to dampen the flames of inflammatory substances spewing into the body 24 hours a day 7 days a week.

Although insulin resistance is the most common hormone problem in the world today, most people don't even know they got it. It is the key factor to obesity, type 2 diabetes, metabolic syndrome, polycystic ovary syndrome, high blood pressure, and cardiovascular disease. Since insulin and leptin resistance go hand in hand, as already mentioned, treatments that help one will naturally help the other a win win situation. In fact most fat cell hormones are linked to insulin resistance, so you can see that obesity is a disease that causes many more diseases.

Insulin resistance makes fat cells dysfunctional in many ways. The normal biological processes that regulate energy balance and metabolism get out of whack. Insulin resistance makes fat cells leak their contents, known as free fatty acids, into the circulation. Its normal to have some free fatty acids in your blood but, if free fatty acids get too high, problems can occur.

Free fatty acids have a toxic effect on the insulin receptor. This is called lipotoxicity, which means the toxic effect of fat. The free fatty acids intensify insulin resistance, in a vicious cycle. Insulin resistance increases levels of free fatty acids, which worsen insulin resistance. The result very high levels of free fatty acids dumb down your insulin to the call let me in.

IS THIS YOU?

All of the following contribute to insulin resistance;

- Genetics - if you have a family history of diabetes or obesity, you are more likely to have insulin resistance
- Physical Activity - lack of exercise is a major risk factor of insulin resistance. Just a few weeks of exercise can improve insulin sensitivity
- Stress - cortisol and epinephrine both promote insulin resistance
- Diet - eating too much sugar is a huge cause of insulin resistance

First off, your blood is not a very sweet beverage. Normal fasting blood sugar is slightly less than one teaspoon of sugar in your five or so litres of blood. What happens when you drink a sugar sweetened drink that contains 10 teaspoons of sugar, like many soft drinks consumed today? It causes a tsunami of an insulin wave where the liver converts most of the sugar into triglycerides and slaps it on your ass, thighs and your stomach! Insulin's goal is to take blood sugar, as its passenger, to various locations in your body that want it. It helps if you are active, as some of the sugar is more likely to be wanted by cells in your body, including your many muscle cells.

In a healthy person, insulin drops 60% of the sugar at your liver, which acts as a warehouse, converting the blood sugar to glycogen for storage. Insulin is released by your pancreas in two phases. The first phase is from insulin that is already made and stored in your pancreas, which is just waiting for some food to come along. This is your first insulin burst coming to pick up the first set of blood sugar passengers. The release of this insulin triggers your pancreas' beta cells to start making more insulin to deal with the rest of the meal.

As you are eating, some of the insulin transports blood sugar to your white adipose tissue, or stored fat. The blood sugar is taken up by fat cells, activating their metabolism, in turn producing the hormone leptin. Leptin now enters your blood and begins traveling up to your brain. The more you eat, the more insulin you make, and the more leptin you make.

When leptin levels get high enough, meaning you have eaten enough, then leptin permeates into your brain and tells your subconscious brain you are full. At the same time, the higher levels of leptin also tell your pancreas that you are full, which turns off the beta cell production of insulin, as no more insulin is required.

If you ate the right amount of food for your physical activity level, then blood sugar always has some place healthy to go; insulin rises and falls in a controlled manner, as does leptin. When insulin is too high, and cells don't need any sugar, then insulin stimulates the production of triglycerides, which can become stored fat. This is how you gain weight through a high carbohydrate diet, along with low activity levels. Unfortunately, as triglycerides elevate in your blood they get in the way of leptin getting into your brain. This keeps you eating more than you need to because you don't yet have a full signal, a problem called leptin resistance. This encourages even further insulin driven triglyceride formation, making it more likely you will gain weight.

If you continually eat too much and gain weight, then cells get tired of seeing insulin and reject entry into the cell. The reason for this rejection of insulin is rather simple. If the cells take in blood sugar when they can't use it, because they already have enough, then the extra sugar will kill the cell. Rejecting insulin is a self defensive measure. This is the mechanism behind basic insulin resistance at the cellular level.

When insulin levels are elevated, the system shifts to fat storage. As insulin levels fall back to normal, fat can leave fat cells and be used as fuel throughout the body. And, remember as insulin rises, growth hormone lowers, but timing of carbohydrates are essential because as mentioned earlier you need insulin to transport nutrients into cells, including IGF1 which is derived from growth hormone. This is covered in habit 9 on nutrient timing.

Fat cells don't make any decisions independently. They must be told when their stored fat energy is required. Hormones monitor this situation carefully, and when more energy is needed, insulin is the messenger that communicates with each fat cell about what action is necessary. When insulin levels are high, they tell fat cells to keep fat locked up and not to release it.

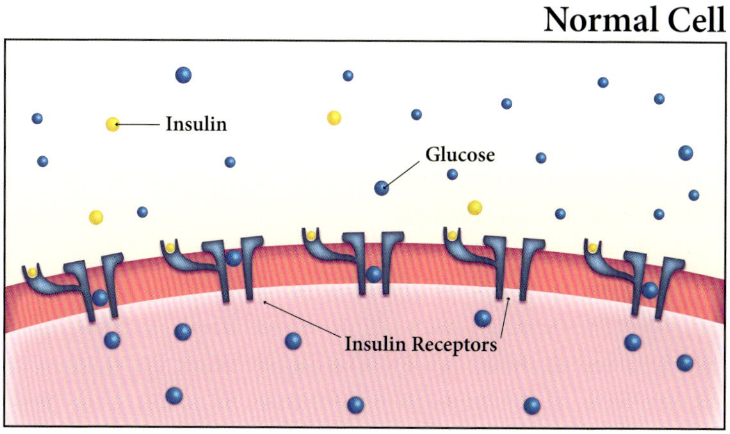

A Normal Cell contains some 20,000 receptor sites

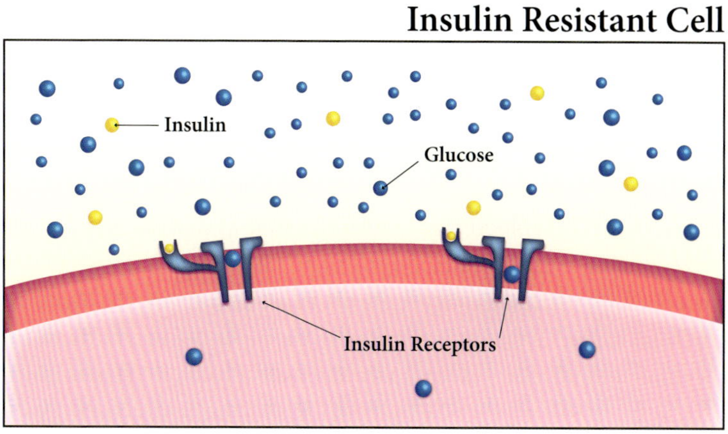

The Insulin Resistant cell has only 5,000 receptors, causing excess free-floating insulin and glucose.

The fat storing hormone that farmers also depend on is insulin. Animals are not usually fed a wide variety of foods. However, significant changes occur when they go from grass fed to corn fed. When you crowd animals together so they can't move around, just like they do in feedlots, so they expend less energy, and then most importantly take them from their natural grass fed diet to one which is now derived from corn. As corn is digested, it is converted into sugar which, as we know, is a potent signal for our fat storage hormone insulin to come and do its job of keeping the fat storage switch on.

This is a very effective method for making cattle bigger - after all the farmer gets paid more money the heavier the animal. This type of feeding and environment increases fat storage whilst simultaneously keeping the fat already in the fat cells from being released. Our bodies work exactly the same way. This is very similar as to why humans are getting fatter: less exercise and wrong food choices.

Insulin and glucagon are oppositional hormones

Insulin is both lipogenic (fat storage) and anabolic (muscle builder), whilst glucagon is both lipolytic (fat burning) and catabolic (muscle breakdown). When insulin goes up glucagon goes down and vice versa, so it is imperative to fat loss that you get these two hormones working for you and not against you if you want to be lean and healthy. The human body wants blood glucose (blood sugar) maintained in a very narrow range. Insulin and glucagon are the hormones which make this happen. Both insulin and glucagon are secreted from the pancreas, and thus are referred to as pancreatic endocrine hormones. Insulin and glucagon are hormones secreted by islet cells within the pancreas. They are both secreted in response to blood sugar levels, but in opposite fashion!

Insulin is normally secreted by the beta cells (a type of islet cell) of the pancreas. The stimulus for insulin secretion is a HIGH blood glucose; it's as simple as that. Insulin has an effect on a number of cells, including muscle, red blood cells, and fat cells. In response to insulin, these cells absorb glucose out of the blood, having the net effect of lowering the high blood glucose levels into the normal range. Glucagon is secreted by the alpha cells of the pancreatic islets in much the same manner as insulin... except in the opposite direction. If blood glucose is high, then no glucagon is secreted.

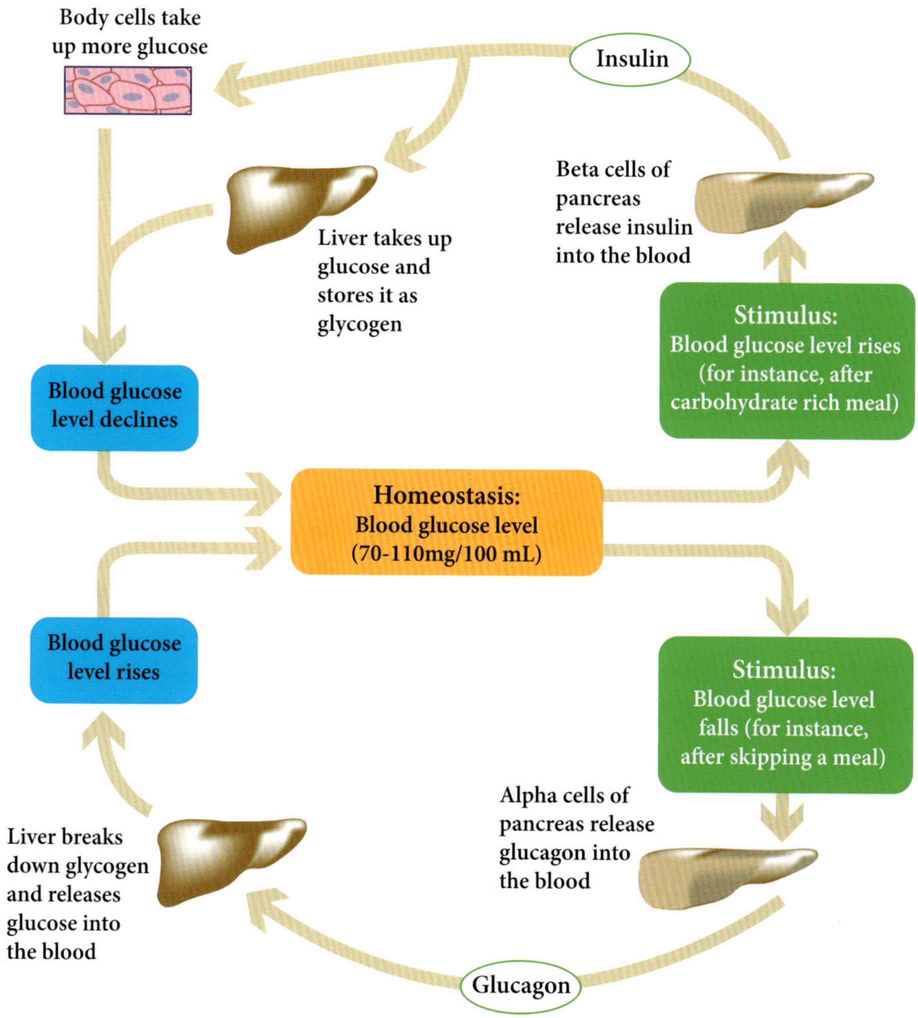

When blood glucose goes low, however, (such as between meals, and during exercise) more and more glucagon is secreted. Like insulin, glucagon has an effect on many cells of the body, but most notably the liver. The effect of glucagon is to make the liver release the glucose it has stored in its cells into the bloodstream, with the net effect of increasing blood glucose. Glucagon also induces the liver (and some other cells such as muscle) to make glucose out of building blocks obtained from other nutrients found in the body (eg, protein). The effect of insulin and glucagon on body fat is well illustrated by a study published in the journal of comparative and physiological psychology in 1978. In this study researchers injected a group of rats with insulin and another group of rats with glucagon. The rats that received insulin injections gained body fat whilst the rats that received glucagon injections lost body fat.

The fact is that with high insulin levels you can't lose fat, and with insufficient insulin you can't build muscle that will help you burn fat. With high glucagon levels you will lose body fat but also muscle as well. So managing the yin and yang of insulin and glucagon is very important in maintaining a healthy body fat percentage. The key word here is timing - knowing when you want high levels of either hormone to manipulate building lean muscle tissue and burning fat.

It is helpful to think of insulin as a storage hormone and glucagon as the key to open the storage room up to release the nutrients to be used as fuel. In addition to insulin being a storage hormone, it is also an anabolic hormone because not only does it shuttles sugar into muscles, but amino acids and other nutrients too. So insulin enhances muscle growth, recovery, and repair by delivering to the muscles everything it needs for muscle growth.

Glucagon mobilizes fat for use as energy; in order for this to happen you must ensure the liver isn't full of glycogen as the body will use this source of glucose first before glucagon can convince the fat cells to give up their stash of fat. As a fat burning hormone glucagon is obviously important in helping you lose excess body fat. However, just like insulin is a double edged sword so is glucagon. For example if you are on a high protein low carbohydrate diet then glucagon will be high and after the liver glycogen stores have been exhausted, the glucagon will simply break down muscle tissue in a process known as gluconeogenesis (the process by which glucose is made, primarily in the liver, from non-carbohydrate sources) and convert to glucose.

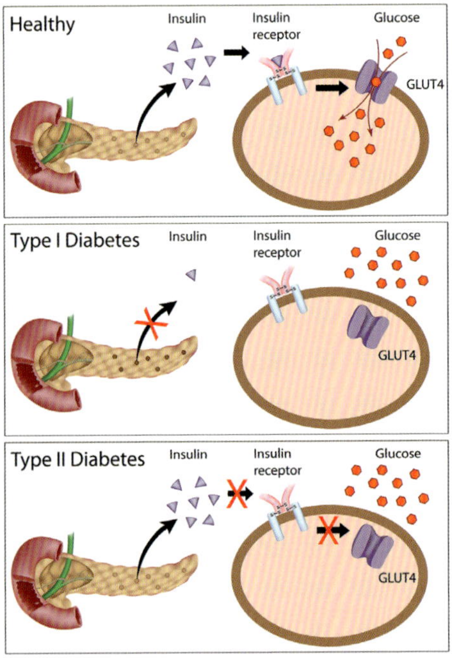

Here's a diagram to show the mechanisms affecting the body in Type I & Type II diabetes. In type I diabetes insulin is not secreted from the pancreas. In Type II diabetes, the cell receptors have gone deaf to insulins message.

I recommend for those people who do not exercise regularly or intensely around 100 - 120 grams of carbohydrate a day to inhibit catabolism (muscle breakdown). Carbohydrate is the primary trigger for insulin secretion and protein is the primary trigger for glucagon secretion. However, protein also exerts a weak stimulatory effect on insulin approximately 30% of the effect of carbohydrate on insulin. If you are wondering about fat, it does not elicit a response either way when consumed alone. When fat is added to a protein or carbohydrate meal it either has no effect on insulin response or slightly increases the insulin response but it does not blunt it.

Carbohydrates will only be converted into body fat when both the muscles and liver are saturated with glycogen (stored carbohydrate), and also if you are insulin resistant. Therefore, to avoid sticking that bread roll on your ass, you must make sure that the cells are sensitive to insulin and there is room for the carbohydrates to be stored.

However, the ketogenic diet will prevent muscles from being used as a fuel and is one of the most efficient ways I know of dropping body fat safely, effectively and for the long term. I discuss the ketogenic diet in great detail in habit 9.

Carbohydrate needs are activity dependent which means lots of activity = lots of carbohydrates needed, little activity = little carbohydrates needed - now it don't get much simpler than that.

Unless you have moved over to a ketogenic diet where you will draw your energy from fat instead of carbohydrates. The only time I do not advocate a ketogenic diet, as you will read in habit 9, is if you are an elite athlete involved in power sports like rugby, boxing and weight lifting and also, if you want to build significant amounts of muscle then you need to know how to time your carbohydrates so insulin can increase lean muscle mass through it's anabolic actions.

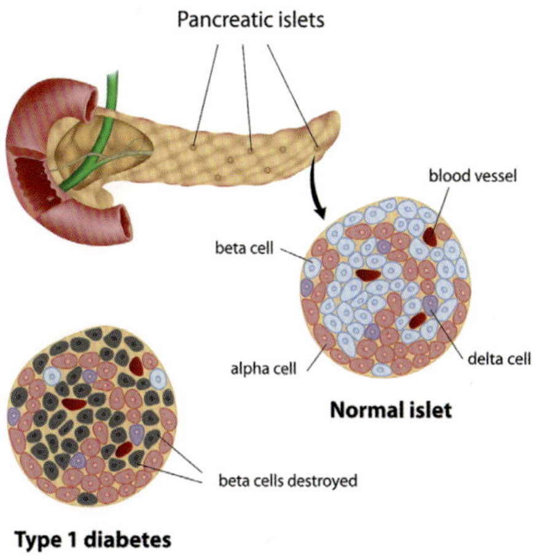

A Norwegian study in 2005 showed that exercise and diet were more effective for type-2 diabetes than insulin therapy. Those treated with lifestyle changes lost more weight, improved their blood sugar, blood pressure and triglyceride levels. The group receiving insulin therapy actually increased in weight and saw some of their metabolic parameter worsen.

To begin increasing your glucose sensitivity there are many things that you can do. First, eat low glycaemic load (GL) foods - to do this you need to cut out simple sugars and switch to low GL foods which do not cause large blood sugar spikes. Low GL foods include foods such as oats and berries. You can also combine carbohydrates with proteins which slows down their digestion and therefore further stabilises blood sugar levels.

A 2005 study comparing low GL diets to a conventional low-fat, low-calorie diet found that, after 6 months, those following the low GL diet lost more weight, had lower levels of LDL cholesterol, triglycerides and fasting glucose levels. The researchers concluded that "implementation of a low GL diet is associated with substantial and sustained improvements in abdominal obesity, cholesterol and blood sugar control".

Research on the Keto Diet for Diabetes

A study published in the journal Nutrition and Metabolism in 2005 evaluated a ketogenic diet in 21 people with type 2 diabetes over 16 weeks. They improved their blood sugar control by 16 percent, on average, and had weight loss of more than 6 percent, and 17 of the participants were able to discontinue or reduce their diabetes medications.

More recent research, involving only animals, noted that limiting both protein and carbohydrates in type 2 diabetes reduces blood sugar dramatically, reverses diabetic complications, and seems to have no adverse effects on heart health.

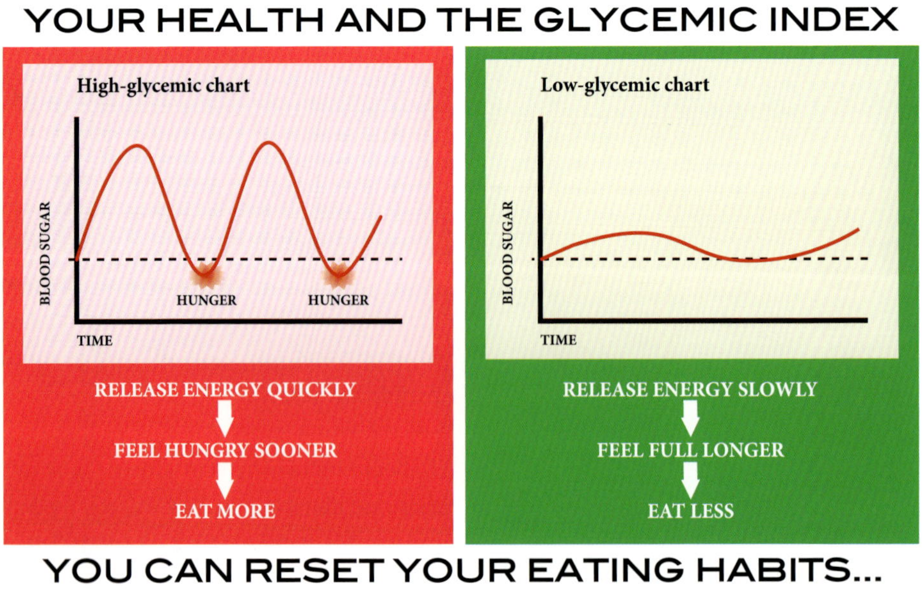

The Bottom Line

The bottom line rule of successful diabetes treatment is to stabilize and reduce blood sugar and control insulin fluctuations. A ketogenic diet makes this task much easier, while at the same time improving the health markers which normally worsen in a situation of uncontrolled diabetes.

This hyperlink http://www.nmsociety.org/diabetes-research.html has at least 55 other studies which support the use of a low carb diabetic diet to improve diabetic health outcomes.

Two diets - one severely restricting (http://diabeteshealth.com/browse/food/low-carb/) carbohydrate intake but with no limit on calories, and the other emphasizing low-glycaemic carbohydrates and (http://diabeteshealth.com/browse/food/low-calorie-and-low-fat/) low calories - allowed high percentages of obese (http://diabeteshealth.com/browse/community/type-2-issues/) type 2 patients in a University study to reduce or even eliminate their (http://diabeteshealth.com/) diabetes medications (95.2 percent of the patients on the extreme low-carb diet and 62.1 percent of the patients on the low-glycaemic diet).

Researchers at Duke University Medical Center assigned 84 patients to one of two diets over a 24-week period. The first, called a "ketogenic diet," restricted carbohydrate intake to 20 or fewer grams per day.

In a ketogenic diet, the body is forced to use fat to provide energy, a process that produces a metabolic product called ketones.

The other diet stressed the consumption of low-glycaemic foods, which are absorbed slowly by the body and do not cause spikes in (http://diabeteshealth.com/browse/monitoring/blood-sugar/) blood sugar levels. The diet also severely restricted daily caloric intake to 500 calories. That drastically low number came about because the study was designed to test intense approaches to treating obese people with diabetes whose previous forms of diet and management had not worked.

Although both diets produced substantial improvements in patients, the ketogenic diet was clearly more effective. While Duke researchers did not always spell out the actual measurements produced by each diet, they said that the ketogenic group enjoyed greater (http://diabeteshealth.com/browse/fitness/weight-loss/) weight loss, and a larger increase in "good" (http://diabeteshealth.com/browse/complications-and-care/lipid-problems/) cholesterol compared to the low-glycaemic group.

The medical center quoted Dr. Eric C. Westman, who led the study, as saying, "It's simple. If you cut out the carbohydrates, your blood sugar goes down and you lose weight, which lowers your blood sugar even further. It's a one-two punch." In fact, reports Reuters, the Duke researchers concluded that "lifestyle modification using low carbohydrate interventions is effective for improving and reversing type 2 diabetes."

High fibre from non starchy fruits and vegetables slow down the passage of carbohydrates through your intestines. This slows blood sugar rises and so will have the effect of improving insulin sensitivity and pull out toxins and excess oestrogen.

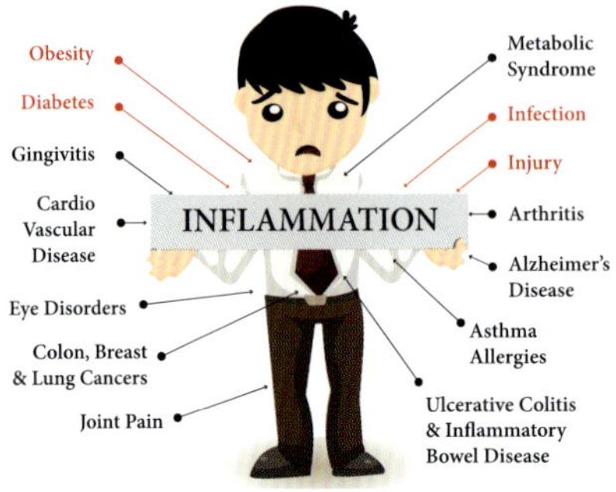

Inflammation promotes insulin resistance and so must be reversed in order to increase insulin sensitivity. To do this you need to balance your omega-3 to omega-6 ratio as mentioned in habit 4. Remember the worst culprits of omega 6 fats are vegetable oils which are usually promoted as health foods when in reality nothing could be further from the truth.

On August 1, 2006 the American Chemical Society published research that showed conclusively that methylmercury induces pancreatic cell apoptosis and dysfunction. Mercury is a well-known toxic agent that produces various types of cell and tissue damage yet governmental health agencies diminish this fact exposing billions of people worldwide to levels of mercury harmful to pancreatic health. In the case of diabetes mercury is especially telling for it affects the beta cells, the insulin itself, and the insulin receptor sites setting off a myriad of complex disturbances in glucose metabolism.

Nutritional Supplements for improving insulin sensitivity

The following nutrients and supplements can help reduce insulin resistance and inflammation in the body:

Omega-3 fatty acids

Omega-3 fatty acids contained in fish oil help in numerous ways to fight inflammation. Omega-3s effectively reduce the inevitably elevated triglycerides of metabolic syndrome, raise HDL, and reduce inflammation. Of all their benefits, the triglyceride-reducing power of omega-3s represents their most powerful effect, which is likely responsible for the dramatic reduction in heart attack and stroke seen with supplementation.

The results of a double-blinded trial published in the July 2013 issue of *Singapore Medical Journal* show positive effects for the omega-3 fatty acid eicosapentaenoic acid (EPA) in overweight type 2 diabetics.

Mahmoud Djalali and his associates at Tehran University of Medical Sciences randomized 26 men and 41 women with diabetes to receive 2000 milligrams EPA or a corn oil placebo for twelve weeks. Blood samples collected before and after treatment were analyzed for hemoglobin A1c (HbA1c, a marker of long term glucose control), fasting plasma glucose and fasting serum insulin.

While plasma glucose, HbA1c, and serum insulin levels had increased by 4%, 3% and 4% in the control group by the end of the study, they declined by 11%, 8% and 3%, respectively, in those who received EPA. Insulin resistance also improved among those who received EPA. The authors note that, in contrast with the findings of other studies with shorter durations, the current study's length could account for the improvement observed in HbA1c, which represents average glucose concentration over the previous months.

In their discussion of the findings, the authors remark that omega-3 fatty acids' anti-inflammatory property could be one mechanism involved in their ability to improve insulin resistance. They note that omega-3 increases the fluidity of skeletal muscle membrane, resulting in improved glucose uptake. Furthermore, genes associated with insulin resistance could be positively affected by omega-3 fatty acids.

USDA scientists have identified unique compounds in cinnamon bark that increase in vitro sugar metabolism "20-fold." According to one government expert, "These polyphenolic polymers found in cinnamon may function as antioxidants, potentiate insulin action, and may be beneficial in the control of glucose intolerance and diabetes."

Cinnamon is rich in bioactive compounds that help regulate blood sugar levels. This isn't the cinnamon you'd use to flavor your cappuccino, by the way. It's a related species called Cinnamomum cassia (**as found in PRP's Cognitive Care**)—and scientists around the world are now discovering its glucose-lowering power. Extract of this form of cinnamon triggers cell signalling proteins inside the pancreas, bringing the secretion and regulation of insulin levels into greater balance. This helps to restore your body's natural ability to control blood sugar as you age.

Cinnamon also acts as an insulin sensitizer, triggering proteins that lower insulin resistance at the cellular level. It has also been shown to thwart advanced glycation end products (AGEs) which are implicated in diabetic complications, atherosclerosis, and Alzheimer's disease. A recent in vivo study found cinnamon accomplishes this anti-glycation effect in part through its antioxidant scavenging capabilities.

Cinnamon also triggers genes in muscle and fatty tissue that transfer glucose out of the bloodstream and into energy producing cells, effectively lowering blood glucose. This quenches the highly reactive oxidant and inflammatory inferno in your body stoked by chronic glucose overexposure. An abundance of animal studies published in 2010 confirm that cinnamon polyphenols can significantly reduce fasting glucose levels, improve pancreatic function, and enhance insulin sensitivity—even in diabetic models.

Curcumin is another nutrient which influences key hormones, supports major body organs, and regulates inflammatory signaling all in ways that help correct or prevent metabolic problems. Curcumin helps lower inappropriately high levels of leptin (reducing leptin resistance) while boosting the all-important levels of the adiponectin protein hormone that modulates metabolism including glucose and fatty acid catabolism. High levels are associated with low body fat. (which lowers insulin resistance). **Curcumin helps activate the fat-burning gene signal PPAR gamma, which also helps to make more new, metabolically-fit fat cells.**

Curcumin directly reduces major inflammatory events from occurring inside white adipose tissue (tumor necrosis factor alpha, interleukin-6, and monocyte chemotactic protein-1). When these inflammatory signals are excessively activated in white adipose tissue they keep sending "EMERGENCY" messages to immune cells around your body to come to the white adipose tissue and join in the inflammatory party. By lowering such inflammation, the source of overweight-induced disease is stopped.

Curcumin also acts directly on liver cells to help prevent them from becoming fatty. And it works directly on pancreatic beta cells to help them produce insulin normally. By helping the liver and the pancreas, curcumin is taking stress off the two most important organs whose function declines before the onset of type 2 diabetes. (This is another reason why I added curcumin to both PRP's Super Digestive Enzymes and Cognitive Care)

Chromium has long been known to play a central role in healthy glucose metabolism at the cellular level. **It sensitizes cells to insulin and increases the number of insulin receptors in cells.** Chromium works by interacting with cell-signaling receptors that enhance the body's response to insulin. In the presence of chromium cells require less insulin to become activated, resulting in greater overall insulin sensitivity and enhanced glucose control.

Chromium also aids in the transfer of glucose from the blood into cells by activating insulin-sensitive glucose transport molecules. Its central role in regulating glucose is underscored by the hallmark signs of chromium deficiency which manifest as elevated fasting glucose and insulin blood levels. Some chromium-deficient patients have even developed diabetes that could not be reversed through insulin injections, but subsided when supplemented with chromium. The body absorbs dietary chromium poorly, highlighting the need for supplementation.

The more efficient your insulin metabolism, the more amino acids get inside the cells and the more muscle you can make. Chromium appears to make insulin function more efficient by enhancing the uptake of glucose from the blood into the cell. Chromium increases the number of insulin receptors on the cell membrane and enhances insulin binding to cells.

The result from chromium therefore is improved glucose transport into muscle, fat and liver tissue, and therefore better glucose control. Although chromium is present in such foods as whole grains, cheese, liver and meat, the typical Western diet is much lower than the recommended 50–200 mcg per day and if you exercise a lot then you need much more than this. The average intake in the typical Western diet is said to be in the region of 28–35 mcg. One reason for the such low amounts of chromium is processing of foods removes the chromium - another reason to stay away from processed junk foods.

Chromium picolinate also has anabolic effects.

Dr Muriel Gilman at Bemidji State University gave 200mcg of chromium picolinate per day to half of a group of students who had enrolled in weight training classes. The study run double blind for six weeks. Students not receiving any chromium made negligible gains, those on the chromium gained an average of 3.5lbs of lean body mass. That's a massive increase in six weeks, even for beginners who have not exploited their muscle growth potential. Also a larger study was then done with trained football players to validate it. Over six weeks intensive weight training, the football players receiving chromium picolinate gained 5.7lbs of lean body mass compared with 4lbs for the control group. In addition, the chromium group lost **3.6%** of body fat compared with 1% for the control group.

Of all the trace minerals, chromium may be the most beneficial to diabetes patients. It's an insulin potentiator, so it makes the body's own insulin production go further.

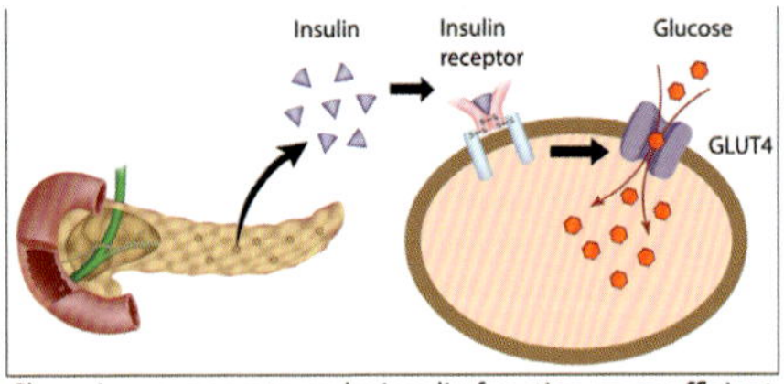

Chromium appears to make insulin function more efficient by enhancing the uptake of glucose from the blood into the cell. Chromium increases the number of insulin receptors on the cell membrane and enhances insulin binding to cells.

The results of several studies suggest that chromium may play a role in controlling diabetes and heart disease. For example, in one study, 180 people with type 2 diabetes were randomly assigned to receive 100 mcg elemental chromium, 500 mcg elemental chromium, or a placebo. Four months later, those taking either dose of chromium scored significantly lower on their fasting and two-hour insulin level tests, indicating improvement in their disease. Those taking the higher amount of chromium were also found to have lower total cholesterol levels.

The average adult body contains between 0.4 and 6 mg of chromium and older people usually have lower levels. There is a wide geographical variation in chromium levels and population studies suggest that the incidence of diabetes and heart disease is lower in areas where chromium intakes are relatively high. In double blind studies, just the addition of chromium supplementation, with no other dietary changes, alters the body fat composition to increase non fat body mass.

One factor affecting chromium stores in the body is the amount of sugar that an individual consumes. Once chromium has acted as a cofactor in insulin response, it is excreted in the urine. With the high sugar diet of today, the turnover rate of chromium is quite high.

Magnesium Cannot Function Properly Without Insulin & Vice Versa

Without insulin, magnesium doesn't get transported from our blood into our cells where it is most needed. When Dr. Jerry Nadler of the Gonda Diabetes Center at the City of Hope Medical Center in Duarte, California, and his colleagues placed 16 healthy people on magnesium-deficient diets, their insulin became less effective at getting sugar from their blood into their cells, where it's burned or stored as fuel. In other words, they became less insulin sensitive or what is called insulin resistant.

There is a strong relationship between magnesium and insulin action. Magnesium is important for the effectiveness of insulin. A reduction of magnesium in the cells strengthens insulin resistance.

A less known fact is that insulin also stores magnesium. But if your cells become resistant to insulin, you can't store magnesium so you lose it through urination.

Intracellular magnesium relaxes muscles. What happens when you can't store magnesium because the cell is resistant? You lose magnesium and your blood vessels constrict. This could lead to cardiovascular problems. **This causes an increase in blood pressure and a reduction in energy since intracellular magnesium is required for all energy producing reactions that take place in the cell.**

But most importantly, magnesium is also necessary for the action of insulin and the manufacture of insulin. When you raise your insulin, you lose magnesium, and the cells become even more insulin resistant. Blood vessels constrict and glucose and insulin can't get to the tissues, which makes them more insulin resistant, so the insulin levels go up and you lose more magnesium. **Magnesium is also vital for converting glycogen into glucose for use as the body's fuel.**

Insulin secretion requires magnesium: magnesium deficiency results in impaired insulin secretion while magnesium replacement restores insulin secretion. Furthermore, experimental magnesium deficiency reduces the tissues sensitivity to insulin.

Subclinical magnesium deficiency is common in diabetes. It results from both insufficient magnesium intakes and increase magnesium losses, particularly in the urine. In type 2 diabetes, magnesium deficiency seems to be associated with insulin resistance.

In several studies, daily oral magnesium supplementation substantially improved insulin sensitivity by 10% and reduced blood sugar by 37%. The Women's Health Study including nearly 12,000 participants showed that people who fail to take the recommended adequate intake of magnesium of 320-420 mg/day are more prone to have both metabolic syndrome and increased C - Reactive Protein (CRP).

R-Lipoic Acid also significantly increases insulin sensitivity, enhances glucose transport, increases metabolic rate and reduces the gain in body fat from aging. This is why I combined magnesium, chromium and R-lipoic acid in my Magnesium Relax so that I get a product that enhances insulin sensitivity.

On the basis of my research I developed a supplement called Magnesium Relax.

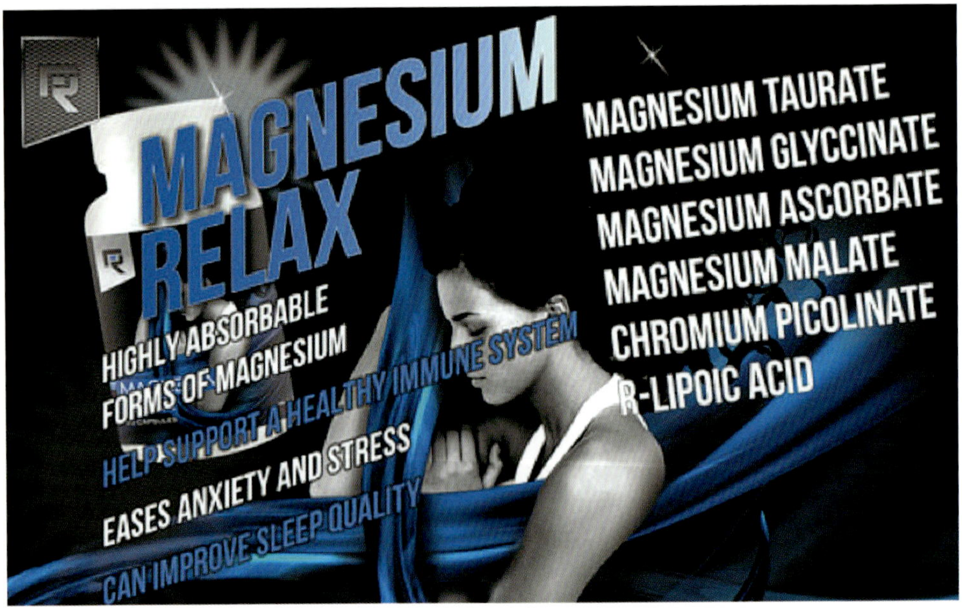

The Power Of Sunlight And Vitamin D To Enhance Your Health & Help Drop Excess Body Fat.

The sun is the ultimate giver of all life and one of the most important anti cancer, anti obesity tools by providing the nutrient Vitamin D. Yes of course respect the sun but ignoring its incredible health and benefits is not the wisest thing to do. Vitamin D is not a vitamin but in fact a hormone. It is unique in that it is made in the skin as a result of exposure to sunlight. The skin has a large capacity to make vitamin D. Exposure of a person with minimum clothing on for than 15-20 minutes on a very sunny day in the UK in June or July at between 12 - 3 p.m. can expect to get a 20,000 IU dose of vitamin D the lighter the skin the less time in the sun required to get this dose.

A major study conducted by researchers at the Karolinska Institute in Sweden found that women who avoid sunbathing during the summer are twice as likely to die as those who sunbathe every day. The epidemiological study followed 30,000 women for over 20 years and "showed that mortality was about double in women who avoided sun exposure compared to the highest exposure group."

Researchers concluded that the conventional dogma, which advises avoiding the sun at all costs and slathering on sunscreen to minimize sun exposure, is doing more harm than actual good. That's because overall sun avoidance combined with wearing sunscreen effectively blocks the body's ability to produce vitamin D3 from the sun's UVB rays, which is by far the best form of vitamin D.

Ironically, vitamin D deficiency can lead to aggressive forms of skin cancer. A ground-breaking 2011 study published in Cancer Prevention Research suggests that optimal blood levels of vitamin D offers protection against sunburn and skin cancer.

The stages of malignant melanoma

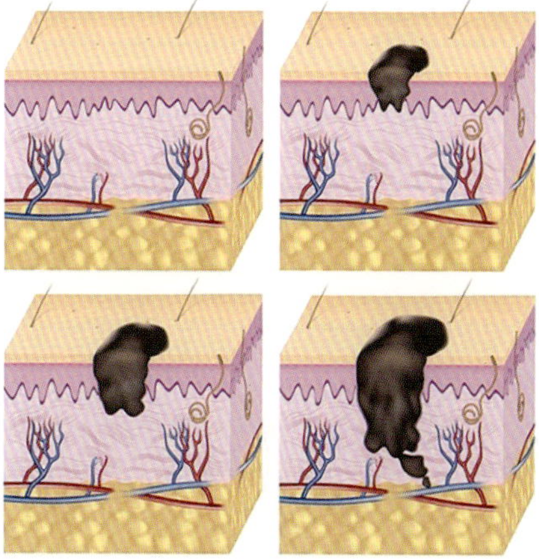

Additionally, vitamin D protects the body from diseases like multiple sclerosis, rickets (in the young), tuberculosis, inflammatory bowel disease, type 1 diabetes, inflammatory bowel disease, rheumatoid arthritis, systemic lupus erythematosus and Sjogren's syndrome and, according to the Vitamin D Council, researchers at the University of Alabama at Birmingham recently reported that "lack of sun exposure may lead to cognitive decline over time."

Bernard Ackerman, MD, (deceased 2008) was one of the world's foremost authorities on the subject of skin cancer and the sun, sunscreens and melanoma skin cancer risks. Below are Ackerman's views excerpted from an article in *The New York Times* (July 20, 2004), titled "I BEG TO DIFFER; A Dermatologist Who's Not Afraid to Sit on the Beach":

> ***"The link between melanoma and sun exposure (dermatology's dogma) is unproven.There's no conclusive evidence that sunburns lead to cancer.There is no real proof that sunscreens protect against melanoma.There's no proof that increased exposure to the sun increases the risk of melanoma."***

British doctors R Marks and D Whiteman are unconvinced also of the sunlight/melanoma link. They point out that:

- Melanoma can be found on ovaries
- Melanoma occurs less frequently on sun-exposed areas
- In Japan forty percent of pedal melanomas are on the soles of the feet
- There is 5-times more melanoma in Scotland on the feet than on the hands
- And melanoma in Orkney and Shetland is ten times that of the Mediterranean islands.

Other clinicians agree. Karnauchow says: "The simplistic idea of a sun/melanoma relationship is based more on a belief than science.....As with other neoplasms, the cause of melanoma remains an enigma and most probably the sun has little, if anything, to do with it."

Think twice before you rub the sunscreen on your skin. A 2000 Swedish study concluded that higher rates of melanoma occurred in those who used sunscreen versus those who did not.

Elizabeth Plourde, PhD, is a California-based scientist who authored the book Sunscreens – Biohazard: Treat as Hazardous Waste, which extensively documents the serious life-threatening dangers of sunscreens **not only to people but to the environment as well.**

Dr. Plourde provides proof that malignant melanoma and all other skin cancers increased significantly with ubiquitous sunscreen use over a 30-year period. She emphasizes that many sunscreens contain chemicals that are known carcinogens and endocrine-disrupting chemicals (EDC).

The Dietary Connection & Skin Cancer

In the 1970s, when kidney transplantation was pioneered, doctors first encountered the problem of tissue rejection. To combat it, they gave their transplant patients linoleic acid. This suppressed their immune systems very effectively, preventing their transplanted kidneys being rejected. But it also caused a large increase in cancers and this treatment was stopped.

Since then, linoleic acid and oils that contain it, have been shown time and again to increase the risk of several types of cancer, including skin cancers. Linoleic acid is the major fatty acid in all polyunsaturated vegetable margarines and cooking oils:

- Polyunsaturated margarines are around 40% linoleic acid
- Sunflower, safflower, corn and soya oils are all more than 50% linoleic acid.

Doctors B.S. and L.E. Mackie, working on Australia's Sunshine Coast, have a great deal of experience in skin cancers. They say: "In view of the work of Black and Erickson in mice and our own work in humans, we believe that human subjects who are at high risk of melanomas and other solar-induced forms of skin cancer should be advised to be moderate in their intake of dietary polyunsaturated fats." It's usually saturated animal fats that get the blame for all diseases today. They are not the culprits - 'healthy so called' vegetable oils are too blame.

Numerous exciting reports about vitamin D's myriad of beneficial effects include recent observations that vitamin D deficiency contributes to insulin resistance and raises blood pressure (by increasing the blood pressure-raising hormone renin). Vitamin D deficiency is exceedingly common, particularly in northern climates, where up to 90% of people have moderate-to-severe deficiency. In sun-deprived climates, 5,000–10,000 IU/day of Vitamin D supplementation may be required to raise blood levels to normal, occasionally more. However, adequate sun exposure does not necessarily guarantee optimal vitamin D levels. Vitamin D status can be assessed by having one's blood tested.

High-dose vitamin D supplements may help increase the body's sensitivity to insulin, thus reducing the risk of diabetes, researchers have found. In the current study, conducted by researchers from Massey University, and published in the British Journal of Nutrition, researchers randomly assigned 81 South Asian women between the ages of 23 and 68 to take either a placebo or 4,000 IU of vitamin D once per day. All participants suffered from insulin resistance at the start of the study, but none were taking diabetes drugs or vitamin D supplements larger than 1,000 IU per day. At the start of the study, the average participant had vitamin D blood levels of approximately 50 nanomoles per liter. **After six months, women in the vitamin D group exhibited significantly more insulin sensitivity and less insulin resistance than women who had received a placebo. The largest effect was seen in women whose vitamin D blood levels had reached 80 to 119 nmol/L.**

According to the Vitamin D Council, blood levels should be at least 125 nmol/L for optimal health.

A 2009 meta-analysis published in the Journal of Clinical Endocrinology & Metabolism found that higher blood levels of vitamin D lowered diabetes risk. Likewise, in a study published in the journal Diabetic Medicine, researchers from the Sitaram Bhartia Institute of Science and Research in New Delhi found that a large dose of vitamin D significantly improved insulin sensitivity after meals in 71 men who were healthy except for central obesity.

Vitamin D stimulates the production of insulin from insulin producing cells in the pancreas. Scientific evidence now exists to show that proper vitamin D supplementation can prevent Type 1 diabetes. One such study comes from Finland. This study begun in 1966 when a total of 10,821 children born in northern Finland were enrolled in the study. Frequency of vitamin D supplementation was recorded during the first year of life. At that time the recommended dose of vitamin D for infants in Finland was 2000 IU's per day. These children were then followed for 31 years for the development of type 1 diabetes. Researchers made the amazing discovery that those children who received the daily recommended dose of 2000 IU of vitamin D during the first year of their life, had an almost 80% reduction in the risk for the development of Type 1 diabetes compared to those children who received less! If a drug could get the same results trust me it would be plastered all over the media and doctors surgeries but I guess vitamin D is cheap and no profits for big pharma!

This was a ground-breaking study that was published in 2001 in the British Medical Journal but has obviously been ignored by the medical profession. Johns Hopkins University Medical School conducted a ten-year epidemiological study that showed exposure to full-spectrum light (including the ultraviolet frequencies) is positively related to the prevention of breast, colon and rectal cancers. How does this work? There is in fact a scientific answer. The sun stimulates production of a hormone in your skin. Ultraviolet B rays, the kind of rays that give you sunburns, interact with a special cholesterol in unblocked skin. Once stimulated, this cholesterol triggers your liver and kidney to make vitamin D3.

Vitamin D3 can then drastically improve your immune system function. Vitamin D 'triggers and arms' the immune system. In particular it triggers and arms the body's T cells, the cells in the body that seek out and destroy any invading bacteria and viruses. Scientists at the University of Copenhagen have discovered that Vitamin D is crucial to activating our immune defences and that without sufficient intake of the vitamin, the killer cells of the immune system – T cells – will not be able to react to and fight off serious infections in the body.

For T cells to detect and kill foreign pathogens such as clumps of bacteria or viruses, the cells must first be 'triggered' into action and "transform" from inactive and harmless immune cells into killer cells that are primed to seek out and destroy all traces of invaders. The researchers found that the T cells rely on vitamin D in order to activate and they would remain dormant, 'naïve' to the possibility of threat if vitamin D is lacking in the blood.

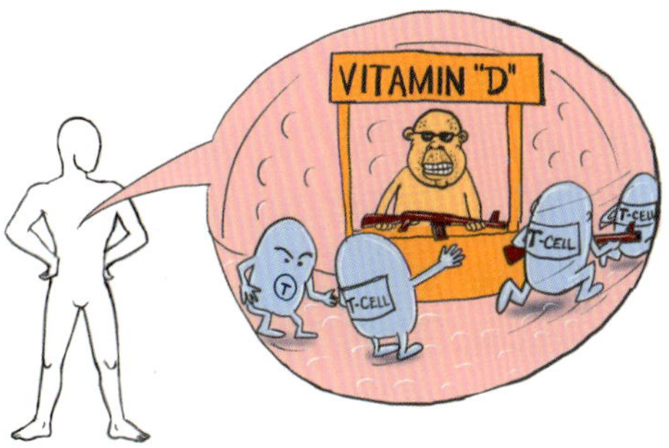

Vitamin D help can help boost your body's defence system by arming your body's T-cells.

Professor Carsten Geisler from the Department of International Health, Immunology and Microbiology, said: "When a T cell is exposed to a foreign pathogen, it extends a signalling device or 'antenna' known as a vitamin D receptor, with which it searches for vitamin D. This means that the T cell must have vitamin D or activation of the cell will cease. If the T cells cannot find enough vitamin D in the blood, they won't even begin to mobilise. "

Yes - you can now see how moronic the advice is to stay out of the sun. Sensible advice would be get enough sun exposure that your skin colour takes, then cover up. Vitamin D from all sources (sunlight, sun lamps, or supplements) reduces the incidence of respiratory infections. Dutch children with the least sun exposure are twice as likely to develop a cough and three times more likely to develop a runny nose compared with children with the most sun exposure.

When Russian athletes were given sun lamps to stimulate vitamin D synthesis in the body, there were 50% fewer respiratory infections and far fewer days of absence. In Russia, a full-spectrum lighting system was installed in factories where colds and sore throats had become commonplace among workers. This lowered the bacterial contamination of the air by 40%-70%. Workers who did not receive the full-spectrum light were absent twice as many days as those who did.

Breast cancer is the most common form of cancer in women, causing about 370,000 deaths annually worldwide. Each year some 220,000 women in Europe and 180,000 women in North America are diagnosed with the disease. About 15,000 British women die of breast cancer annually, a death rate that is higher than elsewhere in Western

Europe. One in 12 British women will develop breast cancer at some time in their lives and, as we have already seen, the incidence of breast cancer is increasing. The reasons for this are not altogether clear, but lack of sunlight could be a factor. In 1989 the Drs Garland, together with Dr Edward Gorham, published the first ever epidemiological work on the relationship between sun exposure and breast cancer.

Their research demonstrated that, as in the case of colon cancer, there was a strong negative correlation between available sunlight and breast cancer death rates. The chances of women from areas of the United States with less available sunlight dying of breast cancer were 40% higher than those of women who lived in Hawaii or Florida.

Vitamin D is also gaining recognition as a crucial modulator of inflammation. A University of London study demonstrated a dramatic reduction in the inflammatory proteins CRP and matrix metalloproteinase (MMP), after supplementation in 171 healthy adults, with a startling 68% reduction in MMP.

It is nearly impossible to get adequate amounts of vitamin D from your diet. Sunlight exposure is the only reliable way to generate vitamin D in your own body. A person would have to drink ten tall glasses of vitamin D fortified milk each day just to get minimum levels of vitamin D into their diet. The further you live from the equator, the longer exposure you need to the sun in order to generate vitamin D. Canada, the UK and most U.S. states are far from the equator.

People with dark skin pigmentation may need 20-30 times as much exposure to sunlight as fair-skinned people to generate the same amount of vitamin D, as we have already discussed. Sufficient levels of vitamin D are crucial for calcium absorption in your intestines. Without sufficient vitamin D, your body cannot absorb calcium, rendering calcium supplements useless. Chronic vitamin D deficiency cannot be reversed overnight: it takes months of vitamin D supplementation and sunlight exposure to rebuild the body's bones and nervous system. Even weak sunscreens (SPF=8) block your body's ability to generate vitamin D by 95%. This is how sunscreen products actually cause disease -- by creating a critical vitamin deficiency in the body.

The sunscreen industry doesn't want you to know that your body actually needs sunlight exposure because that realization would mean lower sales of sunscreen products. It is impossible to generate too much vitamin D in your body from sunlight exposure: your body will self-regulate and only generate what it needs. Vitamin D is "activated" in your body by your kidneys and liver before it can be used. Having kidney disease or liver damage can greatly impair your body's ability to activate circulating vitamin D.

Even though vitamin D is one of the most powerful healing chemicals in your body, your body makes it absolutely free. No prescription required.

On the issue of sunlight exposure, by the way, it turns out that super antioxidants greatly boost your body's ability to handle sunlight without burning. Astaxanthin is one of the most powerful "internal sunscreens" and can allow you to stay under the sun twice as long without burning. Other powerful antioxidants with this ability include the super fruits like Acai, Pomegranates, blueberries, etc.

According to a new review of research, evidence suggests that adequate treatment of vitamin D deficient athletes could dramatically improve their performance. Activated vitamin D is a steroid hormone which regulates more than 1,000 human genes. Researchers reviewed the world's literature for evidence that vitamin D affects physical and athletic performance. Numerous studies, particularly in the German literature in the 1950s, show vitamin D-producing ultraviolet light improves athletic performance. A study in 1945 found that UV radiation for up to 2 minutes, three times a week, improved cardiovascular fitness scores by 19% compared to 2% of students who did nothing.

Vitamin D also increases the size and number of fast twitch muscle fibers. Most cross-sectional and randomized controlled studies show that vitamin D levels are directly associated with musculoskeletal performance. Vitamin D also increases levels of testosterone, which may boost libido. In one study, overweight men who were given vitamin D supplements had a significant increase in testosterone levels after one year.

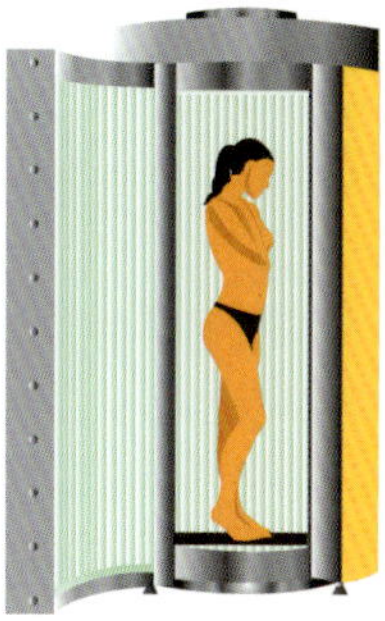

Recent studies from the U.K. show that low levels of vitamin D3 (cholecalciferol) are associated with increased risk of depression and panic. Researchers from the Children's Hospital and Research Center in Oakland, California, defined the role of vitamin D in neurological health, pointing out the wide distribution of vitamin D throughout the brain. The vitamin affects portions of the brain involved in learning and memory, as well as motor control.

Vitamin D is very much involved in production of serotonin, the molecule of will power, and delayed gratification. Decreased serotonin activity can lead to an inability to create and act on well-formed plans. There are many vitamin D receptors in the brain. Bright light going through the eyes increases serotonin production – sunglasses block this effect – and sunscreen blocks the vitamin D formation in the skin.

Studies with rats show that the production of serotonin is directly related to duration of bright sunlight. Sunbathing and exposure to bright light during the day can have a similar effect to antidepressants and of course are far safer. Calcitriol, the hormonally active form of vitamin D, accumulates in the adrenals, and this stimulates the production of the gene for tyrosine hydroxylase, which is involved in serotonin production. Serotonin synthesis is thought to be dependent on the duration of light exposure the previous summer.

How Much Vitamin D Do You Need?

Dr. John Cannell, MD, is the president of The Vitamin D Council, a nonprofit group that advocates higher vitamin D intake. According to Dr. Cannell, adults need to take 5,000 IU a day of vitamin D to put the vast majority of them (97.5%) above the 50 ng/mL level.

For each receptor for vitamin D there are two receptors for vitamin A on every cell. A relative balance of these two nutrients is essential for health. For example if you take large amounts of vitamin D you will create a vitamin A deficiencies which will be catastrophic for health.

Recent research from Spain indicates that vitamin A is necessary for both vitamin D binding and vitamin D release to receptor sites. It also turns out that vitamin D is the most potent protector of omega 3 oils, as mentioned previously.

Vitamin D from sunlight acts as a pro-hormone, rapidly converting in your skin into 25-hydroxyvitamin D, or vitamin D3. Using a safe home tanning bed to achieve similar results as that from natural sunlight exposure. I use a UVB sunbed three times per week for two minutes each time.

Here are some important tips on getting the most out of the sun without risking sunburn.

- Most important: the best protection is a natural suntan.
- DO try to develop a moderate natural suntan unless you have extremely sensitive skin and burn easily.
- DO build up a tan slowly over, say, a week. Aim for no more than a slight pinkness each day. You should never tan so much that your skin peels off.
- DO remember that sunlight is strongly reflected from sand, snow, ice, and concrete and can increase your direct sunlight exposure by 10 to 50%.
- DO cut down on the amount of polyunsaturated fat and oil in your diet.
- DO see your doctor if you spot any unusual moles or growth on your skin —

particularly if they are irregular in shape, bleed, itch, or appear to be changing. Most skin cancers can be cured if caught in time.

- DO NOT sunbathe in the early morning or late afternoon sun as recommended by health authorities. If the sun is low in the sky, you will only receive UVA rays, which is counter-productive. Yes, UVA tans, but it also reduces the body's vitamin D stores.
- DO NOT use a sunscreen loaded with chemicals you cannot pronounce. The best sunscreen is a hat and a shirt. No chemicals for the skin to absorb, no questions about whether the product works and no bogus claims like sunblock. These healthier sunscreens contain Titanium Dioxide and Zinc Oxide as a more natural form of sunblock, but do your research because even these two ingredients have some side effects.
- Some of the best foods and supplements to protect your skin include; Resveratrol (red wine, blueberries and red grapes), Astaxanthin, Catechins (green and white tea), Vitamin E (pumpkin seeds, almonds, and asparagus) and beta-carotene (carrots and red bell peppers).
- DO NOT shower in the morning before going out to sunbathe. The oils naturally produced by your body during the night are a good protection.
- DO NOT shower for at least an hour after you have sunbathed. Vitamin D formed by the action of the sun on oils on the skin need time to be absorbed.
- Forget 'after sun' products. They are expensive and unnecessary if you have followed this advice and not allowed your skin to be burnt. But after you have showered, do use a moisturiser.
- DO NOT wear sunglasses that filter out 100% of the ultraviolet light. They may protect you against the development of cataracts, but they stop UV entering the eyes - and that is much more important as UV through the eyes prevents cancer.

Vitamin K2 is essential for Vitamin D synthesis

Before you start consuming Vitamin D supplements in high dosages read the following very carefully Dr. Kate Rheaume-Bleue, a naturopathic physician has authored an incredible book which alerted me to the importance of combining K2 with Vitamin D in my Ultimate Fish Oil Blend. Her book is titled Vitamin K2 and the Calcium Paradox: How a Little Known Vitamin Could Save Your Life.

"K2 is really critical for keeping your bones strong and your arteries clear," Rheaume-Bleue says. This is a really crucial point: If you opt for oral vitamin D, you need to also consume in your food or take supplemental vitamin K2. "There are so many people on the vitamin-D-mega-dose bandwagon, taking more and more of vitamin D. And it could absolutely be causing harm if you are lacking the K2 to complete the job to get the calcium where it's supposed to be,"

Rheaume-Bleue warns."We don't see symptoms of vitamin D toxicity very often. But when we do, those symptoms are inappropriate calcification. That's the symptom of vitamin D toxicity. And it is actually a lack of vitamin K2 that can cause that..." While the ideal or optimal ratios between vitamin D and vitamin K2 have yet to be elucidated, Rheume-Bleue suggests about 150-200 micrograms of K2 will meet the need for the "average" healthy person. We discuss vitamin K2 in much greater depth in habit 8.

This is why PRP Ultimate Fish Oil is in my opinion unmatched by any other product on the market. Why? Take a look at what you get with one serving.

Active Ingredients: per 5ml serving:

- Fish oil 2103.75mg (Providing 440mg actual EPA and 315mg actual DHA)
- Borage oil 2102.5mg (Borago officinalis seed Providing 420mg actual GLA)
- Mixed Tocopherols 200mg of actual Vitamin E
- CoEnzyme Q10 50mg
- Sweet Orange Oil
- Lemon Oil
- Vitamin D 1000iu
- Vitamin A 1000iu
- Vitamin K2 75 mcg

Conclusion

There is a very synergistic relationship between the awesome foursome growth hormone, insulin, sleep and sunshine. This habit alone if you follow by enhancing growth hormone, getting insulin working for you and not making you fatter, getting good sleep and adequate sunshine can have a dramatic effect on your health and ability to lose fat. Hopefully though you can see that the 10 habits is like a jigsaw puzzle you need all of the pieces to complete the jigsaw and for maximum fat loss to be initiated.

In researching for these topics, some of the books that I read included;

- "The Fat Resistance Diet" - Leo Galland
- "The Vitamin D Solution" - Michael Holick
- "The Liver Cleansing Diet" - Dr Sandra Cabot
- "Grow Young with HGH" - Dr Ronald Klatz
- "The Insulin Factor" - Anthony Haynes
- "Life Extension Revolution" - Philip Miller
- "The Primal Blueprint" - Mark Sisson
- "Enzymes for Health and Healing" - Ellen Culter & Dr Jeremy Kaslow
- "The Blood-Sugar Solution" - Mark Hyman
- "Power of Vitamin D" Sarfraz Zaidi
- "Natural Health & Fat Loss" Barry Groves

HABIT 8

NUTRITIONAL CARDIOLOGY

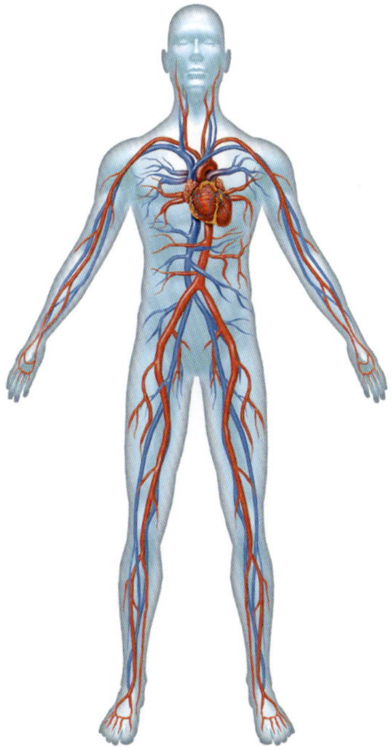

"The best and most beautiful things in the world cannot be seen or even touched - they must be felt with the heart."

Helen Keller

There are not many books that I know on fat loss that would devote so much information about the cardiovascular system. The reason why I wanted to include information about the heart, blood vessels and blood is quite simple - there is no point being lean and dead. With heart disease being the biggest killer in Westernised countries, I wanted to share with you my knowledge on how to have a very healthy and functional cardiovascular system. Collectively, heart and circulatory diseases cause more than one in three of all deaths in the UK, accounting for more than 191,000 deaths each year at an estimated cost of £30 billion to the economy.

There are many causes of heart disease as the below picture shows but because we only hear about cholesterol as being the biggest danger which as you will read in this chapter is completely false we then fail to address the real perpetrators of heart disease.

THE 20 CAUSES OF HEART DISEASE

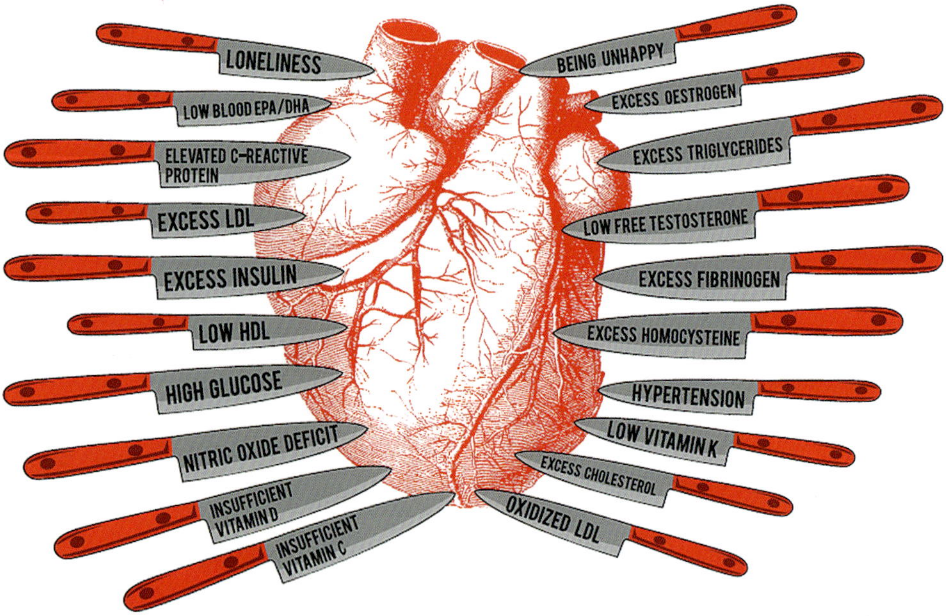

The cardiovascular system is also the transportation system of our nutrients, oxygen and hormones. Nutritional cardiology is essential for the health of our heart, blood vessels and blood. For our 50+ trillion cells to be kept well nourished, we need a fully functioning cardiovascular system which also must be well nourished for it to function at maximum efficiency.

In this habit we will look more closely at the cholesterol myth and the obsession by many in the medical and pharmaceutical industry to demonise this essential nutrient and falsely educate the public to cut cholesterol levels to a level where they simply sell more statins. I will pull no punches in this habit on the insanity of low fat, low cholesterol foods and the real dangers of statin drugs.

Your Heart is the Key

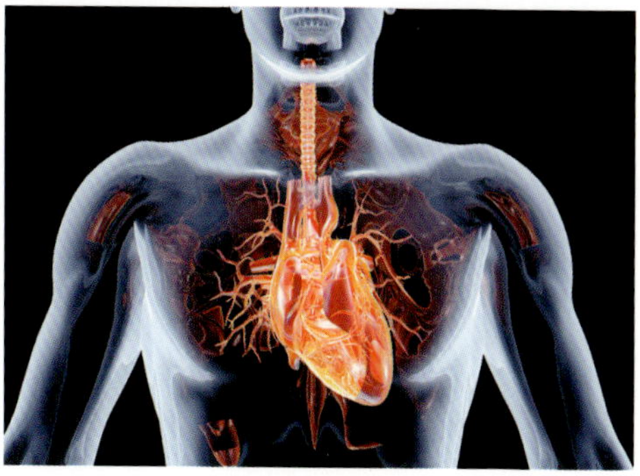

Your heart is a key organ and needs to be nourished, cared for and exercised to function optimally.

Love is the most essential ingredient for the heart.

Most of us think of the heart as a pump that propels blood around the body. This is true, of course, but researchers at the leading edge of science are telling us that it is so much more than a mere pump.

Traditionally, we think of the brain as the central computer of the body. It receives information from the five physical senses which are smelling, seeing, hearing, tasting and feeling and sends information signals to the body to produce the desired actions and to drive physiological functions. I suspect that not many of you know that your heart is an organ that can learn, remember, feel and sense independently of your brain. It's true. There are countless studies that have shown a link between mind and body diseases.

In a twenty five year follow-up study involving 255 University of North Carolina medical students, Dr. John Barefoot found those who scored highest in hostility on a standard personality test were nearly five times as likely to die of heart disease as their less hostile classmates. They were seven times more likely to die by the age of fifty.

The Heart can Remember: a heart transplant story

There are some fascinating stories coming from heart transplant recipients, such as those from Dr Paul Pearsall's book, "The Heart's Code".

In one example, Pearsall tells of an eight year old girl who received a heart transplant from a ten year old girl who was murdered. After a successful operation, the eight year old began having nightmares about the man who had killed her donor.

Distressed, the girl's mother took her to see a psychiatrist, who after a couple of sessions, began to think the girl might not just be having a stress response to her life threatening health problems and the major life change of her receiving a new heart. The psychiatrist could not deny what she was being told by the child. The girl's mother too came to suspect that perhaps this information might be useful to the police. It took some time but she finally overcame her resistance and called the appropriate authorities who came and talked to the girl.

Astonishingly, armed with a description of the man and other information about the murder weapon and circumstances of the crime that the little girl gave them, the police were able to find the murderer, who was eventually convicted.

One day, a poor boy who was selling goods from door to door to pay his way through school, found he had only one thin dime left, and he was hungry. He decided he would ask for a meal at the next house. However, he lost his nerve when a lovely young woman opened the door.

Instead of a meal he asked for a drink of water. She thought he looked hungry so brought him a large glass of milk.

He drank it slowly, and then asked, "How much do I owe you?"

"You don't owe me anything," she replied. "Mother has taught us never to accept pay for a kindness."

He said, "Then I thank you from my heart."

As Howard Kelly left that house, he not only felt stronger physically, but his faith in God and man was strong also. He had been ready to give up and quit.

Year's later that young woman became critically ill. The local doctors were baffled. They finally sent her to the big city, where they called in specialists to study her rare disease.

Dr. Howard Kelly was called in for the consultation. When he heard the name of the town she came from, a strange light filled his eyes. Immediately he rose and went down the hall of the hospital to her room.

Dressed in his doctor's gown he went in to see her. He recognized her at once. He went back to the consultation room determined to do his best to save her life. From that day he gave special attention to the case.

After a long struggle, the battle was won. Dr. Kelly requested the business office to pass the final bill to him for approval. He looked at it, then wrote something on the edge and the bill was sent to her room.

She feared to open it, for she was sure it would take the rest of her life to pay for it all. Finally she looked, and something caught her attention on the side of the bill. She began to read the following words:

"Paid in full with one glass of milk.
Signed, Dr. Howard Kelly."

In 1993, a paper published by the Institute of Heartmath documented the fact that the information coded in our emotions plays a key role in the way the heart tells the brain which chemicals (hormones, endorphins and immune enhancers) to produce in our body at any given time. More precisely, our emotions tell our brains what we believe we need in that moment. This heart-brain communication is well documented in the open literature and generally accepted in the progressive medical community.

Studies by the Institute of Heartmath also show that feelings associated with beliefs (heart-centered beliefs) are transmitted into the heart's electrical and magnetic waves that not only affect our bodies but are also sent out and interact with the physical world. Recurring feelings of frustration, worry, stress, and anger cause heart rhythms to become unbalanced and disordered. On the other hand, forgiveness, appreciation, and love create coherent, harmonious heart rhythms and affect the physical heart's electrical output, as seen in an ECG.

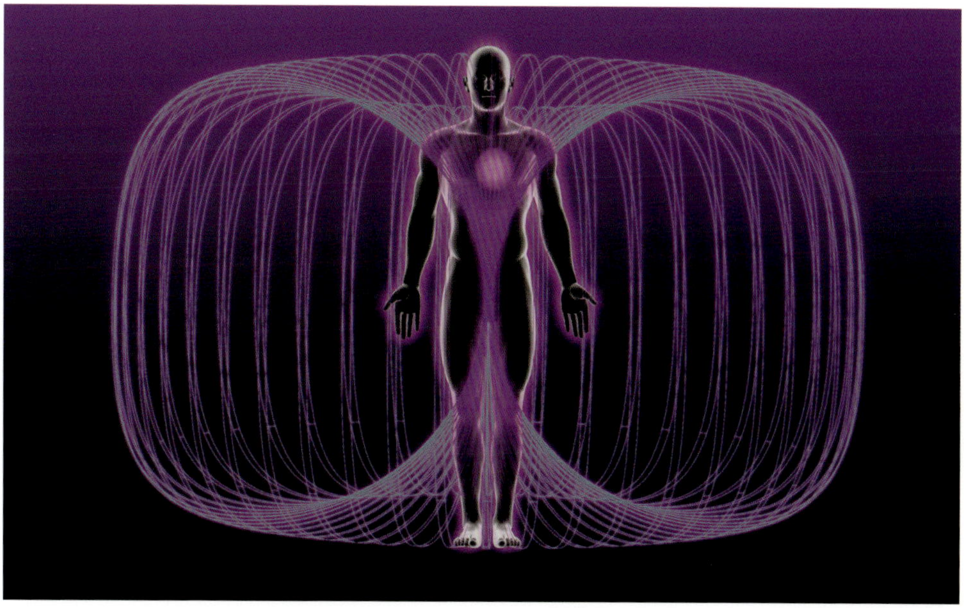

The most important thing for your heart is love :)

"Hatred paralyzes life; love releases it.
Hatred confuses life; love harmonizes it.
Hatred darkens life; love illuminates it."
Martin Luther King Jr.

The most extensive studies on heart disease have shown that a lack of happiness is one of the greatest risk factor for developing heart problems. Even remembering an upsetting experience can reduce the heart's pumping efficiency by 5-7% and decrease the immune system's potency for many hours.

Never hold grudges against anyone it will destroy you far more than it will destroy them and especially your heart.

A 9 year study in Finland showed that hostility is a major risk factor and predictor of coronary heart disease. Hostile people were more than **three times** likely to die from cardiovascular disease than those with a non-hostile approach to life. In the book "The Emotional Wellness Way to Cardiac Health", a study on the role of anger is discussed. It found that among 1,600 patients who had previously suffered a heart attack, the risk of another heart attack after an episode of anger was increased by **200%.**

A study at the Johns Hopkins School of Medicine tracked 1,337 male medical students for 36 years after medical school and found that students who became angry quickly under stress were three times more likely to develop premature heart disease and five times more likely to have an early heart attack. Angry young men, it appears, turn into angry old men with heart problems

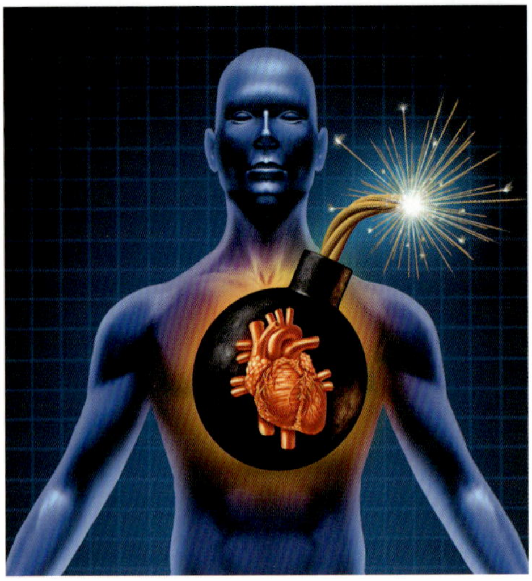

Hostility cripples the heart.

A Harvard study concluded that men who showed high hostility at the start of an eight-year investigation exhibited significantly poorer lung function at the end of it. "This research shows that hostility is associated with poorer [lung] function and more rapid rates of decline among older men," notes Rosalind Wright, an assistant professor at the Harvard School of Public Health.

The biggest surprise that I personally had during my research on finding the most important nutritional factors that cause cardiovascular disease was that the media's and medical professions obsession with cholesterol when, in reality, that is a myth. Stress is undoubtedly the biggest killer when it comes to cardiovascular deaths. But i guess there is no money for big pharma to be made out of stress management like meditation and yoga!

Yoga and medication are excellent for heart health.

Of course, you must get good nutritional habits in place, as well as sensible lifestyle factors, but the most important factor is managing your stress factor if you do not want to become another heart disease statistic. Remember, you do not catch heart disease; you build it. You build it with the food you eat, your thoughts and the people you live with. Take every opportunity in life to have fun as this is the most therapeutic thing for the heart.

The Heart: a non-stop worker

The world's most perfect pump is at this very moment right in your chest. The human heart is approximately the size of a fist, and is a pump made of muscle. With its non-stop beating, the heart sends all of your blood around your body some **1,000** times during the course of a single day.

The heart's most important feature is being able to work without stopping, contracting around 40-70 times a minute (**about 37 million times a year**). It beats on average around 2.5 billion times during the average human lifespan and pumps approximately 300 million litres of blood. That is the equivalent of the amount of liquid it would take to fill 10,000 oil tankers. Even while you sleep, your heart pumps some 340 litres of blood. To put it another way, your heart could fill a car's petrol tank **9 times** over every hour.

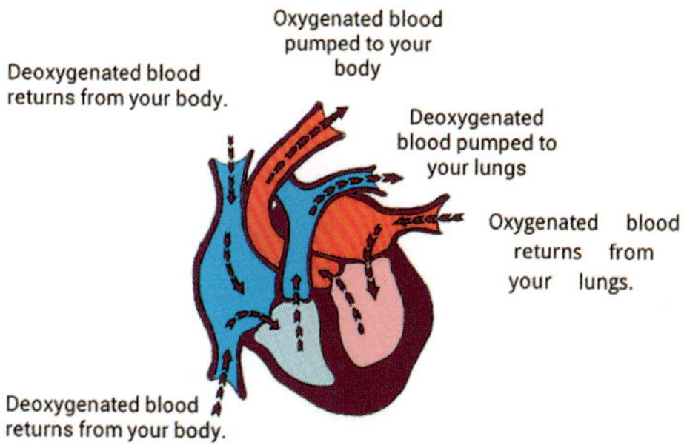

Your heart is a non-stop worker. It pumps deoxygenated blood from the body to the lungs, and then it pumps oxygenated blood, it receives from the lungs, around the body.

Many of the processes that take place within your body are linked to the circulatory system, thanks to an exceedingly complex structure. A network of arteries and veins nourish the 50 trillion or so cells in your body, visiting every one individually. Many of the needs in all living things - such as carrying nourishment and gases like oxygen to the cells, and eliminating waste products from the body - are met by substances carried by the circulatory system. In human beings, the liquid that performs all these functions is the blood. Every single cell in your body, from a skin cell on your fingertip to the specialized retinal cells in your eyes, depends on what blood provides.

The mechanical stress of this non-stop work is a particular challenge to the millions of cells which make up the heart. These cells need an optimum supply of nutrients to ensure their proper functioning and the general health of the heart. It's all about ATP the energy currency of the body. Hearts, skeletal muscles, and every other tissue in our bodies have an absolute requirement for adenosine triphosphate, or ATP, as their primary energy currency. ATP molecules are both synthesized and recycled within the body, and supply all of the body's energy.

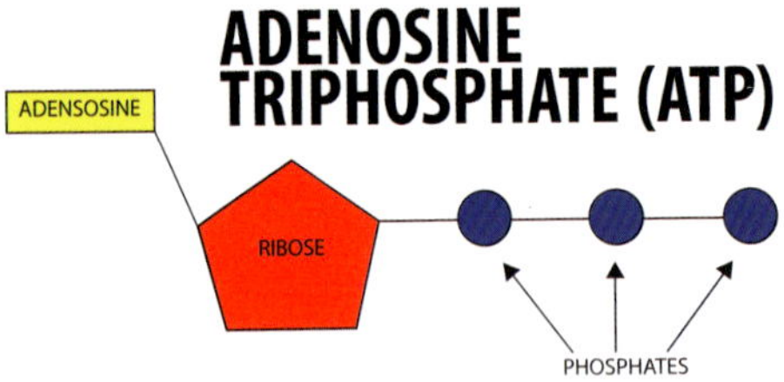

Adenosine triphosphate (ATP) is the energy used by an organism in its daily operations. It consists of an adenosine molecule and three inorganic phosphates. After a simple reaction breaking down ATP to ADP, the energy released from the breaking of a molecular bond is the energy we use to keep ourselves alive.

Both the total pool of ATP in the cell and the cell's ability to recycle these compounds are fundamental to healthy energy metabolism and cell function. If you give your cells the ability to make optimal levels of energy, they can use it to do whatever they want: build and renew cell membranes, create and maintain cell structures, and replicate and protect cell information. In fact it's impossible to think of any physiological function that is not linked in some way to our energy supply.

Joanne Ingwell, a professor of physiology at Harvard University and an expert on energy metabolism of the heart, informs us that every event in the myocyte (heart cell) requires ATP. Diseased hearts are energy-starved, which means they lack ATP to fuel healthy cardiac function. Failing hearts lack adequate energy to drive pump function. As the heart is one of the most responsive organs in the body for targeted nutritional supplementation, practicing "nutritional cardiology" is a must.

By enhancing ATP synthesis and recycling, and promoting more efficient metabolism in mitochondria, the correct nutritional support helps ailing hearts recover. Nutritional cardiology aims to build up and maintain ATP stores in the heart, and ultimately enhance heart health, by providing the body with the nutrients it needs to make ENERGY. This information was first brought to my attention following the excellent work of American cardiologist Dr. Steven Sinatra.

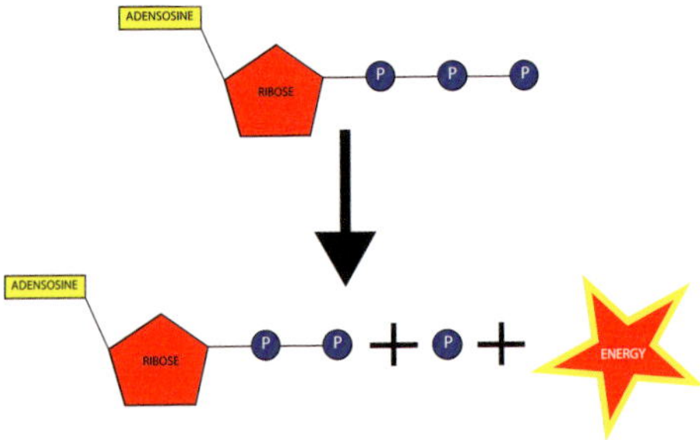

ATP is like a battery containing stored energy within a cell. When the cell requires energy, the bond between the 2nd and 3rd phosphate is broken, releasing some of the stored energy.

People with heart disease often exhibit CoQ10, L-carnitine, D-ribose, and/or magnesium deficiencies.

CoQ10 - The Essential Heart Nutrient

As a nutrient essential to ATP production in all cells of the body, coenzyme Q10 (CoQ10), is a VIP (very important particle) within your body. **With the potential to help heal almost all cardiovascular conditions, it is one of the best nutrients you can feed your heart.** In fact, tissue levels of CoQ10 are usually ten times higher in the healthy heart than any other organ of the body this simply emphasises how essential CoQ10 is to heart. Heart muscle requires an incredible amount of CoQ10 to circulate oxygenated and nutrient-rich blood through your body. CoQ10 can be synthesized within the body. There are, however, circumstances where the body does not make sufficient amounts. When deficiency occurs the heart may be the most affected leading to serious problems. Why? **Because the heart has such high metabolic (energy) demands.**

Often called the "miracle nutrient" or the "universal antioxidant," CoQ10 exists in the mitochondria of our cells, and scavenges and destroys free radicals that cause cardiovascular problems and heart disease. Hundreds of studies have documented the actions of CoQ10 and how they improve heart health. CoQ10 molecules perform a vital role in the production of the body's ATP. This is the key reason CoQ10 is probably the single best nutrient you can take for your heart. CoQ10 is an important part of the inner membranes of the mitochondria where the actual production of ATP occurs. Here electrons (negatively charged particles in atoms) are passed around in what is known as the electron transport chain. CoQ10's job is to collect and transfer these electrons along the chain, which helps power the production of ATP.

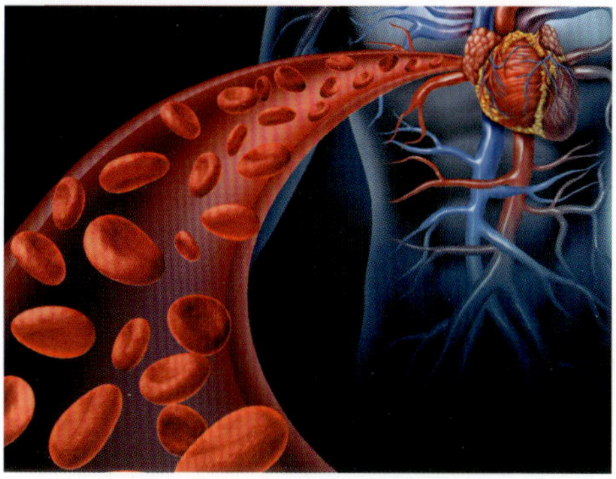

CoQ10, D-ribose, L-carnitine and magnesium all increase the power of the heart to pump blood efficiently.

It is believed that CoQ10 is the key nutrient for generating up to 95% of the total energy required by the human body. Your heart muscle consumes huge amounts of oxygen and energy. CoQ10 essentially recharges the energy system in the heart, enabling the heart muscle to pump blood more efficiently. One of the most serious heart conditions caused by a CoQ10 deficiency is congestive heart failure.

Congestive heart failure (CHF) is the inability of the heart to pump blood effectively to the body. Congestive heart failure does not mean that the heart has stopped working completely, but does mean that the heart is not pumping as strongly as it should. As a result, some of the blood that is normally pumped out of the heart backs up into the lungs and other parts of the body, causing a build-up of fluids in the body (resulting in swelling), shortness of breath and fatigue.

A significant link has been found to exist between low levels of CoQ10 and congestive heart failure. The lower the levels of CoQ10, the more severe the heart failure. Depriving the heart of CoQ10 is like removing a spark plug from your engine - it just won't work. Low levels of CoQ10 are implicated in virtually all cardiovascular diseases, including angina, hypertension, cardiomyopathy and congestive heart failure.

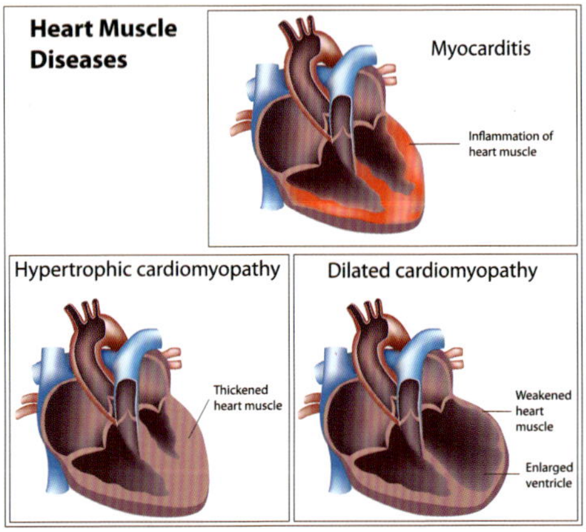

CoQ10 pioneer Karl Folkers claimed that the primary source of CoQ10 in man is biosynthesis. Folkers argues that suboptimal nutrient intake in man is almost universal, causing subsequent secondary impairment in CoQ10 biosynthesis. This means that average or "normal" levels of CoQ10 are really suboptimal and the very low levels observed in advanced disease states represent only the tip of a deficiency iceberg. In the early 1980's, Karl Folkers collaborated with Peter Langsjoen, of the Scott and White Clinic in Temple, Texas, in the first well controlled cardiomyopathy (a weakening of the heart muscle or another problem with the heart muscle) study of CoQ10. The effect of CoQ10 on nineteen patients, all of whom were expected to die of heart failure were astounding. They made an **"extraordinary clinical improvement"**, the researchers said. Heart size decreased and blood pumping improved, regardless of the form of cardiomyopathy.

If mitochondria are little engines, which use oxygen to burn the organic fuels that come from foodstuffs, then you may think of CoQ10 as the part of the engine that provides the spark for this process. No other substance will substitute for CoQ10. Without CoQ10, there is no spark and therefore no production of energy for the cell. And, without energy, there is no life.

CoQ10 Distribution in the Body

The concentration of coenzyme Q10 in the body decreases year by year, indicating that it has a close relationship with ageing.

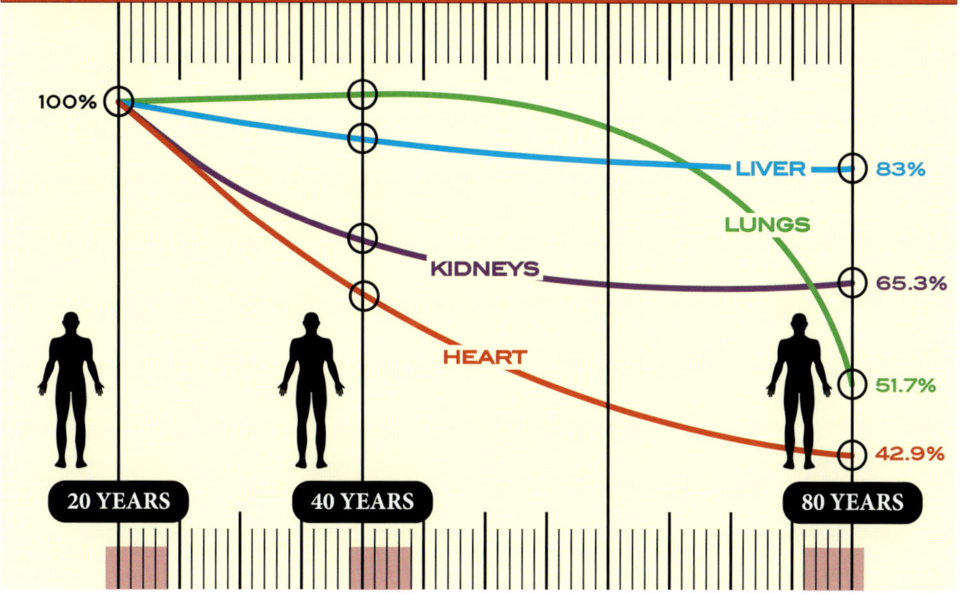

Also, if you exercise strenuously you are using your body's supply. High intensity exercise has been shown to lower CoQ10. This is most probably due to the consequence of an excess of free radicals caused by increased metabolic demands of chronically exercising muscles. In a double-blind, placebo-controlled study published in 2008 in the Journal of the International Society of Sports Nutrition, Baylor University scientists found that supplements of 100 and 200 milligrams increased CoQ10 levels in muscles and prolonged the length of exercise in healthy adults. Another double-blind, placebo-controlled study from researchers at the University Graduate School of Medicine, Osaka, Japan, published in 2008 in Nutrition, showed that 300 milligrams of CoQ10 helped exercise bikers achieve higher velocities for longer periods of time and recover from fatigue more rapidly.

CoQ10 is also known as ubiquinone. That simply means it is found everywhere (in every cell) of our bodies. This fact alone should give us a feel for how important it is to our survival and proper health!

CoQ10 plays many vital roles in numerous bodily processes such as: cellular energy production; cell membrane stabilization; prevention of LDL (Low-density lipoprotein: one of the five major groups of lipoproteins) oxidation. CoQ10 also plays an important role in reducing platelet size, distribution, stickiness and limiting platelet aggregation and activation. As well as these it also helps prevent blood clot formations. Research indicates that if levels of CoQ10 decline by 25% our organs may become deficient and impaired. If levels decline by 75% serious tissue damage and even death may occur.

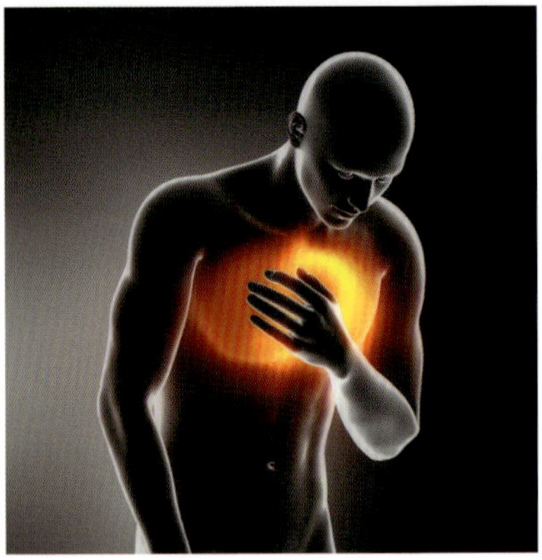

Poorly nourished hearts often become diseased hearts. You need to give the heart a constant supply of oxygen and usable energy.

Studies have shown that nutrients and supplements can strengthen the heart muscle, with fewer side effects than the powerful pharmaceuticals often used to treat the condition. CoQ10 is one of the most powerful. Present in high quantities throughout the heart muscle, CoQ10 has many beneficial effects, including energy production (Awata N et al 1980; Crane FL et al 1997; Nakamura Y et al 1982; Nayler WG 1980), an antioxidant effect (Frei B et al 1990), and stabilizing the heart membrane (Ondarroa M et al 1986).

Heart muscle requires an incredible amount of CoQ10 to circulate oxygenated and nutrient-rich blood through your body.

Studies at the University of Ancona in Italy have provided evidence that CoQ10 supplementation reduces blood levels of epinephrine (adrenalin) and other catecholamine's this is believed to be partly responsible for the drop in blood pressure and may also explain why CoQ10 is effective in reducing the incidence of certain types of arrhythmias.

Yes, CoQ10 truly is an essential nutrient for the heart so why on earth does big pharma and misinformed medical professionals push statins and low cholesterol diets? In truth, statins are extremely dangerous and have the potential to cause a host of adverse effects not often mentioned by the establishment. Among the most prominent adverse effects is heart failure due to a lack of CoQ10, as well as myopathy, a type of disease that affects muscle tissue. These and other conditions are documented in the independent literature as being linked to statin use, and consumers need to beware.

CoQ10 depletion is a genuine potential issue in those who take statins, and CoQ10 supplementation should at least be considered by those who take statins or have taken them.

Look at the diagram below and you can see that statins not only reduce cholesterol but unfortunately and what big pharma doesn't want you to know it also drops your CoQ10 levels along with testosterone and vitamin D which as you will remember from habit 6 & 7 are crucial for heart health as well as fat loss. Yes in a word INSANE!

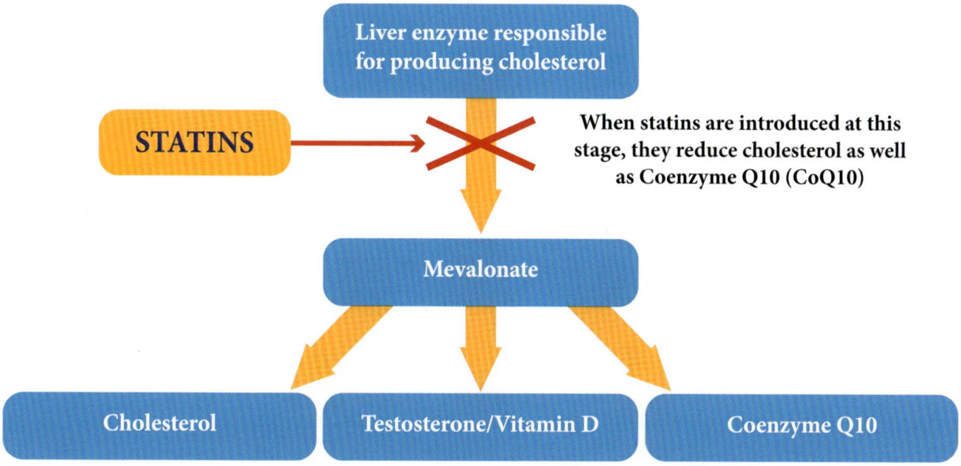

It's well known among integrative cardiologists that heart failure (HF) patients have low blood concentrations of CoQ10. Although CoQ10 is made naturally in the body, production falls off as we age. It is also blocked by certain medications, including statin drugs. A group of New Zealand doctors tested the hypothesis that CoQ10 blood levels are a predictor of total mortality in HF. They took blood samples from 236 hospitalized HF patients and then followed them for an average of 2.7 years. The researchers concluded that CoQ10 concentration in the blood is an independent predictor of mortality and that a deficiency is indeed associated with worse outcomes in HF.

A study conducted at Japan's Toyama University Hospital followed 29 patients with significant coronary artery disease (CAD), none of whom had overt HF. All 29 received either 5 or 10 mg of a well known statin drug once daily for three months. At the end of the study, the researchers found that most participants had a lower blood level of CoQ10 than they had at the trial's start. They noted that as cholesterol goes down, so does CoQ10. The greater the reduction in cholesterol levels, the more significant the drop in vital CoQ10 levels. This study reconfirms that regular treatment with statins depletes CoQ10.

- More than 35 controlled clinical trials in Japan, Europe and the U.S. have proven that CoQ10 therapy is highly effective in treatment of congestive heart failure, angina and ischemic heart disease, and myocardial infarction.

Getting your daily need of CoQ10

You can get your CoQ10 through foods you eat such as meat, poultry and fish in that order. 3 ounces of beef for instance will get you about 2.6 mg. of CoQ10. 3 ounces of oily fish such as herring will get you 2.3 mg and 3 ounces of chicken will get you 1.4 mg (nuts, seeds and whole grains also contain CoQ10 to a lesser degree).

It is estimated that most people don't get more than 10 mg from foods. Since cells will absorb and utilize CoQ10 made available in the blood, consuming foods and supplements with CoQ10 can make up for deficiencies caused by age, malnutrition, or drug interference. A healthy, youthful human body can make its own CoQ10. Endogenous production or biosynthesis of CoQ10 has 17 steps, requiring at least seven vitamins (vitamin B2 - riboflavin, vitamin B3 - niacinamide, vitamin B6, folic acid, vitamin B12, vitamin C, and pantothenic acid) and several trace elements.

Researcher Dr. John Ely, of the University of Washington, holds that CoQ10 supplementation is essential in the aged. Most people make approximately 500 mg of Coq10 daily in the body, at least up until age 21.

However, between ages 21 and 30, levels of CoQ10 begin to drop, perhaps because of aging. This causes the degeneration of cells, which may contribute to age-related diseases and conditions such as high blood pressure, arthritis, heart disease and the breakdown of skin tissue. Statin drugs and deficiencies in several other vitamins also cause blood levels of CoQ10 to drop. To reiterate; statin drugs, (as well as tricyclic antidepressants and beta blockers) deplete CoQ10 and if CoQ10 is not given at the same time as these drugs, cardiomyopathy or CHF may result.

Relatively good food-based sources of CoQ10 include animal products such as beef, pork and chicken with organ meats such as the heart ranking highest. But as you can see from the above you do not get a lot from food sources and that's why I personally take 200 mg CoQ10 every day.

CoQ10 Typical Daily Dosages

- 90 - 250 mg daily for the prevention of cardiovascular and periodontal diseases;
- 180 - 360 mg daily if you have hypertension and heavy exerciser;
- 300 - 600 mg daily for those with CHF (Start with 180 mg and work up to 300+ mg over three weeks);
- 600 - 1,200+ mg daily for people with Parkinson's disease and other debilitating illness such as cancer

Recommended dose: Take at least 100–300 mg of CoQ10 daily if you have any form of heart disease (the most serious cases and those people taking a statin to lower LDL cholesterol levels may require even more). For best results, take CoQ10 in divided doses with your meals. It's more readily absorbed with food (especially some fat). Always consult with your healthcare provider before taking any supplementation.

High cholesterol is a warning to you to control inflammation, not to go on a statin or to start eating those idiotic low fat low cholesterol foods. Inflammation in the body generates C-reactive protein, which in turn causes the body to respond with soothing, repairing, life-saving cholesterol. C-reactive protein is a measure of the body's history of inflammation and a far better predictor of heart attacks than cholesterol levels.

Vitamin C and fish oil have both been proven to reduce your C-reactive proteins better than statin drugs ever will! Tufts University, Berkeley, Seattle's University of Washington School of Medicine, Linus Pauling Institute and others have beaten statin drug statistics with as little as 500 mg a day of vitamin C. When studied, heart attack rates in vitamin C groups have fallen but the statin drug users still had "heart events", fatal heart attacks, and the usual accompanying diabetes risk.

Peter H. Langsjoen, MD has said, *"We are now in a position to witness the unfolding of the greatest medical tragedy of all time - never before in history has the medical establishment knowingly created a life threatening nutrient (CoQ10) deficiency in millions of otherwise healthy people".*

One in three people over the age of 45 in the UK currently takes statins. That's a staggering 7 million people. It costs the National Health Service £450 million per year to fulfill these prescriptions... which goes straight into the pockets of the drug companies and their consultants in the medical establishment. And I would like to know how many of those 7 million not only know the potential dangers of statins but also know if they are taking the statin then they MUST, in my opinion, take CoQ10.

All kinds of other problems can occur as well when your cholesterol levels get too low, including episodes of violent behaviour, depressive symptoms, hormonal imbalances, memory loss, stroke, violent behaviour, suicide and even Parkinson's disease. This is why keeping your cholesterol levels higher may actually help you to prevent disease as many studies confirm this. In 2007 a meta-analysis of over 41,000 patient records found that people who take statin drugs to lower their cholesterol as much as possible may have a higher risk of cancer, and research since has confirmed the significant association between low cholesterol and cancer mortality.

Since we cannot possibly eat enough cholesterol to use for our bodies' daily functions, our bodies make their own. When we eat more foods rich in this compound, our bodies make less. If we deprive ourselves of foods high in cholesterol -- such as eggs, butter, and liver — our body revs up its cholesterol synthesis. The end result is that, for most of us, eating foods high in cholesterol has very little impact on our blood cholesterol levels.

The way the body transports fats and cholesterol into the body is really interesting according to senior research scientist Stephanie Senaff, from the Massachusetts Institute of technology's Computer Science and Artificial Intelligence Laboratory. "The fat & cholesterol doesn't go directly into the bloodstream from the gut. Instead, it gets shipped through the lymph nodes and it arrives at the big vein that goes to the heart. Basically, it wants to direct cholesterol and fat toward the heart to give it first dabs. The body has to make sure the heart gets plenty of this first because it knows the heart needs fat and cholesterol, and the gut stands ready to give it to the heart. That's got to be by design to tell us that the heart needs cholesterol and fat. Everything else just goes straight to the liver before being used elsewhere in the body".

Stress can also increase cholesterol. Why? Cholesterol is needed to make stress-fighting hormones such as cortisone and cortisol. A body under excessive stress (from internal or external sources) may produce extra cholesterol to increase the anti-stress hormones.

L-Carnitine, Fat and the Heart

Combining CoQ10 with another nutrient called L-Carnitine is very effective at improving the heart's function. L-carnitine is a compound produced by the liver and kidneys from the biosynthesis of the amino acids lysine and methionine. To form L-carnitine you also need adequate levels of folic acid, vitamin C, B6, niacin, and iron. The name carnitine is derived from the Latin 'camus' for flesh as carnitine was first isolated from meat sources. Carnitine is the gatekeeper for fat burning, it picks up fat and dumps it into the mitochondria for burning to create ATP. The more carnitine present, the more fat burnt.

The heart is a fat hog and this is essential for the heart to fire on all cylinders. Since the heart is our hardest-working muscle, it is no surprise that carnitine improves myocardial metabolism. This is evidenced by increased fatty-acid uptake by the mitochondria, and higher concentrations of ATP and creatine phosphate (a storage form of ATP) in the heart tissue after carnitine supplementation.

A normal heart muscle derives 60-70% of its fuel from fat. That means anyone with heart disease or a weak heart will have a hard time getting better without addressing the problem of fat delivery inside the heart muscle. There is also the well-documented finding that L-Carnitine lowers triglycerides, and this alone dramatically lowers the risk of heart disease. Lower plasma triglycerides means that blood is less thick with fats, and can move more easily even through the narrow capillaries. And since carnitine also raises HDL cholesterol, blood vessels stay cleaner, again improving blood flow. L-carnitine is also a vasodilator meaning it opens blood vessels and increases blood flow to your heart, muscles and other tissues, resulting in better overall oxygen use by your body.

L-Carnitine is essential for our mitochondria to burn fat and as tthe heart contains the highest amount of motochondria than anywhere else in the body it is essential we have adequate supplies of L-Carnitine to give the heart the fuel it thrives on. YES FAT!

Studies have shown that patients with congestive heart failure (CHF) who take L-carnitine have improved ejection fraction (Goa KL et al 1987; Mancini M et al 1992; Pucciarelli G et al 1992). In a study published in April, 2003 - L-Carnitine was found to help protect the heart from lack of oxygen and from oxygen free radicals. Taking carnitine at 1.5 to 6 grams per day for up to one year resulted in fewer deaths and less heart failure episodes in heart attack patients. Compared to placebo, carnitine use was found to slow heart enlargement over time. In one human trial, carnitine also improved exercise tolerance and the strength of respiratory muscles in COPD (Chronic Obstructive Pulmonary Disease) patients; levels of the metabolic by-product lactate, which causes fatigue, were also reduced (Borghi-Silva A et al 2006).

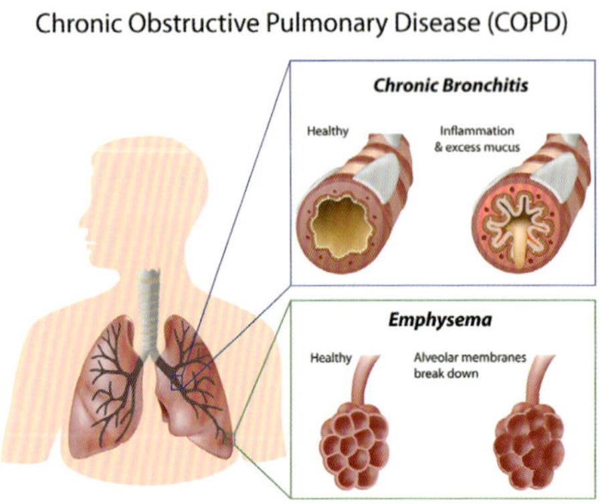

Equally important, carnitine transports waste material out of the mitochondria, such as toxic metabolites that could otherwise disturb the burning of fats and cause disruption inside of cells. The human body is a high energy machine. It creates a lot of toxic waste and accumulates outside toxins as well. **In the interest of getting rid of the gunk and maintaining good health over a lifetime, carnitine gives you a huge detoxification weapon.**

The typical non-vegetarian, Western diet provides around 100-300 mg of carnitine per day. The amount has decreased by an estimated 20% over the last decade, mainly as a result of people eating less red meat. Ovo-lacto-vegetarians (egg and dairy eating vegetarians) have an intake of about 10-40 mg, and strict vegetarians, maybe around 1-4 mg. When you truly understand the nutritional requirements of the body you will soon come to the conclusion that a vegan/vegetarian is simply not going to deliver optimal health.

Food sources of carnitine include meat, poultry, fish, and dairy products are the richest sources of L-carnitine. Grains, fruits, and vegetables contain little or no carnitine.

Research indicates that when your muscles are loaded with carnitine, it can help reduce the breakdown of amino acids that make up your muscle proteins for energy production. So preventing the use of amino acids for energy reduces the breakdown of muscles. When you exercise, if your body uses amino acids for energy, breakdown of muscle mass invariably occurs. In addition to proper protein intake, higher amounts of carnitine in your muscles can deter the use of amino acids for energy production during exercise, and therefore help protect against muscle breakdown and damage.

Studies have shown that, at doses of 1-3 g, carnitine reduces blood triglycerides. Carnitine combines with enzymes found in the mitochondrial membrane to transport fatty acids into the interior of the mitochondria, where they are oxidized to provide fuel for the generation of energy. In the absence of carnitine, fatty acids are not oxidized, but, instead, are transformed into dangerous triglycerides.

According to Robert Crayhon (author of "The Miracle of Carnitine") due to high consumption of red meat, the Stone Age hunter probably got at least 500 mg of carnitine a day, and possibly as much as 2 grams. Today the average carnitine intake is estimated at a mere 30 to 50 mg a day. Strict vegetarians consume practically no carnitine.

Giving your heart the nutrients it needs such as CoQ10, carnitine, D-ribose and magnesium will help keep it stronger for many years to come.

D-Ribose

Studies have shown that supplemental D-ribose can increase exercise tolerance, especially in those with cardiovascular problems.

While coenzyme CoQ10 and L-carnitine both directly support ATP recycling, the most efficient means of cardiac energy metabolism, D-ribose helps ensure there's enough original ATP synthesized for your mitochondria to recycle. Some exciting studies have emerged showing how D-ribose affects active human heart tissue and its function. Investigators have shown how increased ATP levels translate into improved heart muscle function & better blood flow.

Pauly DF, Pepine CJ. Ischemic heart disease: metabolic approaches to management. Clin Cardiol. 2004 Aug;27(8):439-41. Pauly DF, Johnson C, St Cyr JA. The benefits of ribose in cardiovascular disease. Med Hypotheses. 2003 Feb;60(2):149-51

There's excellent science to back up the idea that D-ribose is good for working muscles. Exercise physiologists have shown that supplementing the muscles with D-ribose increases the total amount of ATP produced by up to four-fold, providing a substantial "bank" of energy that could be called on for use when needed. When physiologists in Missouri provided D-ribose to working muscles, they demonstrated as much as a six-fold rise in the rate at which ATP components were recycled for use (recycling ATP is much faster and more efficient than building it from scratch).

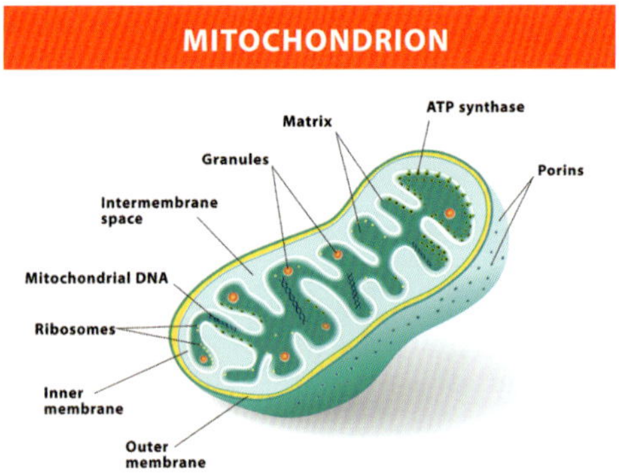

Humans "burn" an amount of ATP equivalent to their own body weight every day!

What Exactly is D-Ribose

D-ribose is a 5-carbon monosaccharide (sugar) molecule found in every living organism which facilitates the production of cell energy. D-ribose is a part of the ATP molecule which is used as the energy currency of cells. The body can manufacture ribose from glucose in something called the Pentose Phosphate Pathway [PPP]- this is a slow process which requires an enzyme called glucose-6-phosphate dehydrogenase (G- 6-PDH), an enzyme that is typically in short supply. The Pentose Phosphate Pathway is variable between organs and Glucose-6-phosphate dehydrogenase (G- 6-PDH) is an enzyme that has limited expression in the heart with significant delay in the production of ribose via glucose if there is injury to the heart. Supplemental ribose by-passes this enzymatic step to rapidly replenish ATP levels in heart and muscle.

Dosage - How much D-Ribose do you need?

How much D-ribose do you need? That question can only be answered with another question, "What do you want it to do for you?"

- 5 grams two to three times a day can be used for heart conditions or peripheral vascular disease.
- 5 grams pre and post-exercise can also be used to help supply and restore ATP levels
- 10-15 grams daily for most patients with heart failure, other forms of ischemic cardiovascular disease, or peripheral vascular disease, for individuals recovering from heart surgery or heart attack, for treatment of stable angina, and for athletes working out in chronic bouts of high-intensity exercise
- 15-30 grams daily for patients with advanced heart failure, dilated cardiomyopathy, or frequent angina, for individuals awaiting heart transplant, and for people with fibromyalgia or neuromuscular disease.

Strenuously exercised muscle may have lowered levels of ATP by 20% and it may then take 3 - 4 days to replenish these ATP levels. Supplementing with ribose can increase the replenishment of ATP by up to 4 times. Human cells can manufacture D-ribose. However, when muscle has been stressed by injury or due to high energy demands, the cells may not be able to produce enough D-ribose for ATP production. In other words, the cells have trouble keeping up with the demand for this simple sugar.

Red meat, particularly veal, contains the highest dietary concentration of D-ribose, but not significant enough to provide any meaningful nutritional support, especially to unwell individuals.

Every cell in the human body makes some of this simple sugar molecule, but only slowly and to varying degrees, depending on the tissue. The liver, adrenal glands, and fat tissue produce the most—enough to serve their purpose of making compounds involved in the production of hormones and fatty acids.

> ***"We cannot overstate the effect of D-ribose supplementation on maintaining energy levels. Any tissue that relies heavily on aerobic energy metabolism, such as the heart and muscles, will be severely affected by any amount of oxygen deprivation. The problem is ATP drain. The solution is to give it back!"***
>
> **Dr Stephan Sinatra & Dr James Roberts**

Supplemental D-ribose absorbs easily and quickly through the gut and into the bloodstream. About 97% gets through. Studies have shown that any amount of D-ribose you give to energy-starved cells gives them an energy boost. At the University of Missouri, researcher Ronald Terjung has shown that even very small doses (the equivalent of about 500 mg) of D-ribose increase energy salvage in muscles by more than 100%. Larger doses increase the production of energy compounds by 340-430%, depending on the type of muscle tested, and improve the salvage of energy compounds by up to 650%. Most amazing is that when muscles are supplemented with D-ribose, they continue to add to their energy stores even while they actively work! Until this study was reported, it was thought that muscle energy stores were only refilled in muscles at rest.

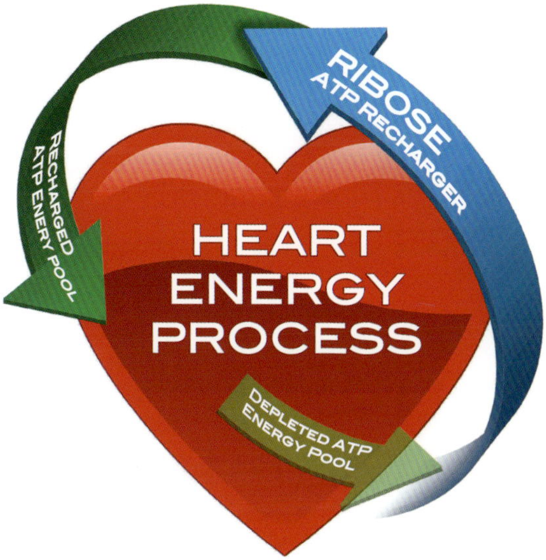

6 Kilograms (13.2lbs) of ATP are needed for the 86,400 beats your heart produces each day. This recycles the ATP pool 10,000 times.

Ribose helps recharge depleted ATP energy.

The D-ribose connection to cardiac function was made by the physiologist Heinz-Gerd Zimmer at the University of Munich. In 1973, he reported that energy-starved hearts could recover faster if D-ribose was given prior to, or immediately following, ischemia (oxygen deprivation). Five years later, he reported the same effect in skeletal muscle and also showed for the first time that the energy-draining effects of drugs that make the heart beat more strongly (inotropic agents) could be lessened if D-ribose was given along with the drug. Zimmer and his research colleagues later proved that D-ribose was the limiting element in energy recovery in ischemic tissue and that energy synthesis could not occur without it.

A clinical study from Zimmer's group in Munich in 1992 showed that D-ribose administration to patients with severe, stable coronary artery disease increased exercise tolerance and delayed the onset of moderate angina. Several other notable papers were published in 2003. One study showed that D-ribose improved diastolic functional performance of the heart, increased exercise tolerance, and significantly improved the quality of life of heart patients.

Patients with arterial and heart disease who chronically choke off oxygen delivery to their tissues need to take a higher dosage simply to allow enough of it to work its way through the clogged vessels into the energy-parched portions of the heart.

A study published in the International Journal of Cardiology stated: *"Ribose, a pentose monosaccharide, has shown to replenish low myocardial energy levels, improving cardiac dysfunction following ischemia, and improving ventilation efficiency in patients with heart failure."*

In studies of healthy athletes, supplying fatigued muscle cells with D-ribose quickly restored cell energy to normal levels. *Am J Physiol Regul Integr Comp Physiol. 2004 Jan;286(1):R182-8.*

D-ribose can also lower blood glucose levels; therefore, insulin-dependent diabetics should check with their physicians before starting on the supplement.

As you can see, D-ribose is a very important component of our ATP and so, therefore, an important part of our bodies.

Magnesium Is Essential For Heart Function

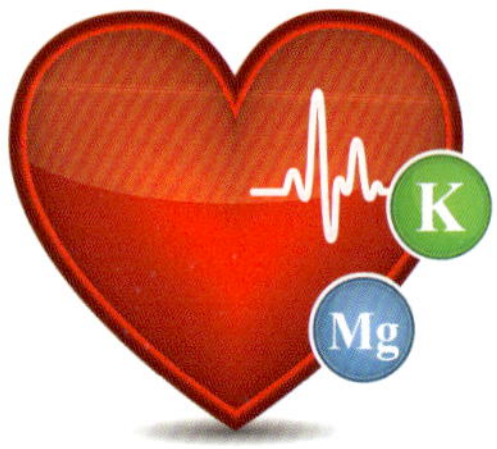

Since all enzymatic reactions involving ATP have an absolute requirement for magnesium, it makes perfect sense to include magnesium to any program which wants to enhance heart function. Magnesium is vitally important in regulating what goes into and what comes out of all the body's cells. If the level of magnesium within cells fall below normal, calcium and sodium rush inside while potassium and magnesium leak out.

If this occurs in heart cells, normal function is impaired and there is a tendency towards excess contraction which can cause big problems for the heart. Magnesium can reduce your risk of sudden cardiac death by nearly 40%, according to a study out of the University of Minnesota. Researchers measured the serum levels of magnesium in more than 14,000 patients. In that group, those who had the highest level of magnesium reduced their risk of sudden cardiac arrest (heart attack) by 38%.

Magnesium can also be amazingly effective at calming down erratic and excitable heartbeats, a leading cause of sudden cardiac arrest. A ten-year study of 2,182 men in Wales found that those eating magnesium-low diets had a 50% higher risk of sudden death from heart attacks than those eating one-third more magnesium.

With insufficient magnesium the muscles stay tense and, through the years, may cause a cramp in the muscle. This could happen when you have too much calcium or too little magnesium. Too much calcium causes the heart to go into a spasm and this can cause a heart attack.

Magnesium has a stabilizing effect on cell membranes, particularly in heart muscle. A healthy heart generates stable, predictable electrical impulses. Lack of magnesium permits unstable electrical impulses in the heart to emerge, generating abnormal heart rhythms. The beneficial effects of magnesium in preventing heart disease relate to its ability improve energy production within the heart; dilate the coronary arteries resulting in improved delivery of oxygen to the heart; reduce peripheral vascular resistance resulting in reduced demand on the heart; inhibit platelets from aggregating and forming blood clots; and improve heart rate.

Many patients with CHF have a magnesium deficiency. The level of magnesium in the blood correlates with the ability of the heart muscle to manufacture enough energy to beat properly. Many disorders of heart rhythm are related to an insufficient level of magnesium in the heart muscle.

The real dangers of Beta Blockers

Beta-blockers are drugs commonly used in the treatment of high blood pressure and congestive heart failure. They work primarily by blocking the neurotransmitters norepinephrine and epinephrine (adrenaline) from binding to beta receptors, thereby dilating blood vessels, which reduces your heart rate and blood pressure.

Until recently, the European Society of Cardiology (ESC) also recommended using beta-blockers in patients undergoing non-cardiac surgery.

An article published in *Forbes Magazine* **(Forbes January 15, 2014)** highlights how medical guidelines based on questionable science may have resulted in the death of hundreds of thousands of patients in just a few years: *"British researchers provoked concern when they published a paper raising the possibility that by following an established guideline UK doctors may have caused as many as 10,000 deaths each year,"* **(Forbes July 31, 2013)** Larry Husten, editorial director of WebMD professional news, writes.

"Now, they have gone a step further and published an estimate that the same guideline may have led to the deaths of as many as 800,000 people in Europe over the last five years **(European Heart Journal 2014: 35(3); 131-137)**. *The 800,000 deaths are comparable in size to the worst cases of genocide and mass murder in recent history."*

Magnesium is a natural beta blocker and may reduce blood pressure in people with high blood pressure, according to new findings.

A study adds to data from epidemiological studies that have reported more magnesium, potassium, and calcium may reduce your risk of hypertension.

Researchers recruited 155 people to take part in a double-blinded, placebo-controlled, randomized trial. The subjects were randomly assigned to receive either daily supplements of magnesium oxide or a placebo for 12 weeks.

At the end of the study, no significant differences were at first observed. However, when the researchers looked specifically at hypertension, significant decreases in both systolic and diastolic blood pressure were observed in the magnesium group.

One out of three people have hypertension, or high blood pressure. This is a common and serious health concern, as uncontrolled hypertension can cause heart disease and increase your risk of having a stroke. It's especially dangerous because it often has no warning signs or symptoms.

You are generally diagnosed with pre-hypertension if your blood pressure is between 120/80 and 140/80, and anything above 140/80 is generally diagnosed as hypertension. The first number is your systolic pressure, which should typically be below 120. The second number is your diastolic pressure, which should typically be below 80. If either your systolic or diastolic number is higher than the typical 120/80, you may get a diagnosis of hypertension or pre-hypertension.

Fortunately many people who have hypertension can normalize their blood pressure through lifestyle modifications, and making sure you're getting enough magnesium would be a good start.

Why Magnesium Is Important for Healthy Blood Pressure and Heart Function

The above study found significant decreases in both systolic and diastolic blood pressure among people with hypertension after taking a magnesium supplement for just 12 weeks.

This lends further support to the immense role this mineral plays in your health. In fact, magnesium is the fourth most abundant mineral in your body and is responsible for the function of over 350 enzymes in your body, including the:

- Creation of ATP (adenosine triphosphate), the energy molecules of your body
- Action of your heart muscle
- Proper formation of bones and teeth
- Relaxation of blood vessels
- Promotion of proper bowel function
- Regulation of blood sugar levels

In your heart, magnesium is particularly important, and doctors have been prescribing magnesium for heart disease since the 1930s.

A review of seven major clinical studies showed that IV magnesium reduced the odds of death by more than half in patients suffering from a heart attack.

One study, LIMIT-2, developed a protocol for giving magnesium as soon as possible after onset of the heart attack and before any other drugs. If those criteria were followed, heart muscle damage was greatly reduced, and neither hypertension nor arrhythmia (abnormal heartbeat) developed.

Magnesium may offer these benefits because in your heart it helps:

- Dilate blood vessels
- Prevent spasm in your heart muscle and blood vessel walls
- Counteract the action of calcium, which increases spasm
- Dissolve blood clots
- Dramatically lessen the site of injury and prevent arrhythmia
- Act as an antioxidant against the free radicals forming at the site of injury

Signs You May Not Be Getting Enough Magnesium

It's been estimated that up to 80 percent of the population is deficient in this important mineral, according to Carolyn Dean, MD, ND, author of *The Miracle of Magnesium*. Further, there has been no lab test that will give an accurate reading of the magnesium status in your tissues. Only one percent of magnesium in your body is distributed in your blood, making a simple sample of magnesium from a blood test often highly inaccurate.

That's why most doctors who rely on blood tests for magnesium, and not magnesium deficiency signs and symptoms and the realization that up to 80 percent of the population is deficient, will miss an important diagnosis.

With that in mind, some early signs of magnesium deficiency to keep an eye out for include:

- Loss of appetite
- Nausea and vomiting
- Fatigue and weakness

An ongoing magnesium deficiency can lead to:

- Numbness and tingling
- Muscle contractions and cramps
- Seizures
- Personality changes
- Abnormal heart rhythms
- Coronary spasms

The Most Common Cause of High Blood Pressure

Magnesium deficiency may contribute to high blood pressure, but the most common underlying cause is typically related to your body producing too much insulin. **As your insulin levels rise, it causes your blood pressure to increase.**

Research published in 1998 in the journal *Diabetes* reported that nearly two-thirds of the test subjects who were insulin resistant also had high blood pressure.

This crucial connection between insulin resistance and hypertension is yet another example of how wide-ranging the debilitating effects of high insulin and blood glucose levels really are.

I recommend you get a fasting insulin level test done by your doctor, especially if you're struggling with high blood pressure. The level you want to strive for is about 2 or 3. If it's 5, or over 10, you have a problem and you ***MUST*** lower your insulin levels to lower your risk of high blood pressure and other cardiovascular problems.

Fortunately, there are a few very simple techniques that will lower your insulin levels as discussed multiple times throughout this book and from a dietary perspective nothing is more effective than going on a ketogenic diet.

An alternative approach is to use magnesium supplements, because calcium and magnesium both compete for the same receptor sites in smooth muscle. When calcium lands in those sites it induces spasm, but magnesium doesn't. If high enough levels of magnesium are maintained in the blood, the magnesium will land in those sites in place of the calcium and prevent the spasms in the same way that calcium blockers do. This supports the idea that magnesium supplements can play a role in preventing heart disease.

Foods rich in magnesium include fish and seafood, leafy green vegetables, soy products, brown rice, bananas, apricots, seeds and nuts. The foods highest in magnesium include kelp, tofu, figs and pumpkin seeds.

Taurine

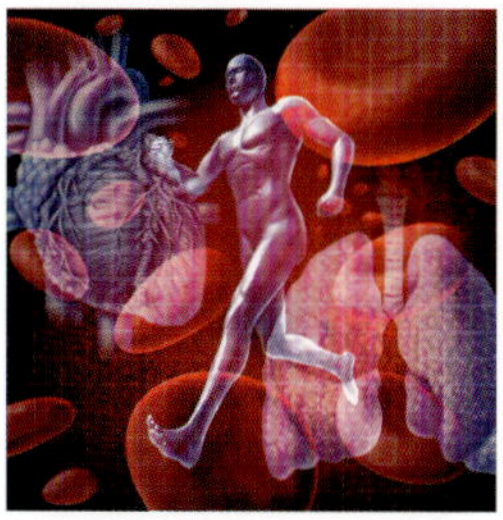

Taurine is the most abundant amino acid in the heart and has been shown to improve nitric oxide production in the vascular endothelium, which is essential to optimal blood flow, maintaining already normal blood pressure, and overall cardiovascular functioning. Taurine is an important amino acid in our body. It is found mostly in our central nervous system, skeletal muscle, and in greater concentration in our heart and brain. It is made from two sulphur containing amino acids called methionine and cysteine which are found in egg yolk and meat as well. Taurine is commonly found in animal protein and not in vegetable protein. Vegetarians with a low intake of protein may have difficulty producing taurine in their bodies

In the cell, taurine keeps potassium and magnesium inside the cell while keeping excessive sodium out. In this sense it works like a diuretic. But unlike prescription diuretics, it is not a cellular poison. There have been studies showing the positive effectiveness of taurine on heart failure. Aside from having diuretic properties, taurine is able to strengthen the heart muscles and maintain proper calcium balance. Together with Coq10 and carnitine, taurine is able to regulate the heart's contractility.

Working together with magnesium, taurine also is able to regulate heart rhythm and help to stabilize it, At high taurine concentrations, any excess fluid in your blood and tissues surrounding your heart is flushed out, leading to lower blood pressure and reduced cardiac stress. Taurine also inhibits the action of angiotensin II, the hormone that increases blood vessel constriction. Increased taurine concentration allows blood vessels to expand which further reduces your blood pressure and your risk of strokes and coronary heart disease.

Taurine is found in abundance in the myocardium of the heart. It helps to modulate the low voltage-dependent calcium channel which allows the transmission of action potential whereby triggering contraction of heart muscles. Low taurine levels can reduce the strength of heart muscle contraction and cardiac output. Sustained deficiency can increase your risk of cardiomyopathy Taurine also partners with magnesium to maintain proper heart rhythm, and has been used as an effective treatment for cardiac arrhythmia.

Research on taurine suggests that it may be beneficial for those patients with congestive heart failure conditions. In a clinical trial with 14 patients where the patients served as their own control group via a crossover study design, 79% improved with 4 weeks of taurine supplementation compared to 21% on placebo.

Taurine must also be present to make bile acid, which enables fat and cholesterol metabolism. Supplementation with taurine has been used in combination with coenzyme Q10 to prevent and treat atherosclerosis and hyperlipidemia.

Hawthorn - The Wonder Berry For Your Heart

Another nutrient called hawthorn works with CoQ10 to increase energy in the heart muscle, improves circulation in the coronary arteries and helps to regulate blood pressure. The extract of hawthorn can increase blood flow to the heart muscle itself. In pharmacological tests on both animals and humans, hawthorn has been shown to improve the contractility of the heart muscle (which can lead to a stronger pumping action of the heart), increase cardiac performance and output, lower the peripheral vascular resistance (reducing the workload of the heart), steady the heartbeat (anti-arrhythmic effect), as well as increasing the heart's tolerance to oxygen deficiency, such as might happen during stress or excitement, or in diseases where the arteries are partially blocked.

A four year study on the benefits of hawthorn, commissioned by the German Ministry of Health, found that it improves contractions in the veins and heart while dilating the heart. This increases blood flow in the heart as well as flow speed throughout the body for increased circulation to organs and musculature. The researchers concluded that hawthorn is best used for low heart function, congestion, arrhythmia and tightness in the chest and no side effects were noted (Hoffmann 1995).

A German clinical trial with 18 healthy patients found that hawthorn lowered heart rate and blood pressure during exercise and maintained resting heart rate while elevations were noted in the control group (Hellenbrecht, et. al. 1990). Chinese laboratory and clinical trials have reported that hawthorn lowers cholesterol and triglycerides by improving excretion (Chang & But 1986). Hawthorn is also reported to increase urination (Hoffmann 1995), often an important modality in heart conditions.

A recent scientific review of all double-blind controlled studies on hawthorn (of which there are many) found a "significant benefit in symptom control and physiologic outcomes from hawthorn extract as an adjunctive treatment for chronic heart failure." Hawthorn was shown to improve the heart's maximum workload, which resulted in improved exercise tolerance. Shortness of breath and fatigue were significantly improved, and the heart's ability to use oxygen was enhanced. These are very significant findings for a dietary supplement. ***Hawthorn Helps Heart Failure Cochrane Database of Systematic Reviews Pittler MH, Guo R, Ernst E.***

On the back of all this research I developed a product called Cardio Fuel:

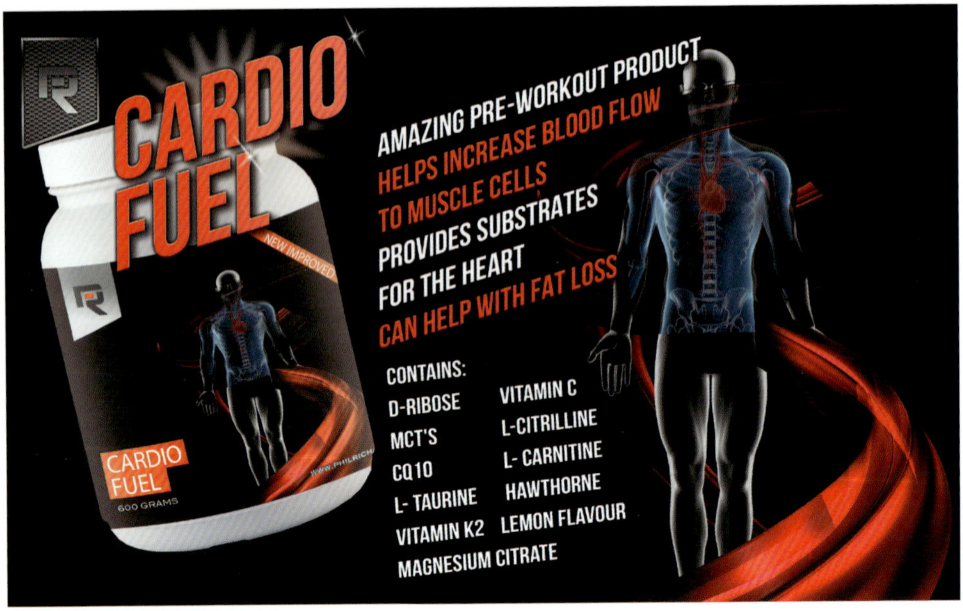

Omega-3 and heart disease prevention

I have talked extensively about the benefits of omega-3 but here is just another sampling, this time in regards to the health of the cardiovascular system:

- Anti-arrhythmic: counteracting or preventing cardiac arrhythmia
- Anti-thrombotic: tending to prevent thrombosis (a blood clot within a blood vessel)
- Anti-atherosclerotic: preventing fatty deposits and fibrosis of the inner layer of your arteries from forming
- Anti-inflammatory: counteracting inflammation (heat, pain, swelling, etc.)

Makes you wonder why the medical profession do not prescribe pharmaceutical grade fish oil instead of warfarin (rat poison) when the fish oil does the same thing but without the toxicity and side effects of rat poison. The medical profession really need to WAKE UP because what they are doing presently SIMPLY DOES NOT WORK!

Omega-3s also improve endothelial function: a major factor in promoting the growth of new blood vessels. Researchers have found that omega-3 oils stop the buildup of fatty deposits in the arteries, which is why oily fish and fish oils protect against heart disease and stroke.

Researchers at the University of Edinburgh suggest that fish oils prevent the platelet activation involved in the formation of atherosclerotic lesions and blood clots (thrombosis). A study in The European Journal of Clinical Nutrition found that increasing the omega-3's from fish and fish oil reduce the risk of heart failure by 25%.

Studies have shown that omega-3 fatty acids combat the development and progression of vascular disease via multiple mechanisms including, lowering triglycerides, lowering blood pressure, improving endothelial function and raising HDL levels ***(Robinson, 2006).*** In another study involving 563 elderly men, 2.4 grams per day of omega-3 fatty acid supplementation was found to improve arterial elasticity ***(Hjerkinn, 2006).***

High levels of pro-inflammatory omega-6 fatty acids relative to anti-inflammatory omega-3 fatty acids create an environment that fosters inflammation and contributes to vascular disease. It has been shown that lowering the omega-6:omega-3 ratio significantly decreases atherosclerotic lesion size and reduces numerous measures of inflammation (Wan, 2010).I recommend maintaining a blood omega-6:omega-3 ratio of less than 4:1.

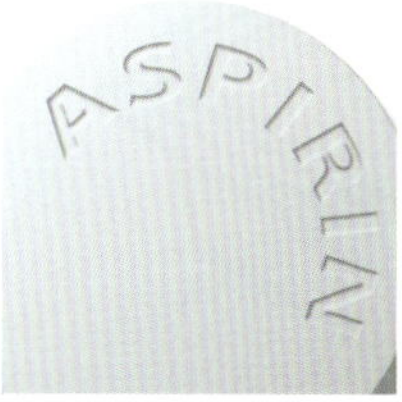

People who are diagnosed with heart failure and follow a treatment regimen that includes blood thinners such as aspirin or coumadin could be putting their health into more danger.

Researchers stated that just because heart failure patients stand a greater chance of experiencing a heart attack or stroke doesn't automatically make them appropriate candidates for antithrombotic therapy.

Study Comparing Blood-Thinning Therapies to no Antithrombotic Therapy

Participants included 279 patients who were diagnosed with heart failure that required diuretic therapy

Participants were divided into three groups, aspirin therapy, warfarin therapy and no antithrombotic therapy

Results of the Study

Aspirin and warfarin didn't provide the patients with any valuable health benefits

There didn't appear to be any substantial differences of incidences of death, nonfatal heart attacks or nonfatal stroke in the three groups of the study

Patients in the aspirin group had increased chances of experiencing serious gastrointestinal problems

Cases of minor bleeding complications were primarily seen among the aspirin and warfarin group

Patients in the aspirin therapy group were twice as likely as the patients in the warfarin group to face hospitalization for cardiovascular complications, particularly worsening cases of heart failure during the first 12 months following the study

Based on the results from this study, experts said that treatment of heart failure involving a multitude of drugs that proved to be ineffective should be eliminated as a treatment option.
American Heart Journal July 2004;148(1):157-64option.04;148(1):157-64

Believe it or not Margarine is BAD for our hearts!

Vegetable oils (and margarine, made from these oils) are oils extracted from seeds like the rapeseed (canola oil) soybean (soybean oil), corn, sunflower, safflower etc, all these oils are polyunsaturated fats which are exceptionally high in omega 6 fats which if you remember from habit 4 is a proinflammatory fat. They were practically non-existent in our diets until the early 1900s when new chemical processes allowed them to be extracted.

Remember margarine has no place in any humans' diet that values their health and well being!

Unlike butter or coconut oil, these vegetable oils can't be extracted just by pressing or separating naturally. They must be chemically removed, deodorized, and altered. These are some of the most chemically altered foods in our diets, yet they get promoted as healthy. Vegetable oils are found in practically every processed food, from salad dressing to mayo. These oils are some of the most harmful substances you can put into your body, no doubt about it! Vegetable oil was practically non-existent in its current form in the early 1900s.

Until that time, most people got their fats from animal sources like meat, tallow, lard, butter, eggs, cream, etc.

The overall amount of fat consumed has not changed much since then (it has decreased slightly) but the type has changed dramatically. In 1900 the amount of vegetable based oils that people consumed was basically none. Today, people consume, on average, many pounds of vegetable oils throughout the year through cooking and spreading this shit on their breads etc. Butter consumption at the turn of the century was eighteen pounds per person per year, and the use of vegetable oils almost nonexistent. Yet cancer and heart disease were rare. Today butter consumption hovers just above four pounds per person per year while vegetable oil consumption has soared–and cancer and heart disease are endemic. Since the 1950's these vegetable oils and their derivatives have been increasingly used in processed foods and for frying or cooking. They are marketed as healthy because they contain monounsaturated fats and some level of Omega 3 fatty acids.

The journal Epidemiology published a study called, "Margarine Intake and Subsequent Coronary Heart Disease in Men." Authors of the study followed participants of the Framingham Heart Study for 20 years and recorded their incidence of heart attack. They also tracked both butter and margarine consumption. The researchers discovered that as margarine consumption increased heart attacks went up. As butter consumption increased heart attacks declined. The study also divided the data into ten year increments. What they discovered is that during the first ten years, there was little association between margarine consumption and heart attacks. However, during the second decade of follow-up, the group eating the most margarine had 77% more heart attacks than the group eating none!

Since vegetable oils are chemically produced, its not really surprising that they contain harmful chemicals. Most vegetable oils and their products contain BHA and BHT (Butylated Hydroxyanisole and Butylated Hydroxytoluene) which are artificial antioxidants that help prevent food from oxidizing or spoiling too quickly. These chemicals have been shown to produce potential cancer causing compounds in the body, and have also been linked to liver/kidney damage, immune problems, infertility or sterility, high cholesterol, and behavioral problems in children. Vegetable oils also contain residues of the pesticides and chemicals used in their growth and manufacture and most often come from genetically modified sources.

Seriously, do not eat this crap. Either throw it or give it to someone you do not like!

You may be interested in a list of the ingredients that may be present in butter and margarine:

Butter:	Margarine:
• milk fat (cream), • a little salt,	• Edible oils, • edible fats, • salt or potassium chloride, • ascorbyl palmitate, • butylated hydroxyanisole, • phospholipids, • tert-butylhydroquinone, • mono- and di-glycerides of fat-forming fatty acids, • disodium guanylate, • diacetyltartaric and fatty acid esters of glycerol, • Propyl, octyl or dodecyl gallate (or mixtures thereof), • tocopherols, • propylene glycol mono- and di-esters, • sucrose esters of fatty acids, • curcumin, • annatto extracts, • tartaric acid, • 3,5,trimethylhexanal, • ß-apo-carotenoic acid methyl or ethyl ester, • skim milk powder, • xanthophylls, • canthaxanthin, • vitamins A and D.

The first process in the manufacture of margarine is the extraction of the oils from the seeds, and this is usually done using petroleum-based solvents. Although these are then boiled off, this stage of the process still leaves about ten parts per million of the solvents in the product. The oils then go through more than ten other processes: degumming, bleaching, hydrogenation, neutralization, fractionation, deodorisation, emulsification, interesterification that include heat treatment at 140-160C with a solution of caustic soda; the use of nickel, a metal that is known to cause cancer, as a catalyst, with up to fifty parts per million of the nickel left in the product; the addition of antioxidants such as butylated hydroxyanisol (E320). These antioxidants are again usually petroleum based and are widely believed to cause cancer.

The hydrogenation process, that solidifies the oils so that they are spreadable, produces trans -fatty acids that rarely occur in nature.

The heat treatment alone is enough to render these margarines nutritionally inadequate. When the massive chemical treatment and unnatural fats are added, the end product can hardly be called either natural or healthy.

Look at the diagram below to give you an indication on how margarine is processed then passed on as a health food - it is a total con in my book.

MARGARINE MANUFACTURING PROCESS

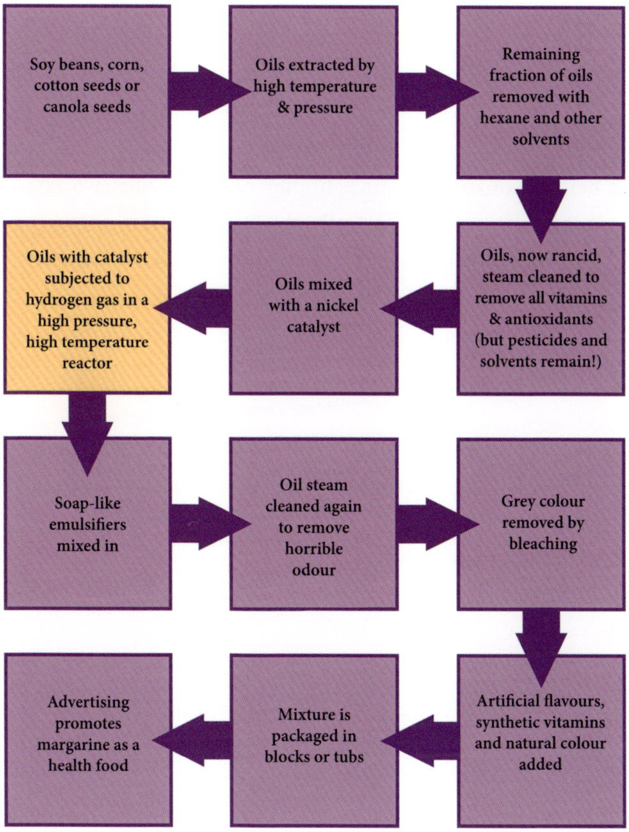

There are many problems with vegetable oil consumption, and in my opinion, no amount is safe. To understand why, let's look at a few of the biggest problems with vegetable oils.

The fat content of the human body is about 97% saturated and monounsaturated fat, with only 3 % polyunsaturated fats. Half of that three percent is Omega-3 fats, and that balance needs to be there. Vegetable oils contain very high levels of polyunsaturated fats, and these oils have replaced many of the saturated fats in our diets since the 1950s.

As we know the body needs fats for rebuilding cells and hormone production, but it has to use the building blocks we give it. When we give it a high concentration of polyunsaturated fats, instead of the ratios it needs, it has no choice but to incorporate these fats into our cells during cell repair and creation. The problem is that polyunsaturated fats are highly unstable and oxidize easily in the body (if they haven't already oxidized during processing or by light exposure while sitting on the grocery store shelf). These oxidized fats cause inflammation and mutations in cells. In arterial cells, these mutations cause inflammation that can clog arteries. When these fats are incorporated into skin cells, their mutation causes skin cancer. When these oils are incorporated into cells in reproductive tissue, some evidence suggests that this can spur problems like endometriosis and PCOS. In short, the body is made up of saturated and monounsaturated fats, and it needs these for optimal health.

I've talked before about how the body needs Omega-3 and Omega-6 fats in balance, preferably a 1:1 ratio. Most people consume a much higher ratio of Omega-6 fats, and this can lead to problems. Vegetable oils contain a very high concentration of Omega 6 fatty acids and polyunsaturated fats, which cause an imbalance of these oils in the body. Omega 6 fats are easily oxidized with heat or light exposure. This is another reason that when these types of fats/oils are incorporated into tissue like skin cells, the heat and light from sun exposure can increase skin cancer risk.

In one study performed at the University of Western Ontario, researchers observed the effects of ten different dietary fats ranging from most saturated to least saturated. What they found is that saturated fats produced the least number of cancers, while omega-6 polyunsaturated fats produced the most. Numerous other studies have also shown that polyunsaturated fats stimulate cancer while saturated fat does not and that saturated fats do not break down to form free radicals.

In another study, Dr. Vivienne Reeve, PhD, Head of the Photobiology Research Group at the University of Sydney irradiated a group of mice while feeding different groups of them polyunsaturated and saturated fats. She discovered that the mice that consumed only saturated fat were totally protected from skin cancer. Those in the polyunsaturated fat group quickly developed skin cancers. Later in the study, the mice in the saturated fat group were given polyunsaturated fats. Skin cancers quickly developed.

The 3% of our body that is made up of polyunsaturated fats is approximately half Omega-3 fatty acids and half Omega-6 fatty acids and our body needs this balance. Omega-3s have been shown to reduce inflammation and be protective against cancer, while too much Omega-6 fats cause inflammation and increase cancer risk. Remember vegetable oils are primarily omega 6 fats and in my opinion have no place in the diet of the human who seeks optimum health and well being.

Oils and Fats to Avoid:

Vegetable Oils and their fats should be avoided completely. There are much healthier alternatives and there is no reason or need to consume these types of fats. The main culprits to watch out for are:

- Canola Oil
- Corn Oil
- Soybean Oil
- “Vegetable” oil
- Peanut Oil
- Sunflower Oil
- Safflower Oil
- Cottonseed Oil
- Grapeseed Oil
- Margarine
- Shortening
- Any fake butter or vegetable oils products

So read the ingredients before you consume these damaging fats simply DO NOT consume or if so in small amounts.

Oils and Fats to Use Freely:

There are so many wonderful and healthy fats that are beneficial to the body, so there is no reason to consume the unhealthy ones above. Fats that can be consumed freely for optimal health are:

- Coconut Oil as discussed in habit 5 is filled with Medium Chain Fatty Acids and Lauric Acid, coconut oil is an all star of the saturated fats. Since the fat composition in cells in the body is largely saturated fat, it is important to get enough of it from healthy sources. Coconut oil does not oxidize easily at high temperatures or go rancid easily, making it a good choice for cooking and baking. It also makes a great natural moisturizer and can be substituted for butter.
- Meats – Meat, especially red meat, has gotten a bad rap, and unfortunately, the animals we eat have been as mistreated nutritionally as we have. Meats like grass fed beef and free range chicken has a very different nutritional profile than their feedlot counterparts. Grass fed and free range meats have higher nutrient levels, healthy forms of saturated fats and even omega-3s. If possible, consume these forms of meat.
- Butter- This one food is usually the one people are happiest to start using again. Butter tastes delicious, and pastured grass fed butter is an excellent source of fat soluble vitamins, healthy saturated fat and other nutrients. In contains a compound that Weston A. Price called Activator X, known to improve nutrient absorption and have preventative benefits against disease.
- Organic Cream- also a good source of healthy saturated fat, organic heavy cream is essentially liquid butter, and is great served whipped on top of fruit, in desserts or in cream based recipes.
- Olive Oil- High in monounsaturated fats and low in polyunsaturated fats, olive oil is a great oil for salad dressings, homemade mayo, and cold recipes. It shouldn't be used for cooking since its high monounsaturated fat content makes it susceptible to oxidation at high temperatures.
- Palm Oil- Has a high saturated fat content and is also heat stable.
- Avocados and Avocado Oil- A good source of monounsaturated fats and great on salads or in guacamole.
- Fish- Fish are naturally high in Omega-3 fatty acids and can help improve the Omega-3/Omega-6 balance in the body. Look for sustainable wild caught sources, and stick to small fish like tuna, sardines, salmon, etc to minimize mercury.
- Eggs- Another all-star in the healthy fats community, eggs are loaded with vitamins, healthy fats and necessary cholesterol. Consume them daily from free range sources.

Blood Vessels

Blood vessels are structures that carry the blood from the heart to all the tissues of the body and then back to the heart. As such, they must be constructed for carrying fluids over long distances, allowing for exchange of materials to and from the blood, and for vasoconstriction/vasodilation to alter blood flow.

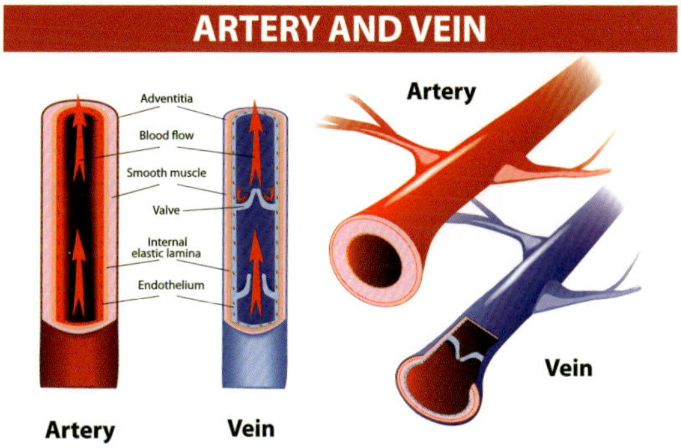

Our arteries carry oxygenated blood and our veins carry deoxygenated blood.

If you took all of the blood vessels out of an average adult, and laid them out in one line, the line would be around 60 000 - 100 000 miles long!

There are three varieties of blood vessels: arteries, veins, and capillaries. Arteries carry blood full of oxygen, picked up in the lungs after you inhale, away from the heart to every tissue of the body. As the blood travels further from the heart, the arteries get smaller and smaller. Soon they are so tiny, they are just one cell thick. Now they are called capillaries. There are capillaries lying right next to all of the tissues in the body. They will give off their oxygen and nutrients then take on carbon dioxide and wastes for excretion. Now the blood is "oxygen poor" and will start its trip back to the heart. The blood travels back to the heart in veins.

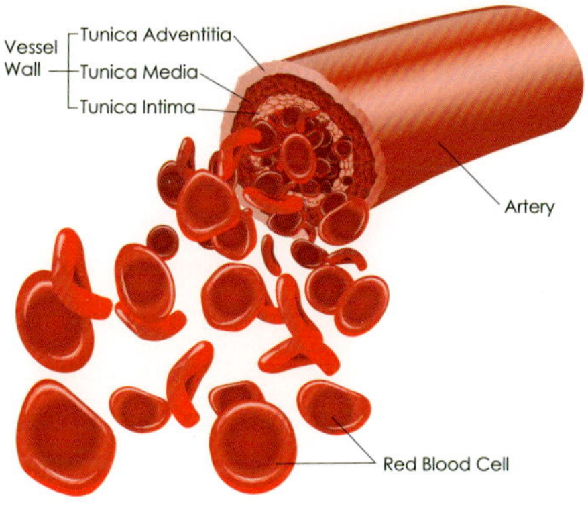

The different components of artery walls. Our arteries are the blood vessels which carry oxygenated blood around the body.

Probably the major underlying condition leading to cardiovascular disease is atherosclerosis, also known as hardening of the arteries. In time, this degenerative disease can narrow or block arteries in the heart, brain, and other parts of the body. It may begin early in life. The linings of the arteries become thickened and roughened by deposits of fat, cholesterol, fibrin (a clotting material), cellular debris, and calcium. As this build up on the inner walls becomes hard and thick, arteries lose their ability to expand and contract. The blood moves with difficulty through the narrowed channels. This makes it easier for a clot to form that will block the channel (lumen) and deprive the heart, brain, and other organs of the necessary blood supply.

Every second man and woman in the industrialized world dies from the consequences of atherosclerotic deposits in the coronary arteries (leading to heart attack) or in the arteries supplying blood to the brain (leading to stroke).

The endothelial cells form the barrier or protective layer between the blood and the blood vessel wall moreover, these cells contribute to a variety of metabolic functions, such as optimum blood viscosity. The smooth muscle cells produce collagen and other reinforcement molecules, providing optimum stability and tone to the blood vessel walls.

When the intercellular glue in your arteries becomes watery due to the lack of vitamin C, the first step of atherosclerosis has taken place. In contrast, a continuous and generous supply of vitamin C to the arterial linings keeps the ground substance in it's healthy, gel like state. As cardiologist Dr. Thomas Levy put it, *"The solitary root cause of all coronary arterial blockages is a vitamin C deficiency in the coronary arteries".*

Homo Sapiens, like the guinea pig, fruit bat and the high-order primates, cannot synthesize vitamin C because of a missing enzyme. Our ancestors lost this ability generations ago when an enzyme that was needed to convert sugar molecules (glucose) into vitamin C became defunct. This change in the molecules of inheritance (genes) of our ancestors had no immediate disadvantage since, for thousands of generations, they relied primarily on plant nutrition such as vegetables and fruit, which provided the daily minimum intake of vitamins for them. So we must obtain the vitamin in the diet.

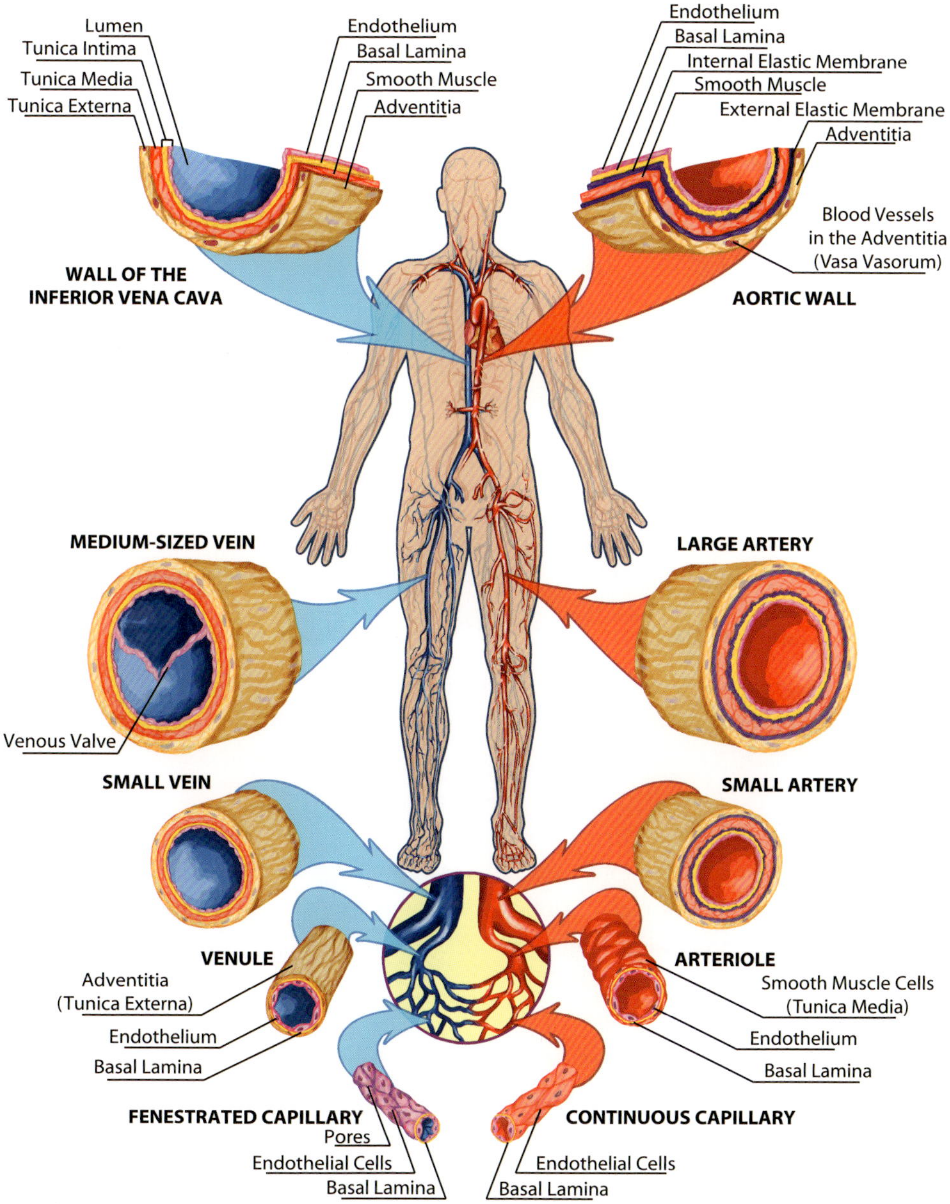

Our blood vessels are the "pipes" which carry all of our blood throughout the body. Rather than just having one layer, like a plastic pipe, these blood vessels have different layers as you can see. Damage to the inner layers can cause plaque buildup which can then lead to various cardiovascular related health issues.

Damage to the innermost lining of an arterial wall can lead to a buildup of plaque which can then restrict blood flow. The chances of this occurring are increased when there is insufficient vitamin C and the amino acids lysine and proline the body. Why? Vitamin C, lysine and proline are essential for collagen production which is the cement that builds healthy blood vessels.

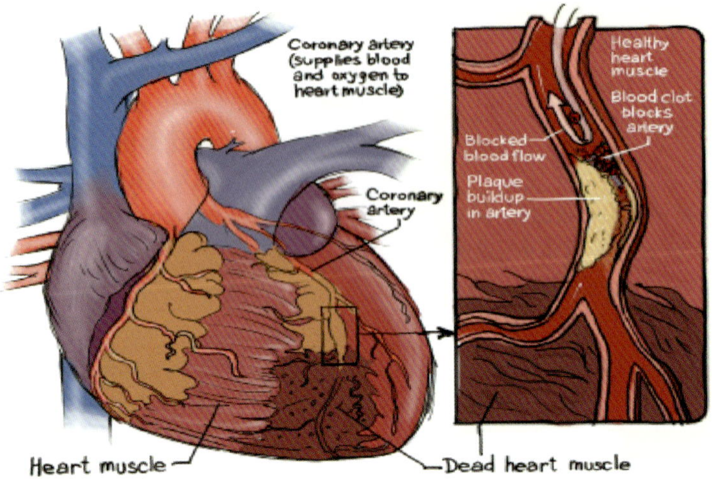

Damage to the innermost lining of an arterial wall can lead to a buildup of plaque which can then restrict blood flow. The chances of this occurring are increased when there is insufficient lysine, proline and vitamin C in the body.

Nutritional habits and dietary intake of vitamins have changed considerably in this century. Today, most people do not receive sufficient amounts of vitamins in their diet. To make matters worse, food processing, long-term storage and overcooking destroy most vitamins in the food.

A mere 10 mg of vitamin C prevents acute scurvy in humans resulting in the long-held hypothesis that ascorbic acid is a vitamin, required only in minuscule amounts. Those few species that fail to synthesize vitamin C all suffer similar heart disease, a form of the disease that is not prevalent in other species. The arterial intima is especially prone to this localised deficiency. Whenever any toxins are released into the blood, the inner lining of the arteries is logically one of the first destinations for the toxins to gather and start neutralizing local vitamin C stores, at least partially explaining why arterial scurvy is probably the most common form of focal scurvy.

The anatomy of the artery is fairly straightforward. The thickness of the arterial wall is composed of three basic layers: **the intima, the media and the adventitia.** Another important point about the anatomy of the arterial wall is that all three layers in the wall require the normal formation and maintenance of collagen in order to be an anatomically normal structure. Vitamin C is absolutely essential for the normal formation of collagen throughout your body. Collagens are the most abundant proteins in the human body, constituting about 30% of the body's total protein content. Linus Carl Pauling was an American chemist, bio chemist, peace activist, author, and educator. He was one of the most influential chemists in history and ranks among the most important scientists of the 20th century. Pauling was one of the founders of the fields of quantum chemistry and molecular biology. For his scientific work, Pauling was awarded the Nobel Prize in Chemistry in 1954. In 1962, for his peace activism, he was awarded the Nobel Peace Prize. This makes him the only person to be awarded two unshared Nobel Prizes. He is one of only four individuals to have won more than one Nobel Prize. He is also one of only two people to be awarded Nobel Prizes in different fields, the other being Marie Curie (Chemistry and Physics). So you can hardly say Linus Pauling was a rogue scientist, though you will find him getting a battering by the medical profession on many fronts for his theory on Vitamin C and heart disease. You can understand why, as Vitamin C costs pennies. Heart disease drugs and treatments are some of the biggest businesses in the world.

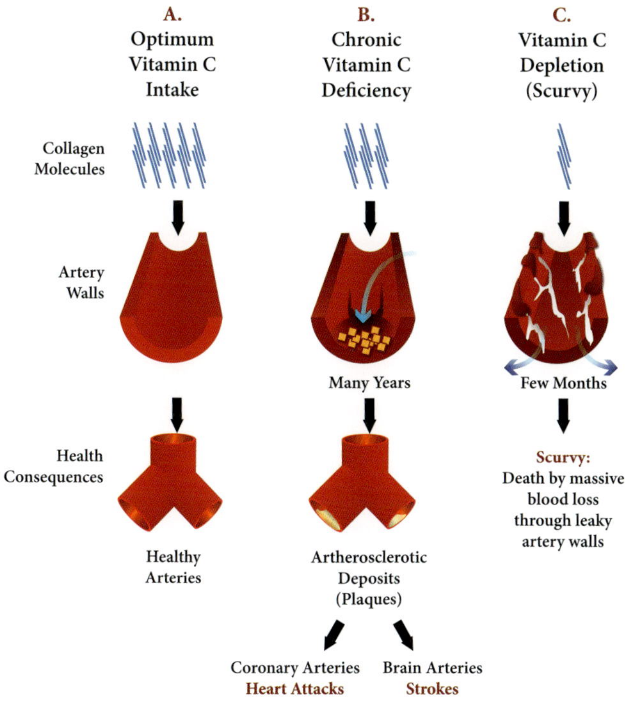

Thanks to the incredible work of Linus Pauling & Dr. Mathias Rath is this information available on the essential role vitamin c has on the prevention of heart disease!

Pauling's revolutionary concept is that lipoprotein-(a) cholesterol in the blood is an evolutionary adaption for, and a symptom of, low vitamin C. After crucial experiments, Dr. Pauling believed that the vitamin C/lysine protocol would save lives by: a) Preventing chronic scurvy, b) Strengthening and healing blood vessels, c) Keeping Lp(a) blood levels low and d) Inhibiting the binding of Lp(a) molecules to blood vessel walls. Due to the build up of damaged collagen, the Lp(a) and other blood clot forming factors increase at the site of damage as well. When this collagen damage continues to grow, so too does the size of the internal scab or plaque that is there to protect the vessel.

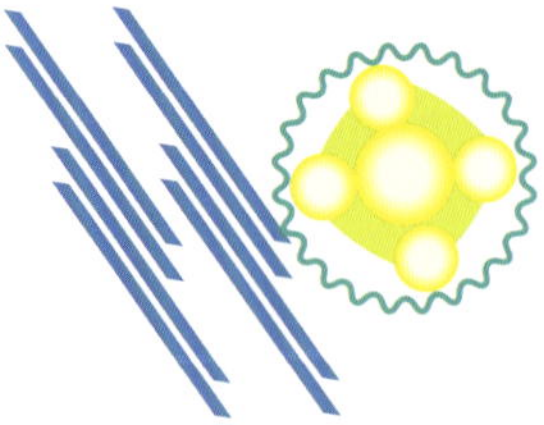

1
Millions of lipoprotein (a) particles accumulate inside the vitamin deficient artery walls by attaching to collagen and other connective tissue molecules.

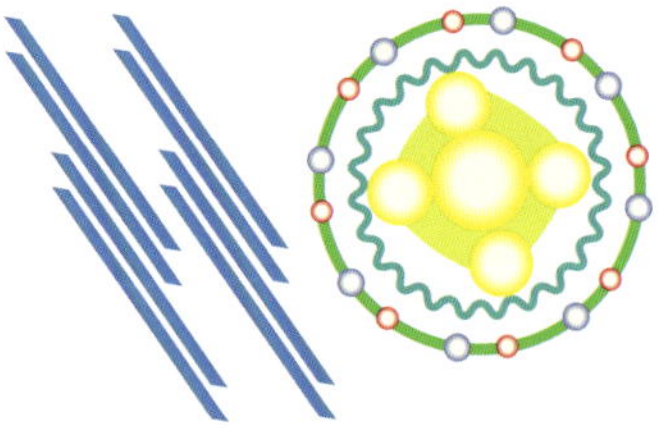

2
The natural amino acids lysine (◦) and proline (◦) form a 'Teflon' layer around the lipoproteins, which prevents further fat deposition in the artery walls. Moreover, fat molecules are detatched from their anchor sites inside the artery walls.

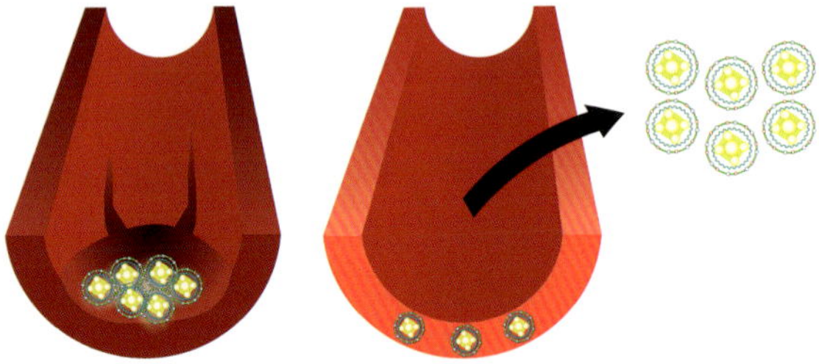

3
The lipoprotein (a) fat molecues are gradually released from the artery wall deposits, leading to the natural reversal of artherosclerosis and cardiovascular disease.

Pauling's crucial insight is that our diets lead to heart disease, but not in the way most people think. Our diets have sufficient vitamin C to prevent scurvy, but less than what we need to function optimally and keep our blood vessels flexible and strong. The result is a subclinical form of scurvy, i.e., chronic scurvy. The Lp(a) binding inhibitors became the Pauling Therapy for heart disease only at high doses, between 3 to 18 g ascorbic acid (Vitamin C) and 3 to 6 glysine.

An optimum supply of lysine, proline, and vitamin C is a decisive factor for the optimum regeneration of the connective tissue in the artery walls and, therefore, for a natural healing of cardiovascular disease.

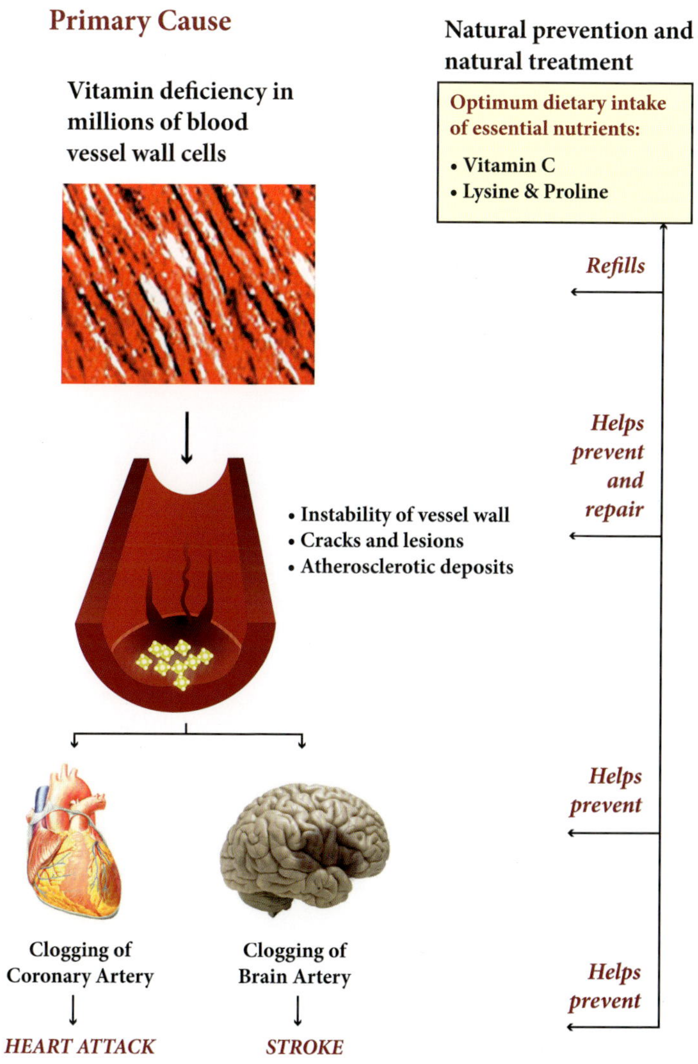

In 1970, Dr. Pauling published his first book "Vitamin C and the Common Cold". Following this, vitamin C consumption in the U.S. rose by 300%. Mortality from heart disease then decreased by 30% making the U.S. the only country with a significant drop in heart disease fatalities.

> ***"Now I've got to the point where I think we can get almost complete control of cardiovascular disease, heart attacks and strokes by the proper use of vitamin C and lysine. It can prevent cardiovascular disease and even cure it."***
>
> **Linus Pauling, British Journal of Optimum Nutrition (JON), Aug. 1994**

> ***"You need lysine to be alive, it is essential, but you can take lysine, pure lysine, a perfectly non toxic substance in food [as supplements], and that puts extra lysine molecules in the blood. They enter into competition with the lysyl residues on the walls of arteries and accordingly count to prevent lipoprotein-(a) from being deposited or even will work to pull it loose and destroy atherosclerotic plaques."***

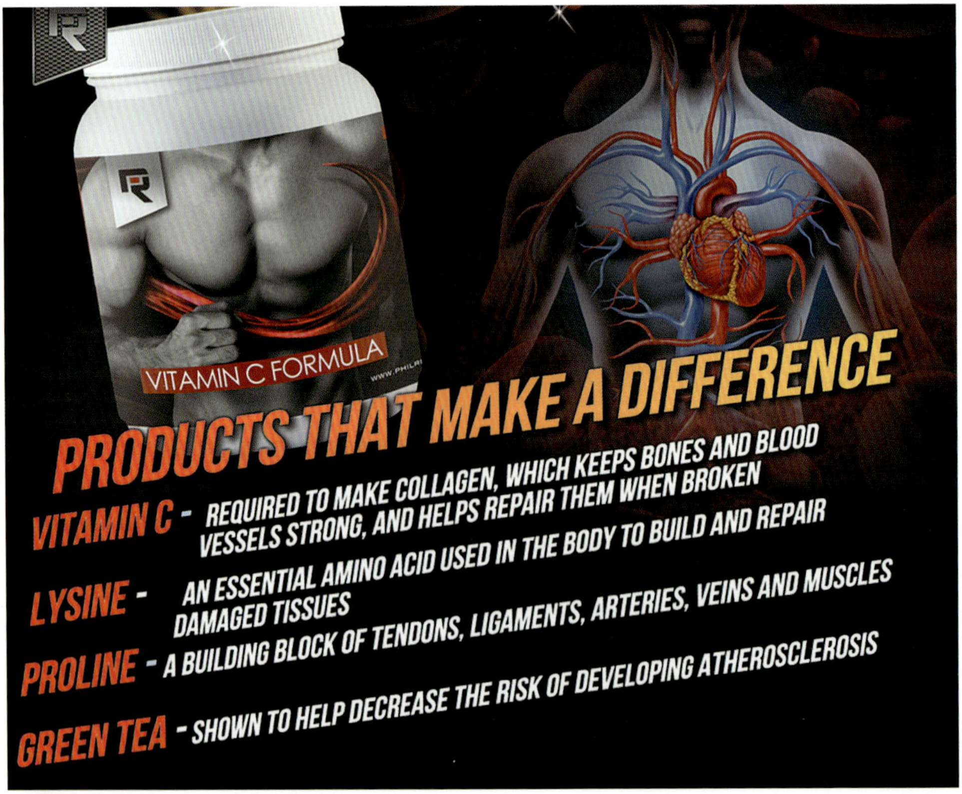

Matthias Rath, M.D. is an internationally renowned scientist was a close research associate and personal friend of the late Nobel Laureate Dr. Linus Pauling. Shortly before his death in 1994, Dr. Pauling stated that Dr. Rath's discoveries would later be seen among the most important of the 20th century. Dr. Rath, along with Pauling, is the scientist who discovered the close connection between cardiovascular disease and vitamin C deficiency: the common denominator of both health conditions is the instability of the blood vessel wall due to impaired supply of micronutrients to millions of cells of the vascular wall.

According to Dr. Rath, the arteries, veins and capillaries in our body are a pipeline that is 60,000 miles long. But this pipeline fails in 90% of the cases at one specific spot: The coronary arteries, with the length of only one billionth of the total vascular pipeline. If bad water quality - e.g. high cholesterol - would cause damage to this pipeline, it would clog everywhere, not just at one spot. Obviously, elevated cholesterol can not be the cause of coronary artery disease.

Why are all important risk factors for CVD closely connected to ascorbate deficiency, including, diabetes, hyperlipdemia, homocysteinuria and others? The common denominator of these metabolic disorders is to provide compensatory stability for the vitamin deficient vascular wall. This is also the reason, why vitamin C deficiency increases fibrinogen and thromboxane levels while decreasing endothelial derived relaxing factor (NO) and prostacyclin.

Let's turn to key evidence for the scurvy / heart disease connection. The guinea pig, like man, cannot synthesize ascorbate endogenously. In published research it was demonstrated that, when guinea pigs are fed vitamin C only at the level of the human RDA they develop atherosclerosis. These vascular lesions are histologically indistinguishable from human atherosclerotic plaques. In contrast, the control animals receiving Vitamin C levels of one teaspoon vitamin C per day have clean arteries.

1997 British Medical Journal: "Vitamin C deficiency, as assessed by low plasma ascorbate concentration, is a risk factor for coronary heart disease." Men who were deficient in vitamin C had 3.5 times more heart attacks than men who were not deficient in vitamin C.

In one study, researchers at the University of California found that participants who took 500 milligrams of vitamin C supplements per day saw a 24% drop in plasma C-reactive protein (CRP) levels after two months. Other researchers have suggested that CRP may be a better predictor of heart disease than cholesterol levels. *"C-reactive protein is a marker of inflammation, and there is a growing body of evidence that chronic inflammation is linked to an increased risk of heart disease, diabetes and even Alzheimer's disease"* said Dr. Gladys Block, UC Berkeley professor of epidemiology and public health nutrition and lead author of the study.

Dr. James Enstrom from the University of California studied the vitamin intake of over 11,000 people for 10 years. He found that 300 mg of vitamin C a day reduced risk of heart disease by 50% in men and 40% in women. Doctor G. C. Willis found that people taking 1,500mg of vitamin C a day for 12 months reversed plaque while those who didn't take vitamin C had worsening plaque. It is clear that vitamin C is necessary for vascular health.

Coronary Artery Disease

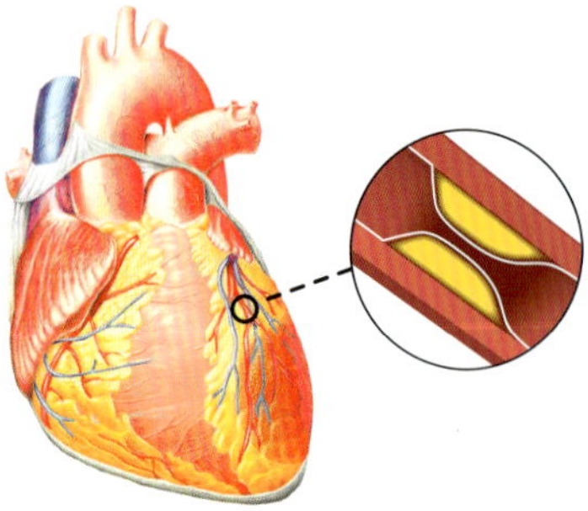

Peripheral Artery Disease

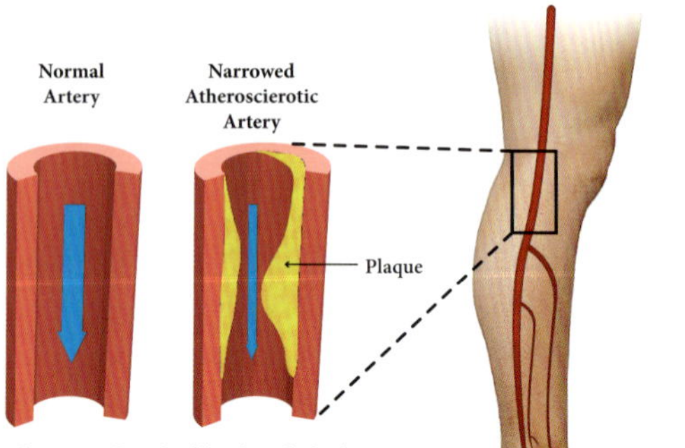

Low levels of vitamin C in the blood are linked to a more severe form of peripheral artery disease, an often painful condition in which the leg blood vessels become blocked.
Circulation Journal of the American Heart Association

Richard T. Lee, MD, and his colleagues at the Harvard Medical School, tested 880 chemical compounds for their effect on embryonic stem cells derived from mice. The stem cells were pretreated so that they would emit a green color if they grew into heart muscle cells. Of all 880 compounds, which are approved for use in people, only one promoted activity in the stem cells, and that was vitamin C.

Human Stem Cell Applications

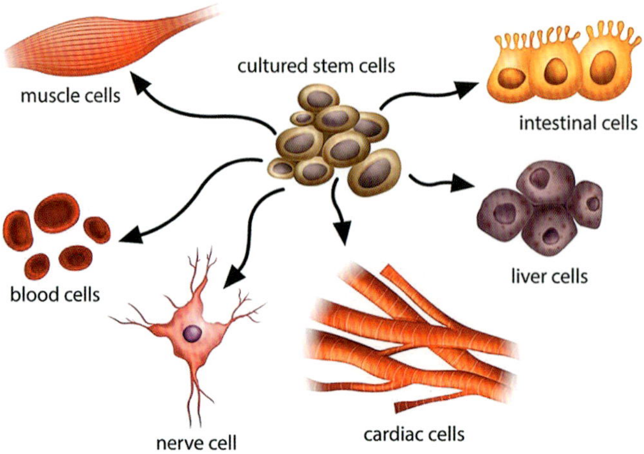

In the experiment, Lee and his colleagues treated embryonic stem cells with vitamin C for 12 days. During this time, large numbers of the stem cells began transforming into heart muscle cells called myocytes. The cells even began to beat rhythmically, as normal heart cells do. In addition, vitamin C prompted the expression, or activation, of several cardiac genes, which would have further directed the behavior of the heart cells. *(Takahashi T, Schulze C, Lord B, et al. Ascorbic acid enhances differentiation of embryonic stem cells into cardiac myocytes. Circulation, March 31, 2003.)*

Cholesterol and Vitamin C Deficiency

- Studies show that arterial blockages will start and grow with a vitamin C deficiency alone in the total absence of cholesterol elevations. *(Willis G, An experimental study of the intimal ground substance in atherosclerosis" Canadian Medical Association Journal 1953 69:17-22.*
- Serum cholesterol levels increase with a vitamin C deficiency. *(Maeda N, et al, "Aortic wall damage in mice unable to synthesise ascorbic acid" Proceedings of the National Academy of Sciences of the United States of America 2000 97(2):841-846*
- Vitamin C supplementation lowers serum cholesterol even with a high cholesterol diet. *(Sitaramayya C, Ali T, "Studies on experimental hypercholesterolemia and atherosclerosis" Journal of Physiology and Pharmacology 1962 6:192-204*
- Vitamin C supplementation protects arteries from plaque build - up, even in the presence of high serum cholesterol. *(Datey K et al, "Ascorbic acid and experimental atherosclerosis" Journal of Physicians of India 1968 16(9):567-570*
- These studies add further proof that vitamin C is essential for maintaining the health of the coronary arteries. The build – up of cholesterol-containing plaque is simply part of the body's response to a weakening of the arterial wall initiated by a lack of vitamin C. In the presence of a continuing deficiency of vitamin C, a progressive arterial breakdown occurs that triggers further formation of vessel – narrowing plaque.

Collagen is the cement for our blood vessel walls

The collagen molecules in our bodies are proteins composed of amino acids. Collagen molecules differ from all other proteins in the body in that they make particular use of the amino acids lysine and proline. We already know that vitamin C stimulates the production of collagen in the cells of the artery wall. An optimum supply of lysine, proline and vitamin C is a decisive factor in the optimum regeneration of the connective tissue in the artery walls and therefore the natural healing of cardiovascular disease.

In almost every case the cause of low vitamin C levels in the arterial linings is a significant daily toxin exposure. These toxins keep neutralizing (oxidizing) the body's stores of vitamin C, making the maintenance of active vitamin C levels in the various tissues of the body a tough task. Vitamin C has a short half-life in the blood. A "half-life" is the amount of time it takes for half of the vitamin C to be depleted from the bloodstream. The half-life of vitamin C in the blood is 30 minutes. This means that, every 30 minutes there is only one-half of the vitamin C left! For example, let's say you have an amount of vitamin C in your blood, we'll say this number is 100 (don't worry about any units). After 30 minutes, if you do not consume any more, you will only have 50 left. After another 30 minutes you would only have 25 left and so on and so on until you take on board more vitamin C.

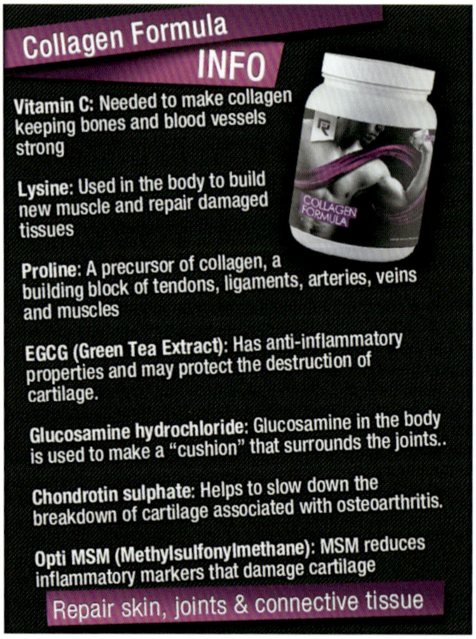

That's why I personally take vitamin C in multiple doses throughout the day and especially first thing in the morning. Why? It helps with cortisol production and my adrenals need all the help they can get.

Make sure if you are taking vitamin C supplements that you understand the following in regards to how to take it. Glucose and vitamin C use the same cell receptor, meaning that if the glucose concentration is too high in the blood, these two molecules compete for access (Ottoboni F, Ottoboni A. J Orthomol Med 2005;20:179-83). So if there are carbohydrates in your meal, DO NOT take your vitamin C at the same time. Take it in between meals, best in divided doses throughout the day. If you are on a ketogenic diet then you can take it with meals as there is no glucose from the meal to compete with vitamin C at the cell receptor.

A study conducted at the University of Maryland School of Medicine examined the effects of a high dose of vitamin C on the functioning of the endothelium. Healthy volunteers were given either (a) a single high fat meal consisting of 50 grams of fat, (b) a low – fat meal with 0 grams of fat, or (c) a high fat (50 grams) meal after taking 1000 mg vitamin C and 800 IU of vitamin E. In the high fat meal group without the anti oxidants, measurements with ultrasound scans showed that the enormous fat intake interfered with the normal dilation of their arteries and their blood flow, known as the endothelium dependent artery vasodilation **for up to four hours**. The group eating the same fat laden meal but taking the vitamins did not experience any such negative effects. These individuals had normal dilation and normal blood flow to the heart. As the researchers concluded, a single high fat meal reduced endothelial function for up to four hours in healthy people with normal cholesterol levels. This decrease can be blocked by taking high dose vitamin C & E.

Another study led by nutrition researchers from Arizona State University found that too little vitamin C in the blood stream correlates with increased body fat and waist measurements. The scientists report that the amount of vitamin C in the blood stream is directly related to fat oxidation – the body's ability to use fat as a fuel source – during both exercise and at rest. The controlled four-week study involved 20 obese men and woman. Half of the participants were given a 500 mg vitamin C capsule daily and the control group took placebos

Cholesterol - here we go again!

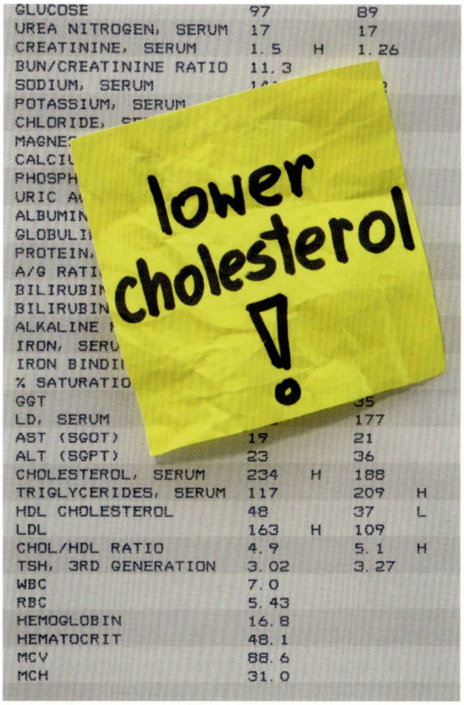

As we have seen, heart disease IS NOT caused by high cholesterol or a statin deficiency it is caused by INFLAMMATION to the endothelium which lines our blood vessel walls. Cholesterol will always be found at the crime scene in this case the site of inflammation not because it caused the inflammation because it's a repair material. It's a bit like you always find an ambulance at the scene of an accident but the ambulance did not cause the accident and this is the case with cholesterol.

Rather than being the cause of plaque buildup in the circulatory system, cholesterol is actually the healing agent the body sends to sites that have been damaged by inflammation. In other words, if you have too much cholesterol buildup in your arteries, your real problem is too much inflammation rather than too much cholesterol, and a whole different mitigatory approach is required to address the problem.

THE CRIMINAL CHOLESTEROL?

Innocent Until Proven Guilty

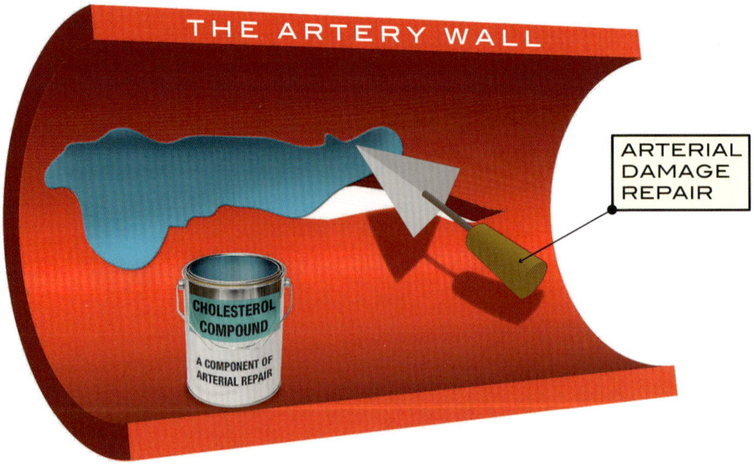

Cholesterol didn't cause the tear, it's simply a component in its repair. The true threat to the artery in not the repair mechanism, but the original cause of the damage.

"It's the inflammation in the vessels that starts the lesion," says Dr. Beverly Teter, a lipid biochemist from the University of Maryland who has been researching fats and their effect on the human body for many years, as quoted by CBN.com. "The body then sends the cholesterol like a scab to cover over it to protect the blood system and the vessel wall from further damage." This runs completely contrary to the prevailing medical dogma, which still maintains that saturated fat and cholesterol are silent killers that can lead to heart disease, diabetes and other forms of chronic illness. As a result, millions of people have been duped into avoiding these necessary nutrients to their own demise, while they instead eat unhealthy vegetable oils, trans fats, sugars, grains, and idiotic low-fat/cholesterol foods.

The gigantic MONICA study, sponsored by the World Health Organization, analyzed the relation between cardiovascular mortality and blood cholesterol in 27 countries, in much the same way as the Seven Countries Study. The results are similar, showing that countries like Japan and China have low mortality and low cholesterol levels, and countries like Finland have high mortality and high cholesterol levels. Yet countries like France, Germany, Switzerland, and Luxembourg have a low mortality rate and yet a high blood cholesterol value. This so-called "French paradox" is not a paradox at all, when examination of the data reveals great disparities in mortality between different regions with the same cholesterol levels. Similarly the residents of Corfu have a 5 fold greater mortality than residents of

Crete, despite identical dietary practices and identical cholesterol levels. Residents of the North Karelia regions of Finland have mortality rate of 493/100,000 and those in Fribourg France have mortality rate of 102/100,000, yet the cholesterol levels are identical at 245 mg/dl in both regions.

The longest running study of cardiovascular disease in a population was initiated in Framingham, Massachusetts in 1948 and continues to this day. This landmark longitudinal study identified important major risks for disease, especially smoking, lack of exercise, age, male gender, and elevated cholesterol levels in younger men. In spite of the great emphasis on cholesterol levels, the Framingham study made several critical observations that refute the "diet-heart" hypothesis. In the first place, dietary cholesterol has no relation to cholesterol levels in the blood, and dietary cholesterol has no relation to the risk of developing cardiovascular disease. This observation was confirmed by multiple large studies from Chicago, Puerto Rico, Honolulu, Netherlands, Ireland, and the massive Lipid Research Clinics study of US citizens. The next astounding finding was that elevated cholesterol was not a risk factor for women of any age or for men over age 47. Furthermore, both total mortality and cardiovascular mortality in Framingham participants increases in those with LOW cholesterol levels. This finding has been confirmed by multiple studies from Canada, Sweden, Russia, and New Zealand. These contradictory findings have been ignored, distorted, and incorrectly reported by supporters of the "diet-heart" hypothesis.

If you value your health and want to be lean & healthy eliminate added sugar from your diet immediately!

A research study team from New Zealand's University of Otago, publishing in The American Journal of Clinical Nutrition, has conducted a review and meta-analysis of a large cohort of dietary studies comparing the effects of higher and lower added sugar consumption on blood pressure and lipids, both of which are important cardiovascular risk determinants. Lead study author, Dr. Lisa Te Morenga and her students have uncovered solid and documented evidence that eating sugar has a direct effect on risk factors for heart disease, and is likely to negatively impact blood pressure and blood lipids. Dr. Te Morenga noted, "Our analysis confirmed that sugars contribute to cardiovascular risk, independent of the effect of sugars on body weight."

The scientists analyzed a total of 49 nutritional intervention trials conducted between 1965 and 2013. Comparing diets where the only intended differences were the amount of sugars and non-sugar carbohydrates consumed by the participants allowed for the measurement of the effects of these diets on lipids and blood pressure. 37 trials reported the effects of dietary sugars on lipid metabolism while another 12 yielded results on blood pressure. The team then pooled the available data to determine the impact on measurable risk factors that affect human health. The team noted that some of the data provided by the studies was skewed as the research was funded by the food/sugar industries. When they factored out those biased results, they found a startling pool of data conclusively demonstrating the negative impact of high-sugar diets on cardio-metabolic risk factors. Small increases in blood pressure, as little as 20 mm Hg systolic and diastolic, **can double the risk of a heart attack.**

Here is some scientific evidence on the effect of the DANGERS of low cholesterol:

1) A 1992 study of over three hundred fifty thousand men, aged thirty-five to fifty-seven, followed for twelve years, found that higher cholesterol levels were associated with lower death rates;
2) A five-year study published in 1989 found that low cholesterol increases the risk of death by at least 340% in elderly women; a twenty-year study published in 2001 found that those with the lowest cholesterol levels have a 35% increase in death rates compared to those with the highest cholesterol levels;

A full English Breakfast is more healthy for you than a bowl of breakfast cereal which in reality is a bowl of sugar!

3) A 1998 study found that low cholesterol levels are associated with higher rates of many infectious diseases including hepatitis, appendicitis, digestive and liver infections, kidney and urinary tract infections, venereal disease and musculo-skeletal infections.
4) Low cholesterol levels predict death in patients with bacterial in the blood. ***Richardson, JP et al. "Risk factors for the development of becteremia in nursing home patients". Archives of family medicine. 1995 Sep;4(9):785 - 9***
5) Violence, anti-social behaviour and premature death associated with low cholesterol levels. ***Repo-Tiihonen, E et al. "Total serum cholesterol level, violent criminal offences, suicidal behaviour, mortality and the appearance of conduct disorder in Finnish male criminal offenders with anti - social personality disorder". European Archives of Psychiatary and Clinical Neuroscience. Volume 252, Number 1, 8 - 11.***
6) Heart failure patients with low cholesterol levels have a 240% increased risk of urgent transplant and death. ***Afsarmanesh, N et al. "Total cholesterol levels and mortality risk in nonischemic systolic heart failure". American Heart Journal. 2006 Dec;152(6):1077-83***
7) The conclusion that lower cholesterol levels carry an increased risk of premature death was borne out by the Bezafibrate Infarction Prevention (BIP) study. The study looked at nearly 11,000 individuals and found that those with initial cholesterol readings of 160 mg/dL or less were more than twice as likely to die of non-cardiac diseases than those with levels above 160 mg/dL. Ironically, the risk of dying of a heart attack was the same in both groups.

A diet that is low in fat is not the one that is optimal for heart health. You need to include foods such as full-fat, unprocessed dairy products. This will ensure you achieve your nutritional needs for things such as vitamin K2.

Eliminating saturated fat from your diet doesn't help decrease cholesterol either as much of the misinformed medical profession and food industry will have you believe, because the liver will make cholesterol out of sugar and starch. It's that necessary for life. Saturated fat and cholesterol rich foods are absolutely essential for our health and well being as I have mentioned numerous times throughout this book!

The cholesterol/saturated fat/heart disease hypothesis is based on the theory that dietary cholesterol levels clog the arteries which progresses to heart disease as I have pointed out on a number of occasions in this book this simply isn't true. So let's look at a few studies to show this to be the case:

- Harvard pathologist finds high blood cholesterol is NOT the cause of blocked arteries: *(Lande KE, Sperry WM. Human atherosclerosis in relation to the cholesterol content of the blood serum. Archives of pathology 1936; 22:301 – 312.)*
- Research team reveal cholesterol levels have NO correlation with clogged arteries: *(Mathur KS et al Serum cholesterol and atherosclerosis in man. Circulation 1961; 23: 847 – 852)*
- Analysis of 1,700 patients finds NO association between the level of cholesterol in the blood and the incidence of heart disease: *(H. Edward Garrett, MD; Evan C. Horning, MD Serum Cholesterol Values in Patients Treated Surgically for Atherosclerosis. Journal of the American Medical Association. 1964; 189(9) : 655 – 659)*
- Another study finds that cholesterol levels are NOT connected to clogged arteries: *(Jose Mendez et al Relationship between Serum Lipids and Aortic Atherosclerotic Lesions in Sudden Accidental Deaths in Guatemala City. American Journal of Clinical Nutrition. Vol 20, 1113 – 1117.)*
- As saturated fat and cholesterol increase in the diet, then rates of heart attack and death decrease: *(Frantz ID et al Test of effect of lipid lowering by diet on cardiovascular risk. The Minnesota Coronary Survey. Arteriosclerosis. 1989 Jan – Feb; 9(1):129 - 35)*
- Diets high in cholesterol and saturated fat lower the risk of heart disease and diabetes: *(Bermudez O et al Dietary and plasma lipid, lipoprotein, and apolipoprotein profiles among elderly Hispanics and non – Hispanics and their association with diabetes. American Journal of Nutrition. 2002 Dec; 76(6) : 1214 – 21)*
- High cholesterol diet results in LESS heart disease risk for both men and women: *(Hernon KL et al High intake of cholesterol results in less atherogenic low density lipoproteins particles in men and women independent of response classification. Metabolism 2004 Jun; 53(6) : 823 -30.)*
- Vegetarians have a higher risk of heart disease compared to meat eaters: *(Kwok T et al Vascular Dysfunction in Chinese Vegetarians: An Apparent Paradox? Journal of the American College of Cardiology. 2005; 46 : 1957 – 1958)*
- Red meat gives protection from heart disease: *(Mamo JC et al A low protein diet exacerbates postprandial chylomicron concentration to a lean red meat protein enriched diet. European Journal of Clinical Nutrition 2005 Oct: 59(10) : 1142-8)*
- Men given "HEALTHY LIVING" advice and cholesterol lowering drugs are twice as likely to die: *(Miettenen TA et al Multifactorial Primary Prevention of Cardiovascular Diseases in Middle – aged Men. Journal of the American Medical Association. 1985; 254(15) : 2097 – 2012)*
- High saturated fat diet can lower the risk of heart disease and stroke: *(Wood AC et al Dietary Carbohydrate Modifies the Inverse Association Between Saturated Fat Intake and Cholesterol on Very*

Low Density Lipoproteins. Lipid Insights. 2011 Aug 23; 2011(4): 7-15.)

- Low fat/high carbohydrate diets implicated in heart disease: *(Weintraub MS et al Clearance of chylomicron remnants in nonmolipidaemic patients with coronary artery disease: case control study over three years. British Medical Journal. 13 April 1996; 312 :935)*

Less than one half percent of humans are born with a much higher cholesterol level than the rest of us. This abnormality, named familial hypercholestremia is a genetic aberration. All cells are able to take up cholesterol which also shows you how important cholesterol is! To take up the cholesterol the cells use the LDL receptor. However in that tiny % of people who have familial hypercholesterolimia the receptor is malfunctioning and this is why their blood cholesterol is higher than normal people!

The British Heart Foundation have teamed up with Flora pro.activ to raise awareness of heart disease amongst women and get more women thinking about how they can help reduce their risk with simple lifestyle changes such as lowering cholesterol through diet.

As part of our partnership Flora pro.activ will donate £750,000 over the next three years in support of our life-saving work.

Together, we're launching the 'Love your heart' campaign in September 2012 and will reach women through a variety of communications including press and television advertising, news coverage, social media, lots of information online and special packs of Flora pro.activ spreads. I personally find this ironic from the research that I did margarine not only doesn't prevent heart disease it can actually encourage it.

This is the dietary advice given out by the British Heart Foundation and I will leave you draw your own conclusion:

Fats

To help look after your heart health it is important to make sure you choose the right type of fats.

So to help keep your heart healthy:

- Replace saturated fats with small amounts of mono and polyunsaturated fats
- Cut down on foods containing trans fats.
- It's also important to remember that all fats and oils are high in calories, so even the unsaturated fats should only be used in small amounts.

Saturated fat

Too much saturated fat can increase the amount of cholesterol in the blood, which can increase the risk of developing coronary heart disease.

Unsaturated fats

Unsaturated fats, which can be monounsaturated fats (for example olive oil, rapeseed oil, almonds, unsalted cashews and avocado) or polyunsaturated fats (including sunflower oil and vegetable oil, walnuts, sunflower seeds and oily fish) are a healthier choice.

This advice goes 100% against the research but I guess having Flora Margarine fund you then you got to keep the heart/diet hypothesis a lie still going to keep the donations coming in.

With all the claims by margarine manufacturers on the benefits of their vegetable oils, let's focus our attention on the magic of plant sterols which are promoted heavily as something that is also beneficial to our health and especially our heart.

There are several types of plant cholesterol and together they are referred to as plant sterols. Human and plant cholesterol compete for uptake in the gut. If you eat much plant cholesterol (as found in these idiotic margarines) your intake of normal cholesterol goes down. And this fact got margarine manufacturers very excited because it allowed them to get an even bigger slice of the cholesterol myth making them more profit on an item which is not even a food.

It is correct that cholesterol goes down if we eat more plant sterol, but that doesn't mean that it is able to prevent heart disease, because no one, as far as I know from my research, has done such a scientific experiment. What unfortunately happens is that our cholesterol is exchanged with a foreign type of cholesterol, not only in our blood but also in our cells and cell membranes.

Several studies have shown that even a mild elevation of plant sterols in the blood is a risk factor. (Weingartner O and others. Eur Heart J 2009;30:404-9), and the findings in people with a rare inborn disease named sitosterolemia are in accord.

As we now know, statin treatment lowers blood cholesterol that there is no denying, but at the same time it raises plant sterols. In the 4S – trial about 25% of the patients had a mildly elevated level of plant sterols before treatment. In this group statin treatment resulted in a further increase of plant sterols and the number of heart attacks was twice as high compared with the patients with the lowest plant sterol levels. So, another reason to grab that margarine and put it straight in the garbage bin where it belongs.

Some more interesting things about cholesterol and blood:

- Red blood cells are 7 microns in diameter (quite small), yet they slither through capillaries that are only 5 microns in diameter. How can they do that? They fold and bend upon themselves – provided they have 23% cholesterol in their outer membranes.
- Lower than that, and the red blood cells lose their flexibility, becoming lodged in the capillaries, creating little mini-strokes.
- Cholesterol inactivates or inhibits bacterial "hemolytic activity" (boring holes into red blood cells, such that the contents leak out, producing death of the cell). This is particularly notable in the microbe Mycoplasma pulmonis. ***FEMS Microbiol Letter, May 1995 128 (2): 213-18.***
- Cholesterol was found to detoxify a very potent poison called cholera toxin. A rather complex reaction, but it detoxifies a toxin that is lethal to humans. Pretty powerful protector. ***Biochemistry Mar 12, 1991, (10) p 2563-70***
- "In reviewing 33 studies, we determined that a 7 mg% reduction in cholesterol resulted in a 70% increase in cancer risk." And the best part was the conclusion: "This does not justify concern that lowering serum cholesterol might cause cancer." ***Cancer Causes and Cures – Vol. 2 1991***

Aspirin increases risk of heart disease and stroke

Why do most medical professionals still keep prescribing and recommending aspirin for both prevention and treatment in those who have cardiovascular problems do they not read their own medical journals?

Lets look at this study (Belch J et al.) which was published in the British Medical Journal in 2008. The objective of this Scottish study was to determine whether aspirin and antioxidant therapy are more effective than a placebo in reducing the development of cardiovascular events in patients with diabetes and peripheral arterial disease. The study involved 1,276 patients aged 40 or more with diabetes who were assigned aspirin, antioxidants or placebo. Jill Belch, professor of vascular medicine from the University of Dundee let the study.

The study found;

There was a 23% increased risk of coronary heart disease or stroke in those who took aspirin compared to those who did not take the aspirin.

Your Brain Needs Cholesterol To Work!

A study conducted in Finland reported that deaths from heart attacks and strokes were 46% higher in those taking cholesterol lowering drugs!

Think about it, for the last 5 decades we have somehow become convinced that saturated fat represented a threat to our health. When in fact fat has been a critical macronutrient for humans and our forebears for at least 2 million years. But suddenly, fat became responsible for every health woe you could think of. And as it specifically relates to dementia, research clearly shows us that individuals eating more of the "dreaded" fat actually have a substantial risk reduction for becoming demented while those with diets favouring carbohydrates the risk for dementia dramatically increased.

The brain needs cholesterol to thrive. Why? The brain contains the highest concentration of cholesterol in your body. The brain needs cholesterol to thrive. Cholesterol is a critical brain nutrient essential for the proper function of brain cells. It plays a fundamental role as a building block of the cell membrane. Most importantly, cholesterol is actually an essential fuel for brain cells. The carrier protein LDL has been given the derogatory title of "bad cholesterol" however, in reality LDL is not a cholesterol molecule at all. The role of LDL in the brain is to capture cholesterol from the blood and transport it to the brain cell, where it performs critical functions. What researchers are now finding is that when cholesterol levels are low, the brain simply doesn't work well. And individuals with low cholesterol are at a much greater risk for dementia and other neurological problems.

Research by an Iowa State University scientist suggests that cholesterol-reducing drugs known as statins may lessen brain function. Yeon-Kyun Shin, a biophysics professor in the department of biochemistry, biophysics and molecular biology, says the results of his study show that drugs that inhibit the liver from making cholesterol may also keep the brain from making cholesterol, which is vital to efficient brain function.

"If you deprive cholesterol from the brain, then you directly affect the machinery that triggers the release of neurotransmitters," said Shin. "Neurotransmitters affect the data-processing and memory functions. In other words, how smart you are and how well you remember things."

High cholesterol levels are associated with higher intelligence cognitive tests were administered to 789 men and 1,105 women who were free of dementia and stroke and were then followed over a 16 – 18 year period. Those with the highest cholesterol levels scored 80% higher in the cognitive tests compared to those with the lowest levels. ***(Elias, PK et al. "Serum Cholesterol and Cognitive Performance in the Framingham Heart Study". Pyscosomatic Medicine. 67:24-30 2005)***

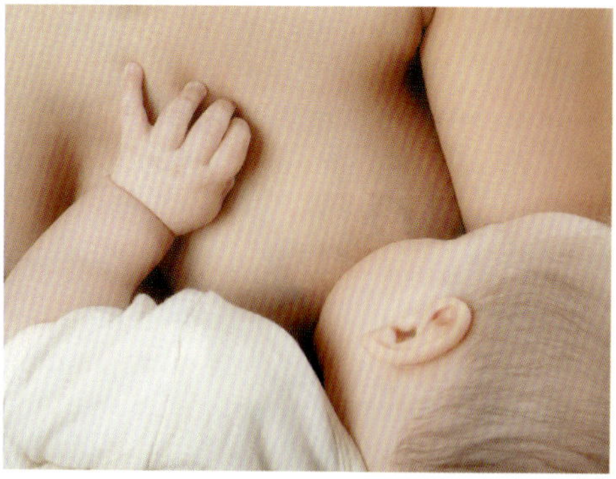

Early exposure to the high cholesterol content of breastmilk may improve fat metabolism in later life. In which case, there may be a strong argument for the content of formula feeds to match that of human milk. The highest concentrations of cholesterol are found in breast milk, where it is essential for infant nourishment and brain development. Why would nature's most perfect food contain such a deadly toxin like cholesterol? Because cholesterol, far from being a toxin, is absolutely essential to life!

Low cholesterol is also a very frequent finding in criminals, in homicidal offenders, and in people with violent or aggressive behaviour and there is a strong association between depression, suicide and low cholesterol. In a Swedish study, for example, the suicide rate was FIVE times higher than normally among those with the lowest cholesterol. And unfortunately I could go on with countless more scientific examples of studies which clearly show the absolute misinformation we the public are given on the pretence of obtaining health when in reality it makes us become diseased all in the name of science and sales of pharmaceutical drugs.

Inflammation - the real cause of heart disease.

The fixation on cholesterol as the cause of heart disease is not only completely wrong when inflammation, the real cause of elevated cholesterol is treated, cholesterol becomes what it should be - a non-issue in heart disease. It is not the reason millions are dying from heart disease. As we have already touched on, one of the biggest contributing factors is that of inflammation.

In 2000, doctors at Harvard University published the first of a series of landmark studies revealing the central role of inflammation in cardiovascular disease (CVD). People with the highest level of C - Reactive Protein (CRP) had **five times** the risk of developing CVD and **four times** the risk of a heart attack or a stroke compared to individuals with the lowest level.

Inflammation increases with weight gain, and weight gain promotes inflammation. The result is a vicious cycle of metabolic lethargy and increased insulin resistance. Medical evidence suggests that obesity-related insulin resistance may be due, in part, to chronic inflammation.

In obese people, CRP can be chronically elevated. **This is because fat cells produce pro-inflammatory signalling molecules called cytokines that in turn stimulate production of CRP.** A high CRP means that inflammatory processes are active in your body.

Overweight and obese individuals have stubbornly elevated C-reactive protein levels as one study showed the following:

Percent with Elevated C-Reactive Protein (>1 mg/dL)

- Normal Weight Individuals 25%
- Overweight Individuals 51%
- Obese Individuals 75%

Visser M, Bouter LM, McQuillan GM, Wener MH, Harris TB. Elevated C-reactive protein levels in overweight and obese adults. JAMA. 1999 Dec 8;282(22):2131-5.

These grim findings correlate well with the increased risks of cancer, stroke, heart attack, and dementia that occur as people accumulate excess body fat.

Increased CRP (>3.0 mg/L) triples heart attack risk, regardless of LDL levels. When CRP is high, coronary atherosclerotic plaque is more prone to rupture, the feared event that triggers a heart attack. When high CRP occurs in the company of small LDL particle size, one of the phenomena associated with insulin resistance a lipoprotein measure, the risk of a heart attack risk is nearly **seven-fold greater.**

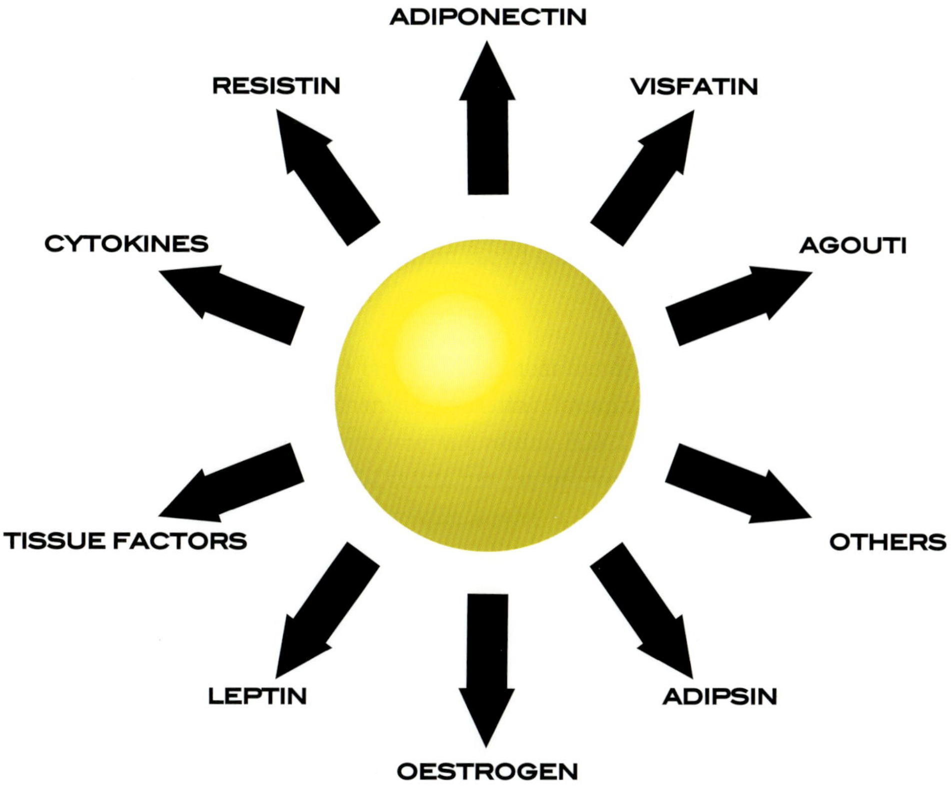

The adipocyte (fat cell) spews out a varity of substances and many of them are harmful to our health.

The high-sensitivity C-reactive protein (hs-CRP) blood test is the best method for measuring the body's general level of inflammation. It does not, however, identify the cause of inflammation. The levels can be elevated in patients with metabolic syndrome, insulin resistance, food allergies, toxicity and a host of other diseases. **People with high CRP levels typically have problems losing weight.**

C-reactive protein is released into the blood by the liver shortly after the start of an infection or inflammation. CRP is an early indicator of these problems because its levels usually start to rise in the blood before symptoms, such as fever and pain, appear.

- If CRP level is lower than 1.0 mg/L, a person has a low risk of developing cardiovascular disease.
- If CRP is between 1.0 and 3.0 mg/L, a person has an average risk.
- If CRP is higher than 3.0 mg/L, a person is at high risk.

C-reactive protein must be viewed in the context of other measures of health and disease. If elevated, the risk of multiple conditions escalates. C-reactive protein (CRP) is a protein produced by the liver when there is inflammation somewhere in the body.

Mounting evidence underscores the critical role that inflammation plays in the development and continuation of diabesity. In fact, those who have a high C-reactive protein blood level have a 1,700% increased probability of developing diabetes.

Supplements to help reduce CRP levels naturally

Vitamin E and CoQ10 have been found to lower CRP by an average of 30% in research with baboons fed a high fat and high cholesterol diet. Another study has shown that women with high levels of EPA and DHA fatty acids in their blood had 56% lower CRP.

A University of California at Berkeley study finds Vitamin C reduces C-Reactive Protein they give participants 1000 mg vitamin C daily and started out with C-reactive protein levels greater than 2.00 mg/L had 34% lower levels compared with the placebo group after only two months of the Vitamin C supplementation.

Vitamin E has been shown to decrease lipid peroxidation and inhibit smooth muscle cell proliferation, platelet aggregation, monocyte adhesion, oxidized LDL uptake, and cytokine production—all of which occur during sclerotic vascular disease (Munteanu A et al 2004; Harris A et al 2002). In cultured arterial endothelial cells, vitamin E increased the production of prostacyclin, a potent vasodilator and inhibitor of platelet aggregation (Wu D et al 2004). Most vitamin E supplements come in the form of alpha tocopherol, but it is also important to supplement with around 200 mg of gamma tocopherol to gain vitamin E's comprehensive benefits.

In a seven-year follow-up study of more than 334,000 postmenopausal women with no previous heart disease, greater intake of dietary vitamin E consisting predominantly of gamma tocopherol was strongly associated with a lower risk of death from cardiovascular disease. The data did not appear to demonstrate a similarly protective role for supplemental alpha tocopherol (Kushi, 1996). Numerous animal studies likewise suggest that gamma tocopherol may provide powerful protection for the heart. In laboratory rats, supplementation with gamma tocopherol reduced platelet aggregation and clot formation even more effectively than alpha tocopherol (Saldeen, 1999). In addition, gamma tocopherol at physiological doses was more effective than alpha tocopherol in enhancing the activity of superoxide dismutase (SOD), an antioxidant enzyme that may help reduce the risk of cardiac events (Li, 1999).

Researchers have found that populations with the highest amount of vitamin E in their blood plasma had the lowest death rate from heart disease. The most dramatic study to date attesting to the benefits of Vitamin E was performed on patients who had already been diagnosed with one heart attack. The Cambridge Heart Antioxidant Study was a double blind, placebo controlled study of 2,002 people with diagnosed heart disease. Patients were either given Vitamin E 400 – 800 IU supplements or a placebo. Within 510 days, researchers found that patients who had been taking the vitamin E had an amazing 77% fewer heart attacks than those who did not take the vitamin E.

In a study of 3,920 people, subjects who ingested the most dietary fiber were found to have a 41% lower risk of elevated C-reactive protein levels, compared with those who ate the least fiber. The doctors who conducted this study concluded: "Our findings indicate that fiber intake is independently associated with serum CRP concentration and support the recommendation of a diet with a high fiber content. ***(Ajani UA, Ford ES, Mokdad AH. Dietary fiber and C-reactive protein: findings from national health and nutrition examination survey data. J Nutr. 2004 May;134(5):1181-5.)***

Homocysteine & heart disease

Homocysteine is a type of protein, produced by the body and found in the blood that, ideally, should be present in very low quantities. However, if you are not optimally nourished, homocysteine can, and does, accumulate, increasing risk of over 50 diseases, including heart attacks, strokes, certain cancers, diabetes, depression and Alzheimer's disease.

Homocysteine is produced from the amino acid methionine, which is found in normal dietary protein. The trouble is, if you don't have optimal amounts of B vitamins in your diet, the enzymes that then turn homocysteine into either glutathione, which is the body's most important antioxidant, or SAMe (s-adenosyl methionine), which is the body's most important 'methyl donor', a very important type of 'intelligent' nutrient for both brain and body, don't work well enough, so homocysteine levels go up.

Also, it has been discovered that one in ten people have an inherited genetic mutation that makes them more prone to high homocysteine. This means that the Methylene-tetrahydrofolate reductase (MTHFR) enzyme that converts homocysteine into SAMe doesn't work so well. This means one in ten people need much larger daily intakes of B12 and folic acid to stay healthy.

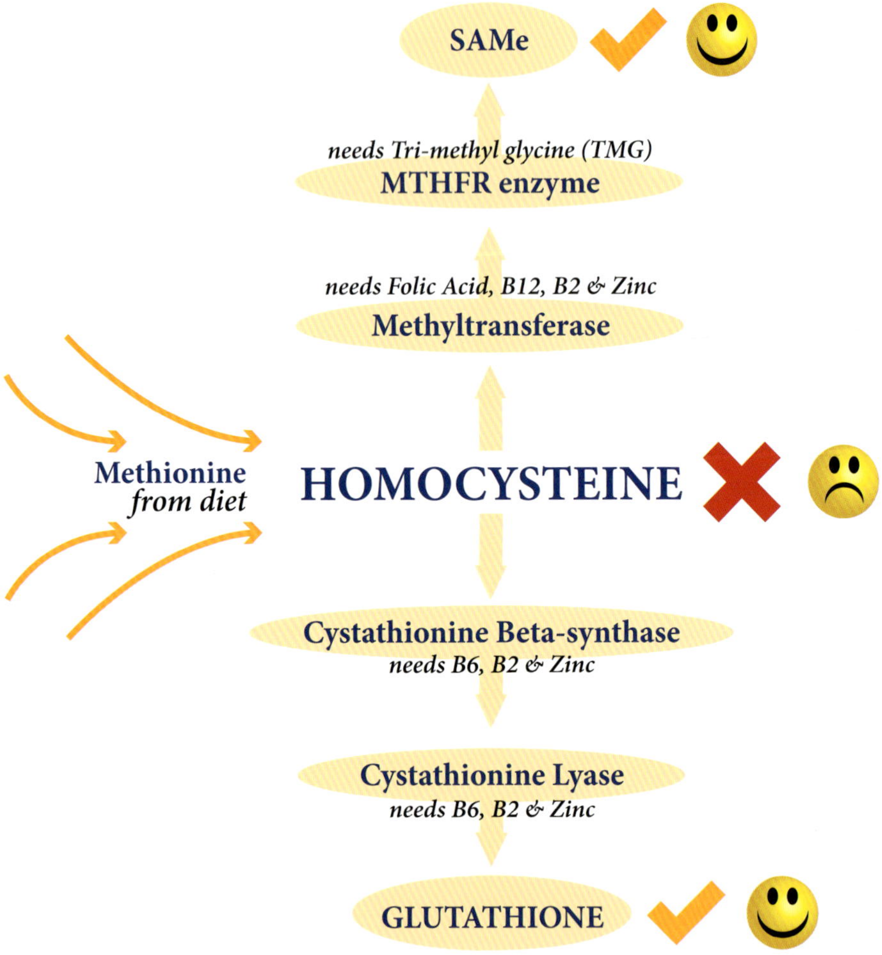

There is a significant and growing body of evidence that the biggest culprit responsible for oxidizing cholesterol and producing atherosclerosis, and therefore heart disease is homocysteine, a substance that in 1969 heart researcher Kilmer S. McCully, M.D., published in the American Journal of Pathology regarding homocysteine as the possible cause of heart disease and not cholesterol. Dr. McCully proposed that homocysteine could, when allowed to accumulate to toxic levels, degenerate arteries and produce heart disease.

Homocysteine Molecule

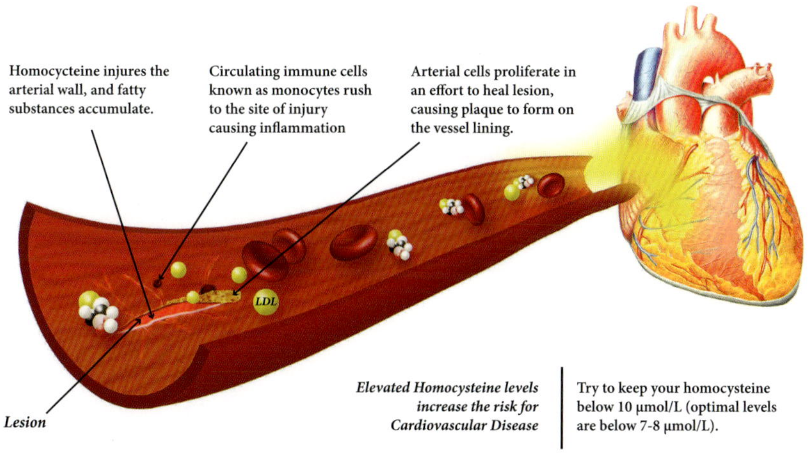

A German study (1991) looked at the coronary arteries of 163 males with chest pain and concluded that the arterial narrowing was due more to blood levels of homocysteine than of cholesterol.

While the importance of antioxidants is now well established, an important new concept in medicine is 'methylation'. The ability for the body to maintain chemical balance hinges upon its ability to add or subtract molecules called methyl groups. This is how the body turns one thing into another.

It has been found that, with every five unit increase in homocysteine measured in the blood, the risk of heart disease went up 42% in those with the MTHFR gene mutation and 32% in those without. The risk for strokes went up 65% in those with the genetic mutation and 59% for those without. The researchers concluded that these *"highly significant results indicate strong evidence that the association between homocysteine and cardiovascular disease is causal"*. ***Wald DS and Morris JK. Homocysteine and cardiovascular disease: evidence on causality from a meta-analysis.BMJ. 325: 1202. 2002.***

This means that having a high homocysteine level isn't just associated with higher risk, it actually causes heart disease – a conclusion that is also being reached by other research groups. ***(Lerk M et al. 'MTHFR 677C>T Polymorphism and Risk of Coronary Heart Disease'. JAMA. Vol. 288(16): 2023-2031. 2002.)***

This also means that if you can lower your homocysteine level (your H score) you remove a key cause, and hence diminish the risk. While the average homocysteine level is around 10 units, an ideal level is below six units. Those with a history of cardiovascular disease often have a level above 15 units. Lowering a high homocysteine from 16 to six units – a 10 point drop – could cut risk significantly! And you can do this by increasing your B6, B12 & Folate intake with both supplementation and food intake.

LOWERING HOMOCYSTEINE LEVELS NATURALLY

Extraordinary findings from a comprehensive research study at the University of Bergen in Norway were published in 2001 in the *American Journal of Clinical Nutrition*. They measured the homocysteine levels of 4,766 men and women aged 65 to 67 back in 1992, and then recorded any deaths over the next five years, during which 162 men and 97 women died. They then looked at the risk of death in relation to their homocysteine levels. Remarkably, they not only reconfirmed the relationship between heart attacks, strokes and high homocysteine, but also found that "a strong relation was found between homocysteine and all causes of mortality". In other words, homocysteine is an accurate predictor of how long you are going to live, whatever the eventual cause of death may be! ***(Vollset SE et al. 'Plasma total homocysteine and cardiovascular and noncardiovascular mortality: the Hordaland Homocsyteine Study'. American Journal of Clinical Nutrition. 74(1): 130-136. 2001.)***

With every five-point increase in H score, researchers found:

- 49% increased deaths from all causes;
- 50% increase in cardiovascular mortality;
- 26% increase in deaths from cancer;
- 104% increase in deaths from any causes other than cancer or heart disease.

If you are already in your fifties or sixties, you might be tempted to think I'm too old to change but by simply taking a few supplements could potentially not only add years to your life but also quality of life which is what comes with improved health.

Measuring Your Homocysteine

Your homocysteine level is easy to measure at home. Yorktest Laboratories in the UK offer a home test kit that works from a pin prick of blood. You put a drop of blood onto a card, which separates and stabilizes the plasma portion of the blood. You then send in your card and you'll know your H score within days.

Homocysteine is measured in mmol/l. It used to be thought that a 'high' level was above 15 units. This is what increases your risk of a heart attack and doubles your Alzheimer's risk. But now, levels as low as 7 units are being linked to increased disease risk. The average level in Britain is 10.5. What you want is a level below 6 units. This equates to having good health.

A study published in the British Medical Journal (Wouter de Ruijter et al, British Medical Journal, 9th January, 2008) showed that your homocysteine level predicts risk of death from cardiovascular disease in older people better than any conventional measure of risk including cholesterol, blood pressure or smoking. A Norwegian study discovered that in 587 patients with coronary heart disease, the risk of death within four years was proportional to total plasma homocysteine level. The risk rose from 3.8% with homocysteine below 9 micromoles per liter to 24.7% in patients with homocysteine levels above 15 micromoles per liter.

A study analysed blood levels of homocysteine and C-reactive protein in heart attack patients compared with a control group who had no symptoms of heart attack. The groups were matched for serum cholesterol, HDL, triglycerides, age, sex, body mass index, and blood pressure. The results showed that compared with the control patients:

- 32% more heart attack patients had homocysteine levels above 10 µmol/L
- 500% more heart attack patients had homocysteine levels above 15 µmol/L
- 572% more heart attack patients had C-reactive protein levels above 3.00 mg/L

This study demonstrates the importance of keeping homocysteine below 10 µmol/L (optimal levels are below 7-8 µmol/L) and C-reactive protein as low as possible (optimal levels are below 0.55 mg/L for men and 1.5 mg/L for women). ***Jarosz A, Nowicka G. C-reactive protein and homocysteine as risk factors of atherosclerosis. Przegl Lek. 2008;65(6):268-7223***

Supplementing with the amino acid taurine can protect against coronary artery disease by favourably modulating blood levels of homocysteine. Research suggests that taurine can block methionine absorption from the diet, thereby reducing available substrate for homocysteine synthesis (Zulli A 2009). A study of 22 healthy middle-aged women (33 to 54 years) found that after taurine supplementation (3g per day for 4 weeks), plasma homocysteine levels exhibited a significant decline, from 8.5 µmol/L to 7.6 µmol/L. The investigators concluded that sufficient taurine supplementation might effectively prevent cardiovascular disease (Ahn 2009).

A growing body of research on marine lipids, rich in omega-3 polyunsaturated fatty acids (PUFAs), has also revealed that omega-3 rich fish oil supplementation can reduce elevated homocysteine levels.

I strongly recommend a high strength multi vitamin and mineral loaded with B vitamins to help reduce homocysteine levels and PRP's Multi Vitamin & Mineral Formula in my opinion is an outstanding product for achieving that goal.

Very effective product for methylation due to it's high content of B6, B12 & Folic Acid

Nitric Oxide - A Miracle Molecule?

Nitric oxide was named "Molecule of the Year" in 1992 and 1998, the Nobel Prize was awarded to three Americans (Robert Furchgott, Ferid Murad and Louis Ignarro) for their work in the discovery of nitric oxide as a key messenger in the cardiovascular system. They had discovered that several important functions relating to the health of the lining of the arteries were initiated by nitric oxide signals. They had also found that nitric oxide was produced in the cells that line the arteries (endothelium). Nitric oxide released by the endothelium works to prevent red blood cells from sticking together, or aggregating, and attaching to the vessel wall. It can also work to control vascular tone, allowing the arteries to relax and stay clear. Nitric oxide is one of the most powerful vasodilators occurring naturally in humans, making it one of the best ways to naturally lower your blood pressure and improve your arterial health.

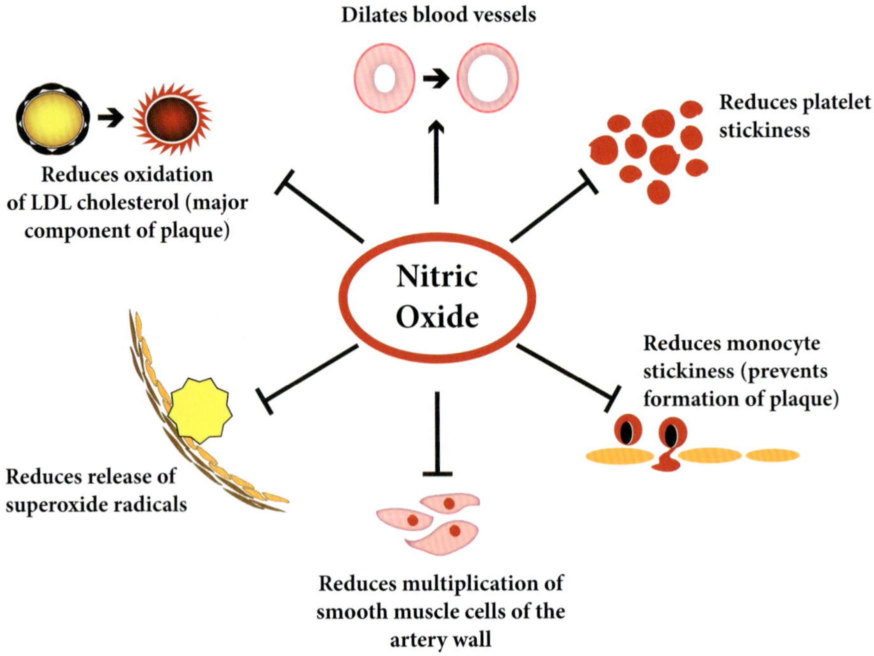

How to increase nitric oxide in your body

The most common way to increase nitric oxide is through exercise. When you run or lift weights, your muscles need more oxygen which is supplied by the blood. As the heart pumps with more pressure to supply the muscles with blood, the lining in your arteries releases nitric oxide into the blood, which relaxes and widens the vessel wall, allowing for more blood to pass through. As we age, our blood vessels and nitric oxide system become less efficient due to free radical damage, inactivity, and poor diet, causing our veins and arteries to deteriorate.

From reading the research, the main nutritional strategy to increase nitric oxide seems to focus on L – Arginine, an amino acid the triggers e–NOS (the enzyme endothelial nitric oxide synthase) to make more nitric oxide.

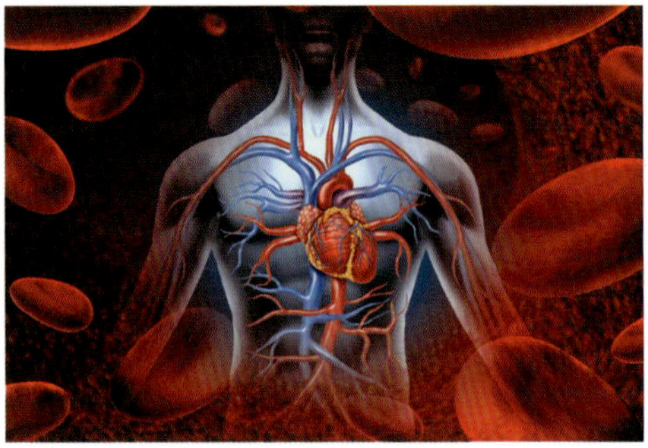

The most common way to increase nitric oxide is through exercise. When you run or lift weights, your muscles need more oxygen which is supplied by the blood.

L-Citrulline is an amino acid that turns into L-Arginine in the body and evidence from Dr. Nathan Bryan and other scientists shows that L-Arginine made from L-Citrulline is much more effective in raising nitric oxide levels than taking L-Arginine directly.

That's because the L-Arginine made from L-Citrulline is directed toward the nitric oxide making pathway-whereas when you take an L-Arginine supplement, there are eight different metabolic pathways the amino acid can wander down, with only about 3% of the L-Arginine used for Nitric Oxide production. To summarize by providing L-Citrulline the supplement allows the body to more effectively use L-Arginine to produce Nitric Oxide.

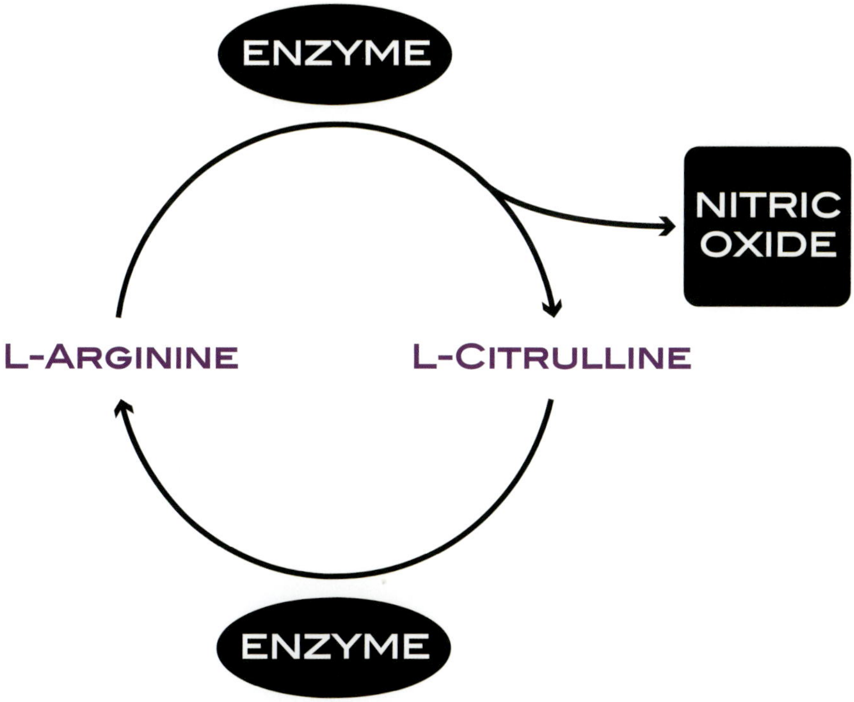

Clinical trials in universities in California have established the effective amount of L-citrulline at 1,000 mg per serving. These studies showed that L-citrulline is critical in the production of nitric oxide because it acts like a catalyst when combined with L-arginine and extends the body's production of nitric oxide to over twenty hours. Compared to just 30 min – 2 hours with just using L-Arginine.

Enzymes that convert arginine to citrulline, and citrulline to arginine need to function optimally for efficient nitric oxide production. We can protect those enzymes and nitric oxide by consuming healthy foods and antioxidants, like fruit, garlic, vitamins C and E, Co-Q10, and alpha lipoic acid, allowing you to produce more nitric oxide. Nitric oxide only lasts a few seconds in the body, so the more antioxidant protection it can get the more effective it can become.

Increasing nitric oxide has also become the new secret weapon for athletes and bodybuilders. Athletes are now taking supplements with L-arginine and L-citrulline to support the flow of blood and oxygen to the skeletal muscle. They also use them to facilitate the removal of exercise-induced lactic acid build-up which reduces fatigue and recovery time. Since arginine levels become depleted during exercise, the entire arginine - nitric oxide - citrulline loop can lose efficiency, causing less-than-ideal nitric oxide levels and higher lactate levels. Supplements can help restore this loop allowing for better workouts and faster recovery from workouts.

Those who are looking to burn off body fat may want to think carefully about the benefits of nitric oxide. One study conducted by the American Journal of Endocrinology and Metabolism looked at the impact of the NO precursor L-arginine on glucose metabolism during exercise. They had nine endurance trained males cycle for 120 minutes total which was then followed by a 15 minute max effort cycling period. During this time glucose levels were measured in the body and it was noted that those who had taken the L-arginine had a significantly higher glucose rate of appearance, glucose rate of disappearance, and glucose clearance rate. This demonstrates that these athletes were taking up the glucose faster into the muscle cells as the exercise persisted. In addition to this, the supplement also supported the increase of nonesterified fatty acid concentration as well as glycerol in the body, potentially pointing to the burning up of fat as fuel. So those who are looking to burn body fat may have a slight advantage when using this process in terms of using up available glucose in the body and then burning off fat tissues.

It's best also to take a product like PRP Nitric Oxide Generator before retiring to bed. Our vascular endothelial cells produce less Nitric Oxide during sleep than when we are awake and moving around. Most heart attacks occur at night, during the early hours of the morning when we produce the least amount of Nitric Oxide.

WARNING: If you have an existing heart condition or abnormal blood pressure, please consult your healthcare professional before taking supplements to increase nitric oxide levels

We now know there are pathways in the body that are not dependent on L-Arginine to generate Nitric Oxide. These pathways can convert foods rich in nitrate and nitrites such as kale, spinach, broccoli & beetroot into nitric oxide. Dark green leafy vegetables are among the foods richest in nitrate and nitrite, two dietary compounds that create NITRIC OXIDE in the body. Research has shown that Leafy greens have been shown to lower heart disease by 18 % and the risk of stroke by 21%.

Dark green leafy vegetables are among the foods richest in nitrate and nitrite, two dietary compounds that create NITRIC OXIDE in the body.

Fish oil also boosts Nitric Oxide. In a study conducted by researchers at the University of Kansas 29 people took fish oil and had an increase in their excretion of nitrate, a sign of increasing NO production. Fish oil stimulates nitric oxide production which suggests another mechanism where fish oil prevents heart disease.

Ways to Naturally Boost Nitric Oxide:

- **Eat more beetroot** - You can juice beets if you don't care for raw or cooked beets, but use organic and throw in the roots, fruit, and even the leaves. Beets naturally boost the production of nitric oxide in the body and help to support energy levels, largely due to the large amount of nitrates found within the root vegetable.
- **Consume hawthorn extract** - Hawthorn is often used to prevent heart disease because it prevents arterial walls from becoming coated with plaque, acts as a calcium-channel blocker and helps the endothelial cells that line our blood vessels to secrete nitric oxide.
- **Exercise every day** - When you work harder physically, the heart has to pump harder to supply oxygen to the body. The additional pressure against the arterial walls – from more blood passing through, causes more nitric oxide to be released.

- **Eat more L-Arginine and L-Citrulline** - Nuts and fruits are the best vegetarian sources of these amino acids, but they also exist in much higher quantities in meat and dairy.
- **Get enough sunlight** - Researchers in University of Edinburgh recently found out that when sunlight hits your skin, your body will instantly release nitric oxide into the bloodstream. Another reason to include sunshine into your life.
- **Supplement with Alpha Lipoic Acid** - In a controlled trial, 58 patients were randomized into two groups. The first group received 300 milligrams of oral Alpha Lipoic Acid daily, the another one got placebo. At the end of the study researchers noted that the ALA group had improved their blood flow by 44% compared to the placebo group. There's also bunch of other studies that all come to this same conclusion: ALA is a very potent vasodilator and likely will boost nitric oxide levels.
- **Reduce your intake of fructose** - Studies suggest that fructose, normally occurring sugar found in fruits is capable of generating a massive decline in nitric oxide production. So if you want to boost nitric oxide naturally steer away from fructose and especially high fructose corn syrup!
- **Use Ginkgo biloba** - there is a lot of studies on pubmed about ginkgo biloba and all of them state the same thing, ginkgo biloba increases nitric oxide production and makes veins more flexible.
- **Make sure you get your vitamin C** - Vitamin C can relax arteries by a different mechanism: it protects your precious nitric oxide from being destroyed by free radicals. Further evidence of Vitamin C's powers in this regard are it's ability to lower blood pressure and reduce arterial stiffness.
- **Eat raw cocoa or dark chocolate** - The flavonoids in dark chocolate or raw cocoa can significantly raise nitric oxide levels. For example, one study gave 44 hypertensive seniors just 30 grams of dark chocolate - a fraction of the typical chocolate bar - and found that it significantly lowered their blood pressure.

Vitamin K2 & heart disease

There are three kinds of vitamin K: K1, K2, and K3. Vitamin K is generally classified as a fat soluble vitamin. This means in order to absorb vitamin K it`s necessary to consume some dietary fat along with your Vitamin K source. Vitamin K`s are distinguished by their side chains, the basic compounds of which they are made.

- Vitamin K1 is made of *phylloquinone* compounds.
- Vitamin K2 is essentially comprised of a group of compounds called *manaquiones.* With K2, there are different manaquione side chain lengths manifesting different characteristics. The MK7 variety is the most readily metabolized and abundant form of K2.
- Vitamin K3 is comprised of *menadione*, which is a synthetic version of vitamin K. It`s used primarily for intravenous medical interventions with infants, sometimes with toxic side effects. K3 won't work as a nutritional supplement!

Arteries with no plaques have a 20 to 50 fold increase in Vitamin K2 concentration when compared to arteries with arterial plaques. The high K2 content arteries were noted to be more flexible and elastic than arteries lacking K2. Lack of Vitamin K2 causes calcium to fail to be deposited in bones where it belongs and to be deposited instead in arteries, aorta, soft tissues including muscle, breast, kidneys and in heel spurs.

A protein called osteocalcin transports calcium to bone. Vitamin K2 is used to solidify this calcium into the bone matrix. When Vitamin K2 is lacking the calcium remains in the blood and ends up getting deposited in the walls of arteries and other sites which is very undesirable. Vitamin K2 is a critical nutrient for patients with arteriosclerosis as it has the potential to prevent and remove calcium from arteriosclerotic plaques thus making plaques easier to dissolve and less dangerous..

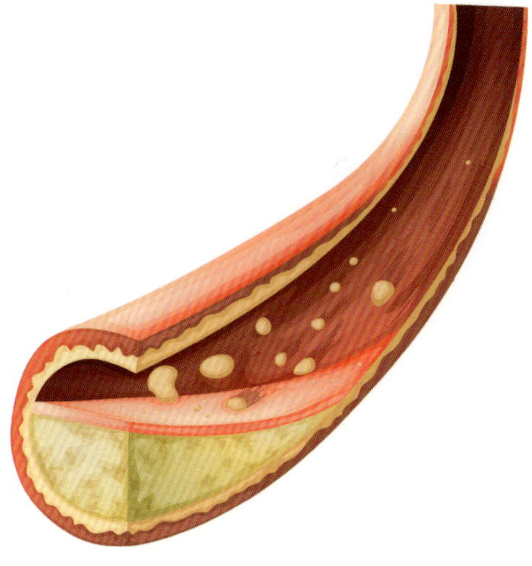

Vitamin K2 helps to decalcify blood vessels.

A large epidemiological study from the Netherlands illustrates this point well. The researchers collected data on the vitamin K intakes of the subjects between 1990 and 1993 and measured the extent of heart disease in each subject, who had died from it and how this related to vitamin K2 intake and arterial calcification. **They found that calcification of the arteries was the best predictor of heart disease.** Those in the highest third of vitamin K2 intakes were 52% less likely to develop severe calcification of the arteries, 41% less likely to develop heart disease, and 57% less likely to die from it. ***(Geleijnse et al., 2004, pp. 3100-3105)*** However, intake of vitamin K1 had no effect on cardiovascular disease outcomes.

It was once erroneously believed that intestinal bacteria are a major contributor to vitamin K status. However, the majority of evidence contradicts this view. Most of the vitamin K2 produced in the intestine are embedded within bacterial membranes and not available for absorption. Thus, intestinal production of K2 likely makes only a small contribution to vitamin K status. ***(Unden & Bongaerts, 1997, pp. 217-234)***

On the other hand, fermented foods, however, such as sauerkraut, cheese and natto (a soy dish popular in Japan), contain substantial amounts of vitamin K2. Natto contains the highest concentration of K2 of any food measured; nearly all of it is present as MK-7, which research has shown to be a highly effective form. One study demonstrated that MK-7 increased the percentage of osteocalcin in humans three times more powerfully than did vitamin K1. ***(Schurgers & Vermeer, 2000, pp. 298-307).***

Foods high in vitamin K

- Natto
- Hard cheese
- Soft cheese
- Egg yolk
- Butter
- Chicken liver
- Salami
- Chicken breast
- Ground beef

Blood: The River Of Life

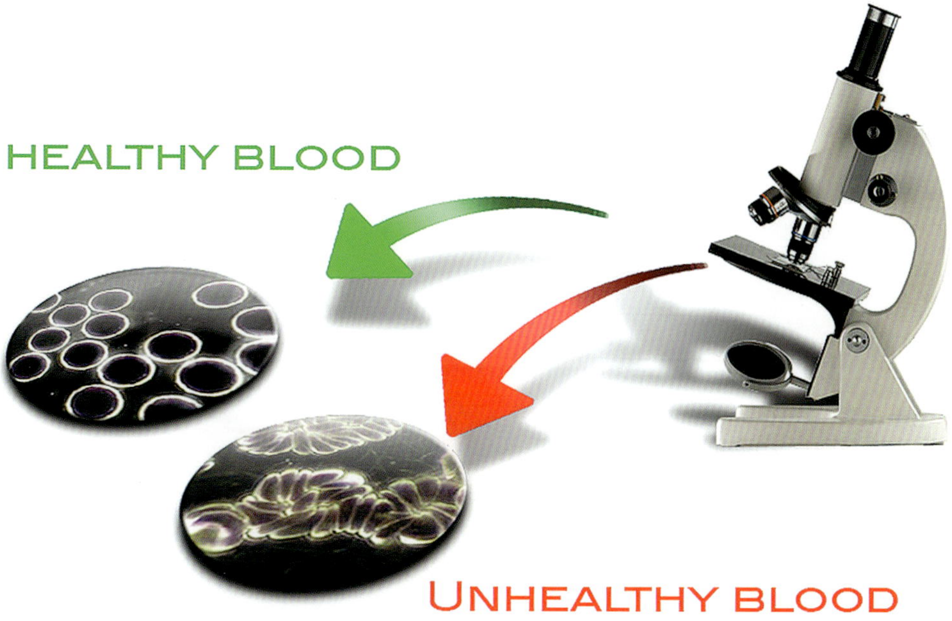

Over the last several years I have analysed hundreds of people's blood using nutritional microscopy which is looking at blood through a very high powered microscope and it never ceases to amaze me what one drop of blood can tell me about someone's health and well being.

The production of red blood cells involves the coordinate interaction of two organ systems in the body. The first is the bone marrow which produces red cells. The second is the kidney which produces the hormone erythropoietin. Hypoxia (low oxygen) of the kidney prompts synthesis and release of erythropoietin. The erythropoietin then travels to the bone marrow via the blood circulation where it activates new red blood production. This increases the blood's oxygen carrying capacity and corrects the hypoxia which was the primary stimulus to erythropoietin production .

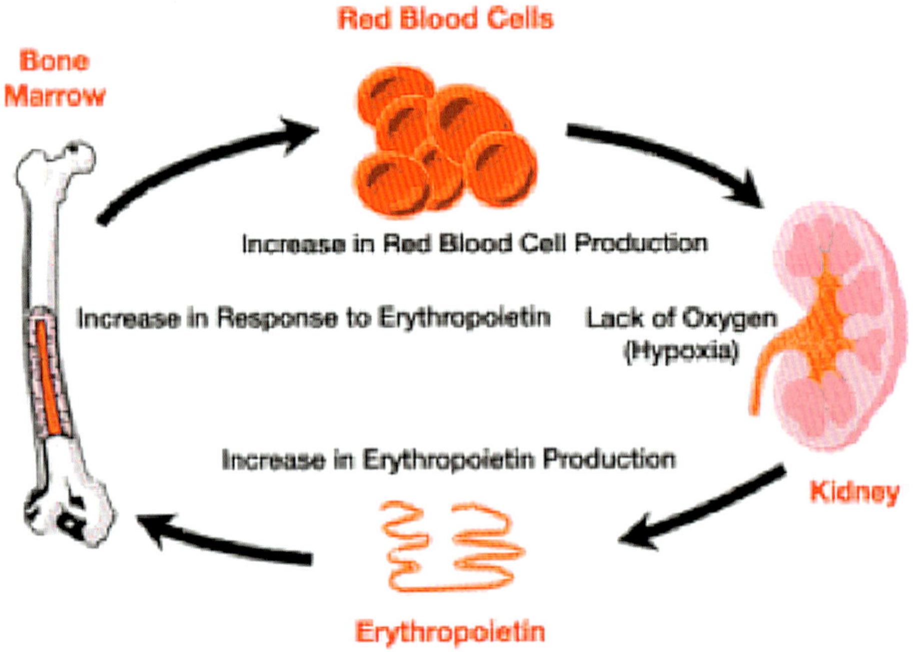

Erythropoietin therefore is part of a finely-tuned feedback circuit that controls red blood cell levels. The best analogy is a thermostat and a furnace. The thermostat senses the temperature and the furnace produces heat to eliminate the chill. Once the proper temperature is reached, the thermostat signals the furnace to cease heat production. Testosterone deficiency also causes anaemia because the hormone helps stimulate kidneys and bone marrow to produce erythropoietin and stem cells. If you don't have enough red blood cells, the tissues and organs of your body may not be getting enough oxygen. This leads to the symptoms of anaemia.

This is another key reason to have optimal testosterone and again another reason to drop all that idiotic nonsense on eating low fat/low cholesterol shite and I genuinely pitty anyone taking statin drugs as discussed in this book they will drop testosterone levels and therefore probably red blood cell production. Message to big pharma you will never beat nature unless you work with her using natural substances!

There are simple ways of increasing the number of red blood cells though. For example, studies have shown that moderate to high intensities of aerobic exercise increases the hematocrit (hematocrit is the proportion, by volume, of the blood that consists of red blood cells), or blood cell volume in people who exercise regularly and intensely.

Hyperbaric oxygen therapy saturates the blood plasma and haemoglobin with oxygen. The red blood cells become more malleable as well, increasing their ability to penetrate restricted blood vessels. Healing time is reduced significantly, and athletes get back into play faster. Breathing high levels of oxygen under hyperbaric conditions causes greater uptake of oxygen by the bodily fluids and so more can reach areas where the circulation is diminished or blocked and therefore improve recovery.

Sunlight also increases both the oxygen content of human blood and its capacity to deliver oxygen to the tissues; in much the same way that exercise does. Essential fatty acids (EFA's) have tremendous oxygenating capabilities. The presence of EFA's in the cell membrane is especially important because they are there to help absorb oxygen.

Anaemia occurs when your blood doesn't have enough haemoglobin. Normal levels are 120 - 160 g/L for women and 140-180 g/L for men. There are around 25 trillion red blood cells in our bodies. Stretched end to end, these cells would form a tower 50,000 kilometres (or 31,070 miles) high .

The importance of blood

Blood is the fluid of life, transporting oxygen from the lungs to body tissue and carbon dioxide from body tissue to the lungs. Blood flows through the arteries and veins that interpenetrates the body like a transport network or river delta, visiting every single corner of the body. During its travels through the arteries, that river carries numerous substances that the cells require.

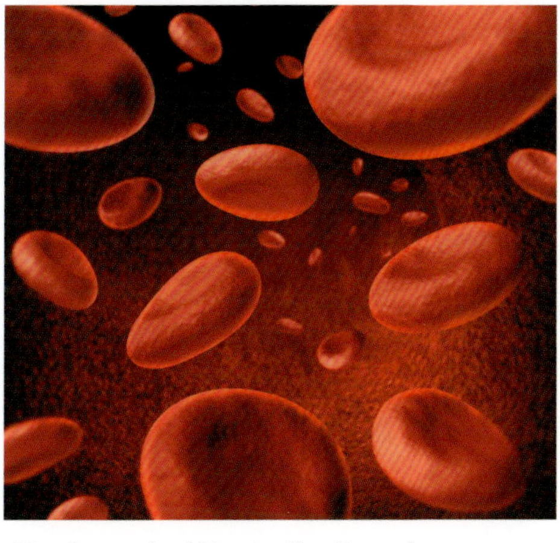

The shape of red blood cells allows them to carry up to 300 million molecules of hemoglobin.

Substances of all kinds that the body requires are carried to the relevant organs by the blood such as hormones, cholesterol, glucose, amino acids, vitamins and minerals and most importantly, oxygen are just a few of these. In addition, the blood works like a waste disposal system, collecting unwanted substances from every cell. And each one of our 50 trillion or so cells in the body produces waste products as a result of its daily functions. These waste products, including such potentially toxic compounds as carbon dioxide and urea, are removed from the cells by means of the bloodstream.

THE ELEMENTS OF BLOOD

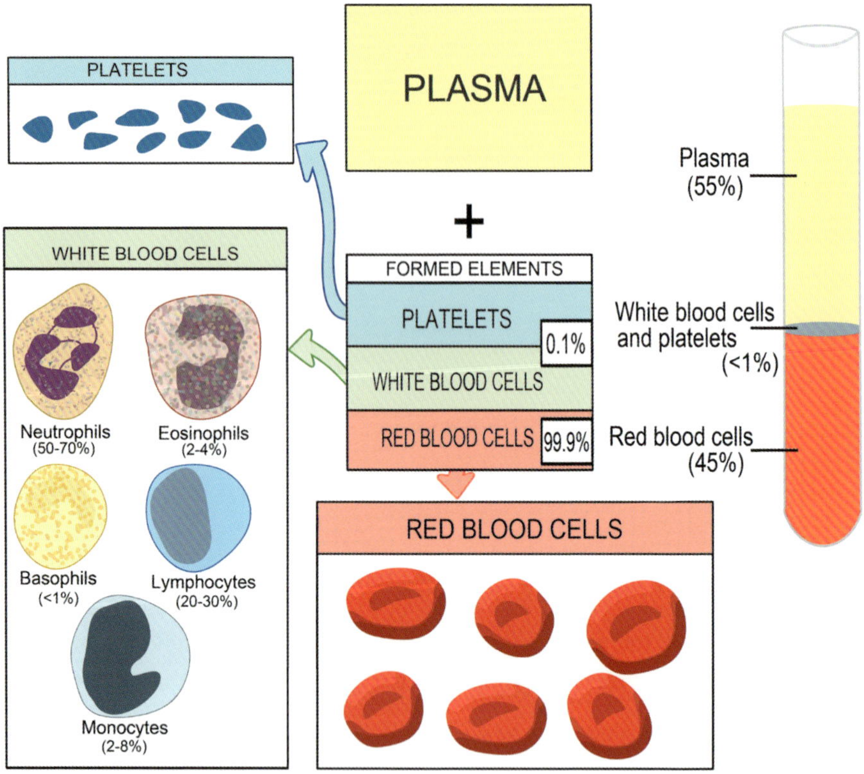

The blood carries the non-gaseous wastes to the kidneys, where they are distilled. The carbon dioxide produced in the cells is carried to the lungs, from where it is expelled from the body. It is unconscious blood cells that do all this. However, these cells can, in a very conscious manner, distinguish between waste and useful substances carried in the blood, and know which are to be deposited where. For example, they never carry toxic gasses to the kidneys, nor metabolic by-products to the lungs.

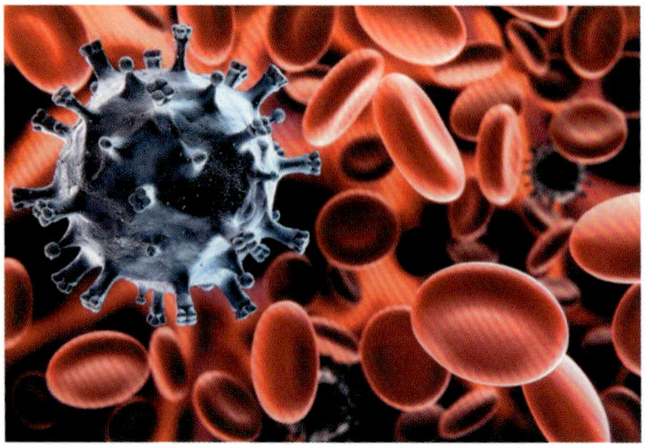

Your blood plays a huge role in making sure that any foreign bodies that enter the blood are neutralised.

Another of the blood's duties is to carry the cells of the immune system that fight disease. Any foreign bodies like viruses and bacteria that enter the body are neutralized by the antibodies and leukocytes in the blood. In addition, immune system cells patrol the bloodstream and so monitor the entire body.

The blood also constitutes one of the body's main avenues of communication. There is a magnificent communications system among the cells in the human body. They exchange information with one another, just as if each one were truly conscious. The cells send to one another chemical messages in the form of hormones and cytokines carried by the blood.

One of the blood's most miraculous features is its clotting mechanism. Thanks to this clotting, or coagulation, blood loss from a damaged vessel is reduced to the minimum possible. During the clotting process, dozens of proteins, enzymes and vitamins serve in regimented order.

One of the vital cargo packages carried by the blood is heat. Arteries filled with blood spread heat through the body, just like the piping that carries hot water throughout a building. But unlike the pipes in a building, the body's heat source is not a single boiler, but all the many cells in the body. Thanks to the blood, heat produced by each cell is distributed equally to all the others. Were there no heat distribution system in your body, you would experience grave problems. As the result of any muscular activity you perform running for instance, or carrying a heavy load your legs or arms would overheat, and other regions of your body would remain close to room temperature—an imbalance that would inflict serious damage on your metabolism. For that reason, the equal distribution of heat is of the greatest importance.

Structurally, the blood is very different to the other fluids in the body. **In one sense, blood is actually a tissue, just like bone or muscle.** However, while the cells that comprise these other tissues are bound tightly together, cells composing the blood are not attached to one another. Individual blood cells—known as erythrocytes (red blood cells), leukocytes (white blood cells) and thrombocytes (platelets) move freely distributed within the blood plasma. Blood consists of 55% plasma and 45% blood cells. Water comprises from 90 to 92% of the plasma, the rest consisting of plasma

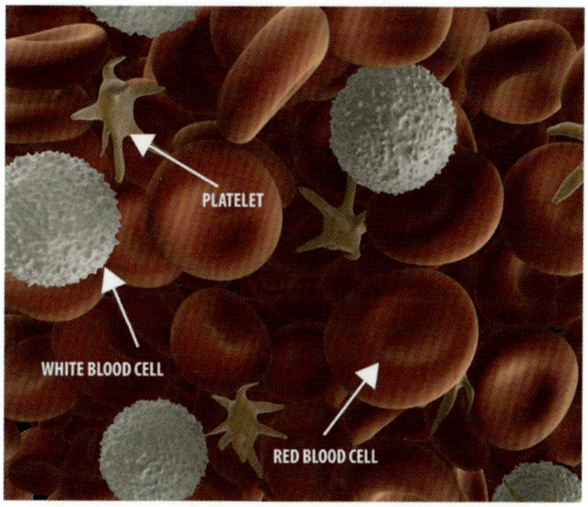

A closer look at some of the components of our blood.

proteins, amino acids, carbohydrates, fats, hormones, urea, uric acid, lactic acid, enzymes, alcohol, antibodies, and elements such as sodium, potassium, iodine, iron and bicarbonate. The blood cells float in this complex fluid.

Under normal circumstances, some 2.5 million erythrocytes are produced in the body every second. It is not enough for the body's transportation system for red blood cells to be flat. Erythrocytes that carry oxygen would be pointless if they could not offer it to the cells in a usable manner. The cells of the body require molecules to bind oxygen to them—molecules that must combine with the oxygen in the ideal manner, in a three-dimensional form, and carry the oxygen safely. However, they must not bind too tightly to the oxygen, and when they arrive at the cell to which they will release the oxygen, they must separate from it with no difficulty. In short, in order for the oxygen to be transported and used where necessary, a very special molecule with a most particular creation is needed. That molecule is haemoglobin, which gives the erythrocyte and thus, the blood itself its red colour.

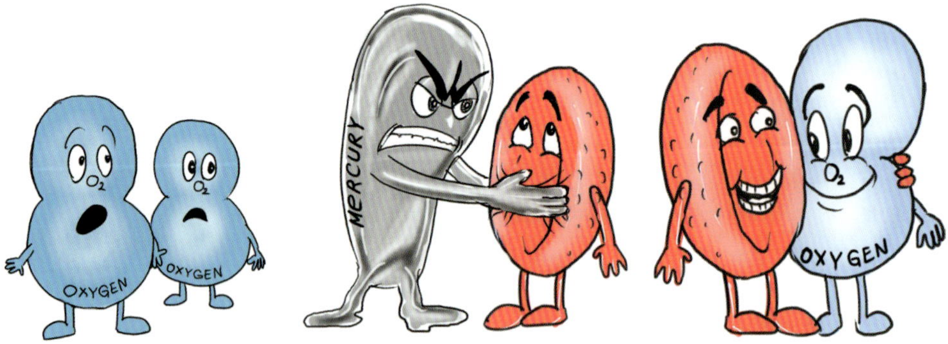

Red blood cells carry oxygen around the body. The oxygen molecules are attracted to red blood cells and are attached to them to be transported around the body. However, mercury can suffocate red blood cells and reduce their ability to carry oxygen molecules.

> ***Mercury from amalgam fillings has been shown to be neurotoxic, embryotoxic, mutagenic, teratogenic, immunotoxic and clastogenic. It is capable of causing immune dysfunction and auto-immune diseases.***
>
> **- Dr. Robert Gammal**

Since haemoglobin performs two entirely separate functions, it has been described as an extraordinary molecule. As haemoglobin deposits carbon dioxide in the lungs, it takes up oxygen and moves from there to the muscles, which oxidize nutrients and produce carbon dioxide. When the haemoglobin reaches the muscles, it carries out a reverse procedure, depositing oxygen and taking up carbon dioxide - all in a seemingly conscious and disciplined manner.

What are the effects of low oxygen?

- Low oxygen levels are associated with poor health:
- Poor concentration and forgetfulness
- Easily stressed and anxious
- Shortness of breath when walking short distances
- Cramping of leg muscles
- Swollen ankles
- General fatigue, particularly after eating
- Recurrent chest infections
- Blueness of fingertips and lips

In 1996, scientists discovered that in addition to carrying oxygen, the haemoglobin molecules in the erythrocyte structure also carried another molecule of vital importance: nitrogen monoxide. There is a very important reason why haemoglobin carries this gas. With the assistance of nitric oxide, haemoglobin monitors how much oxygen is to be provided to the tissues. Therefore, haemoglobin transportation of nitrogen monoxide is of the very greatest importance to human health.

Haemoglobin does not only carry oxygen; when it passes by a muscle in urgent need of oxygen, it also immediately realizes that it must deliver that oxygen, and acts in the knowledge that it needs to collect the carbon dioxide being released, and heads directly for the lungs to deposit its new load. The haemoglobin never confuses oxygen and carbon dioxide, and always moves to the correct destination. An average of 900 million erythrocytes are produced in the human body every hour, and each erythrocyte cell contains some 300 million haemoglobin molecules.

Pernicious Anaemia

Pernicious anaemia is a condition in which the body does not make enough red blood cells (erythrocytes) due to a lack of vitamin B12 in the body. It usually occurs in people whose bodies have lost the ability to absorb vitamin B12 from food. In pernicious anaemia, the blood cells do not divide normally and are too large. They have trouble getting out of the bone marrow. The problem is due to a lack of vitamin B12 in

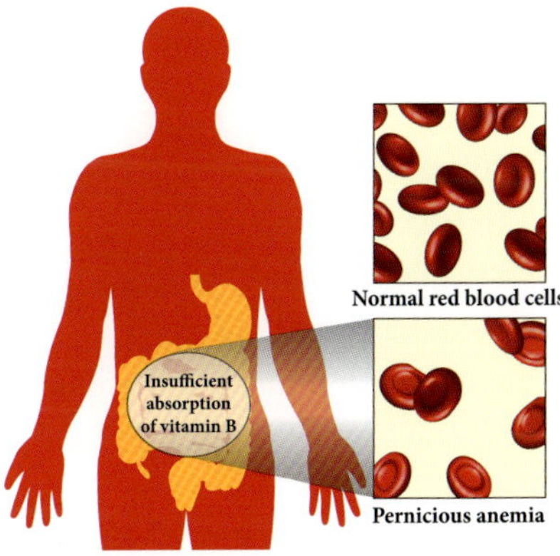

the body. People who have pernicious anaemia often feel tired and weak because the body is not getting enough oxygen.

B12 deficiency attacks the nerves, stripping them of their protective myelin coating and disrupting the communication between cells in the brain or other parts of the nervous system. B12 deficiency can affect your nervous system in other ways as well. Because the nerve cells in your brain control how you feel, think, and behave, B12 deficiency can cause severe mental illness, including depression, paranoia, and even symptoms resembling schizophrenia. B12 plays a crucial role in melatonin production, which is another reason it is important to make sure you're receiving an adequate amount of this vitamin into your blood.

B12 and folic acid also increases the production of a product that fights the depression called SAMe (S-adenosylmethionine, pronounced "Sammy") which has shown in many studies to actually be as effective as the western medicine antidepressant drugs without the often associated side effects of antidepressants.

True pernicious anaemia refers specifically to a disorder of atrophied parietal cells leading to absent intrinsic factor, resulting in an inability to absorb B12.

Besides a lack of intrinsic factor, pernicious anaemia can be caused by Crohn's disease, stomach surgery, or a strict vegetarian diet. Breast-fed infants of vegan mothers are particularly at risk of vitamin B12 deficiency. Vitamin B12 deficiency is certainly the etiology of the macrocytic anaemia, macrocytic red blood cells are a common finding in people who drink alcohol to excess..

Vitamin B12 deficiency can be slow to develop, causing symptoms to appear gradually and intensify over time. It can also come on relatively quickly. Given the array of symptoms it can cause, the condition can be overlooked or confused with something else. Symptoms may include:

- strange sensations, numbness, or tingling in the hands, legs, or feet
- difficulty walking (staggering, balance problems)
- anemia
- a swollen, inflamed tongue
- yellowed skin (jaundice)
- difficulty thinking and reasoning (cognitive difficulties), or memory loss
- paranoia or hallucinations
- weakness
- fatigue

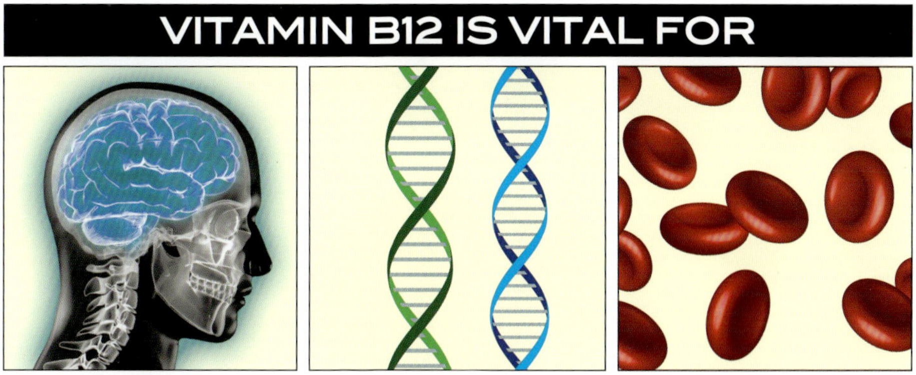

Neurological Function | DNA Synthesis | Red Blood Cell Formation

Best food sources of Vitamin B12

Some of the best sources of B12 include shellfish, liver, caviar, and fish, such as herring and salmon. Clams alone can provide 98.9 micrograms of the vitamin per a 100g serving, a whopping 1648% of the RDA. Lamb liver provides 85.7 micrograms per 100g serving (1428%), and fish eggs offer up 54.6 micrograms per 100g serving (940%). Salmon and herring give 302% and 312% respectively.

Ovo-lacto vegetarians can obtain B12 from eggs and dairy products, such as yogurt, cheese, and milk. While these animal products offer less of the vitamin than meat sources, regular intake can still provide necessary quantities of the vitamin. A breakfast of one cup of yogurt and two eggs, for example, provides you with over 100% of the RDA. Many ovo-lacto vegetarians can also benefit from B12 fortified foods or supplements.

Unfortunately, for strict vegetarian and vegans, B12 is not so easy to come by. Since the vitamin only forms naturally in animal products, vegetarians and vegans who don't consume eggs or dairy products should add B12 supplements to their nutrition plan.

Other B vitamins

The body cannot make Haemoglobin without Vitamin B6 Pyridoxine. Not only does the body need Vitamin B6 Pyridoxine to make Haemoglobin, but Vitamin B6 Pyridoxine will help Haemoglobin to carry more oxygen. Studies also show that pyridoxine deficiency impairs vitamin B12 absorption and reduce the function of this essential nutrient for blood formation. Exercise and a high protein diet increases demand for vitamin B6 (pyridoxine).

Folate is also essential for the formation of both red blood cells (erythrocytes) and white blood cells in the bone marrow, and for their development. Folate deficiency greatly affects red blood cell formation.

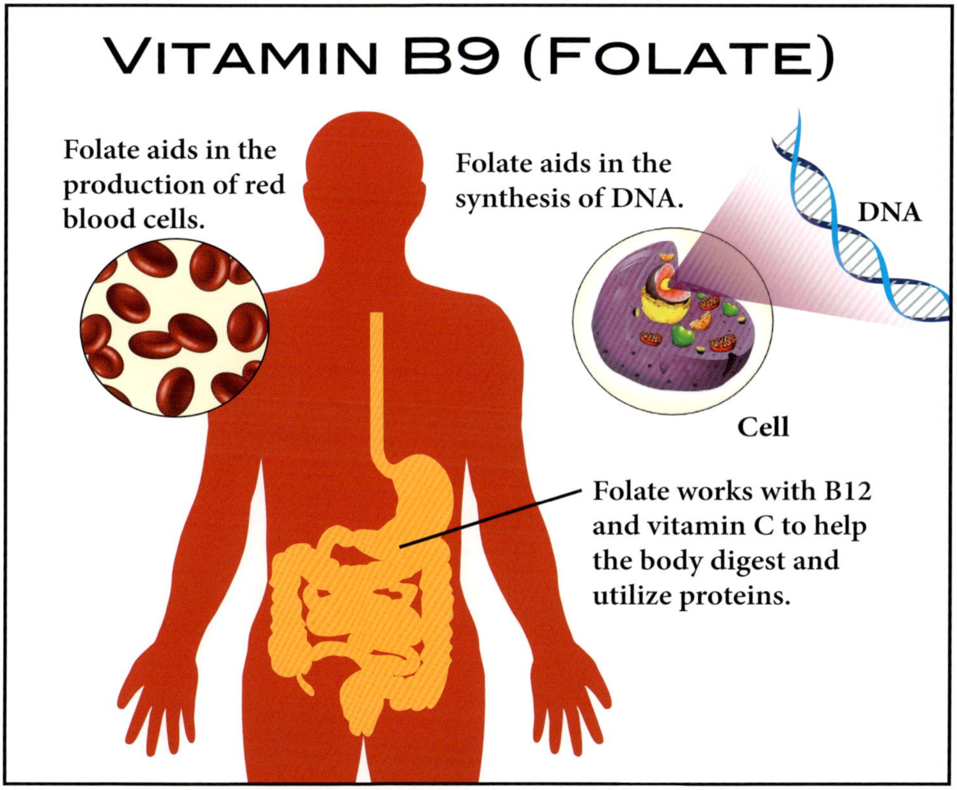

The Importance of Iron

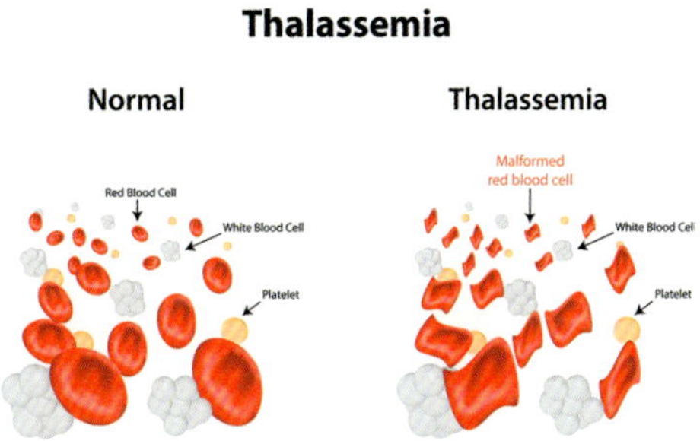

The distribution of body iron stores shows the importance of iron to red cell production. Normally, about 70% of iron is found in the circulating erythrocytes. Approximately 20% of iron is stored as ferritin, primarily in the liver. Smaller amounts of iron are coupled with enzymes, myoglobin and other proteins. The high iron content of erythrocytes reflects the fact that iron is an integral part of hemoglobin. Hemoglobin comprises over 95% of the protein in red cells. Low grade bleeding (for instance, due to hookworm infection) is the most common cause of iron deficiency worldwide. No physiological means of iron excretion exists. Iron absorption from the gastrointestinal tract is the sole means of regulating iron stores.

Iron is an essential part of the diet and is absorbed from the duodenum and proximal jejunem. The iron is rapidly transferred to the carrier protein transferrin which delivers it to all the cells in the body. About 80% of absorbed iron is delivered to the bone marrow. A feedback exists such that iron absorption increases when more red cells are produced by the bone marrow. Ironically, some patients with extremely active marrow red cell production can develop iron overload. This occurs in some forms of thalassemia, for instance.

The body has no means of excreting iron. The obligatory daily iron losses are approximately 1-2 mg. The primary modes of iron loss are epithelial shedding from the GI tract. In females, menstruation accounts for approximately 1 mg of iron loss per day on average.

Erythropoiesis involves the close interaction of iron and erythropoietin. In essence, erythropoietin is the accelerator that drives erythropoiesis. Iron is the fuel for the production of new red blood cells. When the two are coupled, red cell production moves briskly and efficiently. If one component is absent (e.g., iron deficiency) anemia results. Even when both components are available, they must be coordinately delivered to the bone marrow for proper action. For instance, if iron arrives on the scene 6 hours after erythropoietin reaches the bone marrow, red cell production will be suboptimal. The erythropoietin would have spent itself on cells that were unable to respond. Little or none of the erythropoietin would be left when the iron finally arrived.

Evidence of the interplay between iron and erythropoietin has existed for a number of years. For instance, subjects who needed surgery for GI bleeding but refused transfusion because of religious beliefs sometimes developed extremely low hematocrits due to very severe iron deficiency. Replacement of iron by intravenous infusion dramatically increased blood cell production. In some reports, hemoglobins rose from 3 g/dl to 9 g/dl over the course of 14 days (Dudrick, et al,. 1985). These studies were performed before plasma erythropoietin levels could be determined. However, we can extrapolate from current data that the subjects had extremely high erythropoietin levels. The only block to new red cell production was their iron deficiency. When the two components iron and erythropoietin are brought together, bone marrow activity surges tremendously.

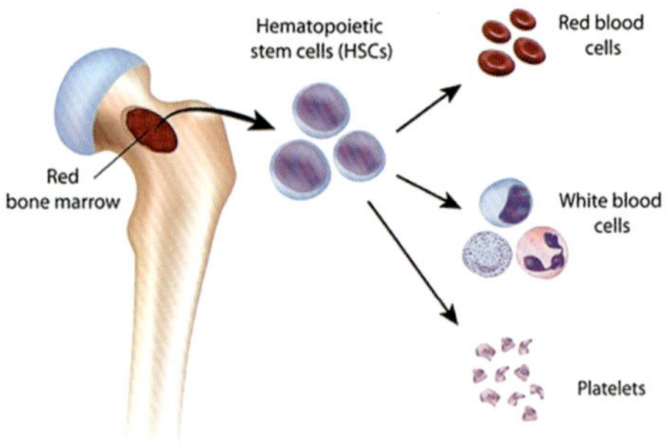

Iron is essential for red blood cell production.

Heme iron is from meat sources and non-heme iron is from plant sources, such as cereal grains, legumes, and leafy greens. If you are vegetarian/vegan and/or are diagnosed anaemic, then you may want to place some restrictions on your tea drinking. Here's why: Tannins chelate non-heme iron. Iron is essential for making haemoglobin, a mere 10% drop in haemoglobin levels can decimate endurance by 20–25%. That doesn't sound like much until you understand that only 10% of the iron in a good diet is bioavailable. So to get sufficient iron, a male athlete in heavy training needs to eat a minimum of 35 mg of iron, and a female 40 mg – every day.

But how exactly does this mineral affect peak physical performance? When a person operates without adequate iron, less oxygen is delivered to the muscles, maximal oxygen consumption (VO2max) drops, and physical performance suffers. Additionally, too little iron may impair immune and other physiological functions.

The Iron Depletion Process

Although iron depletion is a continuous process, it can be categorized into three stages:

- depletion of iron stores (but with functional iron unchanged)
- early functional-iron deficiency without anemia
- iron deficiency anemia

In the first two stages, hemoglobin stores appear normal and iron depletion can easily go undetected or is often dismissed as being insignificant; nevertheless, low iron stores can be detrimental to athletic performance.

The final stage of iron deficiency is anemia, which is defined as a low hemoglobin concentration in the blood, regardless of the cause. Clinical symptoms and the overall effect on performance capacity can vary between individuals at each stage of the iron depletion process, but symptoms may eventually include reduced endurance capacity, lethargy, poor concentration, irritability and increased risk of injury.

Testing Iron Depletion

Iron status is determined by blood testing. If a client's initial test indicates low iron status, the client should be considered at potential risk for developing iron deficiency anemia (Burke & Deakin 2000).

First and foremost, any athlete with low iron status should be referred for additional blood tests and further evaluation. As a preventive measure, an array of biochemical measures can be conducted to further evaluate iron status *(Burke & Deakin 2000)*. Routine indicators include serum iron, ferritin, transferrin, transferrin saturation and hemoglobin; a full blood count should also be taken (Burke & Deakin 2000). Repeated measurements, combined with other diagnostic tools (such as clinical and dietary assessment), would give a better assessment of the athlete's true iron status *(Burke & Deakin 2000)*.

Iron Losses In The Active Body

Elite and recreational athletes who train hard will deplete their iron stores much faster than less physically active people. An athlete can lose iron through sweat, urine and the gastrointestinal tract. Female athletes are at greater risk of iron deficiency anemia because of the added losses through menstruation. Adolescent athletes are also at high risk of iron deficiency anemia often have difficulty meeting iron requirements through diet.

While the stress of exercise is a significant factor, dietary choices cause most cases of iron depletion. Vegetarian and vegan athletes are especially vulnerable in this regard, because they avoid animal sources of dietary iron, known as heme iron, which is more effectively absorbed than the non-heme iron from plant sources. In fact, heme iron provides up to one-third of all absorbed dietary iron.

Athletes who regularly restrict their caloric intake in order to lose or maintain a certain weight are also probably getting inadequate iron, which can result in iron deficiency anemia, unless they are specifically focusing on eating foods that are rich in iron.

Achieving Adequate Iron

Unfortunately, the body cannot manufacture its own iron and is thus dependent on food or supplements or both for an adequate supply. Good food sources of iron are the foods the cholesterol retards warn us against eating red meat, liver and egg yolks. Yes, these are foods crucial for building red blood cells so don't shy away from them unless you want low cholesterol levels, feel like shit and have the endurance of a brick wall.

Research indicates that vitamin C increases iron absorption when iron is needed. It seems to increase excretion of iron when there is an excessive amount of iron. Therefore, vitamin C might be a good treatment of Hemochromatosis.

The effect of mercury on our blood

Mercury destroys red blood cells yet many dentists still keep putting this poison in people's mouths every day and vaccine manufacturers still add it to certain vaccines as if it is a harmless substance! Mercury in the bone marrow becomes incorporated into the haemoglobin of the red blood cells and also inhibits the synthesis of the constituent molecule, heme. This is an absolute disaster for our health and well being and will cause a host of health problems and you have no idea that the culprit is mercury. Mercury vapour is attracted to, and can enter, the red blood cells. So it accumulates within the red blood cells and can destroy their membranes causing rupture and the formation of blood clots (thrombi).

Researchers have determined that exposure to low levels of mercury can encourage clotting of red blood cells, a dangerous condition called thrombosis that contributes to cardiovascular disease. In short, the research shows that red blood cells, when dying after exposure to mercury, release proteins that encourage blood cells and platelets to clot and clump together or coagulate inside vessels. The increased clots can worsen existing cardiovascular disease and raise its risk in others.

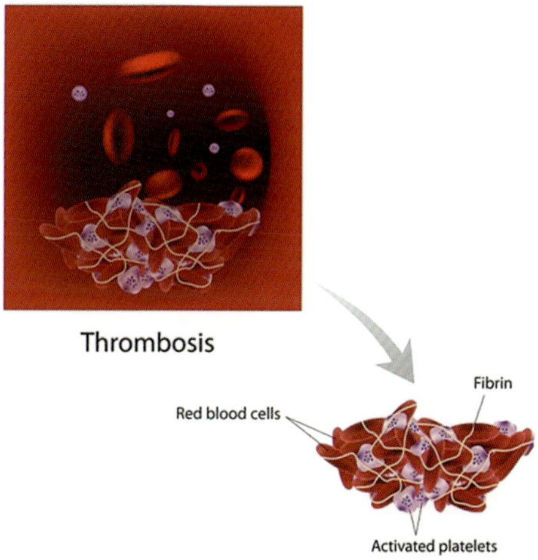

The laboratory study is the first to identify the specific cell responses that may play a role in why exposure to the metal elevates the risk of heart and circulatory disease. The results validate that changes seen in red blood cells exposed to very high levels of mercury also occur in cells exposed to low levels of the metal.In the study, the authors collected blood, isolated the red blood cells, exposed them to low levels of mercury and examined effects in various ways alone, in blood plasma, in tissue samples and in rats. They determined cell shape differences, measured release of proteins key to clotting and analyzed how well the cells stuck to the inside of vessel walls.

They used relatively low concentrations of mercury - 0.25 to 5 micro molar (uM) - which is within the upper range typically measured in blood of those exposed through contaminated fish consumption and found that this caused the red blood cells exposed in culture dishes to change shape and release fragments of their outer cell membrane, results of a process called programmed cell death. The changes are consistent with the process of blood clotting and are a likely way that mercury exacerbates heart disease.

The authors found similar results in rats. The 0.5 – 2.5 milligram per kilogram (mg/kg) doses increased the formation of blood clots and the same protein changes.

HEMOGLOBIN

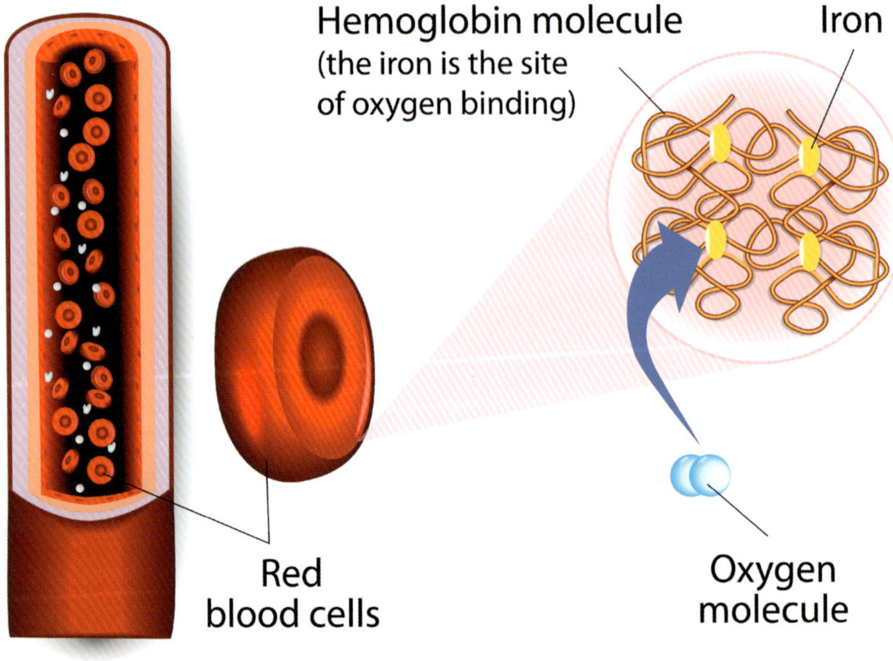

Mercury binds with haemoglobin, which is located inside the red blood cell and carries oxygen for transport to tissues. Mercury bound to haemoglobin results in less oxygen carrying capacity of the red blood cell and therefore less oxygen will reach the tissues. The body senses the need for more oxygen and compensates for this by increasing more red blood cell production which can increase the viscosity of blood leading to circulation problems.

An average filling contains an estimated 800 milligrams of amalgam, with the average middle-aged adult having 8 fillings. The average adult has 3.2 grams or mercury (8 fillings x 800 mg per filling x 50% of total amalgam is mercury) of potential mercury vapour to go into the lungs, blood, and brain from dental fillings alone! That's going to cripple your cardiovascular system. A single dental amalgam filling can release as much as release 15 micrograms of mercury

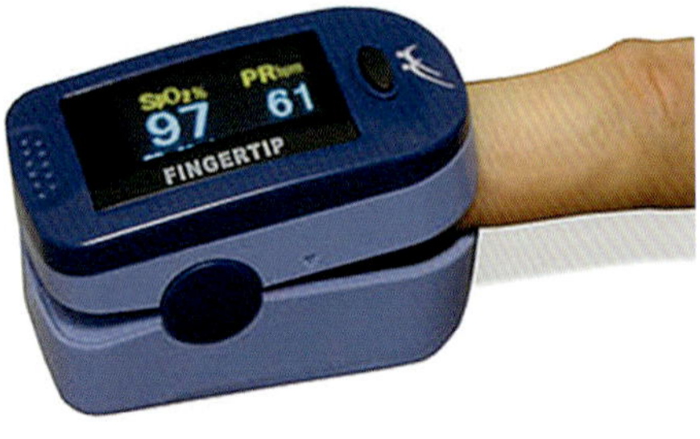

You can purchase an oximeter which you can use as a quick measure of the oxygen levels in your blood.

per day. The average individual who has eight amalgam fillings and could absorb up to 120 micrograms of mercury per day.

- Mercury from amalgams can cause a weakening in the wall of the small blood vessels (micro-angiopathies) – this results in a reduction of blood supply to the tissues resulting in reduced function and/or cell death. *Stortebecker, P.. The Lancet, May 27, 1989.*
- Heart function may be affected by mercury and electrical currents from amalgam. *Silver Dental Fillings - The Toxic Time Bomb, Aurora Press, New York 1984. The Missing Link by Dr Michael F Ziff DDS & Sam Ziff*
- Some reports suggest that elevated cholesterol levels are related to mercury in the body. It has been noted that cholesterol levels drop after removal of amalgam fillings. *Sam Queen; Chronic Mercury Toxicity; New Hope Against an Endemic Disease. Huggins H., It's All In Your Head. 1990*

The first requirement for effective mercury detoxification is boosting your glutathione levels. Most forms of oral glutathione are not effective because they are destroyed in the digestive process. But you can consume foods that contain the precursors of glutathione so that your body can make more of it — specifically, cysteine-rich foods as garlic, onions, parsley and cruciferous vegetables are particularly helpful in addition to avocados, squash and tomatoes. The absolute best source though is high quality whey protein. This whey must come from the "clean" milk of organically raised cows, and not have been overly processed, which denatures the fragile proteins.

Another potent detoxifier of mercury and heavy metals are beneficial bacteria. Their cell membranes tend to bind very effectively to the metals and they are typically excreted in the stool. One of the best ways to provide your body with this resource is with probiotic supplements.

Plasma

Plasma proteins constitute 7-9% of plasma. Plasma is the liquid portion of the blood. Blood cells like red blood cells float in the plasma. Plasma distributes the substances it contains as it circulates throughout the body.

There are three types of plasma proteins: albumins, globulins, and fibrinogen

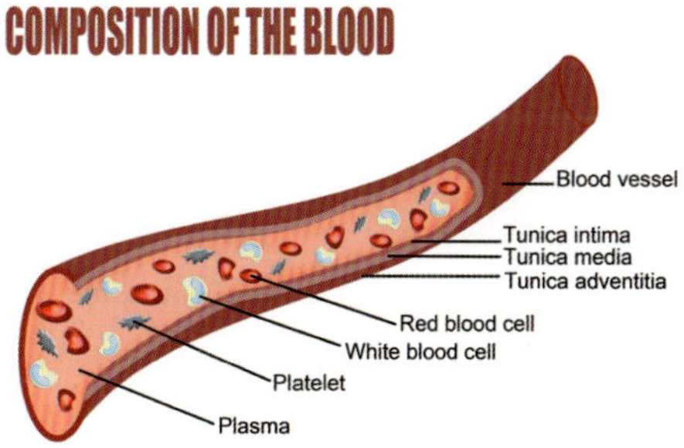

- Albumin - accounts for 60-80%; creates colloid osmotic pressure that draws H20 from interstitial fluid into capillaries to maintain blood volume & pressure
- Globulins - carry lipids; gamma globulins are antibodies
- Fibrinogen - serves as clotting factor; converted to fibrin.

Also dissolved in plasma are electrolytes, nutrients and vitamins (absorbed from the intestines or produced by the body), hormones, clotting factors, and proteins such as albumin and immunoglobulins (antibodies to fight infection).

Fibrinogen is a protein found in blood plasma which plays a vital role in blood clotting. This protein is produced by the liver. Fibrinogen is thought to play a direct role in coronary artery thrombosis. Ideally, therefore, when fibrinogen levels are high, reducing those levels should be the goal of therapy. Elevated fibrinogen levels have also been associated with a number of other diseases, including cancer, diabetes and hypertension. ***(N Engl J Med, 1987, 317: 521; The Framingham Study. JAMA, 1987, 258: 1183)***

When a blood clot forms, fibrinogen is converted to fibrin, which forms the structural matrix of a blood clot (Koenig W 1999). Fibrinogen also facilitates platelet adherence to endothelial cells (Massberg S et al 1999). People with high levels of fibrinogen are more than twice as likely to die of a heart attack or stroke as people with normal fibrinogen levels (Wilhelmsen L et al 1984; Packard CJ et al 2000). In a review which included data for over 154,000 patients, every 100 mg/dL increase in fibrinogen levels was associated with a significantly increased risk of developing coronary heart disease, stroke, and with vascular related mortality.

In one study, those patients with the lowest one-third fibrinogen levels (mean 236 mg/dL) were much less likely to suffer a stroke, develop cardiovascular disease, or die of other vascular related causes when compared to those with the highest one-third fibrinogen levels (mean 374 mg/dL) (Danesh, 2005). This risk goes up even more in the presence of hypertension (Bots ML et al 2002). Fibrinogen levels should be kept between 295 to 369 mg/dl.

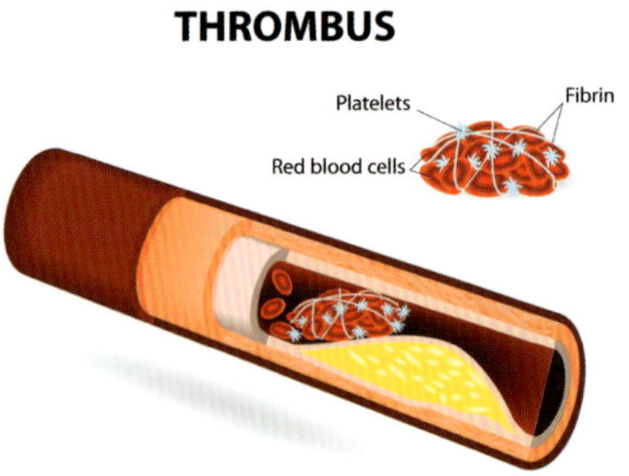

Reducing fibrinogen

Fish oil taken in daily doses of 3000 mg or greater has been shown to lower fibrinogen levels. It may be no coincidence that fish oil has also been shown to reduce heart attack risk.

Excessive homocysteine blocks the natural breakdown of fibrinogen by inhibiting the production of tissue plasminogen activator (tPA). Folic acid, trimethylglycine (TMG), vitamin B12, and vitamin B6 reduce elevated homocysteine levels.

Vitamin C may also help reduce fibrinogen. In one study, heart disease patients were given either 1000 or 2000 mg a day of vitamin C to measure the fibrinogen breakdown effect. At 1000 mg a day, there was no detectable change in fibrinolytic activity or cholesterol. At 2000 mg a day of vitamin C, there was a 27% decrease in the platelet aggregation index, a 12% reduction in total cholesterol, and a 45% increase in fibrinolysis (fibrinogen breakdown) activity.

Platelets

Platelets are tiny cells that circulate in the blood and whose function is to take part in the clotting process. What happens when we are stressed to affect the heart? Adrenaline and cortisol are known to increase stickiness of platelets which tend to be blood clotting fragments. Stress causes the blood to clot more, this serves you well if it's a life or death situation like being in battle, you want more clotting as this can slow down any potential wounds inflicted in battle.

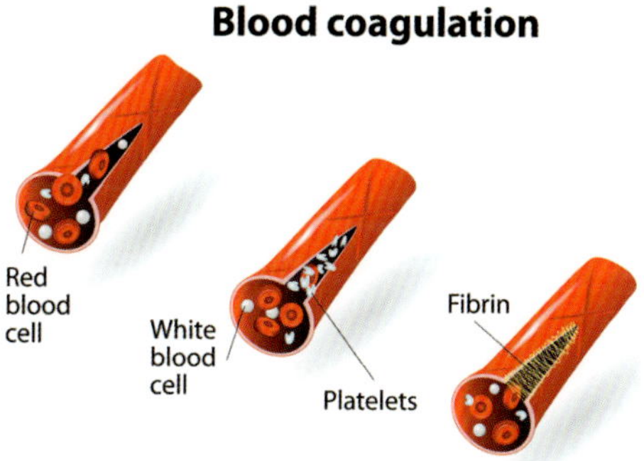

However, constantly being in a stressed scenario (be it through financial, relationship or excess toxicity) causes the blood to become more of a consistency similar to red ketchup rather than a vintage red wine, an analogy created by cardiologist Kenneth R Kensey, a pioneer in the study of blood viscosity as a risk factor for CVD. The thicker and stickier the blood becomes, the greater the risk for cardiovascular disease. How can we improve the viscosity of our blood?

Researchers at the University of Edinburgh suggest that fish oils prevent the platelet activation involved in the formation of atherosclerotic lesions and blood clots (thrombosis).

Vitamin C increases the production of prostacyclin, a small molecule that not only relaxes the blood vessel walls, but also keeps blood viscosity at optimum levels.

Immune Function

Today we all need a vibrant, healthy immune system, probably more so than at any other time during our existence, as we are faced with so many potential immune system attackers.

Your ability to interact with the world around you and remain healthy is dependent to a large extent on the healthy functioning of your immune system. Your immune system is responsible for fighting foreign invaders to your body, like pathogenic bacteria and viruses, and also for destroying cells within your body when they become cancerous. Poor nutrition has been shown to result in increased infections, to slow healing from injury and infections, and to increase susceptibility to symptoms and complications from immune system dysfunction.

Science has shown that immune function often decreases as we age, and due to toxicity and a poor diet. Medical science has established that one of the most important factors in supporting a healthy, balanced immune system is good nutrition. Research studies show that healthy eating can help in keeping your immune system ready and capable of functioning properly when necessary.

What is my immune system?

Your immune system is like a finely tuned army whose purpose is to defend your body from unhealthy insults from the world around you, like the thousands of man-made toxins we discussed in habit 1. Like an army, your immune system contains many different units that work harmoniously together with one goal, protecting you from foreign insults that can cause damage to your body. And, like an army, the different

Organs of the Immune System

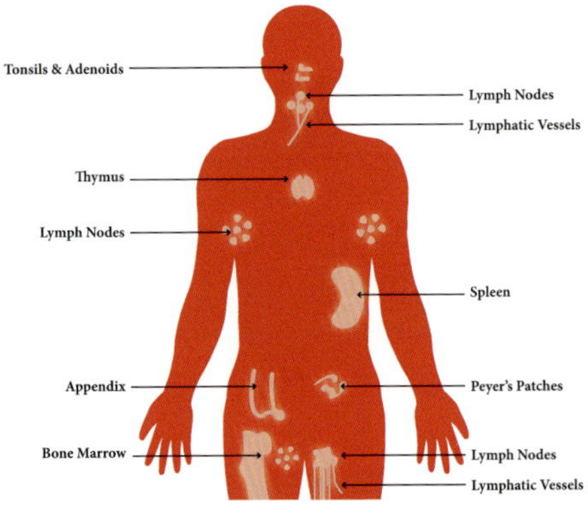

parts of your immune system must be present, play their part at the right time in the fight against the enemy, and then stop when they have completed their function.

The main parts of your immune system are the immune cells, the structural barriers in your body in which the majority of these cells are localized, and the specific messenger molecules that call the cells to action or tell them to stop.

CELLS OF THE IMMUNE SYSTEM

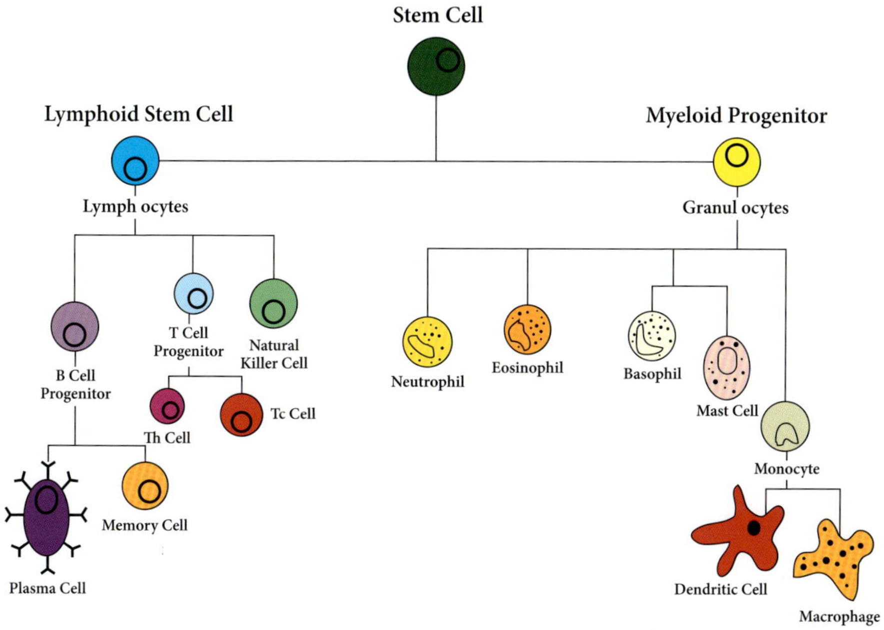

The cells of your immune system are quite varied, and include the *lymphocytes*, or *T-cells*, which fight invading molecules directly, and the *B-cells*, which form *antibodies* that can respond to invading molecules or toxins. The antibodies produced by the B-cells can bind with a potentially damaging molecule or to the surface of a virus or bacteria, thereby targeting it for removal by other immune cells. Your immune system also includes the *phagocytic cells*, such as *macrophages* and *neutrophils*, which remove the debris created from destroying cells and tissue at the site of an infection.

The cells of your immune system are found circulating in your bloodstream or in the lymph nodes, which are located throughout your body; therefore, the immune cells themselves are spread throughout your tissues and can travel quickly when called upon. This way, your immune system is positioned so that it can minimize the entrance into your body of foreign invaders that can cause infection and disease and can quickly respond to any invaders that do manage to gain entrance into your body.

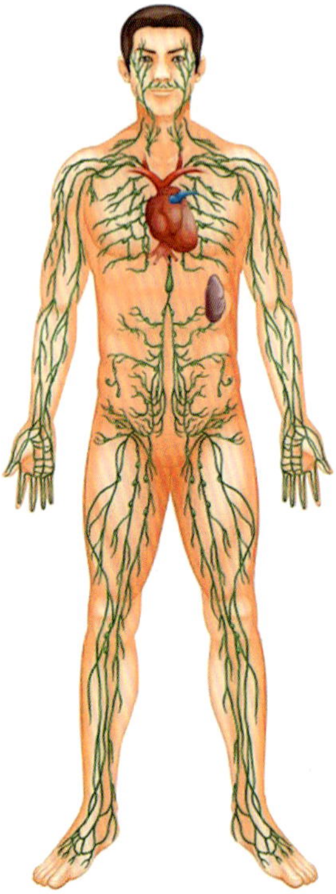

This is the lymphatic system which is essential for immune function.

Your immune system also relies upon specific structures in your body that provide a foundation for defence. The most important structures are the barriers between the inside of your body and the outside. These barriers keep unwanted organisms and molecules from entering your body where they can do damage. Since your skin is in contact with the outside world, it is probably not surprising that your skin is an important barrier; however, it is only one part of your defensive barrier. Your gastrointestinal tract is actually the largest barrier between you and the outside world.

Your immune system also includes molecules called *soluble factors*. These are molecules that can recognize when your barrier has been compromised by a foreign invader or toxin and then try to heal the area of damage and remove the insult from your body rapidly. Factors such as the *complement cascade*, a complex group of proteins, can form an immediate response to an insult.

Your immune system also can deploy signalling molecules, which are soluble factors that send messages to the immune cells located further inside the tissue that has been compromised, or into your bloodstream. These messenger soluble factors call immune cells to the site of damage and activate the cells, bringing them in full force to the infected area. These messenger molecules are called *cytokines*.

Your *cytokines* not only signal immune cells to take up action, but they also often promote an inflammatory response. The inflammatory response at a site of infection is one way your body secludes, or walls-off, an infected area. So, when we talk about the immune system, it is not one organ; it is really the types of immune cells, structures, and soluble factors, like cytokines, which are present throughout all your organs that constitute the immune system. And, your immune system gets help from your inflammatory response.

Nutritionally supporting your immune system means supporting all these sections in the army. Like an well functioning army marches on its stomach a well functioning immune system also needs good nutrition to ensure it can beat invading enemies.

Maintaining a healthy gastrointestinal barrier is essential for optimal immune function.

Of the physical barriers between your internal organs and the outside world, your gastrointestinal tract is of primary importance. The gastrointestinal tract is like an internal skin, but it has about 150 times more surface than does your outside skin. It also contains the largest number of immune cells of your whole body, constituting approximately 60% of your entire immune system. It may be surprising that the gastrointestinal tract has more of your immune system localized within it than any other organ in your body; however, it has a very difficult role. Your gastrointestinal tract comes into contact with the largest amount and number of different molecules, toxins and organisms of any organ in your whole body. Just as an example, the average person ingests more than 25 tons of food over his or her lifetime.

And, unlike your skin or even your lungs, your gastrointestinal tract must figure out how to keep out damaging molecules and pathogenic organisms, while still letting in the nutrients and food components your body needs to survive. So, it has to be selective in its protection. The gastrointestinal mucosal layer has the unique role of keeping out damaging molecules and organisms, like harmful bacteria and viruses, while allowing in only the health-promoting nutrients, molecules and substances. In a perfect scenario, only the beneficial nutrients and phytonutrients are absorbed into the body, while non-beneficial substances and organisms never make it across this barrier and are excreted from your body.

The foods you eat can provide support for this barrier or cause damage to it. For instance, alcohol consumption is known to irritate the gastric (stomach) mucosal barrier. Some drugs, for example the non-steriodal anti-inflammatory drugs like aspirin and ibuprofen, also can harm this barrier.

What nutrients support my immune system cells?

Maintaining healthy cells within the tissues that constitute your barriers, including your gastrointestinal tract is vital for optimal health. Vitamin A plays an important role in supporting the cells of the skin, gastrointestinal tract and lungs which constitute the main barriers that separate you from the external environment. Plus, vitamin A promotes the formation of the protective mucous in your gastrointestinal tract.

Many nutrients like phosphatidylcholine are particularly beneficial in supporting a healthy gastrointestinal barrier since phosphatidylcholine is one of the components of the protective mucosa that lines your intestinal tract and provides the first barrier defence. Phosphatidylcholine is a component of your cell membranes, and therefore choline-rich foods also support healthy cell membranes. Essential fatty acids, such as those found in cold-water fish, and a healthy range of monounsaturated fatty acids, such as those in olive oil, can also support healthy gastrointestinal cells by promoting healthy membranes.

Finally, foods high in fiber, such as fresh fruits and vegetables, promote a healthy gastrointestinal system in several ways. They are fermented by the friendly bacteria in your colon to short-chain fatty acids (SCFAs), which are used as a fuel by gastrointestinal tract cells. Studies have shown that fibers that promote SCFAs also promote a healthy gastrointestinal barrier. Fiber also promotes the removal of toxins that can adversely affect your gastrointestinal tract cells and supports healthy digestive function overall.

Research studies have shown that deficiency of high-quality protein can result in depletion of immune cells, inability of the body to make antibodies, and other immune-related problems. In addition, animal studies have shown that the immune system can be significantly compromised with even a 25% reduction in adequate protein intake.

Glutamine is an important amino acid that may help to maintain muscle, boost the immune system, support gastrointestinal health, and sustain healthy growth hormone levels. Of the 20 amino acids needed for protein synthesis, glutamine is the most abundant, making up 50% of all amino acids in the blood and 60% of those in the body. It is found in high concentrations in skeletal muscle, lung, liver, brain, and stomach tissue. The best dietary sources of glutamine include poultry, beef, fish, cabbage, beets, and dairy products. Because glutamine fuels white blood cells, it is essential in supporting the body's immune system and immune response. Trauma, surgery, viral infections, and chemotherapy have all been shown to deplete glutamine levels. It has been suggested that diminished plasma glutamine levels may lead to suppressed immune function.

Endurance athletes also have decreased plasma glutamine concentrations after prolonged, strenuous exercise. Post-exercise glutamine depletion and associated immunosuppression may render the athlete more susceptible to infection. In one study, a group of 151 elite runners and rowers were given two drinks containing either glutamine or a placebo immediately after and two hours after exercise. Over the following seven days, the percentage of infection-free patients was significantly higher in the glutamine group (81%) than in the placebo group (49%).

Enterocytes, which are epithelial cells lining the small intestine, use glutamine as their primary metabolic fuel. Glutamine is thus essential in maintaining the structural integrity of the intestinal lining. Insufficient glutamine may lead to a loss of gut mucosal integrity, which can allow toxins and infectious agents to be absorbed. This condition, known as increased intestinal permeability, may be associated with health problems such as allergies, skin disorders, and Crohn's disease. By helping guard against increased intestinal permeability, glutamine may have applications in the management of these and other conditions.

The essential vitamins for healthy immune function

As discussed above, your body uses a variety of responses to maintain its defence against harmful pathogenic organisms in the environment; therefore, it may not be surprising that nearly all of the vitamins are necessary to maintain and promote some aspect of your immune function. Some vitamins have received more attention in the research literature since they are particularly important to a healthy immune system.

Much has been written about the role of vitamin C in supporting the immune system, in part because it has been promoted as an immune stimulant by the noted scientist and Nobel Prize Laureate, Linus Pauling. Vitamin C appears to support a decrease in the length of time and severity of symptoms associated with upper respiratory viral infections, promote phagocytic cell functions, and support healthy T-cell function.

A very large body of work, much of it taking place over a half-century ago, has clearly established that the vigorous dosing and administration of vitamin C can cure most acute infections, viral or otherwise, and promptly neutralize most toxin exposures - including many life-threatening health issues.

Behind the scenes, vitamin C is more than 'just' an antioxidant. Why mainstream medicine refuses to embrace the life-saving abilities of vitamin C remains unclear but no doubt in my opinion big pharma does not want the public to know about the incredible powers of Vitamin C. Why? They can't make money from it! But, the validity of the scientific data is absolutely inescapable.

In addition to its role as the premier antioxidant circulating throughout the body, the scientific literature has clearly established vitamin C to directly promote and stimulate a number of very important functions of the immune system. These functions include the following:

1) Enhanced antibody production (B-lymphocytes, humoral immunity)
2) Enhanced interferon production
3) Enhanced phagocytic (scavenger cell) function
4) Enhanced T-lymphocyte function (cell-mediated immunity)
5) Enhanced B-lymphocyte and T-lymphocyte proliferation
6) Enhanced natural killer cell activity (very important anti-cancer function)
7) Enhanced prostaglandin formation
8) Enhanced nitric oxide production by phagocytes

Red blood cells have roughly the same concentration of vitamin C as the surrounding plasma. Heart cells and kidney cells, which are very metabolically active cells, have about 13-fold more vitamin C than the plasma, an impressive concentration difference. This is certainly consistent with the continual need for electrons in such active cells. Phagocytic white blood cells (granulocytes) have 25-fold more vitamin C than the plasma. Since these cells need an abundance of energy to consume and digest pathogens and cellular "debris," this concentration of vitamin C makes a lot of sense as well. The king of the vitamin C concentrators, however, is the circulating monocyte, which becomes known as a macrophage, another cell with phagocytic functions, when it settles into the tissues. This cell has more than an *80-fold* increased concentration of vitamin C inside it relative to the plasma. Few, if any, other examples of a circulating nutrient/vitamin being so selectively concentrated in a given cell type exist.

Whenever inflammation develops, oxidative stress is increased, and vitamin C stores of the inflamed areas are acutely depleted to absent. The first cells that the immune system mobilizes to areas of acute inflammation are the monocytes. As a hypothetical possibility, then, it would appear that this early, initial function of the immune system is to compensate for the inflamed area depleted of vitamin C with a vitamin C 'delivery system': the monocyte. This concept also meshes quite well with the fact that many other immune cells have significantly increased concentrations of vitamin C as well.

Donation of electrons at the molecular level, which is the ultimate positive impact of any therapeutic protocol, is the antioxidant effect. You always want more electron donation and less electron depletion (oxidation). Vitamin C, while not the only good antioxidant you can supplement, performs this electron donation/flow better than anything else available, and it still remains very affordable, in spite of repeated attempts to make it more expensive and market it as a "vitamin C complex" or "natural" vitamin C.

Many of the B-vitamins are also very important in supporting a healthy immune system. For example, vitamin B5 (pantothenic acid) promotes the production and release of antibodies from B-cells, and deficiency of vitamin B5 results in reduced levels of circulating antibodies. Folic acid deficiency leads to a decrease in T-cells and can result in reduced effectiveness of the soluble factors as well.

Vitamin B6 deficiency consistently impairs T-cell functioning and results in a decrease in blood lymphocyte counts. Deficiencies in vitamins B1 (thiamin) and B2 (riboflavin) may impair normal antibody response, and low vitamin B12 appears to inhibit phagocytic cells and possibly T-cell function.

Vegetables are particularly beneficial since they are excellent sources of many of these immune-supporting vitamins. In particular, Romaine lettuce is a rich source of vitamins B1, B2, C, and folate. Turnip greens and spinach are excellent sources of folate, vitamin B6 and vitamin C. Cauliflower happens to be an excellent source of vitamin C, folate, vitamin B6, and pantothenic acid. Red bell peppers are an excellent source of vitamin C and B6

The fat-soluble vitamins, vitamin A, vitamin E and vitamin K are also important to overall health. Vitamin A deficiency has been shown to impair antibody function and T-cell activity. Vitamin E is an important antioxidant and supports a healthy inflammatory response. Vitamin E is also an important component of all cell membranes and promotes healthy cellular functioning overall. T-cells and B-cells from vitamin E-deficient animals show depressed responses, and tumours have been shown to grow faster in vitamin-E deficient animals.

Vitamin K supports a healthy blood-clotting ability in your body, and this is necessary for seclusion of areas of infections and injury in the healing process.

Minerals that support your immune system

Zinc is one of the minerals in food that has received the most attention for its ability to support immune function. Zinc is a potent immunostimulant, and its deficiency can result in profound suppression of T-cell function.

Many other minerals are important in supporting immune function. Clinical research studies have shown that iron deficiency results in impaired response to antibodies, and defective phagocytic cell functioning.

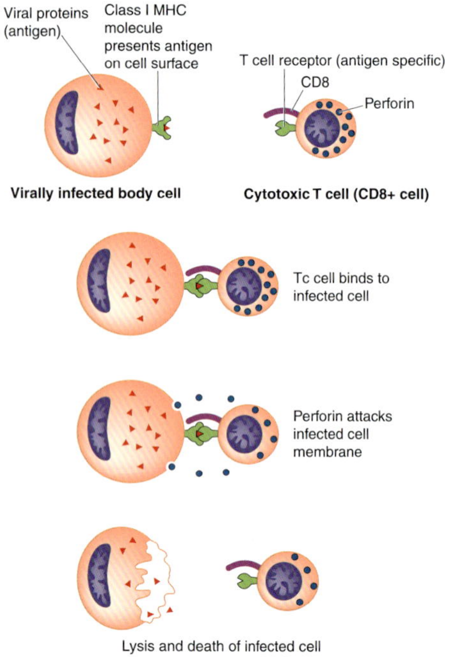

Copper deficiency is associated with an increase in infections and may impair development of immune cells such as T-cells and the phagocytic cells. Selenium and manganese are important for supporting healing from inflammation and may be immunostimulants. Selenium can be obtained from fish, foods grown in selenium rich soils and shellfish, as well as supplements. Excellent sources of copper include sesame seeds, cashews, mushrooms, turnip greens, beet greens, spinach, asparagus, Swiss chard, mustard greens, kale, and summer squash.

Are there foods that are bad for my immune system?

Your immune system is not just involved in fighting invaders like bacteria, but also becomes activated when you eat foods to which you are intolerant or allergic. Reactions to allergenic foods can be quick, like the anaphylactic reaction often seen with peanut or shellfish allergies, but food allergy reactions can also be delayed and cause a number of symptoms like headaches, fatigue, muscle aches, rashes and other systemic (whole body) effects. The most common allergenic foods include peanuts and shellfish, cow's milk, wheat, and soy; however, everyone is unique in their food intolerances and allergies.

Processed foods and foods produced with pesticides or not grown organically may also be problematic for your immune function. Toxic metals such as cadmium, lead and mercury are immunosuppressive. Some pesticides and preservatives can negatively affect the gastrointestinal lining. Food additives can also have untoward effects on the nutrient content of the food. For example, sulfites destroy thiamin-vitamin B1 in foods to which they have been added.

The omega-3 fatty acids, which are produced in your body from the essential omega-3 fat 'alpha-linolenic acid ' have been studied for their effects on the immune system and inflammatory response. Diets low in omega-3 fatty acids are associated with chronic inflammatory conditions and autoimmune diseases. In order to achieve a more beneficial ratio of omega-3 fatty acids in your body, it is important to decrease the amount of omega-6 fatty acids in your diet, while increasing the amount of omega-3 fatty acids.

Red Peppers

Cruciferous Vegetables

Mushrooms

Kale

Berries

Oats

TOP IMMUNE BOOSTING FOODS

Eggs

Cinnamon

Grass Fed Derived Whey

Carrots

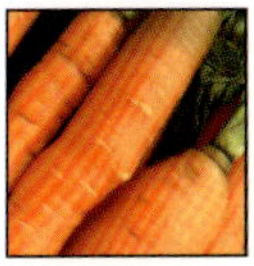

Grapefruit

Walnuts

Garlic

30 MINUTES BEFORE MEALS (UNLESS TRAINING)	BREAKFAST	LUNCH	DINNER	1 HOUR BEFORE BED ON AN EMPTY STOMACH
1 Teaspoons of Alkalising Salts In 500ml of water	1 x Ultimate Multivitamin & Mineral Formula	1 x Ultimate Multivitamin & Mineral Formula	1 x Ultimate Multivitamin & Mineral Formula	2 Scoops of Nitric Oxide Generator
2 x Super Digestive Enzymes (60 minutes before meals)	1 x Oestro Detox Formula	1 x Oestro Detox Formula	1 x Oestro Detox Formula	3 x Magneisum Relax
	2 x Ultimate Fish Oil Capsules	2 x Ultimate Fish Oil Capsules	2 x Ultimate Fish Oil Capsules	
	1 Tablespoon of Collagen Formula	1 Tablespoon of Collagen Formula	1 Tablespoon of Collagen Formula	
	1 x Iodine Forte Capsules	1 x Iodine Forte Capsules	1 x Iodine Forte Capsules	
	1 x Corydceps Plus	1 x Corydceps Plus	1 x Corydceps Plus	
	1 x Probiotic Gut Health	1 x Probiotic Gut Health	1 x Probiotic Gut Health	

BETWEEN MEAL TIMES:
In between breakfast, lunch & evening meals drink 1 pint of still mineral water with ONE heaped TABLESPOONS of Ultimate Greens Powder.

SUPPLEMENT PLAN
Immune system health

What can I do to support and maintain a healthy immune system?

- Provide support for the physical barriers in your body.
- Support a healthy digestive process.
- Consume adequate protein and healthy fats.
- Provide for balanced immune and inflammatory functions. Clinical studies have shown that maintaining a healthy balance between omega-3 and omega-6 fatty acids is one way to support balance in your immune and inflammation responses system. Research indicates a ratio of omega-3 to omega-6 fats of 1:4 is health-promoting.
- Provide micronutrients and phytonutrients that support healthy immune function.
- Decrease intake of allergens and toxins. Eating fresh, organically grown fruits and vegetables, wild-caught fish, and meat and eggs from organically raised animals is one way to minimize the intake of toxins and unhealthy molecules that can inhibit your immune system's ability to protect your health.
- Maintain a healthy body fat percentage and get healthy amounts of sunshine as Vitamin D is a potent immune enhancer as discussed in habit 7.

Conclusion

I hope you know understand just how important it is to have a healthy cardiovascular system and more importantly how to build a healthy heart, blood vessels and blood. This is a habit which I believe is the key for all the other habits to function efficiently. On the back of the research that I did for this habit I developed a number of products which I believe are fundamental for heart, blood vessel and blood health. Remember also the key to a healthy cardiovascular system is happiness and we all deserve to be happy.

I highly recommend the books written by Barry Grove PhD, Uffevnskov, MD,PhD, books by Dr. Thomas E. Levy, a book written by Owen Fonorow called "Practising without a licence" and one by Matthias Rath entitled "Eradicating Heart Disease".

HABIT 9
NUTRIENT TIMING & RECOVERY

"The man who moves a mountain begins by carrying away small stones."
Confucius

In this habit I want to cover the importance of breakfast, ketogenic diets, pre-, during and post-workout nutrition, as well as rest and recovery from training. If you get these factors right then everything else falls into place and you can train with much more intensity, which will increase your metabolism and enhance fat loss. You will also increase your ability to recover, so you can train more frequently and effectively.

If you cannot get your training nutrition right, you are significantly inhibiting the results you will get from your time in the gym. You need to fuel your muscles with the energy they need to train and then provide the building blocks they need to grow and recover. You must get your nutrition, and its timing, right in order to; meet energy requirements for training, achieve and maintain optimum level of body fat composition changes, practice any competition nutrition strategies and maintain optimal immune function.

Visualise how you want to look and get there with hard training and the correct nutrition and lifestyle plan.

It never ceases to amaze me the amount of people I see train really hard and then ignore eating a quality breakfast and not consuming any pre-, during or post-workout nutrition. This will eventually make progress very slow or can make you fatter. Yes, exercise can make you fat if you don't get everything else right. Exercise is stress and if you have lots of stressors in your life then adding another stressor into the mix will add more problems than benefits. That's why I am a huge believer that to get any benefits out of exercise, you have got to be healthy first.

Eat Like a Sumo Wrestler if you want to look like one

Sumo wrestling is an ancient Japanese sport; where the heavier you are the better! Here are some Sumo Wrestlers' tricks for getting big:

Don't eat breakfast: Sumo wrestlers never eat breakfast. This is a great way to slow your metabolism way down and will definitely ensure overeating later in the day.

Eat only 1-2 meals each day: Sumo wrestlers get up early, work out and then don't eat until late in the day. This way they will be starving and will eat anything they can grab and in enormous amounts. This ensures a great calorie surplus and maximum weight gain. When you eat a large amount of calories in one sitting, the body will use up what it can and then fill your extra energy reserves for later. When your storage gets full, everything left over is stored directly as fat.

Eat out: Many studies have found that people eating in a restaurant will eat 40% more food and 30% more fat then they would if they were at home.

Sleep after eating: When they finish their large meals, the wrestlers will take a long nap. Going to sleep on a full stomach forces the body to store most of the calories as fat because it doesn't have the ability to metabolize large amounts of food while sleeping. This is another reason why eating late at night makes you gain weight.

When I first work with an athlete/client I explain to them that I want them to concentrate on chasing one rabbit at a time. They usually reply, "why?", I then reply, "what happens if you try to catch two rabbits at a time?" The athletes/clients who have a functional brain will reply, "you catch none". If you zone in on one thing and ignore the others and put all your effort into one rabbit, the chances of you catching it will improve enormously. I look at nutrition, lifestyle and exercise like this; you must decide what rabbit is going to give you the biggest bang for your buck for the effort you put in. With nutrition it is getting the first meal of the day right, which usually sets you up to for how you will eat for the rest of the day.

The Importance of Breakfast

Let's look at breakfast and its importance in setting our brain chemistry and hormones for the day. I can't emphasize enough that you must get your first meal right for the day if you want to drop fat, be healthy and perform at a high level physically and mentally.

Still think this is the best breakfast choice?

If you eat a very high carbohydrate breakfast, typical of most breakfast cereals and milk, then you are most likely to become fat, sleepy and go into fat storage mode. Why? Breakfast cereals and milk are full of sugar which increases insulin. Insulin is a fat storage hormone and, when high, inhibits the body from burning fat, it will also increase tryptophan levels in the brain which increases serotonin which can leave you feeling sleepy. Not a great way to start the day but that's what millions of people do, including children whose parents have been brainwashed into thinking that breakfast cereal is healthy. You can't blame the perception that breakfast cereals are healthy on parents. It is a multi million pound industry and the food industry aggressively pedal their drug-like foods on uninformed consumers. If I wanted to get fat I would eat breakfast cereal every morning and follow it with a nice big glass of orange juice (AKA sugar in a glass).

This in reality is diabetes in a bowl.

If you look at the typical breakfast in the UK which usually consists of a bowl of cereal and milk, both consisting of both gluten (wheat protein) and casein (milk protein) which is also very problematic to a lot of people due to their highly allergenic properties . These 2 proteins can, no doubt, increase your likelihood of becoming sick, tired and overweight. Most breakfast cereals are nothing more than a bowl of sugar and to add insult to injury we add milk (usually skimmed or semi skimmed) which is also high in lactose which is milk sugar and to really make sure we are giving ourselves the best chance of being a diabetic and obese patient we add sugar to the sugar. This is another reason we have a obesity diabetes explosion in our society and big pharma must be rubbing their hands and thanking the food industry for doing such an incredible job at making sure that the sales of diabetes drugs become as big as another pharmaceutical con statins.

The best breakfast is no doubt a high fat, medium protein and low carbohydrate meal. This type of breakfast will not spike blood sugar and force the body to access its fat burning hormones instead of it's fat storage hormones. I regularly have a full English breakfast cooked in coconut oil (no baked beans though as these are usually loaded with sugar), to help get me lean.

PHIL SAYS
Breakfast

The following would be a typical breakfast for myself or one of my athletes on a non training day. Below is also a breakfast schedule that I would suggest for a training week, where high performance and reducing body fat % are the aims.

Non-training day

- Fried Wild Salmon in cast iron pan with 2 tablespoonís of Coconut Oil
- 2 Fried Eggs also cooked in coconut oil
- Steamed Vegetables (Full fat organic butter with the vegetables)
- 1 tablespoon of extra virgin oil

Now isn't that simple - takes about 12 minutes to prepare and will have huge effect on enhancing brain chemistry and stabilizing blood sugar for hours. So, come mid morning you will not be attacking the snack box looking for a sugar fix.

I would also take a number of supplements with my breakfast, as would my athletes. During this habit, there are lots of example nutrition and supplement plans you can look at.

With nutrient timing, from a breakfast perspective, if I'm going to do High Intensity Interval Training or a Cardio session in the morning I always do this loaded on amino acids (PRP Amino Work Capacity, Cardio Fuel and 3 PRP Metabolic Enhancer capsules). This increases the hormone glucagon and opens the door to use my fat stores during the session instead of stored glycogen as fuel which will accelerate fat loss. And the high intensity workout increases growth hormone significantly which again forces my body to use my own fat stores as fuel because there is no glycogen in the tank to burn and If my last meal was 11-13 hours previous (e.g. 6p.m. evening meal) and I do my HIIT or cardio session at 7 am the following morning, this ensures that my liver glycogen levels are very low as well. This is important as otherwise the liver will release glucose during the session decreasing fats being used for fuel. That's also another reason why the evening meal should be very low in carbohydrates.

If I am doing a strength/hypertrophy workout then I like to have a bit of fuel in the tank from primarily fat and make sure my body is fully awake before I push myself to the limit in the gym from my research one the best time to do weights is late afternoon due to the testosterone cortisol ratio so I usually have breakfast first with my supplements then I have my lunch and then I hit the gym about 3 - 4 hours later. Again, I load with Amino Work Capacity and 3 PRP Metabolic Enhancer capsules and train as hard as I possibly can for 45 - 60 minutes. I will give you some examples of my workouts in Habit 10 that I personally use for both hypertrophy gains and fat loss.

Another essential point to make about breakfasts is to rotate them regularly. Remember, we evolved on a massive variety of food choices and we are still, genetically, a hunter gatherer. Eating the same breakfast every morning is probably the quickest way to build allergies to the food sources you are eating. Have a look at the food table in this chapter which shows you the wide variety of foods available and how to rotate those foods. Try not to have the same breakfast every day. Just keep adding variety and different food choices at every opportunity just - like our hunter gatherers ancestors did.

Take a look at the table below to see how I always got lots of variety into the nutrition plan for a Champion Boxer.

DAY 1	DAY 2	DAY 3	DAY 4	DAY 5	DAY 6	DAY 7
Stir Fry Vegetables Fish Choice 1-2 TBSP Coconut Oil Nuts & Seeds	Greens/Veggie Choice Dairy Choice 1 TBSP Extra Virgin Olive Oil	Greens/Veggie Choice Meat Choice 1 TBSP Extra Virgin Olive Oil	Greens/Veggie Choice Poultry Choice 1 TBSP Extra Virgin Olive Oil	Stir Fry Vegetables Fish Choice 1 TBSP Coconut Oil	Greens/Veggie Choice Meat Choice 1 TBSP Extra Virgin Olive Oil	Porridge Coconut Milk 1 TBSP of Coconut Oil
Fruit Choice	Fruit Choice	Fruit Choice	Fruit Choice	Fruit Choice	Fruit Choice	Fruit Choice
SUPPLEMENTS	SUPPLEMENTS	SUPPLEMENTS	SUPPLEMENTS	SUPPLEMENTS	SUPPLEMENTS	SUPPLEMENTS

I will always remember taking over as Head of Strength & Nutrition at a very famous rugby team. One of the promising young players there was about to get his contract terminated because of his constant injury problems. Whilst working with this player I got him to fill in a seven day nutrition and lifestyle diary (which is found at the end of this habit and you can purchase on my website).

As I analysed the content of the players food diary, my jaw nearly hit the floor. He ate the same breakfast every day, and had done so for the last five years on the recommendations he had been given by a nutritionist. To make things more interesting, the breakfast might look quite nutritious to the layperson as it consisted of scrambled eggs followed by a big bowl of porridge. Now the twist to this is still to come - the breakfast was also cooked in the microwave.

I explained to the player that if I wanted to make someone fat, sick and injury prone I would prescribe that exact breakfast. We started our nutritional plan, which was no different to the nutrition plans in this book and the results were absolutely incredible; from nearly being told to leave the club, the player returned within weeks to full fitness, with no injuries (apart from the obvious ones you would pick up from contact in professional rugby). He was leaner than he had ever been in his life and played for another 10 years as a professional rugby player. And the biggest change was, no doubt, getting his breakfast right and respecting the healing benefits that the right nutrients can have on health and performance.

As the old saying goes eat breakfast like a king, lunch like a prince, and dinner like a pauper and this is so appropriate if you want optimum health and fat loss. But we have developed a culture where we do it completely opposite where we rush breakfast and in most cases this could be a bit of toast on the run, then we grab a sandwich lunchtime with a cup of tea/coffee then by the time we get home from work we could eat a horse and usually do metaphorically speaking of course. And this is a disaster for our ability to lose excess body fat. So make a conscious effort of getting breakfast right. You will be grateful in a few weeks when you start to see the difference not only from a body fat perspective but also from a mood perspective also.

Food diary template and monitoring information

Date

Bedtime last night?

Did you wake refreshed this morning? (Circle one face)

Wake up time today?

What did you have for breakfast?

FOOD	FLUIDS	SUPPLEMENTS / MEDICATION

Snack

FOOD	FLUIDS	SUPPLEMENTS / MEDICATION

What did you have for lunch?

FOOD	FLUIDS	SUPPLEMENTS / MEDICATION

Snack

FOOD	FLUIDS	SUPPLEMENTS / MEDICATION

What did you have for dinner?

FOOD	FLUIDS	SUPPLEMENTS / MEDICATION

Snack

FOOD	FLUIDS	SUPPLEMENTS / MEDICATION

How were your stress levels today?

How were your energy levels today?

pH score

Hydration score

Body weight

Oximeter

Resting Heart Rate

Body fat %

Comments:

Thermogenesis - the science of using foods to increase metabolism and help burn fat

Thermogenesis (or thermic effect) refers to the calorie burn associated with digestion and assimilation of food. When you sweat after eating a big meal that's thermogenesis kicking in right there and you will notice it more the higher the protein content of the food.

The thermogenic effect of food peaks within one hour after a meal is consumed, and can be quite substantial in terms of the amount of energy dissipated. The magnitude of the thermogenic effect of food ranges between 10–35% of ingested nutrients, and varies depending on the type of food eaten.

Of the three macronutrients, protein is the frontrunner when it comes to thermogenesis then it's carbohydrates and then fat. Protein outdistances itself from carbohydrate and fat due to the caloric cost incurred in processing amino acids.

Protein is the most thermogenic of all the macronutrients. But, remember, you cannot absorb more than 30-50g per serving. So, don't try to eat elephant portions at each serving or you will end up looking like one!

A meal of pure protein elicits a thermogenic effect amounting to approximately 30% of the meal's total calories, about twice as much as carbohydrate and more than three times as much as fat. So you can now see the value from a fat loss perspective to including high quality protein to each meal. Now, before you try to consume a whole cow with your baked potato and vegetables, your body will not be able to use more than 30–50 grams of protein per meal, anymore than this can be used to create more body fat.

Fruits and vegetables are also thermogenic because non-processed carbohydrates are moderately thermogenic, but fiber is highly thermogenic. Cruciferous vegetables like broccoli and cauliflower are very thermogenic and therefore should be consumed often.

Medium-chain fatty acids (such as those in coconut oil) have been found to increase metabolism by between 48-65% in obese patients. This thermogenic effect also lasted 24 hours after ingesting medium-chain fatty acids. Experts agree that, on average, medium-chain fatty acids triple the rate of metabolism compared to long-chain fatty acids that come from polyunsaturated fats. This means that medium-chain fatty acids aren't just a healthy energy source, they also help burn off stored fat. That's why I cook in coconut oil regularly, to get my MCT's. Plus, coconut oil is excellent for immune and thyroid health. I strongly advise all my athletes to use coconut oil daily.

Glycaemic Index

The glycaemic index is a measure of the degree to which foods raise blood sugar levels. Consuming fewer high-glycaemic index carbs has been found to promote weight loss and improve insulin sensitivity.

In studies, mice fed a high-GI diet developed 40% more body fat compared to those on a low-GI diet.

A 2008 study in mice found that after 40 weeks on a high-glycaemic-index diet - 40% more body fat was developed and insulin resistance was twice as bad compared to a low-glycaemic-index diet. The mice were also seen to be more lethargic and their physical activity was lower by 45%. This again shows the devastating effect that processed sugar has on increasing our body fat, much more so than saturated fat could ever do.

This bowl of porridge and fruit might look healthy but in reality IT IS NOT!

A group of scientists published a review of the metabolic downside of carbohydrates at breakfast time in the British Journal of Nutrition. One thing they observed with people eating a breakfast full of carbs, is that muscles have a hard time burning fat for the rest of the day.

Research from the University of Texas Southwestern Medical Center. Researcher fed healthy people breakfast drinks containing three different "sugar combinations" followed by a carefully controlled lunch. They did this over several weeks. In one test, the breakfast drink contained 100% glucose; in another the drink was half glucose, half fructose (which is what you'd find in ordinary sugar). In the third condition, the subjects got a drink that was 25% glucose and 75% fructose. The researchers were interested in two things, both of which should interest you. One, they wanted to measure how fast the sugars in the drink turned to fat in the liver. Two, they wanted to see how that morning sugar-meal influenced how people metabolized foods eaten later in the day (for example, lunch).

The findings were disturbing. For one thing, the researchers found that fructose got "made" into fat way more quickly than other sugars. And for the second thing, they found that when fructose was eaten with fat (as is often the case with processed and junk foods e.g. soda with your burger) the fat was much more likely to be stored rather than burned. "*Our study shows for the first time the surprising speed with which humans make body fat from fructose*", said lead researcher Elizabeth Parks, PhD.

Nutrient timing for athletes is different than nutrient timing for fat loss

You need to deliver the right nutrient mixture, at the right time to enhance recovery from exercise and to improve muscle growth, strength and power. Nutrient timing consist of three phases that you need to maximise during a 24-hour growth cycle. These three phases are what I learnt from the excellent book nutrient timing referenced at the end of this habit.

A) Energy phase: Ensuring you have enough available energy to power your workouts and these can come from all three macronutrients protein, fat and carbohydrates..
B) Anabolic phase: 0 – 45 minute window following a workout; with right combination of nutrients initiates repair of damaged muscle protein if you want fat loss go with just amino acids, if you are a competitive athlete and you are already at a very lean body fat% go with combination of protein, carbohydrates, glutamine and creatine.
C) Growth & Recovery phase: from the end of the anabolic phase to the beginning of the next workout, being really smart with quality of meals and lifestyle choices. Again here if you want fat loss DO NOT snack between meals if you are a competitive athlete and again happy with your body fat% levels then snack between meals.

But it is important to remember that the three phases, and what you should consume during them, differ for high end athletes (for whom fat loss is not a priority), compared to those of us whose priority is to shift excess body fat. So, in this habit I will give you what I use with my professional athletes as well as for those whose priority is dropping excess body fat.

Studies have found that delaying nutrient (protein and carbohydrate) consumption for athletes after a workout can greatly reduce the rate of glycogen restoration and protein synthesis. In fact, the rate of glycogen synthesis is reduced by 50% if nutrients aren't consumed immediately after a workout ***(Maehlom et al. 1977, Blom et al. 1987, Ivy et al. 1988).***

It is important to remember here though that you know what is relevant in terms of nutrient timing for your activity levels. If you train a little, eat a little. If you train a lot, eat a lot. If fat loss is your goal drop the carbs and increase your fat intake, if performance is your goal and you do not want to go on a ketogenic diet (which we'll talk about shortly) then up your carbs to a level which you feel is optimum for you.

You can't justify eating 6 times per day with a copious supply of carbohydrates when you only train 3 times per week. I have spent 30 years training people, from soldiers who wanted to join special forces, professional athletes in multiple sports and members of the public, and trust me, if you are a member of the public and you exercise 3–5 days a week, just make sure you get your pre- and post-workout nutrition right. Then get your breakfast right, don't eat within 3 hours before bedtime and stay well hydrated and happy. If you apply all this; results will happen, unless you have a major health/hormonal issue or are living with someone you don't like!

High Carbohydrate Diets For Fat Loss is like the trying to force the square peg in the round hole!

The reason why so many diet and exercise programs fail to drop body fat is quite simple, because they never can access their fat stores because of a continuous supply of glucose from carbohydrate food sources. Unless you are training with massive intensity and duration then your fat cells will keep its stores of fat quite safely locked up. I used to advocate carbohydrates at breakfast and post workout for fat loss to all I consulted for, but for those of us who are not training 10-14 times a week; go high fat, medium protein and low carbohydrate if you want to drop excess body fat. Otherwise you will never access stored body fat due to a continuous supply of glucose which will inhibit fat being used as the primary fuel. This is different to my elite endurance athletes, professional rugby players and professional boxers who are doing a phenomenal amount of training with a phenomenal amount of stress as well. They need carbohydrates, as well as protein and a shit load of fat, just to keep functioning and performing. With some of the professional boxers that I have worked with though, who really struggle to make weight, I have put them on a very low carbohydrate, high fat diet and it works every time for not only reaching their fighting weight but also for enhancing performance.

Studies have shown that humans can effectively use fat for fuel and from an evolutionary perspective have done so for more than 2 million years very effectively.

Doctors Volek and Phinney who are true experts on the ketogenic diet have conducted a research study in which they measured the athletic performance of 5 cyclists before and after a period of 5 weeks on a very low carbohydrate diet. During the 5 weeks period, the cyclists consumed approximately 20 grams of carbohydrates per day while the rest of the calories came mainly from fat and a moderate amount from protein.

The cyclists did not show a decrease in performance. Rather, they showed a dramatic reduction in glucose oxidation (production of energy from glucose), which means they were using mostly fat as fuel. The bottom line, their performance was not affected in any way the researchers concluded.

Ketogenic Diet

So how do we force our body to burn fat when we exercise and even when we are not? One word KETOSIS!

Eating fat enhances your body's ability to burn fat. From a biochemical level a low-fat, high-carbohydrate diet doesn't make sense. It simply doesn't condition the body

ACHIEVING THE OPTIMAL FAT BURNING STATE

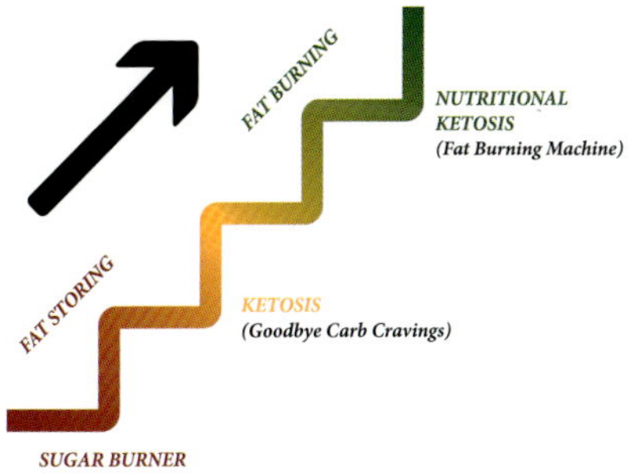

to be efficient at burning fat. Instead, it will ramp up the enzymatic machinery in your body so it becomes efficient at burning carbohydrates. Remember your body has a very limited capacity to store carbohydrates and it is very easy to reach that capacity from eating too much processed foods and the 5 - 11 servings of starchy foods recommended by the standard government food table.

Yes, a product could say low to zero fat on it's packaging but the body doesn't read or understand that packaging advice. Why? When the cells have all the glucose it needs, insulin, which is usually stimulated very highly in low-fat foods, promotes lipogenesis (conversion of carbohydrates to fats and mobilization of these fat into adipocytes) and it suppresses lipolysis, which is the release of fat from the adipose tissue.

It is interesting to note a normal blood sugar represents less than one teaspoon of sugar dissolved in the blood of the human body. YES just one teaspoon (slightly more if you are pre-diabetic)! The point here is that it's a miniscule amount and we have a very limited storage capacity for carbohydrates as I have already mentioned. When you realise something considered 'healthy' like freshly squeezed orange juice contains approximately 51 grams of sugar then you quickly realise why it is easy to become obese and diabetic in our culture today.

It is interesting to note a normal blood sugar represents less than one teaspoon of sugar dissolved in the blood of the human body.

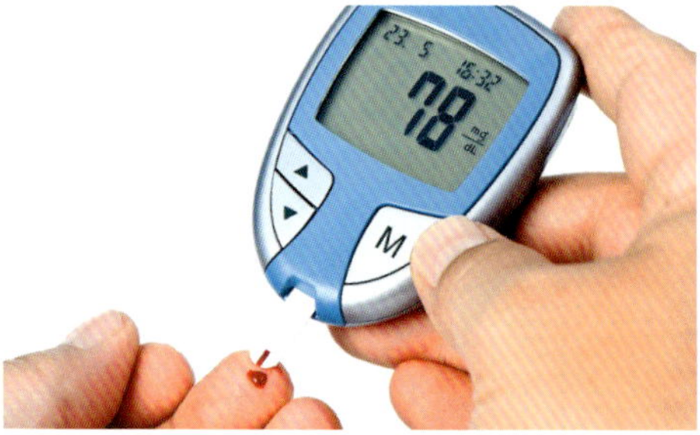

Measuring blood glucose is an excellent way to ensure you are in a fat burning or storing zone!

Measuring your blood sugar levels along with your ketones is a sure way to shift you into the fat burning zone, you can purchase a home testing blood glucose monitor and simply take your blood sugar levels from a pin prick of blood from your finger and see the levels of glucose in your blood.

Blood Glucose Levels

	HbA_{1c} Test Score	MEAN BLOOD GLUCOSE mg/dL	MEAN BLOOD GLUCOSE mmol/L
ACTION REQUIRED	14.0	380	21.1
ACTION REQUIRED	13.0	350	19.3
ACTION REQUIRED	12.0	315	17.4
ACTION REQUIRED	11.0	280	15.6
ACTION REQUIRED	10.0	250	13.7
ACTION REQUIRED	9.0	215	11.9
GOOD	8.0	180	10.0
GOOD	7.0	150	8.2
EXCELLENT	6.0	115	6.3
EXCELLENT	5.0	80	4.7
EXCELLENT	4.0	50	2.6

Sugar causes testosterone deficiency

Is your sugar habit making you testosterone deficient?

Research presented at The Endocrine Society's 91st Annual Meeting in Washington D.C found that sugar ingestion can cause a man's testosterone level to drop by up to 25 percent. The number of men affected by abnormally low testosterone levels is literally becoming an epidemic, along with prescriptions for testosterone capsules, creams and implants. It is well known that overweight men and diabetic men are prone to testosterone deficiency and this population is rapidly rising.

Previous research has also shown that elevated blood levels of insulin correlate with low testosterone. Blood insulin levels rise as we know when you eat sugar, flour, grains, cereals or starches (basically high carbohydrate foods). You are also likely to have high insulin levels if you have a big waist; for men that means a waist greater than 37 inches (94 centimetres).

In the current study researchers gave 74 men a glucose tolerance test, which involved consumption of a sugar solution and subsequent blood tests. Of the 74 men, 42 had normal blood sugar levels, 23 had pre-diabetes (insulin resistance) and 9 had type 2 diabetes. Interestingly the glucose solution lowered testosterone levels by up to 25 percent in all of the men regardless of whether they were diabetic, pre-diabetic or had normal blood sugar levels.

Based on this study, the authors recommend that when men have a testosterone blood test it should be a fasting test, in order to give the most accurate results.

That may be true, but the problem is we consume sugar, and foods that are rapidly digested into sugar (such as breakfast cereals, potatoes, bread, pasta and rice) all day, every day. This means they have suppressed levels of testosterone all the time. So this is another reason to go HIGH FAT – LOW CARB, and drop the booze which elevates insulin very quickly!!

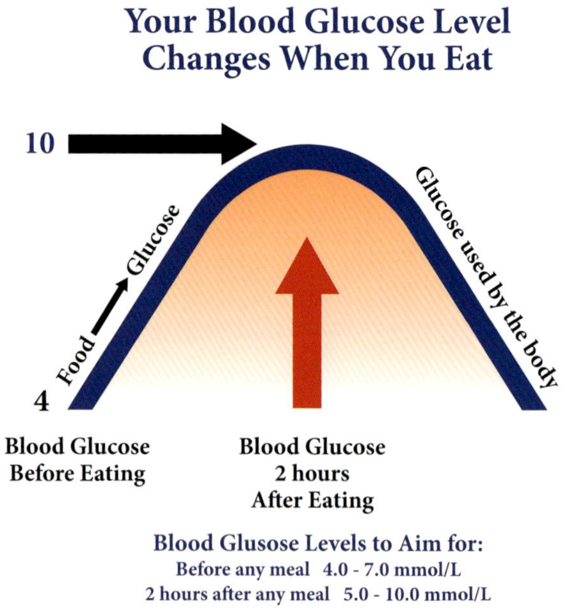

Lower fat diets can also have negative impacts on adipokines which impact fat loss. Adipokines are hormones released specifically from your fat cells. One such hormone, adiponectin, which we have already spoken about in this book, is a true fat-burning hormone that works to enhance your metabolism and increase the rate in which fats are broken down, curbing your appetite. Lower-fat diets lead to lower levels of adiponectin.

When your body senses that there is plenty of fat in the diet, it is quite happy to give up what's stored in your fat cells. Plus, with the ketogenic diet your fat burning hormones - glucagon, testosterone and growth hormone - are working at maximum efficiency whilst your fat storage hormone insulin is pretty much told to shut up and behave itself. This means that the pancreas can take a break from spewing out a ton of insulin.

How do ketogenic diets work?

When carbohydrate containing foods are digested, they are broken down into blood sugar (glucose) in the body. The more carbohydrates we eat, the more glucose is made. As diabetics know, high blood sugar is toxic to the body. Eating more fats and protein and less carb causes our internal biochemical pathways to switch to using our stored fat for fuel instead of burning sugar. This switch produces ketone bodies while at the same time reducing blood sugar levels. As glucose drops and ketone body levels rise in the bloodstream, the heart, muscle and brain stop burning sugar and instead use the ketones as an alternative fuel. This is called being "in nutritional ketosis."

Once the body is using ketones as a main fuel source, all sorts of beneficial effects become apparent. A ketone producing, high fat, low carb diet is terrific for weight reduction, slowing the aging process and addressing health issues such as heartburn, fatty liver and achy joints.

However, these diets are much more powerful than those popular uses would suggest. In fact, being in ketosis can alleviate many serious diseases. The antioxidant and anti-inflammatory effect of nutritional ketosis is potent. In fact, nutritional ketosis and ketone bodies themselves are being studied extensively as a treatment for many metabolic diseases. For instance, there is strong research evidence that ketotic diets can:

- Act as an extremely effective diabetes treatment plan; in some cases, just switching to a ketogenic diet can reverse prediabetes and type 2 diabetes.
- Help reverse cancer with right treatments and lifestyle changes.
- Improve epilepsy treatment outcomes by reducing, and in some cases, eliminating seizures.
- Help patients with Alzheimer's disease regain memory and thought function.
- Reverse heart disease and improve cardiovascular risk factors shown on blood tests.

- Alleviate the symptoms of autism.
- Reverse PCOS.
- Treat severe outbreaks of acne.
- Provide mitochondrial support for a wide variety of neurological disorders such as Parkinsons Disease and ALS.
- Eliminate gluten allergy symptoms and relieve the symptoms of other allergic conditions associated with autoimmune reactions
- Treat metabolic energy disorders such as glucose transporter type 1 (GLUT1) deficiency, pyruvate dehydrogenase complex deficiency (PDHC), McArdle disease, and mitochondrial myopathies.

In other words, the ketogenic diet is not a "fad." It is a potent regulator of metabolic derangement, and when formulated and implemented correctly, it can be extremely effective.

How You Burn Body Fat

We covered some of this information in habit 7 but lets delve a little bit deeper so you truly can understand why the recommendations by governments and most dieticians of getting 60 - 70% of our calories from carbohydrates is so flawed it is embarrassing. Lets look at how we tap into the fat energy stored in our adipose tissue. A key step in this process is removing the fatty acid from the glycerol backbone also known as lipolysis. This is achieved by our best fat busting enzyme known as hormone sensitive lipase. Although many factors can stimulate the activity of hormone sensitive lipase (like adrenaline, noradrenaline, growth hormone and ACTH, thyroid hormone), fat breakdown is principally controlled by one single hormone that inhibits its activity. That hormone is INSULIN and what do you think a diet consisting of multiple servings of carbohydrate rich foods does? Yes - make us fatter than a friggin hippopotamus. In other words, insulin is the primary gatekeeper of body fat. If your insulin levels are consistently high, FAT STORAGE IS EFFECTIVELY BLOCKED.

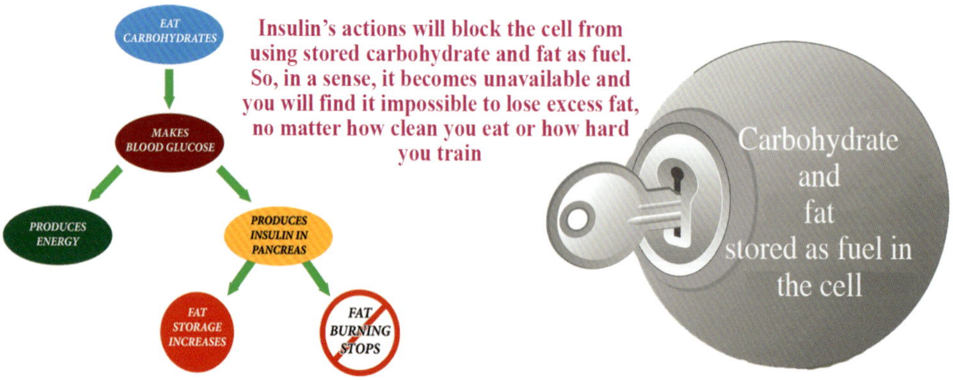

At least two studies, one from Duke University, and one from Cambridge University have shown that reducing carbohydrate consumption and increasing saturated fat intake helps the liver shed excess fat in as little as three days. When the body can access fat immediately, it burns it. Medium Chain Triglycerides oil (which is found in very high quantities in coconut oil) ingestion triggers ketone production, which is not easy to do with diet alone. Ketones help fuel the cells of the nervous system, as well as other tissue in the body, when quick energy is needed from fat molecules. MCT can also represent the idea of a negative caloric load. In *Obesity Research* and in the *International Journal of Obesity and Related Metabolic Disorders*, researchers demonstrated that by simply adding MCT oil into the diet, it increased fatty acid oxidation. Eating fat, they found, burns fat.

What does the ketogenic diet look like?

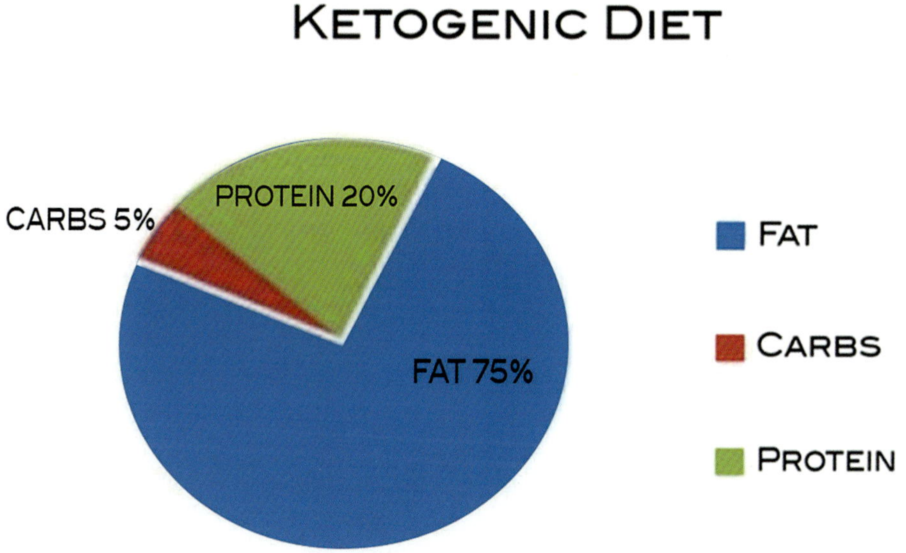

The nutrient intake on a ketogenic diet typically works out to about 70-75% of calories from fat (mainly saturated and monounsaturated fats with a low % from polyunsaturated fats), 20-25% from protein, and 5-10% from carbohydrate on a daily basis.

Why high fat and moderate protein? Fats have no effect on blood sugar and insulin levels. Protein does affect both blood sugar and insulin, if large quantities are consumed. If you overeat protein, about 56% of any excess protein will be converted to glucose (sugar) in the body, and that extra glucose hanging around will increase insulin, and put the brakes on the body's ability to release and burn fatty acids (go into ketosis).

It's not just about losing weight - studies showing health benefits of high-fat diet

Research shows that a diet with less than 40% of energy as fat (and that mainly from animal sources, i.e. saturated) lead to a decrease in testosterone levels. *J Steroid Biochem. 1984 Jan;20(1):459-64.*

Director of the world's longest running heart study says that those that eat more cholesterol and fat weigh the least and are the most physically active. *Castelli WP Archives of Internal Medicine. 1992; 152(7) :1371 - 1372*

High fat diets reduce dangerous C - Reactive Protein levels by 52.6%. *McAuley KA et al Comparison of high fat and high protein diets with a high carbohydrate diet in insulin resistant obese women. Diabetolgia. 2005 Jan; 48(1) :8-16*

A study of healthy young men (only 10 participants), but well-controlled, measured post-meal blood triglycerides as a risk factor. The research showed that butter, which is higher in saturated fats, induced the lowest rise in post-meal triglycerides when compared with olive oil or sunflower oil. *2002 Journal of Nutrition Dec: 132 (12) : 3642-9*

A large epidemiological study of 1 million men in different parts of India revealed that those in regions where fat consumption (mainly animal fats) was 19 times higher, had a decreased incidence of heart disease – 7% less. *1967 British Heart Journal 29, 895*

The fat in human mother's milk is 54 percent saturated fat. Why? Because it is essential for HEALTH!

How much carbohydrate and protein can I eat on the ketogenic diet?

If you consume too much protein the body will convert a lot of the amino acids into glucose in a process called gluconeogenesis so aim for around no more than 1 gram per pound of lean body mass. Stick to no more than 30 - 50 grams of protein per meal.

Evidence for protein needs of athletes has been accumulating since 1974. Dr. I. Gontzea and colleagues at the Institute of Medicine in Bucharest were the first to show that exercise causes the body to use protein at a much faster rate. In one study they instructed their athletes to stop exercising and remain sedentary for two weeks. They were given a daily ration of 1.0 grams per kilogram bodyweight (33% over the RDA). As long as they remained sedentary, this level of protein intake maintained a positive nitrogen balance. Then, when they were given workouts of 2 hours per day, nitrogen balance dropped to negative within 2 days - meaning they were in a catabolic state.

Gontzea fed another group of athletes a higher level of protein at 1.5 grams per kilogram of bodyweight (twice the RDA) as long as they remained sedentary, nitrogen balance was positive. But, when they were given the same 2 hour workouts as the first group, nitrogen balance dropped to negative within 4 days.

Endurance athletes can need as much protein as strength athletes.

Excellent studies that simulated the Tour De France show that, if you increase the intensity and duration of endurance exercise, protein needs increase even further. The Tour De France cyclists doing five hours of intense riding per day, required up to 1.8 grams per kg of bodyweight to remain in nitrogen balance.

During a study analyzing Romanian Weightlifters over three months of training, the weightlifters increased their protein intake from 2.2 g/kg/bw/ per day to 3.5 g/kg/bw per day. Even though these athletes were already near the top of their potential, they made huge gains of 6% in muscle mass and 5% in strength.

Before you start guzzling protein, you must remember that they were training 5 times per day. If you want gains, exercise is the key that creates the demand for new structure. Protein does nothing to stimulate growth, it simply provides the building materials.

Estimate of daily protein requirements for athletes depending on class – class 1 is sports that demand strength first, class 2 demands speed first and class 3 is endurance first. Source from Optimum Sports Nutrition Dr. Michael Colgan.

Bodyweight	Sports Training Category		
Kg	1	2	3
40	80	68	56
50	100	85	70
60	120	102	84
70	140	119	98
80	160	136	112
90	180	153	126
100	200	170	140
110	220	187	154
120	240	204	168

Ancestors Diet

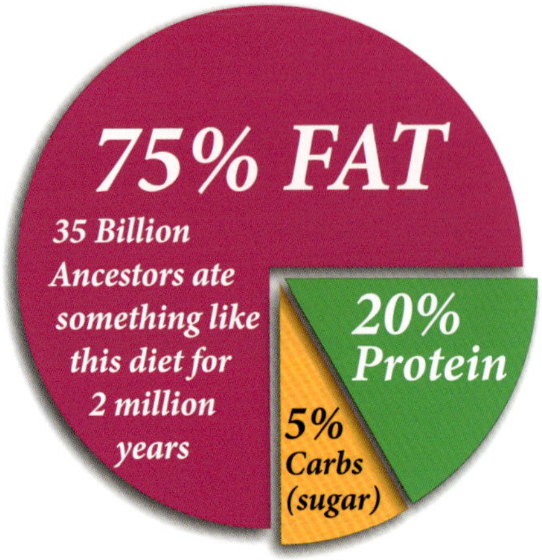

You inherited a human body model programmed from this diet. A very small amount of fat supplies a huge amount of calories. Sugar was almost unavailable much of the year. Ancestors Diet has been proven as an automatic 'fix diet' for *Obesity & Diabetes.*

Recommended by most Government Dieticians

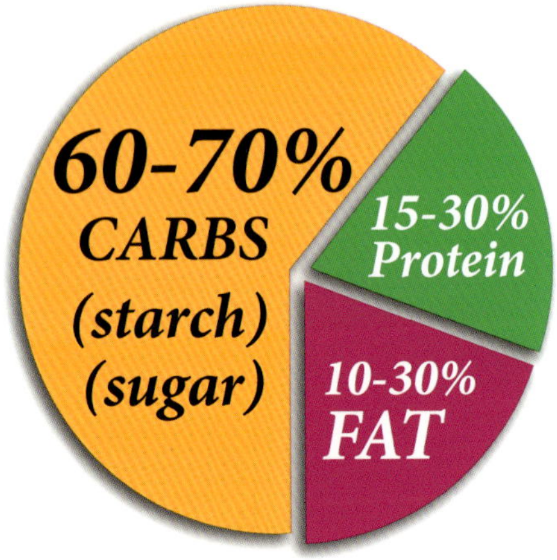

This is the diet which literally goes completely against our genetic design and you only have to look around us today and you can see the mass obesity and disease that it has caused

If you consume more than 30 grams of carbohydrates in a day, then your body will automatically switch back to using glucose for energy. The 30 gram limit varies from person to person some people shift to ketosis on higher amounts too, but 30 grams is considered the maximum dose of carbohydrates if ketosis is to be achieved.

Even when you are aiming for 30 grams of carbohydrates, you should actually try NOT to consume any carbohydrates or at least limit it considerably because 30 grams of carbohydrates can easily slip into your diet without you even realising it. The most important carbohydrates allowed on a ketosis diet is green leafy vegetables which is a bonus as a ketosis diet is quite acidic and as we know green leafy vegetables are alkalising foods. You can add small amounts of berries and other low GL fruits but be careful you don't add too much and, if you are not in the ketosis zone, cut back.

Also if you need a break from the ketogenic diet have a cheat day every 21 days followed the next day with a very high intensity training session aimed at depleting as much glycogen as you possibly can and this will help to switch you back into ketosis mode. I have included some example diet plans and provided a comprehensive food choices table later in this habit.

Why calorie restricted diets don't work!

Most diets that try to lose weight focus on calorie restriction. That's why the diet industry always have repeat custom. Why? IT NEVER WORKS LONG TERM AND THE CUSTOMER KEEPS COMING BACK! Calorie restriction may give you short term weight loss and some of that will be fat but, unfortunately, some will be your metabolic boosting muscle as well. Less muscle means slowed metabolism which makes losing weight much more difficult and it increases the ease with which the weight is put back on as millions of dieters worldwide can attest to.

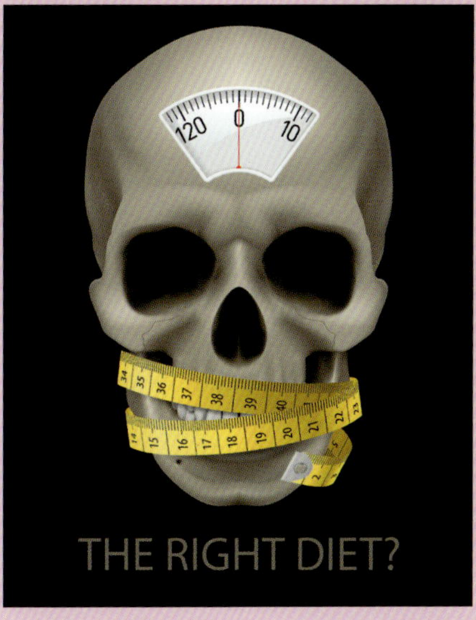

- Low adherence.
- 21% of dieters dropped out in the first 2 months, 45% had quit by the end of the year *(Tufts-New England Medical Center, JAMA Jan 5, 2005)*. 90-95% of people who lose weight with diet gain most of the weight back within 3 to 5 years.
- Most diets restrict your caloric intake so much that metabolism slows down.
- Drastically reducing calories can slow your metabolism and hinder the weight loss process *(Leibel, Rosenbaum & Hirsch 1995)*.
- Dieter's body becomes highly efficient at conserving calories and storing them as fat.
- Lowered metabolism increases likelihood dieter regains even more weight particularly when old eating habits are resumed.
- Often times, more body fat, or weight is gained back due to yo-yo dieting.
- Frequent changes of weight increases risk of heart disease and premature death *(Brownell & Rodin 1994; Lissner et al. 1991)*.

Attaining Ketosis

The ketogenic diet relies upon us reaching a state called ketosis. Ketosis is a state at which the body has an extremely high fat-burning rate. Even the brain can run on fat, via ketone bodies. These are energy molecules in the blood (like blood sugar) which become fuel for our brains after being converted from fat by the liver.

When the body must use its fat stores for energy the fat cells begin to release the stored fatty acids into the blood to be used as fuel, these fatty acids travel to the liver where they are literally cut into two carbon fragments called ketoacids. They are then burned by many tissues in the body as fuel and what is left are called ketones, and they spill into the urine and are then eliminated when you take a pee.

When the body is in the fat burning state where it has no carbohydrate to burn and is breaking down body body fat for fuel we enter the state of ketosis. This is the only metabolic pathway for fat breakdown (lipolysis). Therefore there is no lipolysis without ketosis and no ketosis without lipolysis. To encourage ketone production, the amount of insulin in your bloodstream must be low. The lower your insulin, the higher your ketone production. And when you have a well-controlled, sufficiently large amount of ketones in your blood, it's basically proof that your insulin is very low – and therefore, that you're enjoying the maximum effect of your low-carbohydrate diet. That's what's called optimal ketosis.

What level of Ketosis is optimal?

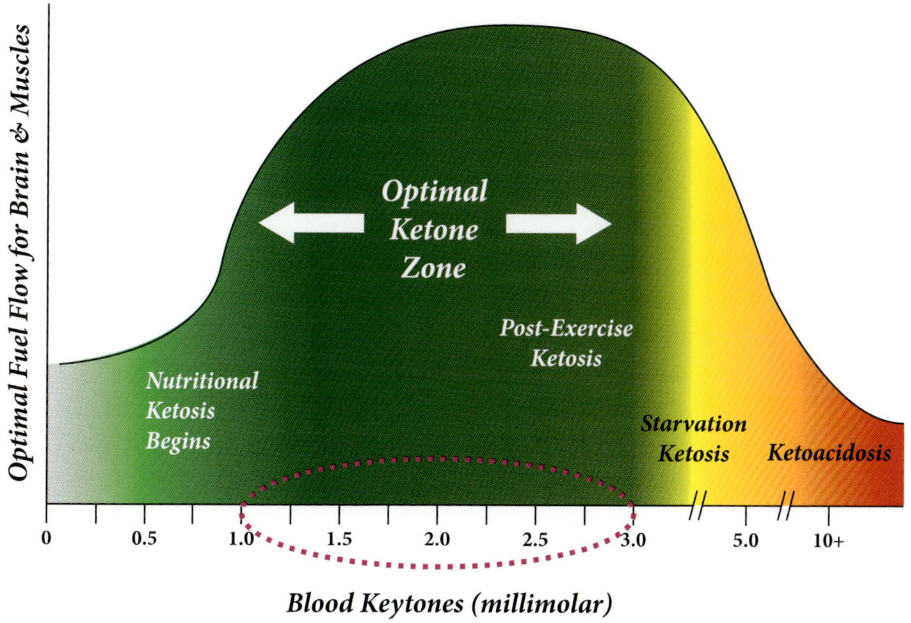

Measuring ketones

One of the ways to check to see if you are in a state of ketosis is to measure your ketone levels. Today, there are reasonably-priced products available for measuring ketone levels at home. One needle prick of the finger, and in just a few seconds you'll know your blood ketone level.

Blood ketones are best measured on a fasted stomach in the morning (before breakfast, that is). Here are a few pointers on how to interpret the result:

- Below 0.5 mmol/L is not considered "ketosis". At this level, you're far away from maximum fat-burning.
- Between 0.5-1.5 mmol/L is light nutritional ketosis. You'll be getting a good effect on your weight, but not optimal.
- Around 1.5 – 3 mmol/L is what's called optimal ketosis and is recommended for maximum weight loss.
- Values of over 3 mmol/L aren't necessary. That is, they will achieve neither better nor worse results than being at the 1.5-3 level. Higher values can also sometimes mean that you're not getting enough food. For type 1 diabetics, it can be caused by a severe lack of insulin.

Ketone levels can also be measured in a more old-fashioned way, with urine test sticks. Ketone sticks give less reliable results for several reasons, and the above recommendations can't be straightforwardly applied to them. They are, however, much cheaper.

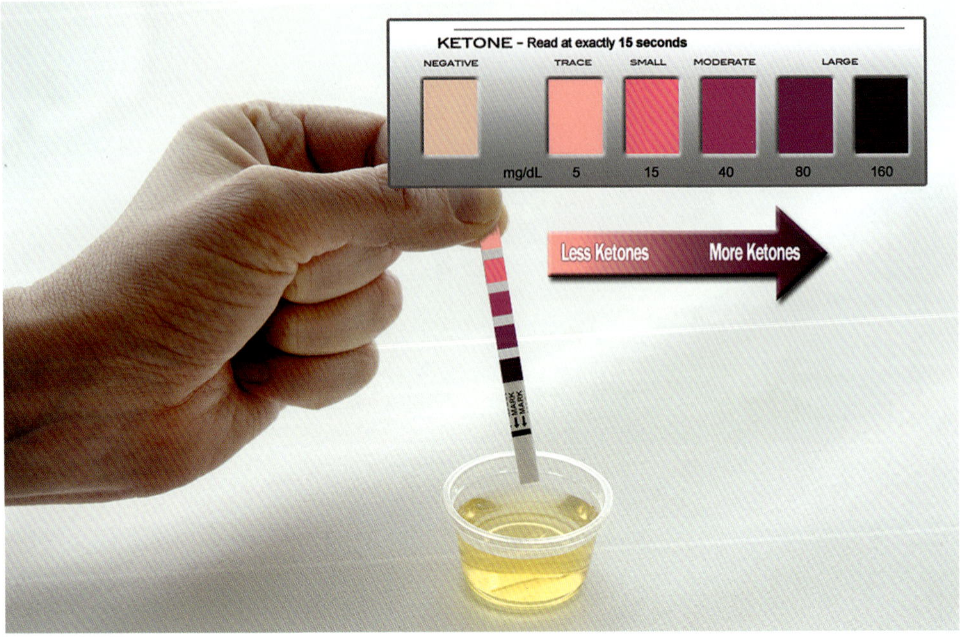

You can also use a ketone breath analyser if you want more accurate and a quicker way to ensure you are in ketosis. The exhaled breath of people who are burning fat contains comparatively high levels of the gas acetone. That's because when fatty acids are broken down, one of the end products is acetone, which is released into the blood and through the lungs in breath. By monitoring acetone concentration, dieters could get a more accurate sense of whether their efforts are working.

I personally use a product called Ketonix which has a few benefits over urine and blood measures.

- Urine strips indicate the excess concentration of acetoacetate in the urine. Ketonix indicates the acetone in your breath. Acetone is produced from the breakdown of acetoacetate in blood. Measurement units are not the same, the concentration of acetoacetate in blood is higher due to less volume (higher density) and is typically measured in mmol/l. The concentration of acetone in breath is lower due to much more volume (lower density) and is measured in PPM. Again, urine strips measures acetoacetate in urine, blood meters measures beta-hydroxybutyrate in blood and Ketonix measures acetone in breath (air).

- Urine strips can only be used once. Ketonix is reusable and can be used over and over again.
- Urine strips show a historical value of the excess production. Ketonix shows a real-time value of what's in the blood right now!
- Urine strips tests need urine and somewhere to do the test. You can perform tests using Ketonix wherever you can access a powered USB port. We don't recommend using Ketonix in vehicles (or in any motion).
- Urine strips need to be disposed.
- Urine strips cost per test. Ketonix is a one-time investment!
- Blood ketone meters measures beta-hydroxybutyrate in blood, not acetoacetate or acetone.
- Blood ketone measure requires strips which are expensive
- Blood ketone measure sometimes fails and cost you twice!
- Blood ketone meter values differ between devices, even when it is the same model and brand.
- Blood values are measured in mmol/l, and gas ranges in PPM. This is of course due to the higher density of blood than air. Therefore the blood ketone concentration of beta-hydroxybutyrate is not the same as the concentration of acetone in breath. Just as the concentration of acetoacetate in urine is not the same as concentration of beta-hydroxybutyrate in blood.

General Tips To Watch Out For When Measuring Ketones

- Generally, ketone concentrations are lower in the morning and higher in the evening. For this reason, it is advisable that you test yourself before bed.
- Keep in mind there are daily fluctuations caused by changes in hormone levels. Don't get discouraged!
- Another aspect that affects the level of ketones is the amount of fat in your diet. Some of you may show higher concentration of ketones after a high-fat meal. Coconut oil contains MCTs that will help you boost ketones.
- Ketone levels tend to be higher after extensive aerobic exercise as your body depletes glycogen stores. Exercise may help you get into ketosis faster.
- Ketogenic "fruity" breath is not pleasant for most people. To avoid this, drink a lot of water, mint tea and make sure you eat foods rich in electrolytes. Avoid too many chewing gums and mints, as it may put you out of ketosis; there may be hidden carbs affecting your blood sugar.

How to achieve optimal ketosis

Many who firmly believe they are eating a strict low-carb diet are surprised when they measure their blood ketones. They may be at around only 0.2 or 0.5 – quite far off from the sweet spot! Why? The trick here is not only to avoid all obvious sources of carbohydrate (sweets, bread, breakfast cereals, spaghetti, rice, potatoes), but also to be careful with your protein intake. If you eat large amounts of meat, eggs, protein shakes etc., the excess protein will converted into glucose in the body. Large amounts of protein can also raise your insulin levels somewhat. This compromises optimal ketosis.The secret to getting around this is usually to eat your protein with *more fat*. For example, if you have a steak with vegetables add 1 tablespoon of organic butter and 1 tablespoon of extra virgin olive oil to the vegetables.

More fat in your food will fill you up more. The hormonal and metabolic benefits of eating more fat are great, but one of the best benefits might be the satiating effects of fat. Nothing is worse than eating a high carbohydrate, lower-calorie diet that leaves your hungry all the time. This is traditionally a huge problem in diets which deny you foods with a higher fat content such as eggs, meats, nuts, fatty fish, cheese, and avocado. Satiating fat leaves you feeling full. When the fat you eat hits your small intestine, it sets off a cascade of signals which includes the release of hormones such as CCK and PYY. These two hormones play a major role in appetite regulation and satiety; they leave you feeling full and satisfied. The more satiated you are, the less likely that you're going to sneak in snacks between meals or pile on a second helping. This will also ensure you eat less protein, and even less carbohydrate during your meals. Your insulin will drop and, hopefully, you'll be able to reach optimal ketosis. And that's when many a stubborn weight plateau is overcome.

If ketosis doesn't work

Being in optimal ketosis for a prolonged period of time (say, a month) will ensure that you experience the maximal hormonal effect from eating a low-carb diet. If this doesn't result in noticeable weight loss, you can be certain that too many carbs are NOT part of your weight issue and not the obstacle to your weight loss. There are, in fact, other causes of obesity as outlined in this book and being overweight as you now know it could be toxicity, thyroid, low testosterone, high oestrogen etc. So you need to be your own health and fat loss detective and solve your own problems.

Ketogenic Diet FAQs

Low carbohydrate diets have been show to decrease thyroid function so what can I do to prevent this?

One concern with a very low carbohydrate diet is the function of the thyroid gland and, as you know from habit 5, you DO NOT want the thyroid becoming dysfunctional as this will crash your metabolism and ability to drop fat. So make sure you follow the advice given in habit 5 to keep the thyroid working at full speed and with the right nutrition and supplementation as outlined in this book and with the amount of coconut oil consumed I'm personally confident your thyroid will become even more efficient.

Will ketosis ruin my athletic performance?

Glucose is usually called the body's 'preferred fuel' because, if it is available, our bodies have been conditioned from birth to use it first. But it is not the best fuel. That distinction belongs to fats. Before the mitochondria can use either glucose or fatty acid as a fuel, it has to be transported into the mitochondria. Fatty acids are transported into the mitochondria as completely intact molecules. Glucose, on the other hand, can be transported only after it has been broken down first into pyruvate by the process of glycolysis. This is then used anaerobically to produce energy with lactate as a by-product.

Let's look at a real athlete. It was 1968 at the Mexico City Olympic Games. The spectators at the marathon went wild as a relatively unknown Ethiopian, Degaga (Mamo) Wolde, won the marathon. Not only was the thirty-six-year-old runner the oldest man ever to win this prestigious event.

So what was Wolde's secret?

Wolde was a member of the Oromo or Galla, a traditionally pastoral tribe who live in West and South Ethiopia and part of Kenya. Traditionally the Oromo were nomadic herders like their neighbours, the Maasai and Samburu tribes. His life consisted of herding and running after and hunting wild game on foot. His diet, like other similar tribes, was one high in animal meat and fat, with practically no carbohydrate. Subsequent tests showed that Wolde's body, under conditions of physical load, readily burned fat as its main energy source. Wolde had no concept of 'hitting the wall'. It had never happened to him.

Are there any studies comparing low carb vs low fat for weight loss and health?

Here are 10 studies comparing high fat/low carb diets to high carb/low fat diets.

Study 1

Details: 132 individuals with severe obesity (mean BMI of 43) were randomized to either a low-fat or a low-carb diet. Many of the subjects had metabolic syndrome or type II diabetes. The low-fat dieters were calorie restricted. Study duration was 6 months.

Weight Loss: The low-carb group lost an average of 5.8 kg (12.8 lbs) while the low-fat group lost only 1.9 kg (4.2 lbs). The difference was statistically significant.

Conclusion: The low-carb group lost significantly more weight (about 3 times as much). There was also a statistically significant difference in several biomarkers:

- Triglycerides went down by 38 mg/dL in the LC group, compared to 7 mg/dL in the LF group.
- Insulin sensitivity improved on LC, got slightly worse on LF.
- Fasting blood glucose levels went down by 26 mg/dL in the LC group, only 5 mg/dL in the LF group.
- Insulin levels went down by 27% in the LC group, but increased slightly in the LF group.

Overall, the low-carb diet had significantly more beneficial effects on weight and key biomarkers in this group of severely obese individuals.

Samaha FF, et al. A low-carbohydrate as compared with a low-fat diet in severe obesity. New England Journal of Medicine, 2003.

Study 2

Details: 30 overweight adolescents were randomized to two groups, a low-carb diet group and a low-fat diet group. This study went on for 12 weeks. Neither group was instructed to restrict calories.

Weight Loss: The low-carb group lost 9.9 kg (21.8 lbs), while the low-fat group lost 4.1 kg (9 lbs). The difference was statistically significant.

Conclusion: The low-carb group lost significantly more (2.3 times as much) weight and had significant decreases in Triglycerides and Non-HDL cholesterol. Total and LDL cholesterol decreased in the low-fat group only.

Sondike SB, et al. Effects of a low-carbohydrate diet on weight loss and cardiovascular risk factor in overweight adolescents. The Journal of Pediatrics, 2003.

Study 3

Details: 53 healthy but obese females were randomized to either a low-fat diet, or a low-carb diet. Low-fat group was calorie restricted. The study went on for 6 months.

Weight Loss: The women in the low-carb group lost an average of 8.5 kg (18.7 lbs), while the low-fat group lost an average of 3.9 kg (8.6 lbs). The difference was statistically significant at 6 months.

Conclusion: The low-carb group lost more weight (2.2 times as much) and had significant reductions in blood triglycerides. HDL improved slightly in both groups.

Brehm BJ, et al. A randomized trial comparing a very low carbohydrate diet and a calorie-restricted low fat diet on body weight and cardiovascular risk factors in healthy women. The Journal of Clinical Endocrinology & Metabolism, 2003.

Study 4

Details: 60 overweight individuals were randomized to a low-carb diet high in monounsaturated fat, or a low-fat diet based on the National Cholesterol Education Program (NCEP).

Both groups were calorie restricted and the study went on for 12 weeks.

Weight Loss: The low-carb group lost an average of 6.2 kg (13.6 lbs), while the low-fat group lost 3.4 kg (7.5 lbs). The difference was statistically significant.

Conclusion: The low-carb group lost 1.8 times as much weight. There were also several changes in biomarkers that are worth noting.

- Waist-to-hip ratio is a marker for abdominal fat. This marker improved slightly in the LC group, not in the LF group.
- Total cholesterol improved in both groups.
- Triglycerides went down by 42 mg/dL in the LC group, compared to 15.3 mg/dL in the LF group.

- LDL particle size increased by 4.8 nm and percentage of small, dense LDL decreased by 6.1% in the LC group, while there was no significant difference in the LF group.

Overall, the low-carb group lost more weight and had much greater improvements in several important risk factors for cardiovascular disease.

Aude YW, et al. The national cholesterol education program diet vs a diet lower in carbohydrates and higher in protein and monounsaturated fat. Archives of Internal Medicine, 2004.

Study 5

Details: 120 overweight individuals with elevated blood lipids were randomized to a low-carb or a low-fat diet. The low-fat group was calorie restricted. Study went on for 24 weeks.

Weight Loss: The low-carb group lost 9.4 kg (20.7 lbs) of their total body weight, compared to 4.8 kg (10.6 lbs) in the low-fat group.

Conclusion: The low-carb group lost significantly more weight and had greater improvements in blood triglycerides and HDL cholesterol.

Yancy WS Jr, et al. A low-carbohydrate, ketogenic diet versus a low-fat diet to treat obesity and hyperlipidemia. Annals of Internal Medicine, 2004.

Study 6

Details: A randomized, crossover trial with 28 overweight/obese individuals. Study went on for 30 days (for women) and 50 days (for men) on each diet, that is a very low-carb diet and a low-fat diet. Both diets were calorie restricted.

Weight Loss: The low-carb group lost significantly more weight, especially the men. This was despite the fact that they ended up eating more calories than the low-fat group.

JS Volek, et al. Comparison of energy-restricted very low-carbohydrate and low-fat diets on weight loss and body composition in overweight men and women. Nutrition & Metabolism (London), 2004.

Study 7

Details: 119 overweight individuals were randomized to a low-carb, ketogenic diet or a calorie restricted low-fat diet for 6 months.

Weight Loss: The low-carb group lost 12.9 kg (28.4 lbs), while the low-fat group lost only 6.7 kg (14.7 lbs).

Conclusion: The low-carb group lost almost twice the weight and experienced less hunger.

McClernon FJ, et al. The effects of a low-carbohydrate ketogenic diet and a low-fat diet on mood, hunger, and other self-reported symptoms.Obesity (Silver Spring), 2007.

Study 8

Details: 13 diabetic and 13 non-diabetic individuals were randomized to a low-carb diet or a "healthy eating" diet that followed the Diabetes UK recommendations (a calorie restricted, low-fat diet). Study went on for 3 months.

Weight Loss: The low-carb group lost 6.9 kg (15.2 lbs), compared to 2.1 kg (4.6 lbs) in the low-fat group.

Conclusion: The low-carb group lost more weight (about 3 times as much).

Dyson PA, et al. A low-carbohydrate diet is more effective in reducing body weight than healthy eating in both diabetic and non-diabetic subjects. Diabetic Medicine, 2007.

Study 9

Details: 40 subjects with elevated risk factors for cardiovascular disease were randomized to a low-carb or a low-fat diet for 12 weeks. Both groups were calorie restricted.

Weight Loss: The low-carb group lost 10.1 kg (22.3), while the low-fat group lost 5.2 kg (11.5 lbs).

Conclusion: The low-carb group lost almost twice the amount of weight as the low-fat group, despite eating the same amount of calories.

This study is particularly interesting because it matched calories between groups and measured so-called "advanced" lipid markers. Several things are worth noting:

- Triglycerides went down by 107 mg/dL on LC, but 36 mg/dL on the LF diet.
- HDL cholesterol increased by 4 mg/dL on LC, but went down by 1 mg/dL on LF.
- Apolipoprotein B went down by 11 points on LC, but only 2 points on LF.
- LDL size increased on LC, but stayed the same on LF.

- On the LC diet, the LDL particles partly shifted from small to large (good), while they partly shifted from large to small on LF (bad).

Volek JS, et al. Carbohydrate restriction has a more favorable impact on the metabolic syndrome than a low fat diet. Lipids, 2009.

Study 10

Details: 322 obese individuals were randomized to three diets: a low-carb diet, a calorie restricted low-fat diet and a calorie restricted Mediterranean diet. Study went on for 2 years.

Weight Loss: The low-carb group lost 4.7 kg (10.4 lbs), the low-fat group lost 2.9 kg (6.4 lbs) and the Mediterranean diet group lost 4.4 kg (9.7 lbs).

Conclusion: The low-carb group lost more weight than the low-fat group and had greater improvements in HDL cholesterol and triglycerides.

Shai I, et al. Weight loss with a low-carbohydrate, Mediterranean, or low-fat diet. New England Journal of Medicine, 2008.

Could a ketogenic diet eventually be a "standard of care" drug-free treatment for cancer?

The premise is that since cancer cells need glucose to thrive, and carbohydrates turn into glucose in your body, then lowering the glucose level in your blood though carb and protein restriction literally starves the cancer cells into oblivion.

In 1931, the Nobel Prize was awarded to German researcher Dr. Otto Warburg, who discovered that cancer cells have a fundamentally different energy metabolism compared to healthy cells, and that malignant tumours tend to feed on sugar. More recently, researchers discovered that while cancer cells feed on both glucose and fructose, pancreatic tumor cells use fructose specifically to divide and proliferate.

Dr. Thomas Seyfried is one of the leading pioneer academic researchers in promoting how to treat cancer nutritionally. He's been teaching neurogenetics and neurochemistry as it relates to cancer treatment at Yale University and Boston College for the past 25 years. He's written over 150 peer-reviewed scientific articles and book chapters, and has also published a book, *Cancer as a Metabolic Disease: On the Origin, Management, and Prevention of Cancer.*

Dr. Seyfried's work confirms that sugar is the primary fuel for cancer, and that by restricting sugar and providing an alternate fuel, namely fat, you can dramatically reduce the rate of growth of cancer. He explains:

"When we're dealing with glucose and [cancer] management, we know from a large number of studies that if respiration of the tumor is ineffective, in order to survive, the cells must use an alternative source of energy, which is fermentation. We know that glucose is the primary fuel for fermentation. Fermentation becomes a primary energy-generating process in the tumor cell. By targeting the fuel for that process, we then have the capability of potentially managing the disease."

The strategy Dr. Seyfried suggests is a low-carb, low to moderate protein, high-fat diet, which will effectively lower your blood sugar. This is an easily measurable parameter that you can check using a diabetic blood glucose meter. This type of diet, called a ketogenic diet, will also elevate ketone bodies, as fat is metabolized to ketones that your body can burn in the absence of food. When combined with calorie restriction, the end result will put your body in a metabolic state that is inhospitable to cancer cells.

Dr. Seyfried uses ketones and glucose as the measures of this new metabolic state. The parameters associated with an ideal state are ketone levels equal to or higher than the glucose level in your blood.

"There's a high ratio of glucose to ketones. But in a fasted or therapeutic state, this ratio is actually reversed. Ketones can actually become higher than glucose," he says. "What they can do is they can get their blood sugars down to 2.5 to 3 millimolar [equivalent to about 55-65 mg/dl], and then their ketones to up to 3 or 4 millimolar, where the ratio is now reversed. It's this state that now brings the body into this new physiology."

Ketogenic food choices

Here is a comprehensive list of food choices coming from fats, protein and low carbohydrate foods then I will give you some examples on my diet plan. Use the following food charts to create your meal plans to get into a ketogenic state if that's your desired goal and included in this habit as well I will give examples on including carbohydrates in your plan if you feel a ketogenic diet is not for you. I have got many athletes shredded not using a ketogenic diet plan and one female bodybuilder I consulted for a number of years had to have carbohydrates in her diet to help her drop body fat so nothing is set in stone, find out what works for you.

Fats and Oils

Since the majority of calories on a ketogenic diet will come from dietary fats, choices should be made with digestive tolerance in mind. Most people cannot tolerate eating a large amount of vegetable oil, mayonnaise or even olive oil over time. And this is a good thing, since vegetable oils are high in polyunsaturated Omega-6 fatty acids.

The Omega-6 fatty acids (found in nut oils, margarines, soybean oil, sunflower oil, safflower oil, corn oil, and canola oil) should be limited due to the inflammatory effect they trigger within the body. Most nuts (with the exceptions of macadamias and walnuts) are high in Omega 6 fatty acids as well, so go easy on them). Your intake of polyunsaturated fats should be balanced between Omega 6 and Omega 3 types. Eating wild salmon, tuna and shellfish will provide balancing Omega 3 fatty acids and are important part of a low carb food list. If you don't like seafood, then consider taking small amounts of a fish oil supplement.

Saturated and monounsaturated fats such as butter, macadamia nuts, coconut oil, avocado and egg yolks are tolerated more easily by most people, and since they are chemically stable, they are less inflammatory. Fats and oils can be combined in sauces, dressings, and other additions to basic meals. Over time, it will become a habit to add a source of fat to each meal.

Avoid hydrogenated fats such as margarine to minimize trans fats intake. If you use vegetable oils (olive, canola, sunflower, safflower, soybean, flaxseed and sesame oils) choose "cold pressed." Keep cold pressed oils like almond and flaxseed refrigerated to avoid rancidity. Avoid heating vegetable oils. Use clean non-hydrogenated lard, beef tallow, coconut oil, ghee and olive oil for frying, since they have high smoke points.

- Avocado (very high in fat, so I'm including it here)
- Avocado oil
- Almond oil
- Beef tallow, preferably from grass fed cattle
- Butter: try to find organic sources
- Chicken fat, organic
- Coconut oil (always go for extra virgin)
- Duck fat, organic
- Ghee (butter with milk solids removed)
- Lard such as organic leaf lard (make sure it is NOT hydrogenated)
- Macadamia Nuts
- Macadamia oil
- Mayonnaise (most have carbs, so count them)
- Olives
- Olive oil, organic
- Organic coconut oil, coconut butter and coconut cream concentrate
- Organic Red Palm oil
- Peanut Butter: make sure to use unsweetened products, and limit due to Omega 6 content.
- Seed and most nut oils: Sesame oil, Flaxseed oil, etc. These are higher in inflammatory Omega 6 fats, so limit amounts, and don't heat them.
- 85-90% dark chocolate can be used in small amounts.

	Calories	Fat (g)	Carbs (g)	Protein (g)
Avocado oil, 1 tbsp	124	14	0	0
Avocado, Haas, 3 oz	102	9	7	2
Bacon fat 1 tbsp	116	13	0	0
Butter 1 tbsp	102	12	0	0
Chicken fat 1 tbsp	115	13	0	0
Cocoa butter 1 tbsp	120	14	0	0
Coconut oil 1 tbsp	117	14	0	0
Cream cheese (block)	101	10	1	2
Flaxseed oil 1 tbsp	120	14	0	0
Ghee 1 tbsp	112	13	0	0
Heavy cream 2 tbsp	103	11	1	1
Lard 1 tbsp	115	13	0	0
Macadamia oil 1 tbsp	120	14	0	0
Mayonnaise (full fat) 1 tbsp	99	11	1	0
MCT oil 1 tbsp	100	14	0	0
Olive oil	119	14	0	0
Olives (black) 1 cup	141	13	8	1
Olives (green) 1 cup	193	20	5	1
Red palm oil	120	14	1	1

Good fats vs bad fats

One study investigated the effects of saturated fat (butter) meals and monounsaturated fat (sunflower oil, found in many margarines) meals on the function of the blood vessels in 17 men.

It found that:

a) The rise in (bad) triglycerides was 66% LESS after the butter meal than after the sunflower oil meal.
b) After the sunflower oil meal there was a DECREASE in blood flow and an INCREASE in cell damage.
c) After the butter meal there was NO change in blood flow and NO cell damage.

The study shows how sunflower oil damages the blood vessels , which may lead to heart disease.

Berry SE, Tucker S, Banerji R, Jiang B, Chowienczyk PJ, Charles SM, Sanders TA. Impaired postprandial endothelial function depends on the type of fat consumed by healthy men. Journal of Nutrition 2008 Oct;138(10):1910-4

Eating saturated fat actually improves the blood lipid profile. It raises HDL (the "good") cholesterol and changes the LDL from small, dense LDL (very bad) to Large LDL, which is benign.

High-fat dairy consumption was found to lower the risk of obesity, with no consistent association between dairy fat, cardiovascular disease or other metabolic diseases. *Eur J Nutr. 2013 Feb;52(1):1-24. doi: 10.1007/s00394-012-0418-1. Epub 2012 Jul 19.*

Take home message - eat good quality fats to lose your excess fat and reclaim your weight as well as your health.

Protein

Fattier cuts of meat are better because they contain less protein and well, more fat. Choose organic or grass fed animal foods and organic eggs if possible to minimize bacteria, antibiotic and steroid hormone intake. Below are some great protein choices and are the best choices for a ketogenic diet.

- Meat: beef, lamb, veal, goat and wild game. Grass fed meat is preferred, as it has a better fatty acid profile.
- Offal, liver, heart and kidneys try to get from grass fed and free range. These foods offer incredible nutrients and health benefits.
- Pork: pork loin, pork chops, ham. Look out for added sugar in hams.
- Poultry: chicken, turkey, quail, Cornish hen, duck, goose, pheasant. Free range is better if it's available.
- Fish or seafood of any kind, preferably wild caught: anchovies, calamari, catfish, cod, flounder, halibut, herring, mackerel, salmon, sardines, sole, snapper, trout, and tuna.
- Canned tuna and salmon are acceptable but check the labels for added sugars or fillers. (Exception: Avoid breaded and fried seafood).
- Shellfish: clams, crab, lobster, scallops, shrimp, squid, mussels, and oysters. (Exception: imitation crab meat. It contains sugar, gluten and other additives).

- Whole eggs: These can be prepared in various ways: fried, hard-boiled, omelettes, poached, scrambled, and soft-boiled.
- Bacon and sausage: check labels and avoid those cured with sugar or which contain fillers such as soy or wheat. Specialty health food stores carry most brands of sugar-free bacon.
- Whey protein powders, plus rice, pea, hemp or other vegetable protein powders.

	Calories	Fat (g)	Carbs (g)	Protein (g)
Bacon, cooked 2 slices	92	9	2	4
Beef, ground, 80% lean, cooked 1 oz	74	4	0	7
Duck, roasted, skin eaten, 1 oz	95	8	0	5
Egg, 1 large	72	5	0	6
Pork sausage, cooked, no filler 1.5 oz	102	9	0	7
Pork ribs, plain 1 oz	104	8	0	8
Pork shoulder, roasted, plain , 1 oz	82	6	0	7
Beef, ground, 92%, cooked, 1 0z	45	2	0	7
Beef steak, 1 oz	71	4	0	8
Chicken breast, roasted, no skin, 1 oz	46	1	0	9
Chicken thigh, roasted, no skin, 1 0z	55	3	0	7
Cottage cheese, 1-2%, 0.25 cup	41	1	2	7
Egg whites, 2 large	34	0	0	7
Fish fillet (flounder, sole), no breading, baked, 2 oz	49	1	0	8.5
Salmon fillet (fresh), 1 oz	39	1	0	7
Salmon (tinned), 1 oz	39	1	0	7
Ham, smoked, 1 oz	53	3	1	5
Pork chops, lean, cooked, 1 oz	57	3	0	7
Pork roast, loin, cooked 1 oz	70	4	0	8
Scallops, baked or broiled, 1 oz	38	1	1	6
Shrimp, steamed or boiled, 1 oz	39	1	0	8
Tuna, tinned, 1 oz	33	0	0	7
Turkey breast, roasted, no skin, 1 oz	38	0	0	9
Turkey thigh, roasted, no skin, 1 oz	52	2	0	8

Fresh vegetables

Most non-starchy vegetables are low in carbs. Choose organic vegetables or grow your own to avoid pesticide residues. Avoid the starchy vegetables such as corn, peas, potatoes, sweet potatoes, and most winter squash as they are much higher in carbs. Limit sweeter vegetables such as tomatoes, carrots, peppers, and summer squashes.

- Alfalfa Sprouts
- Any leafy green vegetable
- Asparagus
- Bamboo Shoots
- Bean Sprouts
- Beet Greens
- Bok Choy
- Broccoli
- Brussels Sprouts
- Cabbage
- Cauliflower
- Celery
- Celery Root
- Chard
- Chives
- Collard Greens
- Cucumbers
- Dandelion Greens
- Pickles
- Garlic
- Kale
- Leeks
- Lettuces and salad greens (Arugula, Bok Choy, Boston lettuce, Chicory, Endive, Escarole, Fennel, Mache, Radicchio, Romaine, Sorrel.)
- Mushrooms
- Olives
- Onions (limited amounts, as they are higher in sugar)
- Radishes
- Sauerkraut
- Scallions
- Shallots
- Snow Peas
- Spinach
- Swiss Chard
- Turnips
- Water Chestnuts

	Calories	Fat (g)	Carbs (g)	Fibre (g)	Net carbs (g)	Protein (g)
Asparagus, cooked, 1 cup	46	2	6	4	2	5
Beans, cooked (black, kidney, chick peas, lentils) 0.25 cup	55	0	10	3	7	4
Beans, green, cooked, 1 cup	34	0.5	8	4	4	2
Blueberries, 0.25 cup	21	0	5	1	4	0
Broccoli, cooked, 0.5 cup	27	0	6	3	3	2
Brussel sprouts, raw, 1 cup	38	0	8	3	5	3
Cabbage, raw, 4 oz	23	0	5	2	3	1
Carrots, raw, 2 oz	20	0	6	2	4	0
Cauliflower, cooked, 1 cup	28	0	6	2	4	2
Celery, 1 cup	36	0	7	4	3	2
Cucumber, 10 oz	29	0	6	2	4	1
Garlic, 6 cloves	24	0	6	0	6	0
Kale, 2 oz	28	0	6	1	5	2
Lettuce, 3 cups	24	0	6	3	3	3
Mushrooms, portabella, 4 oz	29	0	6	2	4	3
Onion, white, 0.5 cup	33	0	7	1	6	1
Pepper, bell, 4 oz	23	0	5	2	3	0
Potato, white, cooked, 0.5 cup	95	4	13	2	11	1
Raspberries, 0.5 cup	32	0	7	4	3	1
Rice, white, cooked, 0.25 cup	51	0	11	0	11	1
Shallots, cooked, 2 tbsp	14	0	4	0	4	0
Spinach, raw, 6 oz	38	1	6	4	2	1

Squash, cooked, 1 cup	36	0	8	3	5	2
Strawberries, 0.5 cup	23	0	6	2	4	0
Tomato, 6 oz	31	0	7	2	5	1
Turnips, 4 oz	32	0	7	2	5	1

Dairy products

Raw milk products are preferable; choose organic if raw products are not available.

- Heavy whipping cream
- Full fat sour cream (check labels for additives and fillers. Look for brands such as Daisy which are pure cream with no added milk; carbs and protein will be low.)
- Full fat cottage cheese
- All hard and soft cheeses
- Cream cheese
- Unsweetened whole fat yogurt like Greek yogurt

	Calories	Fat (g)	Carbs (g)	Protein (g)
Cheese, blue 1 oz	100	8	1	6
Cheese, brie, 1 oz	95	8	0	6
Cheese, cheddar, 1 oz	114	9	0	7
Cheese, cottage, 1 oz	41	1	2	7
Cheese, mozzarella, 1 oz	90	7	1	6
Cheese, parmesan, 1 oz	111	7	1	10
Cheese, ricotta, 0.25 cup	107	8	2	8
Cheese, swiss, 1 oz	108	8	2	8
Yogurt, Greek, full fat, 3.5 oz	95	5	4	9
Yogurt, Greek, 0% fat, 3 oz	50	0	3.5	9

Nuts and Seeds

Nuts and seeds are best soaked and roasted to remove anti-nutrients. Avoid peanuts as they are actually legumes.

- Nuts: macadamias, pecans, almonds and walnuts are the lowest in net carbs and can be eaten in small amounts. Cashews, pistachios and chestnuts are higher in carb, so track carefully to avoid going over carb limits. Nuts are also higher in Omega 6 fats, which are inflammatory so don't rely on nuts as your main protein source.

	Calories	Fat (g)	Carbs (g)	Fibre (g)	Net carbs (g)	Protein (g)
Brazil nuts, roasted, 1 oz	186	19	3	2	1	4
Hazelnuts, 1 oz	183	18	5	3	2	4
Walnuts, 1 oz	185	18	4	2	2	4
Chia seeds, 1 oz	140	10	12	10	2	4
Sesame seeds, 1 oz	161	14	7	5	2	5
Coconut butter, 2 tbsp	186	18	8	4	4	2
Coconut, dried, unsweetened, 1 oz	165	15	6	4	2	3
Macadamia nuts, roasted, 1 oz	203	22	4	3	1	2
Pecans, roasted, 1 oz	201	21	4	3	1	3
Almond flour, 1 oz	160	14	6	3	3	6
Feta cheese, 3 oz	120	11	3	1	2	6
Almonds, 1 oz	172	16	5	3	2	6
Cashews, 1 oz	164	14	10	9	10	8
Flax seeds, 1 oz	152	12	8	7	1	6
Pumpkin seeds, roasted, 1 oz	148	12	4	1	3	9
Sunflower seeds, roasted, 1 oz	168	15	6	3	3	6

Spices

Spices do have carbs, so be sure to count them if they are added to meals made using this low carb food list. Commercial spice mixes like steak seasoning usually have added sugar. Sea salt is preferred over commercial salt, which is usually cut with some form of powdered dextrose.

Basil, Black pepper, Cayenne pepper, Chili pepper, dried, Cilantro/Coriander seeds, Cinnamon, ground, Cloves, Cumin seeds, Dill, Ginger, Mustard seeds, Oregano, Parsley, Peppermint, Rosemary, Sage, Thyme, and Turmeric.

Daily plan

This is what 3 days might look like on a ketogenic diet just to give you an idea you will also see a 7 day ketogenic plan in this habit along with a supplement plan I recommend.

Day 1: Ketogenic Diet

Breakfast

- 2 eggs, fried in coconut oil
- Black Pudding
- Steamed broccoli (When on plate put butter on the broccoli)
- 1 oz of full fat organic cheese
- 2 slices of organic bacon
- organic coffee with 1 heaped tsp of coconut oil and heavy cream (Be aware of adding caffeine (coffee) to your diet as this can release insulin and make you insulin resistant. If you must have a coffee put cream, butter or coconut oil in there as well).

Lunch

- Green salad with lots of extra virgin olive oil on
- Fillet steak and onions cooked in coconut oil
- 1 large organic avocado
- 1 celery stalk with cream cheese
- water or PRP detox power (detox power helps detox the liver)

Dinner

- Liver cooked in coconut oil with peppers
- mushrooms sautéed in butter
- broccoli and brussel sprouts
- small bowl of organic raspberries
- water or PRP ultimate greens (ultimate greens is an alkalizing green drink)

Day 2: Ketogenic Diet

Breakfast

- Haggis or black pudding chopped onion cooked in coconut oil
- Poached eggs
- Stir fry low carb vegetables in coconut oil
- Full fat cheese
- small bowl of organic blueberries
- Cup of organic green tea

Lunch

- Fried Salmon in coconut oil
- Spinach, watercress and rocked with extra virgin olive oil
- water or PRP detox power (detox power helps detox the live

Dinner

- Lamb Chops cooked in coconut oil
- Steamed cabbage and cauliflower then butter on top to serve
- Walnuts
- water or unsweetened flavoured sparkling water or other unsweetened beverage
- water or PRP ultimate greens (ultimate greens is an alkalizing green drink)

Day 3: Ketogenic Diet

Breakfast

- Protein shake made with whey protein powder
- 1 tbsp of extra virgin olive oil in the whey
- 1 tbsp of MCT oil in the whey
- 2 tbsps heavy cream in the whey
- 1 pint of clean water preferably reverse osmosis

Lunch

- Chicken stir fried with vegetables in coconut oil
- 1 ounce of parmesan cheese,
- Celery with cream cheese as a dip
- water or ultimate greens

Dinner

- 6 oz salmon topped with parmesan cream sauce and baked
- 2 cups spinach sautéed with onions and garlic
- salad greens with low carb, high fat dressing
- small bowl of organic strawberries
- green tea organic

PHIL SAYS
DAILY SUPPLEMENTS

This is my personal supplement regime. Of course it changes over time but I will give you an example and all the products mentioned are products that I have developed and from my range PRP supplements. But use what supplement range you feel is best suited for you.

Breakfast: 30 minutes before 1 metabolic enhancer (stimulates fat cells to release fat for fuel and decreases appetite)

I take immediately after my breakfast:

- 1 Ultimate Multivitamin & Mineral Formula
- 1 teaspoon Ultimate Fish Oil Liquid
- 3 Iodine Forte (Thyroid Health)
- 2 Probiotic Gut Health (Gut Health)
- 1 Super Digestive Enzyme (help break down food)
- 1 Oestro Detox Formula (decreases oestrogen load)
- 1 teaspoon of Vitamin C Formula (for adrenal and heart health)
- 1 teaspoon of Cognitive Care (for brain, adrenal and liver health)
- 1 Cordycep Plus (for testosterone and ATP production)

Lunch: 30 minutes before 1 metabolic enhancer (stimulates fat cells to release fat for fuel and decreases appetite)

I take immediately after my lunch:

- 1 Ultimate Multivitamin & Mineral Formula
- 1 teaspoon Ultimate Fish Oil Liquid
- 1 Super Digestive Enzyme (help break down food)
- 1 Oestro Detox Formula (decreases oestrogen load)
- 1 teaspoon of Vitamin C Formula (for adrenal and heart health)
- 1 Cordycep Plus (for testosterone and ATP production)

Dinner: 30 minutes before 1 metabolic enhancer (stimulates fat cells to release fat for fuel and decreases appetite)

I take immediately after my dinner:

- 1 Ultimate Multivitamin & Mineral Formula
- 1 teaspoon Ultimate Fish Oil Liquid
- 1 Super Digestive Enzyme (help break down food)
- 1 Oestro Detox Formula (decreases oestrogen load)
- 1 teaspoon of Vitamin C Formula (for adrenal and heart health)
- 1 Cordycep Plus (for testosterone and ATP production)

Before bed 45 - 60 minutes always on empty stomach

- 2 scoops Nitric Oxide Generator (increases growth hormone, helps with liver detoxification, decreases homocysteine levels and helps me have an incredible deep nights sleep.
- 3 Magnesium Relax (helps relax the muscles and enhances insulin sensitivity)

Before training 45 - 60 minutes again on empty stomach

- 3 Metabolic Enhancers (stimulates fat cells to release fat for fuel)
- 2 scoops Amino Work Capacity (signals to my body to release anabolic hormones)
- 2 scoops Cardio Fuel (gives my mitochondria the substrates to make ATP)

During Training I just drink Amino Work Capacity and this allows my muscles not to be used as fuel and forces my body to use either the amino acids in the drink and my stored fat.

After Training I take my Ketogenic Fuel drink which contains branch chain amino acids, glutamine, creatine and D-Ribose with Medium Chain Triglycerides and ZERO Carbs. Why? First of all this is an awesome recovery drink without giving you a massive insulin spike like a lot of the post recovery drinks on the market. This drink forces my stored fat to be utilised in gluconeogenesis. Gluconeogenesis is a metabolic pathway that results in the generation of glucose from non-carbohydrate carbon substrates such as pyruvate, lactate, glycerol, and glucogenic amino acids

Never take your health or time for granted for when they are gone so are you!

And that's it for me and I feel great. I'm leaner than I have ever been since I was 21 (which was a long time ago) and trust me I really struggled to get lean after that no matter how hard I trained, how often I trained and how clean I ate. Like I said at the beginning of this book, my issue was chronic stress and toxicity poisoning from amalgam fillings and when you combine those two suckers there is only one outcome sick, tired and obese regardless of anything you do. Thankfully through trying to solve my myriad of health problems I feel better than at any other time in my life and I'm very grateful to have had the luxury of studying health, nutrition and training full time for 3 decades and I will continue hopefully for another 3 decades.

One thing to point out though: if I want someone to put size on then I 100% WOULD NOT put them on a ketogenic diet. Why? Because INSULIN is the most anabolic of all our hormones. If you know how to time INSULIN you will put quality muscle on instead of a truck load of fat, which is what happens to most people who eat too much carbohydrates at the WRONG time.

So if I'm consulting for a bodybuilder or a rugby player who wants to put size then nutrient timing becomes essential and this simply means when is it best to eat carbohydrates to increase insulin and how to make sure you do not overeat carbohydrates so that you start to also gain fat as well as muscle.

NUTRITION
FOOD CHOICE TABLE
KETOGENIC

MEATS	POULTRY	FISH			NUTS	BEVERAGES
Beef	Chicken	Mackerel	Halibut	Trout	Almonds	Alkalising Salts
Buffalo	Hen	Salmon	Herring	Whitefish	Brazil Nuts	Organic Coffee (caffeinated)
Elk	Duck	Sardine	Mahi-Mahi	Clams	Cashews	Organic Green Tea
Heart	Goose	Abalone	Octopus	Crab	Chesnuts	Reverse Osmosis Water
Kidney	Pheasant	Anchovy	Oysters	Lobster	Macadamia	Mint Choc Greens
Lamb	Quail	Bass (Freshwater)	Perch	Mussels	Pecans	Coco Choc Grrens
Liver (Beef)	Turkey	Sea Bass	Pompano	Shark	Pine Nuts	Ultimate Greens
Pork	Ostrich	Catfish	Rockfish	Squid	Pistachios	Ultimate Greens
Rabbit		Caviar	Roughy	Swordfish	Walnuts	Whey More Growth
Venison		Cod	Shrimps / Prawns	Tuna		
		Crayfish	Scallops	Cockles		
		Grouper	Snapper			*Supplements stated above can be found on the PRP website.

DAIRY & EGGS	GREENS	VEGETABLES		SEA VEGETABLES	OILS & FATS
Eggs (Chicken - whites)	Arugula	Asparagus	Leek	Agar	Avocado oil
Eggs (Chicken - yolks)	Beet Greens	Bamboo Shoots	Olive (all varieties)	Dulse	Beef tallow
Eggs (Duck - whole)	Dandelion Greens	Beet	Onion	Irish Moss	Organic Butter
Feta	Endive	Bok Choy	Radish	Kelp	Chicken fat, organic
Goats Cheese	Kale	Broccoli	Eggplant (Aubergine)	Laverbread	Extra Virgin Coconut oil
Whey Protein Concentrate	Lettuce (Bibb)	Brussel Sprouts	Jicama		Duck fat, organic
Cottage Cheese	Lettuce (Iceberg)	Cabbage	Peppers		Ghee
Milk (full fat)	Lettuce (Romain)	Cauliflower	Rutabanga		Lard
Cheeses (full fat)	Mustard Greens	Celery	Shallot		Olive oil, organic
Greek Yogurt (full fat)	Radicchio	Cucumber	Water Chesnuts		Organic Red Palm oil
Coconut Yogurt (full fat)	Rocket	Fennel	Zucchini (Corgette)		
	Spinach	Garlic	Mushrooms		
	Sprouts (Alfalfa)				
	Sprouts (Bean)				
	Swiss Chard				
	Turnip Greens				
	Watercress				
	Pea Shoots				

Please use this food table to help you to plan your meals with more variety. For example, when you see on the following nutrition plans, "Fish Choice", simply look at the food table and you will see that there are multiple choices of fish. You simply select one and then, next time, when you see "Fish Choice" again, chose another one. This plan gives you so much flexibility in preparing nutritious meals and allows you to have a wide variety of food in you nutrition plan

FRUITS (Limit intake)	HERBS, SPICES & SEASONINGS		
Blackberries	Anise	Curry Powder	Paprika
Blueberries	Celtic Sea Salt	Dill Weed	Parsley
Booysenberries	Basil	Fennel Seed	Pepper (ground black)
Cherries	Bay Leaf	Fenugreek	Peppermint
Cranberries	Caraway	Ginger	Rosemary
Elderberries	Cardamom	Honey	Saffron
Gooseberries	Carob	Horseradish	Sage
Raspberries	Cayenne	Himalayan Salt	Salt (sea, unrefined)
Strawberries	Chervil	90% Org Choc	Savory
	Chili Powder	Marjoram	Ketchup Organic
	Chive	Molasses	Spearmint
	Cinnamon	Mustard	Tarragon
	Cloves	Mustard Seed	Thyme
	Coriander	Nutmeg	Tumeric
	Cumin	Oregano	Wasabi

Remember no more than 60 grams of carbohydrates per day if you want to stay in ketosis so keep a check on blood glucose levels and your ketone levels to ensure you are burning fat and not glucose.

PHIL RICHARDS PERFORMANCE

KETOGENIC DIET PLAN FOR OPTIMUM FAT LOSS

DAY 1	DAY 2	DAY 3	DAY 4	DAY 5	DAY 6	DAY 7
BREAKFAST Meat Choice Dairy Choice Stir Fry Vegetables ☐ Coconut oil & Butter	BREAKFAST Meat Choice Dairy Choice Stir Fry Vegetables ☐ Coconut oil & Butter	BREAKFAST Meat Choice Dairy Choice Stir Fry Vegetables ☐ Coconut oil & Butter	BREAKFAST Meat Choice Dairy Choice Stir Fry Vegetables ☐ Coconut oil & Butter	BREAKFAST Meat Choice Dairy Choice Stir Fry Vegetables ☐ Coconut oil & Butter	BREAKFAST Meat Choice Dairy Choice Stir Fry Vegetables ☐ Coconut oil & Butter	BREAKFAST Meat Choice Dairy Choice Stir Fry Vegetables ☐ Coconut oil & Butter
SUPPLEMENTS	SUPPLEMENTS	SUPPLEMENTS	SUPPLEMENTS	SUPPLEMENTS	SUPPLEMENTS	SUPPLEMENTS
LUNCH Poultry Choice Greens / Veg Choice Herbs & Spices Choices ☐ Butter & Extra Virgin Olive Oil	LUNCH Poultry Choice Greens / Veg Choice Oils & fat choice Herbs & Spices Choices Butter	LUNCH Poultry Choice Greens / Veg Choice Herbs & Spices Choices ☐ Butter & Extra Virgin Olive Oil	LUNCH Poultry Choice Greens / Veg Choice Oils & fat choice Herbs & Spices Choices Butter	LUNCH Poultry Choice Greens / Veg Choice Herbs & Spices Choices ☐ Butter & Extra Virgin Olive Oil	LUNCH Poultry Choice Greens / Veg Choice Oils & fat choice Herbs & Spices Choices Butter	LUNCH Poultry Choice Greens / Veg Choice Herbs & Spices Choices ☐ Butter & Extra Virgin Olive Oil
SUPPLEMENTS	SUPPLEMENTS	SUPPLEMENTS	SUPPLEMENTS	SUPPLEMENTS	SUPPLEMENTS	SUPPLEMENTS
DINNER Fish Choice Greens / Veg Choice ☐ Butter & Extra Virgin Olive Oil	DINNER Fish Choice Greens / Veg Choice Oils & fat choice	DINNER Fish Choice Greens / Veg Choice ☐ Butter & Extra Virgin Olive Oil	DINNER Fish Choice Greens / Veg Choice Oils & fat choice	DINNER Fish Choice Greens / Veg Choice ☐ Butter & Extra Virgin Olive Oil	DINNER Fish Choice Greens / Veg Choice Oils & fat choice	DINNER Fish Choice Greens / Veg Choice ☐ Butter & Extra Virgin Olive Oil
SUPPLEMENTS	SUPPLEMENTS	SUPPLEMENTS	SUPPLEMENTS	SUPPLEMENTS	SUPPLEMENTS	SUPPLEMENTS

- Use the food Table provided to get all the choices you need and ROTATE foods regularly to prevent food intolerances.
- Since the majority of calories on a ketogenic diet will come from dietary fats, make sure to measure your ketones daily to ensure you are in the ketosis zone.
- Measure blood glucose levels to ensure they are at an optimum level.
- Portion size - as much green vegetables as you want (ALWAYS ORGANIC).
- Fattier cuts of meat are better because they contain less protein and well, more fat. Choose organic or grass fed animal foods and organic eggs if possible to minimize toxins as they are usually stored in the fat of animals.
- If you are not reaching the ketosis zone then limit fruit intake further
- ☐ Compulsory Choice*

PHIL RICHARDS PERFORMANCE

SUPPLEMENT PLAN
KETOGENIC DIET PLAN

60 MINUTES BEFORE MEALS (UNLESS TRAINING)	BREAKFAST	LUNCH	DINNER	1 HOUR BEFORE BED ON AN EMPTY STOMACH
1/2 - 1 Teaspoon of Alkalising Salts In 500ml of water	1 x Ultimate Multivitamin & Mineral Formula		1 x Ultimate Multivitamin & Mineral Formula	1 Scoops of Nitric Oxide Generator
	1 Scoop of Vitamin C Plus	1 Scoop of Vitamin C Plus	1 Scoop of Vitamin C Plus	3 x Magneisum Relax
	1 Teaspoon of Ultimate Fish Oil Liquid	1 Teaspoon of Ultimate Fish Oil Liquid	1 Teaspoon of Ultimate Fish Oil Liquid	
	1 x CLA Capsule	1 x CLA Capsule	1 x CLA Capsule	
	1 x Probiotic Gut Health	1 x Probiotic Gut Health	1 x Probiotic Gut Health	
	1x Super Digestive Enzyme	1x Super Digestive Enzyme	1x Super Digestive Enzyme	
	1 x Oestro Detox Formula	1 x Oestro Detox Formula	1 x Oestro Detox Formula	
	2 x Cordyceps Plus	1 x Cordyceps Plus	1 x Cordyceps Plus	
	1 x Iodine Forte	1 x Iodine Forte	1 x Iodine Forte	
	1 x Metabolic Enhancer	1 x Metabolic Enhancer	1 x Metabolic Enhancer	

45-60 MINUTES BEFORE TRAINING ON AN EMPTY STOMACH	DURING TRAINING SESSION	POST TRAINING SESSION
1 - 2 Scoops of Amino Work Capacity 1 - 2 Scoops of Cardio Fuel	1 Scoop of KHIIT Fuel	1 Scoop of KHIIT Fuel
In 750ml of water	In 750ml of water	In 750ml of water

BETWEEN MEAL TIMES:
In between breakfast, lunch & evening meals drink 1 pint of still mineral water with ONE scoop of Coco Choc Greens.

Coconut Oil is High in Medium Chain Triglycerides, Fatty Acids That Boost Metabolism

Coconut oil is vastly different from most other fats in the diet. Whereas most foods contain predominantly long-chain fatty acids, coconut oil consists almost entirely of Medium Chain Fatty Acids. The thing with these medium chain fatty acids, is that they are metabolized differently than the longer chain fats. They are sent straight to the liver from the digestive tract, where they are either used for energy right away or turned into ketone bodies.

In one study, rats were overfed with either long chain or medium chain fats. The rats fed the medium chain fats gained 20% less weight and 23% less body fat. Overfeeding with medium-chain triglyceride diet results in diminished deposition of fat. ***Am J Clin Nutr. 1983 Jan;37(1):1-4.***

One important property of coconut oil is that it is "thermogenic" – eating it tends to increase energy expenditure (fat burning) compared to the same amount of calories from other fats. In one study, 15-30 grams (1 to 2 tablespoons) of medium chain fats per day increased energy expenditure by 5%, totaling about 120 calories per day. Several other studies confirm these findings. When humans replace the fats they are eating with MCT fats, they burn more calories. Therefore, a calorie from coconut oil is NOT the same as a calorie from margarine fats!

Many studies on medium chain fatty acids show that, compared to the same amount of calories from other fats, they increase feelings of fullness and lead to an automatic reduction in calorie intake. This may be related to the way these fats are metabolized. It is well known that ketone bodies (which the liver produces when you eat coconut oil) can have a powerful appetite reducing effect.

Whatever the mechanism is, it works. In one study of 6 healthy men, eating a high amount of MCTs caused them to automatically eat 256 fewer calories per day. ***J Obes Relat Metab Disord. 1996 May;20(5):435-44.***

In another study of 14 healthy men, those who ate MCTs at breakfast ate significantly fewer calories at lunch. *Am J Clin Nutr. 1998 Aug;68(2):226-34.*

So, if coconut oil can boost metabolism and reduce appetite, then it should help you lose fat over the long term. In fact, there are several studies that support this.

A Randomized Double-Blind Trial on the Effects of Coconut Oil on Abdominal Obesity

This trial, published in the journal Lipids, enrolled 40 women with a waist circumference > 35 inches. Twenty were randomized to take 30 ml – two tablespoons – of coconut oil a day (Group C) over a 12-week period. The other 20 took 30 ml soybean oil/day (Group S).

The Group C women taking the coconut oil exhibited a significant reduction in waist circumference (for the statisticians among us the P value was 0.005) with no change in the soybean Group S. And the only thing that the saturated fat-laden coconut oil did to cholesterol levels was to raise HDL cholesterol, the one that advocates of the lipid hypothesis call the "good" cholesterol. (Lipids 2009;44:593-601)

The fat content of coconut oil is 92 percent saturated fat, the highest saturated fat content of any food. I now start each day with two tablespoons of coconut oil.

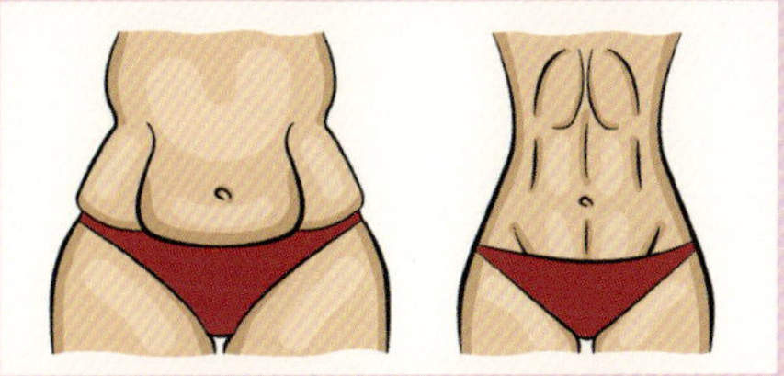

In one study, 40 women were given either 30 grams (2 tablespoons) of either coconut oil or soybean oil for 28 days.

They were instructed to eat fewer calories and walk every day. These were the results:

- Both groups lost weight (about 2 pounds).
- Only the coconut oil group had decreased waist circumference (belly fat) while the soybean oil actually had a mild increase in belly fat.
- The coconut oil group had increased HDL (good) cholesterol levels, while the soybean oil had reduced HDL and increased LDL.

In this study, coconut oil did not cause overall weight loss compared to soybean oil, but it did lead to a significant reduction in belly fat. ***Effects of Dietary Coconut Oil on the Biochemical and Anthropometric Profiles of Women Presenting Abdominal Obesity. Monica L. Assunção, Haroldo S. Ferreira, Aldenir F. dos Santos, Cyro R. Cabral Jr, Telma M. M. T. Florêncio***

Using a non ketogenic approach to fat loss

I am now going to give you some examples of how to get lean using a non ketogenic diet. I have used this approached with many of my athletes, especially those involved in team and endurance sports. But remember, these athletes who I consult for range from international rugby players, world champion boxers through to Olympians. The point is that they do an incredible amount of training and competing and use up an enormous amount of energy. So, once again, mould the diet to suit your metabolic needs and obviously the best way to gage if it's working is simple - are you dropping body fat. If not you've got to keep altering until you start getting leaner!

NUTRITION
FOOD CHOICE TABLE
NON-KETOGENIC

MEATS	POULTRY	FISH			LEGUMES		NUTS	BEVERAGES
Beef	Chicken	Mackerel	Halibut	Trout	Aduki Beans	Pinto Beans	Almonds	Alkalising Salts
Buffalo	Hen	Salmon	Herring	Whitefish	Black Beans	Red Beans	Brazil Nuts	Goats Milk
Elk	Duck	Sardine	Mahi-Mahi	Clams	Black-eyed Peas	Soy Beans	Cashews	Tea (Herbal)
Heart	Goose	Abalone	Octopus	Crab	Fava Beans	Tofu	Chesnuts	Vegetable Juices
Kidney	Pheasant	Anchovy	Oysters	Lobster	Garbanzo Beans	White Beans	Macadamia	Water
Lamb	Quail	Bass (Freshwater)	Perch	Mussels	Green Beans	Chick Peas	Pecans	Coconut Milk
Liver (Beef)	Turkey	Sea Bass	Pompano	Shark	Green Peas		Pine Nuts	Almond Milk
Rabbit	Ostrich	Catfish	Rockfish	Squid	Lentils		Pistachios	Rice Milk
Venison		Caviar	Roughy	Swordfish	Lima Beans		Walnuts	Organic Coffee (caffeinated)
		Cod	Shrimps / Prawns	Tuna	Mung Beans			Wine (Red)
		Crayfish	Scallops	Cockles	Navy Beans			Organic Green Tea
		Grouper	Snapper		Pink Beans			Whey More Growth
								Greens Drinks

DAIRY & EGGS	GRAINS	GREENS	VEGETABLES		SEA VEGETABLES	OILS & FATS
Eggs (Chicken - whites)	Amaranth	Arugula	Artichoke	Onion	Agar	Almond Oil
Eggs (Chicken - yolks)	Buckwheat	Beet Greens	Asparagus	Radish	Dulse	Blackcurrant Oil
Eggs (Duck - whole)	Kamut	Dandelion Greens	Beet	Eggplant (Aubergine)	Irish Moss	Borage Oil
Feta	Millet	Endive	Broccoli	Jicama	Kelp	Coconut Oil
Goats Cheese	Quinoa	Kale	Brussel Sprouts	Parsnip	Laverbread	Evening Primrose Oil
Whey More Growth	Rice (basmati)	Lettuce (Bibb)	Cabbage	Peppers		Fish Oil
Cottage Cheese	Rice (brown)	Lettuce (Iceberg)	Carrot	Peppers (Hot)		Flax Seed Oil
	Rice (white)	Lettuce (Romain)	Cauliflower	Shallot		Hemp Oil
	Spelt	Mustard Greens	Celery	Water Chesnuts		Walnut Oil
	Triticale	Radicchio	Cucumber	Zucchini (Corgette)		Avacado Oil
	Wild Rice	Rocket	Corn	Potato (all varieties)		Almond Butter
	Rice Cakes	Spinach	Fennel	Pumpkin		Brazil Nut Butter
		Sprouts (Alfalfa)	Garlic	Squash (Summer)		Butter (unsalted)
		Sprouts (Bean)	Ginger Root	Squash (Winter)		Extra Virgin Olive Oil
		Swiss Chard	Jerusalem Artichoke	Sweet Potato (Yam)		
		Turnip Greens	Leek	Turnip		
		Watercress	Olive (all varieties)	Mushrooms		
		Pea Shoots				

Please use this food table to help you to plan your meals with more variety. For example, when you see on the following nutrition plans, "Fish Choice", simply look at the food table and you will see that there are multiple choices of fish. You simply select one and then, next time, when you see "Fish Choice" again, chose another one.

FRUITS			HERBS, SPICES & SEASONINGS		
Apples	Gooseberries	Papaya	Anise	Curry Powder	Paprika
Avocado	Grapefruit	Pears	Celtic Sea Salt	Dill Weed	Parsley
Banana	Grapes	Persimmon	Basil	Fennel Seed	Pepper (ground black)
Blackberries	Guava	Pineapple	Bay Leaf	Fenugreek	Peppermint
Blueberries	Figs	Plums	Caraway	Ginger	Rosemary
Boysenberries	Honeydew Melon	Pomegranite	Cardamom	Honey	Saffron
Cantaloupe	Kiwifruit	Prunes	Carob	Horseradish	Sage
Casaba Melon	Kumquat	Raisins	Cayenne	Himalayan Salt	Salt (sea, unrefined)
Cherries	Lemons	Raspberries	Chervil	90% Org Choc	Savory
Coconut	Limes	Rhubarb	Chili Powder	Marjoram	Ketchup Organic
Cranberries	Loganberries	Strawberries	Chive	Molasses	Spearmint
Currents	Mango	Tangerines	Cinnamon	Mustard	Tarragon
Dates	Nectarines	Tomatoes	Cloves	Mustard Seed	Thyme
Elderberries	Oranges	Watermelon	Coriander	Nutmeg	Tumeric
			Cumin	Oregano	Wasabi

This plan gives you so much flexibility in preparing nutritious meals and allows you to have a wide variety of food in you nutrition plan

Food group choices (text colour):

Foods which improve our health

Every opportunity - buy certified organic foods

Consume food from this group only if you digest Legumes well

PHIL RICHARDS PERFORMANCE

NUTRITION PLAN
FOR DETOXIFICATION & FAT LOSS

DAY 1	DAY 2	DAY 3	DAY 4	DAY 5	DAY 6	DAY 7
BREAKFAST Stir Fry Vegetables Fish Choice 1-2 TBSP Coconut Oil Nuts & Seeds	BREAKFAST Greens/Veggie Choice Dairy Choice 1 TBSP Extra Virgin Olive Oil	BREAKFAST Greens/Veggie Choice Meat Choice 1 TBSP Extra Virgin Olive Oil	BREAKFAST Greens/Veggie Choice Poultry Choice 1 TBSP Extra Virgin Olive Oil	BREAKFAST Stir Fry Vegetables Fish Choice 1 TBSP Coconut Oil Nuts & Seeds	BREAKFAST CHEAT BREAKFAST	BREAKFAST Greens/Veggie Choice Dairy Choice 1 TBSP Extra Virgin Olive Oil
Fruit Choice (optional)	Fruit Choice (optional)	Fruit Choice (optional)	Fruit Choice (optional)	Fruit Choice (optional)		Fruit Choice (optional)
SUPPLEMENTS	SUPPLEMENTS	SUPPLEMENTS	SUPPLEMENTS	SUPPLEMENTS	SUPPLEMENTS	SUPPLEMENTS
LUNCH Greens / Veg Choice Poultry Choice 1 TBSP Extra Virgin Olive Oil Grain Choice (optional)	LUNCH Greens / Veg Choice Fish Choice 1 TBSP Avacado Oil Nuts & Seeds	LUNCH Greens / Veg Choice Dairy Choice 1 TBSP Extra Virgin Olive Oill Nuts & Seeds	LUNCH Greens / Veg Choice Poultry Choice 1 TBSP Avacado Oil Grain Choice (optional)	LUNCH Greens / Veg Choice Meat Choice 1 TBSP Organic Butter Nuts & Seeds	LUNCH Greens / Veg Choice Fish Choice 1 TBSP Extra Virgin Olive Oil Nuts & Seeds	LUNCH Greens / Veg Choice Fish Choice 1 TBSP Extra Virgin Olive Oil Grain Choice (optional)
SUPPLEMENTS	SUPPLEMENTS	SUPPLEMENTS	SUPPLEMENTS	SUPPLEMENTS	SUPPLEMENTS	SUPPLEMENTS
DINNER Greens / Veg Choice Meat Choice 1 TBSP Organic Butter Herb choice	DINNER Greens / Veg Choice Poulty Choice 1-2 TBSP Extra Virgin Olive Oil Herb choice	DINNER Greens / Veg Choice Meat Choice 1 TBSP Organic Butter Herb choice	DINNER Greens / Veg Choice Fish Choice 1 TBSP Organic Butter Herb choice	DINNER Greens / Veg Choice Meat Choice 1 TBSP Avacado Oil Herb choice	DINNER CHEAT MEAL	DINNER Greens / Veg Choice Poultry Choice 1 TBSP Organic Butter Herb choice
SUPPLEMENTS	SUPPLEMENTS	SUPPLEMENTS	SUPPLEMENTS	SUPPLEMENTS	SUPPLEMENTS	SUPPLEMENTS

IMPORTANT POINTS:

- Use the food Table provided to get all the choices you need and ROTATE foods regularly to prevent food intolerances.
- The Grains we've provided in the food table are Gluten Free.
- Follow the supplement plan provided for your fluid intake drink in between meals.
- Chew your food properly and I advise you always use super digestive enzymes with each meal.
- Please note Carbohydrate intake depends on exercise intensity & duration. Little exercise = Little Carbs – More Exercise = More Carbs.
- Cheat meal is your choice but no more than 2 glasses of red wine if you do decide to have a drink or it will destroy your hormones that help with fat loss for a few days.
- Portion size as much vegetables as you want but limit root vegetables. Fruit small bowl e.g. berries or 1 piece of fruit (ALWAYS ORGANIC).

SUPPLEMENT PLAN: Mercury Detoxification				
20-30 Minutes Before Meals (Unless Training)	**Breakfast**	**Lunch**	**Dinner**	**1 Hour Before Bed On An Empty Stomach**
1/2 Teaspoons of **Alkalising Salts** In 500ml of water	2 x **Cordyceps**	1 x **Cordyceps**	1 x **Cordyceps**	2 Scoops of **Nitric Oxide Generator**
	1 x **Ultimate Multivitamin** & **Mineral Formula**	1 x **Ultimate Multivitamin** & **Mineral Formula**	1 x **Ultimate Multivitamin** & **Mineral Formula**	
	1 x **Oestro Detox Formula**	1 x **Oestro Detox Formula**	1 x **Oestro Detox Formula**	3 x **Magnesium Relax**
	1 Teaspoon of **Ultimate Fish Oil Liquid**	1 Teaspoon of **Ultimate Fish Oil Liquid**	1 Teaspoon of **Ultimate Fish Oil Liquid**	
	1 x **Iodine Forte Capsule**	1 x **Iodine Forte Capsule**	1 x **Iodine Forte Capsule**	
	2 Scoop **Collagen Formula**	2 Scoop **Collagen Formula**	2 Scoop **Collagen Formula**	
	2 x **Probiotic Gut Health**			

BETWEEN MEAL TIMES:
In between breakfast, lunch & evening meals drink 500ml of reverse osmosis water or still mineral water with TWO heaped TEASPOONS of **Ultimate Greens**.

PHIL RICHARDS PERFORMANCE

NUTRITION PLAN

This is a nutritional plan I used with a world champion triathlete in his age group.

DAY 1	DAY 2	DAY 3	DAY 4	DAY 5	DAY 6	DAY 7
BREAKFAST Stir Fry Vegetables Fish Choice 1-2 TBSP Coconut Oil 1 TBSP Organic Butter Nuts & Seeds	BREAKFAST Greens/Veggie Choice Dairy Choice 1 TBSP Extra Virgin Olive Oil 1 TBSP Organic Butter	BREAKFAST Greens/Veggie Choice Meat Choice 1 TBSP Extra Virgin Olive Oil 1 TBSP Organic Butter	BREAKFAST Greens/Veggie Choice Poultry Choice 1 TBSP Extra Virgin Olive Oil 1 TBSP Organic Butter	BREAKFAST Stir Fry Vegetables Fish Choice 1 TBSP Coconut Oil 1 TBSP Organic Butter	BREAKFAST Greens/Veggie Choice Meat Choice 1 TBSP Extra Virgin Olive Oil 1 TBSP Organic Butter	BREAKFAST Porridge Coconut Milk 1 Desert spoon of Coconut Oil
Fruit Choice with full fat cream	Fruit Choice with full fat cream	Fruit Choice with full fat cream	Fruit Choice with full fat cream	Fruit Choice with full fat cream	Fruit Choice with full fat cream	Fruit Choice with full fat cream
SUPPLEMENTS	SUPPLEMENTS	SUPPLEMENTS	SUPPLEMENTS	SUPPLEMENTS	SUPPLEMENTS	SUPPLEMENTS
LUNCH Greens / Veg Choice Poultry Choice 1 TBSP Extra Virgin Olive Oil 1 TBSP Organic Butter Nuts & Seeds Grain Choice	LUNCH Greens / Veg Choice Fish Choice 1 TBSP Avacado Oil 1 TBSP Organic Butter Nuts & Seeds Grain Choice	LUNCH Greens / Veg Choice Dairy Choice 1 TBSP Extra Virgin Olive Oil 1 TBSP Organic Butter Nuts & Seeds Grain Choice	LUNCH Greens / Veg Choice Poultry Choice 1 TBSP Avacado Oil 1 TBSP Organic Butter Nuts & Seeds Grain Choice	LUNCH Greens / Veg Choice Meat Choice 1 TBSP Organic Butter Nuts & Seeds Grain Choice	LUNCH Greens / Veg Choice Fish Choice 1 TBSP Extra Virgin Olive Oil 1 TBSP Organic Butter Nuts & Seeds Grain Choice	LUNCH Greens / Veg Choice Fish Choice 1 TBSP Extra Virgin Olive Oil 1 TBSP Organic Butter Nuts & Seeds Grain Choice
SUPPLEMENTS	SUPPLEMENTS	SUPPLEMENTS	SUPPLEMENTS	SUPPLEMENTS	SUPPLEMENTS	SUPPLEMENTS
DINNER Greens / Veg Choice Meat Choice 1 TBSP Organic Butter 1 TBSP Coconut Oil Herb Choice Grain Choice Fruit Choice	DINNER Greens / Veg Choice Poulty Choice 1 - 2 TBSP Extra Virgin Oilve Oil 1 TBSP Coconut Oil Herb Choice Grain Choice Fruit Choice	DINNER CHEAT MEAL	DINNER Greens / Veg Choice Fish Choice 1 TBSP Organic Butter 1 TBSP Coconut Oil Herb Choice Grain Choice Fruit Choice	DINNER Greens / Veg Choice Meat Choice 1 TBSP Avacado Oil 1 TBSP Coconut Oil Herb Choice Grain Choice Fruit Choice	DINNER CHEAT MEAL	DINNER Greens / Veg Choice Poultry Choice 1 TBSP Organic Butter 1 TBSP Coconut Oil Herb Choice Grain Choice Fruit Choice
SUPPLEMENTS	SUPPLEMENTS	SUPPLEMENTS	SUPPLEMENTS	SUPPLEMENTS	SUPPLEMENTS	SUPPLEMENTS

Tip! Drink 1 litre of reverse osmosis water per 25kg of body weight daily!

PHIL RICHARDS PERFORMANCE

SUPPLEMENT PLAN
ELITE ENDURANCE ATHLETE

20-30 MINUTES BEFORE MEALS (UNLESS TRAINING)	BREAKFAST	LUNCH	DINNER	1 HOUR BEFORE BED ON AN EMPTY STOMACH
1/2 Teaspoons of Alkalising Salts In 500ml of water	1 x Ultimate Multivitamin & Mineral Formula	1 x Ultimate Multivitamin & Mineral Formula	1 x Ultimate Multivitamin & Mineral Formula	2 Scoops of Nitric Oxide Generator
	1 x Oestro Detox Formula	1 x Oestro Detox Formula	1 x Oestro Detox Formula	3 x Magnesium Relax
	1 Teaspoon of Ultimate Fish Oil Liquid	1 Teaspoon of Ultimate Fish Oil Liquid	1 Teaspoon of Ultimate Fish Oil Liquid	
	3 x Iodine Forte Capsules	1 Tablespoon of Collagen Formula	1 Tablespoon of Collagen Formula	
	1 x Super Digestive Enzymes Capsules	1 x Super Digestive Enzymes Capsules	1 x Super Digestive Enzymes Capsules	
	1 Scoop Cognitive Care	1 Scoop Cognitive Care		
	2 x Probiotic Gut Health			

45-60 MINUTES BEFORE TRAINING ON AN EMPTY STOMACH	DURING TRAINING SESSION	POST TRAINING SESSION
1 1/2 Scoops of Amino Work Capacity 2 Scoops of Cardio Fuel 1-3 x Metabolic Enhancer	1 Scoop of Competition Nutrition per hour	1 Scoop of Anabolic Drive 1 scoop KHIIT Fuel
In 750ml of water	In 750ml of water	In 750ml of water

BETWEEN MEAL TIMES:
In between breakfast, lunch & evening meals drink 1 pint of reverse osmosis water or still mineral water with ONE heaped TABLESPOON of Ultimate Greens.

PHIL RICHARDS PERFORMANCE

NUTRITION PLAN

NON-KETOGENIC APPROACH FOR A FITNESS MODEL

DAY 1	DAY 2	DAY 3	DAY 4	DAY 5	DAY 6	DAY 7
BREAKFAST Stir Fry Vegetables Fish Choice 2 TBSP Coconut Oil 2 TBSP Extra Virgin Olive Oil Nuts & Seeds	BREAKFAST Greens/Veggie Choice Dairy Choice 1 TBSP Full Fat Butter on vegetables 2 TBSP Extra Virgin Olive Oil	BREAKFAST Greens/Veggie Choice Nuts & Seeds Meat Choice 1 TBSP Full Fat Butter on vegetables 2 TBSP Extra Virgin Olive Oil	BREAKFAST Greens/Veggie Choice Poultry Choice 1 TBSP Full Fat Butter on vegetables 2 TBSP Extra Virgin Olive Oil	BREAKFAST Stir Fry Vegetables Nuts & Seeds Fish Choice 2 TBSP Coconut Oil 2 TBSP Extra Virgin Olive Oil	BREAKFAST Greens/Veggie Choice Meat Choice 1 TBSP Full Fat Butter on vegetables 2 TBSP Extra Virgin Olive Oil	BREAKFAST Porridge (Don't microwave) Coconut Oil Coconut Milk
SUPPLEMENTS	SUPPLEMENTS	SUPPLEMENTS	SUPPLEMENTS	SUPPLEMENTS	SUPPLEMENTS	SUPPLEMENTS
LUNCH Greens / Veg Choice Poultry Choice 2 TBSP Extra Virgin Olive Oil	LUNCH Greens / Veg Choice Fish Choice 2 TBSP Extra Virgin Olive Oil	LUNCH Greens / Veg Choice Dairy Choice 2 TBSP Extra Virgin Olive Oill	LUNCH Greens / Veg Choice Poultry Choice 2 TBSP Extra Virgin Olive Oil	LUNCH Greens / Veg Choice Meat Choice 2 TBSP Extra Virgin Olive Oil	LUNCH Greens / Veg Choice Fish Choice 2 TBSP Extra Virgin Olive Oil	LUNCH Grain Choice Meat Choice Fruit Choice
SUPPLEMENTS	SUPPLEMENTS	SUPPLEMENTS	SUPPLEMENTS	SUPPLEMENTS	SUPPLEMENTS	SUPPLEMENTS
DINNER Greens / Veg Choice Meat Choice 2 TBSP Coconut Oil Legumes	DINNER Greens / Veg Choice Poulty Choice 2 TBSP Coconut Oil 2 TBSP Extra Virgin Olive Oil Legumes	DINNER Greens/Veggie Choice Fish Choice 1 TBSP Full Fat Butter on vegetables 2 TBSP Extra Virgin Olive Oil	DINNER Greens / Veg Choice Meat Choice 2 TBSP Coconut Oil 2 TBSP Extra Virgin Olive Oil	DINNER Greens/Veggie Choice Poultry Choice 1 TBSP Full Fat Butter on vegetables 2 TBSP Extra Virgin Olive Oil	DINNER Greens/Veggie Choice Meat Choice 2 TBSP Coconut Oil 2 TBSP Extra Virgin Olive Oil	DINNER TOTAL CHEAT MEAL! As much carbs as you can eat!!
SUPPLEMENTS	SUPPLEMENTS	SUPPLEMENTS	SUPPLEMENTS	SUPPLEMENTS	SUPPLEMENTS	SUPPLEMENTS

PHIL RICHARDS PERFORMANCE

SUPPLEMENT PLAN
FEMALE BODY BUILDER
(who tolerates carbohydrates)

20-30 MINUTES BEFORE MEALS (UNLESS TRAINING)	BREAKFAST	LUNCH	DINNER	1 HOUR BEFORE BED ON AN EMPTY STOMACH
1/2 Teaspoons of Alkalising Salts In 500ml of water	1 x Ultimate Multivitamin & Mineral Formula	1 x Ultimate Multivitamin & Mineral Formula	1 x Ultimate Multivitamin & Mineral Formula	2 Scoops of Nitric Oxide Generator
1 x Metabolic Enhancer	1 x Oestro Detox Formula	1 x Oestro Detox Formula	1 x Oestro Detox Formula	2 x Amino Relax
	1 Teaspoon of Ultimate Fish Oil Liquid		1 Teaspoon of Ultimate Fish Oil Liquid	
	3 x Iodine Forte Capsules	1 Tablespoon of Collagen Formula	1 Tablespoon of Collagen Formula	
	3 x Probiotic Gut Health			
	1 Scoop Cognitive Care	1 Scoop Cognitive Care		

45-60 MINUTES BEFORE TRAINING ON AN EMPTY STOMACH	DURING TRAINING SESSION	POST TRAINING SESSION
1 1/2 Scoops of Amino Work Capacity 2 Scoops of Cardio Fuel	1 Scoop of Competition Nutrition	1 Scoop of Anabolic Drive If struggling to get lean 1 scoop KHIIT Fuel
In 750ml of water	In 750ml of water	In 750ml of water

BETWEEN MEAL TIMES:
In between breakfast, lunch & evening meals drink 1 pint of still mineral water with ONE heaped TABLESPOON of Detox Power for detoxification of the liver and oestrogen.

This is a program that I have recently given to a young rugby player who needs to put on 8kg over the next 12 months for him to have a chance of breaking into professional rugby.

PHIL RICHARDS PERFORMANCE

NUTRITION PLAN
MUSCLE GAIN

DAY 1	DAY 2	DAY 3	DAY 4	DAY 5	DAY 6	DAY 7
BREAKFAST Stir Fry Vegetables Fish Choice Grain Choice ☐ 2 TBSP Coconut Oil ☐ 2 TBSP Extra Virgin Olive Oil SUPPLEMENTS	BREAKFAST Greens/Veggie Choice Dairy Choice Grain Choice ☐ 1 TBSP Full Fat Butter on vegetables ☐ 2 TBSP Extra Virgin Olive Oil SUPPLEMENTS	BREAKFAST Greens/Veggie Choice Meat Choice Grain Choice ☐ 1 TBSP Full Fat Butter on vegetables ☐ 2 TBSP Extra Virgin Olive Oil SUPPLEMENTS	BREAKFAST Greens/Veggie Choice Poultry Choice Grain Choice ☐ 1 TBSP Full Fat Butter on vegetables ☐ 2 TBSP Extra Virgin Olive Oil SUPPLEMENTS	BREAKFAST Stir Fry Vegetables Fish Choice Grain Choice ☐ 2 TBSP Coconut Oil ☐ 2 TBSP Extra Virgin Olive Oil SUPPLEMENTS	BREAKFAST Greens/Veggie Choice Meat Choice Grain Choice ☐ 1 TBSP Full Fat Butter on vegetables ☐ 2 TBSP Extra Virgin Olive Oil SUPPLEMENTS	BREAKFAST Porridge (Don't microwave) Coconut Oil Coconut Milk SUPPLEMENTS
SNACK 2 Scoops of Whey More Growth *Can be found on the PRP website	SNACK 2 Scoops of Whey More Growth	SNACK 2 Scoops of Whey More Growth	SNACK 2 Scoops of Whey More Growth	SNACK 2 Scoops of Whey More Growth	SNACK 2 Scoops of Whey More Growth	SNACK 2 Scoops of Whey More Growth
LUNCH Greens / Veg Choice Poultry Choice Grain Choice ☐ 2 TBSP Extra Virgin Olive Oil SUPPLEMENTS	LUNCH Greens / Veg Choice Fish Choice Grain Choice ☐ 2 TBSP Extra Virgin Olive Oil SUPPLEMENTS	LUNCH Greens / Veg Choice Dairy Choice Grain Choice ☐ 2 TBSP Extra Virgin Olive Oil SUPPLEMENTS	LUNCH Greens / Veg Choice Poultry Choice Grain Choice ☐ 2 TBSP Extra Virgin Olive Oil SUPPLEMENTS	LUNCH Greens / Veg Choice Meat Choice Grain Choice ☐ 2 TBSP Extra Virgin Olive Oil SUPPLEMENTS	LUNCH Greens / Veg Choice Fish Choice Grain Choice ☐ 2 TBSP Extra Virgin Olive Oil SUPPLEMENTS	LUNCH Greens / Veg Choice Grain Choice Meat Choice SUPPLEMENTS
SNACK 2 Scoops of Whey More Growth *Can be found on the PRP website	SNACK 2 Scoops of Whey More Growth	SNACK 2 Scoops of Whey More Growth	SNACK 2 Scoops of Whey More Growth	SNACK 2 Scoops of Whey More Growth	SNACK 2 Scoops of Whey More Growth	SNACK 2 Scoops of Whey More Growth
DINNER Greens / Veg Choice Grain Choice Meat Choice Legumes ☐ 2 TBSP Coconut Oil SUPPLEMENTS	DINNER CHEAT MEAL SUPPLEMENTS	DINNER Greens/Veggie Choice Fish Choice Grain Choice ☐ 1 TBSP Full Fat Butter on vegetables ☐ 2 TBSP Extra Virgin Olive Oil SUPPLEMENTS	DINNER Greens/Veggie Choice Meat Choice Grain Choice ☐ 2 TBSP Coconut Oil ☐ 2 TBSP Extra Virgin Olive Oil SUPPLEMENTS	DINNER Greens/Veggie Choice Poultry Choice Grain Choice ☐ 1 TBSP Full Fat Butter on vegetables ☐ 2 TBSP Extra Virgin Olive Oil SUPPLEMENTS	DINNER CHEAT MEAL SUPPLEMENTS	DINNER Greens/Veggie Choice Meat Choice Grain Choice ☐ 2 TBSP Coconut Oil ☐ 2 TBSP Extra Virgin Olive Oil SUPPLEMENTS

☐ Compulsory choice*

PHIL RICHARDS
PERFORMANCE

SUPPLEMENT PLAN
MUSCLE GAIN

BREAKFAST	LUNCH	DINNER	1 HOUR BEFORE BED ON AN EMPTY STOMACH
1 x Ultimate Multivitamin & Mineral Formula	1 x Ultimate Multivitamin & Mineral Formula	1 x Ultimate Multivitamin & Mineral Formula	2 Scoops of Nitric Oxide Generator
1 x Oestro Detox Formula	1 x Oestro Detox Formula	1 x Oestro Detox Formula	
1 teaspoon Ultimate Fish Oil Liquid	1 teaspoon Ultimate Fish Oil Liquid	1 teaspoon Ultimate Fish Oil Liquid	
1 Tablespoon of Vitamin C Formula	1 Tablespoon of Vitamin C Formula	1 Tablespoon of Vitamin C Formula	
1 x Corydceps Plus	1 x Corydceps Plus	1 x Corydceps Plus	
1 x Probiotic Gut Health	1 x Probiotic Gut Health	1 x Probiotic Gut Health	

45-60 MINUTES BEFORE TRAINING ON AN EMPTY STOMACH	DURING TRAINING SESSION	POST TRAINING SESSION
2 Scoops of Amino Work Capacity 2 Scoops of Cardio Fuel	2 Scoops of Competition Nutrition	1-2 Scoops of Anabolic Drve
In 750ml of water	In 750ml of water	In 750ml of water

Pre-exercise Nutrition

Training on empty

Exercising on an empty stomach has been shown to have a number of health and fitness benefits. This is most easily accomplished if you exercise first thing in the morning, before breakfast. Part of the explanation for why exercising while fasted is beneficial is that this regimen complements your sympathetic nervous system (SNS) along with your capacity to burn fat. Your body's fat burning processes are controlled by your SNS, and your SNS is activated by exercise, and by lack of food. The combination of fasting and exercising maximizes the impact of cellular factors and catalysts (cyclic AMP and AMP Kinases), which force the breakdown of fat and glycogen for energy. This is why training on an empty stomach will effectively force your body to burn fat.

As I have said, I like to pre load with aminos before I train and a product I developed called Metabolic Enhancer which I take along with the amino's in a fasted state usually around 7 A.M. and I'm in the gym about 7.45 - 8 AM ready to train. I want to share with you some of the ingredients in Metabolic Enhancer and why I believe this is a potent fat loss product, providing you follow the information in this book:

Each capsule contains African Mango (300mg), Green Coffee Bean Extract (250mg), Green Tea Extract (150mg) Rasberry Ketones (100mg) and Slendesta® (30mg). That's a pretty powerful punch for a product that can help drop excess body fat lets look at the research behind each ingredient:

African Mango

Fat cells secrete leptin, a hormone that signals the brain that you've eaten enough. But some individuals have become resistant to leptin, resulting in added body fat. An extract from an African mango called *Irvingia gabonensis* has been shown to help increase leptin sensitivity - helping to reduce body fat. ***Lipids Health Dis. 2008 Nov 13;7:44. & Lipids Health Dis. 2009 Mar 2;8:7.***

African mango also helps the body control the rate of carbohydrate absorption from the intestines and, therefore, the caloric impact of starches and sugars. And this extract supports healthy levels of adiponectin, a hormone that regulates metabolism of lipids and glucose. Research indicates it has the ability to promote weight loss. ***Lipids Health Dis. 2009 Mar 2;8:7.***

Green Coffee Bean Extract

The active ingredient in green coffee bean extract are *chlorogenic acids*. In a placebo-controlled, human study, subjects who took 350 mg of green coffee extract, three times daily before meals lost an average of 7.9kg - over 10% of body weight - after just 12 weeks! There was also an average 4.44% reduction in body fat percentage! The conclusion from the study… green coffee extract supports the ability to lose weight. ***Diabetes Metab Syndr Obes. 2012;5:21-7.***

Chlorogenic acid is also has antioxidative activity. It has been suggested that caffeine, chlorogenic acid and other polyphenolic compounds in green coffee bean extract act synergistically to aid fat loss.

Green Tea

Studies have demonstrated that tea catechins produce acute increases in fat oxidation and reduced dietary fat-induced weight gain. In humans, green tea has been found to significantly increase 24-h energy expenditure and reduced 24-h respiratory quotient, indicating an increase in the ratio of fat:carbohydrate oxidized. In a 12-wk study of 240 Japanese men and women with increased visceral adiposity, consumption of a beverage providing 583 mg/d of tea catechins was associated with significantly greater reductions in body weight, body fat, and abdominal fat mass compared with a control beverage.

Raspberry Ketones

Raspberry ketone is an aromatic compound found in raspberries that, when ingested in high doses, is said to increase the body's production of adiponectin, a protein used to regulate your metabolism, as well as the body's breaking down of fat stores. In order to ingest the recommended 100-milligram dosage required to affect these changes, however, one would have to consume 90 pounds of raspberries per day. As a result, the compound is produced synthetically in labs and consumed in pill form.

Researchers became interested in raspberry ketones because of the molecular structure. They noticed that it looked very similar to two other molecules, capsaicin (found in chili pepper) and synephrine (a stimulant). Several studies have shown that these two molecules can boost metabolism, so it was speculated that raspberry ketones could have the same effect. When researchers took isolated fat cells from rats and made them grow in a test tube, adding raspberry ketones to the mix had two effects:

- It increased lipolysis (breakdown of fat), primarily by making the cells more sensitive to the effects of the fat burning hormone norepinephrine.
- It made the fat cells release more of the hormone adiponectin.

Adiponectin as we know is a hormone that is released by fat cells and is believed to play a role in regulating metabolism and blood sugar levels. Thin people have much higher levels of adiponectin than people who are overweight and the levels of the hormone increase when people lose weight. Studies have shown that people with low adiponectin levels are at a higher risk of obesity, type 2 diabetes, fatty liver and even heart diseases. Therefore, it stands to reason that raising adiponectin levels with natural means could help people lose weight and lower the risk of many diseases.

In a recent study using mice, scientists suggested that raspberry ketone increased noradrenaline-induced fat-loss. The researchers concluded that this weight-loss support substance works through the enzyme lipase, which is responsible for freeing fatty acids from the fat cell during the process of fat utilization. When raspberry ketone is present in your system, it has been surmised that levels of this enzyme increase and therefore ups the rate of fatty acid release.

Slendesta®

The potato extract Slendesta is a safe, natural satiety ingredient for weight loss containing Proteinase Inhibitor II (PI2), a protein naturally found in white potatoes. Slendesta enhances the release of Cholecystokinin (CCK), the natural signalling peptide within our body. Once released, CCK travels through the blood and acts on various target organs, including the stomach and brain, where it induces feelings of fullness and satisfaction. This feeling of fullness and satisfaction is known as satiety.

Slendesta is all-natural, derived from potatoes using a water-based, patented process and is completely stimulant-free. It's NOT one of the many so-called "fat burners" on the market today and does not artificially stimulate metabolism or cause jitters, bloating, or other side effects commonly associated with some other weight management ingredients.

Feeding before a workout

In a study published in the British Journal Of Nutrition the effects of exercise before and after meal ingestion on fat metabolism in overweight men was investigated. They found that men performing 60 minutes of walking prior to a meal (fasted state) burned 20% more fat than those who did 60 minutes walking after the meal. And this was just walking! Imagine how much more fat you would burn with higher intensity work.

What I recommend for maximum performance as I have stated in my personal pre workout stack is to load up on amino acids (like PRP Amino Work Capacity and Cardio Fuel). Taken on empty stomach, you will not only burn more fat but, from my research and experience, you will not lose muscle, as would be the case if you exercised regularly in a fasted state. In a purely fasted state, muscles can get broken down to provide fuel during intense exercise. Yes, a form of self-cannibalism and a great way to decrease metabolism and become a smaller fatter version of yourself.

The ultimate combination for pre-workout supplementation, PRP Amino Work Capacity and Cardio Fuel.

Pre-workout drinks are absolutely essential if you are looking for an edge. If training early in the morning, before 8 a.m., then I advise my athletes to drink Phil Richards Amino Work Capacity as it provides the substrates to tell the body you are in a very anabolic state. Why? The consumption of amino acids on empty stomach triggers the release of anabolic hormones - it senses this is an opportunity to grow. The body senses that there are lots of building materials available and that this is a good time to build. This will force the body to use stored body fat as fuel, especially if taken on empty stomach.

I know this to be true not only from the science but also from the feedback from all the elite athletes that have taken this product. One that comes to mind is an elite weightlifter who is also an Olympian. He put 10 kgs on his clean & jerk after consuming 2 scoops of Amino Work Capacity - now that's what you call a RESULT!

It appears that pre-workout amino acid drinks enhance the availability of amino acids to the muscles via enhanced blood flow (from the exercise) during a workout, which prevents, or reduces, the body from breaking down muscle tissue, as it normally does during an intense workout.

The BCAAs leucine, isoleucine, and valine are the most critical group of aminos for muscle growth. They also blunt fatigue and are used by the muscles as a fuel source. Exercise causes an increase in serotonin levels, which are believed to cause fatigue. But BCAAs are believed to reduce serotonin levels, and thus cancel out the fatigue and actually enhance exercise performance. There have been many studies that promote this exact ability: In 1998, subjects ingested either BCAA or a placebo before taking an endurance cycle ride in the heat. The BCAA group cycled 153.1 minutes on average, while the placebo group averaged only 137 minutes. A more recent Japanese study looked at the effects of a BCAA mixture on athletes during a one-month training stint and found that indices of blood oxygen-carrying capacity were increased.

Studies have found improved performance in cyclists when supplementing with BCAAs.

BCAAs are metabolized primarily in skeletal muscles, while other amino acids are metabolized in the liver, which is why some think they must take BCAA supplements if they're engaging in strenuous exercise. With that in mind, BCAAs can help repair damaged muscles, decrease muscle soreness and increase muscle function. Some data shows that BCAA supplementation before (and after exercise) has beneficial effects for decreasing exercise-induced muscle damage and promoting muscle-protein synthesis. A 2006 study concluded that the intake of BCAA may promote an anabolic hormone profile (causing muscle repair after workouts) while also decreasing the likelihood of training-induced muscle damage. A Japanese study examined a group of men and women - some given BCAA supplements and others given a placebo - as they did multiple testing days involving squats, which were used to promote delayed muscle soreness. Both sexes reported less soreness when they were given the supplements. Studies like this one and many others lead experts to believe it's possible to consider BCAA as a useful supplement for muscle recovery.

With my athletes, their pre-workout supplements would depend on the situation e.g. the time of day, any meals already eaten. One of my olympic athletes, who was a 3000m steeplechaser, would train exceptionally early, around 5:30a.m., and he swore by the alkalising salts I developed. He would consume 1 teaspoon of the salts in a pint of reverse osmosis water. Boom - he's on the road and has had tremendous results.

When I was training a world class boxer who had to make weight for fight night I would usually train him twice per day most days. In the first session in the morning I would pre-load him on free form and branch chain amino acids (like my Amino Work Capacity). After training, if we were a few weeks out from the fight I would give him a combination of protein, carbohydrates, creatine and glutamine (like my Anabolic Drive) to ensure maximum recovery. If we were 2 weeks out from fight and he was 5–7 pounds over weight, then I would drop the amount carbohydrates as this would also hold water, and replace it with the free form branch chain drink like my amino recovery drink I developed. This always did the trick for getting bang on the weight come weigh-in, which was the day before the fight.

Many of the rugby teams I worked with usually trained at 10 a.m. and 3 p.m. so the players would have usually had eaten a solid breakfast. There is no point amino loading when there is food in the gut so the emphasis here was their post-workout drink. The players would have lunch and by the time that was digested we were back on the field training - so, again, no point amino loading. When training was complete, they got their recovery drinks and that's it - tomorrow we do it all again. But least I knew their tanks were full so they could be pushed to the max in training.

What if I don't want to take amino acids before training or I can't afford them?

Well I know I've slated coffee during this book but maybe we have found another use apart (from the enema) and that could be the combination of coffee, coconut oil and full fat cream as your pre-workout drink. Yes, all is not loss for those who cannot live without their caffeine fix, but use organic coffee if you can. I have to admit I have used it and I was extremely skeptical at first but it works and you don't just have to use it pre workout but try not to consume after 12 pm or it could affect sleep, as I eluded to in habit 7.

The importance of hydration for health and performance

You can't rely on feeling thirsty as a reminder to replace fluid lost through sweating - one of nature's dirty tricks is that exercise suppresses thirst. Dehydration impairs both physical and mental performance in most types and levels of sport, yet it can be avoided (or at least minimised) by appropriate drinking strategies before, during and after training. When I worked with teams/athletes I monitored their urine with a specialist hydration testing machine. The biggest lesson I learnt was that the athletes thought that they were hydrated but were often not. In one professional rugby team I worked with, the first time I carried out hydration tests, over 90% of the players were dehydrated and this was before the training session. And the players were informed that they were going to be hydration tested that morning and were told drink plenty!!!

Never under-estimate the importance of hydration for performance.

Not everyone can afford to get one of these pieces of kit. However, urine colour can also be used as a guide to measure hydration levels.

You can use urine colour as an indicator of hydration. The darker the urine, the more dehydrated you are. Although, be aware that B vitamins can also alter the colour of your urine, making it darker.

Although sweat rates are highest under conditions of high-intensity exercise in heat and high humidity, total fluid losses can be appreciable in very prolonged events, whatever the conditions. Unless fluid losses are replaced by drinks, sweating causes progressive depletion of circulating blood volume, leading to hypohydration (commonly called dehydration) and a thickening of blood. This places a strain on the cardiovascular system, with a rise in heart rate in order to maintain adequate blood flow to exercising muscles and vital organs. As blood volume depletes, blood flow to the skin is reduced. As a result, sweating decreases and heat dissipation from the skin is impaired, causing body core temperature to rise, potentially leading to heat stress, collapse and even death.

Even low levels of dehydration have physiological consequences. A loss of 2% bodyweight (just 1kg for a 50kg person) causes an increase in perceived effort and is claimed to reduce performance by **10-20%**. A fluid loss exceeding **3-5%** body weight reduces aerobic exercise performance noticeably and impairs reaction time, judgement, concentration and decision making - vital elements in all sports, from pole-vaulting to football. A particular issue for boxers is that dehydration increases risk of brain injury.

The two main factors influencing early fatigue and impaired performance (both physical and mental) in all types of sports and exercise are depletion of body levels of fluids. Maintaining adequate fluid intake optimises training benefits by enabling athletes to train harder and for longer. This can make a difference between winning and losing. The opportunity and ability to eat and drink during training and competition depends on the sport; sports drinks may not be the only feasible option but most of them do provide a convenient supply of carbohydrates and fluid simultaneously, are well tolerated if used appropriately, and can be adapted to suit individual needs in varying circumstances.

Whatever the environmental conditions, sweat losses are probably greater than many athletes appreciate. The highest reported sweat rate was 3.7 litres/hour for Alberto Salazar during the 1984 Olympic marathon. Sweat rates of 2 to 3 litres/hour can be expected during short periods of hard exercise in the heat, and in excess of 1.5-2 litres/hour during endurance events. Even in cooler conditions, losses are appreciable. During a football game on a cool day (10 deg. C), players can lose up to two litres of sweat, and runners are estimated to lose

Marathon runners can lose large amounts of water during races.

around 1.2 litres/hour at 6 minute/mile pace on a cool, dry day (double this amount on a hot, humid day). Additionally, fluid is lost via moisture in exhaled air.

Before any exercise it is important to drink sufficient fluids so as not to be dehydrated. Around 500-750ml of fluid 2 hours before exercise and 300–500ml an hour before then 125-250ml immediately before exercise is one recommended method for endurance training/competition. However, it is of no advantage to drink excess amounts in order to "store" water. This will typically lead to abdominal pains and will probably result in the urge to urinate.

During exercise it is important to limit fluid loss to less than 2% body mass. The best way to do this is through practice. Nude weight before and after training can help you calculate water loss rate (***1 litre water loss = 1kg body mass loss***). Try to consume 1 litre per hour if the training/competition is intense.

Replacing just the water that you have lost is not enough. Studies have shown that around you need to drink around 150% of the fluids lost in order to reach hydration following exercise. Any more than this offers no additional benefits. e.g. lose 1kg replace with 1.5 litres of fluids.

Alkalising Buffer

Researchers from Loughborough University gave sodium bicarbonate to nine elite swimmers, finding that eight of them reduced their time in a 200 meter race by an average of 1.5 seconds. At the 2008 Olympics, the top four swimmers in the men's 200 meter freestyle were separated by just 1.4 seconds. So, in theory, it could be the difference between winning a medal and not. So strong is the effect that athletes can notice the difference in their breathing as more oxygen is carried throughout the system and as more acids are neutralized.

As hydrogen ion concentrations increase the blood and muscle become acidic. This acidic environment will slow down enzyme activity and ultimately the breakdown of glucose itself. By buffering acidity in the blood, bicarbonate draws more of the acid produced within the muscle cells out into the blood and thus reduces the level of acidity within the muscle cells themselves.

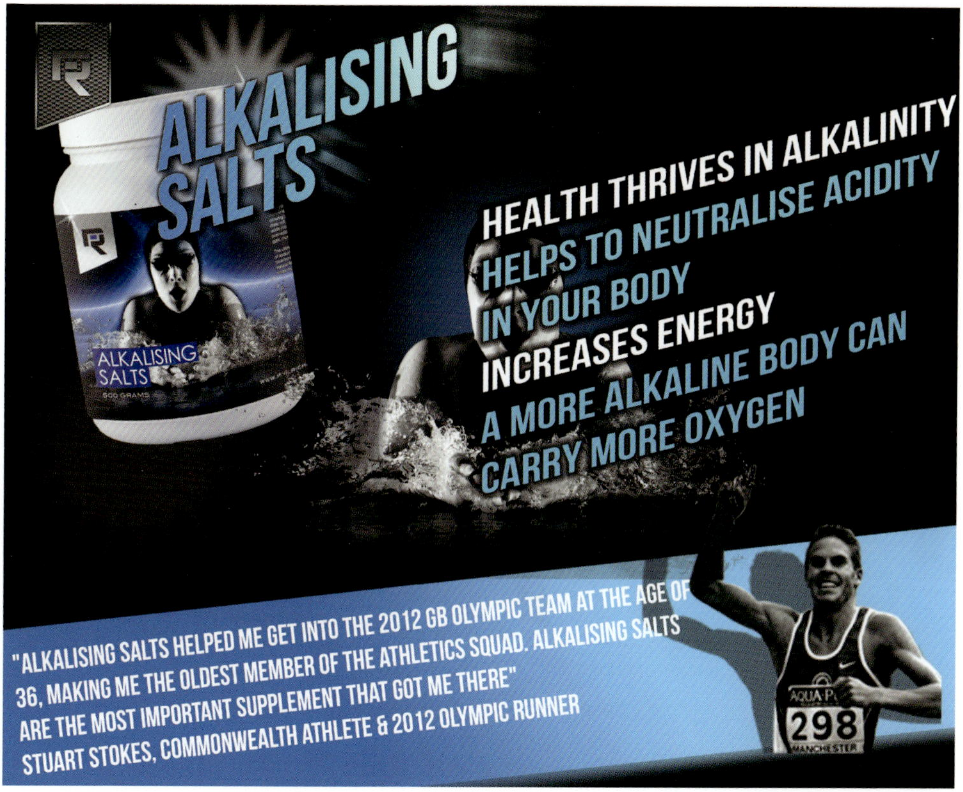

Bicarbonate can be taken frequently throughout the day with half teaspoons amounts, though for long term use lower doses are safer. A mild alkali can absorb 20-100 times more oxygen than a mild acid. When your body becomes too acidic it develops a lack of oxygen, which is the perfect breeding ground for disease. Blood must retain a pH of approximately 7.4 or it can't hold oxygen. The average level of oxygen in the blood is approximately 96% and if this lowers over time, your health can be affected.

During Exercise

It has been shown that when athletes were given a 6% carbohydrate solution during exercise, cortisol levels dropped by almost 80% compared to subjects receiving water. In one study conducted, cyclists drank a fluid containing carbohydrate and protein in a 4:1 ratio, they saw improved endurance of 57% compared with water and 24% compared with a carbohydrate drink. Bishop & colleagues from Loughborough University England showed that carbohydrate alone during exercise could reduce the biochemical markers of inflammation by almost 50%.

So you can start to see how carbohydrates during exercise can increase the quality of the exercise. However, again, each situation warrants its own specific strategy. If you were doing 60 minutes of yoga, then do you think you would need a carbohydrate drink? NO!

What you require during exercise is dependant upon the type and intensity of the exercise as well as your goals.

Research has shown that a carbohydrate intake of 0.8-1.2 grams per 1 kilogram of body weight maximizes glycogen synthesis and accelerates protein repair. However, unless you've had a very long, intense workout and not following the ketogenic diet, 1.2g/kg may be a bit excessive as excess carbohydrate can be converted to body fat. This amount of carbohydrates is what I would recommend to one of my elite endurance athletes, professional boxer or professional rugby players who are training up to 10 - 14 times per week as well as competing at the highest level of their respective sport. However if the boxer was struggling to make his weight a few weeks out from the fight I would not hesitate to go ketogenic with him to drop overall weight as well as body fat. And I have done this many times with professional fighters.

If you are not an elite athlete training multiple times per week drop the carbohydrates during training. To be honest, if you are only training for 45-60 minutes and you have pre-loaded with amino acids(like PRP amino work capacity), then water will be fine. However, if you do train brutally hard and you do not want to fatigue during the workout take my amino recovery which combines BCAA's aka branch chain amino acids, creatine, glutamie and D-ribose this is a phenomenal combination to prevent an energy crash and to continuously supply the body the substrates it needs to recover at

Fuel your exercise appropriately. If you are doing, light-intensity exercise then you do not need to worry about taking on carbohydrates during it.

maximum capacity. Or take a similar product on the market if you can find one or alternative just take BCAA's.

Post Exercise

You've probably heard people talk about the importance of consuming a drink that consists of both carbs and protein post workout. It is generally believed you might need a 2:1 or 3:1 ratio of carbs to protein as soon after working out as possible, or maybe even higher. You might have also heard the carbs need to have a high glycaemic index, meaning they are easy to digest and have the greatest ability to deliver protein to muscle.

However, I believe these are simply supplement company hype combined with misinterpretations of existing studies. In a review published in the *Journal of the International Society of Sports Nutrition*, researchers examined the existing literature on this topic. The researchers focused on the importance of carbs ingested with protein after a workout and also asked whether the carbs need to have a high glycaemic index in order to be most effective as a recovery aid.

The first and foremost reason to ingest carbs post workout is to replenish glycogen stores. Glycogen as we know now is the chemical form of carbohydrates that is stored in the muscles. When you do any kind of exercise that requires you to burn your glycogen stores, it's important you replace the glycogen that was lost.

However, that's not really the issue with a post-workout ratio of carbs to protein. In some workouts, you may burn only a few grams of glycogen for fuel, and in others you may nearly exhaust the glycogen in your skeletal muscle. This all depends on intensity and duration of a workout. You also need protein after exercise to repair and build muscle tissue. Getting enough protein after workouts will help stimulate protein synthesis, which is the creation of new muscle.

The main purpose of a ratio of carbs to protein is to further stimulate protein synthesis. Protein synthesis would theoretically occur as a result of an increase in insulin, which is where the high glycaemic value comes in. When a carbohydrate has a high glycaemic index, it enters the bloodstream quickly and usually stimulates insulin quickly. Insulin is a storage and anabolic hormone as we read in habit 7, meaning it supports the creation of new muscle, generally by improving the uptake of protein and, incidentally, the carbs that come in with the protein.

As it turns out, this extra insulin boost from high-glycaemic carbs is probably not necessary. While insulin is needed for protein synthesis, it seems that the low amounts stimulated by protein alone are sufficient for the creation of new muscle. In fact, the researchers found post-exercise insulin levels that were thirty times higher than resting insulin levels did not seem to affect protein synthesis.

Further, protein degradation caused by exercise is sometimes cited as another reason we need high insulin-promoting carbs after exercise. However, once again, the amount of insulin stimulated by protein alone is sufficient to prevent protein breakdown after exercise.

Consuming even small amounts of carbohydrates after exercise rapidly decreases the release of fatty acids from fat stores and oxidation of fat in the muscle, thereby interfering with keto adaptation, plus also diminishing the beneficial effects of exercise on insulin sensitivitey.

Carbohydrates may be useful for recovery in some scenarios, such as when you need to recover quickly between workouts. However, when it comes to repairing or building muscle through the stimulation of protein synthesis, the researchers said more research is warranted. At present, there is no evidence to support the claim that post-workout carbs in any ratio are needed for protein synthesis. Protein seems to be enough on its own to stimulate an insulin response.

Researchers have used anywhere from 0.2g - 0.4g of protein per 1 kilogram of body weight to demonstrate the effectiveness of adding protein to a post-workout carbohydrate drink (van Loon et al 2000b, Roy et al 1998). Just as you don't need to take in excess protein throughout the day, you also do not need to following exercise. In one study, protein was fed in doses from 0 to 40 g and after resistance exercise and muscle protein synthesis (MPS) was measured. Muscle protein synthesis showed a dose-response increase from 0 to 20 g but, despite doubling the protein intake, at 40 g there was no difference in MPS. Instead, the excess amino acids were oxidised. The conclusion from these data was that an intake of protein of 20 g in larger men (85 kg) was sufficient to maximally stimulate MPS, but that higher intakes would not offer any further benefit and the excess amino acids were oxidized (Moore et al., 2009). This is something you need to consider if you are looking to add a post-workout protein drink into your program. Begin to read labels and check to see how much protein is in the product you take.

Following a glycogen depleting exercise bout, subjects were given either a carbohydrate or a carbohydrate/protein/antioxidant glutamine beverage. Following a 4 hour recovery period, the subjects completed an exercise bout to exhaustion. The subjects who received the carb/

protein/antioxidant/glutamine drink, their performance was 55% better than when they received the carbohydrate only supplement.

Estimate of daily carbohydrate requirements for different bodyweights and training durations. Source from Optimum Sports Nutrition Dr. Michael Colgan.

Bodyweight	Daily Training (Hours)					
Kg	2	3	4	5	6	7
40	200	300	400	500	600	700
50	300	400	500	600	700	800
60	400	500	600	700	800	900
70	500	600	700	800	900	1000
80	600	700	800	900	1000	1100
90	700	800	900	1000	1100	1200
100	800	900	1000	1100	1200	1300
110	900	1000	11000	1200	1300	1400
120	1000	1100	1200	1300	1400	1500

What can BCAA's do for my recovery?

Exercise causes an increase in serotonin levels, which are believed to cause fatigue. But BCAAs are believed to reduce serotonin levels, and thus cancel out the fatigue and actually enhance exercise performance. There have been many studies that promote this exact ability: In 1998, subjects ingested either BCAA or a placebo before taking an endurance cycle ride in the heat. The BCAA group cycled 153.1 minutes on average, while the placebo group averaged only 137 minutes. A more recent Japanese study looked at the effects of a BCAA mixture on athletes during a one-month training stint and found that indices of blood oxygen-carrying capacity were increased.

“BCAAs are metabolized primarily in skeletal muscles, while other amino acids are metabolized in the liver. Some data shows that BCAA supplementation before and after exercise has beneficial effects for decreasing exercise-induced muscle damage and promoting muscle-protein synthesis. A 2006 study concluded that the intake of BCAA may promote an anabolic hormone profile (causing muscle repair after workouts) while also decreasing the likelihood of training-induced muscle damage. A Japanese study examined a group of men and women—some given BCAA supplements and others given a placebo—as they did multiple testing days involving squats, which were used to promote delayed muscle soreness. Both sexes reported less soreness when they were given the supplements. Studies like this one and many others lead experts to believe it's possible to consider BCAA as a useful supplement for muscle recovery.

Glutamine

A high glutamine level in a muscle cell stimulates the entry of other amino acids into the cell. Thus glutamine is anti-catabolic and can be considered an anabolic amino acid. Glutamine functions as a source of energy for the white blood cells. Eric Newsholm, Phd from Oxford University, suggests that glutamine supplementation can lessen the effects of overtraining. This evidence is supported by a study, in which athletes took 5 grams of glutamine in the first two hours after a marathon. **These athletes showed a 32% reduction in infection rate during the seven days following competition.**

Glutamine is classified as a "non-essential amino acid." This label may mislead some people into believing that we don't need it. But, in essence, "non-essential" means that the body can synthesize this amino acid. It does not mean "unimportant". However, there are times when our body may not make sufficient amounts and we may need to supplement.

In fact, glutamine is of crucial importance; we are lucky that we do not have to depend totally on dietary sources. It seems that every cell in the body uses glutamine. Some tissue types, however, depend on glutamine much more than others. Specifically, glutamine is utilized as a source of energy and for nucleotide synthesis by all rapidly dividing cells, such as the cells of the intestinal lining and certain immune cells (lymphocytes and macrophages). **Without sufficient glutamine, the intestines atrophy and the immune function breaks down.**

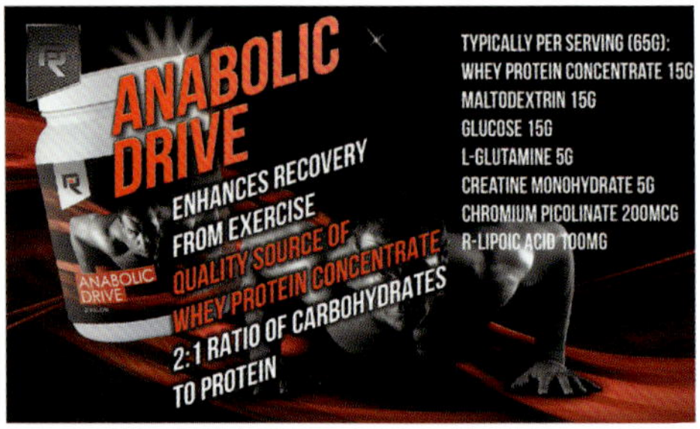

After researching what is needed for post-workout, I included the right substrates in the optimal dosages into this amazing product.

Thus, to say that glutamine is important for our health is an understatement. In view of its multiple functions, it is no surprise that glutamine is the most abundant free amino acid in the serum, muscle and cerebrospinal fluid. It constitutes 50% of all amino acids in the serum, and more than 60% of free amino acids within the body.

Glutamine is plentiful in both animal and plant protein. The typical Western diet provides between 3.5 g and 7 g of glutamine; more is synthesized according to need. Even so, heavy stress, such as strenuous exercise, infectious disease, surgery, burn injury or other acute trauma leads to glutamine depletion with consequent immune dysfunction, intestinal problems and muscle wasting. Consequently, it has been proposed that glutamine should be classified as a "conditionally essential amino acid.

People who use glutamine virtually ensure superior health of their intestinal lining. They need not worry about the "leaky gut syndrome" and all of its troublesome consequences, including allergies, the "leaking out" of pathogens and possible arthritis. In fact, when it was first discovered, glutamine used to be called "intestinal permeability factor." It is by far the most important nutrient for intestinal health. The importance of glutamine for the intestines is enormous - glutamine is the chief source of energy for the cells of the intestinal lining. Most glutamine in the diet (and also most dietary glutamate and aspartate) is metabolized by the intestines, both to serve as intestinal fuel and also to produce glutathione, nitric oxide, polyamines, nucleotides and the amino acids alanine, citrulline and proline, making these available to the rest of the body.

In addition, glutamine is a substrate for glutathione, a tripeptide amino acid that acts as one of our master antioxidants, and also helps enhance the immune function. Though large doses of glutamine stimulate the immune response even under heavy stress, it is important to reduce stress as much as possible. Stress hormones may interfere with glutamine metabolism in the immune cells

Glutamine is very important for those who exercise a lot. In its role as a carbon donor, glutamine helps to replenish glycogen. But actually the function of glutamine as a nitrogen-donor might be even more important. Strenuous exercise such as weight lifting, sprinting & contact sports causes micro-injuries to the muscle tissue. By donating nitrogen, glutamine helps build proteins and repair the muscle. I recommend 5–10 grams of glutamine after high intensity training or competition.

Glutamine is especially useful post-workout when nutrients are at a low until recovery. In this condition research shows glutamine levels are significantly reduced, taking up to one month to return to baseline. In athletes, glutamine has been used as a marker to indicate overtraining. This fall in glutamine is catabolic to muscle tissue. BCAA's [comprising 37% of total muscle] are debranched from skeletal muscle, and the resulting molecules are used to synthesis glutamine.

In the catabolic state, glutamine is the first amino acid used to correct that deficiency. Glutamine drives protein into the muscle cell where it is synthesized for growth[6,8]. This means that additional Glutamine is necessary during periods of stress [such as intense weight training which induces a catabolic state which has been shown to uniformly decrease Glutamine levels by 50%, taking several hours to return to normal levels. Additionally, L-Glutamine also decreases protein degradation [BCAA catabolism], resulting in bigger, stronger muscle cell

Creatine

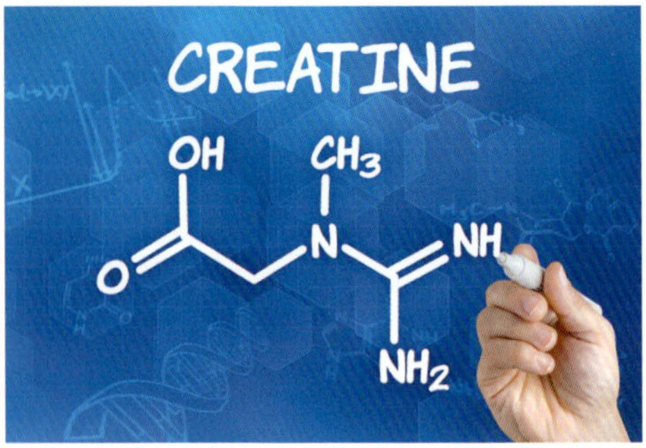

After synthesis in the kidney and liver from amino acids, creatine supplies energy to all cells in the body, not only muscle (although 95 percent of the body's total creatine is found in muscle). It works by increasing the availability/production of ATP, the main fuel source in the cell, by recycling ADP and donating an additional phosphate with aid of the Creatine Kinase enzyme (hence the commonly heard phosphocreatine) to rapidly re-create ATP.

About half of the creatine stored in your body stems from nutrition, meat. Vegetarians actually have lower levels of creatine as vegetables are a poor source of the nitrogenous organic acid. Creatine can either be ingested directly as a supplement or the amino acid building blocks can be consumed (L-arginine, glycine, and L-methionine) and allow the body to make what it needs. Fortunately creatine is easily digestible with up to 80 percent entering circulation. The majority of studies on creatine have used creatine monohydrate, the most digestible and easiest to obtain. Although there are several on the market, none have been studied and proven as effective as creatine monohydrate. It's commonly thought that creatine taxes the organs, especially the liver and kidneys. The most recent meta-analysis of the effects of creatine on these organs have found no adverse reactions and these claims have since been refuted. Since creatine has a short half-life in the body of about three hours, it's important to maintain dosing every three to six hours to maximize the potential benefits. Post ingestion, creatine reaches its peak blood levels in one to two hours. Any additional creatine consumed that cannot be held within the body is excreted as waste.

Creatine is very beneficial when trying to lose fat, due to the fact that it helps you maintain muscle strength and endurance, which will help you maintain more overall muscle mass. You might actually gain strength when you're on creatine, regardless of rather or not you're in a calorie deficit. The end result is a higher muscle to fat ratio, which can improve your fat burning metabolism and help you burn additional calories.

Several studies have shown that oral creatine supplementation in amounts approximately 20-30 grams per day for 5 to 7 days significantly increased intramuscular concentrations of both free creatine and CP during rest and during recovery after intense exercise. You can get excellent results with 5 - 10 grams per day and make sure you keep well hydrated when you take creatine. Many scientific studies have been published and presented about creatine over the past years, and we have never seen any scientific evidence that creatine increases an athlete's chances of experiencing muscle cramps or "pulls." In fact, results from one study conducted at the University of Memphis (entitled "Effects of Creatine Supplementation During Training on the Incidence of Muscle Cramping, Injuries, and GI Distress") revealed no reports of muscle cramping in subjects taking creatine-containing supplements during various exercise training conditions. Among the test subjects were elite junior swimmers, college football players, and trained and untrained endurance athletes.

Some research suggests creatine supplementation may serve as a buffer in the muscle and may decrease muscle lactate accumulation, enhancing performance in sport events dependent on the lactic acid energy system.

One consistent finding in most studies is an increased body mass. A week of creatine supplementation has been found to increase body mass by about 0.9-2.2 kilograms (2.0-4.6 pounds)" (Williams, 1998). In another study, creatine supplementation reduced ATP degradation by 30% and increased work output during two 30 second bouts of maximal isokinetic cycling (Casey, 1996). Paul Greenhaff, a British exercise physiologist said, "Creatine should not be viewed as another gimmick supplement; its ingestion is a means of providing immediate, significant performance improvements to athletes involved in explosive sports" ***(Williams, 1998).***

Surprising benefits to creatine other than strength, performance and fat loss:

Neurodegenerative diseases - Creatine supplementation has been found to increase strength in people with neuromuscular disorders such as ALS, muscular dystrophy, Parkinson's, Huntington's and may ease symptoms of depression.

Hydration - Creatine supplementation was found to improve thermoregulation and endurance through hyper-hydration that can benefit athletes and individuals exposed to prolonged high temperatures.

Cardiovascular - Creatine supplementation has been found to be beneficial to the cardiovascular system by lowering levels of triglycerides and homocysteine, both markers for potential heart disease. It was also found that people with congestive heart failure have low levels of creatine in their heart (remember the heart is a muscle).

Brain power - A placebo-controlled, double-blind experiment found five grams per day supplementation significantly improved short-term memory, fluid intelligence, and even IQ scores as compared with the placebo group. Another study found it improved cognitive ability in the elderly.

Rest & Recovery

Infrared saunas for detox and recovery

One of the tools I have used throughout my career to help athletes recover from training and from injuries is the use of infrared saunas. Regular use of a infrared sauna helps to promote muscle recovery, reducing tension and eliminating performance inhibiting toxic burdens from the body. Far infrared rays are part of the sun's natural spectrum. The radiant energy produced by an infrared sauna is the same as heat from the sun, with the exclusion of the ultraviolet

Infrared saunas are great at helping muscles and joints recover. They are also very effective for detoxification.

rays. A heat source, (usually ceramic heating elements), emits infrared waves that penetrate and relax the body as increased blood circulation warms the skin. The far infrared sauna is far safer and infinitely more tolerable, because it uses a heat energy that penetrates tissues, triggering mobilization of chemicals from subcutaneous fat storage,directly into the sweat. This activating penetration allows for a much lower overall temperature to be used.

Infrared saunas warm the body instead of heating the surrounding air. Traditional steam saunas heat the air and require temperatures ranging from 150 – 200 degrees Fahrenheit to promote perspiration, whereas a heat range of 110 – 140 degrees in an infrared sauna produces the same results. The cooler air temperature is more tolerable to heat-sensitive individuals and allows for sessions of up to 45 minutes, nearly twice as long as in a typical steam sauna session.

Infrared heat can greatly benefit sore, damaged or tired muscles of an athlete. The heat penetrates the muscles, increasing blood circulation and assisting muscle repair. Just as infrared saunas help chronic pain sufferers, they can also help ease joint pain in athletes. The relaxation of the muscles controlling the joints and the increased circulation to the joints enhances healing and repair. I have already talked extensively on the need to eliminate stress levels and cortisol levels but one of the ways in which to do this is through the use of infrared saunas. Scientific evidence shows that infrared sauna therapy helps the body maintain healthy levels of cortisol. While cortisol levels stay the same or rise slightly during a sauna therapy session, they drop immediately afterward.

Massage

With every athlete and club I worked with I always ensured that there were massage therapists available. When I spoke to the late, great Charlie Francis he once told me that 80% of the budget for the Canadian Athletics team was spent solely on massage - that's how powerful he thought it was. There are so many benefits of massage for athletes; reducing stress and anxiety, reducing muscle tension, increasing range of motion, helping to prevent injuries, reducing pain. You can start to see why I have valued it so highly throughout my career.

Many studies have investigated the use of massage to alleviate DOMS. In one such study, carried out by Australian and Japanese researchers, a group of eight men were treated to a 30 minute therapeutic massage on one limb two hours after a 40-minute downhill treadmill walk, loaded with 10% of their body weight via a waist strap. Muscle soreness, tenderness, isometric strength, isokinetic strength and single leg vertical jump height were measured for both limbs on two occasions before the walk and at 1, 24, 72 and 120 house afterwards.

These results showed that, while massage was effective in reducing both soreness and tenderness but there was no difference in the performance tests. Recently, researchers at McMaster University reported that deep massage after an intense workout causes muscles to enlarge and grow new mitochondria, the powerhouses of our cells, which are responsible for converting nutrients into useful energy.For this study, the researchers had men to exercise to exhaustion on stationary bicycles. After the workout, the men had a Swedish-style deep-tissue massage on one leg for 10 minutes. Muscle biopsies were taken from one quadriceps muscle before and after the workout, and from both muscles immediately after a 10 minute massage of one leg, and again two and a half hours later. The deep-tissue massage increased the size and number of new mitochondria more than exercising without massage. Increasing mitochondria can improve endurance performance by increasing the rate that muscles can utilize oxygen.

One of the other benefits of massage is again, much like infrared saunas; they are relaxing and can help reduce stress levels. To further investigate the role of massage in relieving sore muscles, the Ohio State researchers exercised sedated rabbits by triggering a nerve impulse that causes contractions of a leg muscle. They then used a machine to deliver "cyclic compression forces" that simulate 30 minutes a day of Swedish massage (the most common type of sports massage).

Why did they use rabbits? To eliminate the psychological effects of the massage. One of the difficulties when researching the effect of massage is that the subject knows they are being massaged and that it is supposed to help relax them. Rabbits aren't that smart. So what did they find when they analysed the rabbits?

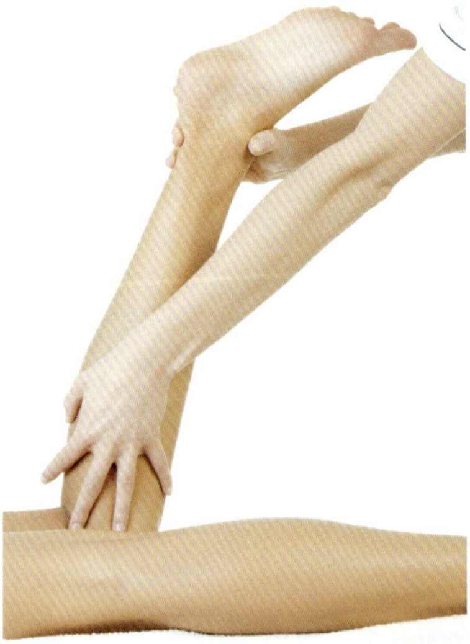

Massage has been found to be effective for alleviating DOMS but result on its effectiveness in terms of recover in performance are mixed.

Rabbits have been used to negate the placebo effect of massage in studies.

The results were clear: Massaged muscles regained 59% of their lost strength after four days, whereas rested muscles regained only 14%. The massaged muscles also had fewer damaged fibres and almost none of the white blood cells associated with muscle damage. The muscles also weighed less, suggesting that massage had helped prevent swelling. Interestingly, the results were much less pronounced if the first massage was delayed for a day after exercise, suggesting that the sooner you get your massage, the better.

Contrast Methods For Improved Recovery

Here is some very interesting information on contrast methods that I think you'll find interesting from the late Dr Mel Siff: Always start with hot and end with cold (unless you plan to go to sleep afterwards, in which case you should end with heat). The duration of each stimulus is 1-5 minutes, but here's the kicker; apparently, the body will adapt to the duration so you must vary it each time. The body should be almost completely submerged (Dr. Siff had an 8-foot deep Jacuzzi) and motion is desirable (particularly in the cold environment, e.g. swim.) The temperature must be appropriate (hot should be very hot, i.e. up to 110 degrees F, and cold should be cold, i.e. as low as 60 degrees F.) Repeat the process 3-4 times.

For contrast showers, Charlie Francis recommended 3 minutes as hot as you can stand followed by 1 minute as cold as you can stand, repeated 3 times to work optimally. This is performed once or twice per day after training sessions or even on recovery days when no training is carried out. It is important to cover the whole body, though, including the head. Although in the past, Siff has pointed out that showers with shower heads located only above the body do not adequately heat up or cool down the lower parts of the body, but not all of us own a deep Jacuzzi and pool so a shower will have to do.

"How much longer coach? My balls are like peanuts".

As well as for recovery, I used to have one premiership rugby player who would take a 3 minute ice bath one hour before every game, and he swore by it. On the other hand I had players who hated ice baths so much it would stress them out. So I would leave the player decide if they wanted to use hot & cold and I would never force them, unless I didn't like them and wanted to see them suffer freezing their nuts off!

Epsom Salt

Epsom salt (also known as magnesium sulphate) is great as a recovery tool when 200-400 grams of is added in a warm/hot bath and the athlete spends 10-20 minutes bathing. This is a very simple and effective way to relax your muscles and decrease inflammation.

A study from the University of Birmingham also found that bathing in a warm Epsom salt bath increases mean blood magnesium levels. This is because magnesium can be absorbed by the skin. We know that magnesium is a very important mineral for athletes, and one that we're often deficient in. Among other things, it helps with muscle relaxation and testosterone production.

Epsom salt baths are an excellent way to recover.

Epsom salt baths also increase perspiration, helping to get rid of toxins and impurities. Magnesium sulphate also stimulates vasodilatation, facilitating blood flow to the muscles and helping reduce inflammation. As a result, these baths can greatly increase the rate of recovery after a hard training session and they reduce muscle and joint pains associated with an excessive inflammatory response.

The Birmingham study found that up to 600 grams of Epsom salt diluted in a normal size bath can be used effectively and without risk. However, they found that levels of 300 to 400 grams are sufficient. This technique should be used two to three times per week for 10 to 20 minutes after particularly gruelling workouts.

Conclusion

You can now see how important it is to get breakfast, as well as pre-, during and post-workout nutrition, right. This is true not only for fat loss, but, also, our overall health. When you get these meals correct, you will get much better results from your exercise program. If you ignore the science on what you have just read, there is a strong likelihood that the exercise that you do will increase body fat and decrease your performance.

Now that we have looked at the science of having a good breakfast, staying hydrated and what to eat before, during and after training I know want to share with you some of the nutrition and supplement plans I used with my athletes. Remember before embarking on any nutrition and supplement plan always consult with your healthcare provider.

Over the years I have read many books that have helped me further my knowledge of nutrition and nutrient timing. In particular, I must give credit to Michael Colgan and his book "Optimum Sports Nutrition" and "Nutrient Timing" by Robert Portman and John Ivy. Remember; never stop reading and never stop learning.

On the next few pages I have included a comprehensive food choices table which shows you the wide variety of foods available to us. I have also included some nutrition plans that I have used with various athletes.

HABIT 10
GETTING THE MOST OUT OF YOUR EXERCISE PROGRAMME

Exercise only works if you get your nutrition, lifestyle and emotions in order. Otherwise, it's just stress on stress!

Phil Richards

The reason why exercise has been left until habit 10 is because if you want to get outstanding results from your exercise/gym program then you must ensure that the other 9 habits are in place. Why? Exercise on it's own will have very little to zero impact of your ability to lose fat I have seen this first hand with not only myself but even with some professional rugby and football players all premiership and international standards training 10 - 14 times per week and still getting fatter over a 10 month season. So for exercise to work, get the 9 habits in place and you will see outstanding results from your efforts in the gym or your chosen activity providing you put the effort in as well. As the saying goes, there is no such thing as a free lunch and exercise is no different.

I have been exercising intensely almost every day for 35 years and I have pushed my body to the limits endless times. This is why I know exercise is not effective for fat loss, as there were many occasions over many years where I simply could not get lean - no matter how hard or how often I trained. In fact, a lot of the times, exercise just made me fatter. Unless you get the 9 habits in this book in place, exercise could be futile for you; especially the older you are or the more obese you are.

In this habit I want to give you the information on Endurance Training, High Intensity Interval Training (HIIT), and Hypertrophy Training. Combine these training methods with a ketogenic diet and you will see truly outstanding results. I cover what I feel you need to know to make the most of your exercise program. If you want further, in-depth knowledge, I have also written a book entitled "Ultimate Strength & Conditioning", which is 250 pages full of information on all aspects of strength & conditioning which you can find on my website.

Learn to love yourself

Most overweight people who attend the gym hate their bodies and go on a mission to try and destroy their body to burn the fat. It would be more beneficial, from a weight loss perspective, to learn to love yourself, your body and realise that the mind and body work together. This, I believe, will help anyone who is overweight lose body fat far more efficiently. For example, I remember training a middle aged man, who was exceptionally overweight. He trained 6 days a week, was an ex-boxer and was trying with 100% effort to lose the fat through exercise. In reality, he had so many anger management issues that I repeatedly told him that until he resolved those issues, the training he did was simply making him fatter. I witnessed him, after 6 months of beasting himself in the gym, gain over 4 kgs in weight. As I have said repeatedly, make sure that you are physically, mentally and emotionally healthy if you want to see the benefits of exercise for fat loss.

The reasons why most exercise programs fail is quite simple: most people exercise whilst they are in an unhealthy condition. I cannot emphasize enough how important it is to have the right lifestyle, nutritional habits, the right thoughts and having people around you who love and care for you. These are essential for any fitness plan to work. The amount of people that I have personally observed over the last 30 years who think they can exercise their fat away but end up failing is astonishing. The reason was always because they did not have the factors listed.

Let's use 2 examples:

Two identical twin sisters (they have identical genes). They are both 45 years of age. Twin A is Lorna. Twin B is Sarah.

I ask them the three questions that I ask all of my athletes to answer when I meet them for the first time are:

1) What are the 5 most stressful things that have happened in your life?
2) How much love and happiness are in your life?
3) What's in your mouth?

Lorna has had a wonderful life; she has 2 children, a loving husband, a beautiful home, no financial worries, has eaten healthily all of her life, has good dental health no mercury fillings or root canals and has healthy body fat levels to start with around 14%.

Sarah also has 2 children, unruly teenagers, a husband who has had numerous affairs. She lives in rented accommodation, her husband is in and out of work and so she has the constant threat of eviction. She has 5 amalgam fillings and a two root canals. She is 20 kgs overweight and as a body fat level of 33% .

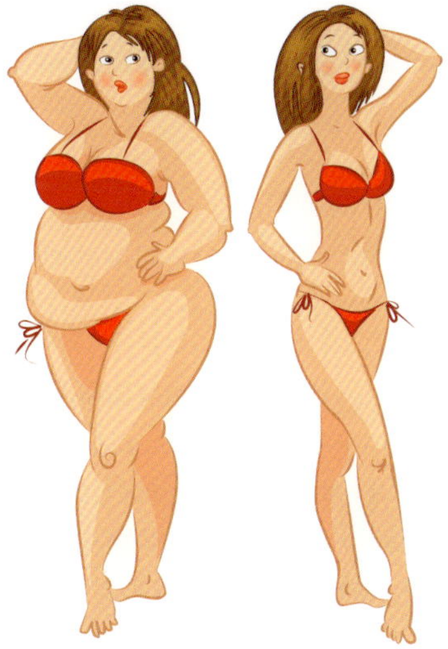

Sarah *Lorna*

Lorna can go straight into an exercise program consisting of HIIT, endurance training and resistance training and, from my experience, can expect to see gains in fitness, sense of well-being and reducing her body fat levels (if that was her goal) very quickly. She could easily exercise 5 mornings a week and benefit from each session.

If Sarah was to try to do this same exercise programme, there would be a strong likelihood that, by the time she gets halfway through week 2, she is realising that she simply cannot keep up with dynamo Lorna. The exercise is making her feel sick, tired and fat, the opposite effect that it is having on Sarah.

I come to the rescue of Sarah. I would advise Lorna to continue what she is doing as she is getting results. My plan with someone like Sarah would be quite simple. From an exercise perspective, I would meet her 3 times a week and take her for a 3-4 mile brisk walk out in nature. Whilst walking with her, I would get her to unload all of her emotional worries and find out what makes her tick. I would also explain the importance of being happy because, without that, every program is doomed to fail.

I would also explain to Sarah that we need to chase one rabbit at a time. We first need to tackle all of her emotional worries to help her reclaim her life. The most important point with Sarah would be to get her to understand that she is in charge of her thoughts, her thoughts are not in control of her. we become what we think about most. This point is invaluable because if you think you are fat and worthless, you become fat and worthless. You must think, "I am lean, happy and healthy. I deserve to be happy". If you keep thinking and believing in these thoughts then they will become a reality.

Once Sarah has managed to get on top of her thoughts, my next step would be to go on the detoxification programme discussed in habit 2. My priority would be removing the amalgam fillings and root canals over a 6 month period with a competent dentist and a very comprehensive nutritional and supplement plan. As the process of the detox protocol was taking place, I would have Sarah using an infrared sauna 3 times a week after a 30 minute walk-jog-sweat-talk programme. I personally would not bring in resistance training with someone like her for around 8-12 weeks. Not until we have gone through emotional and chemical detoxification and nutritional and lifestyle education. I would also begin to educate her on creating the right home environment.

I would also advise Sarah that if, after trying to make it work, her relationship does not improve with her husband then to get out of that relationship. As I have said throughout this book, the most destructive thing to our health is a destructive partner.

When I know all of these factors are in place, it is time to enter the gym. You must remember; exercise is stress. It is pointless putting stress on top of more stress. The exercise will cause more problems than benefits. In Lorna's case, as I see every day in the gyms I train at, the obese clients look the same 12 months later because they don't address nutrition, lifestyle and emotional issues alongside the exercise program. This is a disaster from a fat loss perspective.

The the reason why so many people drop out of their fitness programmes over time - a lack of results.

Don't train, unless you can gain

The reason why I was so successful as a Strength & Conditioning coach in professional sport was my ability to prescribe exercise (stress) to players based on how they could cope and improve from a given exercise (stressor). I could recognise that, when a player was, for example, scheduled in to do a heavy weights session, if his body language was not right, he would benefit more from 1 hour of full body massage than lifting heavy weights. On the flipside, if I had a young player with more testosterone running through his veins than a bull elephant, I know I can push that player to the limits almost every day and he will still keep improving.

EXERCISE FOR FAT LOSS
PHIL SAYS:

This is a program that I have designed for an overweight, 45 year old female, who has done very little exercise in the last 25 years. She has her daughters wedding coming and is desperate to lose 20 pounds in 20 weeks - a sensible weight loss and that is doable. The key to the program is to combine both aerobic and anaerobic exercises in a way that is very achievable. I am trying to enhance the functioning of her mitochondria with the brisk walking and then, with the weight training, my aim is to increase her lean muscle mass, which will raise her metabolic rate.

Starting at about age 25, the average person's metabolism declines between 5 and 10% per decade. So, it is essential to add lean muscle tissue which keeps metabolism high, meaning you do NOT get a drop in metabolism as you age - making it easier to lose and maintain weight!

Each week, I will increase the intensity, if I feel that they can cope with the intensity. You must remember, with exercise, some days you feel great, some days you don't. On the days that you feel great, ramp it up. On the days you don't, you may have to take your foot off the pedal.

Let's take a look at the first 4 week block so that you get a feel of what I would do. Then the second block goes up another gear and I would introduce lots of new exercises to stop her body adapting and would start bringing some High Intensity Interval Training in the second block to speed the fat loss progress up.

Week 1

Monday	Tuesday	Wednesday	Thursday	Friday	Saturday	Sunday
A.M. 20 Minute brisk each morning walk in a fasted state (1 scoop amino work capacity)						
	P.M. All over weights 1		P.M. All over weights 2			P.M. All over weights 3

Week 2

Monday	Tuesday	Wednesday	Thursday	Friday	Saturday	Sunday
A.M. 25 Minute brisk each morning walk in a fasted state (1 scoop amino work capacity)						
	P.M. All over weights 1		P.M. All over weights 2			P.M. All over weights 3

Week 3

Monday	Tuesday	Wednesday	Thursday	Friday	Saturday	Sunday
A.M. 30 Minute brisk each morning walk in a fasted state (1 scoop amino work capacity)						
	P.M. All over weights 1		P.M. All over weights 2			P.M. All over weights 3

Week 4

Monday	Tuesday	Wednesday	Thursday	Friday	Saturday	Sunday
A.M. 40 Min walk/jog		A.M. 40 Min walk/jog		A.M. 40 Min walk/jog		
	P.M. All over weights 1		P.M. All over weights 2			P.M. All over weights 3

The following programs are what I would prescribe to this overweight lady to help drop body fat whilst increasing lean muscle tissue to ramp up her metabolic rate.

All over weights 1

Exercise	Sets	Reps	Rest
A: Bike	1	10 Minutes	
B1: Horizontal Single Arm Pully Rows	3	12	75 Secs
B2: Leg Extension	3	12	75 Secs
C1: Seated Chest Press	3	12	75 Secs
C2: Hip Abductor	3	12	75 Secs
D1: Hip Adductor	3	10	75 Secs
D2: Standing Dumbbell Curls	3	10	75 Secs

All over weights 2

Exercise	Sets	Reps	Rest
A: Rowing	1	10 Minutes	
B1: Smith Machine Squat (Parallel)	3	12	75 Secs
B2: Seated Row	3	12	75 Secs
C1: Pec Dec	3	12	75 Secs
C2: Leg Curl	3	12	75 Secs
D1: Seated Lower Back Extension	3	10	75 Secs
D2: Tricep Extension	3	10	75 Secs

All over weights 3

Exercise	Sets	Reps	Rest
A: Incline Treadmill	1	10 Minutes	
B1: Leg Press	3	12	75 Secs
B2: Seated Shoulder Press	3	12	75 Secs
C1: Dumbbell Step-Ups	3	12	75 Secs
C2: Lateral Raise	3	12	75 Secs
D1: Seated Leg Curl	3	10	75 Secs
D2: Preacher Curls	3	10	75 Secs

Have a look at the complete training, supplementation and nutrition plan that I wrote for a fitness athlete.

This is a 4 week plan for a Miss Bikini/Fitness Competitor. This athlete and her trainer asked me if I would help them with their preparation, yes it's a bit short notice but as she comes from an elite athletic background and her strength & conditioning coach is also of an elite standard I said 'yes' as I thought it would be a great case study for the Ketogenic High Intensity Interval Training Program, along with a intelligent hypertrophy training and supplementation plan.

My brief for preparation for this athlete is as follows:

This is what she has to complete in day 1 of her competition she has to run 800 meters, 400 meters, 200 meters & 100 meters with a series of muscle endurance events between the sprints. As an overview of her background; she is a former GB athlete with her best distances from 100m – 400m. As anyone knows who has done track, 800m is truly a painful distance. She also has to be competent in completing as many full range chins as possible. If there is one thing my 30 years of coaching has taught me it is to stick to the S.A.I.D. principle (Specific Adaptations To Imposed Demands) If you want to be good at something practice it until it's automatic. With this program as well I had to design a weights programs that didn't include exercises like good mornings and lunge & reach we could not afford to have DOMS as this would have ruined the quality of work in the track sessions. She went on and won all her running events.

PHIL RICHARDS PERFORMANCE

TRAINING PROGRAM

WEEK 1

MONDAY	TUESDAY	WEDNESDAY	THURSDAY	FRIDAY	SATURDAY	SUNDAY
A.M Track 5 X 400m 3:1 Rest to Work Ratio	A.M Massage & Swim Recovery	A.M Track 6 X 400m 3:1 Rest to Work Ratio	A.M Massage & Swim Recovery	A.M Track 8 X 400m 3:1 Rest to Work Ratio	A.M Massage & Swim Recovery	REST DAY
P.M All over weights 1	-	P.M All over weights 2	-	P.M All over weights 3	-	REST DAY

WEEK 2

MONDAY	TUESDAY	WEDNESDAY	THURSDAY	FRIDAY	SATURDAY	SUNDAY
A.M Track 4 X 400m 2:1 Rest to Work Ratio	A.M Massage & Swim Recovery	A.M Track 5 X 400m 2:1 Rest to Work Ratio	A.M Massage & Swim Recovery	A.M Track 6 X 400m 2:1 Rest to Work Ratio	A.M Massage & Swim Recovery	REST DAY
P.M All over weights 1	-	P.M All over weights 2	-	P.M All over weights 3	-	REST DAY

WEEK 3

MONDAY	TUESDAY	WEDNESDAY	THURSDAY	FRIDAY	SATURDAY	SUNDAY
A.M Track 2 X 800m 2:1 Rest to Work Ratio	A.M Massage & Swim Recovery	A.M Track 3 X 800m 2:1 Rest to Work Ratio	A.M Massage & Swim Recovery	A.M Track 1 X 800m 1 X 600m 1 X 400m 1 X 200m 1 X 100m	A.M Massage & Swim Recovery	REST DAY
P.M All over weights 1	-	P.M All over weights 2	-	P.M All over weights 3	-	REST DAY

WEEK 4

MONDAY	TUESDAY	WEDNESDAY	THURSDAY	FRIDAY	SATURDAY	SUNDAY
A.M Track 1 X 800m 1 X 400m 1 X 200m 1 X 100m	A.M Massage & Swim Recovery	A.M Power Up Session e.g. Plyos & Med Ball drills nothing fatiguing just keeping the sprint muscles switched on!	A.M Massage & Swim Recovery	A.M Comp Day		
P.M Upper Body	-	P.M Pad & Bag Work	-		-	

PHIL RICHARDS PERFORMANCE

TRAINING PROGRAM

All over 1

EXERCISE	SETS	REPS	TEMPO	REST
A1 Russian High Knee Step Ups	4	6 each leg	1 - 1 - X - 1	60 Seconds
A2 Incline D/Bell Bench Press	4	8- 12	4 - 1 - X - 1	60 Seconds
A3 Under Arm Pull Up	4	6 - 10	1 - 1 - X - 1	60 Seconds
A4 Leg Presses	4	20	2 - 1 - X - 2	60 Seconds
A5 Weighted Press-ups	4	10	3 - 1 - X - 1	60 Seconds

All over 2

EXERCISE	SETS	REPS	TEMPO	REST
A1 Ski Squat	4	5 - 10	2 - 1 - X - 1	60 Seconds
A2 Single arm rows	4	8- 12 (each side)	4 - 1 - X - 1	60 Seconds
A3 Dumbbell lunge	4	6 - 10 (each leg)	1 - 1 - X - 1	60 Seconds
A4 Swiss ball press-ups	4	8 - 12	2 - 1 - X - 2	60 Seconds
A5 Standing cable crunch	4	20	3 - 1 - X - 1	60 Seconds

PHIL RICHARDS PERFORMANCE

TRAINING PROGRAM

All over 3

EXERCISE	SETS	REPS	TEMPO	REST
A1 Box Squat	4	6 - 8	2 - 1 - X - 1	60 Seconds
A2 Towel Chins	4	6 - 10	2 - 1 - X - 1	60 Seconds
A3 Dumbbell lateral step overs	4	10 (each leg)	1 - 1 - X - 1	60 Seconds
A4 Swiss ball reverse crunch	4	20	2 - 1 - X - 1	60 Seconds
A5 Weighted hyper-extension	4	20	3 - 1 - X - 1	60 Seconds

Upper body and Core

EXERCISE	SETS	REPS	TEMPO	REST
A1 Under arm pull up	4	6 - 8	2 - 1 - X - 1	60 Seconds
A2 Weighted press-up	4	10	2 - 1 - X - 1	60 Seconds
A3 Kettlebell rotations	4	10 (each side)	1 - 1 - X - 1	60 Seconds
A4 Tricep press	4	20	2 - 1 - X - 1	60 Seconds
A5 Hanging leg raises	4	20	3 - 1 - X - 1	60 Seconds

PHIL RICHARDS PERFORMANCE

SUPPLEMENT PLAN
KETOGENIC DIET PLAN

20-30 MINUTES BEFORE MEALS (UNLESS TRAINING)	BREAKFAST	LUNCH	DINNER	1 HOUR BEFORE BED ON AN EMPTY STOMACH
1/2 Teaspoons of Alkalising Salts In 500ml of water	1 x Ultimate Multivitamin & Mineral Formula		1 x Ultimate Multivitamin & Mineral Formula	2 Scoops of Nitric Oxide Generator
1 x Metabolic Enhancer	1 x Oestro Detox Formula	1 x Oestro Detox Formula	1 x Oestro Detox Formula	3 x Magneisum Relax
	2 x Probiotic Gut Health	1 Teaspoon of Ultimate Fish Oil Liquid	1 Teaspoon of Ultimate Fish Oil Liquid	
	1 Tablespoon of Collagen Formula	1 Tablespoon of Collagen Formula	1 Tablespoon of Collagen Formula	
	2 x Iodine Forte Capsules			
	1 x Super Digestive Enzymes	1 x Super Digestive Enzymes	1 x Super Digestive Enzymes	

45-60 MINUTES BEFORE TRAINING ON AN EMPTY STOMACH	DURING TRAINING SESSION	POST TRAINING SESSION
1 - 2 Scoops of Amino Work Capacity 1 - 2 Scoops of Cardio Fuel	1 Scoop of Amino Work Capacity	1 Scoop of Ketogenic Fuel
In 750ml of water	In 750ml of water	In 750ml of water

BETWEEN MEAL TIMES:
In between breakfast, lunch & evening meals drink 1 pint of still mineral water with ONE heaped TABLESPOONS of Detox Power.

NUTRITION
FOOD CHOICES TABLE
KETOGENIC

MEATS	POULTRY	FISH			NUTS & SEEDS	BEVERAGES
Beef	Chicken	Mackerel	Halibut	Trout	Almonds	Greens Drinks
Buffalo	Hen	Salmon	Herring	Whitefish	Brazil Nuts	Alkalising Salts
Elk	Duck	Sardine	Mahi-Mahi	Clams	Cashews	Organic Coffee (caffeinated)
Heart	Goose	Abalone	Octopus	Crab	Chesnuts	Organic Green Tea
Kidney	Pheasant	Anchovy	Oysters	Lobster	Macadamia	Reverse Osmosis Water
Lamb	Quail	Bass (Freshwater)	Perch	Mussels	Pecans	
Liver (Beef)	Turkey	Sea Bass	Pompano	Shark	Pine Nuts	
Pork	Ostrich	Catfish	Rockfish	Squid	Pistachios	
Rabbit		Caviar	Roughy	Swordfish	Poppy Seeds	
Venison		Cod	Shrimps / Prawns	Tuna	Pumpkin Seeds	
		Crayfish	Scallops	Cockles	Sesame Seeds	
		Grouper	Snapper		Sunflower Seeds	
					Walnuts	

DAIRY & EGGS	GREENS	VEGETABLES		SEA VEGETABLES	OILS & FATS
Eggs (Chicken - whites)	Argula	Asparagus	Leek	Agar	Avocado oil
Eggs (Chicken - yolks)	Beet Greens	Bamboo Shoots	Olive (all varieties)	Dulse	Almond oil
Eggs (Duck - whole)	Dandelion Greens	Beet	Onion	Irish Moss	Beef tallow
Feta	Endive	Bok Choy	Radish	Kelp	Butter
Goats Cheese	Kale	Broccoli	Eggplant (Aubergine)	Laverbread	Chicken fat, organic
Whey Protein Concentrate	Lettuce (Bibb)	Brussel Sprouts	Jicama		Coconut oil (always go for extra virgin)
Cottage Cheese	Lettuce (Iceberg)	Cabbage	Peppers		Duck fat, organic
Milk (full fat)	Lettuce (Romain)	Cauliflower	Rutabanga		Ghee
Cheeses (full fat)	Mustard Greens	Celery	Shallot		Lard
Greek Yogurt (full fat)	Radicchio	Cucumber	Water Chesnuts		Macadamia oil
	Rocket	Corn	Zucchini (Corgette)		Olive oil, organic
	Spinach	Fennel	Pumpkin		Organic Red Palm oil
	Sprouts (Alfalfa)	Garlic	Mushrooms		Peanut Butter
	Sprouts (Bean)				
	Swiss Chard				
	Turnip Greens				
	Watercress				
	Pea Shoots				

Please use this food table to help you to plan your meals with more variety. For example, when you see on the following nutrtion plans, "Fish Choice", simply look at the food table and you will see that there are multiple choices of fish. You simply select one and then, next time, when you see "Fish Choice" again, chose another one. This plan gives you so much flexibility in preparing nutritious meals and allows you to have a wide variety of food in you nutrition plan

FRUITS (Limit intake)	HERBS, SPICES & SEASONINGS		
Blackberries	Anise	Curry Powder	Paprika
Blueberries	Celtic Sea Salt	Dill Weed	Parsley
Boysenberries	Basil	Fennel Seed	Pepper (ground black)
Cherries	Bay Leaf	Fenugreek	Peppermint
Cranberries	Caraway	Ginger	Rosemary
Elderberries	Cardamom	Honey	Saffron
Gooseberries	Carob	Horseradish	Sage
Raspberries	Cayenne	Himalayan Salt	Salt (sea, unrefined)
Strawberries	Chervil	90% Org Choc	Savory
	Chili Powder	Marjoram	Ketchup Organic
	Chive	Molasses	Spearmint
	Cinnamon	Mustard	Tarragon
	Cloves	Mustard Seed	Thyme
	Coriander	Nutmeg	Tumeric
	Cumin	Oregano	Wasabi

Remember no more than 30 grams of carbohydrates per day if you want to stay in ketosis so keep a check on blood glucose levels and your ketone levels to ensure you are burning fat and not glucose.

PHIL RICHARDS PERFORMANCE

KETOGENIC DIET PLAN FOR OPTIMUM FAT LOSS

DAY 1	DAY 2	DAY 3	DAY 4	DAY 5	DAY 6	DAY 7
BREAKFAST Stir Fry Vegetables Offal Choice 1-2 TBSP Coconut Oil 1 TBSP Organic Butter Small bowl of blueber- ries	BREAKFAST Greens/Veggie Choice Dairy Choice 1 TBSP Extra Virgin 1 TBSP Organic Butter Olive Oil	BREAKFAST Greens/Veggie Choice Meat Choice 1 TBSP Extra Virgin 1 TBSP Organic Butter Olive Oil	BREAKFAST Greens/Veggie Choice Poultry Choice 1 TBSP Extra Virgin 1 TBSP Organic Butter Olive Oil	BREAKFAST Stir Fry Vegetables Fish Choice 1 TBSP Coconut Oil Nuts & Seeds Small bowl of raspber- ries	BREAKFAST Dairy Organic Bacon Watercress & Spinach 1 TBSP Coconut Oil 1 TBSP Organic Butter Peppermint Tea	BREAKFAST Greens/Veggie Choice Dairy Choice 1 TBSP Extra Virgin Olive Oil 1 TBSP Organic Butter
SUPPLEMENTS	SUPPLEMENTS	SUPPLEMENTS	SUPPLEMENTS	SUPPLEMENTS	SUPPLEMENTS	SUPPLEMENTS
LUNCH Greens / Veg Choice Poultry Choice 1 TBSP Extra Virgin Olive Oil	LUNCH Greens / Veg Choice Fish Choice 1 TBSP Avacado Oil Nuts & Seeds	LUNCH Greens / Veg Choice Dairy Choice Meat Choice 1 TBSP Extra Virgin Olive Oill	LUNCH Greens / Veg Choice Poultry Choice 1 TBSP Avacado Oil	LUNCH Greens / Veg Choice Meat Choice 1 TBSP Organic Butter Nuts & Seeds	LUNCH Greens / Veg Choice Fish Choice 1 TBSP Extra Virgin Olive Oil Nuts & Seeds	LUNCH Greens / Veg Choice Fish Choice 1 TBSP Extra Virgin Olive Oil
SUPPLEMENTS	SUPPLEMENTS	SUPPLEMENTS	SUPPLEMENTS	SUPPLEMENTS	SUPPLEMENTS	SUPPLEMENTS
DINNER Greens / Veg Choice Meat Choice 1 TBSP Organic Butter Herb choice Spice Choice	DINNER Greens / Veg Choice Offal Choice 1-2 TBSP Extra Virgin Olive Oil Herb choice Spice Choice	DINNER Greens / Veg Choice Meat Choice 1 TBSP Organic Butter Herb choice Spice Choice	DINNER Greens / Veg Choice Fish Choice cooked in coconut oil 1 TBSP Organic Butter Herb choice Spice Choice	DINNER Greens / Veg Choice Meat Choice 1 TBSP Avacado Oil Herb choice Spice Choice	DINNER Greens/Veg Choice Offal Choice 1 TBSP Organic Butter 1 TBSP Extra Virgin Olive Oil	DINNER Greens / Veg Choice Poultry Choice 1 TBSP Organic Butter Herb choice Spice Choice
SUPPLEMENTS	SUPPLEMENTS	SUPPLEMENTS	SUPPLEMENTS	SUPPLEMENTS	SUPPLEMENTS	SUPPLEMENTS

- Use the food Table provided to get all the choices you need and ROTATE foods regularly to prevent food intolerances.
- Since the majority of calories on a ketogenic diet will come from dietary fats, make sure to measure you ketones daily to ensure you are in the ketosis zone.
- Measure blood glucose levels to ensure they are at an optimum level.
- Portion size - as much green vegetables as you want (ALWAYS ORGANIC).
- Fattier cuts of meat are better because they contain less protein and well, more fat. Choose organic or grass fed animal foods and organic eggs if possible to minimize toxins as they are usually stored in the fat of animals.
- If you are not reaching the ketosis zone then limit fruit intake further

Endurance Training & Fat Loss

We are designed for endurance training or we would not be here today after all our prey didn't come to us we had to hunt it and that often meant running very long distances so that we exhausted our prey! Estimates suggest that hunter-gatherers expended about five times as much energy per day as the average modern Westernised Man. Five times! So let me tell you that three exercise sessions a week is not going to make much difference to your body fat level. When you realise that we are genetically programmed to be much more active than what we are today then I would say you need a minimum of an hour's exercise every day - yes, 7 days a week! So, dont think three 30 minute aerobic sessions on a recumbent bike whilst reading a magazine is going to make a molecule of difference to losing the chubb because it won't.

When you do HIIT you must give 100% effort and leave nothing in the tank!

Let's look at the energy expenditure of modern people collecting food and that of a modern hunter gatherer. Yes we modern people in the West have got it tough when it comes to hunting & gathering; the drive to the supermarket can be incredibly demanding with all those traffic lights to contend with and then the physicality of pushing the trolley around the store. Then, add this to the incredible amount of energy needed to take the shopping out of the trolley and put it into the car. Phew! That must have burnt a whopping 10 calories at most!

A documentary by the BBC filmed in 2001 with David Attenborough looking at Karoha tribesmen showed them doing the Persistence Hunt. From start to finish it took 8 hours of walking, jogging, sprinting through harsh terrain in blistering heat. That 8 hours doesn't even include them then carrying the bull Kudu (which can weigh up to an incredible 315 kg) back to the tribe. The Karoha tribesmen on the hunt were in outstanding physical condition with very low body fat levels after all it would be difficult to do the hunts they do if you are out of condition and obese it simply could not happen.

The point I want to get across here is that we humans are designed to run and that's exactly what allowed us to be such good hunters; we could literally run our prey into the ground as we have the most efficient sweat glands of all mammals allowing us to run exceptionally long distances without overheating. So the next time someone tells you running is a waste of time give them a smile and completely ignore that statement, for we humans would not be here today if we weren't such good endurance runners.

During my time as an elite Strength & Conditioning coach I have had the privilege of training a plethora of athletes; from rugby, soccer, cricket, boxing, triathlon, cage fighting, strongman, cyclists and athletics. A very simple observation is that those who engage in endurance events are absolutely shredded. I will never forget having a few strength coaches interning with me who had been brain-washed at the time into thinking that endurance training makes you fat. At this time I was training Stuart Stokes, a 3000 meter Steeplechaser & Olympian. Half way through the training session, I asked stuart to show them his abs and he lifted his T-Shirt up to show a six pack that would have won any bodybuilding show - he was absolutely shredded at around 5% body fat. That cleared the myth immediately that endurance training is ineffective for fat loss. After all how many fat Tour de France cyclists have you seen? After all this is the toughest endurance event in the world. I also know with myself I get outstanding results with adding endurance training with HIIT and resistance training. You will usually find the more fast twitch fiber a person the less they benefit from endurance and the more slow twitch fiber a person is the more they thrive with endurance part of the conditioning program for fat loss.

Endurance Training & Work Capacity

One of the most effective training methods I used to get my athletes in superb condition, as well as dropping body fat, was field conditioning sessions. I developed hundreds of drills to achieve the task of greater fitness levels and decreased body fat levels. So don't think endurance training is also just plodding on a treadmill or a bike far from it and I have included a few drills in this habit for you.

For example; flipping tyres, dragging sleds, leopard crawls, car pushes, firemans lifts etc., are awesome ways to get in great shape, decrease body fat while acquiring great work capacity. Remember though this type of training is obviously different from targeted hypertrophy training but you can definitely combine the two in one session and let me give you an example program where I do this. This is a typical all over body session I apply with my athletes, which combines both work capacity & hypertrophy in the same session:

- Warm Up = 4 X 20M Prowler Pushes
- A1 = 4 X 6 – 8 Deep Squats
- A2 = 4 X 6 – 8 Weighted Chins
- B1 = 4 X 6 – 8 Incline Bench Press
- B2 = 4 X 20 Leg Press
- B3 = 4 X 8 – 12 T – Bar Rows
- Finish Off With 5 X 1 Min Punch Bag Flat Out With 90 Seconds Rest In Between The Rounds

This is a brutally effective way to train and to achieve outstanding results. More examples are in this habit.

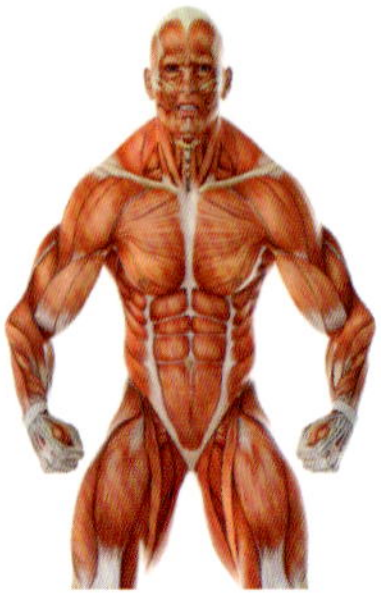

When you exercise correctly, you increase your muscle mass and increase your oxygen intake. These are both important factors in positively effecting your mitochondria. By increasing your muscle mass, you increase the number of cells in your body that contain large numbers of mitochondria. Your muscles have one of the highest concentrations of mitochondria.

This type of training revs up our metabolism and forces our mitochondria to become more efficient at turning food into fuel instead of energy storage so this keeps us lean and healthy. Also, due to the intensity of the Endurance/Work Capacity/HIIT sessions in one training session your growth hormone levels will be high; again enhancing fat loss. For more examples of drills you can purchase my Ultimate Strength & Conditioning book.

What time during the day is best to weight train?

In terms of performance, training in the afternoon or evening is better than the morning. Fluctuations in your body's temperature are one of the reasons that we are stronger and more powerful in the afternoon. Testosterone levels are highest in the morning and decrease by the end of the day. However, while resting testosterone levels are lowest in the evening, the increase in testosterone following exercise appears to be greater in the evening than it is in the morning. ***Michael R. Deschenes, Laurie L. Bronson, Meredith P. Cadorette, Julia E. Powers, and John C. Weinlein "Aged men display blunted biorhythmic variation of muscle performance and physiological responses" J Appl Physiol June 1, 2002 92:(6)***

Resting levels of the hormone cortisol are also higher in the morning and lower in the evening. But the cortisol response to exercise is lower in the evening (7.00pm) compared with the morning (7.00am). ***Jill A. Kanaley, Judy Y. Weltman, Karen S. Pieper, Arthur Weltman, and Mark L. Hartman "Cortisol and Growth Hormone Responses to Exercise at Different Times of Day" JCEM 2001 86: 2881-2889***

In other words, the testosterone-cortisol ratio (when testosterone levels are highest relative to cortisol levels) is higher in the early evening than it is in the morning. This makes the evening the least "catabolic" time to train. For example, in one study, a group of 16 men trained for 10 weeks either before 10.00am (AM group) or after 6.00pm (PM group). Workouts consisted of 45 minutes of weight training followed by 45 minutes of cardiovascular exercise.

The PM group had a 3.2% increase in lean mass, compared with a 0.6% gain in the AM group. Body fat dropped by 4% in the PM group, while it actually increased by nearly 5% in the AM group.

Does that mean you shouldn't train in the morning? Does it mean you won't improve? Of course not! You have to consider practical needs. If you can only train in the morning, train in the morning. If you lose motivation throughout the day and tend to miss afternoon sessions, train in the morning!

So if you look at a typical week of mine you will see that I do not do the same HIIT, Weights or Endurance session in the week as my body adapts very quickly to exercise - after all I've been training for 35 years. So, what I'm going to do here is give you the program details of each of my sessions so it can help you mould a program around your fitness level as well as how much time you have to spare. For example if you can only train 3 times per week combine HIIT, weights and endurance in the same session.

So a typical training week for me can look like this and my aim is very simple drop excess body fat:

Mon	Tue	Wed	Thur	Fri	Sat	Sun
A.m.	P.m.	A.m.	P.m.	A.m	P.m.	A.m.
Hiit 1	Weights 1	Endurance 1	Weights 2	Hiit 2	Weights 3	Endurance 3

If there is a day where I feel I can't give 100% to my training session I will simply not train that day.

The reason I do my HIIT & Endurance training in the morning is that I always do them in a fasted state to encourage more stored fat to be burnt during the session. The reason I do my weights late in the afternoon, normally around 4-6pm, is that you get a much more favourable cortisol to testosterone ratio meaning that you are more anabolic at this time of day, not to mention stronger. You will also see more increases in lean body mass as cortisol levels are not so high compared to early morning training.

My Programs for a typical training week from the table:

Mon = HIIT session 10 min warm up X Country Skier then 30 second all out sprint with 90 seconds recovery. Remember 100% effort is required (so 220 - age plus 5 is the heart rate you are aiming at hitting during the sprints).

Tue = Weights 1

- 10 minute warm up on rowing machine
- A - 6 X 1 - 10 Squats (ass to grass)
- B1 - 4 X 6 - 8 Incline Bench
- B2 - 4 X 8 - 10 Chin Ups
- C1 - 3 X 20 Weighted Hyper Extensions
- C2 - 3 X 20 Hanging Leg Raises

Wed = Endurance and work capacity 1 (Field Conditioning) 20 minute warm up running around field with change of pace.

A1 - Phosphate Runs (see explanation in drills) Repeat three times supersetted with A2 - Tyre Flips X 10 repeat three times.

I will do one set of phosphates which, trust me, if done at the right intensity is brutal. It takes 4 minutes 30 seconds to complete, with the relevant rest periods between sprints. Then I rest up for 5 minutes and then flip a very heavy tyre 10 times as quick as I can. This usually takes around 40 seconds, then rest for 3 minutes.

Thurs = Weights 2

- 10 minute warm up on treadmill
- A1 - 4 X 6 - 8 Dumbbell Lunge & Reach (each leg)
- A2 - 4 X 6 - 8 Flat Dumbbell chest press
- B1 - 4 X 20 Leg Press
- B2 - 4 X 10 Shoulder Press
- C1 - 2 X 20 Standing Cable Crunch
- C2 - 2 X 12 Swiss Ball Leg Curl

Fri = HIIT 2 - 10 minute warm up on bike then 30 second all out sprint with 90 seconds recovery.

I repeat the sprints ten times. If done correctly, this is brutal but extremely effective at dropping body fat.

Sat = Weights 3

- 10 minute warm up on X Country Skier
- A1 - 4 X 10 Dumbbell upright off floor (alternating arms)
- A2 - 4 X 10 Russian High Knee Step Up (each leg)
- B1 - 3 X 15 Leg Extensions
- B2 - 3 X 15 Dumbbell Curls
- C1 - 3 X 15 Dips
- C2 - 3 X 15

Sun = Endurance 2 - 1 hour road run

And the above is a typical week for me. If occasionally I feel that I need a rest day then I will take it. There will be lots more training program examples in this habit for you to look at and then either work with a very qualified and experienced trainer or you can mould a program that works for you. The simplest way to know if what you are doing is right is quite simple - RESULTS!

Now, if you can only manage 3 training sessions per week let me give you an example on how you can combine endurance, HIIT and resistance training so that you still get a big return for your efforts from the training program:

Mon	Tue	Wed	Thur	Fri	Sat	Sun
A.M.	P.M.	A.M.	P.M.	A.M	P.M.	A.M.
HIIT & Weights		Weights & Endurance		Weights & HIIT		

One of the benefits of HIIT and endurance exercise is the increase in mitochondria. The major signal necessary to promote mitochondrial adaptations is the reduction in adenosine triphosphate (ATP) and phosphocreatine, which happens to a greater extent following high intensity interval training than the traditional steady state endurance. Also there seems to be a greater increase in V02max using HIIT over steady state exercise. One study, for example, showed that after six high intensity workout sessions over two weeks, the time that people worked at above VO2 max was increased by 10%, whereas only a 4% increase is seen after 13 weeks of endurance training. So HIIT definitely gives you results, especially if you work to your maximum and follow the habits of this book!

As mentioned in habit 4 exercise increases mitochondrial function and efficiency so lets go over some of what we covered in habit 4 as well as a lot of new information on how to increase our metabolic rate through physical exercise.

Exercise physiologist John Holloszy of the Washington University School of Medicine in St. Louis wanted to show that chronic exercise could put mitochondrial numbers on the upswing. Holloszy simply put one group of lab rats to run on treadmills for up to 120 minutes per day at intensities of about 50-75% of VO2max for a period of 12 weeks, while a second group lolled in their cages. At the end of the 12-week period, Holloszy found that the running rats had increased their mitochondrial densities by approximately 50-60% and had also doubled their concentrations of 'cytochrome c,' a key compound found inside mitochondria which is crucially important in aerobic energy production. ***('Effects of Exercise on Mitochondrial Oxygen Uptake and Respiratory Enzyme Activity in Skeletal Muscle,' The Journal of Biological Chemistry, vol. 242(9), pp. 2278-2282, 1967).***

Of course, exercise physiologists then began wondering which type of training was best for perking up mitochondrial numbers. Should you train fast? Long and slow? Mix fast efforts with slow ones? How long should one exercise be (how many miles per workout and week) in order to optimise mitochondrial density?

Holloszy and his co-workers at Washington University were the first to really tackle this question. In a fairly simple piece of experimental work, the group had one group of rats running 10 minutes per day, another running for 30 minutes, a third group exercising for 60 minutes, and a fourth working for 120 minutes per day. Training took place five days a week for 13 weeks, and training intensity was fixed at about 1.2 mph (or about 32 meters per minute and 313 minutes for the 10K, which is an intensity of around 50-60% VO2max for a healthy lab rat).

Not too surprisingly, the two-hour per day runners turned out to have the best mitochondrial set-ups. For example, compared to sedentary rats, the 10-minute per day exercisers had about 16% more cytochrome c, while the 30-minute workers

boosted cytochrome c by 31%. However, rats who ran for an hour expanded cytochrome c by 38%, and the two-hour rats increased it by 92%!

Holloszy's study provided nice support for the specificity of training principle, too, for during a rugged endurance test staged at the end of the research period, the 10-minute rats lasted 22 minutes, the 30-minute ones for 41 minutes, the hour-long rats ran strenuously for 50 minutes, and the two-hour trainees stayed on the treadmills for a whopping 111 minutes! Of course, run time to exhaustion was directly related to cytochrome c concentration; the more c a rat had, the longer it could run at a tough pace. *('Skeletal Muscle Respiratory Capacity, Endurance, and Glycogen Utilization,' American Journal of Physiology, vol. 228(4), pp. 1029-1033, 1975).*

Intensity is essential for muscle gain and fat loss

Other researchers wanted to explore the intensity question, and Gary Dudley and his colleagues at the State University of New York at Syracuse did just that. Like Holloszy, Dudley had his rats training five times a week and used a variety of different workout durations, from five minutes up to 90 minutes per day. However, unlike Holloszy, Dudley restricted his study to only eight weeks and used a range of different training intensities - 100% VO2max, 85% VO2max, 70% VO2max, 50% VO2max, and 40% VO2max. Dudley also looked at how different intensities and durations influenced different muscle fibre types (fast twitch, aerobic fast twitch or 'intermediate', and slow twitch), which no one had ever done before. *('Influence of Exercise Intensity and Duration on Biochemical Adaptations in Skeletal Muscle,' Journal of Applied Physiology, vol. 53(4), pp. 844-850, 1982).*

In contrast to what Holloszy had found, Dudley was able to show that training beyond about 60 minutes per workout was without benefit in terms of increasing cytochrome c. In other words, a rat training at about 70 to 75% VO2max could upgrade cytochrome c by expanding workout duration from 30 to 60 minutes - but not by increasing workouts from 60 to 90 minutes.

This was true at all intensities studied by Dudley - and also with all three muscle fibre types. Progressing beyond about 60 minutes per workout simply didn't have much value when it came to the mitochondria. However, Dudley's most interesting findings were those related to intensity of training. He was able to show that in fast-twitch muscle fibres, just 10 minutes of fast running (at close to 100% VO2max) per day was enough to roughly **triple cytochrome c concentrations** over an eight-week period. In contrast, running for 27 minutes at 85% VO2max daily only hoisted cytochrome c by 80 per cent, while 60 to 90 minutes at 70 to 75% VO2max nudged cytochrome c upward by just 74%.

So what's the bottom line? As Dudley and his colleagues put it, "an increase in the intensity of training brings about the greatest adaptive response in the mitochondria".

Expressing the importance of intensity another way, Dudley and co-workers said, 'For the same adaptive response, the length of daily exercise necessary to bring about the change becomes less as the intensity of exercise is increased.' **In other words, 10 to 15 minutes of running at 5km pace in a workout can do much more for you than running for 60 to 90 minutes at slower intensities.**

The intensity that you train at also affects the amount of fat and carbohydrate that you metabolise to fuel the exercise. You burn both fat and carbohydrates when you exercise, and the proportion varies with the intensity of exercise.

A very low-intensity activity, like walking, taps mainly into fat stores, whereas high-intensity sprints pull much more heavily from carbohydrate stores. At about 60% of maximum exertion, your body gets about half of its energy from carbohydrate stores and half from fat stores. If you walk off 100 calories, 85 of which come from fat stores, that isn't as effective as spending that time in a moderate run that burns off 200 calories with 100 coming from fat.

And that, in turn, isn't as effective as spending that time doing sprint intervals that burn off 500 calories with 150 coming from fat.

Calories burned while exercising isn't the whole story, though. Studies such as those conducted by Laval University, East Tennessee State University, Baylor College of Medicine, and the University of New South Wales have shown that shorter, high-intensity cardio sessions result in greater fat loss over time than longer, low-intensity sessions. A study conducted by The University of Western Ontario gives us insight into how much more effective it really is. Researchers had 10 men and 10 women train 3 times per week, with one group doing 4-6 30-second treadmill sprints (with 4-6 minutes of rest in between each), and the other group doing 30-60 minutes of steady-state cardio (running on the treadmill at the "magical fat loss zone" of 65% VO2 max). The results: After 6 weeks of training, the subjects doing the intervals had lost more fat. Yes, 4-6 30-second sprints burns more fat than 60 minutes of running on a treadmill. ***Macpherson, R. E., Hazell, T. J., Olver, T. D., Paterson, D. H., & Lemon, P. W. (2011). Run sprint interval training improves aerobic performance but not maximal cardiac output. Medicine and science in sports and exercise, 43(1), 115-122.***

A 1996 study from Baylor College of Medicine (Houston) reported that subjects who performed a high intensity interval training (HIIT) workout on a stationary cycle burned significantly more calories during the 24 hours following the workout than those who cycled at a moderate, steady-state intensity due to a rise in resting metabolism. Why? Since HIIT is tougher on the body, it requires more energy to repair itself afterward.

Research also confirms that HIIT enhances the metabolic machinery in muscle cells that promotes fat-burning and blunts fat production. The Laval University study discovered that the HIIT subjects' muscle fibers had significantly higher markers for fat oxidation (fat-burning) than those in the steady-state exercise group.

And a study published in a 2007 issue of the Journal of Applied Physiology reported that young females who performed seven HIIT workouts over a two-week period experienced a **30%** increase in both fat oxidation and levels of muscle enzymes that enhance fat oxidation.

Moreover, researchers from the Norwegian University of Science and Technology (Trondheim) reported that subjects with metabolic syndrome - a combination of medical disorders that increases one's risk of cardiovascular disease and diabetes - who followed a 16-week HIIT program had a **100%** greater decrease in the fat-producing enzyme fatty acid synthase compared to subjects who followed a program of continuous moderate-intensity exercise.

An Australian study in which 45 women were randomly allocated to either 3 x 40 minutes of moderate intensity cycling a week or three 20 minute sessions of higher intensity cycling. The women who had been allocated to the high intensity group were asked to alternate 8 seconds of sprint cycling with 12 seconds of gentle cycling. They started doing this for just 5 minutes and built it up to 20 minutes per session. At the end of the 15 weeks, both groups had got fitter, as measured by improvements in their VO2 max, but only the high intensity group had lost any weight. They lost on average 2.5 kg, but within the group there were variables. Some of the women lost up to 8kg, a few lost very little. The ones who lost little had little to lose as they were fairly lean starting off. The fatter the women were at the start of the study, the more fat they lost.

Astonishingly the women who did the moderate intensity cycling, despite spending twice as long on their bikes, managed to put on weight and become slightly fatter. Well this shouldn't come as a surprise. For your body to make adaptations and become more efficient at losing fat the stimulus needs to be severe otherwise the body has no reason to change. The women who did the HIIT lost fat not only from their thighs, which you would expect from all the cycling they were doing but they also lost from the stomach. The reduction in abdominal fat was accompanied by a decrease in fasting insulin which was down by as much as 31%.

The same research team then did a similar study with young men, aged around 25, and got them to do three 20 minute sessions a week on an exercise bike. Like the women, after a brief warm up they had to sprint for 8 seconds and cycle easy for 12 seconds. The idea was trying to keep their heart rate at around 80-90 % of maximum while sprinting. After 6 weeks there was not much change in body fat. However, by the end of 12 weeks the young men's aerobic power had increased by 15% and on average they had lost 2kg of fat. Also they had lost

fat from their stomach, which is medically termed visceral fat, and this was down by 17% and they had also put on muscle.

Although the exact mechanisms of how high-intensity cardio trumps steady-state cardio aren't fully understood yet, scientists have isolated quite a few of the factors:

- Increased resting metabolic rate for upwards of 24 hours after exercise.
- Improved insulin sensitivity in the muscles.
- Higher levels of fat oxidation in the muscles.
- Significant spikes in growth hormone levels (which aid in fat loss) and catecholamine levels (chemicals your body produces to directly induce fat mobilization).
- Increased Testosterone levels.
- Post-exercise appetite suppression.

The bottom line is that high-intensity interval training burns more fat in less time than steady-state cardio, and you have the bonus of an increased metabolic rate after the session is over with HIIT compared to almost zero with steady state. But make no bones about it the reason steady state is so ineffective at losing body fat can be summed up in one word INTENSITY for example if you run 10KM as hard as you can trust me you will burn fat and have an increased metabolic rate for a few hours after the run.

When you perform conventional cardio for long periods of time, it's been found to deteriorate muscle tissue and decrease testosterone levels. That's bad, obviously, but things get even worse. A study in The American Journal of Physiology found that steady-state cardio decreases the ability of muscles to absorb glucose after training. Research has also shown that the longer your cardio sessions are, the more they impair strength and hypertrophy. That is, the shorter your cardio sessions are, the more muscle you preserve. So, keeping your cardio sessions short is important when we're talking about maximizing your gains in the weight room, and preserving your muscle. Only high-intensity interval training allows you to do this while still deriving significant benefits from the exercise.

It turns out that HIIT cycling itself has special benefits for adding muscle and strength. These benefits were demonstrated in a particularly interesting study conducted by Stephen F Austin State University. What researchers found is that the TYPE of cardio done had a profound effect on the subjects' ability to gain strength and size in their weightlifting. The subjects that did running and walking for their cardio gained significantly less strength and size than those that cycled. Why? Researchers concluded that it was because cycling involves the use of more of the muscles used in hypertrophy movements (squats, for instance) than running or walking does. That is, it more closely imitates the motions that result in hypertrophy, and thus doesn't impair hypertrophy. ***Gergley, J. C. (2009). Comparison of two lower-body modes of endurance training on lower-body strength development while concurrently training. The Journal of Strength & Conditioning Research, 23(3), 979-987.***

But in reality have you ever seen a fat track sprinter? No, so don't be afraid to get the running shoes on and start banging out the HIIT on the track or a field, as well as including some sprint training to your program I devote a whole chapter on speed and power training in my Ultimate Strength & Conditioning Book if you want more information on this subject.

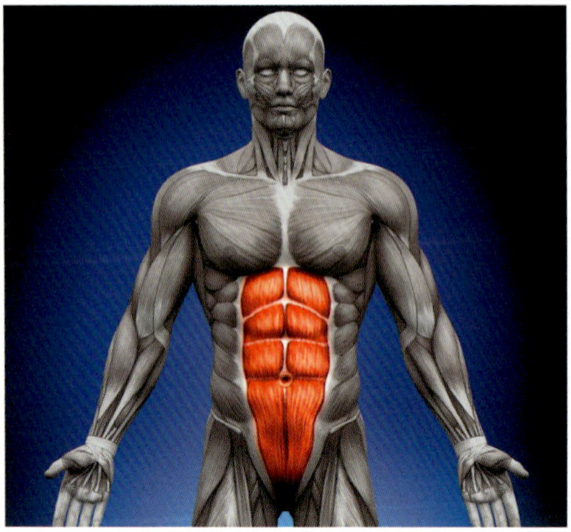

Let's make one thing clear - hard endurance training gets you exceptionally lean. I know from personal experience when I was an elite runner and cyclist I was around 6% body fat so make sure you don't misinterpret 30 minutes sitting on a bike listening to Barry Manilow's greatest hits and training with the intensity that is required for a hamster to take a shit as hard training. You must understand also that endurance exercise is also a strong stimulus for the proliferation of mitochondrial enzymes. The increase in mitochondrial density is associated with an increase in the duration one can perform endurance exercise and the ability to spare total body glycogen stores (Fittz et al., 1975). Generally, more lipids are used to generate ATP as a result of the increased mitochondrial density in response to exercise. A large body of research suggests that the enhancement of mitochondrial density in skeletal muscle is a key component in the development of performance in endurance sport. In a general sense, building more mitochondria allows an athlete to function closer to their potential and burn more fat for fuel instead of carbs or even worse muscle.

PHIL SAYS
WEIGHTS AND CARDIO

"Should I do weights or cardio first?" If you want to up your calorie burn (and who doesn't?), research shows that you should do cardio first.

Published in the Journal of Strength and Conditioning Research, one study examined how many calories exercisers burned doing one of four workout combinations: running only, strength training only, running followed by strength training, and strength training followed by running. Researchers found that while all exercisers experienced a strong "after burn" (a higher rate of calories burned when at rest after exercise) for the two hours after working out, the strength training and run/strength training groups had the highest exercise after burn of all.

So what does this mean? Although it's just one study, the takeaway is that we might burn more calories after working out if we do our cardio first.

From my experience just keep the body guessing alternate from workout to workout and add lots of variety in the program.

HIIT and the cardiovascular system

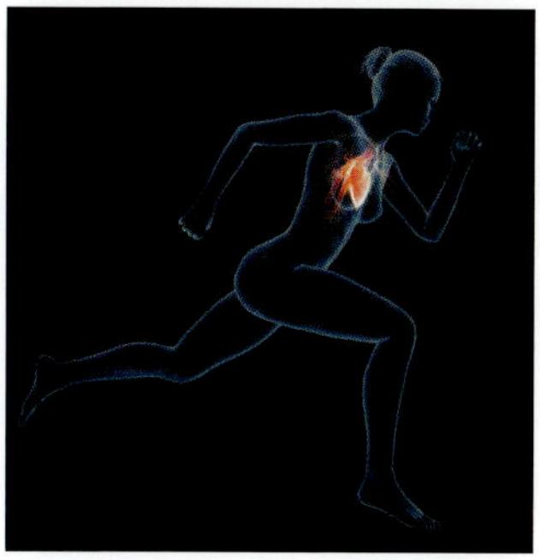

HIIT rapidly increases VO2max (the ability to deliver maximum oxygen during high demand). The improvements in VO2max are greater with HIIT than with moderate intensity training. This has been consistently found in all studies including people with coronary artery disease, congestive heart failure and metabolic syndrome.

Your heart output is controlled by cells in the heart. The speed at which they shorten when the blood is forced out of the heart and relax when the heart refills with blood controls the heart's ability to generate force. This is the contractile of the heart. This force generation is one factor that controls the heart's output. The other is your heart rate. If the force generation of the heart cells is stronger then your heart rate will be lower. This balancing ensures that the same amount of blood is pumped around the body. Following high intensity training, shortening-relaxation rates of heart cells increase by 40% when the body is at rest. The effects of HIIT on heart contractile function is at least 100% greater than moderate intensity training such as jogging. Therefore you will have a bigger reduction in resting heart rate following HIIT than steady state exercise.

HIIT is an exceptionally time efficient way to improve insulin sensitivity. Following just six high intensity training sessions, insulin sensitivity has been shown to improve by 25% in inactive people. This is a much bigger increase in insulin sensitivity in just two weeks compared to traditional exercise programs lasting 8 - 12 weeks.

HIIT gets you leaner and quicker than steady state cardio!

When you do a HIIT session the rate that you break down fat stores from your fat tissue and skeletal muscle fat deposits increases, causing an increase in available fatty acids. These fatty acids can be taken up by skeletal muscles and converted by the mitochondria into adenosine triphosphate (ATP). The length of the HIIT session and the number of sprints in that session will determine the magnitude of fat used during that session.

Two of the hormones that control fat breakdown, adrenaline and noradrenaline, are elevated by as much as 1450% following a HIIT session. The size of this response is much bigger than is seen with steady state exercise such as cycling, swimming, walking or jogging.

But remember this very important point. For HIIT to work, you need to minus your age from 220 and then add 5. For example, for a 47 year old that would be 220 - 47 = 173 then add 5 = 178 beats per minute (BPM). You need to be hitting between 173 - 178 BPM during the intervals for you to see the real physiological benefits. Let me tell you, to hit this range you have to be 100% motivated and committed to seeing results because you will endure pain - make no bones about that.

When you have been participating in a HIIT program specific adaptations occur in skeletal muscles. The most important of these regarding fat metabolism is the increased number of mitochondria found in skeletal muscle. This means that the skeletal muscle has a greater capacity to use fatty acids as a fuel source. As well as increased mitochondria in the skeletal muscle there is also increased mitochondrial protein activity. This is consistently found across all HIIT interventions.

When performing traditional exercise after HIIT there is a 36% increase in the amount of fat used to fuel the exercise. The increased fat use is because there is an increased activity of the protein that is believed to limit the rate that fatty acids can be used by mitochondria. Even at rest there is a lower amount of circulating free fatty acids after two weeks of HIIT. In longer duration HIIT sessions these skeletal muscle adaptations result in a reduction of fat mass of between 10 and 40%. Particularly important is the reduction of abdominal fat. HIIT in various studies has seen a reduction of abdominal fat by as much as 8% in 12 weeks. This is a consistently bigger loss in abdominal fat than is seen with traditional steady state cardio. There is also a bigger loss of fat that is stored under the skin of about 10 to 15% - again this is much higher than what steady state cardio delivers. This loss of fat mass can be associated by improvements in insulin sensitivity, growth hormone and testosterone increases as well as mitochondria increases this equals one thing FAT LOSS!

HIIT in a fasted, ketogenic state

Doing HIIT with a high carbohydrate diet and drinking carbohydrate beverages during and after training is going to have almost zero effect on your current body fat stores, unless you are a very highly trained athlete. This applies even if you are giving 100% effort and your eyeballs are on the floor after the session. (From my observations, most people simply do not understand that for HIIT to really work, 100% effort is required. Anything else and the body has no reason to adapt).

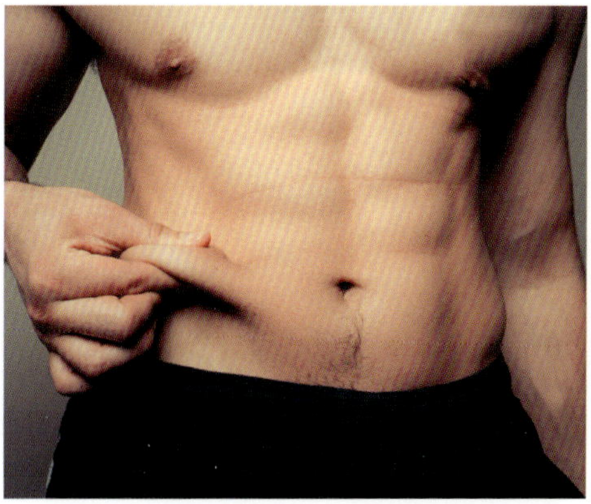

HIIT is a great method at dropping abdominal fat.

The effects of fasting on hormones are multi-faceted. Fasting has a dramatic impact on human growth hormone levels. Increased HGH results in greater endurance with faster muscle repair and growth as well as a slowing of the aging process. One study showed that interval training while fasting increased HGH by **1300%** in women and **2000%** in men. ***Intermountain Medical Center, Eurekalert April 3, 2011***

Like I've said, intelligent fasting would be to have your last meal of the day at around 6pm and then try to exercise the following morning between 7-9am, so you haven't eaten for 13 to 15 hours. Be intelligent with your pre, during and post-workout nutrition, as discussed in habit 9, and this should give you truly outstanding results.

Below are some simplistic HIIT workouts that you can do in your next session:

HIIT Program 1

Warm up	Session
 • 10 minute steady state on X-trainer	• 30 seconds sprint as hard as you can and with the relevant resistance and rest 90 seconds. • Repeat 10 times. • If you are a beginner, start off with 5 sets and work your way up to 10 sets.

HIIT Program 2

Warm up	Session
 • 10 minute steady state on stationary bike	• 30 seconds sprint as hard as you can and with the relevant resistance and rest 90 seconds. • Repeat 10 times. • If you are a beginner, start off with 5 sets and work your way up to 10 sets.

HIIT Program 3

Warm up	Session
 • 10 minute steady state on treadmill	• as hard as you can and with the relevant and rest 90 seconds. • Repeat 10 times. • If you are a beginner, start off with 5 sets and work your way up to 10 sets.

HIIT Program 4

Warm up		Session
	• 10 minute steady state on indoor rower	• 20 seconds sprint as hard as you can and with the relevant resistance and rest 60 seconds. • Repeat 10 times. • If you are a beginner, start off with 5 sets and work your way up to 10 sets.

HIIT Program 5

Warm up		Session
	• 10 minute steady state swimming	• 30 seconds sprint front crawl as hard as you can then rest 90 seconds. • Repeat 10 times. • If you are a beginner, start off with 5 sets and work your way up to 10 sets.

HIIT Program 6

Warm up		Session
	• 10 minute warm up running on field or running track	• Run 400 meters as hard as you possibly can time how long it took you. Rest twice as long as the run. • Repeat 10 times. • if you are a beginner, start off with 5 sets and work your way up to 10 sets.

HIIT Program 7

Warm up		Session
	• 10 minute warm up with kettlebells & punch bag or pads	• 20 kettlebell swings straight into 30 second flat out punch bag or pad work • Repeat 10 times. • If you are a beginner start off with 5 sets and work your way up to 10 sets.

HIIT Program 8

Warm up	Session
• 10 minute warm up running with changes of speed	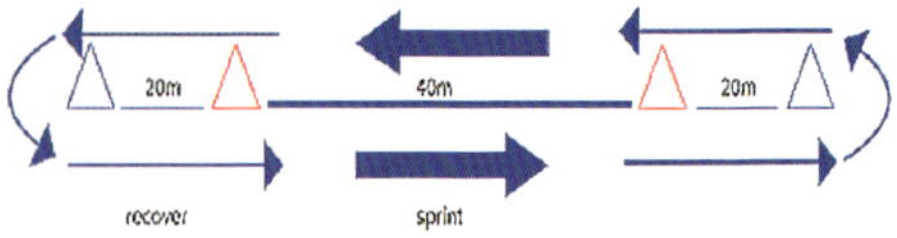 • Mark 40 meters out on field/track with a 20 meter run off either side, which is the recovery run. After you run 40 meters as hard as you can, then jog recovery to designated cone 20 meters away. You will do 40 meters every 30 seconds and go flat out. • If you are a beginner start off with 5 sets and work your way up to 10 sets.

HIIT Program 9

Warm up	Session
• 10 minute warm up with dynamic stretches and down-up movements off the floor	• Shield drill below

HIIT Program 10

Warm up		Session
	• 10 minute warm up with dynamic stretches and down-up movements off the floor	• Prowler push as hard as you can for 30 seconds and rest for 90 seconds. You can also use a car with 2 people pushing and one steering if you haven't access to a prowler. • If you are a beginner start off with 5 sets and work your way up to 10 sets.

HIIT Program 11

Warm up		Session
	• 10 minute warm up stationary bike	• 30 seconds sprint as hard as you can, then straight into 10 pull ups. It doesn't matter if you can't get 10 straight out; rest a little and keep going until you get 10. Then rest 90 seconds. • Repeat 10 times. • If you are a beginner start off with 5 sets and work your way up to 10 sets.

HIIT Program 12

Warm up	Session
 • 10 minute warm up with dynamic stretches and down-up movements off the floor	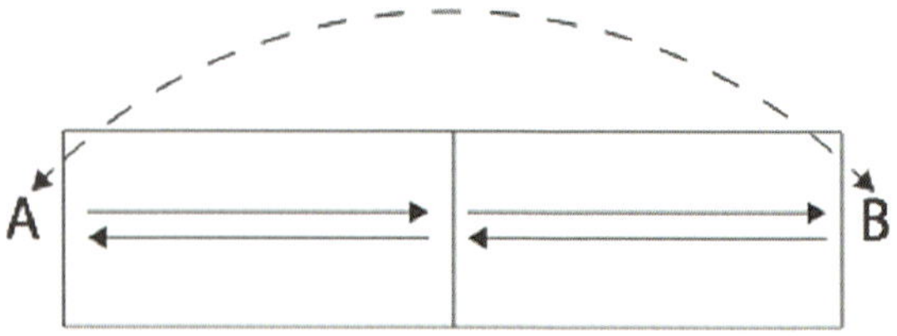 • In pairs, mark out a 10 meter grid with a half way marker. • Stand either side of the grid. One person throws a medicine ball to their partner and immediately sprints forwards to the halfway mark and then backwards to the start. • As soon as their partner gets the ball, they do the same. • The ball is constantly in motion where by the time you sprint backwards to the start, the ball should be arriving for you to throw. • Repeat 10 times. • If you are a beginner start off with 5 sets and work your way up to 10 sets.

Training for hypertrophy (muscle gain)

Muscle tissue is a metabolically active tissue. What that exactly means is that muscle keeps your metabolism elevated. When you have more of it, your body burns more calories at rest. The Colgan Institute of Nutritional Sciences (located in San Diego, CA) run by Dr Michael Colgan PHD, a leading sport nutritionist, explains that in his extensive experience, the most muscle gain he or any of his colleagues have recorded over a year was 18 and 1/4 lbs. Dr Colgan goes on to state that "because of the limiting rate of turnover in the muscle cells it is impossible to grow more than an ounce of new muscle each day." In non-complicated, mathematical terms, this would equate to roughly 23 pounds in a year!

Keep in mind a pound of skeletal muscle will burn between 50-100 calories per day. So it's worth all your hard work trying to gain muscle so you can burn fat even when at rest! Now let's talk about the actual caloric content of muscle. A pound of skeletal muscle is approximately 600 calories. That means if a crocodile ate you they would be eating 600 calories for every pound of your skeletal muscle.

Now fat on the other hand, is much more useless in terms of being metabolically active, it actually burns approximately 9 calories per pound per day so far inferior to muscle tissue. A pound of fat though contains about 3,500 calories! Now that's a lot of energy! The croc would be better off eating your fat (pound for pound) than your muscle.

Doing just aerobic exercise activities does nothing for building muscle tissue and doing too much aerobic exercise will actually eat away at your precious muscle tissue.

More muscle will not only make you stronger, it will help you utilize glucose better because your insulin will have more storage areas (increased muscle) to deposit your glucose. Also the weight training increases growth hormone and testosterone two more fat busting hormones. And last, your body composition will begin to change where you'll fit into those tight clothes that you haven't worn in years.

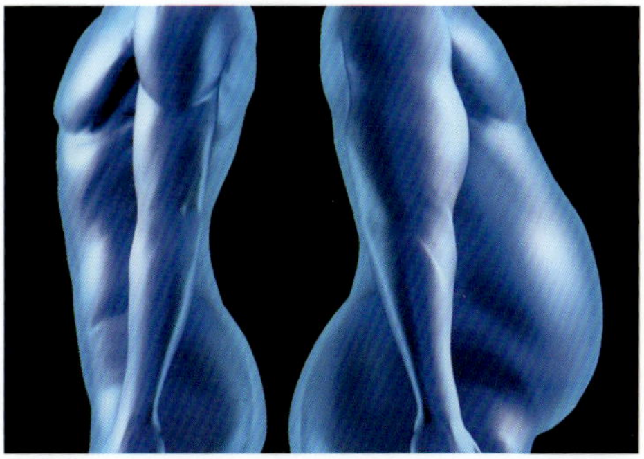

Exercise also increases the number of testosterone and growth hormone receptors in the part of the body being exercised. The exercised area thinks "Okay, I'll get some extra places to receive more guests, more incoming testosterone and growth hormone molecules". This is why it is important to vary your exercises regularly and not do the same exercises week after week, because when you have a big assortment of exercises you will hit the muscles at multiple angles increasing the receptors on the muscles as well as recruiting different fibres each time you use a new exercise. This is why you usually feel sore after the first time you use a new exercise. Then 2 – 4 weeks in, you lose the soreness. This is because the muscles know what's coming that's why you must rotate exercises; so the muscles are always trying to adapt to new stressors and this way they keep getting bigger and stronger whilst you get leaner.

Exercise is a significant, natural optimizer of GH secretion. The type of exercise you do, as well as the intensity and duration of your workouts, all play an important role in determining to what degree your training regimen contributes to GH secretion. A significant release of GH can occur in response to exercise.

Any type of exercise will cause some increase in GH levels. But vigorous exercise like HIIT and lifting heavy weights will cause a greater release than exercise done at a low or moderate intensity.

Exercises that require your body to move through space like chins, dips and squats elicit greater increases in growth hormone than using stationary exercises like a preacher curl. But the key is use multiple exercises to build muscle.

The skeletal muscle all have three levels of strength. The first and weakest is the concentric contraction, then the isometric contraction and finally the eccentric contraction. Considering then that the muscle has three levels of strength, it would seem obvious to exhaust all three levels. To add size and strength, exhaust the muscle in all 3 forms of contraction.

Carrying a set to a point where you are forced to utilize 100% of all three levels of muscular strength (concentric, isometric and eccentric), is one of the most important

Strength training is really a kind of hormone therapy, write researchers at the Spanish University of Extramadura in the European Journal of Applied Physiology. According to the researchers, regular weight training raises testosterone levels by 40%. You must though be careful not to overtrain and always allow your body to recuperate adequately between your workout sessions. If you don't, your circulating testosterone levels can plunge by as much as 40% as was discovered by studies performed at the University of North Carolina. Don't kid yourself though. If you want to add lean muscle tissue then you have to work brutally hard, eat well and rest smartly.

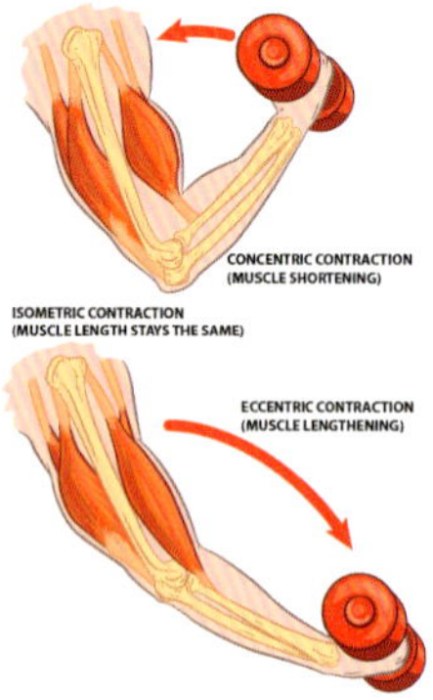

Remember, a muscle can contract in 3 different ways. If you want to strengthen the muscle then you have to take the muscle to failure in all 3 for maximum strength and hypertrophy.

factors in increasing the size and strength of the muscle. I learnt this many years ago from the great contribution that Mike Mentzer brought to bodybuilding training. Working to this point of failure, when another rep is impossible, despite your greatest effort, ensures that you stimulate muscle growth and, in my opinion, anything less than this effort will not increase hypertrophy unless you are a complete beginner and even opening the door to the gym will stimulate growth. But you must fully understand that you need to be extremely motivated to be able to push yourself to this level of muscular failure. You must also blast the muscles from multiple angles, forcing all fibers within that muscle to be stimulated to increase more muscle.

A very effective way to do this is to do giant sets, which is simply doing multiple exercises with very little rest between sets for the same muscle. Let me give you an example on shoulders:

- A1 Lateral Raises X 20
- A2 Seated Machine Shoulder Press X 15
- A3 Bent Over Lateral Raises X 20
- A4 Standing Dumb Bell Shoulder Press X 15
- A5 Front Barbell Raises

You want minimum rest between exercises. When you complete a full giant set you can rest up to 3 minutes. You can also vary tempos on each giant set or within the set itself, the key here is STIMULATION not ANNIHILATION!

You simply can't turn up and do a few sets and expect the muscles to be stimulated enough to grow as this simply won't happen. For humans to carry muscle it is an expensive metabolic demand and this requires energy, as muscle has been reported to be 7 to 8 times more active than fat tissue. Now, this was important during evolution when food supplies were sporadic, muscle was an expensive commodity that would only be added to our frames if it had a bloody good reason to do so. Otherwise it is using vital calories which we didn't have in abundance. So the biggest lesson you can take home here is; if you want to add more muscle you must make sure your motivation is exceptionally high and, again, your nutrition is spot on, stress reduction protocols are in place and rest and recovery become your best friends.

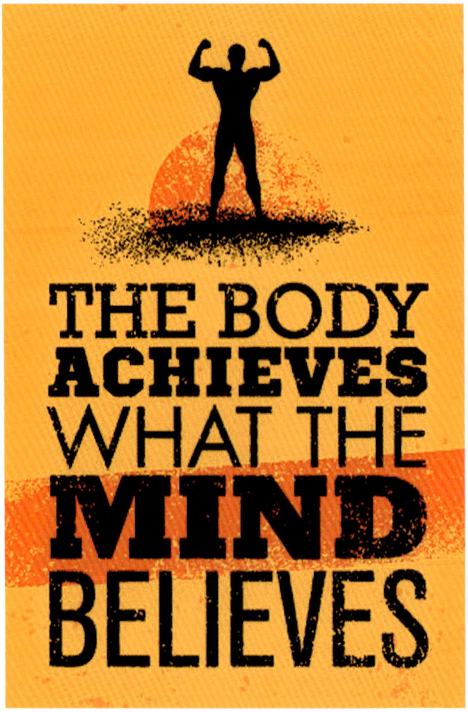

You must concentrate the mind on the muscle being worked for maximum stimulation.

You don't need to do every set to failure you can have build up sets. For example, on the bench press, if you were using this exercise for hypertrophy, the session could look like this:

- First Set 8 reps 60 kg
- Second Set 8 reps 70 kg
- Third Set 8 reps 80 kg
- Fourth Set 8 reps 90 kg
- Fifth Set reps to failure 100 kg.
- It is always wise to use a spotter when going to failure.

Why are multiple sets superior for hypertrophy?

Compared to single sets, multiple sets enhance the intracellular signals and the rate of protein synthesis. Put simply, anabolic signalling proteins remain active for longer following multiple sets, which is causes hypertrophy.

Multiple sets not only make you bigger, they make you stronger. For example, in a study comparing single versus multiple rep training, multiple rep training resulted in a 50% larger increase in 1RM for the squat. ***(KRAMER, J., M. STONE, H. S. O'BRYANT, et al. Effect of single vs. multiple sets of weight training: impact of volume, intensity, and variation. J. Strength Cond. Res. 11:143–147, 1997.)***

For untrained athletes, 3 - 4 sets may generate the optimum gains. However, with trained athletes, more sets can provide more gains. Hypertrophy is also promoted by mechanical damage caused by eccentric loading, which increases protein synthesis. By increasing the time it takes to lower a weight, more mechanical damage is caused resulting in increased hypertrophy, in other words lower your weights under control to cause them more damage to grow.

What I personally make sure of when I'm working with an athlete who has to be very lean and muscular like when I consulted for a female Drug Free Bodybuilder for a number of years who become very successful at her chosen sport was to ensure we rotated exercises frequently but also sets, reps, rest periods, tempo, training days and even training locations. This ensures not only variety so that we don't accommodate to the exercises but also mental stimulation. How many people do you know that train at the same time, same place, do the same exercises and guess what get the same results? **The definition of insanity is doing the same thing over and over again and expecting different results sound familiar? Then change!**

Her program is outlined shortly in this book.

Remember, exercise simply stimulates growth, the body then needs raw materials (nutrients) to start the repair and rebuilding. You then need optimum recovery to allow the muscle to be rebuilt and, if the stimulus was severe enough, then your body will overcompensate by adding more muscle to the frame whilst decreasing body fat. So the story is quite simple from a muscle building perspective;

**Stimulus + Response + Recovery =
Growth = Decreased Body Fat%**

Remember, as you become more advanced, so must the stimulus and the recovery. There are simply no short cuts to muscle gain. Enjoy the journey and keep packing muscle on as it is not only important for sporting performance but also longevity.

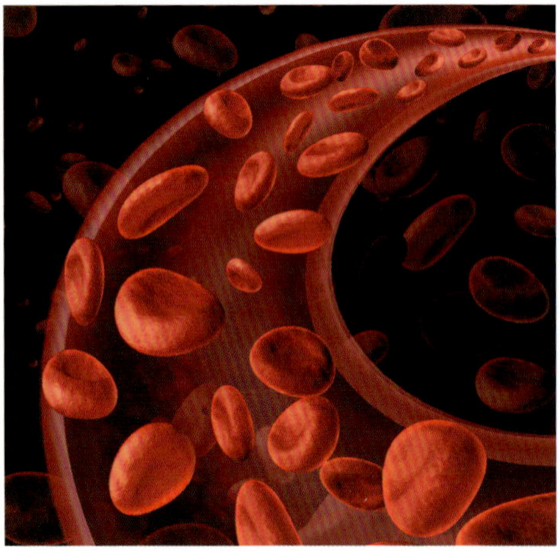

Feed the muscle when you train the muscle. Why? 75% of our blood is transported into the muscles compared to around 10% whilst at rest so nourish the muscles whilst you have this much blood flow there.

Also, although you need to stimulate the muscles whilst training, there is no need to annihilate the muscle! Why? If you keep crushing your body every time you train you will always find yourself in a hole which you can't climb out of and will spend most of your time in a catabolic (muscle wasting) state instead of an (anabolic) muscle building state. Remember, we only have a limited amount of recovery ability so be really intelligent in how you train so you can build your mountain (muscle tissue), so you get in great shape and become a fat burning machine 24/7.

Conclusion

I now want to show you some example programs that I have prescribed with the purpose of decreasing body fat whilst increasing performance. Remember, these sessions are just examples. If they are not relevant for you, your training and your needs then simply use them as a template and find what works for you.

If there are any exercises that you do not know how to do in these programs, or are unsure of the techniques, then speak to a qualified trainer or use the internet, to find the correct method to do the exercises safely and effectively.

Remember, before undertaking any exercise program that you check with a medical professional to ensure that you have no underlying health problems. I realise that, for some people, this may be the first time they have done a weights session in the gym or have seen a program written down. The table below shows you how I set out the programs and what each column means and how to implement it. If you are unsure of anything then speak to a qualified personal trainer who can help.

EXERCISE	This is the order in which to perform the exercises; A, B, C etc. If you see, for example A1 and A2, then this means that you should perform these as a super set. Rather than performing all of the sets for A1, perform one set of A1, then one set of A2. Then repeat for the necessary amount of sets.
SETS	The number of times you will perform each exercise. For example, 6 sets of 6 squats
REPS	How many times you will lift a weight in a single set.
REST	How long you should rest between each set
TEMPO	The tempo of the lift may look like; 3 - 1 - X - 1 The 1st number refers to the eccentric part of the exercise (lowering the bar to your chest on a bench press), the 2nd number refers to the isometric pause in the stretched position (bar is touching your chest), the 3rd number refers to the concentric contraction (pressing the bar up), and the 4th number refers to the isometric pause in the shortened position (bar is locked out over your chest).

% IRM	Approx. No. of Reps	Optimal Total Reps per Workout	Training Effect
95-100%	1-3	4-10	Max Strength
85-95%	3-6	6-14	Strength
75-85%	6-10	10-20	Hypertrophy
65-75%	10-20	12-24	Power, Endurance
55-65%	20-35	18-30	Endurance
45-55%	35-50	50-150	Endurance

Next I've put a 6 week plan that I used with a female fitness model whose main objective was to be exceptionally lean and have a very aesthetically pleasing look which didn't look bulky. This sport requires the athletes to have minimum body fat and have an athletic look. I worked closely with the female bodybuilder who also had a job and was a mum as well and came up with the following 6 week plan leading up to a major competition.

Natural Body Builder

The following program is a 6 week plan I did for drug free, natural female body builder for a major competition. If I was to prepare her again, for another show, it would be slightly different to the one shown here, to prevent adaptation. As she is a teacher and a mum, I had to adapt her training days around her schedule.

Remember, to keep progressing, you must be one step ahead of adaptation so that your body is constantly having to change. In this case the goal was to add lean muscle whilst dropping body fat.

This program worked an absolute treat and the results were truly outstanding. Remember the only way you can judge if something is working is quite simple - RESULTS!

WHEN I FIRST MET PHIL BACK IN SEPTEMBER 2011 I THOUGHT I WAS REASONABLY EDUCATED AND QUITE WELL READ IN THE FIELD OF HEALTH AND NUTRITION HOWEVER, I WAS SOON BLOWN AWAY BY THE KNOWLEDGE I GAINED FROM PHIL BOTH ON A HEALTH AND NUTRITION PERSPECTIVE WHICH HE ALSO WOULD DELIVER IN SUCH A DIGESTIBLE WAY THAT MY UNDERSTANDING AND MY OWN PERFORMANCE PROGRESSED TO ANOTHER LEVEL.

PHIL NOT ONLY TAUGHT ME SOME VALUABLE LESSONS ABOUT HEALTH AND NUTRITION BUT HIS EXPERTISE IN THE FIELD OF STRENGTH TRAINING QUITE SIMPLY TOOK AWAY ALL THE COMPLEXITY THAT IS EASY TO GET TANGLED IN AND SHOWED ME METHODS THAT NOT ONLY MADE SENSE BUT ALSO GAINED PHENOMENAL RESULTS. I HAVE GAINED 3 BRITISH TITLES SINCE WORKING WITH PHIL AND HE HAS NOW GIVEN ME THE CONFIDENCE AND THE KNOWLEDGE TO TAKE OWNERSHIP OF NOT ONLY MY OWN PROGRESS BUT ALSO TO HELP OTHERS REACH THEIR GOALS. PHIL IS A GREAT TEACHER AND WITHOUT HIM WOULD NEVER HAVE MADE THE NECESSARY CHANGES TO REACH INTERNATIONAL LEVEL.

NINA ROSS
MISS FITNESS UK

Week 1	Morning	Evening
Monday	All over weights	1 30 minute run (with fan)
Tuesday		
Wednesday	All over weights 2	30 minute bike (with fan)
Thursday		
Friday	All over weights 3	30 minute row (with fan)
Saturday	Swim – Sauna – Hot Tub	
Sunday		

Week 2	Morning	Evening
Monday	Upper Body 1	Swim – Sauna – Hot Tub
Tuesday		
Wednesday	Lower Body 1	Swim – Sauna – Hot Tub
Thursday		
Friday	Upper Body 2	Swim – Sauna – Hot Tub
Saturday	Lower Body 2	
Sunday		

Week 3	Morning	Evening
Monday	Chest & Back 1	35 minute run (with fan)
Tuesday		
Wednesday	Legs & Abs 1	35 minute bike (with fan)
Thursday		
Friday	Shoulders & Arms 1	35 minute row (with fan)
Saturday		
Sunday		

Week 4	Morning	Evening
Monday	All over weights 4	Swim – Sauna – Hot Tub
Tuesday		
Wednesday	All over weights 5	Swim – Sauna – Hot Tub
Thursday		
Friday	All over weights 6	Swim – Sauna – Hot Tub
Saturday		
Sunday		

Week 5	Morning	Evening
Monday	Upper Body 3	40 minute run (with fan)
Tuesday		
Wednesday	Lower Body 3	40 minute bike (with fan)
Thursday		
Friday	Upper Body 4	40 minute row (with fan)
Saturday	Lower Body 4	
Sunday		

Week 6	Morning	Evening
Monday	Chest & Back 2	Swim – Sauna – Hot Tub
Tuesday		
Wednesday	Legs & Abs 2	Swim – Sauna – Hot Tub
Thursday		
Friday	Shoulders & Arms 2	Swim – Sauna – Hot Tub
Saturday		
Sunday		

Here are the weights programs that were prescribed to get this drug free female bodybuilder as lean as possible and we achieved that goal 100%.

WEEK 1: ALLOVER BODY 1

EXERCISE	SETS	REPS	TEMPO	REST
A1 Snatch Grip Dead Lifts	10	3 - 5	2 - 1 - X - 1	1-3 minutes
ONCE ALL SETS HAVE BEEN COMPLETED REST FOR 3 MINUTES				
B1 Incline D/Bell Bench	4	8 - 12	4 - 1 - X - 1	60 Seconds
B2 Lat Pull Downs	4	8 - 12	3 - 1 - X - 1	60 Seconds
ONCE ALL SETS HAVE BEEN COMPLETED REST FOR 3 MINUTES				
C1 Standing Cable Crunches	3	20	Controlled	60 Seconds
C2 D/Bell Upright Row from floor	3	10 each side	3 - 1 - X - 1	60 Seconds

WEEK 1: ALLOVER BODY 2

EXERCISE	SETS	REPS	TEMPO	REST
A1 Ski Squats (Go Deep)	10	5	2 - 1 - X - 1	1 minute
ONCE ALL SETS HAVE BEEN COMPLETED REST FOR 3 MINUTES				
B1 Lying leg curls	4	8 - 10	4 - 1 - X - 1	60 Seconds
B2 Preacher Curl	4	8 - 12	4 - 1 - X - 1	60 Seconds
ONCE ALL SETS HAVE BEEN COMPLETED REST FOR 3 MINUTES				
C1 Leg Extension	4	15	4 - 1 - X - 2	60 Seconds
C2 Lying Tricep Extension	4	12	3 - 1 - X - 1	60 Seconds
D Incline Sit ups	3	30	3 - 1 - X - 1	90 Seconds

WEEK 1: ALLOVER BODY 3

EXERCISE	SETS	REPS	TEMPO	REST
A1 Rack Bench Press	5	6 - 8	2 - 1 - X - 1	60 Seconds
A2 Leg Press	5	20	2 - 1 - X - 1	60 Seconds
ONCE ALL SETS HAVE BEEN COMPLETED REST FOR 3 MINUTES				
B1 Cable Snatch (Horizontal)	4	15	2 - 1 - X - 1	60 Seconds
B2 Seated Bench Press	4	15	4 - 1 - X - 1	60 Seconds
ONCE ALL SETS HAVE BEEN COMPLETED REST FOR 3 MINUTES				
C1 Hip Abductor	4	20	3 - 1 - X - 1	60 Seconds
C2 Hip Abduction	4	20	3 - 1 - X - 1	60 Seconds

WEEK 2: UPPER BODY 1

EXERCISE	SETS	REPS	TEMPO	REST
A1 Standing Shoulder Press	5	6 - 8	2 - 1 - X - 1	75 Seconds
A2 Supinated Chins	5	6 - 8	4 - 1 - X - 2	75 Seconds
ONCE ALL SETS HAVE BEEN COMPLETED REST FOR 3 MINUTES				
B1 Incline Bench Press	4	8 - 12	3 - 1 - X - 1	75 Seconds
B2 Seated Rows	4	8 - 10	3 - 1 - X - 1	75 Seconds
ONCE ALL SETS HAVE BEEN COMPLETED REST FOR 3 MINUTES				
C1 Pulley Tricep Extensions	3	20	3 - 1 - X - 1	60 Seconds
C2 Pulley Bicep Curls	3	20	3 - 1 - X - 1	60 Seconds
D Sprints Treadmill	5	1 Minute	X - X - X - X	60 Seconds

WEEK 2: LOWER BODY 1

EXERCISE	SETS	REPS	TEMPO	REST
A1 Good Mornings	5	10	2 - 1 - X - 1	1 - 3 Minutes
A2 Backward Sled Drags	5	40 Meters	X - X - X - X	75 Seconds
ONCE ALL SETS HAVE BEEN COMPLETED REST FOR 3 MINUTES				
B1 Leg Press	4	12 -15	3 - 1 - X - 0	75 Seconds
B2 Cable Hyper Extensions	4	20	3 - 1 - X - 0	75 Seconds
B3 Swiss Ball Reverse Crunches	3	20	3 - 1 - X - 1	60 Seconds
ONCE ALL SETS HAVE BEEN COMPLETED REST FOR 3 MINUTES				
C Bike Sprints	6	1 Minute	FLAT OUT	60 Seconds

WEEK 2: UPPER BODY 2

EXERCISE	SETS	REPS	TEMPO	REST
A1 Flat D/B Press	5	8 - 10	4 - 1 - X - 1	75 Seconds
A2 B.O.L.R	5	8 - 10	1 - 1 - 1 - 1	75 Seconds
ONCE ALL SETS HAVE BEEN COMPLETED REST FOR 3 MINUTES				
B1 Seated Bench	4	12 - 15	4 - 1 - X - 1	75 Seconds
B2 Preacher Curls	4	12 - 15	3 - 1 - X - 1	75 Seconds
ONCE ALL SETS HAVE BEEN COMPLETED REST FOR 3 MINUTES				
C1 KBR	4	20	2 - 1 - X - 1	75 Seconds
C2 Over Cable Tricep Ext	4	12	4 - 1 - X - 1	75 Seconds
D Rowing	6 1	Minute	FLAT OUT	60 Seconds

WEEK 2: LOWER BODY 2

EXERCISE	SETS	REPS	TEMPO	REST
A1 Dead Lifts	8	1 - 3	2 - 1 - X - 1	No Rest
A2 Hurdle Jumps	8	5	X - X - X - X	90 Seconds
ONCE ALL SETS HAVE BEEN COMPLETED REST FOR 3 MINUTES				
B1 Leg Extensions	4	15	4 - 1 - X - 1	60 Seconds
B2 Leg Curls	4	15	4 - 1 - X - 1	60 Seconds
ONCE ALL SETS HAVE BEEN COMPLETED REST FOR 3 MINUTES				
C1 Prowler Push	4	50 Meters	FLAT OUT	3 Minutes

WEEK 3: CHEST & BACK 1

EXERCISE	SETS	REPS	TEMPO	REST
A1 Weighted Press Ups	5	8 - 12	3 - 1 - X - 1	60 Seconds
A2 T Bar Rows	5	12	4 - 1 - X - 1	60 Seconds
ONCE ALL SETS HAVE BEEN COMPLETED REST FOR 3 MINUTES				
B1 D/B Bench Press	4	8 - 12	3 - 1 - X - 1	75 Seconds
B2 Any Grip Chin	4	12	4 - 1 - X - 2	75 Seconds
ONCE ALL SETS HAVE BEEN COMPLETED REST FOR 3 MINUTES				
C1 Pulley Curls	4	15	4 - 1 - X - 2	75 Seconds
C2 Tricep Extensions	4	12	4 - 1 - X - 2	75 Seconds

WEEK 3: LEGS & ABS 1

EXERCISE	SETS	REPS	TEMPO	REST
A1 Good Mornings	5	10	3 - 1 - X - 1	60 Seconds
A2 Leg Extensions	5	20	3 - 1 - X - 1	60 Seconds
ONCE ALL SETS HAVE BEEN COMPLETED REST FOR 3 MINUTES				
B1 Leg Press	4	8 - 12	4 - 1 - X - 1	60 Seconds
B2 Cable Crunch	4	20	2 - 1 - 1 - 1	60 Seconds
ONCE ALL SETS HAVE BEEN COMPLETED REST FOR 3 MINUTES				
C1 KBR	4	20	2 - 1 - 1 - 1	60 Seconds

WEEK 3: SHOULDERS & ARMS 1

EXERCISE	SETS	REPS	TEMPO	REST
A1 Standing Shoulder Press	5	10	3 - 1 - X - 1	60 Seconds
A2 Towel Chins	5	8	3 - 1 - X - 1	60 Seconds
ONCE ALL SETS HAVE BEEN COMPLETED REST FOR 3 MINUTES				
B1 Lateral Raises	4	20	3 - 1 - X - 1	60 Seconds
B2 Cable Crossovers	4	20	3 - 1 - X - 1	60 Seconds
ONCE ALL SETS HAVE BEEN COMPLETED REST FOR 3 MINUTES				
C1 Lying Tricep Ext	4	20	2 - 1 - 1 - 1	60 Seconds
C2 D/B Curls	4	15	4 - 1 - 1 - 1	60 Seconds

WEEK 4: ALLOVER BODY

EXERCISE	SETS	REPS	TEMPO	REST
A1 Power Cleans	8	1 - 3	X - X - X - X	1-3 Minutes
ONCE ALL SETS HAVE BEEN COMPLETED REST FOR 3 MINUTES				
B1 Back Squats Deep	5	10	4 - 1 - X - 1	60 Seconds
B2 Any Grip Chin	4	8 - 12	3 - 1 - X - 1	60 Seconds
ONCE ALL SETS HAVE BEEN COMPLETED REST FOR 3 MINUTES				
C1 Standing Cable Crunches	4	20	Controlled	60 Seconds
C2 D/Bell Upright Row from floor	4	10 each side	3 - 1 - X - 1	60 Seconds
D Bike Sprint	8	1 Minute	FLAT OUT	60 Seconds

WEEK 4: ALLOVER BODY 5

EXERCISE	SETS	REPS	TEMPO	REST
A1 Barbell Lunge	5	5 Each Leg	2 - 1 - X - 1	60 Seconds
A2 Dips	5	8 - 10	4 - 1 - X - 1	60 Seconds
ONCE ALL SETS HAVE BEEN COMPLETED REST FOR 3 MINUTES				
B1 Leg Extensions	4	20	3 - 1 - X - 1	60 Seconds
B2 Preacher Curls	4	10 each arm	4 - 1 - X - 1	60 Seconds
ONCE ALL SETS HAVE BEEN COMPLETED REST FOR 3 MINUTES				
C1 Straight Leg Raises	4	20	3 - 1 - X - 1	60 Seconds
C2 Good Mornings	4	10	3 - 1 - X - 1	60 Seconds
D Treadmill	6	1 Minute	FLAT OUT	60 Seconds

WEEK 4: ALLOVER BODY 6

EXERCISE	SETS	REPS	TEMPO	REST
A1 Rack Bench Press	5	10	4 - 1 - X - 1	60 Seconds
A2 Lying Leg Curls	5	12	4 - 1 - X - 1	60 Seconds
ONCE ALL SETS HAVE BEEN COMPLETED REST FOR 3 MINUTES				
B1 Leg Press	4	20	4 - 1 - X - 1	60 Seconds
B2 Cable Tricep Ext	4	20	2 - 1 - X - 1	60 Seconds
B3 Supinated Chins	4	12	4 - 1 - X - 1	60 Seconds
ONCE ALL SETS HAVE BEEN COMPLETED REST FOR 3 MINUTES				
C1 Prowler Push	5	20 Meters	FLAT OUT	90 Seconds
C2 Rowing	5	1 Minute	FLAT OUT	90 Seconds

WEEK 5: UPPER BODY 3

EXERCISE	SETS	REPS	TEMPO	REST
A1 Incline Bench Press	5	6 - 8	4 - 1 - X - 1	1 - 3 minutes
A2 Lateral Raises	5	12 - 15	1 - 1 - X - 1	75 Seconds
A3 Press Up & Twist	5	6 each side	1 - 1 - 1 - 1	75 Seconds
A4 Cable Snatch	5	20	4 - 1 - X - 1	75 Seconds
ONCE ALL SETS HAVE BEEN COMPLETED REST FOR 3 MINUTES				
B Backward Sled Drags	5	50 Meters	FLAT OUT	120 Seconds

WEEK 5: LOWER BODY 3

EXERCISE	SETS	REPS	TEMPO	REST
A1 Ski Squats	5	5	2 - 1 - X - 1	60 Seconds
ONCE ALL SETS HAVE BEEN COMPLETED REST FOR 3 MINUTES				
B1 Russian Step Up	4	6 - 8 each leg	X - X - X - X	60 Seconds
B2 Lateral Step Overs	4	10 each side	3 - 1 - X - 1	60 Seconds
ONCE ALL SETS HAVE BEEN COMPLETED REST FOR 3 MINUTES				
C1 Swiss Ball leg Curls	4	12	2 - 1 - X - 1	60 Seconds
C2 Standing Cable Crunches	4	20	3 - 1 - X - 1	60 Seconds
C3 Cable Pull Throughs	4	20	3 - 1 - X - 1	60 Seconds

WEEK 5: UPPER BODY 4

EXERCISE	SETS	REPS	TEMPO	REST
A1 Cable Snatch	5	15	X - X - X - X	60 Seconds
A2 Incline Bench	5	6 - 8	4 - 1 - X - 1	60 Seconds
ONCE ALL SETS HAVE BEEN COMPLETED REST FOR 3 MINUTES				
B1 Seated Cable Rows	4	12 - 15	4 - 1 - X - 1	60 Seconds
B2 Seated Bench Press	4	12 - 15	3 - 1 - X - 1	60 Seconds
ONCE ALL SETS HAVE BEEN COMPLETED REST FOR 3 MINUTES				
C1 Single Arm Cable Curls	3	12	2 - 1 - X - 1	60 Seconds
C2 Single Arm Tricep Press	3	12	2 - 1 - X - 1	60 Seconds

WEEK 5: LOWER BODY 4

EXERCISE	SETS	REPS	TEMPO	REST
A1 Backward Sled Drags	5	40 Meters	2 - 1 - X - 1	2 Minutes
A2 Lying Leg Curls	5	15	4 - 1 - X - 1	60 Seconds
ONCE ALL SETS HAVE BEEN COMPLETED REST FOR 3 MINUTES				
B1 Leg Extension	4	12	4 - 1 - X - 1	60 Seconds
B2 Lying Leg Press	4	20	4 - 1 - X - 1	60 Seconds
B3 Hip Abductor	4	20	4 - 1 - X - 1	60 Seconds
ONCE ALL SETS HAVE BEEN COMPLETED REST FOR 3 MINUTES				

WEEK 6: CHEST & BACK 2

EXERCISE	SETS	REPS	TEMPO	REST
A1 Thick Grip D/B Bench Press	5	8 - 12	3 - 1 - X - 1	60 Seconds
A2 Single Arms Rows	5	12	2 - 1 - X - 1	60 Seconds
ONCE ALL SETS HAVE BEEN COMPLETED REST FOR 3 MINUTES				
B1 Swiss Ball Press Up	4	10	3 - 1 - X - 1	60 Seconds
B2 Lat Pull Downs	4	12 - 15	2 - 1 - X - 1	60 Seconds
ONCE ALL SETS HAVE BEEN COMPLETED REST FOR 3 MINUTES				
C Rowing	8	1 Minute	FLAT OUT	60 Seconds

WEEK 6: LEGS & ABS 2

EXERCISE	SETS	REPS	TEMPO	REST
A1 Good Mornings	5	10	3 - 1 - X - 1	60 Seconds
A2 Leg Extensions	5	20	3 - 1 - X - 1	60 Seconds
ONCE ALL SETS HAVE BEEN COMPLETED REST FOR 3 MINUTES				
B1 Leg Press	4	20	3 - 1 - X - 1	60 Seconds
B2 Hanging Leg Raises Weighted	4	20	2 - 1 - 1 - 1	60 Seconds
ONCE ALL SETS HAVE BEEN COMPLETED REST FOR 3 MINUTES				
C1 KBR	4	20	2 - 1 - 1 - 1	60 Seconds
D Bike Sprint	6	1 Minute	FLAT OUT	60 Seconds

WEEK 6: SHOULDERS & ARMS 2

EXERCISE	SETS	REPS	TEMPO	REST
A1 Standing Shoulder Press	4	12	3 - 1 - X - 1	60 Seconds
A2 Any Grip Chins	4	12	3 - 1 - X - 1	60 Seconds
ONCE ALL SETS HAVE BEEN COMPLETED REST FOR 3 MINUTES				
B1 Lateral Raises	4	20	3 - 1 - X - 1	60 Seconds
B2 Preacher Curls	4	20	4 - 1 - X - 1	60 Seconds
ONCE ALL SETS HAVE BEEN COMPLETED REST FOR 3 MINUTES				
C1 Lying Tricep Ext	3	12 - 15	2 - 1 - 1 - 1	60 Seconds
C2 Cable Snatch	3	15	2 - 1 - 1 - 1	60 Seconds
ONCE ALL SETS HAVE BEEN COMPLETED REST FOR 3 MINUTES				
D Prowler	4	60 Meters	FLAT OUT	120 Seconds

Champion Boxer

Next, I have included the training plan that I prescribed to a current world champion boxer as I was preparing him for another major fight.

With this fighter in 12 months he lost 9% body fat gained 13.3 pounds of muscle and remained the same fighting weight and that was achieved with 100% dedication, following a detailed nutrition and supplement plan and ensuring every training session counted.

Week 1	Morning	Evening
Monday	Upper Body Weights 1	Bike & Bag Intervals
Tuesday	Swim Recovery & Massage	
Wednesday	Lower Body Weights 1	Prowler & Tyre Work
Thursday	Swim Recovery & Massage	
Friday	All Over Body Weights 1	Bag, Bike & KB Intervals
Saturday	DAY OFF	DAY OFF
Sunday	45 min Run	

Week 2	Morning	Evening
Monday	Upper Body Weights 1	Bike & Bag Intervals
Tuesday	6 x 400m Track	Swim Recovery & Massage
Wednesday	Lower Body Weights 1	Prowler & Tyre Work
Thursday	Swim Recovery & Massage	
Friday	All Over Body Weights 1	Bag, Bike & KB Intervals
Saturday	DAY OFF	DAY OFF
Sunday	45 min Run	

Week 3	Morning	Evening
Monday	Upper Body Weights 1	Bike & Bag Intervals
Tuesday	8 x 400m Track	Swim Recovery & Massage
Wednesday	Lower Body Weights 1	Prowler & Tyre Work
Thursday	Swim Recovery & Massage	
Friday	All Over Body Weights 1	Bag, Bike & KB Intervals
Saturday	Field Conditioning	
Sunday	45 min Run	

Week 4	Morning	Evening
Monday	Boxing Training	Upper Body Weights 2
Tuesday	Swim Recovery & Massage	
Wednesday	Boxing Training	Lower Body Weights 2
Thursday	Swim Recovery & Massage	
Friday	All Over Body Weights 1	All Over Body Weights 2
Saturday	DAY OFF	DAY OFF
Sunday	45 min Run	

Week 5	Morning	Evening
Monday	Boxing Training & Sparring	Upper Body Weights 2
Tuesday	10 x 400m Track	Swim Recovery & Massage
Wednesday	Boxing Training & Sparring	Lower Body Weights 2
Thursday	Swim Recovery & Massage	
Friday	Boxing Training & Sparring	All Over Body Weights 2
Saturday	Field Conditioning	
Sunday	DAY OFF	DAY OFF

Week 6	Morning	Evening
Monday	Boxing Training & Sparring	Upper Body Weights 2
Tuesday	10 x 400m Track	Swim Recovery & Massage
Wednesday	Boxing Training & Sparring	Lower Body Weights 2
Thursday	Swim Recovery & Massage	
Friday	Boxing Training & Sparring	All Over Body Weights 2
Saturday	Field Conditioning	
Sunday	DAY OFF	DAY OFF

Week 7	Morning	Evening
Monday	Boxing Training & Sparring	Upper Body Weights 2
Tuesday	Swim Recovery & Massage	
Wednesday	Boxing Training & Sparring	Lower Body Weights 2
Thursday	Swim Recovery & Massage	
Friday	Boxing Training & Sparring	All Over Body Weights 2
Saturday	Swim Recovery & Massage	
Sunday	45 min Run (if needed for weight)	

Week 8	Morning	Evening
Monday	Swim Recovery & Massage	All Over Body Weights 3
Tuesday	Swim Recovery & Massage	
Wednesday	Boxing Training (Technical Skills)	Lower Body Weights 2
Thursday	DAY OFF	
Friday	Weight In	Light Pad Work
Saturday		FIGHT NIGHT
Sunday		

Here are the weights programs to go with the boxing program as outlined above:

UPPER BODY 1

EXERCISE	SETS	REPS	TEMPO	REST
A1 Viking Press	5	6 - 8	3 - 1 - X - 1	75 Seconds
A2 Cable Snatch	4	12	1 - 1 - 1 - 1	75 Seconds
ONCE ALL SETS HAVE BEEN COMPLETED REST FOR 5 MINUTES				
B1 Incline Bench Press	4	8 - 12	3 - 1 - X - 1	75 Seconds
B2 T-Bar Rows	4	8 - 12	Controlled	75 Seconds
ONCE ALL SETS HAVE BEEN COMPLETED REST FOR 5 MINUTES				
C Med Ball Throws	5	10	X - X - X - X	75 Seconds

LOWER BODY 1

EXERCISE	SETS	REPS	TEMPO	REST
A1 Box Squats	8	1 - 5	2 - 1 - X - 1	1 - 3 Minutes
ONCE ALL SETS HAVE BEEN COMPLETED REST FOR 5 MINUTES				
B1 Prowler Push	4	20 Meters	X - X - X - X	75 Seconds
B2 Lateral Step Overs	4 1	0 each side	X - X - X - X	75 Seconds
ONCE ALL SETS HAVE BEEN COMPLETED REST FOR 5 MINUTES				
C1 Cable Hyper Ext Rows	4	20	2 - 1 - X - 1	75 Seconds
C2 Standing Cable Crunches	4	20	3 - 1 - X - 1	75 Seconds

ALL OVER 1

EXERCISE	SETS	REPS	TEMPO	REST
A1 Log Clean & Press	8	3	X - X - X - X	60 Seconds
ONCE ALL SETS HAVE BEEN COMPLETED REST FOR 5 MINUTES				
B1 Lunge & Reach	4	6 - 8 each leg	2 - 1 - X - 1	75 Seconds
B2 Any Grip Chin	4	8 - 10	3 - 1 - X - 1	75 Seconds
ONCE ALL SETS HAVE BEEN COMPLETED REST FOR 5 MINUTES				
C1 Kettle Bell Rotations	3	20	2 - 1 - X - 1	75 Seconds
C2 Hanging Leg Raises	3	20	3 - 1 - X - 1	75 Seconds

UPPER BODY 2

EXERCISE	SETS	REPS	TEMPO	REST
A1 Dumb Bell Shoulder Press	5	6 - 8	3 - 1 - X - 1	75 Seconds
A2 Dumb Bell Shrug & External Rotation	5	12	1 - 1 - 1 - 1	75 Seconds
ONCE ALL SETS HAVE BEEN COMPLETED REST FOR 5 MINUTES				
B1 Incline Dumb Bell Chest Press	4	8 - 12	3 - 1 - X - 1	75 Seconds
B2 Single Arm Cable Rows	4	8 - 12	Controlled	75 Seconds
ONCE ALL SETS HAVE BEEN COMPLETED REST FOR 5 MINUTES				
C Hurdle Jumps	5	10	X - X - X - X	90 Seconds

LOWER BODY 2

EXERCISE	SETS	REPS	TEMPO	REST
A1 Dead Lifts	8	1 - 5	2 - 1 - X - 1	1 - 3 Minutes
ONCE ALL SETS HAVE BEEN COMPLETED REST FOR 5 MINUTES				
B1 Russian Step Ups	4	10 each leg	2 - 1 - X - 1	75 Seconds
B2 Back Attack	4	20	2 - 1 - X - 1	75 Seconds
ONCE ALL SETS HAVE BEEN COMPLETED REST FOR 5 MINUTES				
C1 Weighted Side Bends	4	12 each side	2 - 1 - X - 1	75 Seconds
C2 Swiss Ball Reverse Crunch	4	20	3 - 1 - X - 1	75 Seconds

ALL OVER 2

EXERCISE	SETS	REPS	TEMPO	REST
A1 Power Cleans	8	1 - 3	X - X - X - X	1 - 3 Minutes
A2 Super Yolk Walks	4	20 Meters	2 - 1 - X - 1	75 Seconds
ONCE ALL SETS HAVE BEEN COMPLETED REST FOR 5 MINUTES				
B1 Rack Bench Press	4	8 - 10	3 - 1 - X - 1	75 Seconds
B2 Lying Tricep Ext	3	8 - 12	2 - 1 - X - 1	75 Seconds
ONCE ALL SETS HAVE BEEN COMPLETED REST FOR 5 MINUTES				
C Pulley Curls	3	20	3 - 1 - X - 1	75 Seconds

ALL OVER 3

EXERCISE	SETS	REPS	TEMPO	REST
A1 Bench Press	4	6 - 8	4 - 1 - X - 1	1 - 3 Minutes
ONCE ALL SETS HAVE BEEN COMPLETED REST FOR 5 MINUTES				
B1 Cable Snatch	4	12	2 - 1 - X - 1	75 Seconds
B2 Reverse Hypers	4	15	3 - 1 - X - 1	75 Seconds
ONCE ALL SETS HAVE BEEN COMPLETED REST FOR 5 MINUTES				
C1 T-Bar Rows	3	8 - 12	2 - 1 - X - 1	75 Seconds
C2 Pulley Curls	3	12	3 - 1 - X - 1	75 Seconds

"PHIL HAS MADE ME DO SESSIONS AND WHEN I HAVE FINISHED THEM I DON'T KNOW WHERE MY HEAD IS. BUT IT IS GOOD TO FEEL LIKE THAT BECAUSE IN A FIGHT I KNOW I WILL FEEL LIKE THAT AT SOME STAGE. I HAVE NEVER FELT THE PAIN OR EXHAUSTION THAT I FEEL WITH PHIL.

"THERE HAVE BEEN SOME SESSIONS THAT HAVE BEEN SO TOUGH, I WANTED TO HIDE IN A CORNER BECAUSE THERE WERE ANOTHER FIVE SESSIONS TO DO.

"HE TAKES YOU TO AN UNCOMFORTABLE ZONE BUT I NEED TO KNOW HOW I FEEL WHEN I AM IN IT. I FEEL MORE FOCUSED THAN EVER, STRONGER THAN EVER, TOO."

AMIR KHAN
WELTERWEIGHT BOXER

Here is a weights diary that I got all my athletes to fill in every time we did a training session to track progress.

Weight session template and monitoring information

What is your motivation like today?
CIRCLE ONE FACE

What is your stress like today?
CIRCLE ONE FACE

TODAY'S GYM SESSION

#	EXERCISE		SETS	REPS	TEMPO		REST	OTHER INFORMATION		
SETS	1	2	3	4	5	6	7	8	9	10
WEIGHT										
REPS										

#	EXERCISE		SETS	REPS	TEMPO		REST	OTHER INFORMATION		
SETS	1	2	3	4	5	6	7	8	9	10
WEIGHT										
REPS										

#	EXERCISE		SETS	REPS	TEMPO		REST	OTHER INFORMATION		
SETS	1	2	3	4	5	6	7	8	9	10
WEIGHT										
REPS										

#	EXERCISE		SETS	REPS	TEMPO		REST	OTHER INFORMATION		
SETS	1	2	3	4	5	6	7	8	9	10
WEIGHT										
REPS										

#	EXERCISE		SETS	REPS	TEMPO		REST	OTHER INFORMATION		
SETS	1	2	3	4	5	6	7	8	9	10
WEIGHT										
REPS										

#	EXERCISE		SETS	REPS	TEMPO		REST	OTHER INFORMATION		
SETS	1	2	3	4	5	6	7	8	9	10
WEIGHT										
REPS										

Comments:

You must create the right training environment for the athlete to flourish! Remember, you become your environment.

You must mentally prepare yourself for any training that you do. You cannot simply turn up to a training session. All of the athletes that I have worked with would mentally prepare themselves for the sessions and go through what they wanted to accomplish from that session.

Whether you think you can,
or you think you can't,
you're right
Henry Ford

So there you have some great information on how best to carry out an exercise program which will deliver results as long as you give 100% effort to each session and follow the other 9 habits in this book. The reason why so many people fail to see results from their training efforts to lose fat and gain lean muscle tissue is quite simple in that they fail to address nutrition, lifestyle and emotional issues. For your training plan to be effective you have to get what you do outside the gym 100% or you will not see 100% results in the gym.

Conclusion

Well I hope you got as much out of reading the Science Of Fat Loss Book as I did in writing it. And may I wish you a very happy healthy life. Thank You :)

Index & Bibliography

Index

A

B

C

D

E

F

G

H

I

K

V

W

Bibliography

Winick M, ed. *Childhood Obesity.* New York, NY: Wiley 1975

Diet, Muscle Glycogen, and Physical Performance, *Acta Physiologica Scandinavica*, vol. 71, pp. 140-150, 1967

Westlund K, Nicholayse R. Scand *J Lab Clin Invest* 1972;127 (S):1-22

American Cancer Society, *Cancer Prevention Study 1959 – 79.* New York, NY: American Cancer Society, 1980

Winick M, ed. *Childhood Obesity.* New York, NY: Wiley 1975

http://www.ncbi.nlm.nih.gov/pubmed/22934546

K. Helme, et al *Diabetogia*, Vol. 29, Number 1/30-33, 1/1/86

Ovetchkine P., *Arch Pediatr*, 8(3):316-20 3/101

Albionico et al, *JAM* 192;9(1)

Pediatrics, Vol. 75, No. 2, Feb 1985

Paediatrics, July, 1992: 89

Diabetologia 1994;37(4):381-387

Fertility and Sterility October 2001;76:723-729

Vimy, M.J., et al. Maternal – Fetal Distribution of Mercury Released from Dental Amalgam Fillings. *American Physiological Society* 258 (1990) R939 – R945

African Journal of Microbiology Research

J Neuropathol Exp Neurol. 1996 Nov;55(11):1115-23.

Trick and Treat by Barry Groves PhD

Newsholme E A. Mechanism for starvation suppression and refeeding activity of infection. *Lancet* 1977; i: 654.

Miller JHD, et al. Double blind trial of linoleate supplementation in the diet in multiple sclerosis. *BMJ* 1973; i: 765-8.

Uldall PR, et al. Unsaturated fatty acids and renal transplantation. *Lancet* 1974; ii: 514.

Pearce M L, Dayton S. Incidence of cancer in men on a diet high in polyunsaturated fat. *Lancet* 1971; i: 464.

American Heart Association Monograph, No 25. 1969.

Nauts HC. *Cancer Research Institute Monograph* No 18. 1984, p 91.

Lahat E, et al. Prevalence of celiac antibodies in children with neurological disorders. *Pediatr Neurol.* 2000 May;22(5):393-6.

Wakefield AJ, et al. Enterocolitis in children with developmental disorders. *Am J Gastroenterol.* 2000 Sep;95(9):2285-95.

J Ped, Dec 2001, Vol. 108

Scandinavian Journal Of Gastroenterology, 2005).

Rolls, B.J. and Miller, D.L. 1997. Is the low-fat message giving people a license to eat more? *Journal of the American College of Nutrition* 16:535

Crozier G. et al. 1987. Metabolic effects induced by long-term feeding of medium-chain triglycerides in the rat. *Metabolism* 36:807-814

Rolls, B.J. et al. 1988. Food intake in dieters and non dieters after a liquid meal containing medium-chain triglycerides. *Am. J. Clin. Nutr.* 48(1):66

Van Wymelbeke, V., et al. 1998. Influence of medium-chain and long-chain triacylglycerols on the control of food intake in men. *Am. J. Clin. Nutr.* 68:226-234

Rizzo AM, Montorfano G, Negroni M, Adorni L, Berselli P, Corsetto P, Wahle K, and Berra B. "A rapid method for determining arachidonic: eicosapentaenoic acid ratios in whole blood lipids:

correlation with erythrocyte membrane ratios and validation in a large Italian population of various ages and pathologies." *Lipids in Health and Disease* 9:7 (2010)

Effects of Exercise on Mitochondrial Oxygen Uptake and Respiratory Enzyme Activity in Skeletal Muscle, *The Journal of Biological Chemistry*, vol. 242(9), pp. 2278-2282, 1967

Skeletal Muscle Respiratory Capacity, Endurance, and Glycogen Utilization, *American Journal of Physiology*, vol. 228(4), pp. 1029-1033, 1975

Influence of Exercise Intensity and Duration on Biochemical Adaptations in Skeletal Muscle,' *Journal of Applied Physiology*, vol. 53(4), pp. 844-850, 1982

Breast Cancer: A Nutritional Approach by Carlton Fredericks, Ph.D.

Iodine: Why You Need It, Why You Can't Live Without It by David Brownstein, M.D.

Yiamouyiannis, J.A. Water Fluoridation and Tooth Decay: Results from the 1986-87 National Survey of U.S. Schoolchildren, *Fluoride*, 23, 55-67, 1990

Colquhoun, J. "Child Dental Health Differences in New Zealand", Community Health Services, *XI* 85-90, 1987

E. A. Mascioli, et al.,*Lipids* 22(6) 421, 1987

Chang 1998; Kupka 2002; Cole 2002; Frye 1999

Lerchbaum E, Pilz S, Boehm BO, Grammer TB, Obermayer-Pietsch B, März W. Combination of low free testosterone and low vitamin D predicts mortality in older men referred for coronary angiography. *Clin Endocrinol (Oxf)*. 2012 Feb 22. doi: 10.1111/j.1365-2265.2012.04371.x.

Akishita, 2007

Malkin, 2010

Militaru, 2010

Turhan, 2007

Khaw, 2007

Corona G, et al. The effect of statin therapy on testosterone levels in subjects consulting for erectile dysfunction. *J Sex Med* 2010;7(4 Pt 1):1547-56

Dobs AS, et al. Effects of high-dose simvastatin on adrenal and gonadal steroidogenesis in men with hypercholesterolemia. *Metabolism2000*;49:1234–8.

Wranicz, 2005; Abbott, 2007; Tivesten, 2006; Dunajska, 2004

Jankowska, 2009

Hoffman J1, Ratamess N, Kang J, Mangine G, Faigenbaum A, Stout J.

Eur J Appl Physiol. 2004 May;91(5-6):628-37. Epub 2003 Dec 18. The effects of creatine supplementation on muscular performance and body composition responses to short-term resistance training overreaching. Volek JS1, Ratamess NA, Rubin MR, Gómez AL, French DN, McGuigan MM, Scheett TP, Sharman MJ, Häkkinen K, Kraemer WJ.

Science & Sports, Volume 26, Issue 5, Pages 272-277 D. Sheikholeslami Vatani, H. Faraji, R. Soori, M. Mogharnasi

Med Sci Sports Exerc. 2001 Feb;33(2):183-8. Creatine supplementation and health variables: a retrospective study. Schilling BK1, Stone MH, Utter A, Kearney JT, Johnson M, Coglianese R, Smith L, O'Bryant HS, Fry AC, Starks M, Keith R, Stone ME.

Zhu, J.S., Halpern, G.M., and Jones, K. (1998): The Scientific Rediscovery of an Ancient Chinese Herbal Medicine: Cordyceps sinensis. Part I. *Journal of Alternative and complementary Medicine* 4(3), pp 289-303 2. Zhu, J.S., Halpern, G.M., and Jones, K. (1998): The Scientific Rediscovery of a Precious Ancient Chinese Herbal Regimen: Cordyceps sinensis. Part II. *Journal of Alternative and complementary Medicine* 4(4), pp 429-457.

Lou Y, Liao X, Lu Y. Cardiovascular pharmacological studies of ethanol extracts of Cordyceps mycelia and Cordyceps fermentation solution. *Chinese Traditional and Herbal Drugs* 1986;17(5):17-21,209-213

Wang WQ. J. Administration *Traditional Chinese Med* 1995;5 (supp;):24

Improvement of physical performance and quality of life, pages 293 – 295

Reported XU C.F et al in ZHU J-S, Halpern GM, Jones K. The Scientific rediscovery of a precious ancient Chinese herbal regimen: Cordyceps sinensis: Part I. *J Alt Comp Med* 1998;4(3):289-303.)

Haesungcharern 1978; Kanwar 1983; Chubb 1985a,b

Zakrzewska 2002

Zakrzewska H, et al. (2002). In vitro influence of sodium fluoride on ram semen quality and enzyme activities. *Fluoride* 35: 153-160.

Chinoy NJ, Narayana MV. (1994). In vitro fluoride toxicity in human spermatozoa. *Reprod Toxicol.* 8(2):155-9

Chubb C. (1985a). Reversal of the endocrine toxicity of commercially produced perfluorochemical emulsion. *Biology of Reproduction* 33(4):854-8

Eur J of Applied Physio, 2004, 91(5-6):698-707

J Appl Physiol, 1988, 65:2406-2412

J of Sports Sciences, 2004, 22(5):465-478

Arwert LI, Deijen JB, Drent ML. Effects of an oral mixture containing glycine, glutamine and niacin on memory, GH and IGF-I secretion in middle-aged and elderly subjects. *Nutr Neurosci.* 2003 Oct;6(5):269-75

St-Onge MP, McReynolds A, Trivedi ZB, Roberts AL, Sy M, Hirsch J. Sleep restriction leads to increased activation of brain regions sensitive to food stimuli. *Am J Clin Nutr* (2012)

Buxton OM, Pavlova M, Reid EW, Wang W, Simonson DC, Adler GK. Sleep restriction for 1 week reduces insulin sensitivity in healthy men. *Diabetes.* 2010;59(9):2126-33

Donga E, van Dijk M, van Dijk JG, Biermasz NR, Lammers GJ, van Kralingen KW, Corssmit EP, Romijn JA. A single night of partial sleep deprivation induces insulin resistance in multiple metabolic pathways in healthy subjects. Deprivation. *J Clin Endocrinol Metab.* 2010 Jun;95(6):2963-8

Pauly DF, Pepine CJ. Ischemic heart disease: metabolic approaches to management. *Clin Cardiol.* 2004 Aug;27(8):439-41. Pauly DF, Johnson C, St Cyr JA. The benefits of ribose in cardiovascular disease. *Med Hypotheses.* 2003 Feb;60(2):149-51

Am J Physiol Regul Integr Comp Physiol. 2004 Jan;286(1):R182-8.

Hawthorn Helps Heart Failure Cochrane Database of Systematic Reviews Pittler MH, Guo R, Ernst E.

Robinson, 2006

Hjerkinn, 2006

American Heart Journal July 2004;148(1):157-64option.04;148(1):157-64

Takahashi T, Schulze C, Lord B, et al. Ascorbic acid enhances differentiation of embryonic stem cells into cardiac myocytes. *Circulation*, March 31, 2003

Willis G, An experimental study of the intimal ground substance in atherosclerosis" *Canadian Medical Association Journal* 1953 69:17-22

Maeda N, et al, "Aortic wall damage in mice unable to synthesise ascorbic acid" *Proceedings of the National Academy of Sciences of the United States of America* 2000 97(2):841-846

Sitaramayya C, Ali T, "Studies on experimental hypercholesterolemia and atherosclerosis" *Journal of Physiology and Pharmacology* 1962 6:192-204

Datey K et al, "Ascorbic acid and experimental atherosclerosis" *Journal of Physicians of India* 1968 16(9):567-570

Richardson, JP et al. "Risk factors for the development of becteremia in nursing home patients". *Archives of family medicine.* 1995 Sep;4(9):785 - 9

Repo-Tiihonen, E et al. "Total serum cholesterol level, violent criminal offences, suicidal behaviour, mortality and the appearance of conduct disorder in Finnish male criminal offenders with anti - social personality disorder". *European Archives of Psychiatary and Clinical Neuroscience.* Volume 252, Number 1, 8 - 11

Afsarmanesh, N et al. "Total cholesterol levels and mortality risk in nonischemic systolic heart failure". *American Heart Journal.* 2006 Dec;152(6):1077-83

Lande KE, Sperry WM. Human atherosclerosis in relation to the cholesterol content of the blood serum. *Archives of pathology* 1936; 22:301 – 312

Mathur KS et al Serum cholesterol and atherosclerosis in man. *Circulation* 1961; 23: 847 – 852

H. Edward Garrett, MD; Evan C. Horning, MD Serum Cholesterol Values in Patients Treated Surgically for Atherosclerosis. *Journal of the American Medical Association.* 1964; 189(9) : 655 – 659

Jose Mendez et al Relationship between Serum Lipids and Aortic Atherosclerotic Lesions in Sudden Accidental Deaths in Guatemala City. *American Journal of Clinical Nutrition.* Vol 20, 1113 – 1117

Frantz ID et al Test of effect of lipid lowering by diet on cardiovascular risk. The Minnesota Coronary Survey. *Arteriosclerosis.* 1989 Jan – Feb; 9(1):129 - 35

Bermudez O et al Dietary and plasma lipid, lipoprotein, and apolipoprotein profiles among elderly Hispanics and non – Hispanics and their association with diabetes. *American Journal of Nutrition.* 2002 Dec; 76(6) : 1214 – 21

Hernon KL et al High intake of cholesterol results in less atherogenic low density lipoproteins particles in men and women independent of response classification. *Metabolism* 2004 Jun; 53(6) : 823 -30

Kwok T et al Vascular Dysfunction in Chinese Vegetarians: An Apparent Paradox? *Journal of the American College of Cardiology.* 2005; 46 : 1957 – 1958

Mamo JC et al A low protein diet exacerbates postprandial chylomicron concentration to a lean red meat protein enriched diet. *European Journal of Clinical Nutrition* 2005 Oct: 59(10) : 1142-8

Miettenen TA et al Multifactorial Primary Prevention of Cardiovascular Diseases in Middle – aged Men. *Journal of the American Medical Association.* 1985; 254(15) : 2097 – 2012

Wood AC et al Dietary Carbohydrate Modifies the Inverse Association Between Saturated Fat Intake and Cholesterol on Very Low Density Lipoproteins. *Lipid Insights.* 2011 Aug 23; 2011(4): 7-15

Weintraub MS et al Clearance of chylomicron remnants in nonmolipidaemic patients with coronary artery disease: case control study over three years. *British Medical Journal.* 13 April 1996; 312 :935

Elias, PK et al. "Serum Cholesterol and Cognitive Performance in the Framingham Heart Study. *Pyscosomatic Medicine.* 67:24-30 2005

Visser M, Bouter LM, McQuillan GM, Wener MH, Harris TB. Elevated C-reactive protein levels in overweight and obese adults. *JAMA.* 1999 Dec 8;282(22):2131-5

Ajani UA, Ford ES, Mokdad AH. Dietary fiber and C-reactive protein: findings from national health and nutrition examination survey data. *J Nutr.* 2004 May;134(5):1181-5

Wald DS and Morris JK. Homocysteine and cardiovascular disease: evidence on causality from a meta-analysis. *BMJ.* 325: 1202. 2002

Lerk M et al. 'MTHFR 677C>T Polymorphism and Risk of Coronary Heart Disease'. *JAMA.* Vol. 288(16): 2023-2031. 2002

Vollset SE et al. 'Plasma total homocysteine and cardiovascular and noncardiovascular mortality: the Hordaland Homocsyteine Study'. *American Journal of Clinical Nutrition.* 74(1): 130-136. 2001

Jarosz A, Nowicka G. *C-reactive protein and homocysteine as risk factors of atherosclerosis.* Przegl Lek. 2008;65(6):268-7223

Geleijnse et al., 2004, pp. 3100-3105

Unden & Bongaerts, 1997, pp. 217-234

Schurgers & Vermeer, 2000, pp. 298-307

Burke & Deakin 2000

Stortebecker, P.. *The Lancet,* May 27, 1989

Silver Dental Fillings - The Toxic Time Bomb, Aurora Press, New York 1984. *The Missing Link* by Dr Michael F Ziff DDS & Sam Ziff

Sam Queen; Chronic Mercury Toxicity; New Hope Against an Endemic Disease. Huggins H., *It's All In Your Head.* 1990

N Engl J Med, 1987, 317: 521; The Framingham Study. JAMA, 1987, 258: 1183

FEMS Microbiol Letter, May 1995 128 (2): 213-18.

Biochemistry Mar 12, 1991, (10) p 2563-70

Cancer Causes and Cures – Vol. 2 1991

Maehlom et al. 1977, Blom et al. 1987, *Ivy* et al. 1988

Samaha FF, et al. A low-carbohydrate as compared with a low-fat diet in severe obesity. *New England Journal of Medicine*, 2003

Sondike SB, et al. Effects of a low-carbohydrate diet on weight loss and cardiovascular risk factor in overweight adolescents. *The Journal of Pediatrics*, 2003

Brehm BJ, et al. A randomized trial comparing a very low carbohydrate diet and a calorie-restricted low fat diet on body weight and cardiovascular risk factors in healthy women. *The Journal of Clinical Endocrinology & Metabolism*, 2003

Aude YW, et al. The national cholesterol education program diet vs a diet lower in carbohydrates and higher in protein and monounsaturated fat. *Archives of Internal Medicine*, 2004

Yancy WS Jr, et al. A low-carbohydrate, ketogenic diet versus a low-fat diet to treat obesity and hyperlipidemia. *Annals of Internal Medicine*, 2004

JS Volek, et al. Comparison of energy-restricted very low-carbohydrate and low-fat diets on weight loss and body composition in overweight men and women. *Nutrition & Metabolism* (London), 2004

McClernon FJ, et al. The effects of a low-carbohydrate ketogenic diet and a low-fat diet on mood, hunger, and other self-reported symptoms. *Obesity* (Silver Spring), 2007

Dyson PA, et al. A low-carbohydrate diet is more effective in reducing body weight than healthy eating in both diabetic and non-diabetic subjects. *Diabetic Medicine*, 2007

Volek JS, et al. Carbohydrate restriction has a more favorable impact on the metabolic syndrome than a low fat diet. *Lipids*, 2009

Shai I, et al. Weight loss with a low-carbohydrate, Mediterranean, or low-fat diet. *New England Journal of Medicine*, 2008

J Obes Relat Metab Disord. 1996 May;20(5):435-44

Am J Clin Nutr. 1983 Jan;37(1):1-4

Am J Clin Nutr. 1998 Aug;68(2):226-34

Michael R. Deschenes, Laurie L. Bronson, Meredith P. Cadorette, Julia E. Powers, and John C. Weinlein "Aged men display blunted biorhythmic variation of muscle performance and physiological responses" *J Appl Physiol* June 1, 2002 92:(6)

Jill A. Kanaley, Judy Y. Weltman, Karen S. Pieper, Arthur Weltman, and Mark L. Hartman "Cortisol and Growth Hormone Responses to Exercise at Different Times of Day" *JCEM* 2001 86: 2881-2889

'Effects of Exercise on Mitochondrial Oxygen Uptake and Respiratory Enzyme Activity in Skeletal Muscle,' *The Journal of Biological Chemistry*, vol. 242(9), pp. 2278-2282, 1967

'Skeletal Muscle Respiratory Capacity, Endurance, and Glycogen Utilization,' *American Journal of Physiology*, vol. 228(4), pp. 1029-1033, 1975

'Influence of Exercise Intensity and Duration on Biochemical Adaptations in Skeletal Muscle,' *Journal of Applied Physiology*, vol. 53(4), pp. 844-850, 1982

Macpherson, R. E., Hazell, T. J., Olver, T. D., Paterson, D. H., & Lemon, P. W. (2011). Run sprint interval training improves aerobic performance but not maximal cardiac output. *Medicine and science in sports and exercise*, 43(1), 115-122

Gergley, J. C. (2009). Comparison of two lower-body modes of endurance training on lower-body strength development while concurrently training. *The Journal of Strength & Conditioning Research*, 23(3), 979-987

Intermountain Medical Center, *Eurekalert* April 3, 2011

KRAMER, J., M. STONE, H. S. O'BRYANT, et al. Effect of single vs. multiple sets of weight training: impact of volume, intensity, and variation. *J. Strength Cond. Res.* 11:143–147, 1997

Tufts-New England Medical Center, *JAMA* Jan 5, 2005

Leibel, Rosenbaum & Hirsch 1995

Brownell & Rodin 1994; Lissner et al. 1991

Effects of Dietary Coconut Oil on the Biochemical and Anthropometric Profiles of Women Presenting Abdominal Obesity. Monica L. Assunção, Haroldo S. Ferreira, Aldenir F. dos Santos, Cyro R. Cabral Jr, Telma M. M. T. Florêncio

Forbes January 15, 2014

Forbes July 31, 2013

European Heart Journal 2014: 35(3); 131-137

Berry SE, Tucker S, Banerji R, Jiang B, Chowienczyk PJ, Charles SM, Sanders TA. Impaired postprandial endothelial function depends on the type of fat consumed by healthy men. *Journal of Nutrition* 2008 Oct;138(10):1910-4

Eur J Nutr. 2013 Feb;52(1):1-24. doi: 10.1007/s00394-012-0418-1. Epub 2012 Jul 19.